CONTEMPORARY PSYCHOMETRICS

Multivariate Applications Series

Sponsored by the Society of Multivariate Experimental Psychology, the goal of this series is to apply complex statistical methods to significant social or behavioral issues, in such a way so as to be accessible to a nontechnical-oriented readership (e.g., nonmethodological researchers, teachers, students, government personnel, practitioners, and other professionals). Applications from a variety of disciplines, such as psychology, public health, sociology, education, and business, are welcome. Books can be single- or multiple-authored, or edited volumes that: (1) demonstrate the application of a variety of multivariate methods to a single, major area of research; (2) describe a multivariate procedure or framework that could be applied to a number of research areas; or (3) present a variety of perspectives on a controversial topic of interest to applied multivariate researchers.

There are currently ten books in the series:

- *What if there were no significance tests?* co-edited by Lisa L. Harlow, Stanley A. Mulaik, and James H. Steiger (1997).
- *Structural Equation Modeling with LISREL, PRELIS, and SIMPLIS: Basic Concepts, Applications, and Programming* written by Barbara M. Byrne (1998).
- *Multivariate Applications in Substance Use Research: New Methods for New Questions,* co-edited by: Jennifer S. Rose, Laurie Chassin, Clark C. Presson, and Steven J. Sherman (2000).
- *Item Response Theory for Psychologists,* co-authored by Susan E. Embretson and Steven P. Reise (2000).
- *Structural Equation Modeling with AMOS: Basic Concepts, Applications, and Programming,* written by Barbara M. Byrne (2001).
- *Conducting Meta-Analysis Using SAS,* written by Winfred Arthur, Jr., Winston Bennett, Jr., and Allen I. Huffcutt (2001).
- *Modeling Intraindividual Variability with Repeated Measures Data: Methods and Applications,* co-edited by D. S. Moskowitz and Scott L. Hershberger (2002).
- *Multilevel Modeling: Methodological Advances, Issues, and Applications,* co-edited by Steven P. Reise and Naihua Duan (2003).
- *The Essence of Multivariate Thinking: Basic Themes and Methods* by Lisa L. Harlow (2005).
- *Contemporary Psychometrics*: A Festschrift for Roderick P. McDonald. Co-edited by Albert Maydeu-Olivares and John J. McArdle (2005).

Anyone wishing to submit a book proposal should send the following: (1) author/title, (2) timeline including completion date, (3) brief overview of the book's focus, including table of contents, and ideally a sample chapter (or more), (4) a brief description of competing publications, and (5) targeted audiences.

For more information please contact the series editor, Lisa Harlow, at: Department of Psychology, University of Rhode Island, 10 Chafee Road, Suite 8, Kingston, RI 02881-0808; Phone: (401) 874-4242; Fax: (401) 874-5562; or e-mail: LHarlow@uri.edu. Information may also be obtained from members of the advisory board: Leona Aiken (Arizona State University), Gwyneth Boodoo (Educational Testing Service), Barbara M. Byrne (University of Ottawa), Patrick Curran (University of North Carolina), Scott E. Maxwell (University of Notre Dame), David Rindskopf (City University of New York), Liora Schmelkin (Hofstra University) and Stephen West (Arizona State University).

CONTEMPORARY PSYCHOMETRICS

A Festschrift for Roderick P. McDonald

Edited by

Albert Maydeu-Olivares
University of Barcelona

John J. McArdle
University of Virginia

2005

LAWRENCE ERLBAUM ASSOCIATES, PUBLISHERS
Mahwah, New Jersey   London

Senior Editor:	Debra Riegert
Editorial Assistant:	Kerry Breen
Cover Design:	Kathryn Houghtaling Lacey
Textbook Production Manager:	Paul Smolenski
Full-Service Compositor:	TechBooks
Text and Cover Printer:	Hamilton Printing Company

This book was typeset in 10/12 pt. Times, Italic, Bold, and Bold Italic.
The heads were typeset in Americana, Americana Italic, and Americana Bold.

Lawrence Erlbaum Associates, Inc., Publishers
10 Industrial Avenue
Mahwah, New Jersey 07430
www.erlbaum.com

Library of Congress Cataloging-in-Publication Data

Contemporary psychometrics : a festschrift for Roderick P. McDonald / edited
by Albert Maydeu-Olivares, John J. McArdle.
    p. cm.—(Multivariate applications book series)
  Includes bibliographical references and index.
  ISBN 0-8058-4608-5 (hardcover : alk. paper)
   1. Psychometrics. I. McDonald, Roderick P. II. Maydeu-Olivares, Albert.
III. McArdle, John J. IV. Series.

  BF39.C594 2005
  150′.1′5195–dc22   2005003324

Printed in the United States of America
10 9 8 7 6 5 4 3 2 1

This book is dedicated to Rod McDonald,
our mentor, colleague, and friend

Roderick P. McDonald

The editors would also like to dedicate the book

A mis padres, Alberto y Margarita (A M-O)
A mi esposa, Carola (JJM)

Contents

Preface

With the approach of Roderick P. McDonald's retirement, a group of former students, colleagues, and friends gathered to honor him celebrating his contributions to psychometrics in the form of this Festschrift volume and a reunion. As Rod had been elected president of the Society of Multivariate Experimental Psychology in 2002, we used this occasion as the date and location of our celebration. "Advances in Psychometrics. A Day to Honor Roderick P. McDonald" took place at the Rotunda of the University of Virginia, Charlottesville, on October 20, 2002. Many of us gathered at a day-long meeting to praise him and present the chapters that now make up this volume. Some of us, like his long-time friend and colleague Colin Fraser, showed up as a surprise.

In many cases, these talks were impromptu, but in all cases, they were inspired. It was clear that each person had a slightly different story to tell, some as colleagues and some as students. However, a common theme emerged clearly—Rod McDonald personally affected both our work and our life. For all of us, this became an inspiring occasion, and, as a collective, we realized we have been trying to follow the strong principles advocated by Rod since we first encountered him. To Rod, it was a very emotion-filled occasion, and in his presentation he cited from classical verse. "I feel," he said, "like an ancient Roman being driven in a chariot for his triumph, and need someone standing behind me whispering, 'Remember, Caesar, that you are mortal.'"

This book is intended as a celebration of the seminal work of Rod McDonald over a career that has spanned more than 40 years and three continents. This work has covered a wide range of topics in psychometrics, and has inspired us in different areas of the field. The chapters included here cover most of the areas Rod has worked on over these years. The chapters are organized in four diverse sections: test theory, factor analysis, structural equation modeling, and multivariate analysis. Yet, a common theme can be found in Rod McDonald's work—the search for a unified framework of psychometric theory. We hope that this volume makes a small contribution toward this goal.

The first section of the book, *test theory*, includes topics such as multidimensional item response theory, the relationship between item response theory and factor analysis, estimation and testing of these models (limited information vs. full information), and a reflection on basic measurement issues that are often neglected. The second section, *factor analysis*, includes topics such as the history and development of the model, issues such as factorial invariance and factor analysis indeterminacy, and Bayesian inference for factor scores and parameter estimates. The third section of the book, *structural equation modeling*, includes a thorough discussion of the reticular action rules for latent-variable structural equation modeling, a survey of goodness-of-fit assessment in these models, resampling methods in structural equation modeling, a discussion of how to compare correlations between and within independent samples, the represention of psychological processes with dynamic factor models based on autoregressive moving-average time series models, and multilevel factor analysis models for both continuous and discrete data. The final section, *multivariate analysis*, includes topics such as dual scaling of ordinal data, model specification, and missing-data problems in time series models, and concludes with a chapter discussing various themes that run through all multivariate methods.

Thus, this book is a thorough, but necessarily incomplete, journey through contemporary psychometrics intended for advanced graduate student's researcher's in the social and behavioral sciences, and methodologists from other disciplines who wish to keep up to date with our discipline.

This volume could not have been completed without the assistance and support provided by many individuals. First, we thank all the contributors for their time and effort in preparing chapters for this volume. We also thank Carlos García-Forero and Uwe Kramp for preparing this volume's indices. Special thanks are due to Avis McDonald for supplying us with Rod's personal history. We are also greatly indebted to Larry Erlbaum for including this volume in the Multivariate Applications Series, and to the Series Editor, Lisa Harlow. Thanks are also due to Debra Riegert, Kerry Breen, and all the wonderful people on the editorial staff at Lawrence Erlbaum Associates, Inc., for their assistance and support in putting together this volume.

—Albert Maydeu-Olivares
—John J. McArdle

Roderick P. McDonald: A Personal History

Roderick Peter McDonald was born on April 16, 1928, in Sydney, Australia. His father was an accountant, his mother a trained nurse. Both very "modern" parents, they quietly encouraged him in academic pursuits and in his developing interests in classical music, swimming, and sailing. He grew up with boats at their waterfront house in an inner suburb of Sydney. At Fort St. Boys' High School, a school selecting on the basis of I.Q. and remarkable for the excellence of its teachers, he was torn between a love of literature and languages and a love of mathematics and physics.

After completing a Master of Science degree in physics at the University of Sydney in 1950, Rod worked first in London and later in Sydney in experimental physics. Wishing to pursue studies for a degree in English literature, he returned to the University of Sydney as a part-time student. He says he was side-tracked into psychology by higher grades, prizes, and the award of the University Medal in that subject. Appointed in 1958 as an instructor in psychology at the University of New England (located in the district of that name in northern New South Wales), he taught and carried out research in experimental psychology, publishing a number of papers in space perception and in learning theory.

Teaching an undergraduate course on abilities, and giving a lecture on the elements of factor analysis, he asked the class—and himself—what would happen to the model if the regression of the test scores on the factors were nonlinear. Contemplating his own question led him to his first set of answers, which became his doctoral dissertation, completed in 1964 under the supervision of John Keats, then at the University of Queensland, and published in 1967 as Psychometric Monograph No. 15. This marked his move from experimental psychology into measurement. The theory of nonlinear factor analysis, supported by the use of harmonic analysis to "linearize" strictly nonlinear models (such as the normal ogive and latent distance models), gave a unified and general treatment of factor theory, item response theory, and Lazarsfeld's latent structure models, accompanied by a set of exploratory techniques for differentiating among the models in applications.

Following completion of his doctorate, Rod spent 1965 on a Fulbright scholarship at the Educational Testing Service in Fred Lord's research group, along with Karl Jöreskog, Walter Kristoff, Mel Novick, and others. Further papers and computer programs resulted from this visit.

Back at the University of New England, he produced a group of papers on psychometric applications of the general eigenproblem, beginning with "A unified treatment of the weighting problem" (1968) and completed by "Alternative weights and invariant parameters in optimal scaling" (1983). The latter reinterpreted optimal scaling as an item response model for unordered category data. This group of papers represented another facet of the generalization and unification of theory that has tended to be the hallmark of Rod's research.

In 1969 he was invited to join the Ontario Institute for Studies in Education of the University of Toronto, where he formed a research group with colleagues and graduate students, some of whose work is represented in this book. Rod found this a very exciting and stimulating period, working with excellent students, a list of whom includes Hari Swaminathan, Gwyn Boodoo, and Bill Krane. He spent 12 years there in the Department of Measurement and Evaluation, teaching alongside such friends and colleagues as Shizuhiko Nishisato and Ross Traub. In this period he worked mainly on a general treatment of covariance structure modeling, introducing, with Swaminathan, a symbolic matrix calculus that simplified the writing of first and second matrix derivatives. The resulting COSAN program, written by Colin Fraser, was the first program capable of fitting nonstandard covariance structures, including, for example, the normal ogive model. The popular NOHARM program was derived from this application of COSAN. Many features of the COSAN program are now included in PROC CALIS as developed by Wolfgang Hartmann.

Rod says that in this period he "regretfully and regrettably" became involved in an ancient debate about the definition and determinacy of latent traits. He came out of it with a strengthened belief that Guttman was right when he declared that common factors/latent traits require infinite behavior domains for their definition. Behavior domain theory accordingly became an important element in his treatment, much later, of test theory.

Another important piece of what he regards as the psychometric jigsaw puzzle was "The simultaneous estimation of factor loadings and scores" (1979). This paper solved a problem, noted by Anderson and Rubin, in connection with earlier work by Lawley. They showed that in Lawley's attempt to get likelihood estimates of structural and incidental parameters, the likelihood did not have a maximum. Rod showed that in such cases, suitable maximum-likelihood-ratio estimators exist when maximum likelihood estimators do not. This theory in turn allowed the development (with Jamshid Etezadi) of a maximum-likelihood-ratio treatment of nonlinear factor models and, in principle, nonlinear structural equation models, using a version of the expectation-maximization algorithm.

In 1981 Rod returned home to Sydney, to the School of Education, Macquarie University. He functioned there as professor of education across a number of fields, including, for example, teaching a course on philosophy of science, an interest he has pursued since his undergraduate years. His textbook *Factor Analysis and*

Related Methods (published by Lawrence Erlbaum Associates Inc., in 1985) from this period surprised some readers by its lack of mathematical complexity.

Rod was elected president of the Psychometric Society in 1984. In his presidential address in Toronto in 1986—which contained cartoons instead of mathematics—he outlined the picture of a general and unified account of psychometric theory that has been the main goal of his research. Work with Harvey Goldstein at the London University Institute of Education while on sabbatical leave there led to the next phase of the search for generality, reported in four papers (1988 through 1993) on general structural models for multilevel/hierarchical data. In 1990 he was awarded a Doctor of Science degree by Macquarie University in recognition of the generality and unity of his oeuvre.

He was invited to join the Quantitative Division of the Department of Psychology, University of Illinois, when mandatory retirement was only a few years ahead in the Australian system. He began work there in 1991. Rod had two main objectives for this (continuing) phase of his career, in the form of books to be written. One has been completed, and the other is still in preparation under contract with Lawrence Erlbaum Associates, Inc. The first, *Test Theory: A Unified Treatment* (published by Lawrence Erlbaum Associates, Inc., in 1999) rather unobtrusively uses the framework established in his first monograph on nonlinear factor analysis to relate classical linear models to the nonlinear models of item response theory, yielding a unified account of measurement. The second, a book on structural models, aims to give a similarly unified and general account of the foundations of structural equation/causal models. Again, Rod enjoyed the stimulation of working with excellent graduate students, such as Albert Maydeu-Olivares and Dan Bolt, and developing his new books with their interests in mind.

Motivated by the desire for a unified treatment of the foundations of structural models, he has also produced a number of articles on basic theory in this recent period. "Path analysis with composite variables" (1996) supplies a rigorous mathematical account of Wold's partial least squares. This algorithm has evoked considerable interest among many applied researchers, whereas its mathematical and logical foundations remained obscure until Rod's investigation. This work also provided a direct link between weighted combinations of variables connected by path models and the special cases treated in his much earlier work on composites yielding eigenvalue treatments.

"Haldane's lungs: A case study in path analysis" (1997) questioned conventional wisdom on the foundational assumptions of path analysis. According to Rod, it was written with some levity after a more solemn and technical account was rejected by reviewers who said that these foundations (in spite of contradictions between theorists) were well understood and could not be questioned.

At a stage in his career where it might seem a daunting task to understand a large literature on a totally new field of applied mathematics, Rod undertook an intensive examination of work on the application to causal modeling of directed acyclic graph theory, with guidance from Judea Pearl, who contributed much of that theory. "What can we learn from the path equations?" (2002) gives an algebraic account of a number of the fundamental results of this theory, thus linking it to the mathematics of structural equations. Each of the last three studies mentioned is regarded by Rod as a piece of the jigsaw puzzle in a general, unified account of structural models, on which he is still working.

At the 2001 meeting of the Society for Multivariate Experimental Psychology, Rod received the Sells Award for outstanding contributions to multivariate experimental psychology, and was also elected president of the Society. Following the 2002 meeting of the Society, many of his former students, friends, and colleagues gathered at the University of Viriginia in a 1-day meeting in his honor. In 2004, at 76, Rod McDonald retired from the University of Illinois and moved back to his beloved Sydney, where he keeps working.

He says that looking back, he is not sorry he was side-tracked from his beloved 16th-century poets into psychology, because poetry and fiction remain as interests and topics of conversation with his wife, Avis, a professor of English literature. He also has continued his enjoyment of swimming and small-boat sailing, and takes every opportunity to snorkel around coral reefs, mostly in Jamaica and Australia. Avis and Rod's home is on the outskirts of Sydney, on the edge of a large river, and needs a boat for access. Rod takes pleasure in having had a number of colleagues and past students visit there. Rod's four children from "life before Avis"—Sallie, Peter, Christine, and Stephanie—are all settled in Australia.

R. P. McDONALD: PUBLICATIONS[1]

Reaction potential and the intervening variable question. *Australian Journal of Psychology*, 1960a, *12*, 149–161.

(with A. J. Yates). Hammer's critique of Eysenck's dimensional psychology. *Australian Journal of Psychology*, 1960b, *12*, 212–218.

Hullian theory and Thurstone's judgment model. *Australian Journal of Psychology*, 1962a, *14*, 23–28.

An artifact of the Brunswik ratio. *American Journal of Psychology*, 1962b, *75*, 152–154.

Apparent interposition in binocular depth perception. *American Journal of Psychology*, 1962c, *75*, 619–623.

Note on the derivation of the general latent class model. *Psychometrika*, 1962d, *27*, 203–206.

A general approach to nonlinear factor analysis. *Psychometrika*, 1962e, *27*, 397–415.

(with Patricia T. O'Hara) Size–distance invariance and perceptual constancy. *American Journal of Psychology*, 1964a, *20*, 276–289.

Factor analytic vs classical methods of fitting individual curves. *Perceptual and Motor Skills*, 1964b, *20*, 270.

Difficulty factors and nonlinear factor analysis. *British Journal of Mathematical and Statistical Psychology*, 1965a, *18*, 11–23.

Numerical methods for polynomial models in nonlinear factor analysis (Research Bulletin RB-65-32), 1965b, Educational Testing Service, Princeton, NJ.

---

[1] An asterisk indicates senior author if not R. P. M.

Some IBM 7090-94 programs for nonlinear factor analysis (Research Memorandum RM-65-11), 1965c, Educational Testing Service, Princeton, NJ.

(with A. J. Yates) Reminiscence as a function of perceptual search. *Australian Journal of Psychology*, 1966, *18*, 137–143.

Nonlinear factor analysis (Psychometric Monographs, No. 15), 1967a.

Numerical methods for polynomial models in nonlinear factor analysis. *Psychometrika*, 1967b, *32*, 77–112.

Some IBM 7090-94 programs for nonlinear factor analysis. *Behavioral Science*, 1976c, *12*, 72–74.

PROTEAN—A comprehensive CD 3200/3600 program for nonlinear factor analysis (Research Memorandum RM-67-26), 1967d, Educational Testing Service, Princeton, NJ.

Factor interaction in nonlinear factor analysis. *British Journal of Mathematical and Statistical Psychology*, 1967e, *20*, 205–215.

Some applications of a unified theory of weighting. *Australian Psychologist*, 1967f, *2*(1).

Towards a unified theory of linear psychometric models. *Australian Psychologist*, 1967g, *2*(1).

(with E. J. Burr) A comparison of four methods of constructing factor scores. *Psychometrika*, 1967, *32*, 381–401.

A CD 3200/3600 program for nonlinear factor analysis. *Behavioral Science*, 1968a, *13*, 513–515.

A unified treatment of the weighting problem. *Psychometrika*, 1968b, *33*, 351–381.

A generalized common factor analysis based on residual covariance matrices of prescribed structure. *British Journal of Mathematical and Statistical Psychology*, 1969a, *22*, 149–163.

The common factor analysis of multicategory data. *British Journal of Mathematical and Statistical Psychology*, 1969b, *22*, 165–175.

Problems of teaching the mathematical foundations of psychology. *International Journal of Psychology*, 1969c, *4*, 239–246.

Three common factor models for groups of variables. *Psychometrika*, 1970a, *35*, 111–128.

The theoretical foundations of common factor analysis, canonical factor analysis, and alpha factor analysis. *British Journal of Mathematical and Statistical Psychology*, 1970b, *23*, 1–21.

Weighted combinations of variables. In J. P. Sutcliffe (Ed.), *Mathematics in the social sciences in Australia* (pp. 517–530). Canberra: Australian Government Publishing Service, 1972.

(with H. Swaminathan) *The structural analysis of dispersion matrices based on a very general model with a rapidly convergent procedure for the estimation of parameters*. Informal publication, Department of Measurement and Evaluation, Ontario Institute for Studies in Education, 1972.

(with H. Swaminathan) A simple matrix calculus with applications to multivariate analysis. *General Systems*, 1973, *18*, 37–54.

Testing pattern hypotheses for covariance matrices. *Psychometrika*, 1974a, *39*, 189–201.

The measurement of factor indeterminacy. *Psychometrika*, 1974b, *39*, 203–222.

(with K. Ahlawat) Difficulty factors in binary data. *British Journal of Mathematical and Statistical Psychology*, 1974c, *27*, 82–99.

A note on Rippe's test of significance in common factor analysis. *Psychometrika*, 1975a, *40*, 117–119.

Descriptive axioms for common factor theory, image theory, and component theory. *Psychometrika*, 1975b, *40*, 137–152.

Testing pattern hypotheses for correlation matrices. *Psychometrika*, 1975c, *40*, 253–255.

A note on monotone polygons fitted to bivariate data. *Psychometrika*, 1975d, *40*, 543–546.

(with J. K. Martin*) Bayesian estimation in unrestricted factor analysis: A treatment for Heywood cases. *Psychometrika*, 1975, *40*, 505–517.

The McDonald–Swaminathan calculus: clarifications, extensions and illustrations. *General Systems*, 1976, *21*, 87–94.

The indeterminacy of components and the definition of common factors. *British Journal of Mathematical and Statistical Psychology*, 1977, *30*, 165–176.

(with A. R. Hakstian* & J. V. Zidek) Best univocal estimates of orthogonal common factors. *Psychometrika*, 1977, *42*, 627–630.

(with W. R. Krane) A note on local identifiability and degrees of freedom in the asymptotic likelihood ratio test. *British Journal of Mathematical and Statistical Psychology*, 1977, *30*, 198–203.

(with S. A. Mulaik*) The effect of additional variables on factor indeterminacy in models with a single common factor. *Psychometrika*, 1978a, *43*, 177–192.

The factor analysis of partial covariance matrices. *Psychometrika*, 1978b, *43*, 121–122.

A simple comprehensive model for the analysis of covariance structures. *British Journal of Mathematical and Statistical Psychology*, 1978c, *31*, 59–72.

Some checking procedures for extension analysis. *Multivariate Behavioral Research*, 1978d, *13*, 319–325.

The definition and determinacy of common factors. In J. P. Sutcliffe (Ed.), *Conceptual analysis and method in psychology: Essays in honour of W. M. O'Neil* (pp. 33–40). Sydney: Sydney University Press, 1978e.

Generalizability in factorable domains: Domain validity and generalizability. *Educational and Psychological Measurement*, 1978f, *38*, 76–79.

(with W. R. Krane*) Scale-invariant estimators in common factor analysis and related models. *British Journal of Mathematical and Statistical Psychology*, 1978, *31*, 218–228.

The structure of multivariate data: A sketch of a general theory. *Multivariate Behavioral Research*, 1979a, *14*, 21–38.

The simultaneous estimation of factor loadings and scores. *British Journal of Mathematical and Statistical Psychology*, 1979b, *32*, 212–228.

(with S. A. Mulaik) Determinacy of common factors: A non-technical review. *Psychological Bulletin*, 1979, *86*, 297–306.

(with Y. Torii & S. Nishisato) Some results on proper eigenvalues and eigenvectors with applications to scaling. *Psychometrika*, 1979, *44*, 211–227.

(with W. R. Krane) A Monte Carlo study of local identifiability and degrees of freedom in the asymptotic likelihood ratio test. *British Journal of Mathematical and Statistical Psychology*, 1979, *32*, 121–132.

A simple comprehensive model for the analysis of covariance structures: Some remarks on applications. *British Journal of Mathematical and Statistical Psychology*, 1980, *33*, 161–183.

The dimensionality of tests and items. *British Journal of Mathematical and Statistical Psychology*, 1981a, *34*, 100–117.

Constrained least squares estimators of oblique common factors. *Psychometrika*, 1981b, *46*, 337–341.

Linear versus nonlinear models in item response theory. *Applied Psychological Measurement*, 1982a, *6*, 379–396.

A note on the investigation of local and global identifiability. *Psychometrika*, 1982b, *47*, 101–103.

Some alternative approaches to the improvement of measurement in education and psychology: fitting latent trait models. In D. Spearitt (Ed.), *The improvement of measurement in education and psychology* (pp. 213–237). Hawthorn: Australian Council for Educational Research, 1982c.

Exploratory and confirmatory nonlinear factor analysis. In H. Wainer & S. Messick (Eds.), *Principals of modern psychological measurement: A Festschrift for Frederick M. Lord* (pp. 197–213). Hillsdale, NJ: Lawrence Erlbaum Associates, Inc., 1983a.

Alternative weights and invariant parameters in optimal scaling. *Psychometrika*, 1983b, *48*, 377–391.

(with J. Etezadi*) A second generation nonlinear factor analysis. *Psychometrika*, 1983, *48*, 315–342.

(with W. F. Velicer) Time series analysis without model identification. *Multivariate Behavioral Research*, 1984a, *19*, 33–47.

Confirmatory models for nonlinear structural analysis. In E. Diday (Ed.), *Data analysis and informatics, III* (pp. 425–432). Amsterdam: Elsevier, 1984.

(with J. J. McArdle*) Some algebraic properties of the reticular action model for moment structures. *British Journal of Mathematical and Statistical Psychology*, 1984, *37*, 234–251.

The invariant factors model for multimode data. In H. G. Law, C. W. Snyder, J. A. Hattie, & R. P. McDonald (Eds.), *Multimode data analysis* (pp. 283–307). New York: Praeger, 1985a.

Factor analysis and related methods. Hillsdale, NJ: Lawrence Erlbaum Associates, Inc., 1985b.

Comments on D. J. Bartholomew, Foundations of factor analysis: Some practical implications. *British Journal of Mathematical and Statistical Psychology*, 1985c, *38*, 134–137.

Unidimensional and multidimensional models for item response theory. In D. J. Weiss (Ed.), *Proceedings of the 1982 Item Response and Computerized Adaptive Testing Conference* (pp. 127–148). Minneapolis: University of Minnesota Press, 1985d.

(with J. R. Balla*) Latent trait item analysis and facet theory—A useful combination. *Applied Psychological Measurement*, 1985, *9*, 191–198.

A survey of some studies in methods for the structural analysis of multivariate data in the social sciences. *Interchange*, 1986a, *17*, 25–40.

Describing the elephant: Structure and function in multivariate data (Presidential address to the Psychometric Society). *Psychometrika*, 1986b, *51*, 513–534.

(with D. J. Bartholomew*) Foundations of factor analysis: A further comment. *British Journal of Mathematical and Statistical Psychology*, 1986, *39*, 228–229.

The first and second laws of intelligence. In A. Watson (Ed.), *Intelligence: controversy and change* (pp. 78–85). Melbourne: Australian Council for Education Research, 1988.

An item response curve for unordered multicategory data. In R. Heath (Ed.), *Current issues in cognitive development and mathematical psychology: John A. Keats Festschrift Conference* (pp. 75–86). Newcastle, UK: Department of Psychology, University of Newcastle, 1988b.

(with H. Goldstein*). A general model for the analysis of multilevel data. *Psychometrika*, 1988, *53*, 455–467.

(with H. W. Marsh* & J. Balla) Goodness-of-fit indexes in confirmatory factor analysis: The effect of sample size. *Psychological Bulletin*, 1988, *103*, 391–410.

(with C. Fraser*). NOHARM: Least squares item factor analysis. *Multivariate Behavioral Research*, 1988, 23, 267–269.

Future directions in item response theory. *International Journal of Educational Research*, 1989a, *13*, 205–220.

An index of goodness-of-fit based on noncentrality. *Journal of Classification*, 1989b, *6*, 97–103.

(with H. Goldstein) Balanced versus unbalanced designs for linear structural relations in two-level data. *British Journal of Mathematical and Statistical Psychology*, 1989, *42*, 215–232.

(with H. W. Marsh) Choosing a multivariate model: Noncentrality and goodness-of-fit. *Psychological Bulletin*, 1990, *107*, 247–255.

(with W. F. Velicer*) Cross-sectional time series designs: A general transformation approach. *Multivariate Behavioral Research*, 1991, *26*, 247–254.

(with W. M. Hartmann) A procedure for obtaining initial values of parameters in the RAM model. *Multivariate Behavioral Research*, 1992, *27*, 57–76.

A general model for two-level data with responses missing at random. *Psychometrika*, 1993, *58*, 575–585.

(with P. M. Parker & T. Ishizuka) A scale-invariant treatment for recursive path models. *Psychometrika*, 1993, *58*, 431–443.

The bilevel reticular action model for path analysis with latent variables. *Sociological Methods and Research*, 1994a, *22*, 399–413.

Testing for approximate dimensionality. In D. Laveault et al. (Eds.), *Modern theories of measurement: Problems and issues* (pp. 63–86). Ottawa: University of Ottawa Press, 1994b.

(with M. Mok*) Quality of school life: A scale to measure student experience or school climate? *Educational and Psychological Measurement*, 1994, *54*, 483–499.

Testing for equivalence of measurement scales: A comment. *Multivariate Behavioral Research*, 1995a, *30*, 87–88.

Not only but also. *Multivariate Behavioral Research*, 1995b, *30*, 113–115.

(with Mok, M.-C.) Goodness of fit in item response models. *Multivariate Behavioral Research*, 1995c, *30*, 23–40.

Latent traits and the possibility of motion. *Multivariate Behavioral Research*, 1996a, *31*, 593–601.

Consensus emergens: A matter of interpretation. *Multivariate Behavioral Research*, 1996b, *31*, 663–672.

Path analysis with composite variables. *Multivariate Behavioral Research*, 1996c, *31*, 239–270.

(with N. G. Waller,* A. Tellegen, & D. T. Lykken) Exploring nonlinear models in personality assessment: Development and preliminary validation of a negative emotionality scale. *Journal of Personality*, 1996, *64*, 545–576.

Goodness of approximation in the linear model. In L. L. Harlow, S. A. Mulaik, & J. H. Steiger (Eds.), *What if there were no significance tests?* (pp. 199–219). Mahwah, NJ: Lawrence Erlbaum Associates, Inc., 1997a.

The normal ogive multidimensional model. In W. J. Van der Linden & R. K. Hambledon (Eds.), *Handbook of item response theory* (pp. 257–269). New York: Springer-Verlag, 1997b.

Haldane's lungs: A case study in path analysis. *Multivariate Behavioral Research*, 1997c, *32*, 1–38.

(with D. M. Bolt) The determinacy of variables in structural equation models. *Multivariate Behavioral Research*, 1998, *33*, 385–401.

Test theory: A unified treatment, Mahwah, NJ: Lawrence Erlbaum Associates, Inc., 1999.

A basis for multidimensional item response theory. *Applied Psychological Measurement*, 2000, *24*, 99–114.

(with J. B. Nitschke,* W. Heller, J. C. Imig, & G. A. Miller) Distinguishing dimensions of anxiety and depression. *Cognitive Therapy and Research*, 2001, *25*, 1–22.

What can we learn from the path equations?: Identifiability, constraints, equivalence. *Psychometrika*, 2002a, *67*, 225–249.

(with M. H. Ho) Principles and practice in reporting structural equation analyses. *Psychological Methods*, 2002b, *7*. 64–82.

Behavior domains in theory and in practice. *Alberta Journal of Educational Research*, 2003, *49*, 212–230.

Respecifying improper structures. *Structural Equation Modeling*, 2004, *11*, 194–209.

The informative analysis of longitudinal data. *Multivariate Behavioral Research*, 2004b, *39*, 517–563.

The specific analysis of structural equation models. *Multivariate Behavioral Research*, in press.

I

Test Theory

Modern test theory revolves around modeling categorical data using nonlinear latent trait models, what has been called in the educational testing literature "item response theory" (IRT). What has now become the standard in IRT modeling seems to be focused on unidimensional models estimated using full-information maximum likelihood estimation (e.g., Lord, 1980). Throughout his career, Rod McDonald has taken a different stance on the topic (e.g., McDonald, 1999). On the one hand, he has empathized with multidimensional models (e.g., McDonald, 2000). On the other hand, he has advocated limited-information estimation and goodness-of-fit testing methods (e.g., McDonald, 1985; McDonald & Mok, 1995). Perhaps the best-known contribution of McDonald to this field is the NOHARM program (Fraser & McDonald, 1988), which is capable of fitting the multidimensional normal ogive model to a virtually unlimited number of items with a virtually unlimited number of latent trait dimensions using limited-information methods.

In the first chapter in this part **Terry Ackerman** provides graphical examples of how multidimensional IRT can be used by testing practitioners to better understand test response data. The chapter begins by reviewing IRT models from both the factor-analytic perspective of McDonald (1999) and the traditional IRT approach of Lord (1980). It concludes with a brief discussion of future directions for multidimensional IRT modeling. In the second chapter, **Daniel Bolt** reviews the main limited-information as well as full-information approaches in IRT estimation and concludes with a presentation of limited- and full-information estimation approaches using Markov chain Monte Carlo.

Albert Maydeu-Olivares deals with the relationship between the common factor model and IRT models. McDonald (1999) showed that in the case of binary data the factor model and a linear IRT model are equivalent when estimated using bivariate information. In this chapter, Maydeu-Olivares considers full-information estimation of the linear IRT model. He shows that no distribution of the latent traits is needed to estimate this model, and that most moments of the latent traits can be estimated. He also points out that a test proposed by Browne (1984) can be used to compare the goodness of fit of factor models and nonlinear IRT models (such as logistic models) to any given data set.

Finally, **John Horn** takes a step back and discusses basic measurement issues that, although they appear in contemporary writings on measurement, are not considered in the everyday research of behavioral scientists. Thus, the chapter discusses how measurement operations determine the shape of distributions and other important properties of measurements, how discriminability is related to distribution form, and how these matters relate to the use of statistics in behavioral science research.

REFERENCES

Browne, M. W. (1984). Asymptotically distribution free methods for the analysis of covariance structures. *British Journal of Mathematical and Statistical Psychology, 37,* 62–83.

Fraser, C., & McDonald, R. P. (1988). NOHARM: Least squares item factor analysis. *Multivariate Behavioral Research, 23,* 267–269.

Lord, F. M. (1980). *Applications of item response theory to practical testing problems.* Hillsdale, NJ: Lawrence Erlbaum Associates, Inc.

McDonald, R. P. (1985). Unidimensional and multidimensional models for item response theory. In D. J. Weiss (Ed.), *Proceedings of the 1982 Item Response and Computerized Adaptive Testing Conference* (pp. 127–148). Minneapolis: University of Minnesota Press.

McDonald, R. P. (1999). *Test theory. A unified approach.* Mahwah, NJ: Lawrence Erlbaum Associates.

McDonald, R. P. (2000). A basis for multidimensional item response theory. *Applied Psychological Measurement, 24,* 99–114.

McDonald, R. P., & Mok, M. C. (1995). Goodness of fit in item response models. *Multivariate Behavioral Research, 54,* 483–495.

1

Multidimensional Item Response Theory Modeling

Terry A. Ackerman
University of North Carolina at Greensboro

The purpose of this chapter is to provide graphical examples of how multidimensional item response theory (IRT) can be used by testing practitioners to better understand test response data. The chapter begins with a review of the unidimensional IRT model from both the factor- analytic perspective of McDonald (1999) and the traditional IRT approach of Lord (1980). These approaches are then extended to the two-dimensional case. Examples of how the two-dimensional model and corresponding graphical displays can help practitioners examine and validate their tests are discussed using item parameter estimates of 15 American College Testing (ACT) Mathematics Usage Test items. The chapter concludes with a brief discussion of future directions for multidimensional IRT modeling.

THE UNIDIMENSIONAL ITEM RESPONSE THEORY MODEL

As its name implies, the unidimensional test is assumed to be a collection of items that are measuring the same latent trait, θ, or common factor, F, even though they may vary in difficulty. Similarly, it is recognized that items differ in their ability to distinguish or discriminate among levels of proficiency of this latent trait. In factor analysis, it is also assumed that items have unique idiosyncrasies that are uncorrelated with the latent trait. This feature contributes to a unique or residual variance of each item. (This is an interesting departure from the traditional IRT model that does not have a residual component. Such residual error variance is "absorbed" in the estimation of the traditional discrimination, a, or difficulty, b, parameters.) These features are combined in the form of Spearman's single-factor model, that represents a scored response to an item i, Y_i, on an m-item unidimensional test by a random examinee as

$$Y_l = \mu_i + \lambda_i f + E_i, \qquad i = 1, \ldots, m, \tag{1}$$

where u_i is the mean score of item i (reflecting differences in item difficulty); f is the examinee's measure on the latent trait F; λ_i is the factor loading, which indicates the degree to which item i can distinguish among levels of the trait; and E_i is an idiosyncratic measure unique to the item. The variance of item i can be expressed as a linear combination of the factor loading and the variance of E (referred to as its *uniqueness*), ψ^2, as

$$\sigma_i^2 = \lambda_i^2 + \psi_i^2. \tag{2}$$

Equation 1 can also be thought of as expressing the regression of the scored responses onto latent ability F. Specifically, this equation can be rewritten as a conditional probability function for a correct response,

$$P\{Y = 1 | F = f\} = \lambda_i f + \pi, \tag{3}$$

where π is the proportion of correct responses.

However, when applied to dichotomously scored data this model has several weaknesses. First, the function is not bounded within the normal $0-1$ range of probability. Probabilities outside the range $0-1$ can occur if f is too small or too large. For example, McDonald (1999, p. 233) obtained the following estimates for Item 2 of the Law School Admissions Test 6 data: $\lambda = .1345$ and $\pi = .709$. For this item, if f is less than -5.27 on the latent ability scale, P is less than 0; if f is greater than 2.164, P is greater than 1.0. Second, the assumption that the error variance is independent of the total test score does not apply for dichotomously scored items. Third, the error of estimate for an item is constant throughout the observable range of F because the function is linear with a constant slope λ. This outcome also does not hold true for dichotomously scored items.

One approach to overcoming these weaknesses is to apply a nonlinear function appropriate for conditional probabilities, that is, to use the normal ogive model as a *link function* joining the probability of correct response to a linear function of the independent variable. Paralleling the conceptual framework of the biserial correlation, it is assumed that for a given dichotomously scored item i, an examinee has a latent response tendency Y_i, where

$$Y_i = \lambda_i F + E_i^*. \tag{4}$$

Because the Y_i are standardized with unit variance and a mean of zero, μ_i is dropped from the equation. If Y_i exceeds the item's threshold τ_i, the response will be scored as correct. If, however, $Y_i \leq \tau_i$, the response will be incorrect. Assuming that F and E_i^* are normally distributed implies that Y_i is also normally distributed. This leads to defining the probability of a correct response as

$$p\{Y_i = 1 | F = f\} = p\{Y_i > \tau_i | F = f\} = \Phi(z), \tag{5}$$

where $\Phi\,()$ is the normal ogive link function, and

$$z = \left[\frac{\lambda_i}{\sqrt{1 - \lambda_i^2}} \right] f - \left[\frac{1}{\sqrt{1 - \lambda_i^2}} \right] \tau_j. \tag{6}$$

McDonald (1999) denoted λ and τ as *common factor parameters* and the traditional IRT parameters a and b as response *factor parameters*. For a given item i, they are related by the formulas

$$b_i = \lambda_i / \sqrt{1 - \lambda_i^2} \tag{7}$$

and

$$a_i = -\tau_i / \sqrt{1 - \lambda_i^2}. \tag{8}$$

Note that the biserial correlation is conceptually equivalent to λ_i, the correlation between Y_i and F. Therefore, these formulas are analogous to the IRT–classical test theory (CTT) relationships given by Lord (1980). In Lord's work, the a and b parameters for a given item i are approximated in terms of the biserial correlation $\rho_{i\theta}$ and the standard normal deviate corresponding to the proportion correct π. McDonald's discrimination parameter b_i is analogous to Lord's a_i parameter. Lord expressed this parameter in terms of the biserial by the equation

$$a_i \cong \rho_{i\theta} / \sqrt{1 - \rho_{i\theta}^2} \ . \tag{9}$$

McDonald's difficulty parameter a_i is actually equivalent to Lord's $-a_i b_i$ formulation. This can be understood by comparing Equation 10 with Equation 7:

$$-ab \cong \left[\frac{\rho_{i\theta}}{\sqrt{1 - \rho_{i\theta}^2}} \right] \left[\frac{z(\pi)}{\rho_{i\theta}} \right] = \frac{z(\pi)}{\sqrt{1 - \rho_{i\theta}^2}}. \tag{10}$$

It must be noted that McDonald chose to follow notation that is common to regression theory, in which a is used for the intercept and b for the slope. This is the opposite of what is traditionally used in IRT. That is, in IRT, a is used to denote an item's discrimination parameter and b the item's difficulty parameter. Throughout this chapter, traditional designations will be followed to avoid confusion with traditional IRT notation.

Whereas many testing practitioners may be familiar with the IRT model, they rarely understand how the ICC gets it characteristic shape from the simple linear regression of the item score onto the latent ability. Figures 1.1 and 1.2 illustrate this relationship (Lord, 1980, p. 32).

The item shown in Fig. 1.1 is highly discriminating, with $r_{bis} = \lambda = .8$ ($a = 1.33$) and a low threshold (i.e., an easy item), $\tau = -.84$ ($b = -1.4$). The

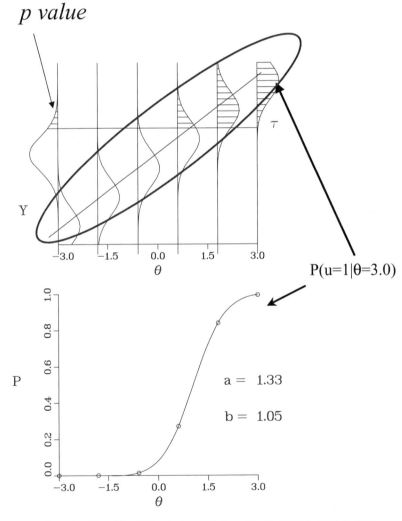

FIG. 1.1. Graphical illustration of the development of the item characteristic curve for a highly discriminating, easy item.

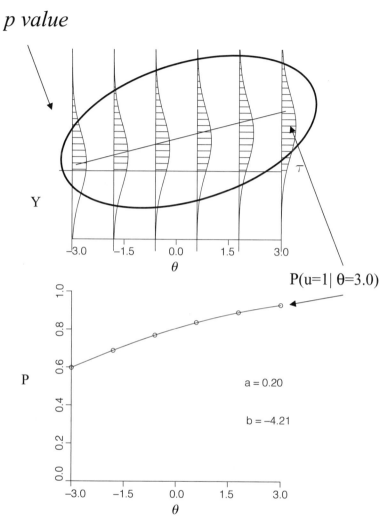

FIG. 1.2. Graphical illustration of the development of the item characteristic curve for a poorly discriminating, difficult item.

item shown in Fig. 1.2 has the opposite configuration, low discrimination with $r_{bis} = \lambda = .2$ $(a = 0.20)$ and a high threshold (i.e., a difficult item), $\tau = .84$ $(b = 0.86)$. The high biserial is portrayed by the narrow ellipse, the low biserial by a wider ellipse. This is equivalent to illustrating different values of a Pearson product–moment correlation in which one would sketch an ellipse enclosing a hypothetical bivariate distribution of values in scatter plot: The higher the correlation, the more linear is the relationship and thus the narrower is the ellipse. Drawn within each ellipse are the conditional normal ogive curves that follow directly from the assumption of simple linear regression. The proportion of the conditional distribution above the threshold line τ, indicated by cross-hatched area in the conditional distribution, corresponds to the proportion of those examinees at proficiency level θ who are expected to get the item correct. Thus, in Lord's notation, the score for item i, U_i, has the following dichotomy:

$$
\begin{array}{llll}
U_i = 1 & \text{if} & Y_i > t_i \\
U_i = 0 & \text{if} & Y_i \le t_i.
\end{array}
\tag{11}
$$

The proportion of the conditional distribution lying above the threshold is given by the traditional IRT normal ogive model formula:

$$
P_i(u = 1 | F = f) = P_i(u = 1 | \Theta = \theta) = \int_{-\infty}^{a(\theta - b)} \frac{1}{\sqrt{2\pi}} \exp\left(-\frac{1}{2}t^2\right) dt, \tag{12}
$$

where the integrand is the expression for the normal curve. The conditional distributions illustrate how the normal curve serves as a link function transforming the linear regression process to be transformed into conditional proportion correct.

In each figure, the corresponding item characteristic curve is plotted at the bottom of the figure. The height of the ICC at a given θ value is the proportion of the corresponding conditional distribution that lies above the threshold. In Fig. 1.2, the difficulty (p value) is quite low. The reader should also notice how the threshold has shifted up compared with Fig. 1.1 and that the ICC is both steeper (more discriminating) and is shifted to the right, indicating it is more difficult. Note further that in both figures, the proportion of the marginal distribution lying above the threshold corresponds to the p value, or the proportion of examinees who would be expected to answer the item correctly. More specifically, this follows because the threshold parameter τ_i is directly related to p value for item i by the formula

$$
\pi_i = \Phi(-\tau_i). \tag{13}
$$

Many practitioners tend to use the logistic form of Equation 12, known as the 2PL (i.e., the two-parameter logistic) IRT model:

$$
p(X = 1 | \theta) = \frac{1}{1 + e^{-1.7a(\theta - b)}}, \tag{14}
$$

where the 1.7 is a scaling constant to make the ICCs from the logistic model (Equation 14) and the normal ogive model (Equation 12) coincide.

THE MULTIDIMENSIONAL ITEM RESPONSE THEORY MODEL

Perhaps the best approach for extending the unidimensional response model to the multidimensional case is to use the factor analytic approach. McDonald extended the work of Christoffersson (1975) by formulating the two-dimensional model in terms of common factor parameters as

$$P\{X_i = 1 \mid F_1 = f_1, F_2 = f_2\} = \Phi\left[(\lambda_{i1}/\psi_i)f_1 + (\lambda_i/\psi_i)f_2 - (t/\psi_i)\right]. \quad (15)$$

In terms of item response function parameters, this can be written as

$$P\{X_i = 1 \mid \Theta_1 = \theta_1, \Theta_1 = \theta_1\} = \Phi\{a_{i1}\theta_1 + a_{i2}\theta_2 + d_i\}, \quad (16)$$

where the discrimination parameters a_{i1} and a_{i2} and the *location* parameter d_i can be expressed in terms of their factor-analytic counterparts as

$$a_{i1} = \lambda_{i1}/\psi_i$$
$$a_{i2} = \lambda_{i2}/\psi_i \quad (17)$$
$$d_i = -\tau/\psi_i.$$

It must be noted that d should not be considered a difficulty parameter, but rather a location parameter. The traditional logistic two-dimensional equivalent of Equation 14 is

$$P(X = 1 \mid \theta_1, \theta_2) = \frac{1}{1 + e^{-1.7(a_1\theta_1 + a_2\theta_2 + d)}}. \quad (18)$$

In this parametrization, there is a discrimination parameter for each latent dimension but only one location parameter. That is, individual location parameters per dimension are indeterminable.

The factor-analytic model offers a better perspective for examining the development of this model because it enables one to determine the correlation between the latent abilities, something the logistic model does not allow for. Specifically, for the two-factor solution where F_1 and F_2 are the two factors or latent abilities, $\rho_{(F_1, F_1)} = \phi_{1,2}$. The underlying composite is then scaled so that the item uniqueness ψ_j can be expressed as

$$\psi_j = \sqrt{1 - \lambda_1^2 - \lambda_2^2 - 2\lambda_1\lambda_2\phi_{12}}. \quad (19)$$

Item parameter estimates derived using Equations 16 and 18 can thus be adjusted to account for the degree of correlation between the latent abilities. For example, an item with common factor parameter values $\lambda_1 = .8$ and $\lambda_2 = .2$ will have IRT parameters of $a_1 = 1.41$ and $a_2 = 0.35$ when $\phi = 0$. However, if $\phi = .5$, a_1 increases to 2.0 and a_2 becomes 0.5. Thus, as the correlation between abilities increases, the error decreases and the IRT discrimination parameters increase. Rescaling a set of item parameters to the metric of another set of item parameters must take differences in correlation into account (Davey, Oshima, & Lee, 1996).

Another advantage is that the factor-analytic approach allows one to assume a confirmatory framework and thus test theoretical assumptions about what specific items are being measured. That is, one can test the fit of whether items measuring certain content, different formats, or dissimilar cognitive characteristics form distinct factors or dimensions, and hence estimate the degree of correlation between them. This flexibility is extremely beneficial because it helps the testing practitioner establish empirical evidence for content or construct validity.

When extending the unidimensional model to the multidimensional case, conceptually things become more complicated to illustrate. Like its unidimensional counterpart, the two-dimensional model is based on the assumption that for each item i there is some threshold τ_i such that the scored response to item i, U_i, can be broken down into a dichotomy of a correct and an incorrect response as expressed in Equation 11.

In the two-dimensional case, the threshold is actually a threshold plane and at each (θ_1, θ_2) location in the latent ability plane there is a conditional normal curve. The area beyond the threshold plane in each normal conditional distribution, as in the unidimensional case, corresponds to the probability of correct response for examinees possessing this two-dimensional composite of proficiency. This relationship is graphically illustrated in Fig. 1.3. Although more complicated, the concept is a direct extension of the unidimensional case. To simplify the extension to the two-dimensional case, each figure is broken down into the progressive steps illustrating the construction of the item response surface (IRS). Beginning in the upper left are the three-dimensional axes $(\theta_1, \theta_2, Y$ [the propensity to answer the given item correctly]). To the right of the axes, the regression plane defined by $Y = a_1\theta_1 + a_2\theta_2$ has been added. In Fig. 1.3a, $a_2 = 0$; in Fig. 1.3b, $a_1 = a_2$; and in Fig. 1.3c, $a_1 = 0$. These correspond to the three type of items to be discussed in Table 1.1. These threshold planes correspond to the regression lines shown in Figs. 1.1 and 1.2. In the center left of each figure, the threshold plane now appears. In each case the threshold has been set to correspond to a p value of .5. In the center right of each figure, a row of condition normal distributions has been added. The cross-hatched portion above the threshold plane corresponds to the proportion of examinees at this (θ_1, θ_2) location expected to answer the item correctly. In Fig. 1.3a, the conditional normal distributions are only drawn in the row where $\theta_1 = -3$; in Fig. 1.3b, they are drawn in a direction where $\theta_1 = \theta_2$; and in Fig. 1.3c, they are drawn in a row where $\theta_2 = -3$. When taken in concert, these proportions form the item characteristic surface (ICS) shown at the bottom left of each figure. The corresponding contour is plotted in the lower right.

A popular computer program for estimating multidimensional item parameters for dichotomously scored data is NOHARM (Fraser, 1988). This program, which uses a nonlinear factor-analytic approach (McDonald, 1967), estimates item parameters in either an exploratory or a confirmatory mode. A user unsure

TABLE 1.1
Two-Dimensional Item Response Theory Parameters for 15 American College
Testing Mathematics Items Presented in McDonald (1999)

Item	a_1	a_2	d
1	1.85472	0.00000	−0.07506
2	1.09184	0.00000	1.24320
3	0.52948	0.00000	0.57740
4	0.94969	0.00000	−0.16195
5	0.63399	0.00000	−0.06536
6	0.00000	0.54265	−1.03832
7	0.00000	0.91077	−0.56462
8	0.00000	0.45358	−0.74148
9	0.00000	0.00120	−0.00130
10	0.00000	0.45701	−0.30624
11	0.68352	0.68727	−1.00375
12	0.64428	0.65880	−0.13430
13	0.63139	0.61552	−0.03351
14	0.36260	0.70894	−0.51545
15	−0.38999	0.63795	−1.16531

of any underlying structure uses the exploratory mode of NOHARM. However, if a particular factor structure is hypothesized, then the confirmatory mode should be used. In this mode, the user specifies which dimension(s) each item is measuring (i.e., simple or complex structure). Unfortunately, NOHARM does not have the capability of estimating individual examinee multidimensional proficiencies.

Over the last decade, NOHARM has emerged as a leading program for estimating item parameters for multidimensional models. Balassiano and Ackerman (1995) and Ackerman, Kelkar, Neustel, and Simpson (2001) investigated the accuracy of the estimation process used by NOHARM. Their research shows that NOHARM is fairly accurate in recovering two-dimensional item parameters from generated data when the correlation between abilities is low, but becomes progressively worse as the correlation between abilities increases to greater than .7.

Graphical Applications of the Two-Dimensional Model

Considerable insight about multidimensional items and tests can be gained using graphical representations. Based on the work of Reckase and McKinley (1985) and Ackerman (1996), testing practitioners can translate the item parameter estimates into figures that help them to better understand what composites are actually being measured by their test.

(a)

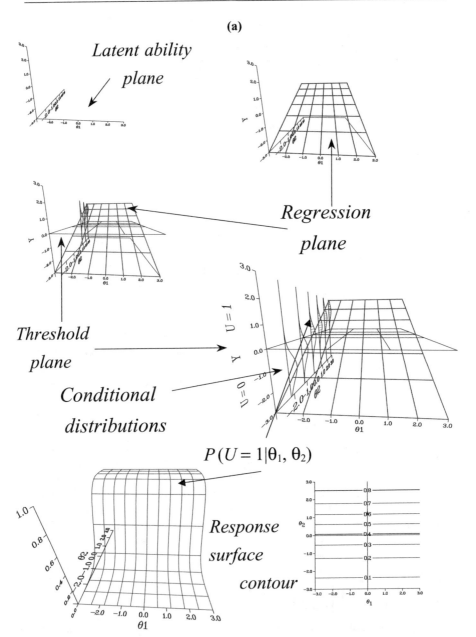

FIG. 1.3. Graphical illustration of the development of a two-dimensional response surface for (a) the item $a_1 = 0.0$, $a_2 = 1.2$, and $d = 0.0$; (b) the item $a_1 = 1.2$, $a_2 = 1.2$, and $d = 0.0$, and (c) the item $a_1 = 1.2$, $a_2 = 0.0$ and $d = 0.0$.

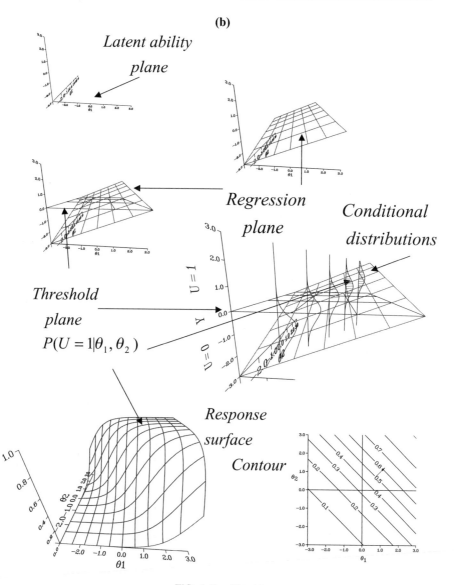

FIG. 1.3. (Cont.)

To begin, consider the parameter estimates computed for a 15-item subset of the ACT Mathematics Usage Test presented in McDonald (1999) and shown in Table 1.1. McDonald specifically chose these parameters because they represent the two-dimensional basis. That is, the first five measure primarily the first factor, the second five measure only the second factor, and the last five are *factorially complex* and load on or measure both factors. These parameter estimates have

(c)

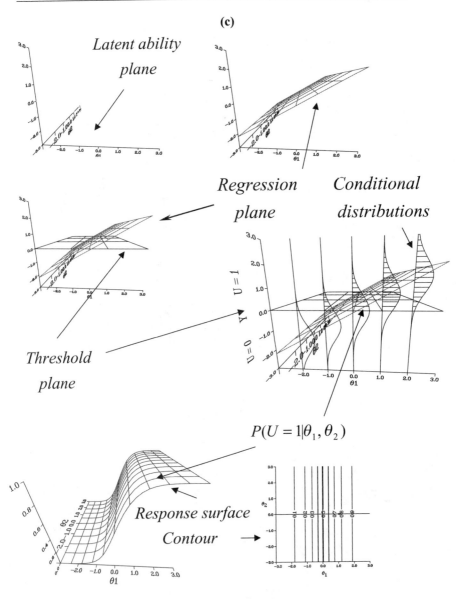

FIG. 1.3. (Cont.)

been converted from McDonald's common factor parameters to two-dimensional IRT parameters using Equation 16.

As previously illustrated, as we move from a single latent skill to the two-dimensional case, the unidimensional ICC becomes the item characteristic surface. This surface represents the probability that an examinee with a given (θ_1, θ_2) composite will correctly answer an item. The ICS for Item 2 ($a_1 = 1.09$, $a_2 = 0.0$,

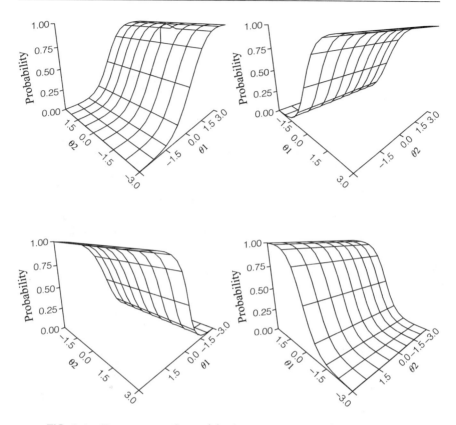

FIG. 1.4.   Four perspectives of the item response surface for Item 2.

$d = 1.24$) is presented in Fig. 1.4. The surface is represented from four different perspectives. This item is only distinguishing among levels of θ_1. Hence, this type of representation is not very informative.

A representation that is more readily interpretable is a contour plot of the ICS. These contours are actually equiprobability contours. That is, all examinees whose (θ_1, θ_2) composites lie on the same contour will have an equal probability of correct response to this item. The contours are parallel and become closer as the slope of the response surface becomes steeper or more discriminating. The contours also help to identify the composite of skills that is being best measured. Specifically, moving across or orthogonal to the contours provides the greatest change in probability of correct response. This direction represents the composite of skills that the item measures best.

A problem that arises with the ICS and contour plots is that they only represent a single item, and thus it becomes awkward to consider several items simultaneously. A more efficient way to represent several items is to represent individual items as vectors. Following the work of Reckase and McKinley (1991), we have each vector represent three item characteristics: discrimination, difficulty, and location. In the Cartesian coordinate system,[1] *discrimination* corresponds to the length of the item response vector (Reckase & McKinley, 1991). This length represents the maximum amount of discrimination, and is referred to as MDISC. For item i, MDISC is given by

$$\text{MDISC} = \sqrt{a_{i1}^2 + a_{i2}^2}, \tag{20}$$

where a_{i1} and a_{i2} are defined in terms of their common factor parameters in Equation 17. The tail of the vector lies on and is orthogonal to the $p = .5$ equiprobability contour. If extended, all vectors would pass through the origin. Because the a parameters are assumed to be positive (i.e., as ability increases, the probability of correct response increases), the item vectors are located only in the first and third quadrants. MDISC is analogous to the a parameter in unidimensional IRT.

Reckase (1985) formally defined multidimensional item difficulty as the signed distance from the origin to the $p = .5$ equiprobability contour. Denoted as D, it can be computed as

$$D = \frac{-d_i}{\text{MDISC}}, \tag{21}$$

where d_i, defined in Equation 17, is the location parameter for item i. The sign of this distance indicates the relative difficulty of the item. Items with negative D values are relatively easy and are located in the third quadrant, whereas items with positive D are relatively difficult and lie in first quadrant. D is analogous to the b parameter in unidimensional IRT.

The third component needed to draw a vector represents the composite the item is best measuring. This is described in terms of the angular direction relative to the positive θ_1 axis (Reckase & McKinley, 1991). For item i, this angle, α_i, is computed as

$$\alpha_i = \arccos \frac{a_{i1}}{\text{MDISC}_i}. \tag{22}$$

A vector with α_i equal to 45 deg is measuring both latent skills equally well. If a vector's angle is greater than 45 deg, the item is a better measure of θ_2 than θ_1, and if α_i is less than 45 deg, the reverse is true.

The vector for Item 11 is plotted on the item's contour in Fig. 1.5. Notice that the tail of the vector lies on and is orthogonal to the $p = .5$ equiprobability

---

[1] The two-dimensional latent ability space is represented on a Cartesian coordinate system despite the fact that most abilities are correlated. It has been suggested by some researchers that the angle between the axes represents the degree of correlation. However, for sake of clarity, an orthogonal axes system is used in which distance measures and vectors can be easily calculated, understood, and interpreted.

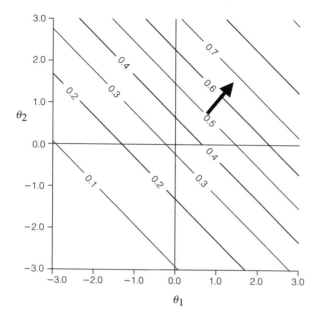

FIG. 1.5. The contour plot and corresponding item vector for Item 11.

contour. The more discriminating an item is, the closer together the contours will be, and hence the longer will be the item vector. Items will always be maximally discriminating at the $p = .5$ contour when there is no guessing.

Once these three components of the items vectors are computed, a plot containing all of the items can be created. These plots can also be used to compare items. For example, items of different content can be represented as different colors. Ideally, items substantively deemed to be measuring the same content would lie in a well-defined sector of the latent ability plane. Figure 1.6 contains the vector plot for the 15-item subset of items. Note that one item, Item 15, actually appears in the second quadrant. This result occurs because a_1 for the item is negative, and thus as an examinee's θ_1 ability increases, the chance of answering the item correctly actually decreases.

Vector plots can be color coded according to content. Such a plot would help to validate whether items substantively identified as measuring different contents indeed measure different ability composites within the latent ability plane. One also could determine whether certain item contents are more discriminating (i.e., longer vectors) or more difficult (i.e., vectors all lie in the first quadrant).

As with the unidimensional case, the individual ICSs can be added to produce the test characteristic surface (TCS). This surface represents the expected-number-correct score for all (θ_1, θ_2) composites throughout the latent ability plane. To be more concise, one can evaluate the contours corresponding to the TCS and determine where the test is best discriminating. Another use would be to evaluate

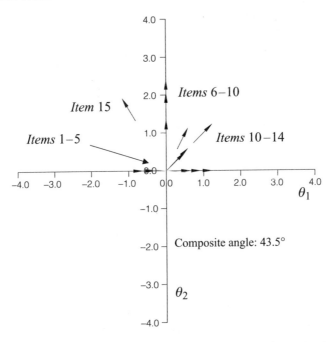

FIG. 1.6. A plot of the item vectors for the 15 ACT Mathematics items.

a particular cut-score and see what composite of the two latent skills would be expected to score greater than the cut-score and so the examinee would be admitted, licensed, or certified (Ackerman, 1994, 1996).

The TCS for the 15-item subset is shown in Fig. 1.7. Unlike the contour plot of the item characteristic surface, the contours denoting composites that would be expected to achieve the same proportion-correct score (i.e., same expected-proportion-correct true score) do not have to be parallel. For this to happen, all items would have to be measuring the exact same ability composite. Note how the contours curve. This is a result of the different composites being measured by Items 1–5 versus Items 6–10 versus Items 11–15.

Contour plots of the TCS are very important in certification or licensure tests that have a cut-score. Once such a cut-score has been determined (e.g., using a modified Angoff procedure), the testing practitioner can examine the contour of the TCS to determine what combinations of $\bar{\theta}_1$ and $\bar{\theta}_2$ are required to score above the established cut-score. This approach would provide insight about the different combinations of skills of those examinees that are being licensed or certified.

Another graphical representation that helps provide validation evidence of score scale consistency is the *centroid plot*. In this plot, the conditional centroid for each raw score, $(\bar{\theta}_1, \bar{\theta}_2 | X = x)$, is analytically computed for a specified underlying bivariate ability distribution and then plotted. It is important that the centroids

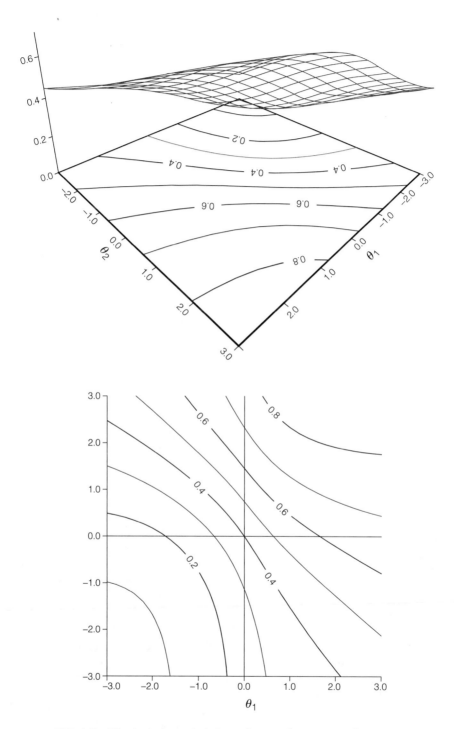

FIG. 1.7. The test characteristic surface and corresponding contour plot for the 15 ACT Mathematics items.

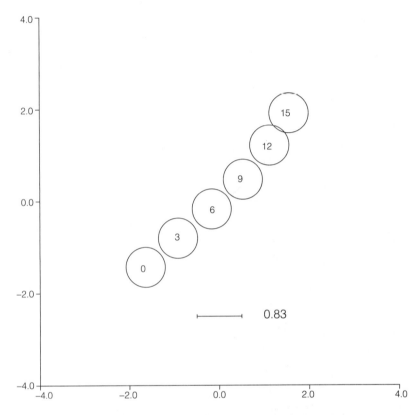

Conditional confidence ellipses

$$\sigma^2_{\theta_1} \quad > \quad \sigma^2_{\theta_2} \qquad \sigma^2_{\theta_1} \quad < \quad \sigma^2_{\theta_2}$$

FIG. 1.8.   Conditional centroids for different number correct scores.

form a straight line. This implies that the (θ_1, θ_2) composite is consistently being measured throughout the observable score scale. Any curvature in the centroids, say something where the centroids are horizontally aligned for low score values and vertically aligned for high score values, implies that differences among low scores represent differences in θ_1, whereas differences in high scores represent primarily differences in θ_2. This outcome could result from a confounding of difficulty with dimensionality (i.e., easy items measure primarily θ_1, difficult items measure primarily θ_2). The centroid plot for the raw scores from 0 to 15 in increments of 3 is shown in Fig. 1.8.

Ellipses about the centroids indicate the size of the θ_1 and θ_2 variances for the different conditional distributions. That is, the variance of the conditional θ_1 distribution corresponds to the x axis of the ellipse and the variance of the conditional θ_2 distribution forms the length of the y axis. The smaller the axis, the more accurate is the estimation of the latent ability. In Fig. 1.8 it appears that the score categories 0–9 have θ_1 being measured more accurately, whereas 10–15 have θ_2 being measured more-accurately. This occurs because the more-discriminating items are also the easiest items and these are measuring only θ_1.

In item response theory, precision is measured using the *information function*. The reciprocal of the information function is the asymptotic variance of the maximum likelihood estimate of ability. This relationship implies that the larger the information function, the smaller is the asymptotic variance and the greater is the measurement precision. Multidimensional information (MINF) serves as one measure of precision. MINF is computed in a manner similar to its unidimensional IRT counterpart except that the direction of the information must also considered. The computational formula is

$$\text{MINF} = P_i(\theta)\left[1 - P_i(\theta)\right]\left(\sum_{k=1}^{m} \alpha_{ik} \cos \alpha_{ik}\right)^2, \tag{23}$$

where α_{ik} represents the angle between the vector representing item i and the θ_1 axis for dimension k. MINF provides a measure of information at any (θ_1, θ_2) value on the latent ability plane (i.e., measurement precision relative to the composite). MINF can be computed at the item level or at the test level (where the test information is the sum of the item information functions).

Reckase and McKinley (1991) developed the *clamshell* plot to represent multidimensional information. This plot bears this name because of the series of vectors representing the amount of information look like a series of clamshells. Specifically, the amount of information provided by a test is computed at 49 uniformly spaced points on a 7×7 grid in the (θ_1, θ_2) space. At each of the 49 points, the amount of information is computed for 10 different directions or ability composites from 0 to 90 deg in 10-deg increments and represented as the length of the 10 lines in each clamshell. Figure 1.9 contains the clamshell plot for the 15 items listed in Table 1.1. θ_1 is measured with more precision than θ_2, with the 10 to 20-deg directions providing the greatest measurement precision. This result is to be expected because the first five items measure on θ_1 and are also the more discriminating items.

One problem with the MINF computation is that it does not account for local dependence in the ability estimation. Hence, MINF should be considered an approximation to the measurement precision for a single multidimensional item at a given (θ_1, θ_2) composite. To overcome this limitation, Ackerman (1992) developed another measure of multidimensional information using the linear composite for two abilities, where the linear composite is defined as $\theta = \beta_1\theta_1 + \beta_2\theta_2$ with $\beta_1 = \cos \alpha$ and $\beta_2 = \sin \alpha$. (Together, β_1 and β_2 provide the angular direction of α.) Then, to find the multidimensional information for a specific composite, the information matrix is inverted to obtain the asymptotic covariance matrix for the (θ_1, θ_2) composite. Once the inverse is computed, the information for a particular

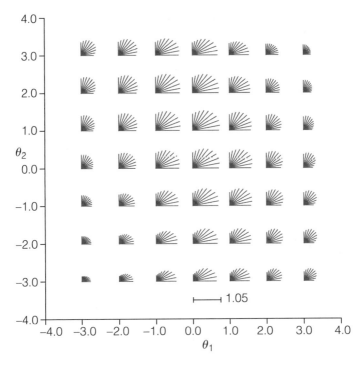

FIG. 1.9. A clamshell plot of the indicating the amount of information in 10 different directions at 49 (θ_1, θ_2) locations.

composite can be calculated as

$$I(\theta_1, \theta_2) = (\cos \alpha)^2 \mathrm{Var}(\hat{\theta}_1 | \theta_1, \theta_2) + (\sin \alpha)^2 \mathrm{Var}(\hat{\theta}_2 | \theta_1, \theta_2)$$
$$+ (2 \sin 2\alpha) \mathrm{Cov}(\hat{\theta}_1 \hat{\theta}_2 | \theta_1, \theta_2), \qquad (24)$$

which is the multidimensional information for a maximum likelihood estimate of ability for the composite given by $\theta = \beta_1 \theta_1 + \beta_2 \theta_2$.

Ackerman (1996) also developed a *number* plot to represent multidimensional information for the composite given by $\theta = \beta_1 \theta_1 + \beta_2 \theta_2$. To create the numbers, the amount of information is computed in 49 uniformly spaced points on a 7×7 grid in the (θ_1, θ_2) space as before. At each of the 49 points, the direction and amount of information are computed in 1-deg increments from 0 to 90 deg. The direction of maximum information is given as a numeric value on the grid. The amount of information is represented by the size of the font for each numeric value (the larger the font, the greater is the information). Figure 1.10 contains the number plot for the six spatial items. These items provide a better measure of θ_1 relative to θ_2, especially in the angular direction between 12 and 28 deg.

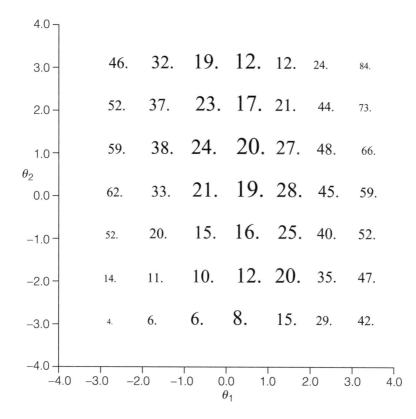

FIG. 1.10.   A plot indicating the direction of maximum information at 49 points in an equally spaced grid of the latent ability plane.

FUTURE RESEARCH DIRECTIONS

Multidimensional item response theory has great potential for solving many problems in educational and psychological assessment. Although many researchers and practitioners believe that educational and psychological tests measure multiple constructs, multidimensional IRT modeling is still in the early stages of development (Reckase, 1997). As a result, research on MIRT theory and applications of MIRT models will become more prevalent in the future.

Multidimensional IRT analyses can help the practitioner to provide evidence that test scores are being properly used and interpreted (Ackerman, 1994, 1996). If the results of a test are reported as a single score, then it is implicitly assumed that all the items are measuring the same skill or same composite of skills. Dimensionality analyses can help establish the degree to which this is true. Response data represent an interaction between examinees and items. There has been a great deal of quality work on verifying the dimensionality of test data by William Stout and his students (e.g., Stout, 1987; Stout et al., 1996). For some examinees, these data may be unidimensional; for others, multidimensional. Thus, dimensionality analyses should be part of a standard set of analyses conducted after each test administration. Dimensionality needs to be separated into valid, replicable traits and construct-irrelevant traits (American Educational Research Association, American Psychological Association, & National Council on Measurement in Education, 1996). This division can help the practitioner decide whether multiple scores should be reported. When multiple scores are reported, vector plots and information plots can support the constructs presented in a table of specifications and provide insight into the relative composite of abilities each item is best measuring.

Another important development uses Markov chain Monte Carlo (MCMC) estimation procedures (e.g., Patz & Junker, 1999). These procedures eliminate some of the complex differentiation algorithms that are currently used and limit researchers in estimating more complex models. Ironically, with MCMC methodology, researchers may begin to develop (and estimate) more-complex models developed from theoretical bases rather than work with limited models because their parameters are estimable. MCMC methodology will greatly advance multidimensional IRT modeling.

REFERENCES

Ackerman, T. A. (1992). A didactic explanation of item bias, item impact, and item validity from a multidimensional perspective. *Journal of Educational Measurement, 29,* 67–91.

Ackerman, T. A. (1994). Using multidimensional item response theory to understand what items and tests are measuring. *Applied Measurement in Education, 7,* 255–278.

Ackerman, T. A. (1996). Graphical representation of multidimensional item response theory analyses. *Applied Psychological Measurement, 20,* 311–330.

Ackerman, T. A., Kelkar, V., Neustel, S., & Simpson, M. (2001). *A simulation study examining NO-HARM's ability to recover two-dimensional generated item parameters.* Paper presented at the annual meeting of the National Council on Measurement in Education, Seattle, WA.

American Educational Research Association, American Psychological Association, & National Council on Measurement in Education. *Standards for educational and psychological testing.* (1999). Washington, DC: Author.

Balassiano, M., & Ackerman, T. A. (1995). *An evaluation of NOHARM estimation accuracy with a two-dimensional latent space.* Unpublished manuscript.

Christoffersson, A. (1975). Factor analysis of dichotomized variables. *Psychometrika, 40,* 5–32.

Computer Associates International, Inc. (1989). DISSPLA 10.0 [Computer software]. Garden City, NY: Author.

Davey, T., Oshima, T. C., & Lee, K. (1996). Linking multidimensional item calibrations. *Applied Psychological Measurement, 20,* 405–416.

Fraser, C. (1988). *NOHARM: An IBM PC computer program for fitting both unidimensional and multidimensional normal ogive models of latent trait theory.* Armidale, Australia: University of New England Press.

Lord, F. M. (1980). *Applications of item response theory to practical testing problems.* Hillsdale, NJ: Lawrence Erlbaum Associates, Inc.

McDonald, R. P. (1967). *Nonlinear factor analysis*. (Psychometric Monographs, No. 15). Chicago: University of Chicago Press.

McDonald, R. P. (1999). *Test theory: A unified approach*. Mahwah, NJ: Lawrence Erlbaum Associates, Inc.

McDonald, R. P. (2000). A basis for multidimensional item response theory . *Applied Psychological Measurement, 24,* 99–114.

Patz, R. J., & Junker, B. W. (1999a). A straightforward approach to Markov chain Monte Carlo methods in item response models. *Journal of Educational and Behavioral Statistics, 24,* 146–178.

Reckase, M. D. (1985). The difficulty of test items that measure more than one ability. *Applied Psychological Measurement, 9,* 401–412.

Reckase, M. D. (1997). The past and future of multidimensional item response theory. *Applied Psychological Measurement, 21,* 25–36.

Reckase, M. D., & Mckinley, R. L. (1985). The difficulty of test items that measure more than one dimension. *Applied Psychological Measurement, 9,* 401–412.

Reckase, M. D., & McKinley, R. L. (1991). The discrimination power of items that measure more than one dimension. *Applied Psychological Measurement, 14,* 361–373.

Stout, W. (1987). A nonparametric approach for assessing latent trait unidimensionality. *Psychometrika, 52,* 589–617.

Stout, W., Habing, B., Douglas, J., Kim, H. R., Roussos, L., & Zhang, J. (1996). Conditional covariance-based nonparametric multidimensionality assessment. *Applied Psychological Measurement, 20,* 331–354.

van der Linden, W. J., & Hambleton, R. K. (1997). *Handbook of modern item response theory*. New York: Springer.

2

Limited- and Full-Information Estimation of Item Response Theory Models

Daniel M. Bolt

University of Wisconsin, Madison

INTRODUCTION

The growth of item response theory (IRT) has been one of the more important trends in psychometrics in the last several decades. Most practitioners are familiar with how the invariance properties of IRT models make them attractive for applications such as test construction, computerized adaptive testing, item bias assessment, and test equating. Perhaps less frequently considered is the equally useful role IRT models can play in test validation. Because most educational and psychological measures are to some degree multidimensional, multidimensional IRT (MIRT) models have become useful in this respect (Ackerman, 1994; chap. 1, this volume). Like the common factor model, a MIRT model can provide the basis for either exploratory or confirmatory investigations of a test's latent dimensional structure. More importantly, because MIRT models assume categorically scored variables and are nonlinear in form, they often provide a better approximation to the examinee/item interaction than the common factor model, which assumes continuous variables and is linear. MIRT is often presented as an outgrowth of two lines of research, one connected to *item factor analysis* (IFA; Christoffersson, 1975; Muthén, 1978), the other an extension of *unidimensional IRT* (Reckase,

27

1997a). IFA defines a model by which factor analysis can be applied to categorically scored items, and is motivated by the known problems of fitting the linear common factor model to the correlation matrices of binary items (see, e.g., Mislevy, 1986). In contrast, the unidimensional IRT approach has sought to extend traditional IRT models to accommodate the presence of more than one latent trait. It has been shown that both the IFA and IRT approaches ultimately lead to algebraically equivalent MIRT models (Takane & DeLeeuw, 1987). However, the two approaches have also contributed to some fundamental differences in how IRT analyses are conducted and interpreted.

One difference—the focus of this chapter—has been the emergence of two approaches to IRT estimation. *Limited-information* (LI) and *full information* (FI) methods can be fundamentally distinguished by the amount of information they use from the item response matrix (i.e., the item score patterns observed for all examinees). To illustrate the difference, suppose we have data from a sample of examinees administered an n-item test in which each item is scored correct/incorrect. We might imagine an n-way contingency table in which each dimension distinguishes examinee scores on an item, so that each cell of the table represents the frequency of a specific item response pattern. For example, the observed frequency of each of the $2^5 = 32$ possible response patterns for a five-item test could be arranged into a table of dimensions $2 \times 2 \times 2 \times 2 \times 2$. LI methods, which follow largely from IFA, consider only marginal frequencies from this table when estimating an IRT model (i.e., frequencies collapsed across other dimensions). The best-known LI methods are *bivariate information methods* in that they are based on only the first- and second-order margins. For binary items, these are the number correct for each item and the joint number correct of each item pair. In contrast, FI methods, which are commonly used in unidimensional IRT estimation, attend to the frequencies of each individual response pattern (i.e., the frequencies within each cell of the contingency table). FI methods are thus sensitive not only to the first- and second-order margins, but also to all third- and higher order margins.

An obvious difference between FI and LI estimation relates to the number of data elements fitted. This difference becomes even greater as the number of items increases. For example, a test containing 20 dichotomously scored test items produces more than one million possible response pattern frequencies ($2^{20} = 1, 048, 576$), but only 210 first- and second-order margins. Therefore, although FI methods maximize use of the data, they also tend to increase the complexity of the model-fitting process. A very practical question (still the focus of research) is whether the additional information used in FI results in any meaningful difference relative to LI, either in terms of the estimates obtained for MIRT model parameters or in the assessment of model fit.

The primary objective of this chapter is to describe and distinguish LI and FI as general approaches to IRT estimation. The focus is on binary items and the multidimensional normal ogive (MNO) model, although in many instances the methods considered can be generalized to items with more than two categories or to models other than the MNO. For a more detailed account of specific IRT estimation methods, particularly as related to unidimensional IRT modeling, the reader is referred to Baker and Kim (2004).

UNIDIMENSIONAL ITEM RESPONSE MODELS

A unidimensional IRT model characterizes the interaction between examinees and items using only one examinee trait parameter, θ. For example, in a test of algebra, we might regard an examinee's performance as being a function of his or her level of algebra ability. Lord (1952) proposed use of the cumulative normal distribution for modeling how θ relates to item performance. The *normal ogive model* is written as

$$\text{Prob}(U_i = 1|\theta) = \frac{1}{\sqrt{2\pi}} \int_{-\infty}^{\alpha_i+\beta_i\theta} \exp\left(-\frac{y^2}{2}\right) dy \equiv N(\alpha_i + \beta_i\theta). \qquad (1)$$

where $\text{Prob}(U_i = 1|\theta)$ denotes the probability of a correct response on item i for an examinee of trait level θ, α_i and β_i denote intercept and slope parameters, respectively, and $N(\cdot)$ is the cumulative normal distribution function. Use of the normal ogive as a model for item responses can be justified through a simple set of assumptions presented by Lord and Novick (1968). Suppose there exists a continuous "latent response propensity," denoted y, underlying each item response, and for which item score is a discrete manifestation; specifically, a correct response occurs provided y exceeds an item-specific threshold corresponding to the difficulty of the item. If we assume that the conditional distribution of y given θ is normally distributed with a mean that is a linear function of θ and a constant variance, then the probability that y is greater than a fixed item threshold value (implying a correct item response) has a relationship with θ that follows a normal ogive. Figure 2.1 illustrates these assumptions and the resulting item response function (see Lord & Novick, 1968, pp. 370–371, for details).

In the normal ogive model, the item intercept and slope parameters represent the difficulty and discrimination, respectively, of the item. Items that are difficult have lower α values and items that are highly discriminating have higher βs. When the θ metric is scaled to have a mean of 0 and variance of 1, items with αs below 0 are more difficult items and items with βs above 1 represent items that are highly discriminating.

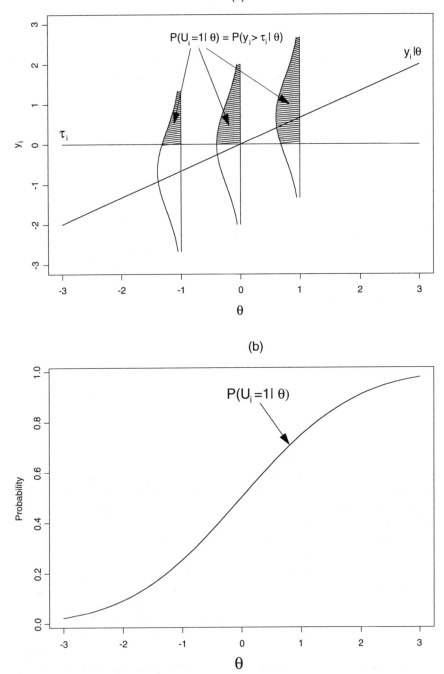

FIG. 2.1. (a) Latent response propensity as function of latent ability, and corresponding regions of correct response under the normal ogive model. (b) Example item response curve for a normal ogive item.

MULTIDIMENSIONAL ITEM RESPONSE MODELS

In a multidimensional model, the examinee/item interaction is modeled by a vector of latent traits, $\theta = (\theta_1, \theta_2, \ldots, \theta_k)$. For example, a mathematics test might measure both geometry and algebra, in which case item performances could be modeled as a function of two skill traits, θ_1 and θ_2. A natural extension of the unidimensional normal ogive model is the *multidimensional normal ogive model*. In the MNO, the probability of correct response is

$$\text{Prob}(u_i = 1|\theta) = \frac{1}{\sqrt{2\pi}} \int_{-\infty}^{\alpha_i + \beta_{i1}\theta_1 + \cdots + \beta_{ik}\theta_k} \exp\left(-\frac{y^2}{2}\right) dy$$

$$\equiv N(\alpha_i + \beta_{i1}\theta_1 + \cdots + \beta_{ik}\theta_k). \tag{2}$$

This model is very similar to Equation 1, but now with a composite of traits, each having its own slope coefficient β_{ik} replacing what had previously been just one trait and one slope coefficient. The β_{ik} function similarly to factor loadings in factor analysis, and the α_i parameters are difficulty parameters, which can be interpreted in the same way as in the unidimensional model. An item response surface for a hypothetical two-dimensional MNO item is illustrated in Fig. 2.2. In this case,

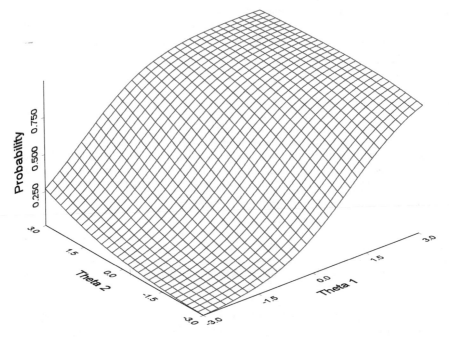

FIG. 2.2. Example item response surface for a two-dimensional MNO item.

the probability of correct response to the item is a function of two θ levels, thus requiring a three-dimensional graphic.

ITEM FACTOR ANALYSIS AND THE MULTIDIMENSIONAL NORMAL OGIVE MODEL

As demonstrated by Takane and DeLeeuw (1987), the MNO model can also be derived from modeling assumptions made in item factor analysis. The common factor model assumes that variables are continuous, and thus is less appropriate for binary items. Mislevy (1986) discussed several problems in applying factor analysis to correlation matrices of binary items (i.e., phi coefficients), including (a) the dependence of the interitem correlations on the means of the items, (b) the inappropriateness of a linear factor/item score relationship due to the bounded item score metric, and (c) the tendency for spurious factors to be extracted. See Maydeu-Olivares (chap. 3, this volume) for a further discussion of these issues.

IFA addresses these limitations by assuming that a vector of continuous variables $\mathbf{y} = (y_1, y_2, \ldots, y_n)$ underlies the n dichotomous item scores $\mathbf{u} = (u_1, u_2, \ldots, u_n)$ achieved by an examinee on a test. We might think of these y variables as similar to the "latent response propensity" variables used to justify the unidimensional normal ogive model. IFA assumes that the covariance structure of the ys is explained by the common factor model. For each item,

$$y_i = \lambda_{i1}\theta_1 + \cdots + \lambda_{ik}\theta_k + \delta_i, \qquad i = 1, \ldots, n, \qquad (3)$$

where δ_i is a residual term distributed Normal $(0, \psi_i)$ that is also independent across items and examinees, $\boldsymbol{\theta} = (\theta_1, \theta_2, \ldots, \theta_k)$ is the examinee trait vector having mean $\mathbf{0}$ and covariance matrix $\boldsymbol{\Phi}$, and $\lambda_i = (\lambda_{i1}, \lambda_{i2}, \ldots, \lambda_{ik})$ is the factor loading vector. One difference between Equation 3 and ordinary applications of the common factor model is that the y_i are not observed. To identify a metric for $\mathbf{y}$, we arbitrarily assign each y_i a mean of 0 and variance of 1. We can then write the conditional distribution of $\mathbf{y}$ given $\boldsymbol{\theta}$ as

$$g(\mathbf{y}|\boldsymbol{\theta}) \sim \text{MVN}(\boldsymbol{\Lambda}\boldsymbol{\theta}, \boldsymbol{\Psi}), \qquad (4)$$

where $\boldsymbol{\Lambda}$ is the factor loading matrix and $\boldsymbol{\Psi}$ is a diagonal matrix (whose diagonal elements are the ψ_i). MVN denotes the multivariate normal distribution.

IFA assumes that each item score is determined by the location of y_i relative to a fixed item threshold parameter τ_i:

$$u_i = \begin{cases} 1 & \text{if } y_i \geq \tau_i \\ 0 & \text{if } y_i < \tau_i. \end{cases} \tag{5}$$

Combining Equations 4 and 5, we obtain for each item

$$\text{Prob}(u_i = 1|\boldsymbol{\theta}) = \text{Prob}(y_i > \tau_i|\boldsymbol{\theta}) = \int_{\tau_i}^{\infty} g_i(y_i|\boldsymbol{\theta})\, dy_i$$

$$= \frac{1}{\sqrt{2\pi}\sigma_{y_i|\theta}} \int_{\tau_i}^{\infty} \exp\left[-\frac{1}{2}\left(\frac{y_i - \mu_{y_i|\theta}}{\sigma_{y_i|\theta}}\right)^2\right] dy_i, \tag{6}$$

where

$$\mu_{y_i|\theta} = \boldsymbol{\lambda}_i'\boldsymbol{\theta} \tag{7}$$

$$\sigma_{y_i|\theta} = \sqrt{\psi_i} = \sqrt{1 - \boldsymbol{\lambda}_i'\boldsymbol{\Phi}\boldsymbol{\lambda}_i}. \tag{8}$$

To reexpress Equation 6 in terms of a standard normal distribution, we first define

$$z_i = \frac{y_i - \mu_{y_i|\theta}}{\sigma_{y_i|\theta}} \tag{9}$$

Then, by substitution,

$$\text{Prob}(u_i = 1|\boldsymbol{\theta}) = \text{Prob}\left(z_i > \frac{\tau_i - \boldsymbol{\lambda}_i'\boldsymbol{\theta}}{\sqrt{1 - \boldsymbol{\lambda}_i'\boldsymbol{\Phi}\boldsymbol{\lambda}_i}}\right)$$

$$= \frac{1}{\sqrt{2\pi}} \int_{\frac{\tau_i - \boldsymbol{\lambda}_i'\boldsymbol{\theta}}{\sqrt{1 - \boldsymbol{\lambda}_i'\boldsymbol{\Phi}\boldsymbol{\lambda}_i}}}^{\infty} \exp\left(-\frac{z_i^2}{2}\right) dz_i \tag{10}$$

$$= N\left(\frac{-\tau_i + \boldsymbol{\lambda}_i'\boldsymbol{\theta}}{\sqrt{1 - \boldsymbol{\lambda}_i'\boldsymbol{\Phi}\boldsymbol{\lambda}_i}}\right), \tag{11}$$

which is equivalent to the MNO subject to a reparametrization. Specifically, Equation 11 is the same as Equation 2, where

$$\alpha_i = \frac{-\tau_i}{\sqrt{1 - \boldsymbol{\lambda}_i'\boldsymbol{\Phi}\boldsymbol{\lambda}_i}} \tag{12}$$

and

$$\beta_{ik} = \frac{\lambda_{ik}}{\sqrt{1 - \boldsymbol{\lambda}_i'\boldsymbol{\Phi}\boldsymbol{\lambda}_i}}. \tag{13}$$

McDonald (1997) referred to the α_i, β_{ik} parametrization of the MNO given in Equation 2 as the model's *latent trait parametrization*, whereas the λ_{ik}, τ_i, ψ_i parametrization in Equation 11 is its *common factor parametrization*. The common factor parameters can be derived from the latent trait parameters as

$$\tau_i = -\frac{\alpha_i}{\sqrt{1 + \beta_i' \Phi \beta_i}}, \tag{14}$$

$$\lambda_{ik} = \frac{\beta_{ik}}{\sqrt{1 + \beta_i' \Phi \beta_i}}, \tag{15}$$

and

$$\psi_i = 1 - \beta_i' \Phi \beta_i. \tag{16}$$

In the IFA model, the λs can be interpreted as standardized factor loadings, and thus represent the correlation between the corresponding factor (trait) and the latent item response propensity, whereas the ψs indicate the uniquenesses (i.e., the proportion of variance in the ys not accounted for by the factors). The τs represent an inverse normal transformation of the classical item difficulty parameter: $\tau_i = N^{-1}(p_i)$, where p_i represents proportion correct for item i. Thus, positive τs represent difficult items, whereas negative τs represent easy items. The common factor parametrization thus has a very natural interpretation for practitioners accustomed to interpreting factor analytic solutions.

Reckase (1985) discussed some appealing aspects of the latent trait parametrization, especially as it relates to the graphical representation of the MNO items illustrated in Fig. 2.2. For example, an item's β vector defines the direction in the latent space along which the item response surface has its maximum rate of increase, and thus also corresponds to the unique composite of traits for which the item is maximally discriminating. The intercept parameter α_i indicates the distance in the latent ability space along the direction vector $\beta_i' \beta_i$ from the origin to the point at which the probability of correct response is .5. This is also the location in the multidimensional ability space at which the item is most discriminating. In this respect, the latent trait parametrization may be attractive to practitioners accustomed to interpreting unidimensional IRT models, where similar interpretations can be given to the slope and intercept parameters.

Besides these differences in parametrization, there are a couple of other ways in which the IFA and IRT approaches differ. Next we look at two differences that are more closely tied to the LI and FI estimation approaches.

STRONG VERSUS WEAK LOCAL INDEPENDENCE

An important concept underlying item response theory is that of local independence. Local independence implies that once the latent space is defined, item responses should be statistically independent conditional on the latent trait. Local independence is thus closely associated with how the dimensionality of a test is determined.

FI and LI estimation methods are connected to different definitions of local independence. FI methods are based on a *strong local independence* (SLI) principle (McDonald, 1981). SLI exists provided

$$\text{Prob}(\mathbf{U} = \mathbf{u}|\boldsymbol{\theta}) = \prod_{i=1}^{n} \text{Prob}(U_i = u_i|\boldsymbol{\theta}) \qquad (17)$$

for all response patterns, where $\text{Prob}(\mathbf{U} = \mathbf{u}|\boldsymbol{\theta})$ denotes the probability of observing response pattern $\mathbf{u}$ from an examinee of ability level $\boldsymbol{\theta}$. SLI implies that this conditional probability can be expressed as the product of the conditional probabilities of each score in the pattern. From the FI perspective, the dimensionality of the latent space has not been fully specified until SLI is achieved. In estimating IRT models, FI methods thus attempt to account for the observed frequencies of each response pattern in the data set.

By contrast, LI methods are connected to a *weak local independence* (WLI) principle (McDonald, 1981). WLI exists when the covariances of all item pairs i, j conditional on the trait are equal to zero, that is

$$\text{Cov}(u_i, u_j|\boldsymbol{\theta}) = 0. \qquad (18)$$

From the perspective of WLI, the latent space is completely specified when the covariances among all item pairs have been accounted for. For binary items, this is equivalent to accounting for the first- and second-order marginals of the item response matrix. In estimating model parameters, LI methods thus employ fitting functions that are sensitive only to recovery of these marginal frequencies.

SLI implies WLI. WLI can exist without SLI, provided the dependence that exists among items only emerges in the third- or higher order marginals of the item response matrix. In theory, these higher order dependences could influence the item parameter estimates. However, because third- and higher order marginals are generally observed to be highly unstable in sampling, their anticipated effects on the estimates, if present at all, are likely small.

The concepts of SLI and WLI are also related to different ways of assessing model fit (McDonald & Mok, 1995). To assess SLI, fit is evaluated by the degree to which the model accounts for the observed frequencies of each response pattern. Statistical tests of fit are $(s - t - 1)$-degree of freedom tests, where s is the number of distinct item response patterns observed in the data and t is the number of model parameters. The causes of misfit are best examined by comparing the observed and expected numbers of each response pattern, which can be quite difficult due to the potentially large number of different response patterns.

From the WLI perspective, model fit is evaluated by the recovery of the first and- second-order marginals of the item response matrix. Goodness-of-fit tests are

$[n(n + 1)/2 - t]$-degree of freedom tests, where n is the number of items. Because $n(n + 1)/2$ will generally be much less than s, statistical tests of fit typically have far fewer degrees of freedom than FI tests. Identifying the causes of misfit is therefore generally also much easier, as residual matrices contain only $n(n + 1)/2$ unique elements. Moreover, because this approach to evaluating model misfit is the same as employed in factor analysis, many previously developed goodness-of-fit indices can be applied in the same way to the MNO model (McDonald & Mok, 1995).

Although the focus of this chapter is on model estimation, it is worth mentioning that the principles of WLI have also affected other aspects of IRT. For example, because most applications of IRT typically assume unidimensionality, tests of the unidimensionality assumption are frequently of great interest. Several statistical tests of unidimensionality have been developed from the concept of WLI. For example, Stout's (1987) DIMTEST procedure tests for essential unidimensionality by evaluating whether the conditional covariances of item pairs within a suspect set of items (believed to possibly measure a different dimension than measured by the rest of the test) differ substantially from zero. Other tests of unidimensionality based on this general idea are considered by Etezadi-Amoli and McDonald (1983) and Holland and Rosenbaum (1986). The concept of WLI has also provided a basis for nonparametric methods of investigating test dimensionality structure. For example, Stout et al. (1996) illustrated two cluster-analytic methods that provide a description of test simple structure using item-pair conditional covariances as measures of item similarity.

It is important to note that the different definitions of local independence used by LI and FI methods need not be viewed as different "assumptions" regarding local independence. Instead, they may be taken to reflect alternative ways of defining dimensionality. As such, it may be more appropriate to regard differences between LI and FI methods as reflecting different ways of thinking about statistical dimensions as opposed thinking of LI methods as having "missed" something in the data.

MARGINAL CONDITIONAL AND UNCONDITIONAL FORMULATIONS OF THE MULTIDIMENSIONAL NORMAL OGIVE MODEL

A second distinguishing feature of LI and FI methods relates to how they characterize response pattern probabilities. Suppose $\pi = (\pi_1, \pi_2, \ldots \pi_{2^n})$ denote the theoretical probabilities of each of the 2^n possible response patterns. Selecting an item response model for the data, such as the MNO, imposes restrictions on the values the πs can take. Assuming the parameters of the MNO model are represented by ϑ, we write $\pi(\vartheta)$ to reflect the dependence of the πs on the MNO model parameters.

Recall that in IFA, the distribution of $\mathbf{y}$, the latent response propensity vector, conditional on θ is assumed multivariate normal. If it is further assumed that $\theta \sim \text{MVN}(\mathbf{0}, \Phi)$, then the unconditional distribution of $\mathbf{y}$ is also multivariate normal. Specifically,

$$f(\mathbf{y}) \sim \text{MVN}(\mathbf{0}, \Lambda \Phi \Lambda' + \Psi). \tag{19}$$

This is the *marginal unconditional density of* $\mathbf{y}$ for an examinee drawn at random from the examinee population. Then the probability of a given response pattern $\mathbf{u}_c$ can be written as

$$\pi_c(\vartheta) = \text{Prob}(\mathbf{u}_c) = \int \ldots \int_{R_c^*} \text{MVN}(\mathbf{0}, \Lambda \Phi \Lambda' + \Psi), \tag{20}$$

where R_c^* denotes an n-dimensional region (each dimension corresponding to the continuous response y underlying a different item) whose bounds are $(-\infty, \tau_i)$ for each dimension corresponding to an item answered incorrectly and (τ_i, ∞) for each item answered correctly. Because Equation 20 is written without reference to the distribution of θ, we refer to it as a *marginal unconditional* formulation of the MNO model.

Alternatively, the probability of each response pattern can be expressed in terms of the MNO model and the distribution of θ. In this case, we write

$$\pi_c(\vartheta) = \text{Prob}(\mathbf{u}_c) = \int \ldots \int_R \text{Prob}(\mathbf{u}_c|\theta) f(\theta) \, d\theta \tag{21}$$

$$= \int \ldots \int_R \left[\prod_{i=1}^{n} [\text{Prob}(u_i = 1|\theta)]^{u_{ci}} [1 - \text{Prob}(u_i = 1|\theta)]^{1-u_{ci}} \right] \times f(\theta) \, d\theta, \tag{22}$$

where $\text{Prob}(u_i = 1|\theta)]$ assumes the form of the MNO given in Equation 2. In this approach, R is now a k-dimensional integration region (each dimension corresponding to a trait) ranging over $(-\infty, \infty)$ for each dimension. Equation 22 is the *marginal conditional* formulation of the MNO because it expresses the probability of the response pattern conditional on θ.

Typically, LI methods use Equation 20 for estimating the MNO. Hence, they commonly assume normality with respect to the latent trait distribution. FI methods typically use Equation 22. Although FI methods frequently assume a normal distribution for θ, they can also readily accommodate other distributions for θ (Mislevy, 1986). Alternatively, the distribution of θ can be estimated along with the parameters of the MNO, in which case no distributional assumption for the traits is made (Mislevy, 1984). Consequently, one practical issue to consider when comparing LI and FI procedures is whether the model parameter estimates will be deleteriously affected by nonnormality of the trait distribution, in which case an FI approach might be preferred.

A second difference between the formulations in Equations 20 and 22 is the explicit specification of the item response function in Equation 22. Reckase (1997a) considered this an important distinguishing feature between the IFA and IRT approaches because it shows how the IRT approach is fundamentally concerned with the item/examinee interaction. Mislevy (1986) also noted the usefulness of this in allowing for alternative expressions for $\text{Prob}(u_{ci}|\theta)$ besides the MNO. For example, the θ distribution could be fixed according to some alternative distributional form (e.g., uniform), and nonparametric item response functions could be estimated.

EXAMPLES OF LIMITED INFORMATION METHODS

In this section, three examples of LI estimation methods are described. The first two are the generalized least squares (GLS) methods of Christoffersson (1975) and Muthén (1978), both of which are based on the item factor analysis model. The third method is the unweighted least squares (ULS) method of McDonald (1967, 1981), which provides a direct approximation to the MNO model.

Christoffersson's Method

Christoffersson (1975) fitted the item factor analysis model of Equations 6–8 to the marginal-proportion-correct and joint-proportion-correct data of an item response matrix. From Equation 6, the proportion correct for each item can be expressed as

$$\pi_i = \text{Pr}(u_i = 1) = \int_{\tau_i}^{\infty} N(y_i; 0, 1)\, dy_i \tag{23}$$

where $N(\cdot; 0, 1)$ denotes the normal density with mean and variance parameters $\mu_i = 0$ and $\sigma_i = 1$, respectively. From Equation 20, the joint proportion correct for items i, j can be expressed as

$$\pi_{ij} = \text{Pr}(u_i = 1, u_j = 1) = \int_{\tau_i}^{\infty} \int_{\tau_j}^{\infty} \text{BVN}(y_i, y_j; 0, 0, 1, 1, \rho_{ij})\, dy_i y_j, \tag{24}$$

where ρ_{ij} represents the correlation between y_i and y_j (i.e., the ijth element in the matrix $\Lambda' \Phi \Lambda$) and $\text{BVN}(\cdot)$ denotes the bivariate normal density having mean and variance parameters $(\mu_i = 0, \mu_j = 0)$ and $(\sigma_i = 1, \sigma_j = 1)$, respectively, and correlation parameter ρ_{ij}. The correlation ρ_{ij} is also referred to as the *tetrachoric correlation* between items i and j. Because the bivariate normal density is symmetric, $\pi_{ij} = \pi_{ji}$.

The π_i and π_{ij} represent theoretical proportions; the corresponding sample proportions are denoted p_i and p_{ij}; respectively. The relationships between the sample and theoretical proportions are

$$p_i = \pi_i + \epsilon_i, \tag{25}$$

$$p_{ij} = \pi_{ij} + \epsilon_{ij}, \tag{26}$$

where ϵ_i and ϵ_{ij} denote error terms. In vector form, we write $\boldsymbol{\pi} = (\pi_1, \pi_2, \ldots, \pi_n, \pi_{21}, \pi_{31}, \pi_{32}, \ldots, \pi_{n,n-1})$, $\boldsymbol{p} = (p_1, p_2, \ldots, p_n, p_{21}, p_{31}, p_{32}, \ldots, p_{n,n-1})$, and $\boldsymbol{\epsilon} = (\epsilon_1, \epsilon_2, \ldots, \epsilon_n, \epsilon_{21}, \epsilon_{31}, \epsilon_{32}, \ldots, \epsilon_{n,n-1})$. The goal is to determine estimates of the model parameters, that is, $\vartheta = \text{vec}(\boldsymbol{\tau}, \boldsymbol{\Lambda}, \boldsymbol{\Phi}, \boldsymbol{\Psi})$, that make the πs close to the ps (i.e., that minimize the ϵs). One possibility is to use ULS estimates, which are chosen to minimize the sum of the squared elements in ϵ. A disadvantage of ULS estimates, however, is that they are not sensitive to differences in the error variances and covariances across items and item pairs, and therefore fail to produce parameter estimates that are efficient.

Christoffersson proposed a GLS procedure in which a consistent estimator of the inverse of the covariance matrix of the errors, denoted S_ϵ, is used as a weight matrix. Christoffersson (1975, Appendix 2) showed how elements of S_ϵ are derived. In addition to the first- and second-order marginals, the third- and fourth-order marginals of the item response matrix are also needed to estimate these elements. Estimates of ϑ are then determined that minimize the fitting function

$$F(\vartheta) = (\mathbf{p} - \boldsymbol{\pi}(\vartheta))' S_\epsilon^{-1} (\mathbf{p} - \boldsymbol{\pi}(\vartheta)), \tag{27}$$

using an adaptation of the Fletcher–Powell method (Christoffersson, 1975). To evaluate $\boldsymbol{\pi}(\vartheta)$, Christoffersson used the tetrachoric function to express each joint proportion correct as an infinite series. A close approximation to $\boldsymbol{\pi}(\vartheta)$ can be obtained from the first 10 terms of the series

$$\pi_{ij} \approx \sum_{s=0}^{9} \xi_s(\tau_i)\xi_s(\tau_j)\rho_{ij}^s, \tag{28}$$

where

$$\xi_s(\tau_i) = \begin{cases} N(\tau_i) & \text{if} \quad s = 0, \\ \frac{1}{\sqrt{s}}\gamma_{s-1}(\tau_i)n(\tau_i) & \text{if} \quad s \geq 1, \end{cases} \tag{29}$$

and

$$\gamma_s(x) = \frac{1}{\sqrt{s!}} \sum_{v=0}^{q} (-1)^v \frac{x^{s-2v}}{2^v v! (s-2v)!}, \tag{30}$$

with $q = s/2$ if s is even and $q = (s-1)/2$ if s is odd.

Christoffersson's method has several positive features. First, it produces parameter estimates that are both consistent and efficient among all estimators fitted only to the first- and second-order marginals of the item response matrix. Second, as a GLS procedure, Christoffersson's method provides a statistical test of model fit. Specifically, $F(\vartheta)$ is asymptotically chi-square distributed under a null hypothesis of model fit. Finally, standard errors of model parameter estimates can be computed, thus allowing hypothesis testing of individual model parameters.

An unattractive feature of Christoffersson's method is its heavy computational demand. In particular, Equations 23 and 24 must be evaluated at each iteration of the estimation algorithm. As mentioned, evaluation of Equation 24 is especially difficult because it involves integration of the bivariate normal density. Moreover, as the number of items increase, the number of item pairs increases exponentially, making Equation 27 increasingly difficult to minimize because it involves inversion of a matrix whose dimensions are determined by the number of item pairs. As a result, Christoffersson's method is only computationally feasible when there exists a relatively small number of items. To address these problems, a similar but less computationally demanding procedure was provided by Muthén (1978).

Muthén's Method

Muthén's (1978) solution is also a GLS solution, but one that is fitted to sample thresholds and tetrachorics rather than the marginal correct and joint correct proportions. Relative to Christoffersson's method, which can be regarded as a one-stage procedure, Muthén's method is a three-stage procedure. A two-stage process is used to convert the p_i and p_{ij} into sample thresholds s_i and tetrachorics s_{ij}. In the first stage, the thresholds are determined using Equation 23; then, with the thresholds held fixed, the sample tetrachorics are estimated in the second stage using Equation 24. Arranged in vector form, we write $s = (s_1, s_2, \ldots, s_n, s_{21}, s_{31}, s_{32}, \ldots, s_{n,n-1})$ and the corresponding theoretical parameters as $\sigma = (\sigma_1, \sigma_2, \ldots, \sigma_n, \sigma_{21}, \sigma_{31}, \sigma_{32}, \ldots, \sigma_{n,n-1})$. Similar to Equations 25 and 26 from Christoffersson's method,

$$s_i = \sigma_i + \delta_i,$$

$$s_{ij} = \sigma_{ij} + \delta_{ij},$$

where $\delta = (\delta_1, \delta_2, \ldots, \delta_n, \delta_{21}, \delta_{31}, \delta_{32}, \ldots, \delta_{n,n-1})$ is an error vector. Through application of a Taylor expansion, Muthén showed that the relationship between s and σ can be approximated as

$$s = \sigma + \Gamma\epsilon + r,$$

where Γ is a matrix of first-order derivatives, ϵ is the error vector with respect to the first- and second-order marginal proportions (as in Christoffersson's method), and r is a rest term vector containing higher order terms. Muthén showed that the asymptotic covariance matrix of δ is $\Gamma S_\epsilon \Gamma'$, where the individual elements of Γ are derived by Muthén (1978, pp. 553–554) and S_ϵ is the same as derived by Christoffersson. Consequently, S_δ also requires the third- and fourth-order marginals of the item response matrix.

In the third step, estimates of the item factor analysis model are determined so as to minimize the fitting function

$$F(\vartheta) = (\mathbf{s} - \sigma(\vartheta))' S_\delta^{-1} (\mathbf{s} - \sigma(\vartheta)). \tag{31}$$

The primary advantage of Muthén's procedure is that Equations 23 and 24 only need to be evaluated once (in computing the sample thresholds and tetrachorics) and not at each iteration of the minimization procedure. Consequently, Muthén's method is less computationally demanding than Christoffersson's method. As a GLS method, it also produces a goodness-of-fit test and standard errors for parameter estimates as well as parameter estimates that are consistent, and asymptotically efficient (among methods using only first- and second-order marginals).

Nevertheless, minimization of Equation 31 still remains a computational challenge for when there is a large number of items. Although the problem of repeatedly recomputing tetrachorics is removed, it is still necessary to invert a very large matrix. Muthén (1978) suggested that the maximum number of items for analysis using this method is about 20.

Other Estimation Methods for Tetrachoric Correlation Matrices

To address these computational difficulties, alternative factor analysis methods can also be considered. For example, unweighted least squares estimates can be obtained by minimizing the fitting function

$$F(\vartheta) = (\mathbf{s} - \sigma(\vartheta))' (\mathbf{s} - \sigma(\vartheta)). \tag{32}$$

Besides being more economical computationally, ULS is also attractive in that it does not require that the correlation matrix be positive definite, which a sample tetrachoric matrix often is not. Muthén (1978) also noted that ULS estimates frequently approximate his GLS solution reasonably well. Thus, although ULS estimates lack the attractive statistical properties of GLS estimates, analysis of a tetrachoric matrix using ULS will probably at least be preferred to factor analysis of phi-coefficient matrices, which, as noted earlier, has several limitations when applied to binary variables.

Other factor-analytic methods (e.g., generalized least squares, maximum likelihood, alpha, principal axis factoring) can also be applied to a tetrachoric matrix (see Knol & Berger, 1991, for several examples). A limitation of the traditional GLS and maximum likelihood solutions (as would be applied to ordinary correlation matrices) is that the tetrachoric matrix is not computed from actual observed variables, and thus the weight matrices used will lead to incorrect standard errors and goodness-of-fit statistics (Knol & Berger, 1991).

However, asymptotically correct standard errors and goodness-of-fit tests can be obtained provided the asymptotic covariance matrix of the tetrachorics is computed, which is possible using computer software such as the PRELIS program (Jöreskog & Sörbom, 1993b). When read into LISREL (Jöreskog & Sörbom, 1993a), the inverse of this matrix is used as a weight matrix for obtaining weighted least squares estimates that will have asymptotically correct standard errors and goodness-of-fit tests. Computation of the asymptotic covariance matrix in PRELIS follows Jöreskog (1994), which for binary variables ends up leading to the same weight matrix as derived for Muthén's method (Maydeu-Olivares, 2002).

McDonald's Method

Unlike Christoffersson's and Muthén's item factor analysis methods, McDonald's method directly approximates the MNO. To understand the method, it is first necessary to distinguish three classes of latent trait models: (a) strictly linear, (b) wide-sense linear, and (c) strictly nonlinear models (McDonald, 1982). McDonald defined strictly linear models as models that are linear both in the coefficients (i.e., the slope parameters) and the latent traits (i.e., θs). The common factor model is an example. Wide-sense linear models are models that are linear in the coefficients but not in the latent traits. A polynomial factor model (of degree greater than one) is an example of a wide-sense linear model. Finally, strictly nonlinear models are models that cannot be written as a wide-sense linear model using a finite number of terms. Most item response models, including the MNO, are examples of strictly nonlinear models.

McDonald (1967, 1982) showed that a strictly nonlinear model can be approximated as closely as desired by a polynomial series using a harmonic analysis. Thus, the basis for McDonald's method is the use of a wide-sense linear model to approximate a strictly nonlinear model. Using harmonic analysis, we can write the MNO as

$$\text{Prob}(u_i = 1|\boldsymbol{\theta}) = N(\alpha_i + \beta_{i1}\theta_1 + \cdots + \beta_{ik}\theta_k) = \sum_{s=0}^{\infty} \zeta_{is}\gamma_s\left(\frac{\boldsymbol{\beta}_i'\boldsymbol{\theta}}{\sqrt{\eta_i}}\right), \quad (33)$$

where γ_s is as defined in Equation 30, $\eta_i = \boldsymbol{\beta}_i'\boldsymbol{\Phi}\boldsymbol{\beta}_i$, and

$$\zeta_{is} = \begin{cases} N\left(\frac{\alpha_i}{\sqrt{1+\eta_i}}\right) & \text{if} \quad s = 0, \\ \frac{1}{\sqrt{s}}\left(\frac{\sqrt{\eta_i}}{\sqrt{1+\eta_i}}\right)^s \gamma_{s-1}\left(\frac{\alpha_i}{\sqrt{1+\eta_i}}\right) n\left(\frac{\alpha_i}{\sqrt{1+\eta_i}}\right) & \text{if} \quad s \geq 1. \end{cases} \quad (34)$$

Over the interval $\boldsymbol{\theta} \in (-3, 3)$, the MNO can be closely approximated by the first four terms of this series (McDonald, 1982). The relationship between the proportion correct and joint proportion correct parameters and the MNO parameters can then be written as

$$\pi_i = \zeta_{i0}, \tag{35}$$

$$\pi_{ij} \approx \sum_{s=0}^{3} \zeta_{is}\zeta_{js} \left(\frac{1}{\sqrt{\eta_i}} \beta_i' \Phi \beta_j \frac{1}{\sqrt{\eta_j}} \right)^s. \tag{36}$$

Estimates of the model parameters are those values that minimize the fitting function:

$$F(\vartheta) = (\mathbf{p} - \pi(\vartheta))'(\mathbf{p} - \pi(\vartheta)). \tag{37}$$

The program NOHARM (for normal ogive harmonic analysis robust method; Fraser, 1988) can be used to implement McDonald's ULS procedure. NOHARM employs a two-stage procedure in which the thresholds are estimated in the first stage, and then in the second stage the slopes are estimated given the estimated item thresholds.

McDonald (1997) discussed the close similarity between his procedure and Christoffersson's method. Both McDonald's and Christoffersson's methods employ the same approximation technique (compare Equation 28 to Equation 36) to fit the first- and second-order marginal proportion correct. However, McDonald's method uses the first 4 terms of the series for the approximation, whereas Christoffersson's method uses the first 10 terms. Both Christoffersson's and McDonald's methods also evaluate model fit according to recovery of the first- and second-order marginal proportions. In this respect, they also differ from Muthén's method, which attends to the recovery of the tetrachoric correlations.

However, McDonald's method also has some advantages relative to Christoffersson's method. Because it does not require inverting large matrices, McDonald's method can generally handle more items than Christoffersson's method. For the same reason, McDonald's method is computationally faster. There are also some disadvantages. First, as a ULS procedure, the estimates it produces are not efficient, nor are there direct standard errors for parameter estimates or statistical tests of model fit. [See Maydeu-Olivares (2001), however, who showed how standard errors and goodness-of-fit tests can be developed using large-sample theory.]

FULL-INFORMATION METHODS

Another approach to addressing the computational limitations of item factor analysis in handling large numbers of items is to use Bock, Gibbons, and Muraki's (1988) full-information procedure.

Bock, Gibbons, and Muraki's Method

Bock and Aitkin (1981) introduced a method of unidimensional IRT estimation that does not require calculation of item correlations and is also not computationally limited by the number of items analyzed. Bock et al. (1988) essentially extended Bock and Aitkin's method to the MNO model. Using the marginal conditional formulation of the MNO in Equation 22, Bock et al.'s (1988) method derives marginal maximum likelihood (MML) estimates of model parameters by integrating the latent trait density out of the likelihood function. Suppose $r = (r_1, r_2, \ldots, r_s)$ denotes the frequencies of each of the s unique response patterns in a data set; then the likelihood of the data for a sample of N examinees can be written as

$$L(r \mid \pi) = \frac{N!}{\prod_{c=1}^{s} r_c} \prod_{c=1}^{s} \pi_c^{r_c}, \tag{38}$$

which is essentially the likelihood expression when sampling N trials from a multinomial distribution. To achieve maximum likelihood estimates, we seek values of the MNO parameters ϑ that maximize this likelihood expression. Although it is not a necessary assumption, for simplicity we assume that $\theta \sim \text{MVN}(\mathbf{0}, \mathbf{I})$, and that an m-dimensional factor solution is of interest. Following Equation 22, we can then write the marginal probability of response pattern $\mathbf{u}_c$ as

$$\pi_c(\vartheta) = \int_{-\infty}^{\infty} \cdots \int_{-\infty}^{\infty} \left\{ \prod_{i=1}^{n} N(\alpha_i + \beta_i \theta)^{u_{ci}} [1 - N(\alpha_i + \beta_i \theta)]^{1-u_{ci}} \right\} \text{MVN}(\theta) \, d\theta, \tag{39}$$

where u_{ci} denotes the 0/1 response to item i in response pattern $\mathbf{u}_c$. To approximate this marginal probability, m-dimensional Gauss–Hermite quadrature (Stroud & Sechrest, 1966) is used. In this approach, Q points are defined along each dimension, which when crossed produce a grid of Q^m points in the latent trait space. Then the marginal probability of response pattern $\mathbf{u}_c$ is approximated as

$$\pi_c(\vartheta) \approx \sum_{q_m=1}^{Q} \cdots \sum_{q_2=1}^{Q} \sum_{q_1=1}^{Q} L_c(\mathbf{X}_q) A(X_{q_1}) A(X_{q_2}) \cdots A(X_{q_m}), \tag{40}$$

where $\mathbf{X}_q = (X_{q1}, X_{q2}, \ldots, X_{qm})$ defines a quadrature point in the m-dimensional ability space, $A(q_k)$ denotes the weight associated with that point (based on the multivariate normal density), which across points sums to 1, and $L_c(\mathbf{X}_q) = \prod_{i=1}^{n} N(\alpha_i + \beta_i X_q)^{u_{ci}} [1 - N(\alpha_i + \beta_i X_q)]^{1-u_{ci}}$. Wilson, Wood, and Gibbons (1998) recommend $Q = 10$ points per dimension for a one-dimensional solution, five per dimension for a two-dimensional solution, and three per dimension for solutions having three or more factors.

To find the maximum likelihood estimate for a model parameter ϑ_i, we need to evaluate

$$0 = \frac{\partial \log L}{\partial \vartheta_i} = \sum_{c=1}^{s} \frac{r_c}{\pi_c} \left(\frac{\partial \pi_c}{\partial \vartheta_i} \right). \tag{41}$$

Assuming conditional independence across items, we find a discrete approximation of this expression:

$$0 = \sum_{q_m=1}^{Q} \cdots \sum_{q_2=1}^{Q} \sum_{q_1=1}^{Q} \frac{\bar{r}_{iq} - \bar{N}_q \text{Prob}_i(X_q)}{\text{Prob}_i(X_q)[1 - \text{Prob}_i(X_q)]} \cdot \frac{\delta \, \text{Prob}_i(X_q)}{\delta \vartheta_i}, \tag{42}$$

where

$$\bar{r}_{iq} = \sum_{c=1}^{s} u_{ci} r_c P(X_q | \mathbf{u}_c, \boldsymbol{\tau}, \boldsymbol{\Lambda}, \boldsymbol{\Phi}, \boldsymbol{\Psi}) \tag{43}$$

is the estimated number of examinees at quadrature point X_q that answer item i correctly,

$$\bar{N}_q = \sum_{l=1}^{s} r_l P(X_k | \mathbf{u}_l, \boldsymbol{\tau}, \boldsymbol{\Lambda}, \boldsymbol{\Phi}, \boldsymbol{\Psi}) \tag{44}$$

is the estimated number of examinees at quadrature node X_q, $P(X_q | \mathbf{u}_c, \boldsymbol{\tau}, \boldsymbol{\Lambda}, \boldsymbol{\Phi}, \boldsymbol{\Psi})$ is the posterior probability that an examinee having score pattern $\mathbf{u}_c$ is at quadrature node X_q, and $\text{Prob}_i(X_q)$ denotes the probability of correct response to item i at quadrature node X_q.

To find item parameter estimates that satisfy Equation 42, an iterative process is followed based on an expectation-maximization (EM) algorithm. Each cycle of the EM algorithm involves the completion of the following two steps:

- The expectation step (E step). In the E step, the current provisional item parameter estimates are regarded as the true item parameters, and $\bar{r}_{iq}$ and $\bar{N}_q$ are estimated from Equation 43 and Equation 44.
- The maximization step (M step): In the M step, the $\bar{r}_{iq}$ and $\bar{N}_q$ from the E step are regarded as the true number correct and number of examinees, respectively, at each quadrature point. Then Equation 42 is solved with respect to the unknown item parameters using Fisher's scoring method. The updated parameter estimates from this step are then the basis for new estimates of $\bar{r}_{iq}$ and $\bar{N}_q$ determined in the next E step.

This iterative process continues until the item parameter estimates computed in the M step no longer change substantially across EM cycles, or until a specified number of EM cycles has been completed.

Bock et al.'s (1988) procedure has several attractive features. First, the resulting estimates are consistent and asymptotically efficient among estimators using full information. Second, a statistical test of fit can be computed. A discrepancy function, similar to the fitting functions described for the LI methods, can be specified as the ratio of the likelihood of the data under the fitted model to the likelihood of the saturated model, with the saturated model being one in which the π_c are equal to the observed proportions (r_c) of each response pattern. This discrepancy function is the basis for a statistical test of fit based on the index

$$G^2 = 2\sum_{l=1}^{s} r_l \ln \frac{r_l}{N\pi_l(\vartheta)}, \tag{45}$$

which follows a χ^2 distribution (under a null hypothesis of model fit) now having $s - t - 1$ degrees of freedom, where s is the number of different item response patterns and t is the number of model parameters. Third, as with Christoffersson's and Muthén's methods, standard errors can be determined, in this case from the inverse of the matrix of second derivatives computed in the final M step.

Another attractive feature of Bock et al.'s (1988) method is the ease with which it can incorporate priors on the model parameters. For example, beta priors might be used for the ψ_i parameters to prevent Heywood cases (instances where the ψ estimates fall below 0 or above 1), or normal priors used for the thresholds to prevent excessively large or small estimates (Wilson, Wood, & Gibbons, 1998). Imposition of priors simply involves multiplying the prior density by the term within the integral in (39).

The primary disadvantage of Bock et al.'s (1988) method is its inability to handle solutions involving large numbers of factors. As the number of dimensions increases, integration over the ability density become increasingly complex, making the method currently intractable for solutions with more than five factors. Mislevy (1986) thus proposed that GLS limited-information methods (e.g., Muthén's method) be preferred for tests with few items but many factors, whereas Bock et al.'s method is better for tests with many items but few factors. Unfortunately, neither method works well when there are both a large number of items and a large number of factors.

Other Full-Information Procedures

Although the FI procedure of Bock et al.'s (1988) is probably the most popular method, other FI methods exist. For example, McKinley and Reckase (1983) developed MAXLOG and Carlson (1987) developed the program MIRTE, both of which are joint-maximum likelihood (JML) methods. Unlike the previous MML method, JML methods search for the maximum likelihood estimates of examinee latent abilities at the same time that the item parameters are estimated. However, for the same reasons that JML has largely been supplanted by MML in unidimensional

IRT, JML methods are not very popular in MIRT modeling. First, they are computationally inefficient because they require inversion of very large matrices. Second, JML estimates lack attractive statistical properties, such as consistency (Baker & Kim, 2004). Later in this chapter, we discuss another FI method based on Markov chain Monte Carlo estimation.

EMPIRICAL COMPARISONS OF FULL- AND LIMITED-INFORMATION PROCEDURES

Various studies have compared FI and LI procedures using simulated and real data. Most commonly, these studies have compared the methods in terms of parameter recovery. Knol and Berger (1991) studied a large number of estimation methods, including the Bock et al. (1988) and McKinley and Reckase (1983) FI methods, McDonald's LI method and several methods for factoring a tetrachoric correlation matrix, including ULS, GLS, maximum likelihood, principal axis, and alpha factoring. Item response data were simulated from one-, two-, and three-dimensional structures for 15- to 30-item tests and sample sizes ranging from 250 to 1,000. Results were evaluated using indices sensitive to both the accuracy of the reproduced parameter estimates and recovery of the item response functions (IRFs). In general, Knol and Berger's results suggest that LI methods, and in particular NOHARM, frequently outperform the FI methods, even on criteria (such as recovery of IRFs) more closely associated with the FI/IRT approach. In addition, despite their poorer statistical properties, the ULS and principal axis analyses of tetrachoric matrices often performed quite well relative to the other, more computationally intensive LI and FI procedures.

Parry and McArdle (1991) compared several LI methods, including McDonald's and Muthén's methods, with ULS estimation applied to both phi and tetrachoric correlation matrices. Their simulation study considered only small sample sizes ($N \leq 200$) and a small number of items ($n = 5$) and also simulated only unidimensional data sets. Their results suggested that neither McDonald's nor Muthén's procedures were clearly superior to the other ULS procedures based on a parameter recovery discrepancy index. Finger (2002) also conducted a simulation study using unidimensional data. He compared the Bock et al. (1988) method (without using any item parameter priors), McDonald's method, and ULS estimation applied to phi and tetrachoric correlation matrices, and found that McDonald's method was the most accurate, whereas the ULS analysis of tetrachorics was approximately equivalent to the ML procedure. Using simulated multidimensional data sets, Gosz and Walker (2002) compared Bock et al.'s method with McDonald's method and found that both approaches performed better in terms of parameter recovery depending on conditions related to the amount and type of multidimensionality present in the data.

FI and LI methods can also be compared in terms of their results for goodness of fit. Using real-data analyses of Law School Admission Test (LSAT) 6 and LSAT 7 data sets, McDonald and Mok (1995) found that both χ^2 tests of fit and goodness-of-fit indices led to similar conclusions for LI and FI estimation methods. They suggested that the instability of the third- and higher order marginals across samples of item response data naturally make them of little consequence in testing fit. Reiser and VandenBerg (1994) considered the problem of response pattern sparseness when applying FI goodness-of-fit tests. In a simulation study, they examined the Type I and Type II error performances of both a Pearson chi-square test of fit and the likelihood ratio test given in Equation 45 as a function of the number of items analyzed. They found that the Type I error rates for the likelihood ratio test became slightly inflated when the number of items was moderate (six or seven items), and then become deflated (due to sparseness) when the number of items was eight or more. Relative to the likelihood ratio test, the Pearson chi-square test maintained more consistent Type I error rates as the number of items increased. Chi-square tests of fit using Christoffersson's method became somewhat inflated as the number of items increased, although serious inflation was not evident until the number of items was nine or higher. Interestingly, the LI tests demonstrated greater power regardless of the number of items analyzed. Thus it would again appear that no useful information regarding lack of fit is lost with LI methods. In addition, as the number of items became large, there was a very substantial difference in power between the LI and FI tests, which could be attributed to sparseness of response pattern frequencies. Indeed, when the number of items was nine or higher, the likelihood ratio test failed to reject a single time in more than 2,000 simulated data sets. Reiser and VandenBerg concluded that LI tests of fit may be expected to perform well when the number of items is small, but LI tests are likely superior to FI methods in terms of power when the number of items is large.

Mislevy (1986) also considered comparisons of the standard errors of model parameter estimates for FI and LI methods as a way of evaluating the practical significance of the information ignored by the LI methods. He cited Gibbons (1984) as providing evidence that the differences in standard errors across methods tend to be very small (less than .01), suggesting very little additional information is provided by the third- and higher order marginals that enhances the precision of parameter estimates.

Many other studies have reported real-data comparisons of FI and LI methods, including those by Bock et al. (1988) and Schumaker and Beyerlein (2000). McDonald and Mok (1995) noted the need for more comparisons using real data because these provide the best comparisons of how the methods perform when the model does not fit. Ideally, such analyses would be performed using large data sets from which multiple samples can be extracted so as to better understand the behavior of the methods under conditions of misfit. Future simulation work is also needed to evaluate the implications of nonnormal trait distributions on LI methods. As noted earlier, this assumption may be more easily relaxed in Bock et al.'s method.

AN EXAMPLE USING ENGLISH
USAGE DATA: ILLUSTRATION
OF SOFTWARE PROGRAMS

Computer software exists for implementing several of the LI and FI methods discussed earlier. This section provides an overview and illustration of four programs: Mplus (Muthén & Muthén, 1998), PRELIS/LISREL (Jöreskog & Sörbom, 1996), NOHARM (Fraser, 1988), and TESTFACT (Wilson et al., 1998). To compare results, a real test data set is analyzed, and both exploratory and confirmatory analyses are performed. The data consist of item responses from 1,000 examinees to 12 items from an English usage section of a college-level English placement test. The test is administered each year at the University of Wisconsin to assist entering freshman in course selection. Example items from the section analyzed here are presented in Appendix A. Each item consists of a sentence in which some type of usage error has been introduced. The examinee selects from several underlined options the sentence part that must be changed to correct the error (or if no error is found, indicates "No Error"). All items are scored dichotomously (correct/incorrect). Previous analyses of similar forms suggested that they possess a multidimensional structure (Bolt, Cohen, & Wollack, 2001).

Exploratory Analysis

Exploratory MNO analyses are motivated by the goal of identifying latent traits or dimensions that account for statistical dependence among the items. For the MNO, such analyses are conducted in largely the same way as exploratory linear factor analyses. Issues related to determining a suitable number of dimensions, rotating solutions, and evaluating model fit are all a part of an exploratory MNO analysis.

Mplus. Mplus (Muthén & Muthén, 1998), the successor to Muthén's previous LISCOMP (Muthén, 1987) program, implements Muthén's three-step GLS procedure. Tetrachoric correlations are estimated based on Muthén (1984). The syntax for an exploratory analysis of the English usage data is straightforward (see Appendix B), and allows for a range of factor solutions to be specified. Besides GLS estimates, alternative methods can also be requested, including unweighted least squares and diagonally weighted least squares, which uses as a weight the inverse of a diagonal matrix having estimates of the asymptotic variances of the tetrachoric correlations along the diagonal (Muthén, du Toit, & Spisic, in press).

Mplus provides a number of criteria that can assist in determining an appropriate number of traits. These include the eigenvalues of the sample tetrachoric correlation matrix and several goodness-of-fit criteria: a χ^2 goodness-of-fit test, the root mean square error-of-approximation (RMSEA) index, and a residual correlation matrix (i.e., the difference between the sample and model-based tetrachoric matrices). Mplus exploratory analyses also provide both Varimax- and Promax-rotated factor solutions, both reported using the common factor parametrization. Although item threshold estimates can be requested in the output (they will not be reported by default), standard errors for parameter estimates (rotated or unrotated) are not available for exploratory analyses. Documentation for the Mplus program is provided by Muthén and Muthén (1998).

NOHARM. The program NOHARM (Fraser, 1988) implements McDonald's ULS procedure. NOHARM can either be run alone, in which case the dichotomous item response matrix is read in directly, or in conjunction with the program PRODMOM, which computes the proportion correct and joint proportion correct for each item and item pair. To find ULS estimates, NOHARM uses either a quasi-Newton or a conjugate gradients algorithm (the choice depends on the size of the problem and the amount of memory required).

To evaluate goodness of fit, NOHARM provides a residual covariance matrix and also reports a root mean square residual (RMSR) and Tanaka's (1993) ULS goodness-of-fit index. A root mean square residual equal to or less than four times the reciprocal of sample size (the typical standard error of the residuals) implies a well-fitting model (Fraser, 1988).

Output from an exploratory NOHARM analysis includes both Varimax- and Promax-rotated solutions reported according to both the latent trait and the common factor parametrizations. Although procedures for computing standard errors and statistical tests of fit have been developed (Maydeu-Olivares, 2001), they have yet to be implemented in the program. The program (including PRODMOM) is available free of charge, and can be downloaded at http://kiptron.psyc.virginia.edu/. Documentation for NOHARM is provided by Fraser (1988).

TESTFACT. The program TESTFACT (Wilson, Wood, & Gibbons, 1998) can be used to conduct both LI and FI exploratory analyses. LI estimation is conducted using a ULS analysis of the tetrachoric correlations. FI estimation is performed using Bock et al.'s (1988) procedure, and uses the LI procedure to determine starting values.

Like Mplus, TESTFACT computes eigenvalues of the sample tetrachoric matrix and a residual correlation matrix. Goodness of fit can be evaluated using the likelihood ratio test in Equation 45. In addition, the frequencies of expected and observed response patterns, the basis for the goodness-of-fit test, are also reported.

TESTFACT performs both Varimax and Promax rotations, and reports solutions according to both latent trait and common factor parametrizations. Relative to Mplus and NOHARM, TESTFACT has been primarily designed for exploratory analyses. Thus, there are a number of other useful features of the program when used in the exploratory mode. For example, TESTFACT can perform a stepwise analysis in which the number of factors is successively increased until the model

TABLE 2.1

Goodness-of-Fit Statistics, Mplus, TESTFACT, and NOHARM, Exploratory Solutions[a]

| | Mplus | | | | TESTFACT | | | | NOHARM | |
Factor	χ^2	df	p	RMSEA	χ^2	df	p	RMSEA	RMSR	Tanaka Index
1	124.33	54	.000	.036	1792.07	533	.000	.049	.00834	.99332
2	76.18	43	.001	.028	1746.14	522	.000	.035	.00618	.99653
3	40.29	33	.179	.015	1713.63	512	.000	.035	.00399	.99890
4[b]	—	—	—	—	1702.33	503	.000	.035	.00285	.99936

[a] RMSEA, Root mean square error-of-approximation index; RMSR, root mean square residual.
[b] Mplus solution not available due to Heywood case.

fits (based on the likelihood-ratio χ^2 test). The user can also specify a model with guessing parameters as well as control other aspects of estimation, including specification of the quadrature points used in EM, priors on model parameters, and estimation of factor scores. Documentation is provided in Wilson et al. (1998).

Results of Exploratory Analysis Using Mplus, NOHARM, and TEST-FACT. Exploratory solutions having one to four dimensions were obtained using Mplus, NOHARM, and TESTFACT. In Mplus, both GLS and ULS solutions were requested. In TESTFACT, both LI and FI solutions were requested. Because the ULS solutions obtained for Mplus and TESTFACT were essentially the same, only the results for Mplus are presented.

The Mplus-estimated tetrachoric matrix had eigenvalues 4.07, 1.21, 1.09, 0.95, 0.76, 0.70, 0.64, 0.59, 0.59, 0.54, 0.50, and 0.36 and an average tetrachoric correlation of 0.27. Table 2.1 displays goodness-of-fit statistics for the Mplus GLS solution and the TESTFACT full-information solution. The Mplus result for the four-dimensional model was an improper solution; thus its results are not reported. One the right-hand side of Table 2.1, the RMSR and Tanaka indices are reported for the NOHARM solutions. As described earlier, the goodness-of-fit tests for the Mplus and TESTFACT solutions contain different numbers of degrees of freedom. Thus, magnitudes of the χ^2 indices differ quite substantially. The RMSEA index also varies across methods, with the FI solution producing a consistently higher index. Interestingly, however, the χ^2-difference tests produce virtually identical results, with the change from one-factor to two-factor solutions producing $\chi^2_D(11) = 48.15$, $p < .001$ and 45.93, $p < .001$, for the Mplus and TESTFACT solutions, respectively. The two- to three-factor comparison results in $\chi^2_D(10) = 35.89$, $p < .001$, and 32.51, $p < .001$, for Mplus and TESTFACT, respectively, and the three- to four-factor comparison produces $\chi^2_D(9) = 11.30$, $p = .256$, for TESTFACT. The NOHARM indices lead to similar conclusions regarding the number of factors. Based on both the RMSR and Tanaka indices, there appears to be a consistent improvement in fit up to the three-factor solution, and then a smaller improvement from the three- to four-factor solution.

Only the three-factor solution produces an RMSR below .004 ($= 4$ divided by sample size), the criterion for a well-fitting model. Thus, each method suggests that improvements in fit are observed up to the three-dimensional solution.

Considering the interpretability of the solutions, however, a two-dimensional solution appeared superior to the three-dimensional solution. The two-dimensional Promax-rotated solutions obtained by each program are displayed in Table 2.2. Also reported is a description of each item type, here defined by the type of error introduced into the sentence.

Once again there appears to be a high degree of similarity among the solutions. (Note that the factor solutions have not been rotated to maximize congruence; hence, some differences may be due to slight differences in rotation.) The loadings in bold identify the factor pattern that generally emerged across solutions. Dimension 1 is most strongly associated with items having errors in word usage, whereas Dimension 2 is associated with items having punctuation errors. There are two items that are exceptions to this: Items 3 and 7, which appear to load on both dimensions. Interestingly, these two items, although having punctuation errors, also contain highly attractive distractors related to word usage. As a result, we might view these items as requiring both word usage and punctuation skill because identifying the correct answer requires recognizing not only that punctuation is the cause of the error in the sentence, but also that the attractive word-usage-related distractor is correctly specified.

Confirmatory Analysis

Based on the exploratory solutions, a confirmatory model was tested. As in linear confirmatory factor analyses, a confirmatory MNO can be fitted by fixing certain slope (loading) parameters to 0 while allowing others to be freely estimated. For the English usage data, a confirmatory model was specified in which Items 1, 4, 5 and 10–12 loaded only on Dimension 1, the "word usage error" dimension, Items 2 and 6–9 only on Dimension 2, the "punctuation error" dimension, whereas Items 3 and 7 loaded on both dimensions. The following discussion considers use of the Mplus, PRELIS/LISREL, and NOHARM programs in fitting this model. It should be noted that recent versions of the TESTFACT program also permit confirmatory analysis, but only for solutions that can be expressed in the form of a bifactor model (Gibbons & Hedeker, 1992). In a bifactor model each item loads on a general factor and exactly one specific factor. The current model cannot be expressed in that form, and so TESTFACT was not used here.

Mplus. Appendix C displays syntax used for the confirmatory analyses. For Mplus, many of the same features discussed for Mplus exploratory analyses apply here also. One difference is that standard errors and confidence intervals for parameter estimates are now reported (provided some type of weighted least squares estimation is used). Additional goodness-of-fit indices are also reported (e.g., the

TABLE 2.2

Exploratory Analysis of English Usage Data: Two-Factor Solutions (Promax Rotated)[a]

Item	Type of Error	Mplus (WLS)				Mplus (ULS)				NOHARM				TESTFACT			
		$\hat{\lambda}_1$	$\hat{\lambda}_2$	$\hat{\psi}$	$\hat{\tau}$	$\hat{\lambda}_1$	$\hat{\lambda}_2$	$\hat{\psi}$	$\hat{\tau}$	$\hat{\lambda}_1$	$\hat{\lambda}_2$	$\hat{\psi}$	$\hat{\tau}$	$\hat{\lambda}_1$	$\hat{\lambda}_2$	$\hat{\psi}$	$\hat{\tau}$
1	Subordination	**.39**	.04	.83	−.97	**.32**	.08	.86	−.97	**.38**	.02	.84	−.97	**.32**	.09	.85	−.97
2	Run-on	−.01	**.65**	.59	−.75	−.05	**.71**	.54	−.75	.01	**.61**	.61	−.75	−.09	**.74**	.53	−.75
3	Punctuation clarity	**.32**	**.43**	.55	−.32	**.30**	**.43**	.57	−.32	**.27**	**.45**	.57	−.32	**.27**	**.44**	.57	−.32
4	Fragment	**.56**	.06	.65	−.83	**.57**	.01	.67	−.83	**.37**	.18	.74	−.83	**.59**	.00	.66	−.83
5	Adverb/adjective	**.54**	−.04	.73	−.68	**.45**	.05	.77	−.68	**.61**	−.11	.71	−.68	**.47**	.04	.76	−.69
6	Comma splice	.07	**.62**	.57	−.27	.15	**.48**	.66	−.27	−.06	**.69**	.57	−.27	.13	**.51**	.64	−.28
7	Punctuation clarity	**.48**	**.24**	.58	.44	**.44**	**.26**	.61	.44	**.55**	**.14**	.58	.44	**.43**	**.24**	.63	.43
8	Punctuation clarity	.04	**.56**	.66	−.27	−.00	**.59**	.66	−.27	.15	**.40**	.73	−.27	−.05	**.62**	.66	−.27
9	Comma splice	.11	**.64**	.51	−.05	.16	**.55**	.57	−.05	−.01	**.70**	.52	−.05	.11	**.58**	.57	−.06
10	Tense	**.53**	.16	.60	.32	**.58**	.09	.60	.32	**.44**	.19	.65	.32	**.59**	.05	.61	.32
11	Subject–verb agreement	**.56**	−.12	.74	.55	**.57**	−.17	.76	.55	**.53**	−.13	.79	.55	**.64**	−.24	.74	.55
12	Adverb/adjective	**.50**	.04	.73	.09	**.43**	.09	.76	.09	**.59**	−.08	.71	.09	**.42**	.08	.77	.09
	Factor correlation	.56				.59				.68				.67			

[a]WLS, Weighted least squares; ULS, unweighted least squares.

Comparative Fit Index (CFI) and Tucker-Lewis Index (TLI)), along with indices reported in exploratory analyses, such as the standard chi-square goodness-of-fit test, the RMSEA index, and the residual tetrachoric matrix. The user can also request computation of modification indices to examine potential causes of misfit in the model.

PRELIS/LISREL. For confirmatory analyses, the PRELIS/LISREL software package can be used to carry out a GLS analysis similar to Muthén's procedure. The analysis is carried out by first using PRELIS to compute (a) the tetrachoric correlation matrix and (b) an asymptotic covariance matrix of the tetrachoric correlations. These two matrices are saved to files that are used in LISREL to fit the confirmatory model. The inverse of the asymptotic covariance matrix of the tetrachoric correlations functions as weights in this analysis. As described earlier, the approach here is equivalent to that used by Muthén (1978).

Like Mplus, LISREL provides standard errors for all estimated parameters as well as a chi-square goodness-of-fit test and a large number of goodness-of-fit statistics. It also reports the tetrachoric residual matrix and modification indices to assist in evaluating causes of misfit. Documentation of this procedure is provided by Jöreskog and Sörbom (1993a, 1993b).

NOHARM. NOHARM functions in much the same way in a confirmatory analysis as in an exploratory analysis, the primary difference being the specification of the factor pattern matrix indicating which loadings are fixed to zero. Estimates will again be reported according to both the latent trait and common factor model parametrizations. As in the exploratory analysis, the residual covariance matrix, the RMSR, and the Tanaka index for ULS solutions are reported for model fit assessment. Besides fixing slope parameters to zero, other types of parameter constraints, including equality constraints and nonzero fixed-value constraints, can also be specified (see Fraser, 1988, for details).

Results of Confirmatory Analysis. Table 2.3 reports the model parameter estimates from the confirmatory analyses. Each of the methods, in this case all LI methods, produce solutions with an even higher degree of similarity in the factor loading, uniqueness, and threshold estimates than was apparent in the exploratory analysis. Across all three solutions, Items 4 and 10 are the most discriminating for the word usage dimension, and Items 6 and 9 are the most discriminating for the punctuation factor.

In terms of goodness of fit, the Mplus solution indicated $\chi^2 = 83.90$, $df = 51$, $p = .003$, with RMSEA = .025, CFI = .951, and TLI = .936. Because this model can be viewed as a constrained version of the exploratory two-dimensional solution, the χ^2 difference between models follows a χ^2 distribution under a null hypothesis of no difference in fit. This comparison produced $\chi^2(D) = 7.72$, $df = 8$, $p > .50$, implying no significant decline in fit. The LISREL Weighted Least Squares fit

TABLE 2.3

Confirmatory Analysis of English Usage Data: Two-Factor Solutions[a]

Item	Type of Error	Mplus (WLS)				LISREL (WLS)				NOHARM			
		$\hat{\lambda}_1$	$\hat{\lambda}_2$	$\hat{\psi}$	$\hat{\tau}$	$\hat{\lambda}_1$	$\hat{\lambda}_2$	$\hat{\psi}$	$\hat{\tau}$	$\hat{\lambda}_1$	$\hat{\lambda}_2$	$\hat{\psi}$	$\hat{\tau}$
1	Subordination	.42		.83	-.98	.41		.83	-.97	.40		.84	-.97
2	Run-on		.61	.63	-.76		.61	.63	-.75		.63	.61	-.75
3	Punctuation clarity	.27	.46	.55	-.33	.27	.46	.55	-.32	.24	.47	.57	-.32
4	Fragment	.61		.63	-.83	.60		.64	-.83	.56		.69	-.83
5	Adverb/adjective	.49		.76	-.70	.50		.75	-.68	.49		.76	-.68
6	Comma splice		.66	.57	-.27		.66	.57	-.27		.63	.61	-.27
7	Punctuation clarity	.47	.22	.58	.43	.47	.22	.58	.44	.50	.18	.59	.44
8	Punctuation clarity		.57	.67	-.28		.57	.67	-.27		.55	.70	-.27
9	Comma splice		.72	.49	-.07		.72	.49	-.05		.68	.54	-.05
10	Tense	.66		.56	.31	.66		.56	.32	.64		.59	.32
11	Subject-verb agreement	.45		.80	.58	.45		.79	.55	.41		.84	.55
12	Adverb/adjective	.53		.72	.08	.53		.72	.09	.50		.75	.09
	Factor correlation	.68				.68				.70			

[a] WLS, Weighted least squares.

indices are nearly identical, with $\chi^2 = 83.51$, $df = 51$, $p = .003$, and RMSEA = .025. Finally, the fit statistics from NOHARM produce RMSR = .0066 and Tanaka index = .99677, also suggesting no meaningful change in fit relative to the two-dimensional exploratory solution.

Table 2.4 reports residual matrices for the Mplus and NOHARM solutions. For Mplus, the elements of the residual matrix represent residual tetrachoric correlations, whereas for NOHARM, the elements are residual covariances. Apart from this difference, the pattern of residuals appears largely the same, and thus a high degree of similarity exists between what these two methods suggest as the primary causes of misfit in the model.

Thus, overall, the exploratory and confirmatory analyses suggest a high degree of similarity between full- and limited-information solutions in terms of both the final parameter estimates and in evaluations of goodness of fit, and only minor differences among LI methods. One difficulty in comparing FI and LI results, however, is that in addition to utilizing different amounts of information, they are also associated with different estimation procedures. The next section provides a brief overview of an alternative estimation methodology that can be implemented in both LI and FI forms, and thus may allow a more direct comparison of the two general strategies.

MARKOV CHAIN MONTE CARLO ESTIMATION

Markov chain Monte Carlo (MCMC) estimation methods have received much attention in item response theory (e.g., Albert, 1992; Patz & Junker, 1999) and are attractive in large part due to the ease with which they can be implemented using computer software. Algorithms for even complex IRT models can often be written in minutes using software programs such as Splus (e.g., Patz & Junker, 1999) and WINBUGS (Spiegelhalter, Thomas, & Best, 2000). Recent examples of the usefulness of this methodology in IRT include applications to multilevel (Fox & Glas, 2001), multidimensional (Bèguin & Glas, 2001; Segall, 2002), and mixture (Bolt et al., 2001) IRT models.

MCMC adopts a perspective of Bayesian inference in which variables are distinguished as observed data, denoted as $\mathbf{Y}$, and unobserved model parameters and missing data, denoted Ω. Given a joint prior distribution for Ω, denoted $P(\Omega)$, and a model for the data, represented by $P(\mathbf{Y}|\Omega)$, we can write the joint multivariate density of the data and model parameters as

$$P(\mathbf{Y}, \Omega) = P(\mathbf{Y}|\Omega)P(\Omega). \tag{46}$$

An application of Bayes's theorem produces the posterior distribution of interest:

$$P(\Omega|\mathbf{Y}) = \frac{P(\Omega)P(\mathbf{Y}|\Omega)}{\int P(\Omega)P(\mathbf{Y}|\Omega)d\Omega}. \tag{47}$$

TABLE 2.4

Residual Matrices for LISREL and NOHARM Confirmatory Solutions

Item	1	2	3	4	5	6	7	8	9	10	11
LISREL											
2	-0.032										
3	-0.010	-0.011									
4	0.033	-0.088	0.018								
5	-0.003	0.008	0.011	-0.089							
6	-0.034	-0.006	0.026	-0.018	-0.044						
7	-0.002	0.009	-0.006	-0.097	-0.030	-0.088					
8	0.007	0.065	-0.003	-0.091	0.013	-0.148	0.059				
9	0.021	-0.034	-0.086	0.078	-0.041	0.009	-0.042	-0.035			
10	-0.131	0.027	-0.067	0.049	-0.039	0.077	-0.025	-0.026	0.011		
11	-0.115	-0.079	-0.064	-0.023	-0.007	-0.019	0.017	-0.114	-0.066	0.020	
12	0.067	0.012	-0.025	-0.138	0.094	-0.064	0.006	0.052	-0.034	-0.087	-0.019
NOHARM											
2	-0.003										
3	0.000	-0.001									
4	0.008	-0.010	0.006								
5	-0.001	0.002	0.003	-0.004							
6	-0.002	-0.001	0.008	-0.002	-0.000						
7	0.000	0.002	0.002	-0.005	-0.006	-0.007					
8	-0.000	0.013	0.005	-0.011	0.001	-0.015	0.010				
9	0.003	-0.003	-0.009	0.009	-0.001	0.004	-0.001	0.004			
10	-0.008	-0.001	-0.008	0.014	-0.001	0.009	0.001	-0.008	-0.001		
11	-0.008	-0.004	-0.002	0.004	-0.003	0.006	0.003	-0.013	-0.000	0.011	
12	0.007	0.003	-0.000	-0.008	0.008	-0.003	-0.001	0.008	0.001	-0.006	-0.003

Estimates of model parameters are derived by estimating this posterior distribution (Gilks, Richardson, & Spiegelhalter, 1996). Specifically, a Markov chain is simulated whose stages represent a sample from the posterior distribution. The key to this simulation process is the creation of a transition kernel for the chain, that is, the probabilistic process of moving from an existing state to a new state at the subsequent stage of the chain, so as to produce a stationary distribution for the chain that is the posterior distribution of interest. Different MCMC strategies are distinguished by the specific method used in defining this transition kernel and carrying out the sampling process. They will not be discussed in detail here; the interested reader is referred to Gilks et al., (1996) for a more comprehensive introduction to MCMC and Patz and Junker (1999) for an introduction of MCMC applications in IRT. We consider one approach below in the next subsection, the so-called Metropolis–Hastings within Gibbs method (Chib & Greenberg, 1995), and illustrate its implementation in both FI and LI estimation of the MNO.

Gibbs Sampling and the Metropolis–Hastings Algorithm

In MCMC, the objective is to simulate observations from the joint conditional posterior distribution of the model parameters (Ω) over stages of the Markov chain. For the MNO, these parameters include both item (slope and threshold) and examinee (latent ability) parameters. Because the total number of parameters is typically quite large, however, the joint distribution of all parameters is typically too highly multivariate to make it practical to sample all parameters at once. Fortunately, it is often possible to group parameters into blocks that can be sampled separately without affecting the convergence properties of the chain (Chib & Greenberg, 1995). For example, in the following examples, we consider the full conditional posterior distributions of each individual item parameter and each individual examinee ability vector, and separately sample from each in the process of estimating their joint distribution.

When the full conditional distributions of the model parameters are of known form (e.g., normal, gamma) they can often be sampled from directly, a process referred to as *Gibbs sampling*. For most item response models, however, the full conditional posterior distributions can often only be determined up to a normalizing constant. As a result, alternative sampling strategies are needed. One possibility is to augment the item response data to include latent responses (similar to the latent response propensities considered earlier). Albert (1992) and Béguin and Glas (2001) showed how such a procedure can be applied with the unidimensional and multidimensional normal ogive models, respectively. Because the full conditional distributions of parameters given the latent responses can be expressed in closed form, Gibbs sampling can then be conducted.

An alternative approach is the *Metropolis–Hastings algorithm* (Hastings, 1970). In the Metropolis–Hastings method, candidate states for the chain are randomly generated from proposal distributions. For example, a candidate state for a model parameter might be generated from a normal distribution whose mean is equal to the current state of the chain. This candidate state is then compared against the current state of the parameter in the chain and accepted (i.e., becomes the next stage of the chain) with probability equal to the ratio of the likelihood of the data given the candidate state to the likelihood of the data given the current state (If the likelihood of the candidate state is higher, it is always accepted). If the candidate state is not accepted, the state of the chain at the previous stage is retained for the next stage. Using this acceptance criterion, it can be shown that the Markov chain will eventually converge to a stationary distribution that represents the posterior distribution of the parameter of interest (Gilks et al., 1996, pp. 7–8). Some experimentation is usually needed to determine suitable variances for the proposal distributions because too small a variance leads to very frequent acceptance of the candidate state and too large a variance leads to infrequent acceptance. Generally, a variance that produces acceptance probabilities of between 20% and 50% is considered desirable.

In all MCMC applications, a starting state (i.e., initial values for all parameters) must be specified for the chain. Because the first several states of the chain are often dependent on the starting state, a number of the initial iterations, referred to as *burn-in iterations*, are discarded. One criterion for determining an appropriate number of iterations to discard is the lag needed between stages before the autocorrelation reaches zero (Geyer, 1992). This lag can be estimated from the stages observed across the entire chain. After this sequence of burn-in stages, the subsequent stages of the chain can be taken to represent a sample from the posterior distribution of the parameter. Because the mean of these iterations represents the mean of the posterior distribution, it is commonly used as an estimate of the model parameter.

The program WINBUGS (Spiegelhalter et al., 2000) can be used for MCMC estimation using Metropolis–Hastings sampling. In WINBUGS, parameters having full conditional posterior distributions that can be expressed in closed form are estimated using Gibbs sampling, whereas the other parameters are sampled using Metropolis–Hastings. The combination of these two procedures is described as the Metropolis–Hastings within Gibbs method. In the WINBUGS program, 4,000 iterations are used to determine suitable variances for proposal distributions prior to simulating stages that are the basis for estimating the model parameters. Further details on Metropolis–Hastings sampling can be found in Patz and Junker (1999) and Spiegelhalter, Thomas, Best, and Gilks (1996).

Simulation studies found MCMC procedures performed comparably to NOHARM and TESTFACT. Béguin and Glas (2001) achieved very similar results for the MNO using Gibbs sampling with data augmentation when compared to NOHARM and TESTFACT. Bolt and Lall (2003) found a Metropolis–Hastings within Gibbs algorithm to be effective in estimating a multidimensional logistic IRT model, although it produced slightly inferior estimates compared to NOHARM.

Analysis of the English Usage Data

Depending on whether the full item response matrix or only marginals are analyzed, an MCMC algorithm can be used as either a full- or a limited-information procedure. In the current analysis, separate FI and LI MCMC routines were designed for an exploratory two-dimensional MNO model using the latent trait parametrization of the model. Both algorithms were applied to the same English usage data analyzed earlier. The same prior distributions were imposed for the model parameters in both methods. The latent ability parameters are assumed to follow a bivariate normal distribution with a means of zero and an identity covariance matrix. The rotational indeterminacy of the two-dimensional solution was resolved by fixing the slope parameter for the first item on the second dimension to zero (i.e., $\beta_{12} = 0$). All other slope parameters were assigned the noninformative priors: $\beta_{i1}, \beta_{i2} \sim \text{Normal}(0, 2)$, whereas the intercept parameters were assigned priors $\alpha_i \sim \text{Normal}(0, 1)$. Taken together, these priors produce full conditional posterior distributions of closed form only for the intercepts. Thus, a Metropolis–Hastings within Gibbs procedure is used in which Metropolis–Hastings sampling is employed for the slope and latent ability parameters and Gibbs sampling is used for the intercepts.

A Full-Information MCMC Algorithm.   In the full-information algorithm, each 0/1 item response is regarded as an outcome from a Bernoulli trial, with probability of success determined by the MNO model and the current states of the item and examinee trait parameters. Thus the data are modeled as

$$u_{ki} \sim \text{Bernoulli}(\text{Prob}_i(U_{ki} = 1 | \theta_k, \alpha_i, \beta_i)). \qquad (48)$$

where u_{ki} denotes the observed 0/1 response to item i by examinee k, and $\text{Prob}_i(U_{ki} = 1 | \theta_k, \alpha_i, \beta_i)$ is the model-based probability of correct response. Independence is assumed across items and examinees. A Markov chain was simulated out to 50,000 iterations, with sampling histories being recorded for each item slope and intercept parameter. The starting state was randomly generated by the WINBUGS program. For the Metropolis–Hastings algorithm, normal proposal distributions were used with variances for the distributions determined from an initial phase of 4,000 iterations.

A Limited-Information MCMC Algorithm.   In the limited-information algorithm, the observed data are the proportion correct (p_i) and joint-proportion-correct (p_{ij}) values. To connect these data back to the MNO model, latent item responses are simulated at each stage of the Markov chain for $N = 1,000$ examinees having latent abilities sampled from a bivariate normal distribution. As for the observed responses in the FI method, the latent responses are regarded as outcomes of Bernoulli trials where the probability of correct response is determined by the MNO model, the latent examinee θs, and the item parameters. In this respect, the LI algorithm is very similar to the FI algorithm, the primary difference being the use of latent as opposed to observed item responses. The latent responses produce π_i and π_{ij}, the marginal proportion correct and joint proportion correct according to the two-dimensional MNO model, respectively. The observed p_i and p_{ij} are regarded as outcomes from normal distributions having these population parameters as means. Specifically,

$$p_i \sim \text{Normal}\left(\pi_i, \sigma_{\pi_i}^2\right), \tag{49}$$

$$p_{ij} \sim \text{Normal}\left(\pi_{ij}, \sigma_{\pi_{ij}}^2\right). \tag{50}$$

For simplicity, the current analysis fixed $\sigma_{\pi_i}^2 = \sigma_{\pi_{ij}}^2 = .001$, although it would also be possible to estimate them or fix them at other values. As in the FI algorithm, a Markov chain was simulated out to 50,000 iterations, with sampling histories being recorded for each item slope and intercept parameter, with the starting state being randomly generated by the WINBUGS program. Normal proposal distributions were again used with Metropolis–Hastings with variances being determined from an initial phase of 4,000 iterations.

Results. Figure 2.3 illustrates examples of the sampling histories and densities of two model parameters, β_{11} and α_1, traced in each of the FI and LI algorithms. Although the lag needed to produce an autocorrelation of zero was about 30 for each run, a conservative 1,000 iterations were omitted as burn-in iterations. The sampling histories in Fig. 2.3 thus illustrate the sampled parameter value at each stage starting at stage 1,001. The estimated densities approximate the accumulated frequencies of the parameter values over the chain, and thus illustrate the estimated marginal posterior distributions of the parameters.

The sampling histories for these parameters (as well as for parameters not shown) suggested the chain converged to its stationary distribution relatively quickly. Moreover, the sampling densities in all cases appear to be unimodal and symmetric, suggesting that the posterior means likely provide reasonable estimates.

Table 2.5 reports the final estimates (unrotated) and standard errors from each analysis. The standard errors are the variances of the estimated posterior distributions. For our purposes, we note that the results observed for the FI and LI algorithms appear to be very similar. The estimates are nearly always the same across methods, whereas the standard errors for the LI method are only slightly higher than those for FI. The results here thus appear consistent with the previous claim that little use appears to be made of third- and higher order marginals when estimating parameters of the MNO. The WINBUGS programs used to produce these results can be obtained from the author.

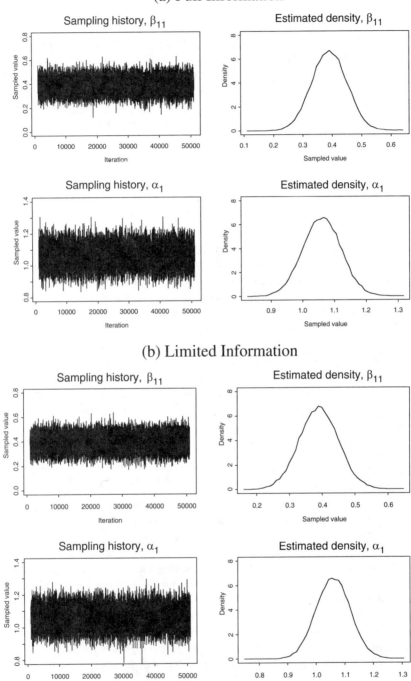

FIG. 2.3. Sampling histories and densities for example parameters using the full-information and limited-information MCMC algorithms.

TABLE 2.5

Two-Factor Markov Chain Monte Carlo Exploratory Solutions: Full and Limited Information (Latent Trait Parametrization)[a]

Item	Type of Error	Full Information						Limited Information					
		$\hat{\beta}_1$	se	$\hat{\beta}_2$	se	$\hat{\alpha}$	se	$\hat{\beta}_1$	se	$\hat{\beta}_2$	se	$\hat{\alpha}$	se
1	Subordination	.39	.06	.00	—	1.06	.06	.39	.06	.00	—	1.05	.06
2	Run-on	.48	.10	.41	.13	1.00	.09	.46	.11	.41	.14	.97	.08
3	Punctuation clarity	.60	.07	.25	.13	.44	.06	.59	.08	.25	.16	.43	.06
4	Fragment	.54	.07	.00	.18	1.02	.08	.52	.07	.01	.19	1.00	.07
5	Adverb/adjective	.50	.06	−.06	.13	.81	.06	.49	.07	−.07	.13	.80	.06
6	Comma splice	.48	.10	.37	.17	.36	.06	.47	.11	.37	.19	.35	.06
7	Punctuation clarity	.60	.05	.07	.14	−.55	.06	.62	.06	.07	.16	−.57	.06
8	Punctuation clarity	.44	.08	.32	.13	.33	.05	.44	.09	.31	.13	.32	.05
9	Comma splice	.53	.09	.39	.14	.08	.05	.52	.11	.39	.16	.07	.05
10	Tense	.58	.06	.02	.18	−.40	.05	.58	.07	.03	.20	−.41	.06
11	Subject–verb agreement	.41	.06	−.16	.15	−.63	.05	.42	.07	−.16	.16	−.63	.06
12	Adverb/adjective	.50	.06	−.05	.13	−.10	.05	.50	.07	−.05	.13	−.11	.05

[a] se, Standard error.

CONCLUSION

Thus chapter focused on applications of limited-information and full-information estimation methods to the MNO model. LI and FI methods can also be generalized to other models and other types of data . For example, both LI and FI methods can be used to modify the MNO to account for guessing effects, as might occur in multiple-choice items. Limited-information methods can account for guessing effects by adjusting the observed proportion correct and joint proportion correct values (Carroll, 1945). These adjusted values can then either be fit directly (as in NOHARM) or used to estimate tetrachoric correlations that are analyzed. Recall that in FI methods, the use of a marginal conditional model formulation allows for straightforward extentions to alternative item response models. Thus, guessing can accommodated by changing the model so that instead of Equation 2 we fit

$$\text{Prob}(u_i = 1|\boldsymbol{\theta}) = g_i + (1 - g_i)N(\alpha_i + \beta_{i1}\theta_1 + \cdots + \beta_{ik}\theta_k), \qquad (51)$$

where g_i is a "guessing parameter" for item i, which represents the lower asymptote of the item response surface.

LI and FI methods can also be generalized to account for items having more than two categories. In item factor analysis (IFA), this is handled by adding a threshold parameter for each pair of successive categories. Under such conditions, the correlation between a pair of ys from different items becomes known as the polychoric correlation. Muthén's method can be easily generalized to accommodate polytomous items, and software programs such as Mplus and LISREL can also be used to compute polychorics. Another approach to handling polytomously scored items in IFA is described by Lee, Poon, and Bentler (1995) and is implemented in the computer package EQS. Among full-information methods, the procedure of Bock, Gibbons, and Muraki has been extended to polytomously scored items by Muraki and Carlson (1995).

Although empirical comparisons of LI and FI methods suggest they perform quite similarly, both approaches have advantages and disadvantages. LI methods are attractive in that they are based on a definition of dimensionality that is more closely aligned with that of factor analysis, and thus is familiar to many test practitioners. This advantage is also apparent when evaluating model fit. Because there are far fewer data values modeled (and thus fewer residuals), isolating the cause of misfit is usually more straightforward. In addition, software programs for LI methods are usually less computationally demanding and much faster than FI methods.

Perhaps the main disadvantage of LI estimation as a general procedure is that many models—for example, latent class models and mixture models—may not be statistically identified from only univariate and bivariate information [but see Maydeu-Olivares (2002; chap. 3 this volume) for examples of other models that are identified using LI].

FI methods are attractive due to the ease with which they can relax modeling assumptions, particularly in relation to the distribution of the latent trait. Through use of a marginal conditional modeling formulation, they also make it easier to accommodate alternative item response models. Computationally, FI methods also offer greater efficiency than most LI methods when there are larger numbers of items, and can also circumvent computational problems associated with analyzing non-positive-definite matrices. Finally, they are also more flexible in accommodating prior distributions on model parameters.

Future simulation work may help in understanding what, if any, distinctions exist between these two approaches.

APPENDIX A. SAMPLE ENGLISH USAGE ITEMS

1. *I, Claudius*, one of television's most lauded series, are being rebroadcast.
              A   B   C   D
   No error.   (Correct Answer: D)
   E

2. Maria, who had just eaten, thought concerning having a candy bar or ice
                  A   B   C   D
   cream. No error.   (Correct Answer: C)
   E

3. Nobody believes that the defendant will be acquitted, even his strongest sup-
            A   B   C
   porters are convinced of his guilt. No error.   (Correct Answer: C)
              D   E

APPENDIX B. MPLUS, NOHARM, AND TESTFACT COMMAND SYNTAX, EXPLORATORY ANALYSIS

Mplus Syntax

```
TITLE:          English Usage data, 12 items
DATA:           FILE is usage.txt;
VARIABLE:       NAMES ARE item1-item12;
                  CATEGORICAL ARE item1-item12;
ANALYSIS:       TYPE = EFA 1 5; ESTIMATOR = WLS;
OUTPUT:         SAMPSTAT;
```

NOHARM Syntax

```
Exploratory Analysis of 12 English Usage Items
12 2 1000 1 1 0 1 0
0 0 0 0 0 0 0 0 0 0 0 0
0.83400 0.65500 0.77200 0.54400 0.52900 0.62500 0.68700 0.63000 0.54000 0.79700
0.64500 0.60300 0.50800 0.62000 0.75300 0.52100 0.51700 0.44800 0.51200 0.47900
0.60700 0.29800 0.29100 0.26300 0.29100 0.28000 0.23800 0.33100 0.52200 0.51900
0.43400 0.49900 0.48200 0.40200 0.25200 0.60600 0.45600 0.45100 0.38300 0.45700
0.41700 0.39200 0.22300 0.37400 0.52000 0.32600 0.32300 0.28000 0.34400 0.31600
0.28200 0.18000 0.26100 0.24600 0.37500 0.24800 0.23500 0.20700 0.25400 0.24100
0.20000 0.13500 0.18400 0.17200 0.15200 0.29000 0.41500 0.38600 0.33300 0.39000
0.39400 0.30800 0.20300 0.32100 0.27700 0.21400 0.16500 0.46400
```

TESTFACT Syntax

```
>TITLE
  English Usage Data
  Exploratory Analysis of 12 Items
>PROBLEM NITEM=12, RESPONSE=3;
>RESPONSE ' ','0','1';
>KEY 111111111111;
>FACTOR NFAC=2,ROTATE=PROMAX;
>FULL QUAD=5;
>INPUT NIDW=3, FILE='usage.txt';
(3A1,T1,12A1)
>STOP;
```

APPENDIX C: MPLUS, PRELIS/LISREL, AND NOHARM COMMAND SYNTAX, CONFIRMATORY ANALYSIS

Mplus Syntax

```
TITLE:      Confirmatory Factor Analysis of English
            Usage Data, 12 Items
DATA:       FILE is c:usage.txt;
VARIABLE:   NAMES ARE item1-item12;
            CATEGORICAL ARE item1-item12;
ANALYSIS:   ESTIMATOR=WLS;
MODEL:      f1 BY item1 item3 item4 item5
             item7 item10 item11 item12;
            f2 BY item2 item3 item6 item7 item8 item9;
OUTPUT:     SAMPSTAT, STANDARDIZED;
```

PRELIS/LISREL Syntax

```
PRELIS Example: English Usage Data
Computing Tetrachoric Matrix for Confirmatory
   Factor Analysis
DA NI=12 TR=LI
RA=c:usage.txt
OR ALL
OU MA=PM PM=c:usage.pm AC=c:usage.acm

LISREL Example: English Usage Data
Confirmatory Factor Model
DA NI=12 NO=1000 MA=PM
PM FI = 'c:usage.pm'
AC FI = 'c:usage.acm'
MO NK=2 NX=12 LX=FU,FI TD=DI,FR PH=ST,FR
FR LX 1 1 LX 3 1 LX 4 1 LX 5 1 LX 7 1 LX 10 1 LX 11 1 LX
   12 1
FR LX 2 2 LX 3 2 LX 6 2 LX 7 2 LX 8 2 LX 9 2
PD
OU
```

NOHARM Syntax

```
Confirmatory Analysis of 12 Items
12 2 1000 1 0 0 1 0
0 0 0 0 0 0 0 0 0 0 0 0

1 0
0 1
1 1
1 0
1 0
0 1
1 1
0 1
0 1
1 0
1 0
1 0
0
1 0
0.83400 0.65500 0.77200 0.54400 0.52900 0.62500 0.68700 0.63000 0.54000 0.79700
0.64500 0.60300 0.50800 0.62000 0.75300 0.52100 0.51700 0.44800 0.51200 0.47900
0.60700 0.29800 0.29100 0.26300 0.29100 0.28000 0.23800 0.33100 0.52200 0.51900
0.43400 0.49900 0.48200 0.40200 0.25200 0.60600 0.45600 0.45100 0.38300 0.45700
0.41700 0.39200 0.22300 0.37400 0.52000 0.32600 0.32300 0.28000 0.34400 0.31600
0.28200 0.18000 0.26100 0.24600 0.37500 0.24800 0.23500 0.20700 0.25400 0.24100
0.20000 0.13500 0.18400 0.17200 0.15200 0.29000 0.41500 0.38600 0.33300 0.39000
0.39400 0.30800 0.20300 0.32100 0.27700 0.21400 0.16500 0.46400
```

REFERENCES

Ackerman, T. A. (1994). Using multidimensional item response theory to understand what items and tests are measuring. *Applied Measurement in Education, 7*, 255–278.

Ackerman, T. A. (2005). Multidimensional item response theory. In A. Maydeu-Olivares & J. J. McArdle (Eds.), *Contemporary psychometrics* (pp. 3–26).

Albert, J. H. (1992). Bayesian estimation of normal ogive item response functions using Gibbs sampling. *Journal of Educational Statistics, 17*, 251–269.

Baker, F., & Kim, S-H. (2004). Item response theory: Parameter estimation techniques (2nd Ed.). New York: Dekker.

Bartholomew, D. J., & Knott, M. (1999). *Latent variable models and factor analysis.* London: Arnold.

Béguin, A. A., & Glas, C. A. W. (2001). MCMC estimation and some model-fit analysis of multidimensional IRT models. *Psychometrika, 66*, 541–562.

Bock, R. D., & Aitkin, M. (1981). Marginal maximum likelihood estimation of item parameters: Application of an EM algorithm. *Psychometrika, 46*, 443–459.

Bock, R. D., Gibbons, R., & Muraki, E. (1988). Full information item factor analysis. *Applied Psychological Measurement, 12*, 261–280.

Bock, R. D., & Lieberman, M. (1970). Fitting a response model for n dichotomously scored items. *Psychometrika, 35*, 179–197.

Bolt, D. M., Cohen, A. S., & Wollack, J. A. (2001). A mixture item response model for multiple-choice data. *Journal of Educational and Behavioral Statistics, 26*, 381–409.

Bolt, D. M., & Lall, V. F. (2003). Estimation of compensatory and noncompensatory multidimensional IRT models using Markov chain Monte Carlo. Applied Psychological Measurement, *27*, 395–414.

Carlson, J. E. (1987). *Multidimensional item response theory estimation: A computer program* (Research Rep. ONR 87-2). Iowa City, IA: American College Testing Program.

Carroll, J. B. (1945). The effect of difficulty and chance success on correlations between items or tests. *Psychometrika, 10*, 1–19.

Chib, S., & Greenberg, E. (1995). Understanding the Metropolis–Hastings algorithm. *American Statistician, 49*, 327–335.

Christoffersson, A. (1975). Factor analysis of dichotomized variables. *Psychometrika, 40*, 5–32.

Embretson, S. E., & Reise, S. P. (2000). *Item response theory for psychologists.* Mahwah, NJ: Lawrence Erlbaum Associates, Inc.

Etezadi-Amoli, J., & McDonald, R. P. (1983). A second generation nonlinear factor analysis. *Psychometrika, 48*, 315–342.

Finger, M. S. (2002, April). *A comparison of full-information and unweighted least squares limited-information item parameter estimation methods used with the two-parameter normal ogive model.* Paper presented at the annual meeting of the American Educational Research Association, New Orleans, LA.

Fox, J.-P., & Glas, C. A. W. (2001). Bayesian estimation of a multilevel IRT model using Gibbs' sampling. *Psychometrika, 66*, 269–286.

Fraser, C. (1988). *NOHARM: A computer program for fitting both unidimensional and multidimensional normal ogive models of latent trait theory.* Armidale, Australia: University of New England, Centre for Behavioral Studies.

Geyer, C. J. (1992). Practical Markov chain Monte Carlo. *Statistical Science, 7*, 473–483.

Gibbons, R. D. (1984). *Multivariate probit analysis: A general model.* Paper presented at the meeting of the Psychometric Society, Santa Barbara, CA.

Gibbons, R. D., & Hedeker, D. R. (1992). Full information item bi-factor analysis. *Psychometrika, 57*, 423–436.

Gilks, W. R., Richardson, S., & Spiegelhalter, D. J. (1996). *Markov chain Monte Carlo in practice.* Washington, DC: Chapman & Hall.

Gosz, J. K., & Walker, C. M. (2002, April). *An empirical comparison of multidimensional item response data using TESTFACT and NOHARM.* Paper presented at the annual meeting of the National Council on Measurement in Education, New Orleans, LA.

Hastings, W. K. (1970). Monte Carlo sampling methods using Markov chains and their applications. *Biometrika, 57,* 97–109.

Holland, P. W., & Rosenbaum, P. R. (1986). Conditional association and unidimensionality in monotone latent variable models. *Annals of Statistics, 14,* 1523–1543.

Jöreskog, K. G., & Sörbom, D. (1993a). *LISREL 8: User's reference guide.* Chicago: Scientific Software International.

Jöreskog, K. G., & Sörbom, D. (1993b). *PRELIS 2: User's reference guide.* Chicago: Scientific Software International.

Haberman, S. J. (1977). Log-linear models and frequency tables with small expected cell counts. *Annals of Statistics, 5,* 1148–1169.

Hoijtink, H., & Molenaar, I. W. (1997). A multidimensional item response model: Constrained latent class analysis using the Gibbs' sampler and posterior predictive checks. *Psychometrika, 67,* 171–189.

Holland, P. W., & Rosenbaum, P. (1986). Conditional association and unidirnensionality in monotone latent variable models. *Annals of Statistics, 14,* 1523–1543.

Jöreskog, K. (1994). On the estimation of polychoric correlations and their asymptotic covariance matrix. *Psychometrika, 59,* 381–389.

Jöreskog, K. G., & Sörbom, D. (1996). *PRELIS2: User's reference guide.* Chicago: Scientific Software International.

Kendall, M. G. (1941). Relations connected with the tetrachoric series and its generalization. *Biometrika, 32,* 196–198.

Knol, D. L., & Berger, M. P. F. (1991). Empirical comparison between factor analysis and multidimensional item response models. *Multivariate Behavioral Research, 26,* 457–477.

Lee, S. Y., Poon, W. Y., & Bentler, P. M. (1995). A three-stage estimation procedure for structural equation models with polytomous variables. *Psychometrika, 55,* 45–51.

Lord, F. (1952). A theory of test scores. *Psychometric Monographs, No. 7.* Chicago, IL: University of Chicago.

Lord, F. M., & Novick, M. R. (1968). *Statistical theories of mental test scores.* Reading, MA: Addison-Wesley.

Maydeu-Olivares, A. (1996). Modelos multidimensionales de repuesta a los items [Multidimensional item response models.] In J. Muñiz (Ed.), *Psicometría* [Psychometrics] (pp. 811–868). Madrid: Universitas.

Maydeu-Olivares, A. (2001). Multidimensional item response theory modeling of binary data: Large sample properties of NOHARM estimates. *Journal of Educational and Behavioral Statistics, 26,* 51–71.

Maydeu-Olivares, A. (2002). *Limited information estimation and testing of discretized multivariate normal structural models.* Unpublished manuscript.

Maydeu-Olivares, A. (2005). In A. Maydeu-Olivares & J. J. McArdle (Eds.), *Contemporary psychometrics* (pp. 73–100).

Maydeu-Olivares, A., Hernández, A., & McDonald, R. P. (2002). *A multidimensional latent trait model for binary attitudinal data.*

McDonald, R. P. (1967). *Nonlinear factor analysis* (Psychometric Monographs, No. 15). Chicago: University of Chicago Press.

McDonald, R. P. (1981). The dimensionality of tests and items. *British Journal of Mathematical and Statistical Psychology, 34,* 100–117.

McDonald, R. P. (1982). Linear versus nonlinear models in item response theory. *Applied Psychological Measurement, 6,* 379–396.

McDonald, R. P. (1985). Unidimensional and multidimensional models for item response theory. In D. J. Weiss (Ed.), *Proceedings of the 1982 Item Response and Computerized Adaptive Testing Conference* (pp. 65–87). Minneapolis: University of Minnesota.

McDonald, R. P. (1997). Normal-ogive multidimensional model. In W. J. van der Linden & R. K. Hambleton (Eds.), *Handbook of modern item response theory* (pp. 257–269). New York: Springer-Verlag.

McDonald, R. P. (1999). *Test theory: A unified treatment*. Mahwah, NJ: Lawrence Erlbaum Associates, Inc.

McDonald, R. P., & Mok, M. C. (1995). Goodness of fit in item response models. *Multivariate Behavioral Research, 54*, 483–495.

McKinley, R. L., & Reckase, M. D. (1983). MAXLOG: A computer program for the estimation of the parameters of a multidimensional logistic model. *Behavioral Research Methods and Instrumentation, 15*, 389–390.

Mislevy, R. J. (1984). Estimating latent distributions. *Psychometrika, 49*, 359–381.

Mislevy, R. J. (1986). Recent developments in the factor analysis of categorical variables. *Journal of Educational Statistics, 11*, 3–31.

Muraki, E., & Carlson, J. E. (1995). Full-information factor analysis of polytomous item responses. *Applied Psychological Measurement, 19*, 73–90.

Muthén, B. (1978). Contributions to factor analysis of dichotomous variables. *Psychometrika, 43*, 551–560.

Muthén, B. (1984). A general structural equation model with dichotomous, ordered, categorical, and continuous latent variable indicators. *Psychometrika, 49*, 115–132.

Muthén, B. (1987). *LISCOMP: Analysis of linear structural equations using a comprehensive measurement model*. Mooresville, IN: Scientific Software International.

Muthén, B. O. (1993). Goodness of fit with categorical and other nonnormal variables. In K. A. Bollen & J. S. Long (Eds.), *Testing structural equation models* (pp. 205–234). Newbury Park, CA: Sage.

Muthén, B. O. (2002). Beyond SEM: General latent variable modeling. *Behaviormetrika, 29*, 81–117.

Muthén, B., du Toit, S. H. C., & Spisic, D. (in press). Robust inference using weighted least squares and quadratic estimating equations in latent variable modeling with categorical and continuous outcomes. *Psychometrika*.

Muthén, B., & Hofacker, C. (1988). Testing the assumptions underlying tetrachoric correlations. *Psychometrika, 53*, 563–578.

Muthén, L. K., & Muthén, B. (1998). *Mplus: Statistical analysis with latent variables*. Los Angeles: Muthén & Muthén.

Parry, C. D. H., & McArdle, J. J. (1991). An applied comparison of methods for least squares factor analysis of dichotomous variables. *Applied Psychological Measurement, 15*, 35–46.

Patz, R. J., & Junker, B. W. (1999). A straightforward approach to Markov chain Monte Carlo methods for item response models. *Journal of Educational and Behavioral Statistics, 24*, 146–178.

Reckase, M. D. (1985). The difficulty of items that measure more than one ability. *Applied Psychological Measurement, 9*, 401–412.

Reckase, M. D. (1997a). The past and future of multidimensional item response theory. *Applied Psychological Measurement, 21*, 25–36.

Reckase, M. D. (1997b). A linear logistic multidimensional model for dichotomous item response data. In W. J. van der Linden & R. K. Hambleton (Eds.), *Handbook of modern item response theory* (pp. 271–286). New York: Springer-Verlag.

Reiser, M., & VandenBerg, M. (1994). Validity of the chi-square test in dichotomous variable factor analysis when expected frequencies are small. *British Journal of Mathematical and Statistical Psychology, 47*, 85–107.

Schumacker, R. E., & Beyerlein, S. T. (2000). Confirmatory factor analysis with different correlation types and estimation methods. *Structural Equation Modeling, 7*, 629–636.

Segall, D. O (1996). Multidimensional adaptive testing. *Psychometrika, 61*, 331–354.

Segall, D. O. (2002). *Confirmatory item factor analysis using Markov chain Monte Carlo estimation with applications to online calibration in CAT.* Paper presented at the annual meeting of the National Council on Measurement in Education, New Orleans, LA.

Spiegelhalter, D., Thomas, A., & Best, N. (2000). WinBUGS (Version 1.3) [Computer program]. Cambridge: MRC Biostatistics Unit, Institute of Public Health.

Spiegelhalter, D., Thomas, A., Best, N., & Gilks, W. (1996). *BUGS 0.5* Bayesian inference using gibbs sampling manual* (Version ii).

Stout, W. (1987). A nonparametric approach for assessing latent trait unidimensionality. *Psychometrika, 52*, 589–617.

Stout, W., Habing, B., Douglas, J. Kim, H. R., Roussos, L., & Zhang, J. (1996). Conditional covariance based nonparametric multidimensionality assessment. *Applied Psychological Measurement, 20*, 331–354.

Stroud, A. H., & Sechrest, D. (1966). *Gaussian quadrature formulas.* Englewood Cliffs, NJ: Prentice Hall.

Tanaka, J. S. (1993). Multifaceted conceptions of fit in structural equation models. In K. A. Bollen & J. S. Long (Eds.), *Testing structural equation models* (pp. 10–39). Newbury Park, CA: Sage.

Takane, Y., & DeLeeuw, J. (1987). On the relationship between item response theory and factor analysis of discretized variables. *Psychometrika, 52*, 393–408.

Wilson, D. T., Wood, R., & Gibbons, R. (1998). *TESTFACT: Test scoring, item statistics, and item factor analysis.* Mooresville, IN: Scientific Software International.

3

Linear Item Response Theory, Nonlinear Item Response Theory, and Factor Analysis: A Unified Framework

Albert Maydeu-Olivares
University of Barcelona

INTRODUCTION

What it is now known as item response modeling [for an overview see van der Linden and Hambleton (1997)] originated as an effort to overcome the limitations of the factor model when applied to test items. Test items are most often categorical in nature, whereas the factor model was designed for continuous data. Unfortunately, over the years item response modeling and factor modeling have developed rather independently from one another. One of the recurring topics in R. P. McDonald's career has been establishing bridges between these two fields (McDonald, 1967, 1980, 1981, 1982a, 1982b, 1985a, 1985b, 1986, 1999, 2001; McDonald & Mok, 1995). Two approaches can be used to relate the nonlinear models used in item response theory (IRT) to the linear model used in factor analysis. One approach is to use harmonic analysis (e.g., McDonald, 1967, 1982a). The second approach is to use link functions (e.g., McDonald, 1999; Moustaki & Knott, 2000).

This chapter focuses on one particular item response model for binary data, the linear IRT model. In this model, the conditional probability of endorsing an item given the latent traits is simply a linear function. McDonald (1999, chap. 12 and 13; see also McDonald, 1969, 1982a) discussed at length the application of the usual IRT theoretical machinery (e.g., information functions) to this model. McDonald (1999) also pointed out that when this model is estimated using bivariate information, it is equivalent to the factor model. In this chapter we explore further the linear IRT model for binary data and its relation to the factor model. We show that with binary data these two models are not always equivalent. In fact, they are only equivalent when the linear IRT model is estimated using only univariate and bivariate information. Thus, in relating the factor model to the linear item response model it is necessary to take into account estimation issues, in particular the use of limited- versus full-information methods. The use of limited- versus full-information estimation methods in IRT is discussed by Bolt (chap. 2, this volume; see also Maydeu-Olivares, 1996), and Krane and Slancy (chap. 5, this volume) provide an useful introduction to the factor model; a more detailed presentation of IRT modeling is given by Ackerman (chap. 1, this volume).

   This chapter is organized as follows. In the next section we discuss the linear item response model within a general presentation of item response models using link functions. The use of harmonic analysis as a unifying framework for both linear and nonlinear item response models is discussed at the end of the section. The third section discusses the factor model and its application to binary data. In that section we relate the factor model to the linear item response model. The fourth section is devoted to estimation and testing. First, we discuss estimation and testing in factor analysis. Next, we discuss estimation and testing in IRT. We close that section by describing some of the challenges currently faced in estimating and testing IRT models and introduce new theoretical results that address these challenges. Several numerical examples are provided in the final section to illustrate the discussion.

THE LINEAR ITEM RESPONSE MODEL FOR BINARY DATA

Item Response Modeling for Binary Data: Nonlinear Models

Consider n binary variables $\mathbf{y} = (y_1, \ldots, y_n)'$, each one with two possible outcomes. Without loss of generality, we may assign the values $\{0, 1\}$ to these possible outcomes. Therefore, the distribution of each y_i is Bernoulli, and the joint distribution of $\mathbf{y}$ is multivariate Bernoulli (MVB).

   All item response models for binary data take on the form (e.g., Bartholomew and Knott, 1999)

$$\Pr\left(\bigcap_{i=1}^{n} y_i\right) = \int_{-\infty}^{\infty} \cdots \int_{-\infty}^{\infty} \gamma_p(\boldsymbol{\eta}) \left\{ \prod_{i=1}^{n} [\Pr(y_i = 1|\boldsymbol{\eta})]^{y_i} [1 - \Pr(y_i = 1|\boldsymbol{\eta})]^{1-y_i} \right\} d\boldsymbol{\eta}, \quad (1)$$

where $\Pr(\bigcap_{i=1}^{n} y_i)$ denotes the probability of observing one of the possible 2^n binary patterns, $\gamma_p(\boldsymbol{\eta})$ denotes the probability density function of a p-dimensional vector of continuous *unobserved* latent traits η, and $\Pr(y_i = 1|\eta)$ is usually denoted as the *item response function* (IRF).

Let $z_i = \alpha_i + \beta_i'\eta$, where α_i is an intercept and β_i is a $p \times 1$ vector of slopes. Two widely used IRFs are

$$\Pr(y_i = 1|\eta) = \Phi_1(z_i) = \int_{-\infty}^{\alpha_i+\beta_i'\eta} \frac{e^{-\frac{t^2}{2}}}{\sqrt{2\pi}}dt, \tag{2}$$

$$\Pr(y_i = 1|\eta) = \Psi(z_i) = \frac{1}{1 + e^{-(\alpha_i+\beta_i'\eta)}}, \tag{3}$$

where $\Phi_1(z_i)$ and $\Psi(z_i)$ denote, respectively, univariate standard normal and standard logistic distribution functions evaluated at z_i. These functions link z_i to the probability of endorsing an item, given a fixed value of the latent traits.

Now, to completely specify Equation 1 we also need to specify the density of the latent traits, $\gamma_p(\eta)$. This is generally assumed to be multivariate normal with mean zero and some correlation matrix Φ, that is,

$$\gamma_p(\eta) = \phi_p(\eta : 0, \Phi). \tag{4}$$

The model given by Equation 1 with Equations 2 and 4 is referred to as the *multidimensional normal ogive model*, whereas the model given by Equation 1 with Equations 3 and 4 is referred to as the *multidimensional two-parameter logistic model*. Note, however, that the IRFs given by Equations 2 and 3 can be coupled in fact with any density function $\gamma_p(\eta)$, for instance, with a nonparametric function. Similarly, the IRF can also be a nonparametric function.

Generally, we require two properties from an IRF:

Property 1. An IRF should be bounded between 0 and 1 because it is a probability.

Property 2. An IRF should be smooth.

In addition, when modeling cognitive test items, we generally also require the following:

Property 3. An IRF should be monotonically increasing.

In the case of attitudinal or personality items, it has been argued (e.g., van Schuur & Kiers, 1994) that Property 3 need not be a reasonable assumption. The IRFs given by Equations 2 and 3 are monotonically increasing. A non-monotonically increasing multidimensional IRF is

$$\Pr(y_i = 1|\eta) = \sqrt{2\pi}\,\phi_1(z_i) = e^{-(\alpha_i+\beta_i'\eta)^2/2}, \tag{5}$$

where $\phi_1(z_i)$ denotes a univariate standard normal density function evaluated at z_i. Maydeu-Olivares, Hernández, and McDonald (2004) recently introduced a model with the IRF given by Equation 5 and normally distributed latent traits, which they denote the *normal PDF model*. The normal ogive, the two-parameter logistic, and the normal PDF models are obtained by simply using the nonlinear functions $\Phi_1(z_i)$, $\Psi(z_i)$, and $\sqrt{2\pi}\phi_1(z_i)$ to link z_i to $\Pr(y_i = 1|\boldsymbol{\eta})$.

The Linear Item Response Model

The linear item response model for binary data discussed in McDonald (1999) simply amounts to using an identity link function $I(z_i)$ instead of a nonlinear link function to specify the IRF. Thus, the IRF of this model is

$$\Pr(y_i = 1|\boldsymbol{\eta}) = I(z_i) = \alpha_i + \boldsymbol{\beta}_i'\boldsymbol{\eta}. \tag{6}$$

The IRF of this model violates Property 1 because it is not bounded between 0 and 1. Thus, for large enough values of the latent traits it yields probabilities larger than 1, and for small enough values it yields probabilities less than 0 (McDonald, 1999). This is a very unappealing property of the model.

On the other hand, the linear model enjoys a very attractive property that has not been noticed, namely, we need not specify a latent trait density. This can be readily seen if we characterize the multivariate Bernoulli distribution using its joint raw moments. In the Appendix we discuss two alternative representations of this distribution: (a) using the set of 2^n binary pattern probabilities $\boldsymbol{\pi}$ and (b) using the set of $2^n - 1$ joint raw moments of this distribution $\dot{\boldsymbol{\pi}}$. We also show that there is a one-to-one relationship between these two representations.

Consider, for example, a unidimensional linear latent trait model for $n = 3$ items. Let κ_i denote the ith raw moment of the latent trait,

$$\kappa_i = E[\eta^i], \tag{7}$$

so that, for instance, the mean of the latent trait is denoted by κ_1. Notice that there are n latent trait moments in a unidimensional linear IRT model for n variables. Using Equations 6 and 7, with Equation A7 of the Appendix, we obtain the univariate moments of the MVB distribution under the linear IRT model as

$$\dot{\pi}_i = E_\eta[\alpha_i + \beta_i\eta] = \alpha_i + \beta_i E[\eta] = \alpha_i + \beta_i\kappa_1. \tag{8}$$

Similarly, using Equation A8, we obtain the bivariate raw moments of the MVB distribution under this model as

$$\dot{\pi}_{ij} = E_\eta[(\alpha_i + \beta_i\eta)(\alpha_j + \beta_j\eta)] = \alpha_i\alpha_j + (\alpha_i\beta_j + \alpha_j\beta_i)E[\eta] + \beta_i\beta_j E[\eta^2]$$
$$= \alpha_i\alpha_j + (\alpha_i\beta_j + \alpha_j\beta_i)\kappa_1 + \beta_i\beta_j\kappa_2. \tag{9}$$

Finally, using Equation A9, we obtain the trivariate moments under this model as

$$\dot{\pi}_{ijk} = \alpha_i \alpha_j \alpha_k + (\alpha_i \alpha_j \beta_k + \alpha_i \alpha_k \beta_j + \alpha_j \alpha_k \beta_i)\kappa_1$$
$$+ (\alpha_i \beta_j \beta_k + \alpha_j \beta_i \beta_k + \alpha_k \beta_i \beta_j)\kappa_2 + \beta_i \beta_j \beta_k \kappa_3. \tag{10}$$

This example illustrates how the moments of **y** under the linear IRT model only depend on the item parameters and on the moments of the latent traits, regardless of the density of the latent traits. This is also true of the cell probabilities because of Equation A5 (see the Appendix).

Not all parameters of the linear IRT model are identified. Fixing any two moments to 0 and 1, respectively, suffices to identify a unidimensional model. These two fixed moments set the location and scale of the latent trait. This can be checked by verifying that $\Delta = \partial \pi (\theta)/\partial \theta'$ is of full rank (Bekker, Merckens & Wansbeek, 1994), where θ denotes the model parameters (i.e., the item parameters and the moments of the latent traits) stacked in a column vector. Thus, if, for instance, (a) the mean and the variance of the latent trait are fixed to 0 and 1, respectively, or (b) the nth- and $(n$th $- 1)$ order moments of the latent trait are fixed to 0 and 1, respectively, then all the item parameters and the remaining moments of the latent trait are identified.

Fewer parameters can be identified when the model is estimated using limited-information methods. For instance, suppose that the model is to be estimated using only univariate and bivariate information. Then third- and higher order moments of the latent traits cannot be identified because they do not appear in Equations 8 and 9. The means and variances of the latent traits cannot be identified either. In this case, the means can be set to 0 and the variances to 1 to identify the model.

In closing our treatment of the linear IRT model, we consider making statements about an individual's location on the latent traits given the individual's binary responses. All the relevant information needed for this is contained in the posterior distribution of the latent traits given the observed binary responses (Bartholomew & Knott, 1999),

$$\varphi_p(\eta|y) = \frac{\gamma_p(\eta) \left\{ \prod_{i=1}^{n} [\Pr(y_i = 1|\eta)]^{y_i} [1 - \Pr(y_i = 1|\eta)]^{1-y_i} \right\}}{\Pr\left(\bigcap_{i=1}^{n} y_i \right)}. \tag{11}$$

Thus, after the item parameters and latent trait moments have been estimated, an individual's location can be obtained, for instance, by computing the mean or the mode of this posterior distribution. The former are known as expected a posteriori (EAP) scores and the latter as maximum a posteriori (MAP) scores. Obtaining MAP scores in general requires an iterative procedure, whereas obtaining EAP scores involves computing

$$\text{EAP}(\mathbf{y}) = \int\limits_{-\infty}^{\infty} \cdots \int\limits_{-\infty}^{\infty} \boldsymbol{\eta}\varphi_p(\boldsymbol{\eta}|\mathbf{y})\,d\boldsymbol{\eta}. \tag{12}$$

It is of interest that in the linear IRT model, although it is not necessary to assume any prior distribution for $\gamma_p(\boldsymbol{\eta})$ to estimate the model parameters, it is necessary to assume some prior distribution to obtain these scores.

Wide-Sense Linear Item Response Models

So far, we have considered linear and nonlinear link functions for obtaining the IRF in item response models. In passing, we point out that a third alternative for obtaining an IRF is to use a wide-sense linear function in the latent traits (McDonald, 1967, 1982a). This is a function that is linear in the item parameters, but nonlinear in the latent traits,

$$\Pr(y_i = 1|\boldsymbol{\eta}) = \alpha_i + \sum_{j=1}^{p} \beta_{ij}\varphi_j(\boldsymbol{\eta}), \tag{13}$$

for some nonlinear functions $\varphi_j(\boldsymbol{\eta})$. A typical example of a wide-sense model is the unidimensional cubic model

$$\Pr(y_i = 1|\eta) = \alpha_i + \beta_{i1}\eta + \beta_{i2}\eta^2 + \beta_{i3}\eta^3. \tag{14}$$

McDonald (1982a) pointed out that wide sense linear models may offer a unified framework for IRFs that encompasses both the linear and nonlinear models as special cases.

It remains to be investigated whether any item response model can be written as a wide-sense model. However, it is easy to show using Hermite polynomials that any item response model with differentiable item response functions and normally distributed latent traits can be expressed as a wide-sense linear model. A Hermite polynomial of degree k, $H_k(x)$, satisfies by definition $H_k(x)\phi(x) = (-1)^k \partial^k \phi(x)/\partial x^k$. The first four terms of this polynomial are

$$H_k(x) = \begin{cases} 1 & \text{if } k = 0, \\ x & \text{if } k = 1, \\ x^2 - 1 & \text{if } k = 2, \\ x^3 - 3x & \text{if } k = 3. \end{cases} \tag{15}$$

For instance, McDonald (1967; see also McDonald, 1997) showed that the unidimensional version of the normal ogive model given by Equation 2 can be written as

$$\Phi_1 (\alpha_i + \beta_i \eta) = \Phi_1 \left(\frac{\alpha_i}{\sqrt{1 + \beta_i^2}} \right) + \phi_1 \left(\frac{-\alpha_i}{\sqrt{1 + \beta_i^2}} \right)$$

$$\times \sum_{k=1}^{\infty} \frac{1}{k!} \left(\frac{\beta_i}{\sqrt{1 + \beta_i^2}} \right)^k H_{k-1} \left(\frac{-\alpha_i}{\sqrt{1 + \beta_i^2}} \right) H_k (\eta). \quad (16)$$

Also, it can be shown that a unidimensional normal PDF model as in Equation 5 can be written as

$$\sqrt{2\pi} \phi_1 (\alpha_i + \beta_i \eta) = \sqrt{2\pi} \left(1 + \beta_i^2 \right)^{-1/2} \phi_1 \left(\frac{-\alpha_i}{\sqrt{1 + \beta_i^2}} \right)$$

$$\times \sum_{k=0}^{\infty} \frac{1}{k!} \left(\frac{\beta_i}{\sqrt{1 + \beta_i^2}} \right)^k H_k \left(\frac{-\alpha_i}{\sqrt{1 + \beta_i^2}} \right) H_k (\eta). \quad (17)$$

A expression for the two-parameter logistic model with a normally distributed latent trait can similarly be obtained, but this does not seem to have been attempted. In any case, we see in Equations 16 and 17 that strictly nonlinear models can be expressed as wide-sense linear models with an infinite number of terms. In practice, they can be well approximated with a small number of terms. For instance, both the normal ogive and normal PDF model can be reasonably approximated by truncating the series in Equations 16 and 17 at $k = 3$.

THE FACTOR MODEL

Description of the Model

Let $\mathbf{y}$ be a $n \times 1$ vector of observed variables to be modeled, η be a $p \times 1$ vector of unobserved latent traits (factors), where $n > p$, and ε be an $n \times 1$ vector of random errors. The factor model assumes that

$$\mathbf{y} = \alpha + \mathbf{B}\eta + \varepsilon, \quad (18)$$

where α is an $n \times 1$ vector of intercepts and $\mathbf{B}$ is an $n \times p$ matrix of slopes (factor loadings). The model further assumes that the mean of the latent traits is zero, that the mean of the random errors is zero, and that the latent traits and random errors are uncorrelated. That is,

$$\mathrm{E}\,[\eta] = \mathbf{0}, \ \mathrm{E}\,[\varepsilon] = \mathbf{0}, \ \mathrm{cov}\,[\eta] = \mathbf{\Phi}, \ \mathrm{cov}\,[\varepsilon] = \mathbf{\Psi}, \ \mathrm{cov}[\eta, \varepsilon'] = \mathbf{0}. \tag{19}$$

Furthermore, the random errors are generally assumed to be mutually uncorrelated, so that $\mathbf{\Psi}$ is a diagonal matrix.

We note two interesting features about this model: First, no assumptions are made on the distribution of the latent traits η nor the errors ε. As a result, no assumptions are made on the distribution of the observed variables y.

The factor model as defined by Equations 18 and 19 has an interesting second feature: It is a partially specified model. By this, we mean the following: Under assumptions 18 and 19, it follows that

$$\mu = \mathrm{E}[\mathbf{y}] = \alpha \tag{20}$$

$$\Sigma = \mathrm{cov}[\mathbf{yy}'] = \mathbf{B}\mathbf{\Phi}\mathbf{B}' + \mathbf{\Psi}, \tag{21}$$

where μ and Σ are the population univariate and bivariate central moments of $\mathbf{y}$, respectively, which depend solely on the model parameters. Moreover, it is a partially specified model in the sense that using only assumptions 18 and 19, we have that the trivariate moments of the observed variables do not depend solely on the model parameters. They also depend, for instance, on the third-order moments of the latent traits. However, these are left unspecified in the factor model. In contrast, item response models are completely specified models in the sense that all the moments of $\mathbf{y}$ are completely specified by the model parameters.

It is not surprising that the factor model is a partially specified model. The objective of factor analysis applications is to model the bivariate associations present in the data: either the central moments (sample covariances) or the standardized central moments (sample correlations). Generally, the mean structure is of no interest, and only the parameters involved in the covariance structure are estimated.

In closing this section, it is interesting that historically it has been frequently assumed that the latent traits η and the errors ε are jointly multinormally distributed. Under this additional assumption (which we do not make here), the distribution of $\mathbf{y}$ is multivariate normal and the factor model becomes a completely specified model because the multivariate distribution is completely specified by its first two moments.

Relationship Between the Factor Model and the Linear Item Response Model

The linear item response model presented here is a model for binary data. In contrast, the factor model does not make any assumptions about the nature of the observed variables. Thus, in principle, it can be applied to binary data. However, when the observed variables are binary, $\text{var}(y_i) = \mu_i(1 - \mu_i)$. Coupling this with Equation 20, we see that when the factor model is applied to binary data it must satisfy

$$\text{var}(y_i) = \alpha_i - \alpha_i^2. \tag{22}$$

where α_i denotes the ith element of α. However, from Equation 21 it must also satisfy

$$\text{var}(y_i) = \beta_i' \Phi \beta_i + \psi_i^2. \tag{23}$$

where ψ_i^2 denotes the ith element on the diagonal of Ψ, and β_i' denotes the ith row of $\mathbf{B}$. As a result, when the factor model is applied to binary data the elements of α and Ψ are jointly underidentified. In other words, when the factor model is applied to binary data one can estimate either $\{\alpha, \mathbf{B} \text{ and } \Phi\}$ or $\{\Psi, \mathbf{B} \text{ and } \Phi\}$. These are two alternative parametrizations of the model. We refer to the former as the α parametrization and the latter as the Ψ parametrization. Using Equation 22 and 23, we obtain the relationship between these parametrizations as

$$\alpha_i = \frac{1 + \sqrt{1 - 4\beta_i' \Phi \beta_i - 4\psi_i^2}}{2}, \tag{24}$$

$$\psi_i^2 = \alpha_i - \alpha_i^2 - \beta_i' \Phi \beta_i. \tag{25}$$

Note that if the factor model is estimated using only the covariance structure (ignoring the mean structure), this identification problem goes unnoticed because α is not involved. Also notice that in estimating a factor model from binary data all the identified model parameters can be estimated using only the covariance matrix. In this case, it seems natural to use the Ψ parametrization, but one can also use the α parametrization. The covariance structure implied by the α parametrization is, from Equation 25,

$$\Sigma = \mathbf{B}\Phi\mathbf{B}' + \text{diag}(\alpha - \alpha^2) - \text{Diag}(\mathbf{B}\Phi\mathbf{B}'), \tag{26}$$

where we use diag $(\mathbf{x})$ to indicate a diagonal matrix with diagonal elements equal to $\mathbf{x}$ and Diag $(\mathbf{X})$ to indicate a matrix where all the off diagonal elements of $\mathbf{X}$ have been set to zero.

Equations 20 and 26 are also the mean and covariance structures implied by the linear item response model. Thus, the factor model applied to binary data and the linear item response model estimated from univariate and bivariate information are equivalent models. In general, they are not equivalent models because the linear item response model can be estimated using full information, and in this case some of the moments of the latent traits can be estimated.

Because the linear item response model and the factor model are equivalent when estimated from bivariate information, a question immediately arises. Can we compare the fit of a factor model and of a nonlinear item response model to a given binary data set? In order to answer this question it is necessary to discuss not only statistical theory for goodness of fit testing but also for estimation in both item response modeling and in factor analysis.

ESTIMATION AND TESTING

Factor Model

Let θ be the q-dimensional vector of parameters to be estimated. Also, let σ be the $t = n(n+1)/2$ -dimensional vector obtained by stacking the elements on the diagonal or below the diagonal of Σ. Finally, let s be the sample counterparts of σ (i.e., sample variances and covariances). A popular approach to estimate the parameters of the factor model is to minimize the weighted least squares (WLS) function,

$$F = (s - \sigma(\theta))' \hat{W} (s - \sigma(\theta)), \tag{27}$$

where $\hat{W}$ is a matrix converging in probability to W, a positive-definite matrix. Now, let $\Delta = \partial\sigma(\theta)/\partial\theta'$ and $H = (\Delta'W\Delta)^{-1}\Delta'W$. Also, let $\xrightarrow{d}$ denote convergence in distribution.

Because $\sqrt{N}(s - \sigma) \xrightarrow{d} N(0, \Gamma)$, then, if Δ is of full rank q and some other mild regularity conditions are satisfied (Browne, 1984), the parameter estimates $\hat{\theta}$ obtained by minimizing Equation 27 are consistent, and

$$\sqrt{N}(\hat{\theta} - \theta) \xrightarrow{d} N(0, H\Gamma H'), \tag{28}$$

$$\sqrt{N}(s - \sigma(\hat{\theta})) \xrightarrow{d} N(0, \Omega), \qquad \Omega = (I - \Delta H)\Gamma(I - \Delta H)', \tag{29}$$

where $(s - \sigma(\hat{\theta}))$ denotes the residual variances and covariances.

Some obvious choices of $\hat{W}$ in Equation 27 are $\hat{W} = \hat{\Gamma}^{-1}$ (minimum variance WLS, or MVWLS), $\hat{W} = (\text{Diag}(\hat{\Gamma}))^{-1}$ (diagonally WLS, or DWLS) and $\hat{W} = I$ (unweighted least squares, or ULS).

Following Browne (1984), when the factor model is estimated by minimizing Equation 27, we can obtain a goodness-of-fit test of the restrictions imposed by the model on the means and covariances of y by using

$$T_B = N(s - \sigma(\hat{\theta}))'\hat{U}(s - \sigma(\hat{\theta})), \qquad U = \Gamma^{-1} - \Gamma^{-1}\Delta(\Delta'\Gamma^{-1}\Delta)^{-1}\Delta'\Gamma^{-1}. \tag{30}$$

T_B is asymptotically distributed as a chi-square distribution with $t - q$ degrees of freedom regardless of the weight matrix used in Equation 27. To obtain standard errors for the parameter estimates and residuals and to obtain an overall goodness-of-fit test using Equations 28–30, we evaluate Δ at the parameter estimates and consistently estimate Γ using sample third- and fourth-order central moments.

Previously, we referred to the estimator obtained by using $\hat{\mathbf{W}} = \hat{\Gamma}^{-1}$ in Equation 27 as the minimum variance WLS estimator. This is because with this choice of weight matrix, the resulting estimator has minimum variance (asymptotically) within the class of estimators based on the sample covariances. In the case of the MVWLS estimator, Equations 28–30 simplify to

$$\sqrt{N}(\hat{\theta} - \theta) \xrightarrow{d} N(\mathbf{0}, (\Delta'\Gamma^{-1}\Delta)^{-1}) \tag{31}$$

$$\sqrt{N}(s - \sigma(\hat{\theta})) \xrightarrow{d} N(\mathbf{0}, \Omega), \quad \Omega = \Gamma - \Delta(\Delta'\Gamma^{-1}\Delta)^{-1}\Delta'. \tag{32}$$

$$T_B = N\hat{F} \xrightarrow{d} \chi^2_{t-q}. \tag{33}$$

Here, we have focused on the weighted least squares discrepancy function 27 (also denoted as the generalized least squares function). Another discrepancy function that is often used to estimate the factor model is the discrepancy function

$$F = \ln|\Sigma(\theta)| - \ln|\mathbf{S}| + \text{tr}((\Sigma(\theta))^{-1}\mathbf{S}) - n, \tag{34}$$

where $\mathbf{S}$ is the sample covariance matrix of $\mathbf{y}$. If $\mathbf{y}$ is normally distributed, minimizing Equation 34 yields maximum likelihood estimates. When $\mathbf{y}$ is not normally distributed, standard errors for the model parameters estimated by minimizing Equation 34 and goodness-of-fit tests can be obtained using Equations 28 and 30, respectively (e.g., Satorra & Bentler, 1994). Another method widely used to assess the goodness of fit when Equation 34 is minimized without a normality assumption and when Equation 27 is minimized using $\hat{\mathbf{W}} \neq \hat{\Gamma}^{-1}$ is to adjust $N\hat{F}$ by its mean (or by its mean and variance) so that the resulting test statistic asymptotically matches the mean (or the mean and the variance) of a chi-square distribution with $t - q$ degrees of freedom (Satorra & Bentler, 1994).

Item Response Models

Let $\pi(\theta)$ denote the 2^n vector of the binary pattern probabilities of Equation 1 expressed as a function of the q mathematically independent parameters θ of an item response model, and let $\mathbf{p}$ be the sample counterpart of π (i.e., cell proportions). Item response models for binary data are commonly estimated by maximizing the log-likelihood function

$$\ln L = N \mathbf{p}' \ln(\pi(\theta)). \tag{35}$$

Thus, the resulting parameter estimates $\hat{\theta}$ are maximum likelihood estimates. Instead of maximizing Equation 35, it is convenient to minimize

$$F_{ML} = \mathbf{p}' \ln\left(\frac{\mathbf{p}}{\pi(\theta)}\right), \tag{36}$$

Now, let $\mathbf{D} = \operatorname{diag}(\boldsymbol{\pi})$. Since

$$\sqrt{N}\,(\mathbf{p} - \boldsymbol{\pi}) \xrightarrow{d} N\,(\mathbf{0}, \boldsymbol{\Gamma}), \quad \boldsymbol{\Gamma} = \mathbf{D} - \boldsymbol{\pi}\boldsymbol{\pi}', \tag{37}$$

then, if $\boldsymbol{\Delta} = \partial\boldsymbol{\pi}(\boldsymbol{\theta})/\partial\boldsymbol{\theta}'$ is of full rank q and some other regularity conditions are satisfied (Agresti, 1990; Rao, 1973), the maximum likelihood parameter estimates are consistent, they have minimum variance (asymptotically), and

$$\sqrt{N}(\hat{\boldsymbol{\theta}} - \boldsymbol{\theta}) \xrightarrow{d} N(\mathbf{0}, (\boldsymbol{\Delta}'\mathbf{D}^{-1}\boldsymbol{\Delta})^{-1}). \tag{38}$$

Also, we have the following result for the residual cell proportions $(\mathbf{p} - \boldsymbol{\pi}(\hat{\boldsymbol{\theta}}))$

$$\sqrt{N}(\mathbf{p} - \boldsymbol{\pi}(\hat{\boldsymbol{\theta}})) \xrightarrow{d} N\,(\mathbf{0}, \boldsymbol{\Omega}), \quad \boldsymbol{\Omega} = \boldsymbol{\Gamma} - \boldsymbol{\Delta}(\boldsymbol{\Delta}'\mathbf{D}^{-1}\boldsymbol{\Delta})^{-1}\boldsymbol{\Delta}'. \tag{39}$$

To obtain standard errors for the parameter estimates and residuals, all matrices are evaluated at the parameter estimates.

The two most widely used statistics to assess the goodness of fit of the model are the likelihood ratio test statistic G^2 and Pearson's X^2 statistic,

$$G^2 = 2N\,\mathbf{p}'\ln\left(\frac{\mathbf{p}}{\boldsymbol{\pi}(\hat{\boldsymbol{\theta}})}\right) = 2N\hat{F}_{ML}, \tag{40}$$

$$X^2 = N(\mathbf{p} - \boldsymbol{\pi}(\hat{\boldsymbol{\theta}}))'(\operatorname{diag}(\boldsymbol{\pi}(\hat{\boldsymbol{\theta}})))^{-1}(\mathbf{p} - \boldsymbol{\pi}(\hat{\boldsymbol{\theta}})). \tag{41}$$

When the model holds, both statistics are asymptotically equivalent and they are asymptotically chi-square distributed with $2^n - q - 1$ degrees of freedom.

We now consider an alternative approach to estimating the IRT parameters that is related to the weighted least squares function in Equation 27 used to estimate the factor model and also to Pearson's X^2 statistic. Suppose $\hat{\boldsymbol{\theta}}$ is obtained by minimizing the generalized minimum chi-square function

$$F = (\mathbf{p} - \boldsymbol{\pi}(\boldsymbol{\theta}))'\,\hat{\mathbf{W}}\,(\mathbf{p} - \boldsymbol{\pi}(\boldsymbol{\theta})), \tag{42}$$

where $\hat{\mathbf{W}}$ is a matrix converging in probability to $\mathbf{W}$, a positive-definite matrix. Then, if $\boldsymbol{\Delta} = \partial\boldsymbol{\pi}(\boldsymbol{\theta})/\partial\boldsymbol{\theta}'$ is of full rank q and some other regularity conditions are satisfied (Ferguson, 1996), $\hat{\boldsymbol{\theta}}$ is consistent, and

$$\sqrt{N}(\hat{\boldsymbol{\theta}} - \boldsymbol{\theta}) \xrightarrow{d} N(\mathbf{0}, \mathbf{H}\boldsymbol{\Gamma}\mathbf{H}'), \quad \mathbf{H} = (\boldsymbol{\Delta}'\mathbf{W}\boldsymbol{\Delta})^{-1}\boldsymbol{\Delta}'\mathbf{W} \tag{43}$$

$$\sqrt{N}(\mathbf{p} - \boldsymbol{\pi}(\hat{\boldsymbol{\theta}})) \xrightarrow{d} N\,(\mathbf{0}, \boldsymbol{\Omega}), \quad \boldsymbol{\Omega} = (\mathbf{I} - \boldsymbol{\Delta}\mathbf{H})\,\boldsymbol{\Gamma}\,(\mathbf{I} - \boldsymbol{\Delta}\mathbf{H})', \tag{44}$$

where $\boldsymbol{\Gamma}$ is given by Equation (37). To obtain the standard error for the parameter estimates and residuals, $\boldsymbol{\Delta}$ and $\boldsymbol{\Gamma}$ are evaluated at the parameter estimates. Some obvious choices of $\hat{\mathbf{W}}$ in Equation 42 are $\hat{\mathbf{W}} = \hat{\mathbf{D}}^{-1}$ and $\hat{\mathbf{W}} = \mathbf{I}$. When $\hat{\mathbf{W}} = \hat{\mathbf{D}}^{-1}$, we obtain asymptotically minimum variance estimators and Equations 43 and 44 reduce to Equations 38 and 39, respectively. Note that in this case we can use $\hat{\mathbf{D}}^{-1} = (\text{diag}(\pi(\hat{\boldsymbol{\theta}})))^{-1}$ or $\hat{\mathbf{D}}^{-1} = (\text{diag}(\mathbf{p}))^{-1}$. The former is the usual minimum chi-square estimator, whereas the latter is the modified minimum chi-square estimator. The two are asymptotically equivalent. When Equation 42 is minimized with $\hat{\mathbf{W}} = (\text{diag}(\pi(\hat{\boldsymbol{\theta}})))^{-1}$, $N\hat{F} = X^2$.

New Developments in IRT Estimation and Testing

Because statistical inference for item response models generally involves full-information procedures, whereas statistical inference for the factor model involves limited-information procedures, the former are generally computationally more involved than the latter. Furthermore, statistical inference for item response models faces several challenges (Bartholomew & Knott, 1999; Bartholomew & Leung, 2001; Bartholomew & Tzamourani, 1999; Reiser, 1996; Reiser & VandenBerg, 1994):

1. In sparse binary tables, the empirical distribution of the overall tests G^2 and X^2 does not match its asymptotic distribution. Therefore, statistical inferences based on these statistics are invalid in sparse tables. Although it is possible to generate the empirical sampling distribution of these statistics using resampling methods (for instance, using parametric bootstrap; Bartholomew and Tzamourani, 1999), the amount of computation involved is substantial, particularly when we are interested in comparing the fit of competing IRT models to data sets with a large number of variables.

2. When G^2 and X^2 indicate a poorly fitting model, one is interested in identifying the source of the misfit. Because the number of cell residuals to be inspected is generally very large, it is difficult if not impossible to draw useful information about the source of the misfit using cell residuals (Bartholomew & Knott, 1999). In recent years it has been advocated (e.g., Bartholomew & Tzamourani, 1999; McDonald & Mok, 1995; Reiser, 1996) to inspect low-order marginal residuals (e.g., univariate, bivariate, and trivariate residuals) to detect the source of any possible misfit. Although it is not difficult to derive the asymptotic distribution of low-order marginal residuals, no overall limited information tests with known asymptotic distribution seemed to be available in the item response modeling literature (but see Bartholomew & Leung, 2001; Reiser, 1996).

3. Several limited-information estimation procedures have been proposed to estimate item response models (e.g., Christoffersson, 1975; McDonald, 1982b; Muthén, 1978; see also Maydeu-Olivares, 2001). These procedures yield limited-information goodness-of-fit tests of known asymptotic distribution that perform well in sparse tables (Maydeu-Olivares, 2001). However, when limited information estimation procedures are used, G^2 and X^2 do not follow their

usual asymptotic distribution (Bishop, Feinberg, & Holland, 1975), and no full-information goodness-of-fit test with known asymptotic distribution had been proposed for these estimators.

Maydeu-Olivares and Joe (in press) recently addressed these challenges by introducing a unified framework for limited- and full-information estimation and testing in binary contingency tables using the joint raw moments of the MVB distribution. These moments can be expressed as a linear function of the cell probabilities $\dot{\pi} = \mathbf{T}\pi$, where $\mathbf{T}$ is a matrix that consists of ones and zeros. Consider now partitioning the vector of joint raw moments of the MVB distribution as $\dot{\pi}' = (\dot{\pi}_1, \dot{\pi}_2, \ldots, \dot{\pi}_n)'$, where $\dot{\pi}_i$ denotes the $\binom{n}{i}$-dimensional vector of ith-order moments (see the Appendix). $\mathbf{T}$ can also be partitioned according to the partitioning of $\dot{\pi}$ as $\mathbf{T} = (\mathbf{T}'_1, \mathbf{T}'_2, \ldots, \mathbf{T}'_n)'$, where $\mathbf{T}_i$ is a $\binom{n}{i} \times 2^n$ matrix of ones and zeros (see the example shown in Equation A3). Consider now the $s = \sum_{i=1}^{r} \binom{n}{i}$, dimensional vector of moments up to order $r \leq n$ $\dot{\pi}'_r = (\dot{\pi}_1, \dot{\pi}_2, \ldots, \dot{\pi}_r)'$, with sample counterpart $\tilde{\mathbf{p}}_r$. Letting $\tilde{\mathbf{T}}_r = (\mathbf{T}'_1, \mathbf{T}'_2, \ldots, \mathbf{T}'_r)'$, we can write

$$\tilde{\pi}_r = \tilde{\mathbf{T}}_r \pi. \tag{45}$$

Then, from Equations 45 and 37, it follows immediately that the asymptotic distribution of the joint sample raw moments up to order r of the MVB distribution is

$$\sqrt{N}\,(\tilde{\mathbf{p}}_r - \tilde{\pi}_r) \xrightarrow{d} N(0, \tilde{\Xi}_r), \qquad \tilde{\Xi}_r = \tilde{\mathbf{T}}_r \Gamma \tilde{\mathbf{T}}_r. \tag{46}$$

Using this result, Maydeu-Olivares and Joe (in press) proposed a unifying framework for limited- and full-information testing in binary contingency tables using

$$M_r = N(\tilde{\mathbf{p}}_r - \tilde{\pi}_r(\hat{\theta}))'\hat{\mathbf{U}}_r(\tilde{\mathbf{p}}_r - \tilde{\pi}_r(\hat{\theta})), \tag{47}$$

$$U_r = \tilde{\Xi}_r^{-1} - \tilde{\Xi}_r^{-1}\tilde{\Delta}_r(\tilde{\Delta}'_r\tilde{\Xi}_r^{-1}\tilde{\Delta}_r)^{-1}\tilde{\Delta}'_r\tilde{\Xi}_r^{-1}, \tag{48}$$

where $\tilde{\Delta}_r = \partial\tilde{\pi}_r(\theta)/\partial\theta'$, and all matrices are evaluated at the estimated parameter values. Maydeu-Olivares and Joe showed that if θ is estimated using any (limited or full information) consistent and asymptotically normal estimator and if $\tilde{\Delta}_r$ is of full rank q (i.e., if the model is locally identified from the moments up to order r), then M_r is asymptotically distributed as a chi-square with $s - q$ degrees of freedom.

M_r is a family of limited information goodness-of-fit test statistics. It includes $M_1, M_2, \ldots$, up to M_n. M_2, for instance, uses only univariate and bivariate information to assess the goodness of fit of the model. Its limiting case, M_n is a full-information statistic because of the one-to-one relation between the set of all marginal moments and the cell probabilities in Equations A4 and A5. Furthermore, Maydeu-Olivares and Joe showed that M_n can be alternatively be written as

$$M_n = N(\mathbf{p} - \boldsymbol{\pi}(\hat{\boldsymbol{\theta}}))'\hat{\mathbf{U}}(\mathbf{p} - \boldsymbol{\pi}(\hat{\boldsymbol{\theta}})), \qquad \mathbf{U} = \mathbf{D}^{-1} - \mathbf{D}^{-1}\boldsymbol{\Delta}(\boldsymbol{\Delta}'\mathbf{D}^{-1}\boldsymbol{\Delta})^{-1}\boldsymbol{\Delta}'\mathbf{D}^{-1},$$
(49)

where all the matrices are to be evaluated at the estimated parameter values. This statistic is asymptotically distributed as a chi-square with $2^n - q - 1$ degrees of freedom for any consistent and asymptotically normal estimator (including limited-information estimators). Also, $M_n = X^2$ when the model is estimated by full-information maximum likelihood.

It is interesting to point out that when applied to binary data, the statistic T_B proposed by Browne (1984) in the context of covariance structure modeling is closely related to the member of the class of Equation 47 where only univariate and bivariate moments are used (i.e., M_2). In fact, with binary data M_2 is asymptotically equal to the T_B statistic. Both statistics are asymptotically chi-square distributed with $t - q$ degrees of freedom for any consistent and asymptotically normal estimator. However, they are not algebraically equal. M_2 is a quadratic form in residual raw univariate and bivariate moments, whereas T_B is a quadratic form in residual covariances (bivariate central moments). Furthermore, the asymptotic covariance matrix of the sample moments used in each statistic is estimated differently. In M_2 this matrix is evaluated at the estimated parameter values, whereas in T_B it is estimated using sample moments. Nevertheless, it is remarkable that since Browne's T_B statistic was proposed in 1984, no one seems to have noticed that if an IRT model is identified from the univariate and bivariate margins, then the T_B statistic can be used to test the goodness of fit of the model.

In closing this discussion on goodness-of-fit statistics, we present an alternative family of test statistics, M_r', introduced by Maydeu-Olivares and Joe (in press), which can also be used to assess the goodness of fit of IRT models and has a greater resemblance to Browne's statistic. This family is

$$M_r' = N(\tilde{\mathbf{p}}_r - \tilde{\boldsymbol{\pi}}_r(\hat{\boldsymbol{\theta}}))'\hat{\mathbf{U}}_r'(\tilde{\mathbf{p}}_r - \tilde{\boldsymbol{\pi}}_r(\hat{\boldsymbol{\theta}})),$$
(50)

where $\hat{\mathbf{U}}_r'$ denotes Equation 48 evaluated as in Browne's statistic, that is, the derivative matrices are evaluated at the estimated parameter values, but $\tilde{\boldsymbol{\Xi}}_r$ is evaluated using sample proportions. Obviously $M_r' \overset{a}{=} M_r \overset{d}{\to} \chi^2_{s-q}$.

In a similar fashion, a unifying framework for limited and full information estimation of IRT models for binary data can be obtained using quadratic forms in joint raw moments of the MVB distribution. Consider the fit function (Maydeu-Olivares & Joe, in press)

$$F_r = (\tilde{\mathbf{p}}_r - \tilde{\boldsymbol{\pi}}_r(\boldsymbol{\theta}))'\hat{\mathbf{W}}_r(\tilde{\mathbf{p}}_r - \tilde{\boldsymbol{\pi}}_r(\boldsymbol{\theta})),$$
(51)

where $\hat{\mathbf{W}}_r$ is a matrix converging in probability to $\mathbf{W}_r$, a positive-definite matrix that does not depend on $\boldsymbol{\theta}$. Some obvious choices for $\hat{\mathbf{W}}_r$ in Equation 51 are $\hat{\mathbf{W}}_r = \mathbf{I}$,

$\hat{\mathbf{W}}_r = (\text{Diag}(\hat{\tilde{\Xi}}_r))^{-1}$, and $\hat{\mathbf{W}}_r = \hat{\tilde{\Xi}}_r^{-1}$, where $\hat{\tilde{\Xi}}_r$ denotes $\tilde{\Xi}_r$ consistently estimated using sample proportions. If $\tilde{\Delta}_r$ is of full rank q and some other mild regularity conditions are satisfied, $\hat{\theta}$ obtained by minimizing Equation 51 is consistent and

$$\sqrt{N}(\hat{\theta} - \theta) \xrightarrow{d} N(\mathbf{0}, \mathbf{H}\tilde{\Xi}_r\mathbf{H}'), \qquad \mathbf{H} = (\tilde{\Delta}'_r\mathbf{W}_r\tilde{\Delta}_r)^{-1}\tilde{\Delta}'_r\mathbf{W}_r, \qquad (52)$$

$$\sqrt{N}(\tilde{\mathbf{p}}_r - \tilde{\pi}_r(\hat{\theta})) \xrightarrow{d} N(\mathbf{0}, \tilde{\Omega}_r), \qquad \tilde{\Omega}_r = (\mathbf{I} - \tilde{\Delta}_r\mathbf{H})\tilde{\Xi}_r(\mathbf{I} - \tilde{\Delta}_r\mathbf{H})'. \qquad (53)$$

To obtain standard errors for the parameter estimates and residual proportions, the derivative matrices may be evaluated at the estimated parameter values, and $\tilde{\Xi}_r$ may be evaluated using sample proportions. Note that when F_n is employed, a class of full-information estimators is obtained. Maydeu-Olivares and Joe (in press) explicitly related the class of estimators F_n to the class of minimum chi-square estimators in Equation 42.

When $\hat{\mathbf{W}}_r = \hat{\tilde{\Xi}}_r^{-1}$ is used in Equation 51, Equations 52 and 53 simplify to

$$\sqrt{N}(\hat{\theta} - \theta) \xrightarrow{d} N\left(\mathbf{0}, \left(\tilde{\Delta}'_r\tilde{\Xi}_r^{-1}\tilde{\Delta}_r\right)^{-1}\right) \qquad (54)$$

and

$$\sqrt{N}(\tilde{\mathbf{p}}_r - \tilde{\pi}_r(\hat{\theta})) \xrightarrow{d} N\left(\mathbf{0}, \tilde{\Xi}_r - \tilde{\Delta}_r\left(\tilde{\Delta}'_r\tilde{\Xi}_r^{-1}\tilde{\Delta}_r\right)^{-1}\tilde{\Delta}'_r\right). \qquad (55)$$

respectively, and we obtain estimators that are asymptotically efficient among the class of estimator using information up to order r. Furthermore,

$$N\hat{F}_r = M'_r \xrightarrow{d} \chi^2_{s-q}. \qquad (56)$$

The estimator proposed by Christoffersson (1975) to estimate the normal ogive model is a member of the family of estimators (51). He estimated the model minimizing $F_2 = (\tilde{\mathbf{p}}_2 - \tilde{\pi}_2(\theta))'\hat{\tilde{\Xi}}_2^{-1}(\tilde{\mathbf{p}}_2 - \tilde{\pi}_2(\theta))$.

NUMERICAL EXAMPLES

We provide two numerical examples to illustrate our discussion using the Law School Admissions Test (LSAT) 6 and LSAT 7 data sets (Bock & Lieberman, 1970). Each of these data sets consists of 1,000 observations on five binary variables.

Comparing the Fit of a Factor Model and of a Logistic Model to the LSAT 6 Data Using Browne's T_B Statistic

In this section we compare the fit of a factor model versus a logistic IRT model applied to the LSAT 6 data. We discussed previously that Browne's T_B statistic can be used to this purpose. We estimated a one-factor model to the LSAT 6 data using unweighted least squares using the sample covariances under the α parametrization in Equation 26. The two-parameter logistic IRT model was estimated using maximum likelihood from Equation 35. The parameter estimates, standard errors, and T_B statistics are shown in Table 3.1. We do not observe that the logistic IRT model outperforms the factor model in fitting these data, as assessed by the T_B statistic.

Notice that Table 3.1 does not report any of the IRT goodness-of-fit statistics for the factor model. This is because under the factor model assumptions in Equations 18 and 19 these statistics cannot be computed. Additional assumptions on third- and higher order moments of the latent trait are needed to compute the expected probabilities under the factor model. These expected probabilities are needed to compute the IRT fit statistics.

Factor Modeling Versus Linear IRT Modeling of the LSAT 6 Data

In the factor model only univariate and bivariate moments are specified. Therefore, this model can only be estimated using univariate and bivariate information. Unlike the factor model, in the linear IRT model all the moments of the latent traits are specified. As a result, the linear IRT model can be estimated using either full information or limited information. Here, we compare the fit of a unidimensional linear IRT model versus the fit of a one-factor model applied to the LSAT 6 data. We assume that the moments of the latent trait in the linear IRT model are fixed constants. The constants chosen are those of a standard normal density. Therefore, the five moments of the latent trait are fixed to

$$\kappa' = (0, 1, 0, 3, 0).$$

(57)

Table 3.1 reports the linear IRT parameters estimated using a variety of full- and limited-information estimators.

Because the factor model and the linear IRT model are equivalent when the latter is estimated using only bivariate information, it is most interesting to compare the last two columns of Table 3.1, where both models are estimated using bivariate information. The results are not identical even though we used the same estimation procedure (ULS). This is because the linear IRT model is estimated from raw moments (marginal proportions), whereas the factor model is estimated using central moments (covariances) and there is not a one-to-one correspondence between both fit functions.

Effects of the Estimation Method and Choice of IRT Model on the LSAT 6 Data

In Table 3.1 we present the results of fitting a two-parameter logistic IRT model to the LSAT 6 data using (a) full-information maximum likelihood and

TABLE 3.1
Parameter Estimates and Goodness-of-Fit Tests for the Law School Admission Test 6 Data

	Logistic IRT Model		Linear IRT Model			Factor Model
	ML (Full)	ULS (Bivariate)	ML (Full)	ULS (Full)	ULS (Bivariate)	ULS (Bivariate)
Parameter estimates						
α_1	2.77	2.84	0.92	0.92	0.92	0.92
	(0.21)	(0.24)	(0.01)	(0.01)	(0.01)	(0.01)
α_2	0.99	0.98	0.71	0.71	0.71	0.71
	(0.09)	(0.09)	(0.01)	(0.02)	(0.01)	(0.01)
α_3	0.25	0.26	0.55	0.56	0.55	0.55
	(0.08)	(0.08)	(0.02)	(0.02)	(0.02)	(0.03)
α_4	1.28	1.27	0.76	0.77	0.76	0.76
	(0.10)	(0.10)	(0.01)	(0.01)	(0.01)	(0.01)
α_5	2.05	2.03	0.87	0.87	0.87	0.87
	(0.13)	(0.12)	(0.01)	(0.01)	(0.01)	(0.01)
β_1	0.83	0.97	0.05	0.05	0.07	0.06
	(0.26)	(0.31)	(0.02)	(0.02)	(0.02)	(0.02)
β_2	0.72	0.63	0.14	0.14	0.12	0.13
	(0.18)	(0.20)	(0.03)	(0.04)	(0.03)	(0.04)
β_3	0.89	1.04	0.18	0.17	0.21	0.19
	(0.23)	(0.36)	(0.04)	(0.05)	(0.05)	(0.03)
β_4	0.69	0.62	0.12	0.10	0.11	0.12
	(0.18)	(0.20)	(0.03)	(0.03)	(0.03)	(0.03)
β_5	0.66	0.55	0.07	0.06	0.06	0.07
	(0.20)	(0.22)	(0.02)	(0.02)	(0.02)	(0.02)
Goodness-of-fit tests						
X^2	18.15	19.62	19.51	20.69	22.47	—
	(0.64)	—	(0.55)	—	—	
G^2	21.47	22.49	22.96	23.96	25.66	—
	(0.43)	—	(0.35)	—	—	
M_n	18.15	18.79	19.51	19.68	19.69	—
	(0.64)	(0.60)	(0.55)	(0.54)	(0.54)	
M_2	4.75	5.07	4.37	4.49	4.70	—
	(0.45)	(0.41)	(0.50)	(0.48)	(0.45)	
T_B	5.06	5.37	4.89	4.83	5.20	4.90
	(0.41)	(0.37)	(0.43)	(0.42)	(0.39)	(0.43)

Note. IRT, Item response theory. Estimators are maximum likelihood (ML) or unweighted least squares (ULS). Information is full or bivariate as indicated. The factor model and the linear item response model estimated from bivariate information are equivalent models. Standard errors are given in parentheses for parameter estimates; p values are given in parentheses for goodness-of-fit tests. When the model is not estimated by full-information maximum likelihood, p values for X^2 and G^2 are not provided because these statistics are not asymptotically chi-squared distributed. There are 21 degrees of freedom for X^2, G^2, and M_n; there are 5 degrees of freedom for M_2 and T_B.

(b) bivariate-information ULS estimation. We also present the results of fitting a linear IRT model to these data using (a) full-information maximum likelihood, (b) full-information ULS estimation, and (c) bivariate-information ULS estimation. Therefore, we can examine the effects of the choice of model and of the choice of estimation method. We can use three statistics to compare the fit of these two models regardless of how they have been estimated: the full-information statistic M_n and the limited-information statistics M_2 and T_B.

Informally speaking, the M_n statistic can be used to assess the fit of these models to the cell proportions. The M_2 statistic can be used to assess their fit to the univariate and bivariate raw moments of the data. Finally, the T_B statistic can be used to assess their fit to the sample covariances. When the model is estimated using full-information maximum likelihood, $M_n = X^2$. Also, when the model is not estimated using an asymptotically efficient estimator, X^2 and G^2 are not asymptotically chi-square distributed and consequently p values are not reported in Table 3.1 in those instances.

Inspecting the relevant goodness-of-fit statistics presented in this table, we see that for these data the difference between estimating a model using full-information maximum likelihood versus bivariate-information ULS is very small. Also, the fit differences between the linear and the logistic models for these data are also rather small. In general, one should expect the logistic model to yield a better fit to binary data than the linear model (see the next example), but for these data the logistic item response functions are so flat that the linear item response model provides a comparable fit. This is illustrated in Fig. 3.1, where we provide the item response functions under both models for a chosen item.

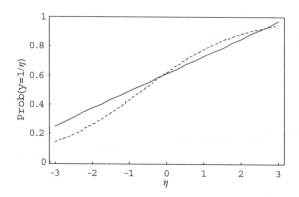

FIG. 3.1.   Item response function of the Law School Admission Test 6 fourth item under the linear and logistic models. The parameter estimates were estimated using full-information maximum likelihood. The parameter estimates are depicted in Table 3.1.

Linear Versus Logistic IRT Modeling of the LSAT 7 Data

We now examine the fit of unidimensional linear and logistic IRT models to the LSAT 7 data. Here we only used full-information maximum likelihood estimation. Initially, we fixed the moments of the latent trait in the linear IRT model at the values of the moments of a standard normal density (see Equation 57). The results are shown in Table 3.2. As can be seen in this table, there is not much difference

TABLE 3.2
Parameter Estimates and Goodness-of-Fit Tests for the Law School Admission Test 7 Data

	Logistic Model	Linear Model A	Linear Model B
Parameter estimates			
α_1	1.86	0.83	0.79
	(0.13)	(0.01)	(0.02)
α_2	0.81	0.66	0.60
	(0.09)	(0.01)	(0.02)
α_3	1.81	0.77	0.71
	(0.20)	(0.01)	(0.02)
α_4	0.49	0.60	0.56
	(0.07)	(0.02)	(0.02)
α_5	1.85	0.84	0.82
	(0.11)	(0.01)	(0.02)
β_1	0.99	0.12	0.14
	(0.17)	(0.02)	(0.02)
β_2	1.08	0.20	0.20
	(0.17)	(0.02)	(0.02)
β_3	1.71	0.20	0.23
	(0.32)	(0.02)	(0.03)
β_4	0.77	0.14	0.17
	(0.13)	(0.02)	(0.02)
β_5	0.74	0.08	0.10
	(0.15)	(0.02)	(0.02)
κ_1	0	0	0.28
	(Fixed)	(Fixed)	(0.07)
Goodness-of-fit tests			
X^2	32.48	46.56	34.09
	(0.05)	(<0.01)	(0.03)
G^2	31.94	42.98	32.11
	(0.06)	(<0.01)	(0.04)
M_2	11.92	10.19	11.27
	(0.04)	(0.07)	—

Note. Standard errors are given in parentheses for parameter estimates; p values are given in parentheses for goodness of fit tests. All models were estimated by full-information maximum likelihood. The number of degrees of freedom for X^2 and G^2 is 21 for the logistic model and linear model A and 20 for linear model B. The number of degrees of freedom for M_2 is 5 for the logistic model and linear model A. The values used to fix the latent variable moments were those of a standard normal density.

TABLE 3.3

Goodness-of-Fit Tests for Some Unidimensional Linear Item Response Models
Applied to the Law School Admission Test 7 Data

Model	G^2	df
All moments fixed	42.98	21
Estimated κ_1	32.11	20
Estimated κ_2	41.86	20
Estimated $\{\kappa_1, \kappa_2\}$	31.76	19
Estimated $\{\kappa_1, \kappa_2, \kappa_3\}$	31.50	18

Note. All models were estimated by full-information maximum likelihood.
The values used to fix the moments were those of a standard normal density.

in how well both models reproduce the bivariate margins of the table. However, the full-information test statistics indicate that the linear model fails to reproduce the observed cell frequencies. An examination of the standardized cell residuals $N(p_c - \pi_c)^2/\pi_c$, where π_c denotes a cell probability as in Equation 1, reveals that the linear model particularly fails to reproduce the patterns (0,1,0,0,0) and (0,0,0,0,0). Their corresponding standardized cell residuals are 13.81 and 7.81, respectively. Thus, these patterns account for 28% and 17%, respectively, of the value of the X^2 statistic.

However, we can improve the fit of the linear IRT model by estimating some of the moments of the latent trait. With five items, up to three moments can be identified. In Table 3.3 we provide the values of the G^2 statistics obtained when some of the moments of the latent trait were estimated. As can be seen in this table, the best unidimensional linear model for these data is obtained by estimating the mean of the latent trait. In Table 3.2 we provide the full set of parameter estimates and standard errors for this model. This model provides a fit to the LSAT 7 data comparable to that of the logistic model, at the expense of an additional parameter. Note that we do not provide a p value for M_2 because this model is not identified from bivariate information.

It should be noted that estimating a high-order moment of a random variable requires large samples, more so, probably, in the case of latent variables. Thus, estimating high-order moments of a latent trait should only be attempted in large samples. If the sample size is not large enough, the linear model may become empirically underidentified (i.e., $\hat{\Delta}$ will not be of full rank).

EAP Scores for the Linear Model

Once the parameters of a linear model have been estimated, we can obtain scores for individual responses. Here we compare the results obtained when computing expected a posteriori scores for the estimated-mean linear model and for the logistic model for the LSAT 7 dataset. The parameter estimates for these models were presented in Table 3.2. For the logistic model, EAP scores were computed using

Equation 12 assuming a prior standard normal density because this is the density we used in estimating the parameters of this model.

For the linear model, although it is not necessary to assume a density for the latent traits to estimate the model parameters, it is necessary to use some prior distribution to obtain the posterior distribution of the latent traits. In the unidimensional case, we have found that the normal prior distribution

$$\gamma_1(\eta) = \phi_1\left(\eta : -\kappa_1, \kappa_2 - \kappa_1^2\right) \tag{58}$$

yields good results. When the EAP scores for the mean-estimated linear model are obtained using this prior distribution, they correlate 0.98 with the logistic EAP scores and 0.95 with the number right scores (i.e., the unweighted sum of the binary scores). Figures 3.2 and 3.3 are plots of the linear EAP scores against the logistic EAP and number-right scores.

Similar results were obtained when we computed EAP scores for the LSAT 6 data using the linear and logistic models estimated by full-information maximum likelihood. The linear EAP scores correlated 0.96 with the logistic EAP scores, and 0.96 with the number-right scores.

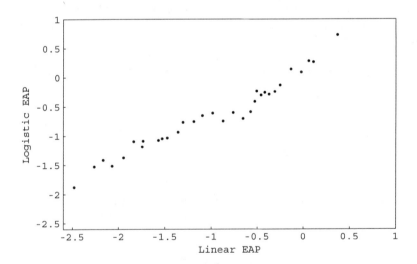

FIG. 3.2. Plot of the expected a posterior (EAP) latent trait estimates under the logistic model and a linear model estimating the mean of the latent trait for the Law School Admission Test 7 data. The parameter estimates were estimated using full-information maximum likelihood. The parameter estimates are depicted in Table 3.2.

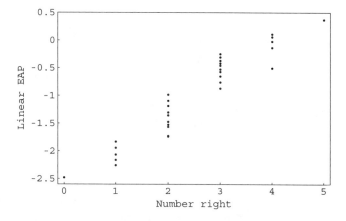

FIG. 3.3. Plot of the expected a posterior (EAP) latent trait estimates under a linear model estimating the mean of the latent trait
versus number-right score for the Law School Admission Test 7
data.

DISCUSSION AND CONCLUSIONS

In this chapter we integrated factor analysis and IRT within a unified modeling
and estimation framework. McDonald (1982a) offered a unified treatment of linear
and nonlinear IRT modeling using Hermite polynomials. He also offered an alternative unified treatment of linear and nonlinear IRT modeling using link functions
(McDonald, 1999). When the latter approach is employed, it is not clear what the
difference is, if any, between a factor model applied to binary data and a linear
item response model for binary data. We discussed that these two models differ in
that the linear item response model is a fully specified model, whereas under the
factor model only the first two moments of the data are specified. As a result, under
the linear item response model, most moments of the latent traits can be identified
when full-information estimation is used.

One attractive feature of the linear item response model is that it does not require
any assumptions on the distribution of the latent traits. Only assumptions on the moments of the latent traits are needed to identify the model. Furthermore, we showed
that high-order moments of the latent traits can be estimated under the linear IRT
model. We illustrated this fact by estimating the first three moments of the latent
trait along with the item parameters of a unidimensional model fitted to the LSAT 7
data. Note, however, that large samples are needed to estimate high-order moments
of any random variable, more so, probably in the case of latent random variables.
Also note that although we have not assumed any prior distribution of the latent
traits to estimate the item parameters, we needed to assume a prior distribution of

the latent traits to obtain the posterior distribution of the latent traits, which is the approach taken here to compute individual scores under the linear IRT model.

An unattractive feature of the linear model is that the item response functions are not bounded between zero and one. Thus, in principle, for low enough values of the latent traits the probability of endorsing the item may be negative, whereas for high enough values of the latent traits the probability of endorsing the item may be greater than one. However, we verified that at the EAP scores computed for the LSAT 6 and LSAT 7 data the item response functions do not fall outside of the [0, 1] range. Also, for these two data sets the linear item response model is a proper model because the cell probabilities are in the range [0, 1].

Although in general we expect nonlinear IRT models to yield a better fit to binary data than the linear model, we also showed using two data sets that in some applications the linear model may provide a good fit to binary data sets. For the LSAT 6 data, a linear model with fixed moments provides a fit comparable to that of the two-parameter logistic model. For the LSAT 7 data, a linear model with fixed moments provides a poor fit to the observed binary pattern frequencies, but a linear model estimating the mean of the latent traits provides a fit comparable to that of a two-parameter logistic model (at the expense of an additional parameter, of course).

In closing, we note that McDonald (1999) pointed out that when the linear IRT model is estimated using only univariate and bivariate information, this model is equivalent to the factor model applied to binary data. However, the factor model is generally estimated using central joint moments (covariances) or standardized joint central moments (correlations), whereas in limited-information IRT estimation raw joint moments (cross-products) are generally used. In any case, the general framework of moment estimators provides a unifying estimation framework for factor analysis (and more generally structural equation modeling) and IRT. We pointed out that Browne's T_B statistic provides a common yardstick for assessing the goodness of fit of a factor model and an IRT model to binary data. This statistic is a quadratic form in the residual covariances with a sample-based weight matrix. Maydeu-Olivares and Joe (in press) recently introduced a similar statistic, M_2. This is also a quadratic form, but in the residual cross-products, where a model-based weight matrix is used instead. The two statistics are asymptotically chi-square distributed for any consistent and asymptotically normal estimator, and so is the full information extension of M_2, M_n. Because M_n is also asymptotically chi-square distributed for any consistent and asymptotically normal estimator it can be used, unlike X^2 or G^2, to assess the goodness of fit of competing IRT models regardless of whether they have been estimated using limited- or full-information methods.

APPENDIX. REPRESENTATIONS OF THE MULTIVARIATE BERNOULLI DISTRIBUTION

The $\binom{n}{1}$ univariate moments of the multivariate Bernoulli distribution are of the form

$$E[y_i] = 1 \times \Pr(y_i = 1) + 0 \times \Pr(y_i = 0) = \Pr(y_i = 1) = \dot{\pi}_i. \qquad (A1)$$

Similarly, each of the $\binom{n}{2}$ bivariate raw moments of $\mathbf{y}$ is of the form

$$E[y_i y_j] = \Pr[(y_i = 1) \cap (y_j = 1)] = \dot{\pi}_{ij}, \quad i < j. \qquad (A2)$$

and so forth. The overall number of raw joint moments of $\mathbf{y}$ is $\sum_{i=1}^{n} \binom{n}{i} = 2^n - 1$. The relationship between the $(2^n - 1)$ vector of moments $\dot{\pi}$ and the 2^n vector of cell probabilities π is linear, say $\dot{\pi} = \mathbf{T}\pi$, where $\mathbf{T}$ is a matrix that consists of ones and zeros (Maydeu-Olivares, 1997).

We illustrate $\dot{\pi} = \mathbf{T}\pi$ for the case of $n = 3$ Bernoulli variables:

$$
\begin{pmatrix} \dot{\pi}_1 \\ \dot{\pi}_2 \\ \dot{\pi}_3 \\ \dot{\pi}_{12} \\ \dot{\pi}_{13} \\ \dot{\pi}_{23} \\ \dot{\pi}_{123} \end{pmatrix}
=
\begin{pmatrix}
0 & 1 & 0 & 0 & 1 & 1 & 0 & 1 \\
0 & 0 & 1 & 0 & 1 & 0 & 1 & 1 \\
0 & 0 & 0 & 1 & 0 & 1 & 1 & 1 \\
0 & 0 & 0 & 0 & 1 & 0 & 0 & 1 \\
0 & 0 & 0 & 0 & 0 & 1 & 0 & 1 \\
0 & 0 & 0 & 0 & 0 & 0 & 1 & 1 \\
0 & 0 & 0 & 0 & 0 & 0 & 0 & 1
\end{pmatrix}
\begin{pmatrix} \pi_{000} \\ \pi_{100} \\ \pi_{010} \\ \pi_{001} \\ \pi_{110} \\ \pi_{101} \\ \pi_{011} \\ \pi_{111} \end{pmatrix},
\qquad (A3)
$$

where, for instance, $\pi_{100} = \Pr[(y_1 = 1) \cap (y_2 = 0) \cap (y_3 = 0)]$.

The relationship between π and $\dot{\pi}$ is one-to-one. To see this, notice in Equation A3 that $\dot{\pi} = \mathbf{T}\pi$ can always be written as

$$\dot{\pi} = (\mathbf{0} \; \breve{\mathbf{T}}) \begin{pmatrix} \pi_0 \\ \breve{\pi} \end{pmatrix} = \breve{\mathbf{T}}\breve{\pi}, \qquad (A4)$$

where $\pi_0 = \Pr[\bigcap_{i=1}^{n} (y_i = 0)]$, $\breve{\pi}$ is used to denote the $(2^n - 1)$-dimensional vector of cell probabilities excluding π_0, and $\breve{\mathbf{T}}$ is an upper triangular square matrix. Then, because $\pi_0 = 1 - \mathbf{1}'\breve{\pi}$, the inverse relationship between $\dot{\pi}$ and π is

$$\pi = \begin{pmatrix} 1 \\ \mathbf{0} \end{pmatrix} + \begin{pmatrix} -\mathbf{1}'\breve{\mathbf{T}}^{-1} \\ \breve{\mathbf{T}}^{-1} \end{pmatrix} \dot{\pi}. \qquad (A5)$$

As a result, we can represent any item response model for binary data using its vector of moments $\dot{\pi}$ rather than its vector of cell probabilities π.

We now present some results for the moments of the multivariate Bernoulli distribution that are valid under any item response model. We make use of these results in the body of the text.

First, we notice that the expected value of a variable given the latent traits simply equals the item response function. This is because

$$E[y_i|\boldsymbol{\eta}] = 1 \times \Pr(y_i = 1|\boldsymbol{\eta}) + 0 \times \Pr(y_i = 0|\boldsymbol{\eta}) = \Pr(y_i = 1|\boldsymbol{\eta}). \qquad (A6)$$

Next, we notice that the univariate moments are simply the expected value of the item response function,

$$\dot{\pi}_i = E_{\eta}[\Pr(y_i = 1|\boldsymbol{\eta})], \qquad (A7)$$

where $E_{\eta}[\bullet]$ is used to indicate that the expectation is to be taken with respect to $\boldsymbol{\eta}$. This result follows immediately from Equation A6 and the double expectation theorem (e.g., Mittelhammer, 1996), $E[y_i] = E_{\eta}[E[y_i|\boldsymbol{\eta}]]$.

Similarly, we notice that the bivariate raw moments are simply

$$\dot{\pi}_{ij} = E_{\eta}[\Pr(y_i = 1|\eta)\Pr(y_j = 1|\eta)]. \qquad (A8)$$

This is because we can write $\dot{\pi}_{ij} = E[y_i \cap y_j] = E_{\eta}[E[(y_i \cap y_j)|\boldsymbol{\eta}]]$. From the assumption of local independence, however, $E[(y_i \cap y_j)|\boldsymbol{\eta}] = E[y_i|\boldsymbol{\eta}]E[y_j|\boldsymbol{\eta}]$. Finally, the trivariate moments are simply

$$\dot{\pi}_{ijk} = E_{\eta}[\Pr(y_i = 1|\boldsymbol{\eta})\Pr(y_j = 1|\boldsymbol{\eta})\Pr(y_k = 1|\boldsymbol{\eta})]. \qquad (A9)$$

Similar expressions result for higher moments.

ACKNOWLDGMENTS

This research was supported by the Dept. of Universities, Research and Information Society (DURSI) of the Catalan Government, and by grants BSO2000-0661 and BSO2003-08507 from the Spanish Ministry of Science and Technology.

REFERENCES

Agresti, A. (1990). *Categorical data analysis*. New York: Wiley.

Bartholomew, D. J., & Knott, M. (1999). *Latent variable models and factor analysis*. London: Arnold.

Bartholomew, D. J., & Leung, S. O. (2001). A goodness of fit test for sparse $2p$ contingency tables. *British Journal of Mathematical and Statistical Psychology, 55*, 1–16.

Bartholomew, D. J., & Tzamourani, P. (1999). The goodness of fit of latent trait models in attitude measurement. *Sociolological Methods and Research, 27*, 525–546.

Bekker, P. A., Merckens, A., & Wansbeek, T. J. (1994). *Identification, equivalent models and computer algebra*. San Diego, CA: Academic.

Bishop, Y., Feinberg, S. E., & Holland, P. (1975). *Discrete multivariate analysis: Theory and practice*. Cambridge, MA: MIT Press.

Bock, R. D., & Lieberman, M. (1970). Fitting a response model for n dichotomously scored items. *Psychometrika, 35*, 179–197.

Browne, M. W. (1984). Asymptotically distribution free methods for the analysis of covariance structures. *British Journal of Mathematical and Statistical Psychology, 37*, 62–83.

Christoffersson, A. (1975). Factor analysis of dichotomized variables. *Psychometrika, 40*, 5–32.

Ferguson, T. S. (1996). *A course in large sample theory*. London: Chapman & Hall.

Maydeu-Olivares, A. (1996). Modelos multidimensionales de respuesta a los items [Multidimensional item response models]. In J. Muñiz (Ed.), *Psicometría* [Psychometrics] (pp. 811–868). Madrid: Universitas.

Maydeu-Olivares, A. (1997). Structural equation modeling of binary preference data. (Doctoral dissertation, University of Illinois at Urbana-Champaign, 1997). *Dissertation Abstracts International, 58*, 5694B.

Maydeu-Olivares, A. (2001). Multidimensional item response theory modeling of binary data: Large sample properties of NOHARM estimates. *Journal of Educational and Behavioral Statistics, 26*, 49–69.

Maydeu-Olivares, A., & Joe, H. (in press). Limited and full information estimation and testing in 2^n contingency tables: A unified framework. *Journal of the American Statistical Association*.

Maydeu-Olivares, A., Hernández, A., & McDonald, R. P. (2002). *A multidimensional unfolding latent trait model for binary attitudinal data*. Manuscript under review. Barcelona: University of Barcelona.

McDonald, R. P. (1967). *Nonlinear factor analysis*. (Psychometric Monographs, No. 15). Chicago: University of Chicago Press.

McDonald, R. P. (1969). The common factor analysis of multicategory data. *British Journal of Mathematical and Statistical Psychology, 22*, 165–175.

McDonald, R. P. (1980). A simple comprehensive model for the analysis of covariance structures: Some remarks on applications. *British Journal of Mathematical and Statistical Psychology, 33*, 161–183.

McDonald, R. P. (1981). The dimensionality of tests and items. *British Journal of Mathematical and Statistical Psychology, 34*, 100–117.

McDonald, R. P. (1982a). Linear vs. nonlinear models in latent trait theory. *Applied Psychological Measurement, 6*, 379–396.

McDonald, R. P. (1982b). Fitting latent trait models. In D. Spearrit (Ed.), *Some alternative approaches to the improvement of measurement in education and psychology* (pp. 213–237). Hawthorn: Australian Council for Educational Research.

McDonald, R. P. (1985a). Unidimensional and multidimensional models for item response theory. In D. J. Weiss (Ed.), *Proceedings of the 1982 Item Response and Computerized Adaptive Testing Conference* (pp. 127–147). Minneapolis: University of Minnesota Press.

McDonald, R. P. (1985b). *Factor analysis and related methods*. Hillsdale, NJ: Lawrence Erlbaum Associates, Inc.

McDonald, R. P. (1986). Describing the elephant: Structure and function in multivariate data. *Psychometrika, 51*, 513–534.

McDonald, R. P. (1997). Normal ogive multidimensional model. In W. J. van der Linden & R. K. Hambleton (Eds.), *Handbook of modern item response theory* (pp. 257–269). New York: Springer.

McDonald, R. P. (1999). *Test theory. A unified approach*. Hillsdale, NJ: Lawrence Erlbaum Associates, Inc.

McDonald, R. P. (2001). A basis for multidimensional item response theory. *Applied Psychological Measurement, 24*, 99–114.

McDonald, R. P., & Mok, M. C. (1995). Goodness of fit in item response models. *Multivariate Behavioral Research, 54,* 483–495.

Mittelhammer, R. C. (1996). *Mathematical statistics for economics and business.* New York: Springer.

Moustaki, I., & Knott, M. (2000). Generalized latent trait models. *Psychometrika, 65,* 391–411.

Muthén, B. (1978). Contributions to factor analysis of dichotomous variables. *Psychometrika, 43,* 551–560.

Rao, C. R. (1973). *Linear statistical inference and its applications.* New York: Wiley.

Reiser, M. (1996). Analysis of residuals for the multinomial item response model. *Psychometrika, 61,* 509–528.

Reiser, M., & VandenBerg, M. (1994). Validity of the chi-square test in dichotomous varible factor analysis when expected frequencies are small. *British Journal of Mathematical and Statistical Psychology, 47,* 85–107.

Satorra, A., & Bentler, P. M. (1994). Corrections to test statistics and standard errors in covariance structure analysis. In A. von Eye and C. C. Clogg (Eds.), *Latent variable analysis: Applications to developmental research* (pp. 399–419). Thousand Oaks, CA: Sage.

van der Linden, W. J., & Hambleton, R. K. (1997). *Handbook of modern item response theory.* New York: Springer.

van Schuur, W. H., & Kiers, H. A. L. (1994). Why factor analysis is often the incorrect model for analyzing bipolar concepts, and what model can be used instead. *Applied Psychological Measurement, 5,* 245–262.

4

Neglected Thinking About Measurement in Behavioral Science Research

John L. Horn
University of Southern California

PRELUDE

This volume testifies to the many important contributions Rod McDonald has made to improving design and analyses in behavioral science research. This chapter deals with measurement, only one of the areas in which McDonald has made notable contributions.

Good measurement is a necessary component of scientific research. Without good measurement, the best of design and data analysis can prove little. Yet measurement is often a weak link in the chain of jobs that must be done. Attending to McDonald's thinking can very much improve measurement and thus strengthen this link. His book, *Test Theory: A Unified Treatment* (McDonald, 1999), is a comprehensive account of the rationale and technology of measurement. It brings together classical true-score theory and item response theory in a unification that also includes invariance analysis, scaling theory and an analysis of variance and common factor integration of generalizability theory. The book is truly a unified treatment of important psychometric theory, much of which is not covered in other texts.

So, the neglected thinking is not here, but this is at the level of theory. At the level of drawing practical implications from principles of measurement important thinking has been neglected. It is thinking about applications that I wish to bring to the fore in this chapter.

I will discuss how item means, variances and intercorrelations determine the shape of the distribution and the discriminability of linear composite measurements. I will make a case for constructing scales that not only have good internal cohesiveness reliability, but also have discriminability well designed to provide good bases for the kinds of decisions that are called for in scientific research and in other uses of psychological measurement. I will also have a word or two to say about how these matters relate to the use of statistics.

MEASUREMENT IN THE BEHAVIORAL SCIENCES

Most measurement in the behavioral sciences is linear composite measurement. That is, measurements are obtained by summing numbers that are assigned a priori to represent responses to stimuli (which I will usually refer to as items). Such measurements are described with the following kind of equation:

$$Y_i = W_1 X_{1i} + W_2 X_{2i} + \cdots + W_j X_{ji} + W_k X_{ki}, \tag{1}$$

where Y_i is the measure of individual i, X_{ji} is the coded-into-number response of individual i on item j, and the W_j are weightings that can be applied explicitly to each X_{ji}.[1]

The variance of such a composite is

$$\mathrm{Var}(Y) = \sum W_j^2 S_j^2 + W_j W_h r_{jh} S_j S_h, \tag{3}$$

where $\mathrm{Var}(Y)$ is the variance, $\Sigma W_j^2 S_j^2$ is the weighted sum (over $j = 1, 2, \ldots, k$ items) of the variances of the individual items, and $W_j W_h r_{jh} S_j S_h$ is the double sum (over j & $h = 1, 2, \ldots, k$) of the products of the item $W_j W_h$ weights, the item correlations r_{jh}, and the item standard deviations $S_j S_h$.

The weights of a linear composite[2] often are, or are assumed to be, equal, in which case the variance is simply sum of the item variances plus the sum of the

---

[1]We could write an alternative to Equation 1 for binary items in terms of a model that represents the probability of a keyed response to item j for a subject with a particular value f of a (common factor) attribute,

$$\hat{X}_j = \lambda_j f + \mu_j = P\{X_j = 1 | F = f\} \tag{2}$$

and develop our arguments in terms of item response theory, but I think I can make the points that need to be made without that theory, and that they are valid when evaluated in terms of the theory.

[2]Nonlinear composites are infrequently used in psychology. These will not be considered here (but see Horn, 1963). The basic principles discussed in this chapter apply as well to nonlinear composites as to linear composites.

item covariances,

$$\text{Var}(Y) = \sum S_j^2 + \sum \sum r_{jh} S_j S_h. \tag{4}$$

Seen in terms of this unweighted linear composite, one general expression for reliability is

$$r_{yy} = \frac{k}{k-1} \frac{\sum \sum r_{jk} S_j S_k}{\sum S_j^2 + \sum \sum r_{jk} S_j S_k}. \tag{5}$$

Often referred to as the internal consistency alpha[3], this is a general form for representing most concepts of reliability for measurements that are in one sense or another composites. That is, stability reliability, split-half reliability, retest reliability and the generic concept of reliability, as well as internal cohesiveness reliability, can be expressed in terms of a ratio of the extent to which the elements of a composite are inter-related (as indicated primarily by the r_{jk}) to the total variance of the composite (a ratio of the covariance to the variance).

These basics are well stated in McDonald's book. I restate them here simply to provide background and lay out the particular symbolism I will use in subsequent discussion.

Whence Come Distributions?

The shape of the distribution of measurements seems often to be assumed to be an intrinsic feature of the attribute measured. For example, Graziano and Raulin (2004) argue that "measurements of most human characteristics, such as . . . intelligence, are distributed normally." Books on research design (Goodwin, 2001) and personality (Mischel, 1993) similarly argue that human characteristics have particular distribution forms. Depression, for example, is said to have a skewed distribution such that within a given year only about 10% to 15% of adult Americans experience it (Blazer, Kessler, McGonagle, & Schwartz, 1994).

However, regardless of what is said or assumed, as in theory, distributions of measurements are determined by operations of measurement (as these play out within particular samplings of subjects). Depending on the operations of measurement, distributions may be of almost any form one can imagine. Distributions for measures of depression, such as are obtained with the Beck Depression Inventory (Beck, Ward, Mendelsohn, Mock, & Erbaugh, 1962), may be symmetric, for

---

[3]McDonald (1999) notes that this coefficient "was first given by Louis Guttman in 1945. He showed that it is a lower bound in the population to the reliability coefficient . . . Coefficient alpha is often incorrectly attributed to a paper by Cronbach in 1951. In view of Cronbach's contributions to our understanding of this coefficient, it is referred to here as the Guttman–Cronbach alpha or G–C alpha."

I will refer to the coefficient as simply "the reliability," and occasionally distinguish between internal cohesiveness and other variations of the concept.

example, whereas distributions of characteristics thought to be symmetric, such as locus of control (Rotter, 1966), may be skewed and saw-toothed (Phares, 1978).

The, shape of the distribution of measurements can be largely under the control of the scale constructor. This is particularly evident in the case of linear composite measurements. Here the operations of measurement amount to putting together a particular set of items in a test construction sample. In this sample, the items will have particular intercorrelations and particular variances and means (the latter for binary items can be written as probabilities of the keyed response, which we will refer to as difficulty levels). The particular selection of these item characteristics determines the shape of the distribution of the measures. Given a proper sample of items to select from, one can make the distribution into any of a variety of forms—almost any form one might like.

It seems that often this is not understood, or at least that nothing is done about it if it is understood. The writing and selecting of items in test construction are done without consideration of how item difficulties and intercorrelations affect the form of the distribution of measures. If the items selected for a measurement device are not chosen by design to yield a particular distribution form, then the distribution obtained with the device is essentially arbitrary.

There is belief that measurements should be normally distributed—that if they are not, something has gone wrong and it is incorrect to use statistical methods such as correlations, analysis of variance, multiple regression, and factor analysis to analyze the data. This belief is not well founded in understanding of principles of measurement or principles of application of statistical theory in scientific research. Normal distributions of measurements are neither required nor desirable in such research.

To make these points I first consider a case in which no measurement at all is obtained with operations of measurement, and I then lay out a few simple examples to illustrate how properties of measurements—and distributions of measurements in particular—are determined. I indicate how the researcher can have control over these determining factors—how a test constructor can write and select items that, at least in the test construction sample, will yield linear composite measurement that have a distribution form that conforms to particular ideas about what the distribution should be. I indicate how particular properties are related to particular objectives that can be more or less important in particular research projects. Along the way I indicate why I think belief that manifest variables should be normally distributed is not warranted, and argue that for many purposes of measurement—in applications as well as in research—a good case can be made for constructing measures for which the distribution is rectangular.

A Case of When Nothing Is Measured

Suppose we have a questionnaire or test made up from 10 two-choice items in which response to one of the choices is scored correct, whereas response to the other choice is scored incorrect. Suppose further that on the response form the two choices occur equally often in one position (say, top) as compared to another position (say, bottom), and that the measurements are obtained (as is most common) as a simple sum of the correct responses. The measure obtained from responses to items of this test is thus a simple unweighted linear composite.

$$Y_i = X_{1i} + X_{2i} + X_{3i} + \cdots + X_{ji} + X_{ki}. \tag{6}$$

Next, suppose that 1,024 people take this test and every participant determines his or her response to each item by flipping a balanced coin, for which the probability of heads equals the probability of tails. If a head comes up, the top response is chosen, and if a tail comes up, the bottom response is chosen.

Under these conditions there are 11 possible linear composite scores, and the frequency of occurrence of each of these scores can be obtained from a symmetrical binomial formula, where the probability of getting each possible combination of responses constituting a score is

$$p_n = \frac{10!}{r!\,(10-r)!}(p)^n(q)^{n-r} \tag{7}$$

and the frequencies f_j of the 11 "measures" of 1,024 subjects have the distribution shown in Table 4.1.

A plot of the binomial frequencies indicates that the distribution is as close to a normal distribution as one can get with only 11 distinct scores. The example illustrates that a normal distribution can result when no measurement at all has been obtained (Fig. 4.1).

TABLE 4.1
Expected Frequencies for Different Intervals for
$N = 1,024$ Persons

Interval	Calculation	Frequency
f_0	$\frac{10!}{0!(10-0)!}(.5)^0(.5)^{10-0}1{,}024$	1
f_1	$\frac{10!}{1!(10-1)!}(.5)^1(.5)^{10-1}1{,}024$	10
f_2	$\frac{10!}{2!(10-2)!}(.5)^2(.5)^{10-2}1{,}024$	45
f_3	$\frac{10!}{3!(10-3)!}(.5)^3(.5)^{10-3}1{,}024$	120
f_4	$\frac{10!}{4!(10-4)!}(.5)^4(.5)^{10-4}1{,}024$	210
f_5	$\frac{10!}{5!(10-5)!}(.5)^5(.5)^{10-5}1{,}024$	252
f_6	$\frac{10!}{6!(10-6)!}(.5)^6(.5)^{10-6}1{,}024$	210
f_7	$\frac{10!}{7!(10-7)!}(.5)^7(.5)^{10-7}1{,}024$	120
f_8	$\frac{10!}{8!(10-8)!}(.5)^8(.5)^{10-8}1{,}024$	45
f_9	$\frac{10!}{9!(10-9)!}(.5)^9(.5)^{10-9}1{,}024$	10
f_{10}	$\frac{10!}{0!(10-0)!}(.5)^{10}(.5)^{10-10}1{,}024$	1

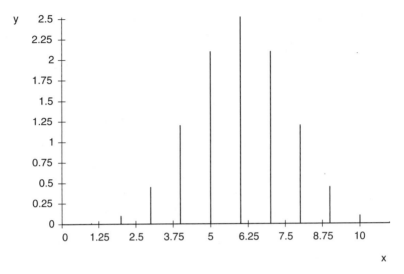

FIG. 4.1. A plot of frequencies indicating graphically that the distribution is as close to a normal distribution as one can get with only 11 scores.

The variance of the linear composites obtained in this case is relatively small,

$$\mathrm{Var}(Y_i) = \sum(.5)_j^2 + \sum\sum r_{j,k}(.5)_j(.5)_k$$
$$= k(.5)^2 + (.5)(.5)(0) = 10(.25) = 2.5,$$

for there is no contribution from the covariance $(r_{j,k}S_jS_k)$ component of the variance because the expected value of the interitem correlations $r_{j,k}$ is zero.[4]

The expected value of the internal cohesiveness version of reliability is also small, indeed, zero

$$r_{yy} = \frac{10}{10-1}\frac{(.5)(.5)\sum\sum r_{j,k}}{k(.5)^2 + (.5)(.5)\sum\sum r_{j,k}}$$
$$= \frac{10}{9}\frac{(.5)(.5)0}{10(.5)^2 + (.5)(.5)0} = 0,$$

for there is no contribution from the covariance $(r_{j,k}S_jS_k)$ component of the variance, and so reliability has an expected value of zero.

---

[4]The variance could be smaller, of course—if the probabilities of "correct" and "incorrect" responses were not equal—but the point is that the variance is in any case small.

Thus (I belabor the point for emphasis) a normal distribution is a chance distribution, not an outcome of measurement. If such a distribution is found, and no information about reliability is given—a not uncommon occurrence in behavioral science research—there is a prima facie case for the claim that no measurement was obtained, that the so-called measurements are numbers generated by chance. It is possible, of course, to get an approximately normal distribution with measurement operations that are reliable, but a normal distribution is not the expected outcome if good measurement operations are applied.[5]

EXAMPLES ILLUSTRATING THE PROPERTIES OF MEASUREMENTS

What kind of distribution should result if good measurement operations are employed? The following four very simple examples provide a basis for answering this question.

I set up a simple generic case in which linear composite measurements are obtained from just two items, X_{1i} and X_{2i}, each scored 0 (incorrect) and 1 (correct),

$$Y_i = X_{1i} + X_{2i}. \tag{8}$$

The possible measurements for Y_i thus will be simply 0, 1, or 2: $Y_i = 0$ will occur when both X_{1i} and X_{2i} are 0; $Y_i = 1$ will occur when either X_{1i} or X_{2i} is 1; and $Y_i = 2$ will occur when both X_{1i} and X_{2i} are 1. I will assume that the proportion correct for one item (say, X_{1i}) is .6 and for the other item (X_{2i}) is .4, and that the total frequency is 100. The following four examples can then be used to illustrate the applications of principles of measurement I wish to call to attention.

Example A: The Case of No Measurement

This is the random-response condition described earlier for a 10-item test. A contingency table for this two-item example of no measurement can be laid out as follows:

Item 1 Response Possibilities→ *Item 2 Response Possibilities↓*	0	1	Σ		0	1	Σ
0	24	36	60		N_{00}	N_{01}	N_{00}
1	16	24	40	=	N_{10}	N_{11}	N_{10}
Σ	40	60	100		N_{00}	N_{01}	N_{00}

---

[5]Indeed, Wilcox (2003) found that good approximations to normal distributions occur only rarely in behavioral science research.

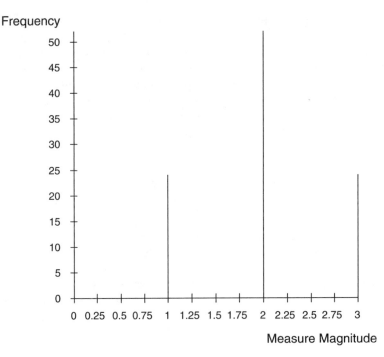

FIG. 4.2.   The distribution of Example A.

from which the product–moment correlation between the two items can be calculated with the phi coefficient,

$$\rho_{12} = \frac{N_{00}N_{11} - N_{10}N_{01}}{\sqrt{N_{0.}N_{1.}N_{.0}N_{.}}} = \frac{(24)(24) - (16)(36)}{\sqrt{(60)(40)(40)(60)}} = 0,$$

and the distribution for the Y_i measures can easily be seen to be as shown in Fig. 4.2.

Here it can be seen that the frequency for the smallest measure ($Y_i = 1$) is 24
(when both X_{1i} and X_{2i} are 0), the frequency the next-largest measure ($Y_i = 2$)
is $16 + 36 = 52$ (when either X_{1i} or X_{2i} is 1), and the frequency for the largest
measure ($Y_i = 3$) is 24 (when both X_{1i} and X_{2i} are 1). We also see clearly that the
shape of the distribution is peaked and symmetric, as normal as a distribution can
get when there are only three possible scores and the marginal distributions are
not the same.

The item intercorrelations are zero and so is the internal cohesiveness reliability,

$$r_{yy} = \frac{2}{2-1} \frac{2(0)\sqrt{(.6)(.4)}\sqrt{(.4)(.6)}}{(.6)(.4) + (.4)(.6) + 2(0\sqrt{(.6)(.4)}\sqrt{(.4)(.6)})} = 0,$$

and the assumption that nothing has been measured is reasonable.

Example B: The Case of Some Reliable Measurement

This case exemplifies conditions commonly found in the behavioral sciences. Typically, items selected for psychological measures have intercorrelations in the range of .15 to .25. Here we consider the case in which the item intercorrelation for a two-item test is .25. The contingency table under these conditions is the following:

Item 1 Response Possibilities→ *Item 2 Response Possibilities↓*	0	1	Σ
0	30	30	60
1	10	30	40
Σ	40	60	100

The correlation and reliability for the two-item measure are, respectively,

$$\rho_{12} = \frac{(30)(30) - (10)(30)}{\sqrt{(60)(40)(40)(60)}} = \frac{1}{4} = .25,$$

$$r_{yy} = \frac{2}{2-1} \frac{2\left(\frac{1}{4}\right)\sqrt{(.6)(.4)}\sqrt{(.4)(.6)}}{(.6)(.4) + (.4)(.6) + 2\left(\frac{1}{4}\right)\sqrt{(.6)(.4)}\sqrt{(.4)(.6)}} = .40,$$

and the distribution for the measures is as seen in Fig. 4.3.

The distribution is flattened relative to a normal distribution. The correlation between the items, which is needed to gain reliability, reduces the peakedness of

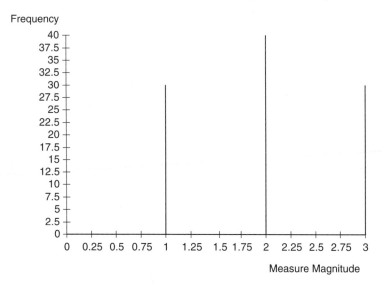

FIG. 4.3. The distribution of Example B.

the distribution. What is desirable for measurement—reliability—does not produce normality; it produces a flattened distribution.

Example C: The Case of Rectangularly Distributed Measurements

If the item intercorrelations are .33 to .40 (for item difficulties in the neighborhood of .2 to .8), the measures will not only be reliable, they will have another quality that can be desirable for measurements: maximum discriminability. Illustrating this application of principle with the present example of item difficulties, is the following contingency table in which the item intercorrelation is .375:

Item 1 Response Possibilities→ *Item 2 Response Possibilities↓*	0	1	Σ
0	33	27	60
1	7	33	40
Σ	40	60	100

The correlation and the reliability for a two-item measure in this case are respectively,

$$\rho_{12} = \frac{(33)(33) - (7)(27)}{\sqrt{(60)(40)(40)(60)}} = .375,$$

$$r_{yy} = \frac{2}{2-1} \frac{2(.375)\sqrt{(.6)(.4)}\sqrt{(.4)(.6)}}{(.6)(.4) + (.4)(.6) + 2(.375)\sqrt{(.6)(.4)}\sqrt{(.4)(.6)}} = .55,$$

and the distribution of the $Y_i + 1$ measures is very nearly rectangular, as seen in Fig. 4.4.

The distribution is as nearly rectangular as it can be for two items with difficulties that are different, .4 and .6. If marginal distributions are all .5 and the item intercorrelations are .33, the distribution will be perfectly rectangular.

Example D: The Case of High Redundancy

Suppose item intercorrelations are as large as they can be. For this case, the contingency table, item intercorrelations, and reliability for our two-item test are as follows, respectively:

Item 1 Response Possibilities→ *Item 2 Response Possibilities↓*	0	1	Σ
0	40	20	60
1	0	40	40
Σ	40	60	100

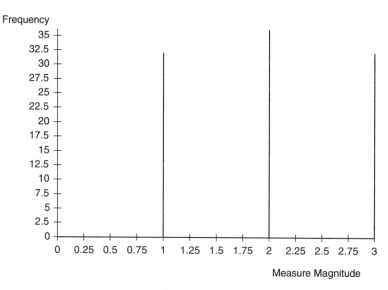

FIG. 4.4. The distribution of Example C.

$$\rho_{12} = \frac{(40)(40) - (0)(20)}{\sqrt{(60)(40)(40)(60)}} = .67,$$

$$r_{yy} = \frac{2}{2-1} \frac{2\left(\frac{2}{3}\right)\sqrt{(.6)(.4)}\sqrt{(.4)(.6)}}{(.6)(.4) + (.4)(.6) + 2\left(\frac{2}{3}\right)\sqrt{(.6)(.4)}\sqrt{(.4)(.6)}} = .8.$$

This product–moment correlation is as large as it can be (.67) when variables have different marginal distributions. The internal cohesiveness reliability in this case is very large (.8) for a two-item test, and the distribution is U-shaped, as seen in Fig. 4.5.

Because reliability is large, this case is sometimes regarded as indicating very good measurement. However, the measure has little breadth—the items are perfectly redundant—and the distribution is bimodal U-shaped.

Summary of the Examples

These examples for binary items and item difficulties evenly distributed from rather high to rather low (here from .4 to .6) illustrate the following general principles for linear composite measurement:

1. If item intercorrelations are near zero, the distribution of the measurements will be approximately normal; the variance of the composite will be small, the internal cohesiveness reliability will be low, and there is good reason to suppose that nothing is measured.

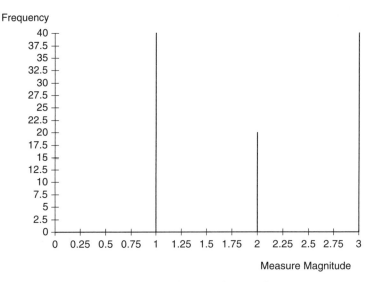

FIG. 4.5.   The distribution of Example D.

2. If item intercorrelations are of the order of .15 to .30, the variance and reliability will indicate some degree of measurement, and the distribution for the measurements will be bell shaped, often regarded as "near normal" (e.g., Goodwin, 2001), but in fact flattened relative to a normal distribution.
3. If item intercorrelations are in a range of about .33 to .40, the variance and reliability will indicate that measurement has been obtained and the distribution of the measures will be approximately rectangular.
4. If item intercorrelations are near the maximum possible, variance and internal consistency reliability will be very large, the measures will be redundantly narrow, and the distribution of the measures will tend toward bimodal, U-shaped.

Example C illustrates an outcome of measurement operations that may be desirable—a rectangular distribution. Such a distribution provides maximum discriminability across the range of measurements. Just as variance and reliability are desirable qualities of measurement, so discriminability is such a quality. Under the conditions of Examples A and D, discriminability across the range of measurements is small. Let us next look at this matter of discriminability in a more analytical fashion.

DISCRIMINABILITY AND MEASUREMENT

Measurements should discriminate. Operations of measurement should identify differences among the objects measured—people, rats, or, in general, subjects.

The operations should provide information about greater than ($>$) and less than ($<$). Only in the context of $>$ and $<$ information can information about equality ($=$) be informative.

Calculating Discriminations

A discrimination in measurement is indicated when the measure of one subject is larger or smaller than the measure of another subject. Each pair comparison of a measure of one subject with a measure of another subject provides a possible instance of discriminability. That is, each such comparison can indicate whether subject S_i's measure is larger than, smaller than, or equal to subject S_j's measure. Thus, in a sample of N subjects, the number of pair comparisons that can independently yield information about larger than, smaller than, or equal to is $\frac{1}{2}(N^2 - N)$.

In this total let us distinguish the frequencies of instances of discriminability from the frequencies of instances of equality. The overall frequencies of the separate measures for the simple two-item test (which yields measures of 0, 1, or 2) can be represented by f_0 for measures of 0, f_1 for measures of 1, and f_2 for measures of 2. The total frequency N is then seen to be

$$N = f_0 + f_1 + f_2, \tag{9}$$

and the total number of pair comparisons for which discriminating information (about $>$, $<$, or $=$) can be expressed in terms of these frequencies as follows:

$$\frac{1}{2}(N^2 - N) = \frac{1}{2}\left[(f_0 + f_1 + f_2)^2 - (f_0 + f_1 + f_2)\right]. \tag{10}$$

Expanding this expression on the right enables us to distinguish between comparisons that provide discriminating information and comparisons that do not provide this kind of information:

$$\frac{1}{2}(N^2 - N) = \frac{1}{2}\left[(f_0^2 + f_1^2 + f_2^2) + 2f_0f_1 + 2f_0f_2\right.$$
$$\left. + 2f_1f_2 - (f_0 + f_1 + f_2)\right] \tag{11}$$
$$= \frac{1}{2}\left[(f_0^2 + f_1^2 + f_2^2) - (f_0 + f_1 + f_2)\right]$$
$$+ \frac{1}{2}(2f_0f_1 + 2f_0f_2 + 2f_1f_2).$$

Here it can be seen that the first two kinds of terms, in which there are no cross-comparisons—the $\frac{1}{2}[(f_0^2 + f_1^2 + f_2^2) - (f_0 + f_1 + f_2)]$ terms—do not provide information about $>$ and $<$ and thus indicate only the number of $=$ frequencies, whereas the last term on the right does have cross-comparisons, $\frac{1}{2}(2f_0f_1 +$

$2 f_0 f_2 + 2 f_1 f_2) = (f_0 f_1 + f_0 f_2 + f_1 f_0 + f_1 f_2 + f_2 f_0 + f_2 f_1)$, that record the inequality relationships of either $>$ or $<$, and thus it does indicate the number of discriminating comparisons.

Because the number of nondiscriminating and discriminating comparisons must add up to the total number of comparisons, another way to express the number of discriminating comparisons is to calculate the difference between the total number of comparisons and the number of nondiscriminating comparisons: Thus,

$$
\begin{aligned}
\text{Discriminating comparisons} &= \frac{1}{2} \left[\left(\sum_j^3 f_j \right)^2 - (f_0 + f_1 + f_2) \right] \\
&\quad - \frac{1}{2} \left[(f_0^2 + f_1^2 + f_2^2) - (f_0 + f_1 + f_2) \right] \\
&= \frac{1}{2} \left[\left(\sum_j^3 f_j \right)^2 - (f_0 + f_1 + f_2) \right. \\
&\quad \left. - \sum_j^3 f_j^2 + (f_0 + f_1 + f_2) \right] \\
&= \frac{1}{2} \left[\left(\sum_j^3 f_j \right)^2 - \sum_j^3 f_j^2 \right],
\end{aligned}
\tag{12}
$$

and this is equal to $(f_0 f_1 + f_0 f_2 + f_1 f_0 + f_1 f_2 + f_2 f_0 + f_2 f_1)$, the other way of expressing the number of discriminating comparisons.

Comparing Discriminations and Nondiscriminations

Applying the partitioning we have just developed to the four two-item examples of our previous discussion, we can see that for distributions that approach rect-angularity, the number of discriminating comparisons is substantially larger and the number of nondiscriminating comparisons is substantially smaller than for distributions that approach normality or U shape (Table 4.2).

Although there are only three measures, the rectangular distribution provides 371 more discriminations than the near-normal distribution and 133 more discrim-inations than the U-shaped distribution.

When there are more than just 3 measures, the differences in number of dis-criminations between rectangular and other distributions are substantially larger than in these 3-measure examples. This is evident for the random response model presented to open this discussion of the origins of distributions—the 10-item test,

TABLE 4.2

A Summary of Discriminations in Four Cases

| | Frequencies | | | Comparisons | |
| | | | | Nondiscriminating | Discriminating |
	f_0	f_1	f_2	$\frac{1}{2}[\sum_j^3 f_j^2 - \sum_j^3 f_j]$	$\frac{1}{2}[(\sum_j^3 f_j)^2 - \sum_j^3 f_j^2]$
Case 1	24	52	24	1,878	3,072
Case 2	30	40	30	1,650	3,300
Case 3	33	34	33	1,617	3,333
Case 4	40	20	40	1,750	3,200

yielding 11 measures. This case, better than the 3-measure examples, more nearly represents the conditions found in the practice of measurement in the behavioral sciences. For this case the rectangular distribution provides 44,715 more discriminations than the near-normal (symmetrical binomial) distribution. Expressed independently of sample size, 91% of the comparisons for the rectangular distribution provide discriminating information as compared to 82% for the near-normal distribution.

Comparing Discriminability Along the Scale of Measurement

Where the difference in discriminability occurs for different distributions is also important. This difference is indicated by comparing the contributions to discriminability obtained for each measure in the near-normal and the rectangular distributions. These contributions are indicated in Table 4.3, which provides a summary of the discriminations—and differences in discriminations—for the near-normal and rectangular distributions of measures for 1,024 subjects.

Here it can be seen that for the smallest and largest measures in the near-normal distribution, the frequency is only 1 and the sum of the discriminations for each of these two frequencies is only 511.5. In contrast, the frequency for the smallest and largest measures in a rectangular distribution is approximately 93 and the sum of the discriminations for each of the extreme measures is 43,291.5.

The differences in discriminations at these end points for the two distributions are substantial: 42,780 more discriminations for the rectangular distribution at both ends of the scale −85,560 discriminations in all. The difference is large, also, for the not-so-extreme measures. For the next-to-the-smallest and next-to-the largest measures, the difference in discriminations is 38,221 at each end, and for the two next-most-extreme measures the differences are 21,264.

For measures near the middle of the distribution, the number of discriminations is larger for the near-normal distribution than for the rectangular one. In general,

TABLE 4.3

Frequencies, Discriminations, and Differences in Discriminations
for Near-Normal and Rectangular Distributions

Measure	Symbol	Frequency Normal	Frequency Rectangular	Discrimination Normal	Discrimination Rectangular	Difference Normal	Difference Rectangular
1	f_0	1	93	511.5	43,291.5		42,780.0
2	f_1	10	93	5,070.0	43,291.5		38,221.5
3	f_2	45	93	22,027.5	43,291.5		21,264.0
4	f_3	120	93	54,240.0	43,291.5	10,948.5	
5	f_4	210	93	85,470.0	43,291.5	42,178.5	
6	f_5	252	94	97,272.0	43,710.0	53,562.0	
7	f_6	210	93	85,470.0	43,291.5	42,178.5	
8	f_7	120	93	54,240.0	43,291.5	10,948.5	
9	f_8	45	93	22,027.5	43,291.5		21,264.0
10	f_9	10	93	5,070.0	43,291.5		38,221.5
11	f_{10}	1	93	511.5	43,291.5		42,780.0
Totals		1,024	1,024	431,910	476,625	159,816	204,531

the number of discriminations for any one measure is largest for the measure that has the largest frequency. In the near-normal distribution this is the measure at the mode (mean and median). At this point the near-normal distribution provides 53,562 more discriminations than is provided by the rectangular distribution. Overall, as mentioned before, the rectangular distribution provides 44,715 more discriminations than the near-normal distribution.

Indices of Discriminability

In the foregoing discussion I used the ratio of the number of discriminations obtained to the total number of pair comparisons to indicate a difference between the near-normal and rectangular distributions. Attneave (1959) and Ferguson (1949) proposed indices of discrimination that are more precisely informative than this simple ratio. A derivation of Ferguson's measure also rather clearly indicates how discriminability relates to distribution form, and so it is useful to develop it here.

Ferguson reasoned that a measure of discriminability should indicate the number of discriminations actually obtainable relative to the number of possible discriminations (rather than the number of pair comparisons, as such). To see the logic of this index, recall that if all f_j are equal, so $f_0 = f_1 = f_2 = \cdots = f_k$ and the distribution is perfectly rectangular, discriminability is a maximum because each of the cross-product indicators of $<$ and $>$ comparisons in $f_0 f_1 + f_0 f_2 + \cdots + f_{k-1} f_k$ is as large as it can be and thus the sum will be a maximum. The equation (12) expression we developed for discriminating companisons, $\frac{1}{2}[(\sum_{j=0}^{k} f_j)^2 - \sum_{j=0}^{k} f_j^2]$, must be a maximum under these conditions.

Also, notice that when all the f_j are equal, each f_j is equal to the average of the frequencies, so

$$f_j = \bar{f} = \frac{\sum_{j=0}^{k} f_j}{k+1} = \frac{N}{k+1}, \tag{13}$$

where, because k is the number of items, there are $k+1$ possible measures. Thus, the maximum number of discriminations (when all f_j are equal) will be the following:

$$
\begin{aligned}
\text{Max}(D) &= \frac{1}{2}\left[\left(\sum_{j=0}^{k} f_j\right)^2 - \sum_{j=0}^{k} f_j^2\right] \\
&= \frac{1}{2}\left[\left(\sum_{j=0}^{k} \bar{f}\right)^2 - \sum_{j=0}^{k} \bar{f}^2\right] \\
&= \frac{1}{2}\left[\left(\sum_{j=0}^{k} \bar{f}\right)^2 - \sum_{j=0}^{k} \bar{f}^2\right] \\
&= \frac{1}{2}\left[(K+1)^2\left(\frac{N}{k+1}\right)^2 - (K+1)\left(\frac{N}{k+1}\right)^2\right] \\
&= \frac{1}{2}\left(N^2 - \frac{N^2}{k+1}\right).
\end{aligned}
\tag{14}
$$

(This indicates that as the number of discriminating items increases, the maximum number of discriminations increases). For any measurement device, the ratio of the number of discriminations achieved to this maximum number is the Ferguson index of discriminability:

$$Df = \frac{\left(\sum_{j=0}^{k} f_j\right)^2 - \sum_{j=0}^{k} f_j^2}{N^2 - N^2/(k+1)}. \tag{15}$$

This index can take on values ranging from zero, when all individuals make the same score (and there is no discrimination) to 1.0, when there is a perfect rectangular distribution, in which case the $(\sum_{j=0}^{k} f_j)^2$ and $\sum_{j=0}^{k} f_j^2$ in the numerator are equal, respectively, to N^2 and $N^2/(k+1)$ in the denominator. For dichotomous items that have difficulties of .50, this maximum occurs when the item intercorrelations are .33.

DETERMINING THE PROPERTIES
OF MEASUREMENTS

We see, then, that the operations of measurement an investigator employs (within the sample that is selected) determine not only the mean, variance, and internal cohesiveness reliability of measurements, but also the distribution form and the discriminability of the measures. This is not say that an investigator can know in advance of experimentation how to select a sample and write the items that produce measures that have particular means, variances, reliabilities and discriminabilities, but it is to say that the overall design of a study can include a design to obtain measurements that have properties appropriate in accordance with the objectives of the research.

Generally, if item difficulties divide the sample at the middle, then as item intercorrelations increase from around 0 to around .20 to around .35 to around .70, the distribution of the linear composite scores goes from nearnormal to flattened bellshaped to rectangular to U-shaped. If item difficulties are themselves distributed in a particular way—say, normally or rectangularly—the distribution of the measurements will mirror this distribution when item intercorrelations are small and become flattened as item intercorrelations become larger. The more nearly the distribution of difficulties is to rectangular, the lower the intercorrelations need to be to ensure a rectangular distribution of the linear composite measurements (Scott, 1972). The smaller the item intercorrelations are, the more nearly the shape of the distribution of measurements mirrors the shape of the distribution of item difficulties. If the item difficulties pile up at a particular point under these conditions, linear composite measurements will peak at that point. Discriminability at this point then contributes more to the overall discriminability than discriminability at any other point. Discriminability can be said to be best at this point (Lord, 1980). As item intercorrelations increase, the peak will be somewhat flattened and discriminability at points somewhat removed from the peak will be relatively increased.

When items are not binary, but multiple response, such as those that are said to be Likert-scale items, what I have referred to as item difficulties are item means, and what are referred to as slopes for item response curves of binary items are item variances, and it is these factors, along with item intercorrelations, that determine the form of distribution and discriminabilities of measurements, as well as their reliability, variance, and mean. It is still the case that if item means are nearly the same, item variances are comparable, and item intercorrelations are near zero, the distribution of the linear composite measurements will approximate a normal distribution, the variance will be small, the internal cohesiveness reliability will be near zero, and the discriminability will be relatively small, particularly for large and small measurements. For items intercorrelating around .30 to .40, on the other hand, reliability and discriminability will be near-optimal across the full range of measure. To the extent that an investigator recognizes that item characteristics determine the properties of measurements, and takes account of them in the design of research, the investigator is in control of the measurement feature of research.

Measurement operations can also be designed to determine the unit of measurement, although this is more difficult than designing operations to determine the variance, internal cohesiveness reliability, shape of distribution, and discriminability. Because the mathematics the investigator most wants to use in the analysis of research data are the mathematics of the real number system, there is desire to measure at the interval or ratio level of measurement. Thinking in this manner is not lacking in the behavioral sciences, but it leads mainly to agonizing because nothing is, and seemingly can be, done about it. However, it may not be quite as bad as that. There are few things an investigator can do that lend some support to a hypothesis that measures are at the internal level.

For example, McDonald (1999) points out that if one can fit a one-parameter logistic (one common factor) model and selects for the scale, items with parallel item response curves, and difficulties spaced at equal intervals, the result can be an internal level scale. For samples of subjects that are representative of the population in which the model fits, the model yields an interval scale for the sets of items chosen for their conformity to it (McDonald, 1999, p. 426). On a more pessimistic note, McDonald points out "that it is not generally expected that items in a homogeneous behavior domain will fit the . . . model" and that different sets of items chosen to fit such a model will not necessarily be linearly related. Still, there are operations of measurement—a model of theory—that can be constructed to test hypotheses about level of measurements.

SUMMARY AND CONCLUSIONS

Measurement is difficult to do well. It is not easy to construct composite measurements that have appropriate measurement properties. Measurement is not simply a matter of presenting participants with stimuli, recording their responses, and adding them up. The stimuli must be well conceived. Appropriate numbers must be assigned for responses. The numbers must be combined in a manner well designed to yield composites that accurately discriminate differences in magnitudes of the attribute being measured. One should think about how magnitudes of the attribute are distributed in particular samples, how these should relate to the magnitudes of the other variables of the research, and how, therefore, the measurement operations should be designed to yield measurement that enable one to best realize the objectives of a research program. The constructor of measurements can, to some extent, control the properties of linear composite measurements and, by doing so, produce measurements that are best for the research at hand.

When operations of measurement produce a normal distribution, there is a prima facie suggestion that no measurement has been attained. If chance is operating to produce the normally distributed numbers that are regarded as measures, the variance and reliability of numbers will be small relative to what it could be for the number of items involved. Even if chance responding is not primarily responsible for the normal distribution, the discriminability of the measures will be relatively small overall, will be concentrated near the middle of the scale, and will be very poor for the high and low measures.

Discriminability across the full range of a scale of measurement is a maximum when the frequency distribution is rectangular. For measures made from binary items, this occurs when item intercorrelations are approximately .33 for items distributed symmetrically around .50 difficulties and for measure made from multiple-choice items, the item intercorrelations should be in a range of .30 to .40 (for items that discriminate in the midrange of an attribute). Scales constructed to have rectangular distributions will have adequate internal cohesiveness reliabilities, although this reliability will not be unduly large.

Items correlated at levels that yield rectangular distributions carry independent information and thus can represent different aspects of an attribute. In contrast, when items are very highly intercorrelated, they are redundant and only a narrow version of the construct is assessed. When operations of measurement are directed at producing very high internal consistency reliability, the measures will lack substantive breadth

Even if in theory an attribute is normally distributed in some conception of a population, there is no necessary reason to require linear composite measurements of that attribute to be normally distributed in samples from the population. Measurements in samples drawn from normal distributions are not normally distributed, particularly if the samples are not representatively drawn (as most often they are not in behavioral science research) and uniform distributions sum to normal distributions in accordance with the central limit theorem. Thus, distributions in samples will not be normally distributed, and there are good reasons why linear composite measurements should not be normally distributed. Internal cohesiveness reliability is better if average of item intercorrelations are such that they flatten the distribution and discrinability will be better across the range of the measure. Error of measurement is normally distributed, but this should not dominate in the manifest variable and render it normally distributed.

Statistical analyses of measurements do not require an assumption that the manifest variable be normally distributed. In statistical theory, variables are random and distributions are normal, but it is precisely this theory that the scientist's substantive theory and research plan are designed to reject. It is not incorrect or a violation of assumptions to do statistical analyses with variables that are not normally distributed. The assumptions of statistical procedures are assumptions for variations due to chance, not assumptions for variations due to measurement. In the use of statistical methods, the assumption is that what is left after the lawful relationships have been taken fully into account and partialed out is error that is normally distributed.

Often in the practice of measurement in the behavioral science the obtained distribution of measurements of an attribute is not particularly indicative of any theory about the distribution of that attribute. It is arbitrary. However, by adroit use of item information—item difficulties, variances, and intercorrelations—a scientist can construct measurement operations that result in measures that have properties that approximate what is specified in theory.

It is not necessarily true that scales that provide many discriminations across the range of measures are better for research in the behavioral sciences than scales that provide fewer discrimination. Similarly, it is not necessarily true that scales that provide relatively many discriminations in the tails of distributions are better than scales that provide most of their discriminations near the midpoint of the measure. However, it is wise to consider where along a scale of measurement discriminations should be made, and strive to construct scales that provide discriminations where they are most needed.

Maximum discriminability across the full range of magnitudes of an attribute can be desirable in research. If it is not known where along the scale of measurement valid relationships with other variables should occur, then it would be wise to ensure there is a reasonable amount of discriminability at every measure. It world seem that this often occurs in behavioral science research. The principal hypotheses simply state that X relates to Y, and there are no clear thoughts about where along the scales of X and Y the relationship occurs primarily—no thought that the relationship occurs in particular parts of the joint distribution. It is thus reasonable to suppose that many discriminations are better than few and that distributions for scales of measurement therefore should be rectangular.

It is not uncommon for the theory of a research to imply that relatively more discriminations should be made at the high and/or low ends of a measure than near the middle of the distribution. Some theories call for relationships between variables at the maladaptive ends, for example; other theories call for relationships at the superior performance ends. Midrange behaviors and performances are often of least interest. Rectangular distributions provide more discriminations for measures that are on the low and high ends of a measurement. In relating one such measure to another, there are many more opportunities to identify relationships at the ends of the scales. Thus, when both the high end and the low end of distributions are of principal interest, scales that yield rectangular distributions are preferred.

When there are good reasons to suppose that the important relationships for a variable occur primarily near particular levels of an attribute, as, for example, when the aim is to identify the indicators and correlates of abnormal conditions, then maximum discrimination should occur at the point along a continuum that distinguishes the abnormal from the normal. In such research when samples are drawn that contain both the abnormal and the normal, measures probably should not be rectangularly distributed. Item difficulties should not hover around the .5 midpoint of a scale, but should hover around the proportion of the abnormal relative to the normal. Items with intercorrelations that are relatively large at this cut-point should be written and selected for the scale. The distribution of the measurements under these conditions should be skewed. Discriminability across the full range of measures should not be large; discriminability at the point that distinguishes the abnormal from others should be a maximum.

In sum do not neglect to think about how item means, variances, and inter correlations affect the measurement distribution, and how discriminability is affected by the distribution of measurements.

ACKNOWLEDGMENTS

I particularly thank Jack McArdle for his contributions to my writing of this chapter. His comments and suggestions on an early draft led me to write something very different from, and much better than, what otherwise would have been presented. I also thank Mitch Earleywine, Nayena Blankson and Charles Reichandt for very helpful comments.

REFERENCES

Attneave, F. (1959). *Applications of information theory to psychology*. New York: Holt.

Beck, A. T., Ward, C. H., Mendelsohn, M., Mock, J. E., & Erbaugh, J. K. (1962). *An inventory for measuring depression*. New York: Guilford.

Blazer, D. G., Kessler, R. C., McGonagle, K. A., & Schwartz, M. S. (1994). The prevalence and distribution of major depression in a national community sample. The National Comorbidity Survey. *American Journal of Psychiatry, 151*, 979–986.

Brogden, H. E. (1946). Variations in test validity with variation in item difficulties, number of items, and degree of their intercorrelation. *Psychometrika, 11*, 197–214.

Ferguson, G. A. (1949). On the theory of test discrimination. *Psychometrika, 14*, 61–66.

Goodwin, J. C. (2001). *Research in psychology: Methods and design*. New York: Wiley.

Graziano, A. M., & Raulin, M. L. (2004). *Research methods: a process of inquiry*. Boston: Pearson.

Horn, J. L. (1963). Equations represnting combinations of components in scoring psychological variables. *Acta Psychologica, 21*, 184–217.

Humphreys, L. G. (1956). The normal curve and the attenuation paradox in test theory. *Psychological Bulletin, 53*, 572–476.

Lonsway, K. A., & Fitzgerald, L. F. (1995). Attitudinal antecedents of rape myth acceptance: A theoretical and empirical reexamination. *Journal of Personality and Social Psychology, 68*, 704–711.

Lord, F. M. (1980). *Applications of item response theory to practical testing problems*. Hillsdale, NJ: Lawrence Erlbaum Associates, Inc.

McDonald, R. P. (1999). *Test theory: A unified treatment*. Mahwah, NJ: Lawrence Erlbaum Associates, Inc.

McGrew, K. S., & Flanagan, D. P. (1998). *The intelligence test desk reference*. Boston: Allyn & Bacon.

Mischel, W. (1993). *Introduction to personality*. New York: Harcourt Brace Jovanovich.

Phares, E. J. (1978). *Locus of control*. In H. London & J. E. Exner, Jr. (Eds.), *Dimensions of personality* (pp. 288–329). New York: Wiley.

Rotter, J. B. (1966). Generalized expectancies for internal versus external control of reinforcements. *Psychological Monographs, 80*, 1–28.

Scott, W. A. (1972). The distribution of test scores. *Educational and Psychological Measurement, 32*, 725–735.

Tucker, L. R. (1946). Maximum validity of a test with equivalent items. *Psychometrika, 11*, 1–13.

Wilcox, R. R. (2003). Applying contemporary statistical techniques. Boston: Academic Press.

II

Factor Analysis Models

A great deal of the work of Roderick P. McDonald has dealt with the most widely studied and most widely used model in psychometrics—the common factor model. His contributions to this area reflect McDonald's versatility as well as the wide range of his interests: nonlinear factor analysis (McDonald, 1967; Etezadi-Amoli & McDonald, 1983), factor scores (McDonald & Burr, 1967) and their indeterminacy (McDonald, 1974), Bayesian estimation of the model (Martin & McDonald, 1975), and a long etcetera. Not surprisingly, McDonald (1985) wrote one of the most widely used textbooks on the topic, widely know as "Old McDonald's FARM."

In this part, **William Krane** and **Kathleen Slaney** examine the history and development of the unrestricted common factor model. Then they discuss the model assumptions, methods of estimation, goodness of fit, standard errors for parameter estimates, and the rotation of factor-analytic solutions.

Roger Millsap's contribution revolves around the study of factorial invariance. The chapter focuses on four of unresolved problems in this topic (the effect-size problem, locating the violation of invariance, invariance with ordinal measures, and modeling noninvariance) and on the prospects for their solution.

Stanley Mulaik provides a fascinating historical tour through the indeterminacy controversies in factor analysis that have sprouted every now and then in this field since the 1920s (with special virulence in the 1970s).

Finally, **Murray** and **Irit Aitkin** approach the problem of Bayesian inference for factor scores and parameter estimates using Markov chain Monte Carlo methods. This approach has clear connections to the expectation-maximization algorithm for maximum likelihood estimation. Interestingly, it also casts some light on the controversy over factor-score estimation and factor indeterminacy.

REFERENCES

Etezadi-Amoli, J., & McDonald, R. P. (1983). A second generation nonlinear factor analysis. *Psychometrika, 48*, 315–342.

Krane, W. R., & McDonald, R. P. (1978). Scale-invariant estimators in common factor analysis and related models. *British Journal of Mathematical and Statistical Psychology, 31*, 218–228.

Martin, J. K., & McDonald, R. P. (1975). Bayesian estimation in unrestricted factor analysis: A treatment for Heywood cases. *Psychometrika, 40*, 505–517.

McDonald, R. P. (1967). *Nonlinear factor analysis* (Psychometric Monographs, No. 15). Chicago: University of Chicago Press.

McDonald, R. P. (1974). The measurement of factor indeterminacy. *Psychometrika, 39*, 203–222.

McDonald, R. P. (1985). *Factor analysis and related methods.* Hillsdale, NJ: Lawrence Erlbaum Associates, Inc.

McDonald, R. P., & Burr, E. J. (1967). A comparison of four methods of constructing factor scores. *Psychometrika, 32*, 381–401.

5

A General Introduction to the Common Factor Model

William R. Krane and Kathleen L. Slaney
Simon Fraser University

A TRIBUTE TO RODERICK P. MCDONALD

The association of the first author (W. R. K.) with Rod McDonald dates back over 30 years. It began with a telephone conversation in 1972 in which I spoke to Rod about the possibility of attending one of his graduate courses on multivariate analysis at the Ontario Institute for Studies in Education. I found the enthusiasm with which he described his course and his obvious passion for his subject matter irresistible. I was hooked. And so began one of the most intensive and rewarding periods of my life. I was now a member of Rod's growing band of graduate students, which he called the "G.R.O.U.P." (General Research on Understanding Psychometrics). We held weekly meetings on Fridays at a local restaurant. One of my most vivid memories of that time is engaging in an animated conversation with Rod and others over a pitcher of beer and steak sandwiches while he scribbled mathematics with a black felt pen on Steak 'n Burger napkins. If the truth were told, many of Rod's manuscripts from the 1970s began in this form.

I am extremely proud to be known as a student of Rod McDonald. I have no doubt that each of us who had the privilege of studying with him feels the same way. One of the main reasons that I have such respect, admiration, and affection for Rod is that he never made us feel like students, but rather like colleagues whose abilities he openly acknowledged and demonstrably valued. Rod has the wonderful capacity to challenge his gifted students with significant problems and issues, and yet support and mentor those who sometimes struggle with psychometric concepts. He is always generous with his ideas. Rod holds high standards and is as critical of his own work (to the point of chastening himself in print) as he is of others. He typically writes for himself, arguing that the best way to advance knowledge and for others to derive the greatest benefit from your work is to present *your* understanding of an issue as honestly and lucidly as you can. Unquestionably, Rod was the professor and colleague who had the greatest influence on the development of my academic career. He taught me my scholarly values, how to argue logically and rigorously, and how to face controversial topics with conviction. (As we know, Rod never shied away from controversy.) For these lessons, and all his sage counsel over the years, I will be forever grateful.

I believe that we, as psychometricians, accrue benefits from our discipline that many of our colleagues in psychology and the social sciences, in general, do not. I speak of the longevity that much psychometric work enjoys. Typically, the fruits of our labor last far beyond what others can reasonably expect from theirs. It is not unusual for us to cite classic works published more than 50 years ago. Given the breadth, depth, and volume of Rod's career contributions to our field, there can be no doubt that his influence will endure for generations to come. This is a fitting legacy for someone who has accomplished and contributed so much. Rod's career has truly been a magnificent one.

INTRODUCTION

The term factor analysis is often used to describe a set of procedures whose general aim is to account for the observed covariation among a set of measured variables. As a category of techniques, it includes both statistical models that, in some cases, yield testable hypotheses and other techniques that are strictly data analytic in nature (McDonald, 1985). Throughout its almost 100-year history, factor analysis has enjoyed both controversy and prestige. It has been misunderstood and misused by many. On the other hand, it is a powerful descriptive and inferential tool that has opened up a world of opportunities to researchers and paved the way for a new class of analytic procedures whose use is becoming more and more commonplace in social science research.

The origins of factor analysis can be traced to the efforts of Galton and Mendel in the late 19th century to discover the principles of inheritance (Mulaik, 1972) and to the work of Karl Pearson on "the method of principal axes" in the early 20th century (Harman, 1976). However, it is Charles Spearman who is most often credited as the originator of the method. Spearman hypothesized the existence of a general ability that he believed could account for the observed correlations among scores on several different tests of cognitive abilities (Mulaik, 1972). In his seminal 1904 work "General Intelligence, Objectively Determined and Measured," Spearman first introduced the foundations of what he called his "Two-Factor" theory.[1] It posited that the correlations among observed variables could be explained by the existence of a general factor, g, common to all the variables and other factors specific to each.

It soon became apparent that Spearman's single-factor model was not appropriate for describing many batteries of psychological tests, and subsequently multiple-factor analysis was born. Unlike Spearman's model, which focused on explaining covariation in terms of one common factor and several specific factors, multiple-factor analysis accounted for the relationships within a set of variables by positing more than one common factor along with factors unique to each variable.[2] Although the origins of the concept of multiple factor analysis have been traced to the work of Garnett (Harman, 1976), the development and popularization of the technique in the United States is without question due to the efforts of L. L. Thurstone. His emphasis on multiple factors brought the concept of rotation in the factor space to the forefront, and led him to formulate the notion of "simple structure" as a criterion for adopting a particular factor-analytic solution (Bartholomew, 1995).

Prior to World War II, factor analysis was predominantly theory driven for two reasons: its origin from the discipline of psychology (as opposed to statistics), and the computational limitations of the time. As Bartholomew (1995) noted, factor analysis is "a sophisticated multivariate statistical method which was born before its time" (p. 216). World War II marked the beginning of a period of dramatic developments in factor analysis, primarily driven by advances in computer technology and the influences of statistical theory on the technique. Its use accelerated substantially in the postwar period. Mulaik (1972) described the 1950s and early 1960s as "the era of blind factor analysis," in which the procedure was applied to many different kinds of data with little or no attention paid to theoretical considerations. In the latter half of the 1960s, theory and practice came face to face as factor analysts turned away from using the method in a strictly mechanical fashion and began to treat it as a device for testing hypotheses about covariances.

This chapter focuses exclusively on issues about the unrestricted common factor model, not only to meet the constraints of limited space, but because it may be considered a paradigm example of the general class of factor models.

---

[1]Because Spearman (1904, 1927) emphasized the existence of two types of factors that could account for observed correlations (i.e., the general factor g and specific factors unique to each variable), he named his theory the "Two-Factor" theory. However, it has become known as the *single*-factor model, which posits that the observed relationships among the measured variables are wholly attributable to the existence of one underlying factor.

[2]As Bartholomew (1995) noted, arguing that a multiple-factor interpretation for a particular set of measured variables is better than a single-factor interpretation must rest on theoretical considerations about "usefulness" or "meaningfulness" when there is no statistical basis for distinguishing between them.

THE COMMON FACTOR MODEL

The common factor model is based on the notion, first introduced by Spearman, that for a given set of variables, what is observed can be accounted for by something *common* to all variables as well as something *unique* to each of the variables. Formally, the common factor model is a model about "hypothetical variables" that account for the linear relationships among observed variables. These hypothetical variables are characterized by a number of properties: (a) They form a set of linearly independent variables, that is, no one hypothetical variable can be derived as a linear combination of the others; (b) They can be divided into two types: (i) *common factors*, each having more than one observed variable with a nonzero regression (or factor loading) associated with it, and (ii) *unique factors*, which are distinguished, conversely, by each one having only one variable with a nonzero regression (or unique loading) associated with it; (c) common factors are assumed to be uncorrelated with unique factors, and unique factors are assumed to be mutually uncorrelated; and (d) it is typically assumed that the number of unique factors equals the number of observed variables, but the number of common factors is less than the number of observed variables (Mulaik, 1972).

For a given set of observed variables, we cannot uniquely determine an individual's common or unique factor scores, but we can obtain estimates of the factor loadings and the variances of the unique factors because the common factor model imposes a known structure on the covariances (or correlations) among the observed variables. In other words, the characteristics of the foregoing hypothetical variables imply a certain structure for the linear relationships among the observed variables that can be expressed in terms of the factor loadings and the variances of the unique factors.

Another way to describe the basic premise of the common factor model is to say that the covariances (or correlations) that exist among a set of observed variables are accounted for, or explained, in terms of a smaller number of unobserved variables or factors (Lawley & Maxwell, 1971). That is, once the common factors are taken into account, the remaining covariances among the observed variables vanish. This notion may be formally expressed as the *principle of local independence*. According to this principle, there exists a random variable f (or a set of variables $f_1, f_2, \ldots, f_m$) such that all the partial correlations among the observed variables are zero when f (or $f_1, f_2, \ldots, f_m$) is held constant.

Suppose **x** denotes a $(p \times 1)$ random vector of observed variables with mean $\mu = 0$ and covariance Σ. The common factor model may be expressed as

$$x = \Lambda f + \varepsilon, \tag{1}$$

where $\Lambda = (\lambda_{jk})$ is the $(p \times m)$ matrix of factor loadings (i.e., the regression weights of the jth observed variable on the kth factor for $j = 1, \ldots, p$ and $k = 1, \ldots, m$), **f** is the $(m \times 1)$ random vector of common factors, and ε is the $(p \times 1)$

random vector of unique factors of the p variables. Assume that

$$E(\mathbf{f}) = \mathbf{0}, \qquad E(\varepsilon) = \mathbf{0}, \qquad E(\mathbf{f}\varepsilon') = \mathbf{0} \tag{2}$$

and

$$E(\varepsilon\varepsilon') = \boldsymbol{\Psi}^2, \tag{3}$$

where $\boldsymbol{\Psi}^2$ is a $(p \times p)$ diagonal matrix with diagonal elements $\psi_1^2, \ldots, \psi_p^2$. The diagonal elements represent the variances of the unique factors and are often referred to as the unique variances or, simply, uniquenesses. If it is further assumed that the m factors are mutually uncorrelated, that is,

$$E(\mathbf{f}\mathbf{f}') = I_m, \tag{4}$$

then it can be shown that the covariance structure for $\mathbf{x}$,

$$E(\mathbf{x}\mathbf{x}') = E[(\boldsymbol{\Lambda}\mathbf{f} + \varepsilon)(\boldsymbol{\Lambda}\mathbf{f} + \varepsilon)'],$$

implied by the common factor model of Equation 1 and the assumptions in Equations 2–4 is

$$\boldsymbol{\Sigma} = \boldsymbol{\Lambda}\boldsymbol{\Lambda}' + \boldsymbol{\Psi}^2. \tag{5}$$

This form of the model, which relies explicitly on Equation 4, is known as the *orthogonal* common factor model.

Expressing the model of Equation 5 in scalar terms shows that the off-diagonal elements of the covariance matrix $\boldsymbol{\Sigma}$ take the form

$$\lambda_{i1}\lambda_{j1} + \lambda_{i2}\lambda_{j2} + \cdots + \lambda_{im}\lambda_{jm}$$

for $i = 1, \ldots, p$; $j = 1, \ldots, p$; $i \neq j$; and the diagonal elements take the form

$$\lambda_{j1}^2 + \lambda_{j2}^2 + \cdots + \lambda_{jm}^2 + \psi_j^2$$

for $j = 1, \ldots, p$.

Thus, the common factor model yields a testable hypothesis. It states that a given covariance matrix has the structure specified by Equation 5, for a prescribed number of factors. Ideally, we would like the number of common factors to be small relative to the number of observed variables. As we shall see, it is possible to test this hypothesis by measuring the fit of the model to sample data with certain indices.

METHODS OF ESTIMATION

The population covariance matrix Σ of the p observed variables may be estimated by the sample covariance matrix, which we will denote by S. If the off-diagonal elements of S (or the corresponding sample correlation matrix[3] R) are small, then it is unlikely that the observed variables are linearly related to each other. In this case, factor analysis will not yield much useful information for either data-analytic or inferential purposes. However, if the off-diagonal elements of S depart from zero, indicating that linear relationships do exist among the variables, then factor analysis may be used to determine whether those relationships may reasonably be explained by a factor (or set of factors) common to all the variables.

Like other estimation problems, estimates of the parameters of the common factor model must be obtained from sample data. In our case, S provides the sample information for this purpose. For the orthogonal factor model, there are $pm + p$ population quantities that need to be estimated: the pm factor loadings and the p unique variances, which are elements of the parameter matrices Λ and Ψ^2, respectively. Early factor analysts invented a variety of approximate methods of estimation, which were necessitated, in part, by the significant computational difficulties that they faced. However, such methods have largely been replaced by modern procedures, which take a formal approach to estimating the parameters of the model by directly fitting them to the sample data.[4]

Approximate Estimation Methods

In general, classical approximate estimation methods yield estimates of the factor loadings and unique variances whose statistical properties are not fully known. The basic approach employed by these techniques is to make some "guesses" about the values of the communalities (i.e., the variance of the variables that is attributed to the common factor or factors) and then "extract" the factors one by one until the "residuals" (i.e., the differences between the sample covariances and those reproduced from the factor solution) are small enough to be considered negligible. These methods, some of which are described here, do produce a factor solution that is calculated directly from the sample covariance matrix, but they do not require a priori specification of the number of common factors.

---

[3] It should be noted that although most factor-analytic theory has been developed for the analysis of covariance matrices, researchers are typically interested in making inferences about population correlations rather than covariances, and hence often conduct analyses of correlation matrices. Unfortunately, this practice may lead to incorrect results and gives rise to several thorny technical issues (e.g., Krane & McDonald, 1978; Swaminathan & Algina, 1978; Yuan & Bentler, 2000).

[4] McDonald (1985) maintained that the existence of these two very different approaches to "estimating" the parameters of a factor model has contributed to confusion in the literature about samples versus populations, measures of fit versus methods of fitting, and concepts central to factor-analytic theory versus arithmetic devices that may be employed in the course of conducting an analysis.

One commonly used strategy for obtaining approximate estimates of the factor loadings is the "principal axes" method, in which the principal components of the sample covariance matrix are regarded as substitutes for the common factors. As it turns out, an iterative variant of this technique does yield estimates that are known to be consistent and asymptotically normal. Other classical approximate methods include (a) using the residual variance of each variable about its regression on the remaining $p - 1$ variables as an approximation to its unique variance, (b) using principal components of the partial images of the variables (i.e., regression estimates of each variable on the remaining $p - 1$ variables) as common factors (Kaiser, 1970), (c) using "reduced" partial anti-image variances (i.e., the residual variance about the regression estimates of each variable on the remaining $p - 1$ variables) as unique variances (Jöreskog, 1962), and (d) using the triangular decomposition of the sample covariance matrix (sometimes with its diagonal elements modified), also known as the "diagonal method" of factoring, to obtain a factor solution in lower echelon form (Harman, 1976; Mulaik, 1972).

Recently, several investigators have proposed approximate estimation methods whose properties are known (e.g., Bentler & Dijkstra, 1985; Cudeck, 1991; Hägglund, 1982; Ihara & Kano, 1986; Jennrich, 1986; Kano, 1990). The Ihara and Kano (1986) procedure yields a closed-form estimator for the unique variances that is simple and inexpensive to compute. The estimates that it produces are consistent and asymptotically normal (but not asymptotically efficient).

Approximate estimation methods enjoy some advantages: (a) They are computationally efficient; (b) they are able to accommodate analyses with a large number of observed variables whose size may exceed the limitations of available computer programs; (c) they may provide a good starting point for other computationally intensive methods that rely on complex procedures with multiple iterations to obtain a factor solution; and (d) they typically do not yield Heywood cases[5] (i.e., inadmissible estimates of the unique variances). Also, in some cases, the estimates produced by approximate methods possess the appropriate statistical properties (such as consistency and asymptotic normality) that allow them to be used in evaluating the goodness of fit of the model to the data; that is, they provide a statistical basis for inferring whether the covariance matrix reproduced from a given factor solution constitutes a reasonable fit to the sample covariance matrix. Theory on weighted least squares estimation developed by Browne (1984) may be applied to calculate significance tests of fit for such approximate estimates. Browne showed that, under mild assumptions and for a suitably large sample size $n + 1$, $n \times \hat{F}$ is distributed as chi-square with $\frac{1}{2}[(p - m)^2 - (p + m)]$ degrees of freedom, where

$$\hat{F} = (\mathbf{s} - \sigma(\hat{\theta}))'\hat{\Gamma}^{-1}(\mathbf{s} - \sigma(\hat{\theta})),$$

[5]McDonald (1985) noted that this "advantage" should be considered with certain degree of care because Heywood cases often signal something important about the quality of the data (e.g., not enough variables being included to define each factor adequately).

where $\mathbf{s} = (s_{11}, s_{21}, s_{22}, s_{31}, \ldots, s_{pp})'$ and $\boldsymbol{\sigma} = (\sigma_{11}, \sigma_{21}, \sigma_{22}, \sigma_{31}, \ldots, \sigma_{pp})'$ are vectors with $p^* = \frac{1}{2}p(p+1)$ components consisting of the elements in the lower triangle of the sample covariance matrix $\mathbf{S}$ and the estimated population covariance matrix $\boldsymbol{\Sigma}(\hat{\boldsymbol{\theta}})$ obtained via Equation 5, respectively; $\hat{\boldsymbol{\theta}}$ is a vector whose $p(m+1)$ components are the approximate estimates for the elements of $\boldsymbol{\Lambda}$ and $\boldsymbol{\Psi}^2$; and $\hat{\boldsymbol{\Gamma}}$ is a consistent estimate of $\boldsymbol{\Gamma}$, the $(p^* \times p^*)$ asymptotic covariance matrix of the elements of $\mathbf{s}$.

Modern Iterative Estimation Methods

Contemporary approaches to estimating the parameters of the common factor model stem from the view that the model represents a statistical hypothesis that prescribes the structure of the population covariance matrix and the number of common factors (of which the observed variables are manifestations). It is this a priori specification of the model (by identifying the number of factors) that differentiates modern procedures from some of the approximate methods described previously. Once estimates of the factor loadings contained in $\boldsymbol{\Lambda}_m$ and the unique variances in $\boldsymbol{\Psi}^2$ are obtained, the covariance matrix implied by the model given in Equation 5 can be estimated as

$$\hat{\boldsymbol{\Sigma}}_m = \hat{\boldsymbol{\Lambda}}_m \hat{\boldsymbol{\Lambda}}'_m + \hat{\boldsymbol{\Psi}}^2.$$

(Henceforth, unless required for clarity, the subscript m will be dropped.) Given this characterization of the model, any number of methods may be used to obtain "best" estimates of the population factor loadings and unique variances. We describe four of the most commonly used iterative estimation procedures: unweighted least squares, generalized least squares, maximum likelihood, and weighted least squares.

In the context of unweighted least squares (ULS) estimation, "best" means choosing values for the factor loadings and unique variances in such a way that the sum of squared differences between the observed and fitted (i.e., model-implied) covariances is as small as possible. That is, when ULS estimation is applied in factor analysis, we obtain estimates $\hat{\lambda}_{jk}$ and $\hat{\psi}_j^2$ of λ_{jk} and ψ_j^2, the factor loading of the jth variable on the kth factor and the unique variance of the jth variable, respectively, so that the elements of the matrix of residuals $\mathbf{S} - \boldsymbol{\Sigma}$ are, collectively, as small as possible. In formal terms, the ULS estimates of $\boldsymbol{\Lambda}$ and $\boldsymbol{\Psi}^2$ are defined as those that minimize the discrepancy function

$$F_{\text{ULS}} = \frac{1}{2}\text{tr}[(\mathbf{S} - \boldsymbol{\Sigma})^2] = \frac{1}{2}\text{tr}[(\mathbf{S} - \boldsymbol{\Lambda}\boldsymbol{\Lambda}' - \boldsymbol{\Psi}^2)^2], \tag{6}$$

where, as before, $\mathbf{S}$ is the sample covariance matrix and $\boldsymbol{\Sigma}$ is defined by Equation 5. By differential calculus, we find that the necessary conditions under which F_{ULS}

is a minimum are

$$(\mathbf{S} - \mathbf{\Lambda}\mathbf{\Lambda}' - \mathbf{\Psi}^2)\mathbf{\Lambda} = \mathbf{0} \qquad (7)$$

and

$$\text{Diag}(\mathbf{S} - \mathbf{\Lambda}\mathbf{\Lambda}' - \mathbf{\Psi}^2) = \mathbf{0}. \qquad (8)$$

Unfortunately, we cannot obtain a closed-form solution for this system of equations and, hence, must resort to iterative numerical algorithms to find the values of $\mathbf{\Lambda}$ and $\mathbf{\Psi}^2$ that make F_{ULS} a minimum. There are two general approaches for obtaining such estimates: (a) iteratively obtain values of $\mathbf{\Psi}^2$ that approach the required minimizing values and, at each iteration, use these values to produce an estimate of $\mathbf{\Lambda}$ that satisfies Equation 7, and (b) find values of $\mathbf{\Lambda}$ that successively approach the minimizing values and, at each iteration, use these values to obtain an estimate of $\mathbf{\Psi}^2$ that satisfies Equation 8. In the former approach, obtaining the estimate of $\mathbf{\Lambda}$ requires the calculation of the eigenvalues and eigenvectors of $\mathbf{S} - \mathbf{\Psi}^2$ at each iteration of the process. The best-known implementation of the latter approach is the MINRES procedure, which was introduced by Harman and Jones (1966). It employs the straightforward solution to Equation 8, namely $\mathbf{\Psi}^2 = \text{Diag}(\mathbf{S} - \mathbf{\Lambda}\mathbf{\Lambda}')$, at each iteration, in the process of minimizing the sum of squares of the off-diagonal elements of the residual covariance matrix, which is the equivalent of Equation 6.

One advantage of ULS estimation is the intuitively appealing way in which the notion of "fit" is defined for it (and made optimal). In addition, ULS estimation produces estimates that are consistent and asymptotically normal, without relying on assumptions about the distributional properties of the observed variables (e.g., Bollen, 1989). These properties allow Browne's (1984) methods to be used to test the goodness of fit of the ULS estimates and to obtain the standard errors of the estimates from normal theory. However, there are disadvantages to employing ULS estimation in factor analysis. Most notable among these are that (a) it does not yield asymptotically efficient estimators of the model's parameters and (b) it is neither scale free (Swaminathan & Algina, 1978) nor scale invariant (Krane & McDonald, 1978). Consequently, the values of F_{ULS} will change with any rescaling of the observed variables, such as when correlations are analyzed instead of covariances.

Another potential problem with the ULS method is that it weights all the elements of the residual matrix $\mathbf{S} - \hat{\mathbf{\Sigma}}$ the same and ignores differences in the asymptotic variances and covariances of the elements of $\mathbf{S}$. This deficiency can be overcome by applying a set of differential weights to the residuals. Jöreskog and Goldberger (1972) proposed weighting the residuals by the inverse of the sample covariance matrix, $\mathbf{S}^{-1}$. In their approach, estimation is accomplished by minimizing a "generalized" least squares (GLS) discrepancy function of the form

$$F_{\text{GLS}} = \frac{1}{2}\text{tr}[\{\mathbf{S}^{-1}(\mathbf{S} - \mathbf{\Sigma})\}^2] = \frac{1}{2}\text{tr}[(\mathbf{I} - \mathbf{S}^{-1}\mathbf{\Sigma})^2], \qquad (9)$$

where $\mathbf{S}$ and $\mathbf{\Sigma}$ are the same as in Equation 6. (We omit stating the necessary conditions for a minimum of Equation 9 and for the other methods of estimation to be discussed below because they are similar in form to Equations 7 and 8.) The GLS estimates of the elements of $\mathbf{\Lambda}$ and $\mathbf{\Psi}^2$ are those values that minimize this quantity. The estimates of the factor loadings and unique variances produced by this method are consistent and asymptotically efficient, and their asymptotic standard errors can be computed from well-known theory if the observed variables have a multivariate normal distribution. These properties also make it possible to conduct simple tests of fit for large samples.

Although both ULS and GLS estimation methods are in common use, another procedure, known as the method of maximum likelihood (ML), is perhaps the most frequently employed to estimate the parameters of the common factor model. In the 1940s, D. N. Lawley made breakthroughs in the development of maximum likelihood estimation procedures (e.g., Lawley, 1940, 1943). However, at the time, Lawley's methods were too computationally intensive for the kinds of data sets to which psychological researchers were accustomed. However, with the advent of electronic computers in the 1950s and 1960s, computationally complex methods like Lawley's became feasible options for analyzing multivariate data.

ML is a general procedure for estimating the values of population parameters (in our case, $\mathbf{\Lambda}$ and $\mathbf{\Psi}^2$) that makes the probability of occurrence of a given sample from the population as large as possible. That is, ML estimates are those values of the population parameters that maximize the *likelihood* of our particular sample having been selected. Like many ML procedures devised for the analysis of multivariate data, the ML estimation of factor loadings and unique variances rests on the distributional assumption of multivariate normality for the population. Specifically, both the common and unique factors are assumed to be jointly normal and independently distributed in the population (Fuller & Hemmerle, 1966). It follows from normal theory that the observed variables will also have a multivariate normal distribution.

ML estimates for the elements of $\mathbf{\Lambda}$ and $\mathbf{\Psi}^2$ can be found by maximizing the *likelihood ratio*, which is defined as the ratio of the likelihood of the observed data under the restrictive hypothesis that m factors account for the covariances in the population to the likelihood of the sample data when no restrictions are imposed on the population covariance structure. In practice, we minimize an equivalent quantity, which is a constant times the natural logarithm of the likelihood ratio, namely

$$F_{\mathrm{ML}} = \log|\mathbf{\Sigma}| + \mathrm{tr}(\mathbf{S}\mathbf{\Sigma}^{-1}) - \log|\mathbf{S}| - p, \qquad (10)$$

where p is equal to the number of observed variables (e.g, Lawley & Maxwell, 1971). The reason for this choice of the discrepancy function will become apparent in the next section. Specifically, the ML estimates $\hat{\mathbf{\Lambda}}$ and $\hat{\mathbf{\Psi}}^2$ are those values of $\mathbf{\Lambda}$ and $\mathbf{\Psi}^2$ that make F_{ML} a minimum. The resulting estimates are scale free and scale invariant (Bollen, 1989; Swain, 1975). That is, the estimation equations are independent of the scale of measurement of the observed variables, and the estimated factor loadings for a given observed variable are proportional to the standard deviation of that variable. This means that the ML estimation equations may be expressed in terms of correlations, rather than covariances, if so desired (Krane & McDonald, 1978).

ML estimates possess desirable asymptotic sampling properties; they are asymptotically unbiased, consistent, and efficient. Their standard errors may be computed from normal theory. The ML estimation method also affords an asymptotic statistical test of the fit of the model to the sample data. Thus, it enables researchers to explore specific hypotheses about the number of factors in the population, a topic explored in the next section.

The ML factor analysis has been criticized for relying on what is seen to be a restrictive assumption of multivariate normality. It has been argued that it should not be applied in situations where the distribution of the observed variables is unknown. It is true that if the assumption of normality does not hold, then the likelihood ratio test and the standard errors based on normal theory will not be asymptotically correct. However, in these circumstances, Browne's (1984) results may be applied to derive a statistical test and standard errors of the estimates that are asymptotically correct, despite a lack of normality. As we shall see, ML estimates of the factor loadings and unique variances can be obtained, their fit tested, and their standard errors computed under only mild assumptions about the distribution of the observed variables.

Another approach to estimating the factor loadings contained in $\mathbf{\Lambda}$ and the unique variances in $\mathbf{\Psi}^2$ is to minimize Browne's (1984) weighted least squares (WLS) discrepancy function

$$F_{\text{WLS}} = (\mathbf{s} - \boldsymbol{\sigma}(\boldsymbol{\theta}))' \mathbf{W}^{-1} (\mathbf{s} - \boldsymbol{\sigma}(\boldsymbol{\theta})), \tag{11}$$

where $\mathbf{s}$ and $\boldsymbol{\sigma}$ are $(p^* \times 1)$ vectors defined as before, $\mathbf{\Sigma}(\boldsymbol{\theta})$ is the population covariance matrix obtained from Equation 5, $\boldsymbol{\theta}$ is a vector whose $p(m+1)$ components are the elements of $\mathbf{\Lambda}$ and $\mathbf{\Psi}^2$, and $\mathbf{W}$ is a positive-definite weight matrix, which can be fixed or stochastic. It can be shown that the ULS, GLS, and ML discrepancy functions defined by Equations 6, 9, and 10, respectively, are all special cases of Equation 11. For example, if $\mathbf{W}$ is set to be the identity matrix (i.e., $\mathbf{W} = \mathbf{I}_{p^*}$), then Equation 11 reduces to Equation 6, the ULS discrepancy function. Browne (1984) demonstrated that, under very general assumptions, minimizing Equation 11 for any choice of positive-definite $\mathbf{W}$ will yield consistent estimates of the factor loading and unique variances. He also derived general expressions for their standard errors based on $\mathbf{W}$, the Jacobian matrix for $\boldsymbol{\sigma}$, and $\mathbf{\Gamma}$, the $(p^* \times p^*)$ asymptotic covariance matrix of the elements of $\mathbf{s}$.

If $\mathbf{W}$ is chosen to be a consistent estimate of $\mathbf{\Gamma}$, $\hat{\mathbf{\Gamma}}$ say, then Equation 11 becomes what Browne calls the "asymptotically distribution free" (ADF) discrepancy function,

$$F_{\text{ADF}} = (\mathbf{s} - \boldsymbol{\sigma}(\boldsymbol{\theta}))' \, \hat{\boldsymbol{\Gamma}}^{-1} \, (\mathbf{s} - \boldsymbol{\sigma}(\boldsymbol{\theta})) . \qquad (12)$$

Browne provided a general procedure for calculating $\hat{\boldsymbol{\Gamma}}$ from the fourth-order central moments of the data and the sample covariances. His method may be applied to data obtained from any multivariate distribution satisfying very mild assumptions (including the multivariate normal and elliptical distributions). The ADF estimates obtained by minimizing Equation 12 are asymptotically efficient and yield asymptotically correct tests of fit and standard errors.

The ADF (and more generally WLS) method is very attractive from a theoretical point of view. However, in practice it does suffer from some disadvantages. First, the dimension of the weight matrix $\mathbf{W}$, which is of order $p^* \times p^*$, increases rapidly with the number of variables being analyzed. For large p, the computational requirements are significant. Second, to estimate the fourth-order moments with a reasonable degree of accuracy requires a very large sample size. Otherwise, the calculation of the asymptotic tests of fit and the standard errors may be incorrect. Satorra and Bentler (1994) suggested methods for modifying the tests of fit and standard errors to correct such deficiencies. Finally, Browne's (1984) theory was developed for the analysis of sample covariance matrices. If sample correlations are to be analyzed instead, care must be taken to employ appropriate estimates of the asymptotic covariances of the sample correlations in specifying $\hat{\boldsymbol{\Gamma}}$. The sample correlations have different asymptotic variances and covariances from the sample covariances, even if the data arise from a multivariate normal distribution.

The focus of this section has been to describe methods of estimating the parameters of the common factor model. The modern procedures all share a common feature: The values representing estimates of the population factor loadings and unique variances are chosen so that the estimated covariance matrix $\hat{\boldsymbol{\Sigma}}$, is as close as possible to the sample covariance matrix $\mathbf{S}$. What distinguishes them is how "close" is defined. The next section is concerned with the criteria for determining whether the estimated covariance matrix constitutes a reasonable approximation to the sample data.

ASSESSING FIT

In exploratory factor analysis, often the researcher has little or no notion about which factor model is "best," in the sense of having some nonstatistical basis (informed by theoretical considerations) for choosing a particular factor model to explain the relationships among the observed variables. In such cases, the researcher may employ various factor-analytic procedures or related techniques to decide how many factors to retain. As noted previously, the theory on weighted least squares developed by Browne (1984) may be used in conjunction with some approximate estimation procedures to determine an optimal number of factors to include in the model. However, it is much more common for researchers to rely on one (or more) of the modern iterative methods of estimation because they lend themselves naturally to producing indices of goodness of fit (actually badness of fit) that indicate how well the estimated covariance matrix implied by a model with a particular number of factors approximates the data.

Indices of fit may also be used to perform tests of significance about whether the common factor model holds for a particular population covariance matrix. Formally, the null hypothesis being tested is

$$H_0: \quad \mathbf{\Sigma} = \mathbf{\Sigma}_m = \mathbf{\Lambda}_m \mathbf{\Lambda}'_m + \mathbf{\Psi}^2, \tag{13}$$

where m is the number of common factors, against the alternative hypothesis

$$H_a: \quad \mathbf{\Sigma} = \text{any positive-definite matrix}$$

(Lawley & Maxwell, 1971). In other words, the hypothesis of interest is that the population covariance matrix of the observed variables, $\mathbf{\Sigma}$, is equal to the model, $\mathbf{\Sigma}_m$, specified by Equation 13. Note that Equation 13 prescribes both the structure of the covariance matrix in the population and the number of common factors. Indices of fit can be used to determine whether the null hypothesis is tenable, in the sense that they measure the extent to which $\mathbf{S}$ departs from $\mathbf{\Sigma}_m$.

Because $\mathbf{\Sigma}$ is not available for inspection, the sample covariance matrix $\mathbf{S}$ must be compared to $\hat{\mathbf{\Sigma}}_m$, the estimate of $\mathbf{\Sigma}_m$. The fit between $\mathbf{S}$ and $\hat{\mathbf{\Sigma}}_m$ can be gauged in many different ways. We will first describe the ubiquitous chi-square measure of goodness of fit because it is relatively well known and because it is the default index of fit in many statistical software packages. However, other methods that provide estimates of the error of approximation (of the model to the population covariance matrix) and the overall error (of the fitted model to the population covariance matrix) are considered by many to constitute a more appropriate means of assessing various aspects of the fit of the model to sample data (e.g., Browne & Cudeck, 1992; McDonald, 1999).

Let $\hat{F} = F(\mathbf{S}, \hat{\mathbf{\Sigma}})$ denote the minimum value of the GLS, ML, or ADF discrepancy function defined by Equation 9, 10, or 12, respectively. $\hat{F}$ is obtained by evaluating F at the estimated values $\hat{\mathbf{\Lambda}}$ and $\hat{\mathbf{\Psi}}^2$ for $\mathbf{\Lambda}$ and $\mathbf{\Psi}^2$ via

$$\hat{\mathbf{\Sigma}} = \hat{\mathbf{\Lambda}}\hat{\mathbf{\Lambda}}' + \hat{\mathbf{\Psi}}^2. \tag{14}$$

If the null hypothesis of Equation 13 holds and F is correctly specified in the sense of Browne and Shapiro (1988), then the asymptotic distribution of $n \times \hat{F}$ is chi-square with degrees of freedom given by

$$df = \tfrac{1}{2}[(p-m)^2 - (p+m)], \tag{15}$$

where $n + 1$ is the sample size. For ULS, an adjustment is required to achieve a similar result. The quantity

$$n \times \hat{F} = n \times F_{\mathrm{ADF}}(\mathbf{S}, \hat{\boldsymbol{\Sigma}}_{\mathrm{ULS}})$$

is asymptotically chi-square with degrees of freedom given by Equation 15. Here $F_{\mathrm{ADF}}(\mathbf{S}, \hat{\boldsymbol{\Sigma}}_{\mathrm{ULS}})$ denotes the value of the ADF discrepancy function at the ULS estimate for $\hat{\boldsymbol{\Sigma}}$ that is obtained from Equation 14. We will no longer consider this case explicitly.

In summary, if the data are drawn from a multivariate normal distribution, the null hypothesis specified in Equation 13 holds, and the sample size is sufficiently large, then the GLS, ML, and ADF discrepancy functions all yield test statistics that are approximately chi-square with degrees of freedom given by Equation 15. If the data are drawn from a nonnormal population, then the ADF discrepancy function will be correctly specified and, if the sample size is sufficiently large, the test statistic $n \times \hat{F}$ will follow an approximate chi-square distribution. It is worth repeating that the sample size must be substantial for the latter result to hold; otherwise, the estimates of the fourth-order moments used to calculate $\hat{\boldsymbol{\Gamma}}$ in Equation 12 are too imprecise to produce an approximate chi-square distribution. It should also be noted that the ML discrepancy function can be used without assuming normality by adjusting the distribution of the test statistic $n \times \hat{F}$ so that its mean (or mean and variance) coincides with the mean (or mean and variance) of a chi-square distribution with degrees of freedom given by Equation 15 (Satorra & Bentler, 1994).

In practice, we may calculate the test statistic $n \times \hat{F}$ in any of its forms using a computer program like LISREL (Jöreskog & Sörbom, 1996). Although LISREL does not perform unrestricted factor analysis directly, estimates of the factor loadings and unique variances can be obtained by specifying $\boldsymbol{\Lambda}$ in lower echelon form, with $\frac{1}{2}m(m-1)$ fixed zeros. The factor solution produced under this (identifiability) constraint yields the required minimum value of F, $\hat{F}$.

We have referred to $n \times \hat{F}$ as a "test statistic," and, indeed, this quantity may be used to test the null hypothesis of Equation 13. However, in exploratory factor analysis, the researcher does not make an a priori assumption about precisely how many factors underlie the relationships among the observed variables. Another limitation of hypothesis testing in this context is that the test statistic will always lead to a rejection of the null hypothesis if the sample size is large enough. Moreover, for most applications, the factor model should be considered as an approximation to reality, at best. For these reasons, it is best to recast the statistical testing problem as one of determining how many factors reasonably "fit" the data. That is, the test statistic should be regarded as a measure of the goodness of fit (or, more accurately, the badness of fit) of the model to the data. Typically, a sequential fitting procedure is used in which one begins with a small value for m and calculates estimates of the model parameters under Equation 13 and the observed value of $n \times \hat{F}$. This value is then compared to the number of degrees of freedom for the model (i.e., the theoretical mean of $n \times \hat{F}$), which provides a standard for judging whether the chi-square value is large or small. If the fit is poor, then a $m + 1$ solution is computed and the test statistic is reevaluated, and so on, until a factor solution is found that constitutes a reasonable fit to the data.

The chi-square goodness-of-fit statistic provides a useful overall summary of the extent to which the factor model approximates the data. Inspecting the elements of the residual covariance matrix $S - \hat{\Sigma}$ (perhaps using a stem-and-leaf or Q-plot) will give additional information about the fit of the model with respect to the individual pairs of variables and may give an indication about the source of the misfit of the model if such occurs. "Good" fit is obviously characterized by suitably small residuals. However, because the residuals depend on the units of measurement of the observed variables, it is not always an easy task to judge whether a residual is large or small. To overcome this difficulty, standardized residuals may be computed by dividing the fitted residual by its standard error.

As noted earlier, the assumption that Equation 13 holds exactly in the population is unrealistic in most empirical research situations, and will inevitably lead to the rejection of the factor model in large samples based on the chi-square goodness-of-fit statistic. This potential difference between the factor model of Equation 13 and the actual population covariance matrix, Σ_0 say, is called the error of approximation. Browne and Cudeck (1992) proposed measuring it using McDonald's (1989) estimate of the population discrepancy function,

$$\hat{F}_0 = \text{Max}\left[\hat{F} - \left(\frac{d}{n}\right), 0\right], \tag{16}$$

where $\hat{F}$ is the minimum value of the discrepancy function, d is the number of degrees of freedom for the model given by Equation 15, and $n + 1$ represents the sample size. A confidence interval for F_0 can also be easily calculated. They also suggest using Steiger's (1990) estimate of the root mean square error of approximation (RMSEA),

$$\hat{\varepsilon} = \sqrt{\frac{\hat{F}_0}{d}}, \tag{17}$$

which takes into account the fact that $\hat{F}_0$ generally decreases when parameters are added to the model, as a measure of the discrepancy per degree of freedom. A confidence interval for ε and a significance test of the hypothesis $\varepsilon \leq .05$ (indicating close fit) are also available.

Another problem with the chi-square goodness-of-fit statistic is that it will always decrease in value when parameters are added to the factor model, as is the case when estimates of a model with m factors are compared to those with $m + 1$ factors. Thus, there is the danger of overfitting the sample data if parsimony is not also taken into account. Ideally, we would like a measure that balances fit and parsimony in such a way that it first decreases as additional factors are added to the model, attains a minimum value for the "best" number of factors, and then increases as the model is overfit with additional factors. Browne and Cudeck (1989) proposed a measure that has this property, the expected cross-validation index (ECVI). They showed that this index is related to a measure of "overall error," which is defined as the difference between the elements of the population covariance matrix Σ_0 and the fitted model $\hat{\Sigma}$ given by Equation 14. The ECVI may be approximated by the expectation of the discrepancy function $F(\Sigma_0, \hat{\Sigma})$. This quantity can indeed increase as more factors are added to the model, and is estimated by

$$c = F(\mathbf{S}, \hat{\Sigma}) + \frac{2q}{n}, \tag{18}$$

where $q = \frac{1}{2}[2p(m+1) - m(m-1)]$ is the effective number of model parameters when the identifiability constraints are taken into account. A confidence interval for the ECVI is also available. In the case of ML estimation, Browne and Cudeck (1989) suggested that the estimate c of the ECVI in Equation 18 be replaced by

$$c^* = F_{\mathrm{ML}}(\mathbf{S}, \hat{\Sigma}) + \frac{2q}{n - p - 1}. \tag{19}$$

We now turn our attention to what have been perhaps the most contentious issues surrounding the common factor model—factor rotation and factor score indeterminacy.

FACTOR ROTATION AND FACTOR SCORE INDETERMINACY

For any method of estimation, it is necessary to impose an arbitrary set of constraints initially on the factor loadings to estimate them uniquely. However, the resulting solution can often be difficult to interpret because either (a) the researcher has a priori notions about how the factors should be related to the observed variables, or (b) the analysis is truly exploratory and the researcher's aim is to determine whether there are common factors that can reasonably account for the observed relationships among the variables and what their nature is. More often than not, any conclusions about the population covariance structure based on the pattern of factor loadings from an initial solution will be ambiguous at best. For example, imagine that for a test that included different measures of mathematical and verbal abilities, an initial two-factor solution includes a set of factor loadings that are all positive and moderately large for the first factor and are positive and negative, and also moderately large (in absolute value), for the second factor. What interpretation can be given to this solution? Fortunately, the researcher is not required to consider only the initial solution. A fundamental property of the common factor model known as "rotational" indeterminacy allows the researcher to derive a subsequent solution that may be more easily interpreted and is equivalent to the original solution in the sense that it yields the same estimated covariance matrix of the observed variables. The general process by which such a solution is obtained is known as *factor rotation*.

Rotational indeterminacy arises from the fact that although a solution (for $m > 1$ factors) determines the $m-$dimensional space containing the common factors, it does not determine their exact positions. In what follows, we discuss the issue in terms of population quantities, but the same arguments apply to their estimates. Suppose Λ represents an initial matrix of factor loadings that satisfies Equation 5, that is

$$\Sigma = \Lambda\Lambda' + \Psi^2.$$

Let $\mathbf{T}$ be an arbitrary orthogonal matrix (with the property that $\mathbf{TT}' = \mathbf{I}_m$). We may write

$$\Sigma = \Lambda\mathbf{TT}'\Lambda' + \Psi^2$$
$$= (\Lambda\mathbf{T})(\Lambda\mathbf{T})' + \Psi^2$$
$$= \Lambda^*\Lambda^{*'} + \Psi^2$$

where $\Lambda^* = \Lambda\mathbf{T} \neq \Lambda$. This shows that, for any given Λ that satisfies the common factor model, there exist an infinity of other Λ^* that will also satisfy the same model. Thus, the factor loadings are not unique, because they are determined only up to an orthogonal transformation $\mathbf{T}$. This means that, for any set of observed variables, there exists an infinite number of sets of factor loadings that will yield the same covariance matrix. Consequently, a researcher may choose a particular solution[6] (different from the initial solution) that permits a better interpretation of the factors.

Several different approaches have been suggested to contend with the rotational indeterminacy problem, one of which has been alluded to previously, that is, specifying an identifiability constraint (e.g., $\Lambda'\Lambda$ must be diagonal) that uniquely defines Λ when the condition is imposed (e.g., Schönemann & Wang, 1972; Steiger & Schönemann, 1978). A Λ that satisfies such a constraint is often referred to as the

---

[6]Although we discuss only orthogonal rotation here, in practice, the factor analyst must decide (presumably on theoretical grounds) whether an *orthogonal* or an *oblique* factor rotation is desired. An orthogonal rotation is appropriate for factors that are assumed to be mutually uncorrelated, whereas an oblique rotation should be used for cases in which it is reasonable to suppose that the factors are correlated.

matrix of "unrotated" factor loadings. Another very common device is to choose a solution on the basis of "simple structure." In this case, parsimony of interpretation is sought by having each factor account for the covariances among a small number of observed variables in accordance with a number of criteria [see Thurstone (1947, p. 335; 1954) for a technical definition of simple structure].

Carroll (1953), Saunders (1953), Neuhaus and Wrigley (1954), and Ferguson (1954) were among the first to propose criteria for producing factor solutions consistent with Thurstone's definition of simple structure. Although each was based on a different rationale, they produced similar solutions by orthogonal rotation. Collectively they came to be known as the *quartimax* family (Browne, 2001; Harman, 1976). Each attempts to reduce the "complexity" of the factor pattern (i.e., the number of nonzero elements) so that each variable has a nonzero loading on only one factor.

Later, Kaiser (1958) proposed a method that, in contrast to its quartimax predecessor, was based on simplifying the columns (representing the common factors) of the initial factor solution rather than simplifying its rows (representing the variables). Specifically, the "raw" varimax criterion maximizes the quantity

$$v^* = \sum_{k=1}^{m} \frac{p \sum_{j=1}^{p} \left(\lambda_{jk}^2\right)^2 - \left[\sum_{j=1}^{p} \left(\lambda_{jk}^2\right)\right]^2}{p^2},$$

which represents the sum, over all factors, of the variance of the squared loadings of each factor. Kaiser also proposed maximizing the "normalized" varimax criterion

$$v = \sum_{k=1}^{m} \frac{p \sum_{j=1}^{p} \left(\lambda_{jk}^2/h_j^2\right)^2 - \left[\sum_{j=1}^{p} \left(\lambda_{jk}^2/h_j^2\right)\right]^2}{p^2}, \tag{20}$$

where the factor loadings are divided by h_j^2, which represents the communality of the jth variable. He argued that maximizing this criterion would produce solutions that better reflected simple structure because any variation in the communalities of the observed variables would be "equalized" (Kaiser, 1958). In essence, applying the varimax criterion for simple structure to a factor solution serves to simplify the pattern of loadings so that each factor has only a small number of variables with large loadings on it and thus facilitates greater interpretability of the solution.

The varimax (as well as quartimax) criterion is a member of the *orthomax* family (Harman, 1976) and is the most common rotational device in use. It is the default choice for a rotational method in many statistical packages (Fabringar, Wegnener, MacCallum, & Strahan, 1999; cited in Browne, 2001). However, it should be noted that, for situations in which the factor patterns are very complex, these standard methods might yield poor solutions, in which case less well-known rotational procedures may be preferred. [See Browne (2001), for a thorough explication of various rotational criteria.]

Although the theory for obtaining the standard errors of unrotated and rotated factor loading estimates has been known for some time, particularly in the context of ML estimation (e.g., Archer & Jennrich, 1973; Jennrich, 1974; Lawley, 1967), the algebra is quite complicated (even more so when sample correlations are analyzed) and, consequently, it has largely been unimplemented in factor analysis computer programs. Browne and Du Toit (1992) developed a general procedure for estimating the parameters and testing the fit of nonstandard models for covariance matrices that permits nonlinear equality (and inequality) constraints on the model parameters. It turns out that factor rotation can be defined as a set of such constraints, and the (asymptotic) standard errors of rotated factor loading estimates can be obtained by their methods. [See Maydeu-Olivares (2001) for a related example of this approach.] In addition, Browne, Cudeck, Tatateni, and Mels (1999) produced a computer program called CEFA for performing exploratory factor analysis of correlation matrices (explicitly), which is based on a clever reparametrization of the unrestricted factor model (Jennrich, 1974). It accommodates a variety of methods of estimation and calculates estimates of the standard errors of the rotated factor loadings from normal theory.

It could be argued that the idea of rotating an initial set of factor loadings via an orthogonal transformation to allow a researcher to more easily interpret the factors in terms of the observed variables under study is straightforward in comparison to a second controversial feature of the common factor model—*factor-score* indeterminacy. This issue has instigated decades of passionate debate among theorists who study this topic. This second type of indeterminacy arises from the fact that, for a given common factor model defined by Equation 1, there exists an infinity of sets of factor scores all of which will generate the same factor solution (i.e., the same factor loadings and unique variances) and, hence, the same covariance matrix implied by the model. Therefore, imposing identifiability conditions as a way of contending with rotational indeterminacy and obtaining a determinate factor solution does not make the factor model determinate (Guttman, 1955; Mulaik & McDonald, 1978; Rozeboom, 1988; Schönemann & Wang, 1972), and does not constitute a solution to the more fundamental problem of factor-score indeterminacy. Mulaik discusses this issue extensively in chapter 7 of this volume.

AN ILLUSTRATIVE EXAMPLE OF MODERATE SAMPLE SIZE

We now present the analysis of a data set taken from the literature on human laterality. It is well known that humans display lateral preferences (or sidedness) when they engage in certain kinds of physical tasks, such as throwing a ball or looking through a telescope. Several investigators have suggested that these dextral biases

TABLE 5.1

Correlations Among Human Laterality Measures ($N = 962$)

	Ball	Draw	Eraser	Card	Kick	Pebble	Chair	Keyhole	Bottle	Rifle	Door	Heart	Earphone
Ball	—												
Draw	.80	—											
Eraser	.74	.84	—										
Card	.43	.39	.41	—									
Kick	.63	.53	.58	.40	—								
Pebble	.44	.41	.41	.27	.44	—							
Chair	.34	.32	.31	.24	.37	.30	—						
Keyhole	.25	.25	.23	.17	.26	.21	.23	—					
Bottle	.27	.27	.26	.19	.28	.24	.20	.83	—				
Rifle	.31	.31	.28	.19	.29	.18	.21	.60	.61	—			
Door	.19	.16	.16	.17	.23	.20	.24	.24	.22	.19	—		
Heart	.20	.17	.18	.14	.21	.24	.25	.20	.21	.23	.72	—	
Earphone	.25	.23	.25	.17	.26	.27	.25	.17	.21	.14	.51	.45	—

can be explained by a primary neural or cerebral mechanism. Porac, Coren, Steiger, and Duncan (1980) argued that such a single-factor theory does not adequately describe the processes underlying human laterality. They investigated four types of lateral preferences—handedness, footedness, eyedness, and earedness—in a sample of 962 individuals of widely varying ages, using a behaviorally validated self-report instrument. The inventory contained 13 items, 4 related to handedness and 3 each to footedness, eyedness, and earedness (see Table 5.1 for a list of item labels). An example of one of the handedness items was, "With which hand do you draw?"

The sample correlations among the laterality measures are presented in Table 5.1. They are all positive, suggesting that some common mechanism gives rise to the relationships among the indicators of lateral preference. However, the items related to limb preference are much more highly intercorrelated than they are with any of the measures of sensory laterality. Also, the eyedness items are strongly intercorrelated, as are the earedness items, but they are only weakly related to each other and to the measures of limb preference. These observations suggest that the mechanism underlying lateral preferences may be multidimensional in nature. Porac et al. (1980) confirmed this conjecture by conducting a principal components analysis of the sidedness items. By applying some of the classical rules of thumb for performing factor analysis, they concluded that three components adequately accounted for the observed relationships among the laterality measures. The (rotated) component loadings demonstrated an independent clusters pattern. That is, the limb preference measures all loaded highly on one component, whereas the sensory laterality measures loaded negligibly on the same component; the eyedness items loaded highly on a second component and the rest loaded negligibly; and the earedness items loaded highly on a third component and the rest loaded negligibly.

TABLE 5.2
Indices of Fit for Human Laterality Measures ($N = 962$, $p = 13$)

m	q	df	$\hat{F}$	$\hat{\varepsilon}$	$(\hat{\varepsilon}_L, \hat{\varepsilon}_U)$	c	(c_L, c_U)	$n \times \hat{F}$	Probabilty Exact	Close
0	13	78	6.7420	.292		6.769		6,479.04	.000	.000
1	26	65	2.8596	.207	(.201, .214)	2.914	(2.739, 3.096)	2,748.06	.000	.000
2	38	53	1.2670	.151	(.144, .159)	1.346	(1.232, 1.468)	1,217.62	.000	.000
3	49	42	0.2765	.074	(.066, .083)	0.378	(0.329, 0.436)	265.72	.000	.000
4	59	32	0.0763	.037	(.026, .048)	0.199	(0.177, 0.229)	73.29	.000	.977
5	68	23	0.0482	.032	(.019, .046)	0.190	(0.173, 0.214)	46.34	.003	.985
6	76	15	0.0245	.024	(.000, .042)	0.183	(0.174, 0.201)	23.53	.073	.993
7	83	8	0.0257	.047	(.026, .068)	0.198	(0.187, 0.218)	24.69	.002	.567
8	89	2	0.0139	.077	(.042, .118)	0.199	(0.191, 0.215)	13.40	.001	.098
Sat.	91	0	0.0000	.000		0.189				

Note: m, number of factors (Sat. denotes the saturated model); q, effective number of parameters; df, degrees of freedom; $\hat{F}$, discrepancy function minimum; $\hat{\varepsilon}$, point estimate of root mean square error of approximation (RMSEA), Equation 17; $(\hat{\varepsilon}_L, \hat{\varepsilon}_U)$, 90% confidence interval for RMSEA; c, point estimate of expected cross-validation index (ECVI), Equation 18; (c_L, c_U), 90% confidence interval for ECVI; $n \times \hat{F}$, observed value for chi-squared goodness of fit statistic; Exact and Close denote the exceedance probabilities for the tests of exact and close fit, respectively.

It may be argued that because Porac et al. were interested in explaining the multidimensional nature of the correlations among the laterality measures (rather than their variances), factor analysis would have been a more appropriate method to employ to analyze these data. Their sample correlation matrix was reanalyzed using the computer programs CEFA (Browne et al., 1999) and LISREL (Jöreskog & Sörbom, 1996). The unrestricted common factor model was fitted to the data, with from 0 to 8 factors, using the ML method of estimation. (For this example, the factor model has positive degrees of freedom for up to 8 factors.) The results are summarized in Table 5.2. The first four columns represent the number of fitted factors, the effective number of model parameters (once the identifiability constraints are taken into account), the number of degrees of freedom, and the minimum value of the discrepancy function, respectively. The next four columns contain the point and interval estimates of the RMSEA and ECVI fit measures, defined by Equation 17 and 18. (The special case of ECVI for ML estimation, given by Equation 19, is not implemented in CEFA or LISREL.) The last three columns give the chi-square goodness-of-fit statistic and the exceedance probabilities for testing the hypotheses $\varepsilon = 0$ (exact fit) and $\varepsilon \leq .05$ (close fit), respectively. The first row (where $m = 0$) represents the situation where the laterality measures are mutually uncorrelated and corresponds to the hypothesis that the population correlation matrix, **P** say, is the identity matrix (i.e., $H_0: \mathbf{P} = \mathbf{I}_p$). The last row represents the "saturated" model, where **P** is any positive-definite matrix with $\text{Diag}(\mathbf{P}) = \mathbf{I}_p$.

All the measures of fit exhibit similar behavior: They decrease rapidly in value and then plateau for $m \geq 4$. For $m = 4$, the RMSEA is estimated to be less than .05, with a reasonably tight confidence interval, the confidence interval for the ECVI captures the value for the saturated model (.189), and the hypothesis of close fit cannot be rejected. The evidence seems to suggest that $m = 4$ is the best choice for the number of factors to fit to these data. Unfortunately, the fourth factor turns out to be difficult to interpret. Basically, three of the factors in the four-factor solution replicate the pattern of loadings found by Porac et al. (1980); however, the fourth factor has high loadings with the first three handedness items (but not the fourth) and negligible loadings with the rest. Also, the four-factor solution yields a Heywood case for the second handedness item, that is, the unique variance for the item Draw is estimated to be zero. Finally, the estimated value of RMSEA for $m = 3$, while not ideal, is acceptably low (i.e., less than .08) and the corresponding confidence interval is reasonably narrow. Subjective judgment dictates that we support the original authors' decision to fit and interpret three common factors.

Two other three-factor solutions were obtained using the GLS and ULS methods of estimation. The factor loadings obtained by each estimation method were rotated to simple structure using Kaiser's (1958) normalized varimax criterion. The estimates of the rotated factor loadings and the unique variances obtained by the ML, GLS, and ULS methods and their estimated standard errors are displayed in Tables 5.3 and 5.4, respectively. For these data, the three estimation methods yield solutions that are very similar to one another and to the original loadings obtained by Porac et al. (1980). The standard errors of the factor loadings are similar in magnitude to those of the original sample correlations.

CONCLUDING REMARKS

In this chapter we demonstrated that chi-square goodness-of-fit statistics can be obtained for *any* method of estimation that yields consistent and asymptotically normal estimates of the parameters of the unrestricted common factor model, that is, the factor loading and unique variances, whether the sample data are drawn from a multivariate normal distribution or not. This statement applies not only to rigorous, iterative estimation procedures such as weighted least squares and maximum likelihood, but also to certain classical approximate methods such as "principal axis" factor analysis. Likewise, estimates of the asymptotic standard errors of all the factor model parameter estimates may be calculated whether the sample data are drawn from a multivariate normal distribution or not. Finally, computational methods have developed that allow researchers to compute the asymptotic standard errors of analytically rotated factor loading estimates derived from the analyses of either sample correlations or covariances.

However, a significant problem remains. The software to accomplish these computational tasks is not contained in a single computer program yet. If researchers

TABLE 5.3

Estimates of Rotated Factor Loadings and Unique Variances for a Three-Factor Model of Human Laterality Measures

Laterality Measure	Maximum Likelihood				Generalized Least Squares				Unweighted Least Squares			
	Factor Loadings			Unique Variances	Factor Loadings			Unique Variances	Factor Loadings			Unique Variances
	I	II	III		I	II	III		I	II	III	
Ball	.848	.107	.132	.251	.858	.109	.134	0.234	.865	.099	.134	.225
Draw	.909	.055	.125	.155	.939	.050	.122	0.101	.867	.051	.135	.227
Eraser	.883	.069	.110	.204	.884	.070	.112	0.201	.860	.069	.114	.243
Card	.443	.125	.110	.776	.445	.131	.114	0.772	.467	.119	.108	.756
Kick	.618	.177	.175	.556	.660	.199	.193	0.488	.662	.179	.172	.500
Pebble	.449	.195	.146	.739	.461	.203	.154	0.722	.477	.213	.131	.710
Chair	.337	.239	.152	.806	.344	.247	.158	0.795	.365	.249	.149	.783
Keyhole	.141	.128	.887	.177	.142	.130	.889	0.173	.138	.124	.890	.173
Bottle	.169	.119	.892	.163	.168	.118	.896	0.154	.168	.123	.889	.167
Rifle	.242	.122	.621	.541	.246	.121	.630	0.528	.237	.118	.623	.542
Door	.099	.871	.118	.217	.100	.890	.115	0.185	.093	.869	.117	.223
Heart	.123	.794	.103	.345	.125	.795	.105	0.342	.118	.784	.114	.358
Earphone	.218	.541	.098	.650	.219	.548	.100	0.642	.227	.546	.087	.643

147

TABLE 5.4

Standard Errors for Estimates of Rotated Factor Loadings and Unique Variances for a Three-Factor Model of Human Laterality Measures

Laterality	Maximum Likelihood				Generalized Least Squares				Unweighted Least Squares			
	Factor Loadings			Unique	Factor Loadings			Unique	Factor Loadings			Unique
Measure	I	II	III	Variances	I	II	III	Variances	I	II	III	Variances
Ball	.010	.022	.021	.015	.009	.022	.020	.014	.024	.024	.023	.060
Draw	.008	.021	.019	.013	.006	.020	.018	.013	.025	.024	.023	.061
Eraser	.009	.022	.020	.014	.008	.021	.020	.014	.025	.024	.023	.061
Card	.027	.030	.029	.036	.026	.029	.028	.035	.020	.024	.023	.049
Kick	.020	.027	.025	.027	.018	.025	.024	.023	.022	.025	.024	.052
Pebble	.026	.031	.029	.035	.025	.030	.028	.033	.021	.027	.024	.049
Chair	.030	.033	.031	.037	.029	.032	.030	.036	.021	.028	.025	.048
Keyhole	.020	.021	.014	.022	.020	.020	.013	.022	.018	.023	.044	.084
Bottle	.020	.020	.014	.022	.020	.020	.013	.022	.018	.023	.044	.084
Rifle	.025	.025	.020	.027	.024	.025	.020	.030	.019	.023	.030	.057
Door	.021	.020	.021	.033	.021	.019	.021	.035	.018	.048	.022	.088
Heart	.022	.021	.022	.031	.021	.019	.022	.031	.018	.043	.022	.075
Earphone	.026	.025	.026	.032	.026	.024	.026	.032	.019	.030	.022	.055

wish to take advantage of the full range of factor analytic procedures described here, then they would need to use at least three different programs: LISREL (Jöreskog & Sörbom, 1996), CEFA (Browne et al., 1999), and EQS (Bentler, 1995). One can hope this state of affairs will change in the not too distant future, and exploratory factor analysis will be much the better for it.

REFERENCES

Archer, C. O., & Jennrich, R. I. (1973). Standard errors for rotated factor loadings. *Psychometrika, 38,* 581–592.

Bartholomew, D. J. (1995). Spearman and the origin and development of factor analysis. *British Journal of Mathematical and Statistical Psychology, 48,* 211–220.

Bentler, P. M. (1995). *EQS program manual.* Encino, CA: Multivariate Software.

Bentler, P. M., & Dijkstra, T. (1985). Efficient estimation via linearization in structural models. In P. Krishnaiah (Ed.), *Multivariate analysis VI* (pp. 9–42). Amsterdam: North-Holland.

Bollen, K. A. (1989). *Structural equations with latent variables.* New York: Wiley.

Browne, M. W. (1984). Asymptotically distribution-free methods for the analysis of covariance structures. *British Journal of Mathematical and Statistical Psychology, 37,* 62–83.

Browne, M. W. (2001). An overview of analytic rotation in exploratory factor analysis. *Multivariate Behavioral Research, 36,* 111–150.

Browne, M. W., & Cudeck, R. (1989). Single sample cross validation indices for covariance structures. *Multivariate Behavioral Research, 24,* 445–455.

Browne, M. W., & Cudeck, R. (1992). Alternative ways of assessing fit. *Sociological Methods and Research, 21,* 230–258.

Browne, M. W., Cudeck, R., Tateneni, K., & Mels, G. (1999). CEFA: comprehensive exploratory factor analysis. [Computer program]. URL: http://quantrm2.psy.ohio-state.edu/browne/

Browne, M. W., & Du Toit, S. H. C. (1992). Automated fitting of non-standard models. *British Journal of Mathematical and Statistical Psychology, 41,* 193–208.

Browne, M. W., & Shapiro, A. (1988). Robustness of normal theory methods in the analysis of linear latent variate models. *Multivariate Behavioral Research, 27,* 269–300.

Carroll, J. B. (1953). Approximating simple structure in factor analysis. *Psychometrika, 18,* 23–38.

Cudeck, R. (1991). Noniterative factor analysis estimators with algorithms for subset and instrumental variable selection. *Journal of Educational Statistics, 16,* 35–52.

Ferguson, G. A. (1954). The concept of parsimony in factor analysis. *Psychometrika, 19,* 281–290.

Fuller, E. L., Jr., & Hemmerle, W. J. (1966). Robustness of the maximum-likelihood estimation procedure in factor analysis. *Psychometrika, 31,* 255–266.

Guttman, L. (1955). The determinacy of factor score matrices with implications for five other basic problems of common factor theory. *British Journal of Statistical Psychology, 8,* 65–81.

Hägglund, G. (1982). Factor analysis by instrumental variables methods. *Psychometrika, 47,* 209–222.

Harman, H. H. (1976). *Modern factor analysis* (3rd ed. rev.). Chicago: University of Chicago Press.

Harman, H. H., & Jones, W. H. (1966). Factor analysis by minimizing residuals (MINRES). *Psychometrika, 31,* 351–368.

Ihara, M., & Kano, Y. (1986). A new estimator of the uniqueness in factor analysis. *Psychometrika, 51,* 563–566.

Jennrich, R. I. (1974). Simplified formulae for standard errors in maximum-likelihood factor analysis. *British Journal of Mathematical and Statistical Psychology, 27,* 123–131.

Jennrich, R. I. (1986). A Gauss–Newton algorithm for exploratory factor analysis. *Psychometrika, 51,* 277–284.

Jöreskog, K. G. (1962). On the statistical treatment of residuals in factor analysis. *Psychometrika, 27*, 335–354.

Jöreskog, K. G., & Goldberger, A. S. (1972). Factor analysis by generalized least squares. *Psychometrika, 37*, 243–260.

Jöreskog, K. G., & Sörbom, D. (1996). *LISREL 8: User's reference guide* (2nd ed.). Chicago: Scientific Software International.

Kaiser, H. F. (1958). The VARIMAX criterion for analytic rotation in factor analysis. *Psychometika, 23*, 187–200.

Kaiser, H. F. (1970). A second-generation Little Jiffy. *Psychometrika, 35*, 401–415.

Kano, Y. (1990). Noniterative estimation and the choice of the number of factors in exploratory factor analysis. *Psychometrika, 55*, 277–291.

Krane, W. R., & McDonald, R. P. (1978). Scale invariance and the factor analysis of correlation matrices. *British Journal of Mathematical and Statistical Psychology, 31*, 218–228.

Lawley, D. N. (1940). The estimation of factor loadings by the method of maximum likelihood. *Proceedings of the Royal Society of Edinburgh A, 60*, 64–82.

Lawley, D. N. (1943). The application of the maximum likelihood method to factor analysis. *British Journal of Psychology, 33*, 172–175.

Lawley, D. N. (1967). Some new results in maximum likelihood factor analysis. *Proceedings of the Royal Society of Edinburgh A, 67*, 256–264.

Lawley, D. N., & Maxwell, A. E. (1971). *Factor analysis as a statistical method*. New York: Elsevier .

Maydeu-Olivares, A. (2001). Multidimensional item response theory modeling of binary data: Large sample properties of NOHARM estimates. *Journal of Educational and Behavioral Statistics, 26*, 49–69.

McDonald, R. P. (1985). *Factor analysis and related methods*. Hillside, NJ: Lawrence Erlbaum Associates, Inc.

McDonald, R. P. (1989). An index of goodness of fit based on noncentrality. *Journal of Classification, 6*, 97–103.

McDonald, R. P. (1999). *Test theory: A unified treatment*. Mahwah, NJ: Lawrence Erlbaum Associates, Inc.

Mulaik, S. A. (1972). *The foundations of factor analysis*. New York: McGraw-Hill.

Mulaik, S. A., & McDonald, R. P. (1978). The effect of additional variables on factor indeterminacy in models with a single common factor. *Psychometrika, 43*, 177–192.

Neuhaus, J. O., & Wrigley, C. (1954). The quartimax method: An analytical approach to orthogonal simple structure. *British Journal of Mathematical and Statistical Psychology, 7*, 81–91.

Porac, C., Coren, S, Steiger, J. H., & Duncan, P. (1980). Human laterality: A multidimensional approach. *Canadian Journal of Psychology, 34*, 91–96.

Rozeboom, W. W. (1988). Factor indeterminacy: The saga continues. *British Journal of Mathematical and Statistical Psychology, 41*, 209–226.

Saunders, D. R. (1953). *An analytical method for rotation to orthogonal simple structure* (Research Bull. 53–10). Princeton, NJ: Educational Testing Service.

Satorra, A., & Bentler, P. M. (1994). Corrections to test statistics and standard errors in covariance structure analysis. In A. Von Eye & C. C. Clogg (Eds.), *Latent variable analysis: Applications for developmental research* (pp. 399–419). Thousand Oaks, CA: Sage.

Schonemann, P. H., & Wang, M.-M. (1972). Some new results on factor indeterminacy. *Psychometrika, 37*, 61–92.

Spearman, C. (1904). General intelligence, objectively determined and measured. *American Journal of Psychology, 15*, 201–293.

Spearman, C. (1927). *The abilities of man*. New York: Macmillan.

Steiger, J. H. (1990). Structural model evaluation and modification: An interval estimation approach. *Multivariate Behavioral Research, 25*, 173–180.

Steiger, J. H., & Schönemann, P. H. (1978). A history of factor indeterminacy. In S. Shye (Ed.), *Theory construction and data analysis in the social sciences* (pp. 136–178). San Francisco: Jossey-Bass.

Swain, A. J. (1975). A class of factor analysis estimation procedures with common asymptotic sampling properties. *Psychometrika, 40*, 315–335.

Swaminathan, H., & Algina, J. (1978). Scale freeness in factor analysis. *Psychometrika, 43*, 163–178.

Thurstone, L. L. (1947). *Multiple factor analysis*. Chicago: University of Chicago Press.

Thurstone, L. L. (1954). An analytical method for simple structure. *Psychometrika, 19*, 173–182.

Yuan, K.-H., & Bentler, P. M. (2000). On equivariance and invariance of standard errors in three exploratory factor models. *Psychometrika, 65*, 121–133.

6

Four Unresolved Problems in Studies of Factorial Invariance

Roger E. Millsap
Arizona State University

INTRODUCTION

Interest in the invariance of the factor model with respect to different populations of individuals, different time periods, or even different variables from a domain appeared early in the history of factor analysis. Thurstone (1947) studied how the factor structure for a set of measured variables changes when additional variables are included in the set being analyzed (Little, Lindenburger, & Nesselroade, 1999). Change in the factor structure of a measure taken longitudinally has also been studied, but population differences in factor structure have received the most attention. Technical developments in methods for studying group differences in factor structure have now advanced to the point where studies of invariance can be completed by anyone with a personal computer and access to confirmatory factor-analytic software. As noted by McDonald (1999), the factor model can even be applied to the study of group differences in the factor structure of dichotomously scored items. However, these technical developments have not fully resolved some conceptual or practical problems facing researchers who study factorial invariance. This chapter focuses on four of these unresolved problems and the prospects for their solutions. We begin with a review of definitions of factorial invariance and their relation to broader notions of measurement invariance (Meredith & Millsap, 1992), and follow with sections describing each problem in turn.

DEFINITIONS OF FACTORIAL INVARIANCE

What do we mean by factorial invariance? The modern approach to this topic is to embed the definition of factorial invariance within a broad notion of "measurement invariance." McDonald would approve of this general approach because it is entirely consistent with his unified treatment of psychometric theory (McDonald, 1999). Consider a $p \times 1$ vector of measured variables $\mathbf{X}$, an $r \times 1$ vector of latent variables $\mathbf{W}$, and an $s \times 1$ vector of population indicators $\mathbf{V}$. The latent variables $\mathbf{W}$ represent the variables that $\mathbf{X}$ has been created to measure: $\mathbf{X}$ is intended as a measure of $\mathbf{W}$. The indicators $\mathbf{V}$ include enough information to distinguish the populations of interest. Consider also that $\mathbf{X}$ has some probability distribution that is conditional on $\mathbf{W}$ and possibly on $\mathbf{V}$. For continuous $\mathbf{X}$ this distribution is expressed as a density, and for discrete $\mathbf{X}$ it is a discrete probability function. Let $P(\mathbf{X}|\mathbf{W}, \mathbf{V})$ represent either case, depending on the context in what follows. Then $\mathbf{X}$ is said to fulfill measurement invariance in relation to $\mathbf{W}$ and $\mathbf{V}$ if

$$P(\mathbf{X}|\mathbf{W}, \mathbf{V}) = P(\mathbf{X}|\mathbf{W}) \qquad (1)$$

for all $\mathbf{X}, \mathbf{W}, \mathbf{V}$ (Mellenbergh, 1989; Meredith & Millsap, 1992). This general definition can be specialized to cover different cases. The case of interest here arises when $\mathbf{W}$ represents scores on one or more common factors, with $\mathbf{X}$ fitting a common factor model. When $\mathbf{X}$ is continuous, the standard common factor representation is

$$\mathbf{X} = \boldsymbol{\tau}_k + \boldsymbol{\Lambda}_k \mathbf{W} + \mathbf{u}, \qquad (2)$$

where $\boldsymbol{\tau}_k$ is a $p \times 1$ vector of measurement intercept parameters, $\boldsymbol{\Lambda}_k$ is a $p \times r$ factor pattern matrix, and $\mathbf{u}$ is a $p \times 1$ vector of unique factor scores. The parameters $(\boldsymbol{\tau}_k, \boldsymbol{\Lambda}_k)$ are subscripted to indicate that these parameters correspond to the kth population, and may have different values in other populations. Standard factor-analytic assumptions then lead to

$$\mathbf{E}_k(\mathbf{X}) \overset{\bullet}{=} \boldsymbol{\mu}_k = \boldsymbol{\tau}_k + \boldsymbol{\Lambda}_k \boldsymbol{\kappa}_k \qquad (3)$$

and

$$\mathbf{Cov}_k(\mathbf{X}) = \boldsymbol{\Sigma}_k = \boldsymbol{\Lambda}_k \boldsymbol{\Phi}_k \boldsymbol{\Lambda}_k' + \boldsymbol{\Theta}_k. \qquad (4)$$

Here $\boldsymbol{\kappa}_k$ is an $r \times 1$ vector of means on the common factors, $\boldsymbol{\Phi}_k$ is the $r \times r$ common factor covariance matrix, and $\boldsymbol{\Theta}_k$ is a $p \times p$ diagonal covariance matrix for the unique factors. The symbol E is the expectation operator. The foregoing assumes that a common factor representation is possible in all populations. This assumption may be incorrect, and we will return to this issue.

To return to the measurement invariance question, measurement invariance would imply

$$\mathbf{E}_k(\mathbf{X}|\mathbf{W}) = \tau + \Lambda\mathbf{W} \qquad (5)$$

and

$$\mathbf{Cov}_k(\mathbf{X}|\mathbf{W}) = \Theta, \qquad (6)$$

with no subscripts, indicating that τ, Λ, and Θ are the same in all populations of interest. Equations 5 and 6 indicate that the parameters of interest in invariance studies are the measurement intercepts, the factor loadings, and the unique factor covariance matrix. The factor means κ_k and the factor covariance matrices Φ_k are excluded from consideration, as they denote population characteristics of the common factors, and may vary over populations. Note also that the definition of invariance requires some examination of mean structures in addition to covariance structures because this is the only way to get information on τ. Finally, invariance of τ, Λ, and Θ is necessary but not sufficient for measurement invariance. Measurement invariance requires consideration of the distributional form for $P(\mathbf{X}|\mathbf{W}, \mathbf{V})$ and whether this distribution depends on $\mathbf{V}$. Equations 5 and 6 show that the conditional expectation and covariance matrix are invariant. Under multivariate normality for $P(\mathbf{X}|\mathbf{W}, \mathbf{V})$, invariance of the conditional mean and covariance matrix is sufficient for invariance in distribution. More generally however, Equations 5 and 6 do not imply measurement invariance.

Given the highly restrictive nature of measurement invariance, it is natural to ask whether weaker forms of invariance might exist that are still useful for various purposes. Equation 5 says, for example, that on average, members of different populations who have the same common factor score can be expected to have the same observed score. Equation 6 says that members of different populations who have the same factor score will have the same conditional variability in their observed scores. Taken together, these conditions are less strong than measurement invariance but are still quite useful. Meredith (1993) referred to the combination of the two conditions as an example of "weak measurement invariance," or "strict factorial invariance" in the factor-analytic context. If the condition in Equation 6 is dropped, the remaining condition denotes "strong factorial invariance" in Meredith (1993). This condition has been described elsewhere as combining "metric invariance" and "scalar invariance" (Horn & McArdle, 1992; Steenkamp & Baumgarter, 1998; Vandenberg & Lance, 2000), where metric invariance refers to invariance in factor loadings, and scalar invariance denotes invariance in measurement intercepts. The distinction between "strong" and "strict" factorial invariance turns on the invariance in the unique factor variances. It should be obvious that strict factorial invariance need not imply that the reliabilities of the observed measures are themselves invariant. These reliabilities also depend on the factor covariance matrix Φ_k, which may still differ across groups under strict factorial invariance.

At a still weaker level of restriction, the notion of "partial invariance" permits individual measured variables to differ in the level of invariance that holds for each variable (Byrne, Shavelson, & Muthén, 1989). For example, strong factorial invariance may hold for some subset of the measured variables, but the remaining variables may only fulfill metric invariance due to group differences in their measurement intercepts. Although it is simple to define such conditions in theory, two problems are encountered when evaluating partial invariance in practice. First, it is often difficult to determine which configuration of invariance conditions is correct for the data at hand based on data considerations alone. Second, the implications of partial invariance for the interpretation of the observed measures is sometimes unclear. If the majority of the measured variables have loadings that differ across groups, is it still the case that the measured variables are indicators of the same underlying construct, for example? At what point should we conclude that the measured variables are measuring different constructs in different groups? These questions are taken up later.

Selection-Theory Perspective

A dominant perspective on factorial invariance that has shaped much of the theorizing on invariance is selection theory. Briefly, selection theory concerns how the characteristics of subpopulations depend on characteristics of a parent population from which the subpopulations are selected. The selection mechanisms of interest are not completely random, but depend on one or more "selection variables" that determine who belongs in a given subpopulation. For example, a subpopulation of "graduate school applicants" might depend on a set of variables, including test scores and grade point averages. Lawley (1943) presented theorems governing selection in multivariate systems in which all regressions of interest are linear and homoscedastic. Using these theorems, Meredith (1964) showed that the factor pattern matrix and the unique factor covariance matrix are invariant across subpopulations if those subpopulations were selected via selection variables that satisfy some restrictions. These results can easily be extended to show that invariance must also hold for the measurement intercepts. However, the common factor covariance matrix and the common factor mean vector are not generally invariant under selection. An intriguing aspect of selection theory is that the selection variables themselves need not be measured directly; the only requirement is that subpopulations be created via *some* set of selection variables that fulfill the required restrictions.

Although the selection perspective provides motivation for the study of factorial invariance, one problem with this perspective seems to have gone unrecognized. Let **g** be the vector of hypothetical selection variables used to create the populations under study. We assume that the factor model in Equation 2 holds for $\mathbf{X}$ in the general population, with subpopulations created via selection from this general or parent population. We also need some assumptions about the relations between $\mathbf{g}$ and $(\mathbf{W}, \mathbf{u})$. We assume that in the general population (a) $E(\mathbf{W}|\mathbf{g})$ is linear, (b) $\text{Cov}(\mathbf{W}|\mathbf{g})$ does not depend on $\mathbf{g}$, (c) $\mathbf{g}$ and $\mathbf{u}$ are independent, and (d) $\text{Cov}(\mathbf{u}, \mathbf{e})$ does not depend on $\mathbf{g}$. Here $\mathbf{e}$ is the vector of residual variables in the regression of $\mathbf{W}$ on $\mathbf{g}$. Lawley's theorem then establishes that the parameters (τ, Λ, Θ) will be invariant across subpopulations created from $\mathbf{g}$. What is the relationship between the hypothetical selection variables $\mathbf{g}$ and the indicators $\mathbf{V}$, which directly define the populations under study? The simplest answer to this question is to set $\mathbf{g} = \mathbf{V}$: The selection variables are identical to the indicators $\mathbf{V}$ that define the subpopulations being compared. If so, however, assumptions (b) and (c) would imply that $\Sigma_k = \Sigma$, or that no subpopulation differences exist in the covariance matrices for the measured variables $\mathbf{X}$. This conclusion follows as long as $\text{Cov}(\mathbf{V}, \mathbf{V}) = 0$ within the selected subpopulations. If $\mathbf{V}$ contains the variable "sex" and the subpopulations consist of "male" versus "female," the null covariance condition would hold because each subpopulation is homogeneous in sex. Hence, for the selection perspective to have useful consequences, either the selection variables must be viewed as separate from $\mathbf{V}$ or there must be variability in $\mathbf{V}$ within the subpopulations. If the selection variables are separate from $\mathbf{V}$, what are they? This question remains unanswered in discussions of selection theory as it applies to the invariance problem.

UNRESOLVED ISSUES

The Effect-Size Problem

Full factorial invariance in an exact sense is easily defined in theory and rarely encountered in practice. In most empirical studies, a confirmatory factor analysis is declared to support invariance when the cumulative loss of fit entailed by the various invariance restrictions is below a certain threshold. Current practice in such studies, as in structural equation modeling more generally, is to rely on measures of approximate model fit for deciding when to retain or reject a proposed model. Models that would be rejected by a statistical test of exact fit (e.g., chi-square) are retained if the degree of approximate fit is acceptable by current standards. The implication of this practice is that some degree of violation of invariance is tolerated; the resulting models represent "approximate invariance" rather than exact invariance as defined in theory.

If the use of approximate fit indices is going to continue, invariance researchers must eventually confront the following question: When are group differences in factor structure small enough to ignore? This question should not be approached solely from the viewpoint of indices of model fit. Model fit indices assess some measure of discrepancy between the mean and/or covariance structure as reproduced by the model and the same structure as found either in the sample data or in the population. Unfortunately, there is no clear relationship between these discrepancies and the practical consequences of violations of invariance in actual test use. For example, a group difference in factor loadings of .05 may lead to a meaningful degree of misfit as measured by standard fit indices, yet this difference may have no practically meaningful consequences for the use of the measures in the groups being compared. If we are to decide when group differences in factor structure are meaningful in practical terms, we should do so directly rather than indirectly through measures of model fit.

A starting point for the question of practical consequences is to consider the purpose for the measure being studied. How will the measure be used in practice? What goal is to be achieved in using the measure? If we can answer these questions, we can then ask whether the violations of invariance as found empirically are of sufficient magnitude to impede the use of the measure for its stated purpose. To give an example, suppose that we wish to use scores on the measure as a basis for selection of individuals. In a clinical context, scores on the measure might be used to either refer the person for treatment or declare that treatment is not needed. In education, scores on the measure might be used to determine whether a student is placed in remedial courses or can pursue credit-bearing coursework. Other examples of this situation are common. In all of these cases, a primary objective is accuracy of selection: We wish to minimize the errors of selection, both false positives and false negatives. Furthermore, we would like to maintain accuracy in all groups. If violations of factorial invariance contribute to inaccuracy of selection in one or more groups, these violations have practical consequences. We therefore need to quantify the relationship between the factor structure of the measure and accuracy in the use of the measure for selection purposes.

Millsap and Kwok (2004) illustrated how the relationship between invariance of the factor structure and accuracy in selection can be evaluated. The investigator must first decide on the best-fitting factor solution in each group and obtain estimates for all model parameters. It is assumed that a single-factor model holds within each group. The factor solutions presumably include some parameters that are constrained to invariance and others that have been found to vary across groups. It is assumed that selection is to be based on the sum or average of the scores on the measured variables. The distributions of common factor scores and unique factor scores within each group are assumed to be normal, with means and variances estimated or fixed in each group. Once the distributions of the factor scores are specified, the distributions of the measured variables are determined by the factor structure under the model for a given group. The distribution of the sum of the measured variables is easily derived as well. We have a bivariate normal distribution for the measured sum and the common factor scores, with separate distributions for each group. Assuming that selection is to be considered in the pooled population that combines individuals from each group, we find that the relevant bivariate distribution in the pooled population is a mixture of bivariate normals. This mixture may be differentially weighted to reflect the different sizes of the groups under study.

An example of the foregoing construction will help illustrate the method. Suppose that $p = 6$ measures are taken in each of two groups, with the measures fitting a single-factor model within each group. Suppose also that $\kappa_1 = 0$ and $\phi_1 = 1$ in the first group, and $\kappa_2 = 0.5$ and $\phi_2 = 1$ in the second group. The factor loading estimates in the two groups are

$$\lambda_1 = \begin{bmatrix} .6 \\ .5 \\ .3 \\ .4 \\ .2 \\ .4 \end{bmatrix}, \qquad \lambda_2 = \begin{bmatrix} .6 \\ .5 \\ .3 \\ .5 \\ .4 \\ .5 \end{bmatrix}$$

The intercepts τ in the two groups and the invariant unique factor covariance matrix Θ are given by, respectively,

$$\tau_1 = \begin{bmatrix} .4 \\ .1 \\ .5 \\ .2 \\ .1 \\ .4 \end{bmatrix}, \qquad \tau_2 = \begin{bmatrix} .4 \\ .1 \\ .5 \\ .4 \\ .3 \\ .8 \end{bmatrix}, \qquad \mathrm{diag}[\Theta] = \begin{bmatrix} .3 \\ .3 \\ .4 \\ .2 \\ .3 \\ .2 \end{bmatrix}.$$

These parameter values determine the distribution of the sum of the measured variables in each group. Let $\lambda_1^* = 2.4$ be the sum of the loadings in the first group and $\lambda_2^* = 2.8$ be the corresponding sum in the second group. Similarly, let $\tau_1^* = 1.7$, $\tau_2^* = 2.5$, and $\theta^* = 1.7$ be the intercepts and the unique variance for the sum score, respectively. From these values and the parameters for the distribution of the common factor, we can generate the mean and variance of the sum of measured variables. In the first group, we have $\mu^* = 1.7$ and $\sigma^{2*} = 7.46$. In the second group, $\mu^* = 3.9$ and $\sigma^{2*} = 9.54$. Finally, the correlation between the measured sum score and the common factor score can be calculated using the factor model parameters in each group. This correlation is

$$\rho_k = \frac{\lambda_k^* \sqrt{\phi_k}}{\sqrt{\lambda_k^{*2} \phi_k + \theta_k^*}}. \tag{7}$$

Based on the foregoing parameter values, this correlation is equal to .879 in the first group and .907 in the second group.

Putting this information together, we find the five relevant parameters for Group 1 are $[\mu_1^*, \sigma_1^{2*}, \kappa_1, \phi_1, \rho_1] = [1.7, 7.46, 0, 1, .879]$. In Group 2, the relevant parameters are $[\mu_2^*, \sigma_2^{2*}, \kappa_2, \phi_2, \rho_2] = [3.9, 9.54, .5, 1, .907]$. The pooled population

TABLE 6.1
Partial Invariance Case

Group	TP	FP	TN	FN	SENS	SPEC	PPV
Focal	.0229	.0067	.9352	.0350	.3955	.9929	.7736
Reference	.1134	.0568	.8012	.0284	.7997	.9338	.6663

Note. TP, True positives; FP, false positives; TN, true negatives; FN, false negatives; SENS, sensitivity; SPEC, specificity; PPV, positive predictive value.

consisting of the combination of Groups 1 and 2 is a mixture of bivariate normal distributions. We will consider just the equal-mixture case here. This mixture is not itself a bivariate normal distribution. The next task is to consider selection at a cut-point on the marginal distribution of factor scores. This selection consists in an "ideal" selection of a desired percentage from the marginal distribution of factor scores obtained from the mixture distribution. The selection is ideal in the sense that we will not actually base selection on the factor scores in practice because these are unknown. For example, suppose we want to consider selection at the 90th percentile on this marginal distribution, corresponding to selecting the top 10% based on the factor scores. The cut-point at the 90th percentile is found to be 1.572. The actual selection would be based on the sum of the measured variables. We also need to know the cut-point corresponding to the 90th percentile in the marginal distribution of this sum. This cut-point is found to be 6.845. Taken together, these two cut-points partition the bivariate mixture distribution into four quadrants, and each group-specific bivariate distribution is also split into four quadrants by the two cut-points. In each case, we can identify the four quadrants with four different selection outcomes. *True positives* (TP) are cases that would be selected either using the factor score or the sum of measured variables. *False positives* (FP) are cases that would be selected using the sum of measured variables, but would not have been selected given knowledge of their factor scores. *True negatives* (TN) are cases that would not be selected either using the factor scores or the sum of measured variables. *False negatives* (FN) are cases that would not be selected using the sum of measured variables, but would have been selected using the factor score. We can calculate the proportion of cases in each of these four categories for each group. These proportions are given in Table 6.1 along with some additional quantities to be described.

We can compute some functions of these quadrant proportions that will help reveal their implications. First, the "sensitivity" (SENS) of the sum of measured variables is the proportion of true positives out of the total number of cases that exceed the cut-point on the factor score. Sensitivity can also be viewed as a conditional probability: the probability of being selected based on the sum of measured variables, given that a case exceeds the cut-point on the factor score. From the foregoing proportions, the sensitivity in the focal group is .3955 and in the reference group it is .7997. Next, the "specificity" (SPEC) is the proportion of true negatives out of the total number of cases that fall below the cut-point on the factor score. Specificity is the conditional probability of not being selected based on the sum of measured variables, given that a case falls below the cut-point on the factor score. The specificity in the focal group is .9929 and in the reference group it is .9338. Finally, we can calculate the "positive predictive value" (PPV) of the sum of measured variables as the proportion of true positives out of the total number of cases that exceed the cut-point on the sum of measured variables. In personnel selection, this quantity is known as the "success ratio." It is the conditional probability that a case exceeds the cut-point on the factor score, given that the case is selected based on the sum of measured variables. The positive predictive value in the focal group is .7736 and in the reference group it is .6663. Among these three quantities, the largest discrepancy between the reference and focal groups lies in the sensitivity. Among those who exceed the cut-point on the factor score, we are more certain in the reference group of being selected based on the sum of the measured variables.

For comparison purposes, consider the selection results that would have been obtained if the factor loadings in this example were invariant, with loading values being equal to those found in Group 1. The sum of the loadings in both groups would be $\lambda^* = 2.8$. In this case, the relevant parameter values for the bivariate distributions in each group are [2.5, 9.54, 0, 1, .907] in Group 1, and [3.9, 9.54, .5, 1, .907] in Group 2. The marginal cutpoint for the 90th percentile in the mixture distribution is again 1.572 for the factor scores and 7.261 for the sum of observed scores. We can again calculate the proportions of cases corresponding to each of the four types of selection outcomes, done separately by group. These proportions are given in Table 6.2.

What has changed in Table 6.2 in comparison to Table 6.1? The most obvious change lies in the sensitivity. The two groups are much more similar in Table 6.2 on this measure than in Table 6.1. Given that the only difference in the factor models between Tables 6.1 and 6.2 lies in the invariance constraints on the loadings and intercepts, we can attribute the change in sensitivity to the shift from partial to full invariance in loadings and intercepts. Under partial invariance, a much smaller proportion of the population in the focal group will be selected from among those whose factor scores truly exceed the cut-point. In the fully invariant case, the proportion of cases selected from among those whose factor score exceeds the cut-point is comparable between the reference and focal groups. A further change from Table 6.1 to Table 6.2 is that the positive predictive value of the

TABLE 6.2
Full Invariance Case

Group	TP	FP	TN	FN	SENS	SPEC	PPV
Focal	.0395	.0221	.9198	.0184	.6822	.9765	.6412
Reference	.1018	.0365	.8215	.0400	.7179	.9575	.7361

Note. TP, True positives; FP, false positives; TN, true negatives; FN, false negatives; SENS, sensitivity; SPEC, specificity; PPV, positive predictive value.

procedure shrinks in the focal group under full invariance in comparison to partial invariance: .7736 under partial invariance and .6412 under full invariance. Here the total proportion of the focal group that is above the 90th percentile on the sum of observed measures is .0616 under full invariance and is .0296 under partial invariance. Hence, whereas a greater proportion of these focal group members is selected under partial invariance, the absolute number of focal group members being selected is smaller than in the fully invariant case.

Locating the Violation of Invariance

We say that partial factorial invariance holds when some, but not all, of the model parameters $[\tau_k, \Lambda_k, \Theta_k]$ are invariant (Byrne, Shavelson, & Muthén, 1989). Ordinarily this condition is meant to apply within a given parameter type, such as when some factor loadings in Λ_k are invariant whereas others are not. Partial factorial invariance is typically found to hold after hypotheses that specify complete invariance for a given parameter type are rejected. Following rejection of complete invariance, the goal is to determine which parameters are invariant and which are not. This goal is difficult to achieve if no theory or prior research exists that could suggest which parameters might vary over groups. A further complication is that some model constraints are required for identification purposes, and these constraints typically require that some parameters be invariant. If the parameters chosen for this purpose are *not* invariant, the identification constraints complicate the process of finding which parameters vary. This problem also arises in multiple-group item response theory models (Glas & Verhelst, 1995).

To illustrate this problem, consider a two-group single-factor model in which we have constrained all loadings to invariance and all intercepts to invariance: $\Lambda_1 = \Lambda_2, \tau_1 = \tau_2$. Assume that the single-factor model itself fits well in each group without invariance constraints. The model with invariant loadings and intercepts can be identified by requiring the factor mean and variance in one, group to be equal to zero and one, respectively. If this model is rejected, we would conclude that either $\Lambda_1 \neq \Lambda_2$ or $\tau_1 \neq \tau_2$, or both.

We typically wish to go beyond general inequalities of this type, however, and test hypotheses about which individual parameters might vary across groups. This specific information would be needed to apply the method described here for evaluating the impact of the violation of invariance or to eliminate the items or measures that are the source of the violation. When p is large, the potential number of invariance constraints to be tested individually becomes large, leading to problems of multiple hypothesis testing unless appropriate controls are introduced. Furthermore, at least one invariance constraint on the loadings and one constraint on the intercepts must be maintained for identification purposes. The same measure would typically be used to provide both constraints. If this measure turns out to itself be a source of violation of invariance, the invariance constraint used for identification will distort the parameter estimates in the rest of the model. As a result, we may erroneously reject the invariance constraint for another measure, leading to mistaken conclusions about which measures are responsible for the violation of overall invariance.

The process of locating which measures are responsible for the violations of invariance is a specification search. One model (the fully invariant model) has been rejected, and the correct model representing partial invariance is sought. Controls for the inflation of Type I error rates can be introduced, but these controls do not guarantee the success of the specification search. If the search is guided primarily by data-based local fit indices (e.g., modification indices), the prospects for locating the correct model are known to be affected by several influences. Sample size is an important consideration because larger samples provide more power and greater stability to any data-based indices. The number of misspecified constraints in the original model is a second important influence. The greater the number of incorrect constraints, the more difficult it will be to arrive at the correct model through a series of data-based modifications to the original model (MacCallum, Roznowski, & Necowitz, 1992). The implication is that it will be easier to locate violations of invariance when few measures are responsible. Moreover, present standards for fit evaluation permit models that are rejected by tests of exact fit to be retained if the values of approximate fit indices are acceptable. By these standards, the specification search may never find the correct model because an incorrect model manages to pass the test of approximate fit. All of these problems are common across all forms of specification searches that rely on data-based indices of fit in structural equation modeling. Although it is known that no perfect solution exists for the misspecification problem, some aspects of the problem in the invariance context could be studied in more detail. For example, simulation evidence might shed light on whether the best strategy would be to add constraints to an unconstrained model (forward restriction) or to eliminate constraints sequentially from a fully constrained model (backward relaxation). It is likely that neither strategy is uniformly superior.

The need for at least one invariance constraint each on the loadings and intercepts presents a further source of difficulty. Unless we are confident that the measure chosen for these invariance constraints is truly invariant, we must in some way consider whether the chosen measure lacks invariance. Rensvold and Cheung (2001) presented a search procedure that is designed to locate which measures could be considered invariant and which measures lack invariance. The procedure requires a sequence of fit evaluations in which for each possible pair of measures, the relevant parameters are constrained to invariance while permitting the parameters for the remaining measures to vary. For example, if the parameters under study are the loadings, the procedure would constrain the loadings of a chosen pair of measures to invariance while permitting the remaining loadings to vary across groups. A chi-square difference test is then applied to evaluate the fit of the model with the pair of constrained loadings to the fit of a model with a single invariance constraint on the loadings. In Rensvold and Cheung (2001), both models include a fixed unit loading as one of the invariant loadings, but the procedure could be implemented without fixing the values of any loadings. The chi-square difference is evaluated against a Bonferroni-adjusted critical value. This procedure is repeated for all $p(p-1)/2$ pairs of measures. The goal is to identify subsets of measures whose parameters are invariant. This procedure has been applied to real examples, but it apparently has not been used in simulations where the true model is known and the accuracy of the method can be studied. The procedure's use of chi-square difference tests is also troublesome if weaker models in the sequence leading to the specification search (e.g., configural invariance) are rejected based on the chi-square test. In such cases, we know that the baseline model against which all the models in the search set are compared lacks fit to some extent. Is it still reasonable to base model selection on changes in the chi-square statistics?

Meredith and Horn (2001) suggested an alternative approach to identifying the model in relation to mean structures under partial invariance. This approach applies when invariance in the pattern matrices (metric invariance) has already been established and the focus changes to the measurement intercepts. Ordinarily, one can identify the intercepts in multiple group problems by fixing the latent means in one group to zero and requiring at least r intercepts to be invariant, where r is the number of factors. An alternative to this approach would be to fix all latent means across groups, eliminating the need to impose any invariance constraints on the intercepts for identification purposes. The problem with this option is that it is unclear what values to use for the fixed latent means. Meredith and Horn (2001) suggested that one first fit the factor model without mean structure, checking for invariance of the pattern matrices. Assuming metric invariance holds, one then uses the factor solution to compute estimates of the latent means in each group by applying the Bartlett factor score weights to the means of the measured variables in each group. Specifically, one calculates

$$\hat{\kappa}_k = (\Lambda' \Theta_k^{-1} \Lambda)^{-1} \Lambda' \Theta_k^{-1} (\mu_k - \mu), \tag{8}$$

where μ is the $p \times 1$ vector of grand means for the measured variables across all groups. Having obtained estimates for all of the latent means in each group in this manner, one then includes mean structures in the factor model, fixing the latent means at their estimated values, and proceeds with the means and covariance structure model. The measurement intercepts are identified by the fixed latent means, and so the initial model need not include constraints on these intercepts. The results found with this model may suggest that some intercepts can be constrained to invariance. Constraints on the intercepts are added to simplify the model while maintaining adequate fit. If enough constraints are added (at least r), the latent means can subsequently be freed in all but one group, generating new estimates for the latent means. Meredith and Horn (2001) also noted that the degree-of-freedom values generated by the software will be too high because of the fixed latent means. They recommended that a reduction be applied to the degree of freedom of $r(K-1)$, where K is the number of groups.

This procedure is potentially useful as a way of identifying the mean structure without introducing distortions due to lack of invariance in the measures chosen for identification purposes. Alternative estimators for the latent means could be considered that would employ weights other than the Bartlett weights. It might be expected that the success of the procedure would be related to the sizes of the communalities of the measures, given that high communalities imply stronger associations between factor scores and scores on measures. Further research should focus on the performance of the method under varying data conditions, such as the number of measures, the degress of invariance in the factor means and intercepts, and the sample size.

Invariance with Ordinal Measures

Factor-analytic methods for the analyis of ordered-categorical measures have been available for some time (Bartholomew, 1980; Bock and Aitkin, 1981; Christofferson, 1975; Jöreskog, 1990, 1993; Muthén, 1978, 1984). These methods typically assume that the observed responses on a given measure are determined by the value of a continuous latent response variate X^* in relation to C threshold parameters, with each measure having $C + 1$ possible response categories. For a three-category measure scored $(0, 1, 2)$, we might have

$$
\begin{aligned}
X &= 0 && \text{if} && X^* < \nu_1 \\
&= 1 && \text{if} && \nu_1 \le X^* < \nu_2 \\
&= 2 && \text{if} && \nu_2 \le X^*.
\end{aligned}
\tag{9}
$$

The threshold parameters are ν_1 and ν_2. The latent response variates are in turn given a factor representation,

$$
\mathbf{X}^* = \boldsymbol{\tau} + \boldsymbol{\Lambda}\boldsymbol{\xi} + \boldsymbol{\delta},
\tag{10}
$$

with the usual assumptions holding for the factor model. The latent response variates are assumed to have a multivariate normal distribution with mean $\mu_{X^*} = \mathbf{0}$ and $\mathrm{diag}(\boldsymbol{\Sigma}_{X^*}) = \mathbf{I}$. The latter restrictions on the mean vector and the variances are included for identification, but other choices are possible (see Browne & Arminger, 1995, for examples). The covariance matrix is therefore a polychoric correlation matrix. The parameter estimates $[\boldsymbol{\tau}\boldsymbol{\Lambda}\boldsymbol{\Theta}]$ can be obtained using weighted least squares (e.g., Muthén, 1984).

The extension of this theory to invariance in the multiple-group case is less often discussed in the literature (Browne & Arminger, 1995; Lee, Poon, & Bentler, 1989; Muthén & Christofferson, 1981; Poon, Lee, Afifi, & Bentler, 1990). The definition of factorial invariance for this case must be broadened in comparison to the traditional factor model for continuous measures. In this traditional model, measurement invariance in Equation 1 will hold for continuous $\mathbf{X}$ if (a) $\boldsymbol{\tau}$, $\boldsymbol{\Lambda}$, and $\boldsymbol{\Theta}$ are invariant and (b) the conditional distribution of $\mathbf{X}$ given $\mathbf{W}$ is multivariate normal. In the ordered-categorical case, the invariance of τ, Λ, and Θ would not imply measurement invariance even if the conditional distribution of $\mathbf{X}$ given ξ is multivariate normal, and this normality assumption will not hold in any case because $\mathbf{X}$ is discrete. Invariance of τ, Λ, and Θ is not even sufficient to guarantee factorial invariance in Equations 5 and 6. Weak factorial invariance, as well as measurement invariance, must consider the invariance of the threshold parameters across groups and the distributions of the unique factors in all groups. For example, in the ordered-categorical case we know that for an individual measure X,

$$E_k(X|\xi) = \sum_{c=0}^{C} X_c P(X = X_c|\xi). \tag{11}$$

The probability $P(X = X_c|\xi)$ is the probability that

$$\nu_c \leq X^* < \nu_{c+1}, \tag{12}$$

given the value of ξ, with X^* as in Equation 10. In requiring invariance for the expected value in Equation 11, we must also have invariance in thresholds and in $f(\delta|\xi)$, the conditional density for the unique factor scores. Hence if we wish to investigate factorial invariance for ordered-categorical measures, we must evaluate more conditions in the data than in the continuous measure case.

The addition of threshold parameters to the factor model also introduces some new identification questions. Must all thresholds be invariant if the model is to be identified in the multiple-group case? Can both thresholds and measurement intercepts be included as free parameters in an identified model? The existing literature on the multiple-group case does not clearly describe the constraints needed to identify the model. Millsap and Tein (2004) provided identification conditions for a variety of confirmatory factor analysis models for ordered-categorical measures, along with proofs and examples. When the measures are dichotomous, all thresholds are taken as invariant, and the variances of r latent response variates must be fixed to known, invariant values (e.g., unit values), where r is the number of factors. These conditions assume that if $r > 1$, each measure has a nonzero loading on only one factor. All intercepts are dropped from the model by setting $\tau_k = \mathbf{0}$ for all k. In the polytomous case, we need to constrain only $p + r$ thresholds to invariance. Typically, these constrains would be implemented by fixing the p thresholds for one response category and the thresholds of r measures for a second category. The remaining thresholds are free to vary across groups. The measurement intercepts are all fixed to zero as in the dichotomous case. Here again it is assumed that each measure has a nonzero loading on only one factor if $r > 1$. More-complex models in which this simple loading pattern does not hold are also discussed in Millsap and Tein (2004).

A practical difficulty facing invariance studies of ordered-categorical measures is the sample size required to obtain stable standard error estimates and test statistics. The weighted least squares estimator used traditionally in these applications is known to require very large samples to yield accurate results. For example, simulations reported in Boomsma and Hoogland (2001) reveal that for adequate Type I error performance in the chi-square test statistic, an $N > 1,600$ is required. Boomsma and Hoogland (2001) did not study the multiple-group case, but their results should generalize to this case. Estimation methods that would not require such large samples are needed. The Mplus (Muthén & Muthén, 1999) software program offers some alternative estimators: Weighted Least Squares Mean-adjusted (WLSM) and Weighted Least Squares Mean- and Variance-adjusted (WLSMV). These estimators vary in how the weight matrix is used for parameter estimation and in calculating standard errors and fit statistics (Muthén, duToit, & Spisac, 2002). The WLSM and WLSMV estimations methods are purported to function well in smaller samples than those needed for weighted least squares, but more evaluation of their performance is needed.

Modeling Noninvariance

An open question facing invariance researchers has always been: If invariance is violated, what is the explanation for the violation? A violation of invariance is simply a group difference in one or more factor model parameters. An invariance study will typically stop once a group difference is located and shown to be both meaningful and beyond chance. The further question of the explanation for the group difference is generally outside the scope of the factor analysis. Granting the truth of this point, it is still useful to consider the type of measurement model that might account for the group difference. In differential item functioning (DIF) research, for example, Stout and colleagues (Shealy & Stout, 1993; Stout, 1990) proposed a semiparametric item response theory (IRT) framework in which DIF arises as a consequence of two joint influences: multidimensionality and group differences in the distributions on the multiple latent variables. When the DIF analysis evaluates DIF by conditioning on total scale scores, the imperfect matching due to the multidimensionality, along with the group differences in distributions, leads to rejection of the null hypothesis of "noDIF." In this formulation, DIF is due to the action of additional latent variables, but only when these latent variables have distributions that differ across the groups being compared. In the traditional IRT modeling literature, DIF due to multidimensionality is now a common theme (e.g., Ackerman, 1992).

A similar formulation was presented in a context similar to factor analysis by Camilli (1992). In this paper, a multivariate probit model for scores on dichotomous items was used that is essentially a factor model. Violations of invariance are due to the exclusion of additional common factors from the model that serves as a baseline model in the invariance study. Camilli (1992) demonstrated algebraically that under certain conditions, exclusion of these additional factors will lead to apparent violations of invariance in the smaller common factor solution even though no violation exists in the complete factor space. We might express this idea by splitting $\mathbf{W}$ in Equation 1 into $\mathbf{W} = (\mathbf{W}_1, \mathbf{W}_2)$, where $\mathbf{W}_1$ is the common factor vector included in the invariance study, and $\mathbf{W}_2$ contains the additional common factors. We can understand the results in Camilli (1992) as asserting

$$P(\mathbf{X}|\mathbf{W}_1, \mathbf{V}) \neq P(\mathbf{X}|\mathbf{W}_1) \tag{13}$$

but

$$P(\mathbf{X}|\mathbf{W}_1, \mathbf{W}_2, \mathbf{V}) = P(\mathbf{X}|\mathbf{W}_1, \mathbf{W}_1). \tag{14}$$

Measurement invariance holds in the complete factor space based on $\mathbf{W} = (\mathbf{W}_1, \mathbf{W}_2)$, but fails to hold in the subspace based on $\mathbf{W}_1$. As in Stout's model, the exclusion of $\mathbf{W}_2$ creates the violation of invariance through group differences in the distribution of $\mathbf{W} = (\mathbf{W}_1, \mathbf{W}_2)$.

All of these approaches have a common theme: Violations of invariance occur when additional latent variables are excluded from the model, and the groups under study have different distributions on these excluded latent variables. This account is compelling theoretically, and it is tempting to conclude that all forms of noninvariance can be understood by appealing to the operation of additional latent variables. A logical consequence of this view is that we should seek explanations for noninvariance by studying these additional latent variables. Furthermore, the measures under study do not actually function differently across groups, but only appear to do so due to unequal distributions across groups on the additional latent variables. We may or may not decide to retain the measures in spite of the violations of invariance, depending on our view of the relevance of the additional variables.

However, the explanation of noninvariance through factor models extended by additional factors raises some difficulties. One difficulty lies in the traditional procedure followed in evaluating invariance in the factor model. The procedure begins with some baseline model that specifies a fixed number of factors in each group. This model is the least restrictive model tested in the sequence of models because it includes no invariance constraints apart from the "invariance" in the number of factors. If no baseline model is found to fit adequately, the investigation of invariance for the factor model parameters cannot begin. By implication, a completed investigation of invariance will have employed a baseline model that specifies a fixed number of common factors and will have retained this number of factors in subsequent models. Once violations of invariance are found, to explain these violations as due to additional, unmodeled factors is to argue that the original baseline model was flawed. It seems contradictory, however, to first declare the baseline model to be adequate and then later argue that it is inadequate due to fit evidence that built on that baseline model. Either the baseline model was inadequate to begin with, and all subsequent evaluations of relative fit in comparison to the baseline are ambiguous, or the baseline model was adequate and there was never any need for additional factors.

In response to this dilemma, we might argue that the original fit evaluation of the baseline model may have simply concluded that the model provides a good approximation. An approximate fit may leave room for additional factors, expecially if these factors are "small" in their contributions to the variances in the measures. This position argues that whereas the degree of approximation is good enough to provide a basis for comparison to subsequent models, the approximation is also poor enough to explain the presence of even large violations of invariance that are found subsequently. These two claims do not seem consistent in general, although it may be possible to explain small deviations from invariance in this manner.

A different objection to the "additional latent variables" account is that some violations of invariance may be difficult to represent by the addition of such variables. A thought experiment may help to illustrate this point. Consider a randomized experiment in which the dependent measures are scores on items for a test that has been shown to fit a single-factor model in the population under study. A suitably homogeneous math test would be an example. Examinees are randomly assigned to two groups, a control group and a treatment group. In the control group, examinees take the test under ordinary conditions. In the treatment group, examinees take the test under distraction conditions in which some environmental stimulus (e.g., noise) is present during testing. The distraction is of sufficient intensity to influence performance on the exam. Following the testing, score distributions on many items for the two groups are found to differ. What is the explanation for the score differences? How should the factor model represent the score differences?

The answer to the first question seems obvious; the answer to the second question is not. We can attribute the score difference to the presence of noise, but the representation of noise within the factor model is unclear. Random assignment implies that the two groups are identical in their distributions on all latent variables prior to testing. By the definition of measurement invariance in Equation 1, we should find that the items of the test violate invariance because item score distributions vary whereas latent distributions do not. If we want to explain this violation of invariance by hypothesizing additional latent variables, we must argue that these variables appear suddenly during testing, and that the groups differ in their distributions on these additional variables. In effect, the presence of noise elicits new factors and also creates group differences in distributions on these factors. Yet the noise itself is not a "person" variable. It is a feature of the situation to which all examinees assigned to the treatment group are exposed. Why should we represent the influence of this situational feature as a person characteristic? The traditional factor model does not offer many choices on this point; sources of variation in the model are linked to the measures or to the latent variables. The measures themselves cannot be responsible for the violations of invariance because the same set of measures is taken by examinees in both groups.

The foregoing thought experiment represents a type of violation of invariance that may be best explained without invoking additional factors. It might be argued that the noise affects the expression of existing factors, leading to group differences in factor loadings, for example. If so, we should find that factor models with group-specific loadings provide good fits with the same anticipated number of factors in both groups. The influence that is responsible for the violation of invariance is situational. Whereas the situational feature that is responsible for the violation is obvious in this example, in real applications such "situational" features may not be so obvious. The testing situation may place different perceived demands on members of different demographic groups, for example, leading to influences on test performance that are situationally specific even though no objective differences in the testing situations are present. Present factor-analytic models for studying invariance in such cases are capable of documenting violations of invariance. The models are poorly suited for explaining the origin of the violations, however, unless the conventional view involving additional factors is suspended and alternative origins are sought.

REFERENCES

Ackerman, T. A. (1992). A didactic explanation of item bias, item impact, and item validity from a multidimensional perspective. *Journal of Educational Measurement, 29,* 67–91.

Bartholomew, D. J. (1980). Factor analysis for categorical data. *Journal of the Royal Statistical Society, Series B, 42,* 293–321.

Bock, R. D., & Aitkin, M. (1981). Marginal maximum likelihood estimation of item parameters: Application of an EM algorithm. *Psychometrika, 46,* 443–459.

Boomsma, A., & Hoogland, J. J. (2001). The robustness of LISREL modeling revisited. In R. Cudeck, S. Du Toit, & D. Sorbom (Eds.), *Structural equation modeling: present and future* (pp. 139–168). Lincolnwood, IL: Scientific Software.

Browne, M. W., & Arminger, G. (1995). Specification and estimation of mean and covariance structure models. In G. Arminger, C. C. Clogg, & M. E. Sobel (Eds.), *Handbook of statistical modeling for the social and behavioral sciences* (pp. 185–249). New York: Plenum.

Byrne, B. M., Shavelson, R. J., & Muthén, B. (1989). Testing for equivalence of factor covariance and mean structures: The issue of partial measurement invariance. *Psychological Bulletin, 105,* 456–466.

Camilli, G. (1992). A conceptual analysis of differential item functioning in terms of a multidimensional item response model. *Applied Psychological Measurement, 16,* 129–147.

Christoffersson, A. (1975). Factor analysis of dichotomized variables. *Psychometrika, 40,* 5–32.

Glas, C. A. W., & Verhelst, N. D. (1995). Testing the Rasch model. In G. H. Fischer & I. W. Molenaar (Eds.), *Rasch models: Foundations, recent developments, and applications* (pp. 69–95). New York: Springer-Verlag.

Horn, J. L., & McArdle, J. J. (1992). A practical guide to measurement invariance in research on aging. *Experimental Aging Research, 18,* 117–144.

Jöreskog, K. G. (1990). New developments in LISREL: Analysis of ordinal variables using polychoric correlations and weighted least squares. *Quality and Quantity, 24,* 387–404.

Jöreskog, K. G. (1993). Latent variable modeling with ordinal variables. In K. Haagen, D. J. Bartholomew, & M. Deistler (Eds.), *Statistical modeling and latent variables* (pp. 163–171). Amsterdam: North-Holland.

Lawley, D. N. (1943). A note on Karl Pearson's selection formulae. *Proceedings of the Royal Society of Edinburgh, 2,* 28–30.

Lee, S. Y., Poon, W. Y., & Bentler, P. M. (1989). Simultaneous analysis of multivariate polytomous variates in several groups. *Psychometrika, 54,* 63–73.

Little, T. D., Lindenburger, U., & Nesselroade, J. (1999). On selecting indicators for multivariate measurement and modeling with latent variables: When "good" indicators are bad, and "bad" indicators are good. *Psychological Methods, 4,* 192–211.

MacCallum, R. C., Roznowski, M., & Necowitz, L. B. (1992). Model modifications in covariance structure analysis: The problem of capitalization on chance. *Psychological Bulletin, 111,* 490–504.

McDonald, R. P. (1999). *Test theory: A unified treatment.* Mahwah, NJ: Lawrence Erlbaum Associates, Inc.

Mellenbergh, G. J. (1989). Item bias and item response theory. *International Journal of Educational Research, 13,* 127–143.

Meredith, W. (1964). Notes on factorial invariance. *Psychometrika, 29,* 177–185.

Meredith, W. (1993). Measurement invariance, factor analysis, and factorial invariance. *Psychometrika, 58,* 525–543.

Meredith, W., & Horn, J. (2001). The role of factorial invariance in modeling growth and change. In L. M. Collins & A. G. Sayer (Eds.), *New methods for the analysis of change* (pp. 203–240). Washington, DC: American Psychological Association.

Meredith, W., & Millsap, R. E. (1992). On the misuse of manifest variables in the detection of measurement bias. *Psychometrika, 57,* 289–311.

Millsap, R. E., & Kwok, O. M. (2004). Evaluating the impact of partial factorial invariance on selection in multiple populations. *Psychological Methods, 9,* 93–115.

Millsap, R. E., & Tein, J.-Y. (2004). Assessing factorial invariance in ordered-categorical measures. *Multivariate Behavioral Research, 39,* 479–515.

Muthén, B. O. (1978). Contributions to factor analysis of dichotomized variables. *Psychometrika, 43,* 551–560.

Muthén, B. O. (1984). A general structural equation model with dichotomous, ordered categorical and continuous latent variable indicators. *Psychometrika, 49,* 115–132.

Muthén, B. O., & Christoffersson, A. (1981). Simultaneous factor analysis of dichotomous variables in several groups. *Psychometrika, 46,* 407–419.

Muthén, B. O., du Toit, S. H. C., & Spisac, D. (2002). *Robust inference using weighted least squares and quadratic estimating equations in latent variable modeling with categorical and continuous outcomes.* Unpublished manuscript.

Muthén, L. K., & Muthén, B. O. (1998). *Mplus User's Guide.* Los Angeles: Muthén & Muthén.

Poon, W. Y., Lee, S. Y., Afifi, A. A., & Bentler, P. M. (1990). Analysis of multivariate polytomous variates in several groups via the partition maximum likelihood approach. *Computational Statistics and Data Analysis, 10,* 17–27.

Rensvold, R. B., & Cheung, G. W. (2001). Testing for metric invariance using structural equation models: Solving the standardization problem. *Research in Management, 1,* 25–50.

Shealy, R., & Stout, W. (1993). An item response theory model for test bias and differential test functioning. In P. Holland & H. Wainer (Eds.), *Differential item functioning* (pp. 197–240). Hillsdale, NJ: Lawrence Erlbaum Association, Inc.

Steenkamp, J. E. M., & Baumgartner, H. (1998). Assessing measurement invariance in cross-national consumer research. *Journal of Consumer Research, 25,* 78–90.

Stout, W. (1990). A new item response theory modeling approach with applications to unidimensionality assessment and ability estimation. *Psychometrika, 55,* 293–325.

Thurstone, L. L. (1947). *Multiple Factor Analysis.* Chicago: University of Chicago Press.

Vandenberg, R. J., & Lance, C. E. (2000). A review and synthesis of the measurement invariance literature: Suggestions, practices, and recommendations for organizational resarch. *Organizational Research Methods, 3,* 4–70.

7

Looking Back on the Indeterminacy Controversies in Factor Analysis

Stanley A. Mulaik
Georgia Institute of Technology

ROTATIONAL INDETERMINACY

The common factor analysis model has two forms of indeterminacy: (a) rotational indeterminacy and (b) factor indeterminacy. To discuss these, let us first specify the model equation of the common factor analysis model and the fundamental theorem derived from it. The model equation of common factor analysis is

$$\eta = \Lambda \xi + \Psi \varepsilon, \tag{1}$$

where η is a $p \times 1$ random vector of observed random variables, Λ is a $p \times m$ matrix of factor pattern coefficients (which indicate how much a unit change of a common factor effects a change in a corresponding observed variable), ξ is an $m \times 1$ random vector of latent (hypothetical) common factor variables, Ψ is a $p \times p$ diagonal matrix of unique factor pattern loadings, and ε is a $p \times 1$ random vector of unique factor variances. We will assume without loss of generality that all variables have zero means and that the common factor and unique factor variables have unit variances so that $\{\mathrm{diag}[\mathrm{var}(\xi)]\} = \mathbf{I}$ and $\mathrm{var}(\varepsilon) = \mathbf{I}$, where $\mathrm{var}(\xi)$ denotes the $p \times p$ variance–covariance matrix of the common factor variables. A fundamental set of assumptions of the common factor model, which introduce prior constraints into the model, is that $\mathrm{cov}(\boldsymbol{\xi}, \boldsymbol{\varepsilon}) = \mathbf{0}$ and $\mathrm{var}(\boldsymbol{\varepsilon}) = \mathbf{I}$, which implies that the common factor variables are uncorrelated with the unique factor variables and further that the unique factor variables are also mutually uncorrelated. From the model equation, the additional fact that we assume that $\boldsymbol{\Psi}$ is a $p \times p$ diagonal matrix, and these covariance constraints one can readily derive the fundamental theorem of common factor analysis given by the equation

$$\boldsymbol{\Sigma} = \boldsymbol{\Lambda}\boldsymbol{\Phi}\boldsymbol{\Lambda}' + \boldsymbol{\Psi}^2, \tag{2}$$

where $\boldsymbol{\Sigma} = \mathrm{var}(\boldsymbol{\eta})$ is the $p \times p$ variance–covariance matrix for the observed variables, $\boldsymbol{\Lambda}$ is the $p \times m$ matrix of factor pattern coefficients (as before), $\boldsymbol{\Phi} = \mathrm{var}(\boldsymbol{\xi})$ is the $m \times m$ variance/covariance matrix for the common factors, and $\boldsymbol{\Psi}^2 = \boldsymbol{\Psi}\,\mathrm{var}(\boldsymbol{\varepsilon})\boldsymbol{\Psi} = \boldsymbol{\Psi}\mathbf{I}\boldsymbol{\Psi}$ is a diagonal matrix of unique variances, representing in its principal diagonal the respective variance within each observed variable due to its corresponding unique factor variable. The diagonality of $\boldsymbol{\Psi}^2$, which implies that its off-diagonal elements are all zero, also means that the covariances off the principal diagonal of $\boldsymbol{\Lambda}\boldsymbol{\Phi}\boldsymbol{\Lambda}'$ are only functions of the common factors. So one can conclude that covariances between observed variables represent effects of only the common factors. On the other hand, the total variance of each observed variable in $\boldsymbol{\eta}$, which is its corresponding element in the principal diagonal of $\boldsymbol{\Sigma}$, is the sum of the corresponding diagonal elements in $\boldsymbol{\Lambda}\boldsymbol{\Phi}\boldsymbol{\Lambda}'$ and $\boldsymbol{\Psi}^2$.

Rotational indeterminacy arises from the following fact. Given the model in Equation in 1, we may postmultiply $\boldsymbol{\Lambda}$ by any arbitrary $m \times m$ nonsingular transformation matrix $\mathbf{T}$ and premultiply $\boldsymbol{\xi}$ by $\mathbf{T}^{-1}$, the inverse matrix of $\mathbf{T}$, to obtain

$$\boldsymbol{\eta} = \boldsymbol{\Lambda}\mathbf{T}\mathbf{T}^{-1}\boldsymbol{\xi} + \boldsymbol{\Psi}\boldsymbol{\varepsilon} = \boldsymbol{\Lambda}^{*}\boldsymbol{\xi}^{*} + \boldsymbol{\Psi}\boldsymbol{\varepsilon}, \tag{3}$$

where $\boldsymbol{\Lambda}^{*} = \boldsymbol{\Lambda}\mathbf{T}$ and $\boldsymbol{\xi}^{*} = \mathbf{T}^{-1}\boldsymbol{\xi}$. This equation is also a model equation for the common factor model, but in terms of $\boldsymbol{\Lambda}^{*}$ and $\boldsymbol{\xi}^{*}$. The name *rotational indeterminacy* refers to the fact that the transformation matrix $\mathbf{T}$ and its inverse $\mathbf{T}^{-1}$ transform $\boldsymbol{\Lambda}$ and $\boldsymbol{\xi}$, respectively, into a new factor pattern matrix and corresponding set of common factor variables, which represent corresponding "rotations" or transformations of the original factor pattern matrix and common factor variables. The corresponding variance–covariance matrix for the observed variables in terms of these new factors is given by

$$\boldsymbol{\Sigma} = \boldsymbol{\Lambda}\boldsymbol{\Phi}\boldsymbol{\Lambda}' + \boldsymbol{\Psi}^2 = \boldsymbol{\Lambda}^{*}\boldsymbol{\Phi}^{*}\boldsymbol{\Lambda}^{*\prime} + \boldsymbol{\Psi}^2, \tag{4}$$

where $\boldsymbol{\Lambda}^{*} = \boldsymbol{\Lambda}\mathbf{T}$ and $\boldsymbol{\Phi}^{*} = \mathbf{T}^{-1}\boldsymbol{\Phi}\mathbf{T}^{-1\prime}$. The same covariances are modeled by a different set of common factor variables and factor pattern coefficients.

That $\mathbf{T}$ is arbitrary makes the model equation not unique and the common factors not unique. This is the basis for rotational indeterminacy. Which factors and which factor pattern matrix should one use? Thurstone (1947) solved this problem with the concept of factor rotation to simple structure. He argued that it is reasonable to assume that all of the variables come from a domain in which all of the variables of the domain are various linear functions of the same set of common factors. However, some variables will be linear functions of only subsets of the full set of common factors; in fact, he said it was reasonable to assume that nature is relatively simple in that most observed variables are functions of only a subset of the full set of common factors of the domain. This has a remarkable consequence. If one could plot all the potential observed variables and common factors in an m-dimensional vector space where each variable and each factor is a vector in that space, then the observed variable vectors would tend to fall within m smaller dimensional subspaces of $m - 1$ dimensions of the full m-dimensional common factor space. The observed variables would arrange themselves into a pattern in which there would be large holes in the full-dimensional space containing few or no observed variables, whereas certain subspaces containing all variables dependent on a specific set of $m - 1$ of the common factors would contain a relatively large number of observed variables. The common factors would be at the intersections of these subspaces, representing the fact that they are common factors in $m - 1$ of the subspaces. Even more remarkable is the fact that in any representative selection of observed variables from the full domain of observed variables, the same subspaces could be identified, and in turn the common factors would be identified at their intersections. Thurstone (1947) called finding such a solution the "simple structure" solution because it would be the solution in which the preponderance of the variables were dependent on only a smaller number than the full number of common factors. It would be an objective solution because it would yield almost always the same common factors with different samples of observed variables from the domain. It did not matter what solution one began with for the factor pattern matrix and the common factors; the factor pattern matrix for the factors of the simple structure matrix could be identified by moving around m vectors known as reference axes arbitrarily inserted in the common factor space to find for each reference axis large numbers of distinct sets of observed variables orthogonal to them. Orthogonal to each reference axis would then be a subspace of $m - 1$ dimensions containing a number of observed variable vectors. These subspaces would be the subspaces sought at the intersection of which would be the common factors. The cosines of the angles between observed variable vectors and the reference axis vectors would be analogous to correlations between the observed variables and variables corresponding to the reference axes. From this there would be equations that would directly yield the factor pattern matrix for the simple structure solution and the matrix of correlations among the simple structure common factors. The factor pattern matrix and the matrix of correlations among the common factors of the simple structure solution could then be interpreted to determine the common factors of the domain—or so everyone thought. So, the rotational indeterminacy problem was solved by a solution for the common factors that would be independent of the researcher and the particular set of observed variables sampled from the domain. From that point on it was only a matter of working out computing algorithms for identifying factor pattern matrices of such a simple structure solution. But this is another topic for another occasion.

FACTOR INDETERMINACY

Early History

There is, however, another form of indeterminacy that Thurstone seems not to have paid much heed to. Discussion of it had already taken place in the literature as he put forth his simple structure solution. However, much of that literature was in British journals, and Thurstone and his students and their students tended to ignore the British journals because, I believe, they thought they were the current avant guard in factor analysis and there was nothing much to be gained by reading the old literature on factor analysis, which had been mostly in British journals up to the beginning of World War II in 1939. Furthermore, a number of the British factor analysts in the mid-1930s believed they had finally laid this form of indeterminacy to rest. So, perhaps Thurstone and his students did not think there was another indeterminacy problem to contend with.

This form of indeterminacy is known as *factor indeterminacy*. Even if you know a factor pattern matrix for a simple structure solution, and the corresponding correlations among the common factors, this is not sufficient to uniquely identify the common and unique factors. Mathematically there exists an infinite set of distinct variables that one could construct as having the same pattern of correlations with the observed variables as do the common and unique factors of a given factor analysis solution. So, which variables in the world are the common factors?

E. B. Wilson, a past president of the American Statistical Association, who had edited and published Gibbs's ground-breaking lecture notes on vector analysis (the calculus of vectors) (Wilson, 1901), and who was a public health statistician at Harvard, confronted Charles Spearman's theory of the g factor of intelligence (Spearman, 1927) in a series of articles (Wilson, 1928a, 1928b, 1929), Wilson pointed out that Spearman's model did not uniquely determine what g is. Wilson's argument drew on his sophistication with vectors and his realization that the g variable would correspond to a vector in a space of $p + m$ dimensions for which there would be only p observed equations, each corresponding to an observed variable, by which to determine it. In other words, there were not enough equations to uniquely determine the vector in a space of at least $p + m$ dimensions. Spearman thought he had already overcome that problem in a previous article (Spearman, 1922). There he argued that the g factor variable is determinate if p, the number of observed variables, is infinite. Of course, that is not a very realistic solution. So, in response to Wilson, Spearman (1929) suggested that the indeterminacy in identifying g could be eliminated if one simply found an additional test that was perfectly correlated with g, which seemed feasible.

Piaggio (1931, 1933) showed that if the number of tests satisfying the single-common-factor model could be increased indefinitely (and the added tests each has nonzero absolute correlation with g), then the multiple correlation of the tests with g would approach unity in the limit, and this would make the g factor determinate, because one could perfectly predict its scores from the scores on the observed variables. A variant of this would be to find a finite number of variables whose correlations with g each exceeded a certain absolute magnitude so that their multiple correlation would be unity with the g factor. This is just a variation on Spearman's idea of finding a single variable that has a correlation of unity with g. Spearman (1933, 1934) subsequently argued that the problem with measuring g was just a problem of imprecision and error of measurement, and with a sufficient number of tests one would be able to determine g and scores on g precisely.

Guttman Generates Controversy

As indicated earlier, this may have been why Thurstone and his students did not pay much heed to the factor indeterminacy problem. It was not until Guttman (1955) raised the issue again that the issue received further attention, but only briefly. Guttman argued that the factor indeterminacy problem was not simply an indeterminacy in determining the scores on a common factor, but also a problem of not knowing to which variable a common factor referred in the world.

To understand this, let us establish the following background. The multiple regression equation for predicting a variable from a set of other variables requires that one have only the scores on the predictor variables, the covariances among the predictor variables, and the covariances between predictors and the variable(s) predicted. All of this is available in a common factor analysis. Obviously one has the scores on the observed variables and the covariances among the observed variables. The covariances between the observed variables and the common factors are the coefficients of the factor structure matrix, which is readily obtained from the factor pattern matrix Λ and the matrix Φ of covariances among the common factors of the factor analysis. In other words, given Λ and Φ, the matrix of covariances between observed variables and common factors is given by $\Xi = \Lambda\Phi$. Then the matrix of regression coefficients for predicting the common factors is given by $\mathbf{B} = \Sigma^{-1}\Xi$. Assuming without loss of generality that all variables have zero means, we find the regression equation for estimating the common factor variables from the observed variables as

$$\hat{\xi} = \Xi'\Sigma^{-1}\eta. \qquad (5)$$

The equation gives the corresponding estimated scores $\hat{\xi}$ on the common factors for a given random observation of the random vector of observed scores η. These are not the actual factor scores of the common factors ξ themselves. The accuracy of the population estimate of a common factor variable is given by the predicted variance of the common factor divided by the total variance of the common factor variable, which here is unity by choice. This can be obtained simultaneously for each common factor by first finding the diagonal elements of the matrix of covariances among the estimated common factor variables. That is,

$$\text{var}(\hat{\xi}) = E(\Xi'\Sigma^{-1}\eta\eta'\Sigma^{-1}\Xi) = \Xi'\Sigma^{-1}\Xi = \Phi\Lambda'\Sigma^{-1}\Lambda\Phi. \tag{6}$$

The proportion of total variance of each factor that is predictable from the observed variables is thus given by the diagonal elements of the following diagonal matrix:

$$\Pi = [\text{diag } \Phi]^{-1}[\text{diag } \Phi\Lambda'\Sigma^{-1}\Lambda\Phi], \tag{7a}$$

where [diag C] denotes a diagonal matrix whose principal diagonal elements are the principal diagonal elements of C. We can show Π in more expanded form as

$$\Pi = \begin{bmatrix} \rho_1^2 & 0 & \cdots & 0 \\ 0 & \rho_2^2 & \cdots & 0 \\ \vdots & \vdots & \ddots & \vdots \\ 0 & 0 & \cdots & \rho_m^2 \end{bmatrix}. \tag{7b}$$

The square root of ρ_j^2 for the jth common factor is the multiple correlation coefficient that represents the correlation between $\hat{\xi}_j$, the random estimate of the jth common factor, and ξ_j, the jth common factor itself.

Similar equations can be obtained for estimating the unique factor variables:

$$\hat{\varepsilon} = \Psi\Sigma^{-1}\eta, \tag{8}$$

$$\text{var}(\hat{\varepsilon}) = \Psi\Sigma^{-1}\Psi, \tag{9}$$

$$\Gamma = [\text{diag } \Psi\Sigma^{-1}\Psi]. \tag{10}$$

Guttman argued that the common factors would be determined by the observed variables if the squared multiple correlations for predicting each were unity. But almost always they are not. Guttman realized that a correlation coefficient corresponds to the cosine of the angle between two vectors representing two variables. In this case it is the cosine between a vector representing the regression estimate $\hat{\xi}_j$ and a vector representing the common factor ξ_j itself. Then Guttman noted that interpreting a factor involves examining its factor pattern coefficients in Λ and the correlations among the common factors in Φ. These in turn determine the covariances between observed variables and common factors given by the factor structure matrix Ξ. So, he reasoned, all of the information involved in interpreting a common factor is summarized in the factor structure matrix, and this is also the basis for the estimate of the common factor variable. He then argued that any number of variables might have the same pattern of covariances with the observed variables as do the common factors of the factor analysis. The correlation between any one of these variables ξ_j and the estimate of the common factor $\hat{\xi}_j$ would equal the multiple correlation between the observed variables in η and the common factor ξ_j. Schönemann (1971) and Mulaik (1972, 1976b) illustrated the situation graphically by showing how all possible alternative variables ξ_j' having the same correlation with $\hat{\xi}_j$ could be represented by vectors, and the locus of these variables would form a cone around a vector representing the estimate $\hat{\xi}_j$ of the common factor. The cosine of the angle between any vector in the cone and the vector in the center representing the estimate of the common factor would equal the multiple correlation. This is illustrated in Fig. 7.1.

Guttman then suggested that an index of indeterminacy could be obtained from the worst-case scenario in which two alternative variables chosen as the interpretation of the common factor would correspond to vectors that lie directly opposite one another across the cone. The angle between these two vectors would be twice the angle between any vector in the cone and the vector representing the estimate of the common factor. The correlation between these two alternative variables would then equal the cosine of the double angle between the opposing vectors across the cone. From the well-known trigonometric formula for the cosine of a double angle given the cosine for the single angle, $\cos 2\theta = 2\cos^2 \theta - 1$, and noting that the multiple correlation is the cosine of the angle between the common

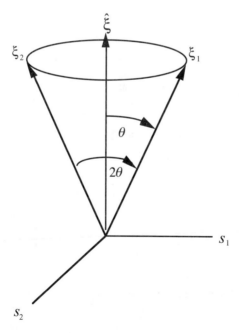

FIG. 7.1. Cone containing all vectors ξ_i having an angle of θ with $\hat{\xi}$, the regression estimate of the common factor ξ, where $\cos \theta = \rho$.

factor and the regression estimate of it, Guttman showed that the correlation between two minimally correlated alternative variables chosen as interpretations of the common factor would be

$$\omega_j = 2\rho_j^2 - 1.$$

Guttman then drew some consequences from this formula. Specifically, if the multiple correlation is less than .7071, then the correlation between minimally correlated alternative solutions for the common factor would be negative. For example, if the multiple correlation were .50, then the minimal correlation between any two candidate variables for the common factor would be $2(.25) - 1 = -.50$, which suggests that two, somewhat contrary variables could each be possible common factors. Guttman suggested that this had negative consequences for the common factor model. McDonald (1974) extracted the crucial criticisms in Guttman's (1955) paper. Guttman (1955) said first, "it seems that the sought-for traits are not very distinguishable from radically different possible alternative traits, for the identical factor loadings" (p. 74). Then Guttman noted that if the squared multiple correlation for estimating a factor from the observed variables is low, "it raises the question of what it is that is being estimated in the first place; instead of only *one* 'primary trait' there are many widely different variables associated with a given profile of loadings" (p. 79). He further concluded, "if more direct observations on the [factor scores] cannot be made than statistical analysis of Σ and η, the Spearman–Thurstone approach may have to be discarded for lack of determinacy of its factor scores" (p. 79).

Guttman also demonstrated that the indeterminacy was not simply a problem of only being able to estimate the scores on the common factor. The problem was that an unlimited number of distinct solutions for the common and unique factors of the common factor model could be *constructed*. In other words, we can construct variables that have the mathematical properties of common factors and unique factors, but we cannot do this uniquely. What follows draws on Guttman (1955), Schönemann and Wang (1972), McDonald (1974), and Mulaik (1976a, 1976b). To construct factor variables, we need a set of s mutually independent random variables, $s \geq p + 1$, arranged in a random vector σ, which has the further properties that $\mathbf{E}(\sigma) = \mathbf{0}$, and var$(\sigma) = \mathbf{I}$, and cov$(\eta, \sigma) = \mathbf{0}$. In other words, σ is uncorrelated with the observed variables in η and furthermore consists of mutually uncorrelated variables with unit variances and zero means. It is not meant to be exhaustive of all possible variables orthogonal to η nor to be the basis for all possible solutions, but simply to demonstrate the possibilities for alternative solutions. From the estimating equations 5 and 8 and the random vector σ we will be able to construct variables that have the properties of common factors and unique factors. The idea is to construct from σ vectors of residual variables to be added, respectively, to each vector of estimated variables. Thus the constructed common factors are given by

$$\mathbf{x} = \Phi\Lambda'\Sigma^{-1}\eta + \mathbf{Ps}, \tag{11}$$

where $\mathbf{P}$ is any $m \times m$ gram factor of the residual covariance matrix for the common factors after the parts of them predictable by linear regression from the observed variables have been partialed out, that is, $\mathbf{PP'} = (\mathbf{\Phi} - \mathbf{\Xi}\mathbf{\Sigma}^{-1}\mathbf{\Xi})$, $\mathbf{s} = \mathbf{T}_1\mathbf{MT}_2\boldsymbol{\sigma}$. Here $\mathbf{T}$, is an arbitrary $m \times m$ orthogonal transformation matrix; $\mathbf{M}$ is an $m \times s$ selection matrix, $\mathbf{M} = [\mathbf{I} : \mathbf{0}]$; and $\mathbf{T}_2$ is an arbitrary $s \times s$ orthonormal transformation matrix. The expression $\mathbf{s} = \mathbf{T}_1\mathbf{MT}_2\boldsymbol{\sigma}$ functions in the following way: $\mathbf{T}_2$ performs an orthogonal rotation on the s-dimensional random vector $\boldsymbol{\sigma}$ and feeds the result to $\mathbf{M}$, which extracts the first m variables of the result and feeds them in turn into the orthonormal $m \times m$ transformation matrix $\mathbf{T}_1$. The matrix $\mathbf{T}_1$, rotates the preceding resulting vector to $\mathbf{s}$, which consists then of mutually uncorrelated variables also, and these are then modified by $\mathbf{P}$ to yield random variables having a covariance matrix equal to the residual covariance matrix of the unpredictable part of the common factors. From the model equation for common factor analysis, Equation 1, we are able also to solve for $\boldsymbol{\varepsilon}$ as $\boldsymbol{\varepsilon} = \mathbf{\Psi}^{-1}(\boldsymbol{\eta} - \mathbf{\Lambda}\boldsymbol{\xi})$. By substituting $\mathbf{x}$ for $\boldsymbol{\xi}$, we obtain

$$\mathbf{e} = \mathbf{\Psi}^{-1}[\boldsymbol{\eta} - \mathbf{\Lambda}(\mathbf{\Phi}\mathbf{\Lambda}'\mathbf{\Sigma}^{-1}\boldsymbol{\eta} + \mathbf{Ps})],$$

which may be simplified to

$$\mathbf{e} = \mathbf{\Psi}\mathbf{\Sigma}^{-1}\boldsymbol{\eta} - \mathbf{\Psi}^{-1}\mathbf{\Lambda}\mathbf{Ps}. \tag{12}$$

Conceiving of s as a rotation and extraction from a much larger dimensional vector of mutually uncorrelated variables $\boldsymbol{\sigma}$ was a contribution of Mulaik (1976a, 1976b), which provided the algebra to show how a cone of alternative solutions could be obtained by orthogonal rotations of a set of variables orthogonal to $\hat{\boldsymbol{\xi}}$. Varying the rotation matrices $\mathbf{T}_1$ and $\mathbf{T}_2$ generates the different solutions for the constructed common factors in $\mathbf{x}$ and the unique factors in $\mathbf{e}$. However, if s is many times larger than $p + m$, numerous alternative vectors $\mathbf{s}_2, \mathbf{s}_2, \ldots$ may be extracted that have the property that $\mathrm{cov}(\mathbf{s}_j, \mathbf{s}_k) = \mathbf{0}$, $j \neq k$. In those cases the correlation between alternative solutions for a common factor will equal the squared multiple correlation for predicting the common or unique factor in question.

Now, one may remain skeptical that arbitrarily constructed $\mathbf{x}$ and $\mathbf{e}$ behave as common and unique factor variables, respectively. We can show that they behave in all respects as common and unique factors for $\boldsymbol{\eta}$. If by the model equation we can show that $\mathbf{\Lambda}\mathbf{x} + \mathbf{\Psi}\mathbf{e}$ equals $\boldsymbol{\eta}$, we establish the first property, that they satisfy the model equation:

$$\begin{aligned}
\mathbf{\Lambda}\mathbf{x} + \mathbf{\Psi}\mathbf{e} &= \mathbf{\Lambda}(\mathbf{\Phi}\mathbf{\Lambda}'\mathbf{\Sigma}^{-1}\boldsymbol{\eta} + \mathbf{Ps}) + \mathbf{\Psi}(\mathbf{\Psi}\mathbf{\Sigma}^{-1}\boldsymbol{\eta} - \mathbf{\Psi}^{-1}\mathbf{\Lambda}\mathbf{Ps}) \\
&= (\mathbf{\Lambda}\mathbf{\Phi}\mathbf{\Lambda}'\mathbf{\Sigma}^{-1}\boldsymbol{\eta} + \mathbf{\Lambda}\mathbf{Ps}) + (\mathbf{\Psi}^2\mathbf{\Sigma}^{-1}\boldsymbol{\eta} - \mathbf{\Lambda}\mathbf{Ps}) \\
&= \mathbf{\Lambda}\mathbf{\Phi}\mathbf{\Lambda}'\mathbf{\Sigma}^{-1}\boldsymbol{\eta} + \mathbf{\Psi}^2\mathbf{\Sigma}^{-1}\boldsymbol{\eta} \\
&= (\mathbf{\Sigma} - \mathbf{\Psi}^2)\mathbf{\Sigma}^{-1}\boldsymbol{\eta} + \mathbf{\Psi}^2\mathbf{\Sigma}^{-1}\boldsymbol{\eta} \\
&= \mathbf{\Sigma}\mathbf{\Sigma}^{-1}\boldsymbol{\eta} - \mathbf{\Psi}^2\mathbf{\Sigma}^{-1}\boldsymbol{\eta} + \mathbf{\Psi}^2\mathbf{\Sigma}^{-1}\boldsymbol{\eta} \\
&= \boldsymbol{\eta}.
\end{aligned}$$

Although tedious, it can be further shown that $\text{cov}(\eta, \mathbf{x}) = \mathbf{\Lambda\Phi}$, $\text{cov}(\mathbf{x}, \mathbf{e}) = \mathbf{0}$, $\text{var}(\mathbf{x}) = \mathbf{\Phi}$, and $\text{var}(\mathbf{e}) = \mathbf{I}$, all properties of common and unique factors, respectively. I leave proof as an exercise for the reader.

It should be noted that prior to his 1955 paper, Guttman (1953) developed his "image analysis" model as a determinate but analogous alternative to the common factor model. There he defined an analogue of the common factor part of a variable as the image of the variable projected onto all of the other variables in a domain of infinitely many variables. The analogue of the communality of the variable was the squared multiple correlation for predicting the variable from all of the other variables in the domain. The image thus is the part of the variable that could be predicted by multiple regression from all the other variables in the domain. The anti-image, on the other hand, was the unpredictable part of the variable that could not be predicted from all the other variables in the domain and was analogous to the unique factor part of the variable. Guttman (1956) then showed that if the common factor model (applied to an infinite number of tests from the domain) were determinate in the domain, so that its common factors would be determinate in the domain, then the image analysis and common factor analysis models would converge to the same model in the infinite domain. For a finite selection of variables from the domain, the "partial image" of a variable was the part of the variable that could be predicted from the $p - 1$ other variables in the selection. The "partial anti-image" was the corresponding residual or unpredictable part. The squared multiple correlation for predicting a variable from the $p - 1$ other variables in the selection was analogous, but a lower bound, to the communality of the variable. Analogous to factoring the reduced covariance matrix $\mathbf{\Sigma} - \mathbf{\Psi}^2$ was factoring the partial image covariance matrix $\mathbf{G} = \mathbf{\Sigma} + \mathbf{S}^2\mathbf{\Sigma}^{-1}\mathbf{S}^2 - 2\mathbf{S}^2$, where $\mathbf{S}^2 = [\text{diag } \mathbf{\Sigma}^{-1}]^{-1}$. His development of image analysis showed his profound commitment to the idea that to be useful, a scientific model or method must produce determinate latent entities. We question this assumption later.

Schönemann

Guttman (1955) made some very serious accusations regarding the common factor model, but these were largely ignored for the next 15 years until Schönemann (1971) published a paper supportive of Guttman's position. Schönemann showed in that paper that alternative constructed solutions for the common and unique factors could be obtained by a linear transformation of a given solution. Schönemann also worked out matrix equations for simultaneously finding for each common factor and each unique factor Guttman's minimum correlation between alternative solutions for the factor. This is given by $\mathbf{T} = [\text{diag}\,(2\mathbf{\Xi}'\mathbf{\Sigma}^{-1}\mathbf{\Xi} - \mathbf{I})]$ for the common factors and by $\mathbf{U} = [\text{diag}\,2(\mathbf{\Psi}\mathbf{\Sigma}^{-1}\mathbf{\Psi} - \mathbf{I})]$ for the unique factors. He then defined the average minimum correlation between equivalent sets of factors as

$$\tau = \frac{1}{m + p}\,(\text{tr}\mathbf{T} + \text{tr}\mathbf{U}),$$

where tr($\bullet$) is the trace of the matrix within parentheses, which is the sum of its principal diagonal elements. If the factors are furthermore uncorrelated, then the factor structure matrix $\Xi = \Lambda$. In that special case he showed that the minimum average correlation between alternative sets of factors is invariant under orthogonal rotations of the factors.

Schönemann and Wang (1972) worked out corresponding equations for the sample case using maximum likelihood estimation, in particular equations for constructing common and unique factor variables equivalent to Equations 11 and 12. They showed that one could construct factor scores by sample analogues of Equations 11 and, 12 using computer-generated random numbers to generate an $m \times N$ score matrix the rows of which are row centered and orthogonalized with respect to other rows. Of special interest is their reanalysis of 13 published common factor analysis studies in which they demonstrated a number of studies in which the smallest obtained minimum correlation between alternative factors was negative, sometimes on the order of $-.466$

McDonald (1974)

Schönemann (1971) and Schönemann and Wang (1972) evidently provoked McDonald (1974) to review Guttman (1955) and other early historical papers on factor indeterminacy. He concluded that Guttman's index of factor indeterminacy, the minimum correlation between alternative factors, was "inconsistent with the foundations of the factor model in probability theory" (McDonald, 1974, p. 203). McDonald's paper, when submitted to and eventually accepted by *Psychometrika* after more than the usual number of revisions, became a focus for controversy among some of the paper's reviewers, McDonald, and the journal's editor, Bert Green. Green seemed not to appreciate the seriousness of the matter. In a review of an early version of Mulaik (1976a, 1976b), Guttman (who revealed his identity after Mulaik's had been inadvertently revealed on the manuscript sent to him for review) quoted Bert Green as having written to him on March 13, 1973, in connection with the turmoil surrounding the reviews and multiple revisions of MacDonald's (1974) paper: "I sometimes get the feeling that we are enthusiastically counting the number of angels dancing on the head of a multidimensional pin." Whereas there were those like Guttman and Schönemann who advocated the cosine of the angle across the diameter of the cone as an index of indeterminacy, others like McDonald advocated the cosine of the angle between the center and circumference.

A major preoccupation of McDonald in that paper was the idea that alternative solutions for the common and unique factors of the common factor model could be constructed as linear transformations of some initial set of variables, making it possible to construct alternative factors that would be diametrically opposite across a cone that was the locus of linearly related alternative factors. McDonald went to considerable trouble to prove that there could be alternative solutions that were not linear transforms of one another. However McDonald did not have $\mathbf{s} = \mathbf{T}_1 \mathbf{M} \mathbf{T}_2 \boldsymbol{\sigma}$ at that point, for it appeared later (Mulaik, 1976b). Defining $\mathbf{s}$ this way, however, makes it easy to demonstrate this point, if one imagines that the s-dimensional space containing the vector $\boldsymbol{\sigma}$ spans at least a countably infinite number of dimensions. Thus, different orthonormal transformations of $\boldsymbol{\sigma}$ are going to present different sets of random variables to be extracted by the filter matrix M, many of which will be mutually uncorrelated. The consequences will be as stated earlier, that $\mathrm{cov}(\mathbf{s}_j, \mathbf{s}_k) = \mathbf{0}$, $j \neq k$, in numerous pairs of cases. McDonald noted that

> There is no clear evidence that any recent writer on this question [of factor indeterminacy] has envisaged the existence of alternative factors or, what is the same thing, arbitrary components, that are not linearly related. Yet, in a certain sense, the latter case is infinitely more numerous than the former. (McDonald, 1974, p. 211)

McDonald (1974) did not establish a proof for the relative numerosity of linear-related to linear-unrelated cases that he asserts. Certainly, the uncorrelated, $\mathbf{s}_j$ and $\mathbf{s}_k$ will each generate uncountably many linearly related alternative sets of common and unique factor variables. All those generated as linear transforms of each $\mathbf{s}_j$ will be mutually uncorrelated with each of the linear transforms of $\mathbf{s}_k$ because linear transforms of vectors within mutually orthogonal spaces are still orthogonal with all vectors in the other space. However, because uncountable infinities are involved, a more rigorous proof would be needed to support this conjecture.

One motivation for establishing that mutually uncorrelated alternative solutions are more common than those that are correlated nonzero is that in those cases the correlation between alternative factors equals the squared multiple correlation. It was the squared multiple correlation that McDonald (1974) believed was the more appropriate index of factor indeterminacy. For example, let $\mathbf{x}_1 = \boldsymbol{\Phi}\boldsymbol{\Lambda}'\boldsymbol{\Sigma}^{-1}\boldsymbol{\eta} + \mathbf{P}\mathbf{s}_1$ be a constructed set of common factors based on $\mathbf{s}_1$ and let $\mathbf{x}_2 = \boldsymbol{\Phi}\boldsymbol{\Lambda}'\boldsymbol{\Sigma}^{-1}\boldsymbol{\eta} + \mathbf{P}\mathbf{s}_2$ be a constructed set of common factors based on $\mathbf{s}_2$. Assume further that $\mathrm{cov}(\mathbf{s}_1, \mathbf{s}_2) = 0$. Then

$$\mathrm{cov}(\mathbf{x}_1, \mathbf{x}_2) = \mathrm{E}[(\boldsymbol{\Phi}\boldsymbol{\Lambda}'\boldsymbol{\Sigma}^{-1}\boldsymbol{\eta} + \mathbf{P}\mathbf{s}_1)(\boldsymbol{\Phi}\boldsymbol{\Lambda}'\boldsymbol{\Sigma}^{-1}\boldsymbol{\eta} + \mathbf{P}\mathbf{s}_2)']$$
$$= \boldsymbol{\Phi}\boldsymbol{\Lambda}'\boldsymbol{\Sigma}^{-1}\boldsymbol{\Lambda}\boldsymbol{\Phi},$$

the diagonal elements of which are just the squared multiple correlations for predicting the common factors from the observed variables in $\boldsymbol{\eta}$. However, even if one could establish that this case is relatively more numerous in some sense than those that are based on linear transformations of a given vector $\mathbf{s}$ and particularly than those cases where the pairs of solutions for $\mathbf{x}$ are opposite one another across a cone, this would not rule out Guttman's index as a description of one aspect of the indeterminacy.

Nevertheless, in commenting on Guttman's criticisms of the common factor model because of the indeterminacy of its factors, McDonald said:

> All of these difficulties rest on the assumed correctness of Guttman's choice of an index of factor indeterminacy. The choice is not immediately compelling. At least the same degree of plausibility pertains to the use of the squared multiple correlation of a factor with the observations, or the equivalent measures used by Spearman, Holzinger, Camp, Piaggio, and Thomson. The commonsensical argument would be that we ordinarily measure statistical determinacy in these ways so it is natural to do so in this context. (McDonald, 1974, p. 215)

However, one could say that Guttman's index of indeterminacy and the squared multiple correlation are not only systematically related, but simply describe different aspects of the same indeterminacy, so it is not a question of which is the correct index, but a question of what aspect of the indeterminacy one describes with one or the other index. Guttman's index has a certain shock value in describing the worst possible case, which may not be a common or typical case.

Be that as it may, McDonald (1974) seemed to recognize that something more was needed to make his position convincing. He believed that the answer would lie in a "deeper analysis of the concept of unobservable random variables." He hoped to show, I believe, that Guttman's conception was somehow inconsistent with fundamental conceptions of random variables. Nevertheless his argument is difficult to follow. Guttman claimed (personal communication, July 14, 1976) that Schönemann's student James Steiger read and reread the section of McDonald's paper containing this argument 100 times and could make no sense of it. Even McDonald is said to have later admitted that the argument was badly formulated. Effectively, McDonald argued that the proponents of Guttman's measure of indeterminacy had the view that a common factor variable simultaneously takes on several mutually exclusive values for any given individual, which is patently absurd. He considered a case with a single common factor and then defined two alternative minimally correlated constructed solutions,

$$\xi^+ = \lambda'\Sigma^{-1}\eta + ps \tag{13a}$$

and

$$\xi^- = \lambda'\Sigma^{-1}\eta - ps, \tag{13b}$$

where λ is a $p \times 1$ factor pattern matrix for the single common factor, p is the standard deviation of the residual, and s is a unit-variance variable uncorrelated with any of the variables in η. Suppose that these minimally correlated alternative versions of the common factor are correlated zero, meaning their individual multiple correlations with the observed variables in η is .7071. McDonald then argued:

> It is not here being denied that given η we can contemplate random variables ξ^+ and ξ^- that are possible solutions of the equations of the model, *i.e.* possible values of

the unobservable common factor score coordinate ξ, and that hence we can compute the correlation between these possible solutions. Certainly ξ^+ and ξ^- are defined as functions of η and $\mathbf{s}$, hence they are two random variables defined on the same sample space. But if they are regarded as alternative solutions of one system of equations, *i.e.* as possible distinct values of one variable ξ, then the only prediction of one of them from the other, ... is the logical disjunction of mutually exclusive events. If an individual is at ξ^+, he is not at ξ^-. That is all there is to it. (McDonald, 1974, p. 218)

The best way I can now make sense of what McDonald was trying to prove here is to suppose that he viewed the common factor model as saying nothing about additional variables σ or any other set of variables. So "constructed factors" constructed from additional variables have no meaning in that context. For him, then, the factor indeterminacy problem was simply an estimation problem. The common factor model presumes the existence of latent variables known as common factors and the task is to try to obtain scores on them, which, unhappily we do not have. What we do have are scores on the observed variables, the correlations among the observed variables, and the correlations between the observed variables and the common factors (the factor structure coefficients). That is sufficient information to compute a regression estimate of the common factor scores. The estimation is not perfect, and the multiple correlation coefficient and the squared multiple correlation coefficient are the usual indices of the uncertainty of estimation. So, Guttman's index of factor indeterminacy seemed bizarre to McDonald. What are these alternative constructed factor variables? In the single-common-factor case there is just one common factor that we are estimating. To suggest that these alternative variables are simultaneously the same factor variable is incoherent. The factor variable is just what it is and not several variables simultaneously. To compute the correlation between them is doubly absurd, particularly to compute the minimum correlation between them. If the common factor is a variable with such and such scores, then we know it cannot have other scores, so, in McDonald's view, it would make no sense to predict one set of scores from the other. But there was another way to look at this.

Mulaik (1976a, 1976b)

In Mulaik (1972), a text on the foundations of factor analysis, I drew on Guttman (1955) for a discussion of factor indeterminacy. I do not believe McDonald had seen my text when his drafts for his 1974 paper were undergoing a series of reviews. He made no mention of it. But in my text I came up with the following analogy: Suppose you are able to get measurements of a variable X_1 and someone else tells you that there is another variable X_2 that has a correlation of .8 with X_1. Can you tell from this information which variable in the world is X_2? The answer is that you cannot. Any number of variables may have correlations of .8 with X_1, and these would all be represented by vectors in a cone having an angle whose cosine equals .8 with the vector X_1 in the axis of the cone. The same situation exists in factor analysis. Instead of a single correlation with a single variable, we have, for a given common factor, a pattern of correlations relating it to each of several observed variables as rendered in the factor structure matrix of the factor analysis. Any variable having this pattern of correlations with the observed variables would be a potential candidate for the common factor. I included in the discussion a figure of a cone like that in Fig. 7.1 to illustrate the nature of factor indeterminacy. All variables with the pattern of correlations with the observed variables yielded by the factor structure matrix of the factor analysis would have a multiple correlation, say, of ρ with them. The estimated scores of the common factor would be a stand-in for the observed variables, for any variables that had the pattern of correlations with the observed variables revealed in the factor structure matrix would have a correlation of ρ with the estimated scores. So all candidates for the common factor would be represented by vectors in a cone or hypercone around the estimated factor scores whose angle with the vector representing the estimated factor scores at the axis of the cone would have a cosine equal to ρ. I noted that two alternative candidate factors could be as minimally correlated as $2\rho^2 - 1$, which is the cosine of the double angle across the cone. These minimally correlated candidate factors would correspond to two vectors directly opposite one another across the cone. Guttman (1955) made it clear that factor indeterminacy was not just a problem of determining factor scores, but of using the same information that a regression estimate would use, to interpret and identify the common factor.

When McDonald's (1974) paper was published I was unaware of the turmoil surrounding its publication. However, I believed that McDonald misunderstood the nature of the factor indeterminacy problem and I decided to write a commentary on his paper that would set things right. The paper was eventually accepted in the spring of 1976. I prepared a paper (Mulaik, 1976a) based on the article to appear in *Psychometrika* later that year (Mulaik, 1976b) for presentation at the Psychometric Society annual meeting held April 1–3, 1976, at Bell Labs in Murray Hill, New Jersey. My paper was joined by papers on the topic of factor indeterminacy by James Steiger, Peter Schönemann's student, who spoke on the history of the factor indeterminacy question, and Rod McDonald, who defended his point of view.

In my talk I began by presenting a diagram of the cone like the one in Fig. 7.1 and presented the simple problem of identifying a variable from knowing only its correlation with a known variable and showing how it was analogous to the factor indeterminacy problem. Then I turned to a critique of McDonald (1974), which I thought sought to make two points (although I said I had difficulty understanding the argument): (a) McDonald believed that those who advocated Guttman's formula based on the cosine of the double angle assumed that all alternative versions of the common factor were simultaneously the factor to be identified, which, he held, is logically impossible. (b) Granting Guttman's position for the sake of argument, McDonald also questioned whether the relative occurrence of minimally correlated solutions is not infinitesimally small compared to the relative occurrence of other pairs of solutions. He therefore recommended use of the squared multiple correlation as an index of indeterminacy.

In tackling the first objection, I argued that there was no need to choose between Guttman's index and the squared multiple correlation, because they described two different aspects of factor indeterminacy. More important was simply to recognize the nature of the indeterminacy problem. My simple problem of identifying a second variable from knowing only its correlation with a first variable recast the indeterminacy problem into one of not having enough information to uniquely determine which of many possible variables in the world might be the common factor. There is one subtle point that should be recognized, however. Guttman, Schönemann, and I had changed the rules. Thinking of how we use the results of a common factor model, we took it for granted, without realizing we were changing the game, that we could introduce additional variables "in the world" into the common factor model, any one of which might be a common factor. The original common factor model makes no mention of these, confining itself to just the variables on which we have scores, and the latent common and unique factors, for which we have no scores. More about this later.

As for the second of McDonald's objections, for the single-factor case, I introduced the device of $\mathbf{s} = \mathbf{MT}\boldsymbol{\sigma}$ as a way of generating "all possible versions" from an indefinitely large random vector $\boldsymbol{\sigma}$ uncorrelated with $\boldsymbol{\eta}$ by the equation $\xi = \boldsymbol{\lambda}'\boldsymbol{\Sigma}^{-1}\boldsymbol{\eta} + (1 - \rho^2)^{1/2}\mathbf{s}$. Here ρ^2 equals the squared multiple correlation for predicting ξ from the variables in $\boldsymbol{\eta}$, $\mathbf{M} = [1 : 0]$, and $\mathbf{T}$ is an orthonormal matrix such that $\mathbf{TT}' = \mathbf{I}$. By varying or rotating $\mathbf{T}$, one generated all versions possible for $\mathbf{s}$ based on $\boldsymbol{\sigma}$ and hence for all corresponding versions of ξ. I noted that in practice researchers rarely seem to have strong disagreements over the interpretation of a given factor. I believed that researchers would provisionally treat the common factors obtained as some varying attribute of something in the world they were familiar with. Each researcher might hypothesize where to look for a common factor variable—perhaps in functioning of certain brain structures such as "working memory" (in the case of intelligence, say, as a factor). The hypothesis could be tested by seeing whether one could measure such an attribute directly and show that it has the appropriate correlations with the original variables of the factor analysis. Each interpretation would correspond to a different version for ξ generated by a different version for $\mathbf{s}$. For a hypothetical population of researchers we could characterize the distribution of different researcher's interpretations of the factor by defining a density function on the surface of an s-dimensional hypersphere generated by all the possible rotations $\mathbf{T}\boldsymbol{\sigma}$. Each point on the surface of this hypersphere would map to one of the alternative versions of the factor by corresponding to a different version for the random variable $\mathbf{s}$. Next I worked out the correlation between alternative versions ξ_a and ξ_b as

$$\rho(\xi_a, \xi_b) = \rho^2 + (1 - \rho^2)\rho(s_a, s_b). \tag{14}$$

The average value of $\rho(\xi_a, \xi_b)$ would be obtained by taking the expected value of Equation 14:

$$E[\rho(\xi_a, \xi_b)] = \rho^2 + (1 - \rho^2)E[\rho(s_a, s_b)].$$

The variance of $\rho(\xi_a, \xi_b)$ is

$$\text{var}[\rho(\xi_a, \xi_b)] = (1 - \rho^2)^2 \, \text{var}[\rho(s_a, s_b)].$$

Under the unrealistic assumption that all researchers would be uniformly distributed across the surface of the s-dimensional hypersphere, I was able to work out, using the gamma distribution, that the mean of the distribution of $\rho(s_a, s_b)$ is zero and the variance of the $\rho(s_a, s_b)$ is $1/s$. The result on the variance of $\rho(s_a, s_b)$ is remarkable because it implies that as the dimensionality $\mathbf{s}$ of the vector σ increases, the variance of $\rho(s_a, s_b)$ converges to zero. Consequently, substituting these values in the previous equations, we get

$$E[\rho(\xi_a, \xi_b)] = \rho^2 \qquad (15)$$

and

$$\text{var}[\rho(\xi_a, \xi_b)] = \frac{(1 - \rho^2)^2}{s} \qquad (16)$$

As the dimensionality s of σ increases without bound, the correlation between alternative versions of the common factor converges in probability to ρ^2. This supported McDonald's second contention that ρ^2 would be infinitely more likely than the Guttman minimum correlation for the correlation between any two versions of the factor. For the more realistic case of a nonuniform distribution of researchers on the surface of the hypersphere, I was able to establish that

$$E[\rho(\xi_a, \xi_b)] \geq \rho^2.$$

However, if all alternative versions were equally likely of being chosen by researchers, it would suggest the gloomy result that all but an infinitesimally small proportion of the correlations between alternative versions of a factor would be equal to ρ^2, meaning there would be practically no agreement between researchers when $\rho^2 < 1$, but practically no cases correlated $2\rho^2 - 1$ as suggested by Guttman either. The more realistic case would be that the distribution is not uniform. In that case the average correlation between alternative versions would be at least ρ^2. I was not able to work out a bound on the variance in this case.

My conclusion was that we did not need to choose between Guttman's index and use of the squared multiple correlation. Both could be retained as descriptive of different aspects of the indeterminacy problem.

At the end of my talk questions were raised from the floor. I particularly remember Darrell Bock's pointing out that the indeterminacy problem is not a fundamental problem because one could simply add more variables and raise the squared multiple correlation. This was the answer that Spearman gave to Wilson, which was supported by Piaggio. I was provoked by that comment to show that this is not a solution to indeterminacy.

Mulaik and McDonald (1978): Debate and Reconciliation

When I returned home from the Psychometric Society meeting I began work on a paper entitled "The effect of additional observed variables on factor indeterminacy in models with a single common factor," which I finished and sent off to *Psychometrika* at the end of April. I also sent a copy to Rod McDonald. In that paper I sought to simplify the problem of additional variables by focusing on a single common factor and the effect of adding further variables to the analysis. The question I raised was

> Given an original study with a specified set of variables, suppose two independent researchers, after seeing the results of the initial analysis of the original set of variables, seize on operationally different conceptions of the factor and construct additional variables that are consistent with the properties of the factor of the original study. Could this sequential process of adding variables to the original variables conceivably converge to different determinate constructs for the original factor? (Mulaik unpublished manuscript.)

In the meantime Mulaik (1976b) was published in June along with a brief note by Green (1976), the editor of *Psychometrika*, on the factor indeterminacy controversy. In that note Green argued:

> I submit that it is more reasonable to claim that the vector of factor score estimates is estimating the entire infinite set of possible factor score vectors. After all, the estimates correlate ρ_g with every one of the z_g^*. All of the z_g^* have exactly the same predictable part, y_g, and that is what is being estimated. The myriad z_g^*'s differ only in their "error" parts (Green, 1976, p. 264).

Green then added that on the basis of my paper ρ_g or ρ_g^2 was the more appropriate index of factor indeterminacy, whereas Guttman's $2\rho_g^2 - 1$ was "grossly unrepresentative". "A better index is the expected correlation between two different score vectors, which is ρ_g^2 " (p. 264). This was ironic because on the one hand Green supported McDonald's recommendation of the use of ρ_g^2, while interpreting factor score indeterminacy as being about how the estimated factor scores estimated simultaneously all the "myriad" alternative versions of the factor. Mc-Donald, I believed then, still believed that there was a domain of variables from which the observed variables were obtained and the common factor was just the common factor of all variables in this domain, and the other myriad so-called factors had no basis in reality. What it would take to get him to see Guttman's version of indeterminacy was to see that in exploratory factor analysis the so-called domain was itself usually not clearly and explicitly defined and there might be several domains one could conceive of from which the variables were drawn and the common factor of which would be a common factor of the original variables.

Be that as it may, back in November 1975 Guttman submitted a paper to *Psychometrika* entitled "The Green–McDonald proof of the nonexistence of factor analysis." Guttman held Green responsible for the publication of McDonald (1974), and with this article sought to expose how, using what he thought were their premises and logic, one would be able to deduce that the common factor model does not exist. In other words, he sought to demonstrate a *reductio ad absurdum*. Guttman sent copies of this paper to several people in 1976. It was never published by *Psychometrika*, but was published as Guttman (1994b). The irony was that Green and McDonald were now categorized as having the same position, which I am sure McDonald would not have accepted.

McDonald returned a version of my paper that he rewrote within his framework. That began a debate in correspondence that was to last from April to September of 1976. I compare the exchange of letters to something like correspondence chess. As each letter arrived from McDonald I would first read it through and have the impression that he finally had me. But then closer inspection of his argument usually revealed a subtle error and I would expose it and send a rebuttal back. Nevertheless, in the process McDonald was bringing an organization to the argument that I lacked, forcing me to think more rigorously. Finally, in September 1976 after receiving a counterexample from McDonald to an example I had sent him earlier, I conceived of a counter-counterexample, using his own counterexample as a basis for my counter-counterexample. He finally saw the point of factor indeterminacy from my and the Guttman point of view. In the meantime in late August I received a letter from the editor of *Psychometrika* saying that they wanted another revision of my paper that I had submitted in April. At that point I no longer felt it was just my paper. McDonald had introduced so many worthwhile new ideas on the topic that I felt honor bound to recognize his contribution to any revision of my paper. I invited him to join me as second author of the paper.

Mulaik and McDonald (1978), like most *Psychometrika* papers, is a difficult paper to read. It consists of a fundamental definition of "the g-factor law" and six theorems with several corollaries. The argument is a very tightly argued mathematical argument with proofs. After a review of the history of the idea of factor indeterminacy, we began our argument where I had in my initial version submitted to *Psychometrika* in April 1976. We focused on an initial set of p random variables

η satisfying the single-common-factor model

$$\eta = \lambda\xi + \Psi\varepsilon.$$

For convenience we assumed that all variables have zero means and unit variances, and all factors are mutually orthogonal. We then considered an augmented vector of observed variables $[\eta', \mathbf{v}_1']$, where $\mathbf{v}_1$ is a $k_1 \times 1$ random vector of additional variables. McDonald had the good judgment to see that we should define a "law" whereby the augmented vector $[\eta', \mathbf{v}_1']$ still satisfies the common factor model in a way consistent with the initial model for η : $[\eta', \mathbf{v}_1']$ satisfies the g-factor law if

$$\begin{bmatrix} \eta \\ \mathbf{v}_1 \end{bmatrix} = \begin{bmatrix} \lambda & \mathbf{P}_0 \\ \mathbf{c}_1 & \mathbf{P}_1 \end{bmatrix} \begin{bmatrix} \xi \\ \xi_1 \end{bmatrix} + \begin{bmatrix} \Psi_0^2 & \mathbf{0} \\ \mathbf{0} & \Psi_1^2 \end{bmatrix}.$$

Here $\mathbf{c}_1$ is a $k_1 \times 1$ vector of factor loadings on the first g-factor. Any element in this vector must range between -1 and $+1$. However, my presentation here is slightly modified from the original to allow that the first set of variables in η may also load on any r_1 additional common factors introduced with the inclusion of $\mathbf{v}_1$ in the analysis. Some of our requirements for what we called the g-factor law were too stringent. It is sufficient, I now believe, that there would be a rotation of the factors that would allow the first set of variables to still have their same loadings on the first general factor. However, to satisfy the g-factor law, there must be no Heywood cases (Heywood, 1931) where the communalities exceed the variances of the observed variables. This requirement would be satisfied if, for the elements of $\mathbf{P}_0$,

$$\sum_{j=2}^{r_1} p_{ij}^2 \le (1 - \lambda_i^2), \qquad i = 1, \ldots, p,$$

and for the elements of $\mathbf{P}_1$,

$$\sum_{j=2}^{r_1} p_m^2 \le \left(1 - c_m^2\right), \qquad m = 1, \ldots, k_1.$$

I think now I would add the requirement that

$$\begin{bmatrix} \Sigma_{00} & \Sigma_{01} \\ \Sigma_{10} & \Sigma_{11} \end{bmatrix} - \begin{bmatrix} \lambda \\ \mathbf{c}_1 \end{bmatrix} [\lambda' \quad \mathbf{c}_1']$$

is nonnegative definite, as we do analogously in a second theorem to be described.

Now, we said, any unit-variance variable X would be a solution for the g-factor of $[\eta', \mathbf{v}_1']$ iff

$$E(\eta X) = \lambda \qquad \text{and} \qquad E(\mathbf{v}_1 X) = \mathbf{c}_1.$$

Furthermore, every unit-variance variable X satisfying the g-factor law would be a one-factor common factor of η. But not every one-factor variable $X = \xi$ of η would satisfy the g-factor law for $[\eta', \mathbf{v}_1']$. This latter assertion follows from the fact that according to Guttman (1955), the correlation ρ_{12} between any two alternative solutions X_1 and X_2 for the common factor of η must satisfy the inequality

$$2\rho_0^2 - 1 \le \rho_{12} \le 1,$$

where ρ_0^2 is the squared multiple correlation for predicting any one-factor of η.

This is the basis for regarding the indeterminacy of the original set of variables as unavoidable. Adding variables does not reduce the original indeterminacy, but simply reduces the possible alternatives in the augmented set.

On the other hand, the correlation ρ_{12}^* between any two unit-variance variables X_1^* and X_2^* satisfying the g-factor law for $[\eta', \mathbf{v}_1']$ must satisfy the inequality $2\rho_{(0+1)}^2 - 1 \le \rho_{12}^* \le 1$. Because η is a subset of the variables in $[\eta', \mathbf{v}_1']$, $\rho_0^2 \le \rho_{(0+1)}^2$. Hence $2\rho_0^2 - 1 \le 2\rho_{(0+1)}^2 - 1$. Hence, whereas any variable X satisfying the g-factor law of $[\eta', \mathbf{v}_1']$ is a one-factor of η, there can exist (by construction) one-factors of η that are not g-factors of $[\eta', \mathbf{v}_1']$, for they would not satisfy the inequality $2\rho_{(0+1)}^2 - 1 \le \rho_{12}^* \le 1$. This implies that the additional variables reduce the set of possible alternative solutions for the g-factors of the augmented set of variables.

Our first theorem showed how for any one-factor X of η we could construct an infinite set of additional variables

$$V_j^* = c_j X + \left(1 - c_j^2\right) E_j^*, \quad -1 < c_j < 1, \quad c_j \ne 0,$$

that, when joined to η as $[\eta', \mathbf{v}^{*\prime}]$, would satisfy the g-factor law and furthermore determine X uniquely with a squared multiple correlation of unity. This was what Piaggio (1933) had established and was the inspiration for Darrell Bock's comment at our presentation at Bell Laboratories that you could add additional variables satisfying the same common factor model and obtain a determinate common factor.

Our second theorem considered two additional sets of variables $\mathbf{v}_1$ and $\mathbf{v}_2$ that each separately satisfied the g-factor law when joined with η, that is, $[\eta', \mathbf{v}_1']$ satisfied the g-factor law with a general common factor and $[\eta', \mathbf{v}_2']$ satisfied the g-factor law with a general common factor. We then considered the conditions under which all three sets of variables would jointly satisfy the g-factor law. That would be the case if

$$\begin{bmatrix} \eta \\ \mathbf{v}_1 \\ \mathbf{v}_2 \end{bmatrix} = \begin{bmatrix} \lambda & \mathbf{P}_0^* \\ \mathbf{c}_1 & \mathbf{P}_1^* \\ \mathbf{c}_2 & \mathbf{P}_2^* \end{bmatrix} \begin{bmatrix} X \\ \xi_{1+2} \end{bmatrix} + \begin{bmatrix} \mathbf{\Psi}_0^{*2} & \mathbf{0} & \mathbf{0} \\ \mathbf{0} & \mathbf{\Psi}_1^{*2} & \mathbf{0} \\ \mathbf{0} & \mathbf{0} & \mathbf{\Psi}_2^{*2} \end{bmatrix}.$$

and if the matrix

$$\begin{bmatrix} \Sigma_0 & \Sigma_{01} & \Sigma_{02} \\ \Sigma_{10} & \Sigma_1 & \Sigma_{12} \\ \Sigma_{20} & \Sigma_{21} & \Sigma_2 \end{bmatrix} - \begin{bmatrix} \lambda \\ c_1 \\ c_2 \end{bmatrix} [\lambda' \quad c_1' \quad c_2']$$

is nonnegative definite, where c_1 and c_2 are the loadings, respectively, of v_1 and v_2 on the g-factor in the cases of $[\eta', v_1']$ and $[\eta', v_2']$, respectively. ξ_{1+2} represents any additional common factors formed by joining v_1 and v_2 with η. Asterisks indicate matrices unique to this case.

Our third theorem showed that if one increased the number of variables in v_1 and v_2 each without bound, and they continued to satisfy the g-factor law of the second theorem, then by Theorem 1, $[\eta', v_1']$ and $[\eta', v_2']$ would each determine a common factor and the correlation between these would be unity, since by the g-factor law, they would be the same variable.

From the previous results we can show without proof that if you constructed v_1 around a solution X_1 for the one-factor of η and v_2 around a solution X_2 for the one-factor of η that was minimally correlated $2\rho_0^2 - 1$ with X_1, and in each case $[\eta', v_1']$ and $[\eta', v_2']$ satisfy the g-factor law, then the determinate factors obtained by increasing the number of such additional variables without bound will be correlated $2\rho_0^2 - 1$ with each other, whereas $[\eta', v_1', v_2']$ does not satisfy the g-factor law.

A couple of our theorems were so esoteric that I will pass over them. But there is one important theorem that McDonald insisted we include in the paper. I state the theorem verbatim without proof.

Theorem 6. Let $v' = [V_1, \ldots]$ be an infinite domain of variables having a determinate factor space with r common factors (r not necessarily finite). Then the following is true: (a) if $[\eta', v_1']$ and $[\eta', v_2']$ are each selections of, respectively, $p + k_1$, and $p + k_2$ variables chosen from the domain such that each conforms to the g-factor law, then $[\eta', v_1', v_2']$ conforms to the g-factor law. (b) In the limit, if k_1 and k_2 increase without bound, the g-factors, respectively, of $[\eta', v_1']$ and $[\eta', v_2']$ and the g-factor of $[\eta', v_1', v_2']$ are each determinate and are the same variable. (c) In the limit if k_1 and k_2 increase without bound, v_1 and v_2 need not share any variables in common, nor need the set $[\eta', v_1', v_2']$ contain every variable in the domain having the specified factor in common. (d) The set of all possible components of v_1 and all possible components of v_2 are the same. (Mulaik & McDonald, 1978, p. 187)

The key to the previous theorem is the assumption that there is a domain with a determinate set of factors in the limit in the domain. Guttman argued that only in this determinate case would the common factor model be defensible. Ordinarily we cannot know this with any selection of variables η, which are usually selected in exploratory factor analysis without any explicit criteria as to what variables constitute members of a domain spanned by a given set of common factors.

In drawing implications from these results we first suggested that one could use the proposition that a particular domain has a determinate factor space as a working hypothesis that could be partially tested empirically. Common factors could be asserted as hypothetical constructs, and variables supposedly determined by these factors could be selected and analyzed by confirmatory factor analysis to see whether they conform to the researcher's expectations. Further confirmation would come from selecting or constructing additional variables and including them with the original variables to determine whether the joint set conforms to the g-factor law. Someone else may believe that the factor is something else and construct additional variables according to that conception and include them with the original core set. If they also satisfy the g-factor law, then the test of whether the two conceptions represent the same factor could be tested by merging both sets of additional variables with the original variables to see whether the three sets of variables jointly conform to the g-factor law. If not, that establishes that each researcher is working indeed with a different conception of the factor. We noted that some writers had suggested that "marker variables" from earlier analyses be included in an analysis to represent a factor. We noted, however, that the marker variables might not

> necessarily define or determine the same factor variable when these marker variables are embedded in different sets of other variables, unless the different sets of other variables, when combined together with the marker variables, jointly satisfy at least the g-factor law. (Mulaik & McDonald, 1978, p. 191) Marker variables would be like a core set in η.

Another implication was the case of selecting homogeneous sets of variables by factor analysis. If we do not have an explicit criterion of what constitutes variables of a defined behavioral domain, we may begin with a small nucleus of items written to measure one construct that all seem to satisfy the one-factor law. Then, merely on the basis of whether additional items conform to the same g-factor law, we may include and retain additional variables and believe that they measure the same construct we thought underlay the original nucleus of items. But the additional items may diverge from that conception in the direction of another. The moral is that factor analysis alone should not be the criterion of homogeneity of items. There must be external criteria of content and/or measurement operations that also serve to guide one to retain or exclude variables from consideration as homogeneous.

A major problem for factor analysts is to develop criteria for variable domains. Such criteria must be external to the factor analysis. They must correspond to some publicly observable mark or characteristic of the variables that allows one to decide whether to include or exclude them from the domain. Even so, such categories applied to experience cannot be given necessary and sufficient conditions. As epistemologists in the 1980s and 1990s discovered, implicit contextual features qualify rules of category membership, so that when the categories are extended to new and unanticipated contexts, the categorization rules need augmentation or revision. For example, the rules of tennis will not be sufficient for a game of tennis to be played outside of a space station in orbit where the pull of gravity is weak. Similarly, one could not play tennis on the surface of Jupiter or the Moon with standard equipment. Guttman's technique of facet analysis (1970, 1977/1994a) was a first step for establishing criteria for behavioral domains and still has an active following (Canter, 1985; Shye, 1978; Shye, Elizur, & Hoffman, 1994). However, not all domains of variables constructed by a facet analysis of the concepts involved would necessarily satisfy the common factor model. Susan Embretson has also developed techniques for constructing items with consistent properties (Embretson, 1998, 1999, 2000) that are reminiscent of definitions of variable domains. The problem is to produce clear definitional criteria for the kinds of items that belong in a domain. This will lend itself, however, to confirmatory factor analysis more than exploratory factor analysis.

After publishing Mulaik and McDonald (1978), McDonald and Mulaik (1979) published a less technical version of the first paper that may be more comprehensible for many psychometricians.

In looking back at Guttman's creation of image analysis as a determinate alternative to common factor analysis and his condemnation of common factor analysis as an indeterminate model, it seems to me that this reflects the empiricist epistemology that was rampant back in the 1940s and 1950s. Empiricism was based on the idea that concepts were meaningful only if they referred uniquely to elements of experience. Even the founders of empiricism like David Hume recognized that such criteria often led to violations of common sense. He could not find the elements of experience to which a causal connection between kinds of impressions could be referred. He could not find the elements of experience that corresponded to the idea of the object that unified a collage of certain kinds of sensory impressions. He could not even locate within himself an impression of a self that united all his thoughts and ideas. He did have the analogy that the mind somehow in mysterious ways joined the simple ideas derived from sensory impressions into complex ideas, just as gravity pulls material bodies together by a mysterious form of attraction. He called these ways the principles of association of the mind. Undeterred by the incoherence of a referential theory of meaning grounded in elements of experience and ideas of associative processes of the mind, empiricism evolved into the logical positivism of the 1920s and the subsequent logical empiricism of the 1930s and 1940s. The late-19th-century Austrian physicist and empiricist philosopher Ernst Mach sought to exclude from science concepts of hidden or unobservable entities as having no referents in experience. Karl Pearson, the founder of modern multivariate statistics, was a dedicated follower of Mach, and preached a similar philosophy of science. Regression equations were only summary descriptions of associations between scores on variables and had no intrinsic reference to entities or forces in nature. Mach had difficulty with the concept of the atom and Pearson with that of the gene because these were in their times unobservables. B. F. Skinner was also strongly influenced by Mach, although it would not be fair to call him a strict empiricist, because he had no confidence in introspectionist accounts of the functioning of the mind, on which empiricist epistemology was based. Like Mach, however, Skinner sought to exclude from psychology reference to unobserved entities such as theoretical constructs. All that was needed was description of what is observed. It was within such a strongly empiricist climate that Guttman (1955) could make a credible case against an indeterministic model like common factor analysis in favor of a deterministic model like image analysis. To what did the common factors refer if they did not refer uniquely?

The climate in philosophy-of-science circles changed radically in the 1960s and 1970s when it was demonstrated in various ways that scientific theories—in fact, empirical concepts generally—are underdetermined from experience. Quine (1960), in developing a behavioristic conception of concept formation, realized that in learning a concept or a foreign language there would always be an ambiguity in that to which words would refer (the inscrutability of reference and the indeterminacy of translation) or in the way that they would be used in certain contexts. Hempel (1965) realized that one could always fit numerous curves to a given set of data points, so if a given curve represented a particular form of inductive generalization from the data, it was not unique. Goodman (1983) introduced his "new riddle of induction," which showed that not all regularities are a basis for predictions or inductive generalizations. Logical empiricism had the ideal that scientific propositions could be formally expressed in the logical syntax of the predicate calculus and the empirical meaning of the propositions achieved by calculating their truth values from the truth values of their symbolic components.

The propositions were just formal strings of symbols governed formally by the logical syntax of the predicate calculus. The truth values of the symbolic components of the proposition would be given empirically by truth functions of reference to entities in the world. This was the basis of what came to be known as "model-theoretic semantics." The philosopher Hilary Putnam (1981) then demonstrated that there was an unavoidable indeterminacy of reference in any such model. [For a clear account and commentary on Putnam's model-theoretic argument see Lakoff (1987, chap 15).] You could reassign the referents for the symbols in such a way as to change the referents and yet maintain the same truth values for the symbols and hence the calculated truth values of the propositions in all situations. So, you could not use the truth values of the symbols or propositions to distinguish the difference in "meaning" produced by changing the referents. Finally, Wittgenstein (1953), by his "private language" argument, knocked out the linchpin of classical empiricism's introspectionistic idea that meaning resides in the assignment of symbols to complexes of privately experienced sensory impressions. Implicit to the empiricist program was the idea that language involved rules for the assignment of meaningless symbols to privately experienced entities of experience. In effect, then, every individual supposedly spoke a kind of private language and only achieved public communication through consensual acts of cooperation. Wittgenstein demonstrated that if one regards following a rule as requiring an objective way of determining whether one is or is not following the rule, and regards language as based on following rules, such as rules to use a certain symbol every time a certain private sensation occurs, then in following a rule of a private language, you will never be able to distinguish when you are right from when you think you are right. So, you are not following a rule, and hence do not have a private language.

Thus, with these demonstrations of unavoidable indeterminacies in programs designed to model the world unambiguously with determinate referents for model entities, Guttman's preferences for a determinate model like image analysis over common factor analysis seem less persuasive now. There are other ways to think about and use the common factor model that do not demand unambiguous referents for the common factors in any given study. Some of my own contributions to this topic are given in Mulaik (1976b, 1986, 1990, 1993a, 1993b, 1994, 1996a, 1996b, 2004).

THE MARAUN COMMENTARY

As editor of *Multivariate Behavioral Research*, I published a commentary on a target paper addressing the issue of factor indeterminacy by Michael Maraun (1996a, 1996b, 1996c). Commentators on the paper were James Steiger (1996a, 1996b), David Bartholomew (1996a, 1996b), William Rozeboom (1996a, 1996b), Peter Schönemann (1996a, 1996b), Stanley Mulaik (1996a, 1996b), and R. P. McDonald (1996a, 1996b). There were two rounds of commentary with rebuttal from Maraun after each round.

Maraun noted that there were two interpretations of factor indeterminacy: (1) the alternative solution position and the posterior moment position. Maraun identified Wilson (1928a, 1928b), Guttman (1955), Schönemann (1971), Schönemann and Wang (1972), Mulaik (1972, 1976a, 1976b), and Steiger and Schönemann (1978) with the alternative solution position, and McDonald (1974) and Bartholomew (1981) with the posterior moment position. Maraun did not cite Mulaik and McDonald (1978) as representative of the alternative solution position, although clearly it was, but linked that paper to what Maraun called the infinite behavior domain position, on the basis of only one of the theorems (Theorem 6) in that paper. Admittedly, Mulaik and McDonald (1978) was a difficult paper to master, and evidently Maraun (1996a, 1996b, 1996c) did not succeed in doing so. What made Maraun's papers a distinct approach was his application of Wittgenstein's conceptions on the nature of following a rule to the establishment of a criterion for a latent common factor. Maraun claimed to simply focus clearly on the rules in mathematics that one used to provide criteria for a latent common factor. He explicitly was unwilling to consider applications or uses for the concept of a latent common factor or strategies to follow as a consequence of factor indeterminacy. They were irrelevant to his analysis of the rules.

Maraun's argument ran like this. Suppose we have a single-common-factor model. In classical exploratory common factor analysis this variable is viewed as but a single variable. As McDonald (1974) put it, the variable cannot simultaneously have multiple values for a given subject. But Maraun then argued that the idea of "oneness" here demands that there be a conceptual criterion of identity for the common factor. If it is one thing, it cannot be another thing. So, to know that it is one thing, one must be able to pick it out from all possible things, by providing a criterion for its identity. We can do that with a principal components analysis model because the observed variables have unique identities. We can put them alongside other variables and know that they are unique and distinct. So, any component variable in the principal components analysis model, by being a specific linear combination $C = \mathbf{v}'\eta$ of the observed variables (where $\mathbf{v}$ is an eigenvector of Σ), also has a unique identity, derived from the observed variables by the unique linear function that gives rise to it. This identity, however, is confined to the principal components analysis model. There is no other criterion for its identity independent of that model. But even this is not the case in exploratory common factor analysis. The common factors are not determinate linear combinations of the observed variables. Although the common factor model provides criteria for common factors—they must have a certain pattern of covariances $\Xi = \Lambda\Phi$ with the observed variables—they do not uniquely give the common factors an identity. They provide no standard of correctness for the claim that "this variable in the world is the common factor." They only provide criteria that a variable could be a common factor. But many variables may meet those criteria. So, confusion arises when one conflates the idea that the common factor variable is a unique variable in the world with the criteria for a common factor provided by the common factor model itself. On the other hand, Maraun argued that Guttman's construction formula $\mathbf{x} = \Phi\Lambda'\Sigma^{-1}\eta + \mathbf{Ps}$, like the construction formula for a principal component, yields a way to generate variables that do satisfy the criteria for variables that are common factors of η. But I must point out that any variables $\mathbf{x}$ whose covariances with η equal Ξ would satisfy criteria for common factors of η, so Guttman's construction formula is not the only way to come upon variables that satisfy the criteria of common factors. It is just a sure way of doing so. Maraun (1996c), however, regarded the construction rule as constitutive of what it means to be a common factor: "The criterion I prescribe for 'LCF to $\mathbf{Y}$' [latent common factor to $\mathbf{Y}$] is a constitutive rule. A variate not constructed as $X_i = \Lambda'\Sigma^{-1}\mathbf{Y} + pS_i$ is not an LCF to $\mathbf{Y}$" (p. 679). In that respect he believed that the alternative solution position was essentially correct.

I believe the alternative solution position only arises out of a subtle changing of the rules of the factor-analytic game. Maraun, as a Wittgensteinian scholar, should have recognized this. The original factor-analytic game is based only on the model equation $\eta = \Lambda\xi + \Psi\varepsilon$ and rules such as $\{\text{diag}[\text{var}(\xi)]\} = \mathbf{I}$, Ψ is a $p \times p$ diagonal matrix, $\text{var}(\varepsilon) = \mathbf{I}$, and $\text{cov}(\xi, \varepsilon) = \mathbf{0}$. These rules are sufficient to allow one to derive such results as $\Xi = \text{cov}(\eta, \xi) = \Lambda\Phi$. However, the common factors are indeterminate from the observed variables. Period. But nowhere does one postulate the existence of additional variables σ having the property that $\text{var}(\sigma) = \mathbf{I}$ and $\text{cov}(\eta, \sigma) = \mathbf{0}$. Their postulation seems to arise out of the discomfort some feel with the lack of identity for the common factors. This drives those so discomforted to construct variables $\mathbf{x} = \Phi\Lambda'\Sigma^{-1}\eta + \mathbf{Ps}$, where $\mathbf{s} = \mathbf{T}_1\mathbf{MT}_2\sigma$, which have properties of common factors—among other things, $\text{cov}(\eta, \mathbf{x}) = \Lambda\Phi$. However, unless the variables of σ have a criterion for identity, the variables in s will lack identity. Even so, one may give them a mathematical identity but not an identity external to the mathematics. On the other hand, identifying σ with a vector of scores generated by a computer's random number generator and assigned arbitrarily to the subjects places the generated s in the world, but such variables would hardly seem to be explanations for the correlations among variables in η, because they do not represent measured quantitative properties of the subjects.

In the original common factor model there is no such thing as a constructed common factor. They only occur if you add additional variables and rules governing their use with respect to other variables in the model. It is like adding additional players into a game with rules governing how they are to play with the other players. But this changes the game. What Guttman did by introducing the notion of constructed factors is play the age-old trick of subtly changing the rules and then declaring that he had new paradoxical results in the old game: Solutions for the common factors can be as minimally correlated as $2\rho_g^2 - 1$. Maraun is playing the same trick of changing the rules of the game and declaring that by (his) rules the posterior moment position is incorrect. But such declarations are meaningful only in the context of the game that Maraun is playing. The moves that lead to constructed factors and factors minimally correlated as $2\rho_g^2 - 1$ are not possible moves in the classical game of common factor analysis. That is why McDonald (1974) found the Guttman–Schönemann position almost incomprehensible and could see no justification for $2\rho_g^2 - 1$ over ρ. It is why Bartholomew finds the alternative solution position so incomprehensible. So Maraun used a rhetorical trick that Wittgenstein would have avoided of playing with a new set of rules without explicitly announcing that he is doing so and then taking someone who is playing by the old rules to court for violating the new, unannounced rules.

So, how do you get someone who is playing the game by an old set of rules to play by a new set of rules that you prefer? There is no easy formula. Essentially you can show them that it is in their interest to do so. They will enjoy the game more. They will derive more benefits from following the new rules. They will avoid punishment. They will function in the world better. And so on.

Why do rules of games change? I suppose that changes result from someone believing that there will be additional benefits from playing the game in the new way. The choice to play by a new set of rules is not governed by rules, even though retrospectively we may seek reasons for the choice. I believe that the constructed-factors rules arose out of attempts to make the common factors have a more concrete reality as somethings in the world. The observed variables and their common and unique factors are better regarded as being embedded in a larger space of variables representing attributes of objects in the world. After all, I contend, factor analysis is a conceptual blend of a mathematical model with our ideas, percepts, and experiences of things in the world. The mathematics is only metaphor, as are the ways of blending the mathematics with things in the world.

Maraun took issue with my arguing that factor indeterminacy is not a major problem because it is just an example of "the pervasive indeterminacy that exists throughout science" (Mulaik, 1990, p. 54), for "it is now recognized by most philosophers of science (Garrison, 1986) that scientific concepts are underdetermined with respect to experience" (Mulaik, 1994, p. 231). This, Maraun claimed, rests on a category error:

> It is a category error in which considerations relevant to empirical investigation are wrongly imported to characterize a conceptual issue. In the first place, concepts are not in any way *determined* [sic] by experience (Wittgenstein, 1953). Concepts instead have rules of correct application, and a concept's meaning is precisely the set of rules that specify its correct application (Baker & Hacker, 1980). Rules, however, are not right or wrong at all. They are not theories or hypotheses. They are not determined or caused. Instead they are standards of correctness, and are *constitutive* for experience (Ter Hak, 1990; Wittgenstein, 1953). They are laid down by people, and may be *formulated*, depending on the domain of application, in a number of different ways. (Maraun, 1996a, p. 534)

This is peculiar because I was not arguing that concepts are caused by experience. That was a belief of the empiricists. Underdetermination does not mean that concepts are caused by experience, even partially. It means what we have been arguing about factor indeterminacy, that many scientific concepts, like common factors, have criteria for their use and application, but not necessary and sufficient conditions in experience that serve as criteria of identity. Like common factors, scientific objects that are concepts that unite diverse observations and are generalized beyond those observations cannot do so with criteria of identity because, among other things, errors of measurement in observation prevent one from uniquely identifying the object. Furthermore, one can formulate any number of concepts for generalizing from a given set of observations, so the observations do not uniquely "determine" the concepts.

If Maraun argued that rules are neither right nor wrong, that should have been his cue to avoid declaring himself in favor of the alternative-variables solution over the unique-variable solution. Each position is based on a different set of rules. The unique-variable solution is limited in being unable to determine scores uniquely on the latent variable from just the observed variables. The alternative-variables solution introduces additional variables, presumably observed, meaning there are criteria of identity for them, and further introduces the rule that they must be uncorrelated with the original set of observed variables. From these one can construct variables that will satisfy criteria for the common factors and also have criteria of identity. But variables so constructed may have little scientific interest. So, if neither set of rules is right nor wrong, we cannot choose between them on the basis that one is righter than the other. Although there may be reasons for the choice, the reasons do not determine the choice and are not rules of right and wrong. One is free to choose however one wishes. That's all I think Maraun can get out of a Wittgensteinian position that focuses just on the mathematics of these positions and ignores the positive benefits of metaphor in the factor-analytic game.

The other contributors to the dialogue with Maraun (and one another) did not reveal much that was new to me or previous contributions to the literature, and I will not extend this chapter to deal with them in detail. I do, however, have a few remarks. I was disappointed that both Maraun (1996a) and Steiger (1996a) both seemed to identify Mulaik and McDonald (1978) with the infinite-behavioral-domain position. I wish they had made clearer that Mulaik and McDonald (1978) was *not* an example of the infinite-behavior-domain position that some use to discount the existence or relevance of factor indeterminacy. It was quite the opposite, a critique and refutation of that position that showed why postulating infinite behavioral domains will not eliminate factor indeterminacy of an original analysis. More than one infinite behavioral domain may be constructed around each of the alternative solutions for the factors. I welcomed, however, Steiger's example of the signal from space received at four stations, and thought his review of the history of Wilson's and Spearman's exchanges in the literature quite enlightening and fair (Steiger, 1996b).

I am pleased to say that in this exchange McDonald and I were pretty much in agreement on the major issues of factor indeterminacy and factor-analytic practice. He did take issue in his second commentary to something I said in my first commentary: "Professor Mulaik interprets me as being/having been 'beguiled' into believing that the infinite behavior domain can solve the problems of exploratory factor analysis in the absence of a (defined) behavior domain. I have never believed any such self-refuting foolishness" (McDonald, 1996b, p. 664) That is not what I said. I noted that it was McDonald who insisted on inclusion of Theorem 6 in Mulaik and McDonald (1978). As already described, it showed that selections of variables η', $[\eta', \mathbf{v}'_1]$, $[\eta', \mathbf{v}'_2]$, and $[\eta', \mathbf{v}'_1, \mathbf{v}'_2]$ from a determinate infinite domain would all satisfy the g-factor law and not yield evidence of alternative factors. I said to Maraun that this theorem:

> reflects, I believe, a mathematical truth that beguiles many a factor analyst into believing there are not alternative solutions for a common factor in exploratory factor analysis. An infinite determinate domain of variables all dependent on the same factor *will* satisfy the g-factor law in all subsets of variables from the domain. I believe it was this idea that beguiled McDonald (1974), and in some form beguiled Bartholomew (1981) (in the single-actor case) into thinking there is but one latent variable to which the common factor of an exploratory factor analysis could refer (Mulaik 1996a, pp. 581–582).

If it was not this that beguiled McDonald, I do not know what it was. But it took several months of sustained correspondence to get him to see the existence of alternative solutions for common factors as a coherent idea. Still, I think in writing this chapter I have come to see how his position in McDonald (1974) was more coherent than we (Steiger, Schönemann, Guttman, or I) believed at the time. We were just playing a different game than McDonald. Today, this is really a small matter and I mention it only to demonstrate our friendly competitiveness in playing the factor-analytic game.

I was intrigued, however, that McDonald went on to say, "Indeed, having been influenced by the early work of Guttman... from the inception of my own work, I have never advocated exploratory factor analysis, and most certainly not of a heap (in the sense of Piaget's) of variables" (McDonald, 1996b, p. 664). I think this is an important point of agreement between us. Questioning the routine use of exploratory factor analysis is perhaps more important than debating the nuances of factor indeterminacy and whether this is fatal to the common factor model. Common factor analysis is based on just one kind of structure among variables, and variables often are generated by quite different kinds of structures, like the simplex, circumplex and other forms, for the awareness of which we are indeed indebted to Guttman. So, exploratory factor analysis ought not to be mindlessly and routinely used as if it will always reveal the underlying structures of any "heap" of variables.

One final point. In commenting on Steiger's signal detection example, McDonald (1996a) noted "The signal is not in any sense a common property of the recordings. It is a common cause. A common cause cannot be a common factor, and will behave like one only accidentally—in this example by a possible accident of geography" (p. 595). I have heard him say that common factors are not common causes but common properties. Perhaps this is something we can debate in the future because obviously we are playing by a different set of rules here.

McDonald is indeed one of the greats among psychometricians of our generation. His contributions on factor indeterminacy are only a small part of his numerous contributions to the field. I note with admiration his models of nonlinear factor analysis, and his cataloging and development of a calculus of matrix derivatives, his development of the COSAN program for analysis of covariance structures, his texts on psychometric theory and factor analysis, and his numerous papers on item response theory, scaling, structural equation modeling, and factor analysis. He also should be famous for his limericks and poems, which in time he may become.

REFERENCES

Bartholomew, D. J. (1981). Posterior analysis of the factor model. *British Journal of Mathematical and Statistical Psychology, 34*, 93–99.

Bartholomew, D. (1996a). Comment on: Metaphor taken as math: Indeterminacy in the factor model. *Multivariate Behavioral Research, 31*, 551–554.

Bartholomew, D. (1996b). Response to Dr. Maraun's first reply to discussion of his paper. *Multivariate Behavioral Research, 31*, 631–636.

Canter, D. (Ed.) (1985). *Facet theory: Approaches to social research.* New York: Springer-Verlag.

Embretson, S. E. (1998). A cognitive design system approach to generating valid tests: Application to abstract reasoning. *Psychological Methods, 3*, 300–396.

Embretson, S. E. (1999). Generating items during testing: Psychometric issues and models. Psychometrika, 64, 407–433.

Embretson, S. E. (2000). Generating abstract reasoning items with cognitive theory. In S. Irvine & P. Kyllonen, (Eds.), *Generating items for cognitive tests: Theory and Practice.* Mahwah, NJ: Lawrence Erlbaum Associates, Inc.

Garrison, J. W. (1986). Some principles of post-positivistic philosophy of science. *Educational Researcher, 15*, 12–18.

Goodman, N. (1983). *Fact, fiction, and forecast* (4th ed.). Cambridge, MA: Harvard University Press.

Green, B. F. (1976). On the factor score controversy. *Psychometrika, 41*, 263–266.

Guttman, L. (1953). Image theory for the structure of quantitative variates. *Psychometrika, 18*, 227–296.

Guttman, L. (1955). The determinacy of factor score matrices, with implications for five other basic problems of common-factor theory. *British Journal of Statistical Psychology, 8*, 65–81

Guttman, L. (1970). *The facet approach to theory development.* Unpublished manuscript, Israel Institute of Applied Social Research, Jerusalem.

Guttman, L. (1956). "Best possible" systematic estimates of communalities. *Psychometrika, 21*, 273–285.

Guttman, L. (1994a). "What is not what" in theory construction. In S. Levy (Ed.), *Louis Guttman on theory and methodology*: Selected writings (pp. 3–20). Brookfield, VT: Dartmouth (Original work published in 1977).

Guttman, L. (1994b). The Green–McDonald proof of the nonexistence of factor analysis. In S. Levy (Ed.), *Louis Guttman on theory and methodology: Selected writings* (pp. 361–369). Brookfield, VT: Dartmouth.

Hempel, C. G. (1965). Aspects of scientific explanation. In C. G. Hempel (Ed.), *Aspects of scientific explanation and other essays in the philosophy of science.* New York: Macmillan.

Heywood, H. B. (1931). On finite sequences of real numbers. *Proceedings of the Royal Society of London, Series A, 134*, 486–501.

Lakoff, G. (1987). *Women, fire and dangerous things: What categories reveal about the mind.* Chicago: University of Chicago Press.

Mc Donald, R. P. (1996a). Latent traits and the possibility of motion. *Multivariate Behavioral Research, 31*, 593–601.

Mc Donald, R. P. (1996b). Consensus emergens: A matter of interpretation. *Multivariate Behavioral Research, 31*, 663–673.

Maraun, M. (1996a). Metaphor taken as math: Indeterminacy in the factor analysis model. *Multivariate Behavioral Research, 31*, 517–538.

Maraun, M. (1996b). Meaning and mythology in the factor analysis model. *Multivariate Behavioral Research, 31*, 603–616.

Maraun, M. (1996c). The claims of factor analysis. *Multivariate Behavioral Research, 31*, 673–690.

McDonald, R. P. (1974). The measurement of factor indeterminacy. *Psychometrika, 39*, 203–222.

McDonald, R. P. (1977). The indeterminacy of components and the definition of common factors. *British Journal of Mathematical and Statistical Psychology, 30*, 165–176.

McDonald, R. P., & Mulaik, S. A. (1979). Determinacy of common factors: A nontechnical review. *Psychological Bulletin, 86*, 297–306.

Mulaik, S. A. (1972). *The foundations of factor analysis.* New York: McGraw–Hill.

Mulaik, S. A. (1976a, April). *Comments on the measurement of factorial indeterminacy.* Paper presented at the joint meeting of the Psychometric Society and the Mathematical Psychology Group, Bell Laboratories, Murray Hill, NJ.

Mulaik, S. A. (1976b). Comments on "The measurement of factorial indeterminacy." *Psychometrika, 41*, 249–262.

Mulaik, S. A. McDonald, R. P. (1977). The effect of additional observables on factor indeterminacy in models with a single common factor, *Psychometrika, 43*, 177–192.

Mulaik, S. A. (1986). *The indeterminacy of common factor analysis as a model of semantic indeterminacy and scientific underdetermination.* Paper presented at of the 78th annual meeting of the Southern Society for Philosophy and Psychology, Knoxville, TN.

Mulaik, S. A. (1990). Blurring the distinctions between component analysis and common factor analysis. *Multivariate Behavioral Research, 25*, 53–59.

Mulaik, S. A. (1993a). Objectivity and multivariate statistics. *Multivariate Behavioral Research, 28*, 171–203.

Mulaik, S. A. (1993b). The critique of pure statistics: Artifact and objectivity in multivariate statistics. In B. Thompson (Ed.), *Advances in social science methodology* (vol. 3, pp. 247–296). Greenwich, CT: JAI.

Mulaik, S. A. (1994). Kant, Wittgenstein, objectivity and structural equation models. In C. R. Reynolds (Ed.), *Cognitive assessment: A multidisciplinary perspective* (pp. 209–236). New York: Plenum.

Mulaik, S. A. (1995). The metaphoric origins of objectivity, subjectivity and consciousness in the direct perception of reality. *Philosophy of Science, 62*, 283–303.

Mulaik, S. A. (1996a). On Maraun's deconstructing of factor indeterminacy with constructed factors. *Multivariate Behavioral Research, 31*, 579–592.

Mulaik, S. A. (1996b) Factor analysis is not just a model in pure mathematics. *Multivariate Behavioral Research, 31*, 655–661.

Mulaik, S. A. (2004). Objectivity in science and structural equation modeling. In D. Kaplan, (Ed.), *Handbook of quantitative methodology for the social sciences.* Thousand Daks, CA: Sage Publications, publisher.

Mulaik, S.A., & McDonald, R.P. (1978). The effect of additional variables on factor indeterminacy in models with a single common factor. *Psychometrika, 43*, 177–192.

Piaggio, H. T. (1931). The general factor in Spearman's theory of intelligence. *Nature, 127*, 56–57.

Piaggio, H. T. (1933). Three sets of conditions necessary for the existence of a g that is real and unique except in sign. *British Journal of Psychology, 24*, 88–105.

Putnam, H. (1981). *Reason, truth, and history.* Cambridge: Cambridge University Press.

Quine, W. V. (1960). *Word and object.* Cambridge, MA: Harvard University Press.

Rozeboom, W. W. (1996a). What might common factors be? *Multivariate Behavioral Research, 31*, 555–570.

Rozeboom, W. W. (1996b). Factor-indeterminacy issues are not linguistic confusions. *Multivariate Behavioral Research, 31*, 637–650.

Schönemann, P. H. (1996a). The psychopathology of factor indeterminacy. *Multivariate Behavioral Research, 31*, 571–578.

Schönemann, P. H. (1996b). Syllogisms of factor indeterminacy. *Multivariate Behavioral Research, 31*, 651–654.

Schönemann, P. H. (1971). The minimum average correlation between equivalent sets of uncorrelated factors. *Psychometrika, 36*, 21–30.

Schönemann, P. H., & Wang, M. M. (1972). Some new results on factor indeterminacy. *Psychometrika, 37*, 61–91.

Shye, S. (Ed.) (1978). *Theory construction and data analysis in the behavioral sciences.* London: Jossey-Bass.

Shye, S., Elizur, D., & Hoffman, M. (1994). *Introduction to facet theory.* Thousand Oaks, CA: Sage.

Spearman, C. (1922). Correlation between arrays in a table of correlations. *Proceedings of the Royal Society of London, Series A, 101*, 94–100.

Spearman, C. (1927). *The abilities of man.* London: Macmillan.

Spearman, C. (1929). The uniqueness of "g." *Journal of Educational Psychology, 20*, 212–216.

Spearman, C. (1933). The uniqueness and exactness of *g*. *British Journal of Psychology, 24*, 106–108.

Spearman, C. (1934). The factor theory and its troubles. IV. Uniqueness of *g*. *Journal of Educational Psychology, 25*, 142–153.

Steiger, J. H. (1996a). Dispelling some myths about factor indeterminacy. *Multivariate Behavioral Research, 31*, 539–550.

Steiger, J. H. (1996b). Coming full circle in the history of factor indeterminacy. *Multivariate Behavioral Research, 31*, 617–630.

Steiger, J. H., & Schönemann, P. H. (1978). A history of factor indeterminacy. In S. Shye (Eds.), Theory construction and data analysis in the behavioral sciences (pp. 136–178). San Francisco: Jossey–Bass.

Thurstone, L. L. (1947). *Multiple factor analysis*. Chicago: University of Chicago Press.

Wilson, E. B. (1901) *Vector analysis*. New Haven, CT: Yale University Press.

Wilson, E. B. (1928a). On hierarchical correlation systems. *Proceedings of the National Academy of Sciences, 14*, 283–291.

Wilson, E. B. (1928b). Review of "The abilities of man, their nature and measurement" by C. Spearman. *Science, 67*, 244–248.

Wilson, E. B. (1929). Comments on Professor Spearman's note. *Journal of Educational Psycholoogy, 20*, 217–223.

Wittgenstein, L. (1953). *Philosophical investigations*. Oxford: Blackwell.

8

Bayesian Inference for Factor Scores

Murray Aitkin and Irit Aitkin
University of Newcastle, UK

INTRODUCTION

Bayesian methods are rapidly becoming more popular with the greatly increased power of Markov chain Monte Carlo (MCMC or MC^2) methods for inference in complex models. Such features as missing or incomplete data, latent variables, and nonconjugate prior distributions can be handled in a unified way. Bayesian methods solve inferential problems that are difficult to deal with in frequentist (repeated-sampling) theory:

- The inadequacy of asymptotic theory in small samples and the difficulties of second-order asymptotics.
- The difficulties of maximum likelihood methods with complex models and partial or incomplete data.

The Bayesian solution of these problems, as for all models, requires a full prior specification for model parameters and all other unobserved variables. Bayesian analysis of the factor model was considered in considerable generality by Press and Shigemasu (1989, 1997), who gave a good coverage of earlier work; in the context of this volume, Bayesian methods have been used for the problem of

Heywood cases by Martin and McDonald (1975). Rowe (2002) gave a comprehensive Bayesian treatment of the factor model. Data augmentation (DA) methods
including MCMC methods are discussed in detail in Tanner (1996), but these have
apparently not been applied to the factor model apart from the maximum likelihood
expectation-maximization (EM) algorithm approach of Rubin and Thayer (1982).
In this chapter we describe the fully Bayesian DA approach.

THE SINGLE-FACTOR MODEL

We adopt the standard notation of upper-case letters for random variables and
lower-case letters for their observed values. For the single-common-factor model
with p test variables Y and a single unobserved factor X,

$$Y|X = x \sim N(\mu + \lambda x, \Psi),$$

$$X \sim N(0, 1),$$

and the marginal distribution of Y is

$$Y \sim N(\mu, \Sigma), \qquad \Sigma = \lambda\lambda' + \Psi,$$

where μ is a length-p column vector of means, λ is a length-p column vector of
factor loadings, and $\Psi = \text{diag}(\psi_1^2, \ldots, \psi_p^2)$ is a $p \times p$ diagonal matrix of specific
variances. We restrict X to be standard normal because of the unidentifiability
of its mean and variance parameters. It follows immediately that the maximum
likelihood estimate (MLE) of μ is $\bar{y}$.

Maximum likelihood methods for the estimation of λ and Ψ from data y_i
$(i = 1, \ldots, n)$, together with large-sample standard errors from the information
matrix, are implemented in many packages, and will not concern us here apart
from the EM algorithm approach of Rubin and Thayer (1982). In this approach,
we regard the unobserved factor variables X_i as missing data; in the "complete-
data" model in which the x_i are counterfactually observed, the complete data
log-likelihood is, omitting constants,

$$\ell^* = \log L^*(\mu, \lambda, \Psi) = -\frac{n}{2}\log|\Psi| - \frac{1}{2}\sum_{i=1}^{n}(y_i - \mu - \lambda x_i)'\Psi^{-1}(y_i - \mu - \lambda x_i)$$

$$-\frac{1}{2}\sum_{i=1}^{n}x_i^2$$

$$= -\frac{n}{2}\sum_{j=1}^{p}\log\psi_j^2 - \frac{1}{2}\sum_{i=1}^{n}\sum_{j=1}^{p}(y_{ij} - \mu_j - \lambda_j x_i)^2/\psi_j^2$$

$$-\frac{1}{2}\sum_{i=1}^{n}x_i^2,$$

which is equivalent to a sum of p separate log-likelihoods from the p regressions of Y_j on x with intercept μ_j, slope λ_j, and variance ψ_j^2. The term $\sum_i x_i^2$ does not involve unknown parameters and can be omitted.

The sufficient statistics in these regressions involve the x_i and x_i^2; in the E step of the algorithm these are replaced by their conditional expectations given the current estimates of the parameters.

Standard calculations give the conditional distribution of X given $Y = y$ and the parameters as

$$X|Y = y \sim N(\lambda'\Sigma^{-1}(y - \mu), 1 - \lambda'\Sigma^{-1}\lambda).$$

Here $\rho^2 = \lambda'\Sigma^{-1}\lambda$ is the squared multiple correlation of the factor X with the variables Y, so the conditional variance of X given $Y = y$ is $1 - \rho^2$.

In the E step of EM the unobserved x_i are replaced by

$$\tilde{x}_i = \lambda'\Sigma^{-1}(y_i - \mu)$$

and the unobserved x_i^2 are replaced by

$$\widetilde{x_i^2} = \tilde{x}_i^2 + 1 - \rho^2,$$

where the parameters are replaced by their current estimates. In the M step of EM new estimates of the parameters are obtained from the p regressions by solving the score equations

$$\hat{\lambda}_j = \sum_i (y_{ij} - \bar{y}_j)x_i \left/ \left[\sum_i \tilde{x}_i^2 + n(1 - \rho^2)\right]\right.$$

$$\hat{\psi}_j^2 = \sum_i (y_{ij} - \bar{y}_j - \lambda_j\tilde{x}_i)^2/n + \rho^2\lambda_j^2.$$

The EM algorithm may converge very slowly if the regression of Y on X is weak, and further numerical work is needed for the information matrix and (large-sample) standard errors for the parameter estimates.

BAYESIAN ANALYSIS

Bayesian analysis of the factor model, as with any other model, requires prior distributions for the model parameters; the product of the joint prior and the likelihood gives the joint posterior distribution (after normalization), and any marginal posterior distributions of interest may be computed by integrating out the relevant parameters.

Prior distributions may be *diffuse*, representing little information, or *informative*, representing real external information relevant to the current sample. *Conjugate* prior distributions are widely used where they exist; by setting the ("hyper-")

parameters in these distributions at appropriate values, they can be made to represent a range of information from diffuse to precise.

Because the factor model is essentially a set of conditionally independent linear regressions, diffuse priors are the same as for a regression model—flat on μ, λ, and log ψ_j^2. Conjugate priors are normal for μ and λ, and inverse gamma for ψ_j^2.

The mean μ is of no inferential interest, so it is convenient to integrate it out immediately from the posterior distribution. The multivariate normal likelihood can be written

$$L(\mu, \Sigma) = \frac{1}{|\Sigma|^{n/2}} \exp\left[-\frac{1}{2}\sum_{i=1}^{n}(y_i - \mu)'\Sigma^{-1}(y_i - \mu)\right]$$

$$= \frac{1}{|\Sigma|^{1/2}} \exp\left[-\frac{n}{2}(\bar{y} - \mu)'\Sigma^{-1}(\bar{y} - \mu)\right]$$

$$\cdot \frac{1}{|\Sigma|^{(n-1)/2}} \exp\left[-\frac{1}{2}\sum_{i=1}^{n}(y_i - \bar{y})'\Sigma^{-1}(y_i - \bar{y})\right].$$

A flat prior on μ leaves this unchanged, and integrating out μ gives directly the *marginal* likelihood

$$M(\Sigma) = \frac{1}{|\Sigma|^{(n-1)/2}} \exp\left(-\frac{n}{2}\operatorname{tr} S\Sigma^{-1}\right),$$

where $S = \sum_1^n (y_i - \bar{y})(y_i - \bar{y})'/n$ is the sample covariance matrix; as in frequentist theory, the analysis of the factor model may be based on this matrix.

Because the structure of $\Sigma = \Psi + \lambda\lambda'$ does not lead to any simple form for the posterior distributions of the λ_j and ψ_j^2, it is simpler to approach the posterior distributions of these parameters indirectly, through the complete-data model. Because, conditional on the x_i, the regressions of y_j on x are independent with unrelated parameters, it follows immediately from standard Bayesian results for regression models that

$$(\mu_j, \lambda_j)|\mathbf{x}, \psi_j \sim N\left((\hat{\mu}_j, \hat{\lambda}_j), \psi_j^2 S_{xx}^{-1}\right)$$

$$(n-1)s_j^2/\psi_j^2|\mathbf{x} \sim \chi_{n-1}^2,$$

where

$$\mathbf{x} = (x_1, \ldots, x_n)'$$

$$\hat{\mu}_j = \bar{y}_j - \hat{\lambda}\bar{x}$$

$$\hat{\lambda}_j = S_{jx}S_{xx}^{-1}$$

$$(n-1)s_j^2 = S_{jj} - S_{jx}S_{xx}^{-1}S_{xj}$$

$$S_{jj} = \sum_i (y_{ij} - \bar{y}_j)^2$$

$$S_{jx} = \sum_i (y_{ij} - \bar{y}_j)x_i$$

$$S_{xx} = \begin{bmatrix} n & \sum_i x_i \\ \sum_i x_i & \sum_i x_i^2 \end{bmatrix}.$$

Because the individual λ_j given $\mathbf{x}$ are conditionally independent, the joint conditional distribution of the λ_j given $\mathbf{x}$ and the ψ_j is multivariate normal with a diagonal covariance matrix, so integrating out the ψ_j, one obtains that the joint distribution of the λ_j given $\mathbf{x}$ is multivariate t, with the marginal distributions of the individual λ_j, given $\mathbf{x}$, being

$$\frac{\lambda_j - \hat{\lambda}_j}{s_j} \sim t_{n-1}.$$

We cannot proceed further analytically—integrating out $\mathbf{x}$ as well gives an intractable marginal distribution for the λ_j and ψ_j because of the complex appearance of $\mathbf{x}$ in the conditioned distributions.

Inference About the Factor Scores

One standard approach to factor score estimation in repeated-sampling theory is to use the conditional mean $\tilde{x}_i$ as the estimate of x_i, the "regression estimate" of the factor score. This estimate requires the MLEs of μ, λ, and Ψ to be substituted for the true values, introducing uncertainty that is difficult to allow for; although the delta method may be used to find large-sample standard errors for nonlinear functions like $\lambda'\Sigma^{-1}$, this does not give reliable representation of uncertainty in small to medium samples.

A further difficulty is that the regression estimate is only the (conditional) *mean* of the factor score distribution—the conditional *variance* is ignored in this representation. This underlies the criticism of regression estimates by Guttman and others, to be discussed later in this chapter.

In the Bayes theory, inference about X, like that about the model parameters, is based on its posterior distribution. The conditional distribution of X given the parameters is normal, as given previously, but in the Bayes analysis we have to integrate out the parameters from this conditional distribution (and not substitute the MLEs for the unknowns) with respect to their conditional distribution given the data.

Unfortunately, integrating out λ and Ψ from the conditional distribution of X given these parameters is intractable, although Press and Shigemasu (1997) showed, in a more general model than ours, that the marginal posterior distribution of $\mathbf{X}$ is asymptotically multivariate matrix T.

The attraction of Bayesian methods is that they can give *exact* (to within simulation error) posterior distributions without asymptotic approximations. We now consider *simulation* methods to obtain these.

Data Augmentation

The close parallel between the EM algorithm approach to maximum likelihood, using the complete data model, and the Bayesian analysis of the same model can be turned to advantage using a simulation approach called data augmentation by Tanner and Wong (1987).

We *augment* the observed data by the unobserved factor $\mathbf{x}$, using the same complete data model as for the EM algorithm. Write $\theta = (\mu, \lambda, \Psi)$ for the full vector of parameters. Then the conditional posterior distribution of θ given $\mathbf{x}$ and $\mathbf{y}$ is $\pi(\theta|\mathbf{x}, \mathbf{y})$ and the conditional distribution of $\mathbf{x}$ given θ and $\mathbf{y}$ is $\pi(\mathbf{x}|\theta, \mathbf{y})$. Our object is to compute the *marginal* posterior distribution $\pi(\theta|\mathbf{y})$ of θ given $\mathbf{y}$ and the *predictive* distribution $\pi(\mathbf{x}|\mathbf{y})$ of $\mathbf{x}$. The DA algorithm achieves this by cycling between the two conditionals, in a similar way to the EM algorithm cycling between the E and M steps. However, in DA we perform not expectations as in the E step, but full *simulations* from the conditional distributions (Tanner, 1996, p. 91), and convergence is *in distribution*, rather than to a function maximum. One full iteration of the DA algorithm consists of the following:

- *Imputation step*: Generate a sample of M values $\mathbf{x}_{[1]}, \ldots, \mathbf{x}_{[M]}$ from the current approximation to the predictive distribution $\pi(\mathbf{x}|\mathbf{y})$.
- *Posterior step*: Update the current approximation to $\pi(\theta|\mathbf{y})$ to be the mixture of conditional posteriors of θ, given $\mathbf{y}$ and the augmented data $\mathbf{x}_{[1]}, \ldots, \mathbf{x}_{[M]}$:

$$\tilde{\pi}(\theta|\mathbf{y}) = \sum_m \pi(\theta|\mathbf{x}_{[m]}, \mathbf{y}) \cdot \frac{1}{M}.$$

- Generate a sample of M values $\theta_{[1]}, \ldots, \theta_{[M]}$ from $\tilde{\pi}(\theta|\mathbf{y})$.
- For each $\theta_{[m]}$, generate a random value $\mathbf{x}_{[m]}$ of $\mathbf{x}$ from $\pi(\mathbf{x}|\theta_{[m]}, \mathbf{y})$.

We repeat these iterations until the posterior distributions of θ and $\mathbf{x}$ converge, or "stabilize." To assess this stability, we track summary statistics of the posterior distributions of the parameters; we illustrate with the medians and quartiles of the model parameters.

These iterations can be carried out with relatively small M, like $M = 50$, to save computing time. Once the posterior distributions have converged, M may be increased to a larger number, like $M = 1,000$, to give the posterior distribution to high accuracy. We use kernel density estimation to give a smooth graphical picture of the posteriors, though the 1,000 values themselves may be used to make any needed probability statements about the parameters.

This process can be substantially accelerated by starting from an approximate posterior for θ based on the MLEs $\hat{\theta}$ and information matrix I of the parameters from a maximum likelihood routine, though it can start from a random starting point, as we show in the example.

At convergence we have the full (marginal over $\mathbf{x}$) posterior distribution of θ and the (marginal over θ) posterior distribution of $X = (X_1, \ldots, X_n)$, so the marginal posterior distribution of any individual factor score X_i follows immediately.

An obvious but fundamental point is that the inference about X_i is its *distribution*, conditional on the observed responses y_{ij}. From the M simulation values of this X, we *could* compute the posterior mean and variance, and these would be corrected for the underestimation of variability in the "plug-in" conditional mean and variance. This is unnecessary, however, because we have the full (simulated) *distribution* of X: The distribution of the simulated values represents the real information about X, that is, it is not a parameter that can be estimated by maximum likelihood with a standard error, but a random variable.

AN EXAMPLE

We illustrate the DA analysis with $n = 200$ observations from a four-variate example, with

$$\mu' = (0, 0, 0, 0), \quad \lambda' = (0.8, 0.6, 0.4, 0.2), \quad \text{diag } \Psi = (0.36, 0.64, 0.84, 0.96).$$

We generate 200 values x_i randomly from $N(0, 1)$, and compute the data values

$$y_{ij} = \mu_j + \lambda_j x_i + e_{ij}, \qquad i = 1, \ldots, 200; \quad j = 1, \ldots, 4$$

where the e_{ij} are randomly generated from $N(0, \psi_j^2)$.

To illustrate the power and capabilities of the DA approach, we do not use a maximum likelihood factor analysis package to get initial estimates of the parameters, but begin with a set of $M = 1,000$ random values of x_{im}, $m = 1, \ldots, M$, generated from $N(0, 1)$ for each observation i. For each m we fit the regression of each y_j on $\mathbf{x}_m$, obtaining MLEs of the model parameters. We then draw, for each m and each j, random values μ_{jm}, λ_{jm}, and ψ_{jm}^2 from the respective current conditional posterior distributions of these parameters given $\mathbf{y}$ and $\mathbf{x}$. The values of all the parameters for each m are conceptually assigned mass $1/M$ in the discrete joint posterior distribution of all these parameters; the updated posterior is the unweighted mean of the M individual conditional posteriors. This completes one "posterior" step of the DA algorithm.

To generate random parameter values from the current marginal posterior, we draw a random integer m' in the range $(1, M)$, and select the corresponding parameter vector indexed m' from the foregoing discrete posterior distribution. Given the parameter vector $(\mu_{[m']}, \lambda_{[m']}, \psi^2_{[m']})$, we compute the posterior distribution of $\mathbf{x}$ given y_{ij}, and draw one random vector $\mathbf{x}_{[m']}$ from this distribution.

We repeat this process of random integer drawing and random generation of $\mathbf{x}$ a total of M times, obtaining $\mathbf{x}_{im'}$, $m' = 1, \ldots, M$. This completes one full iteration of the DA algorithm.

Figure 8.1 shows the median and upper and lower quartiles of the posterior distributions of the factor loadings λ_j and specific variances ψ^2_j for 100 iterations of the DA algorithm. The distributions of the intercepts μ_j are very stable around zero and we do not show them. The 100 iterations, each with $M = 1{,}000$, required about 5 hours of computing time on a Dell workstation. All programming was done in Stata 8.

It is clear that convergence of the algorithm for most of the λ_j requires 10–15 iterations (this is known as the "burn-in" period in the Bayesian literature), but many more iterations are needed for the variances ψ^2_j, especially for ψ^2_1, the smallest variance, and the corresponding λ_1: as for the EM algorithm, convergence of a parameter value near a zero boundary is much slower. The rate of convergence is parametrization dependent, an important issue in large-scale Markov chains for complex models; convergence may be substantially improved by choosing near-orthogonal parametrizations.

From the 1,000 observations on each parameter we compute a kernel density using a Gaussian kernel, choosing the bandwidth to give a smooth density. The kernel densities for all the parameters are shown in Fig. 8.2. The density for ψ^2_1 is shown on the log scale because the kernel method does not restrict the density estimate to the positive values of ψ^2_1.

All posterior densities have the true parameter values within the 95% credible region, though some are near the edges. The densities of the loadings λ_j are slightly skewed and have slightly longer tails than the normal distribution; those for μ_j are very close to normality, and those for ψ^2_j are quite skewed as expected, especially for small ψ^2_j.

We show in Fig. 8.3 the kernel posterior density for x_1 (solid curve), together with the "empirical Bayes" normal density $N(\hat{\lambda}'\hat{V}^{-1}(y - \hat{\mu}), 1 - \hat{\rho}^2)$ (dashed curve) using the maximum likelihood estimates of the parameters from a standard factor analysis routine; these are given in Table 8.1. For reference, the true value of

TABLE 8.1
Maximum Likelihood Estimates of the Parameters

j	$\hat{\mu}_j$	$\hat{\lambda}_j$	$\hat{\psi}^2_j$
1	−0.0337	0.9743	0.0508
2	−0.0137	0.4626	0.7861
3	−0.0553	0.3538	0.8749
4	0.0690	0.3101	0.9038

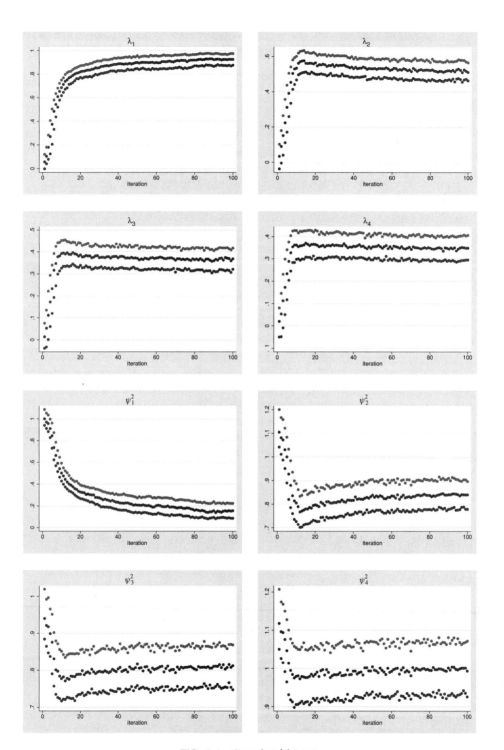

FIG. 8.1. Iteration history.

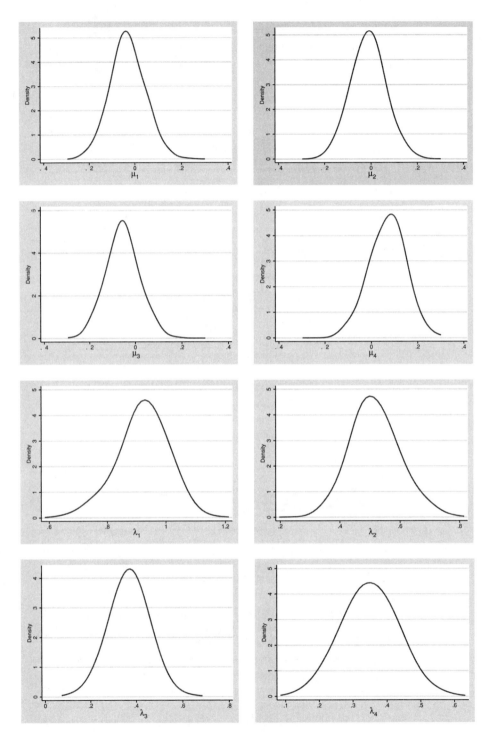

FIG. 8.2. Kernel densities.

216

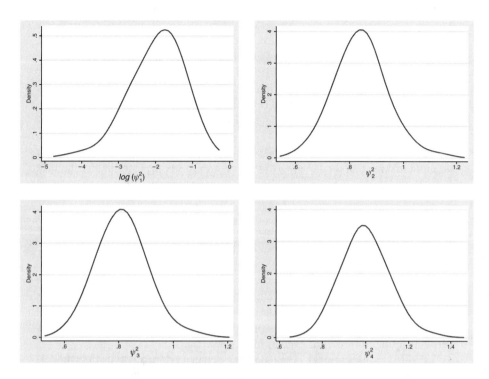

FIG. 8.2. contd.

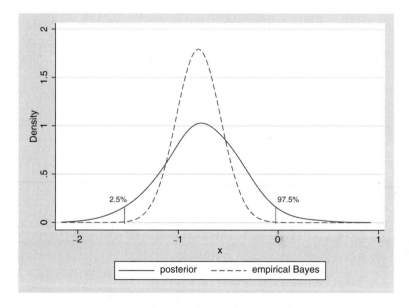

FIG. 8.3. Posterior density of x_1 and empirical Bayes density.

217

x_1 is -1.094. The much greater dispersion of the posterior density is quite marked, showing the importance of allowing correctly for uncertainty in the parameters. The figure also shows the 2.5% (-1.537) and 97.5% (-0.024) points of the x_1 distribution, giving a 95% "credible interval" for x_1 of (-1.537, -0.024). The corresponding values from the "plug-in" normal distribution are -1.234 and -0.363; respectively, the coverage of this interval is only 76% from the true posterior distribution of x_1.

We remark again that preliminary estimates of the parameters are not required; it is quite striking that the DA algorithm converges to stable posterior distributions relatively quickly, given the well-known slow convergence of the EM algorithm in this model.

RELATION TO FACTOR INDETERMINACY

The DA analysis casts light on the controversy over factor score estimation and factor indeterminacy (Guttman, 1955; McDonald, 1974). The standard practice at the time for factor score estimation was to use the mean of the conditional distribution of $X | Y = y$ as a point estimate of x. The estimates of the parameters were substituted for their true values in this approach.

This substitution approach is well documented in modern random effect models as the empirical Bayes approach—the posterior distribution (typically normal) of the random effects, depending on the unknown model parameters, is estimated by the same distribution with the unknown parameters replaced by their MLEs, called "plug-in" estimates. This distribution is used to make full distributional statements about the random effects, not just the mean. The distributional statements are deficient because the uncertainty in the MLEs is not allowed for, and so the true variance of the posterior distribution is underestimated (as in Fig. 8.3).

Guttman was concerned, however, with a different issue, the behavior of the "regression estimate" as a random variable in repeated sampling.

He considered the sampling distribution of the regression estimate, averaged over the distribution of Y. Conditionally on $Y = y$,

$$X | Y = y \sim N(\lambda' V^{-1}(y - \mu), 1 - \rho^2),$$

but if we average the distribution of

$$\tilde{X} = \lambda' V^{-1}(y - \mu)$$

over Y, we have

$$\tilde{X} \sim N(0, \lambda' V^{-1} \lambda),$$

which is $N(0, \rho^2)$. So the *unconditional* distribution of $\tilde{X}$, averaged across varying sample values of Y, has zero mean but variance ρ^2, not 1.

If regression estimates were really estimates of the factor scores, then it seemed axiomatic that they should have the "right" distribution, that of the true factor scores. They clearly failed this requirement.

Guttman expressed this failure through a conceptual simulation experiment: given the true values of all the parameters, generate a random error term ϵ from $N(0, 1 - \rho^2)$ and add this to the regression estimate, giving a new estimate $Z_1 = \tilde{X} + \epsilon$. Then the unconditional distribution of Z_1 would be $N(0, 1)$ like that for X.

Now imagine two such error terms with opposite signs: given ϵ, we could equally well have observed $-\epsilon$, and this could have been used to obtain $Z_2 = \tilde{X} - \epsilon$ (with the same ϵ). The correlation of Z_1 and Z_2, in repeated random generations, would be

$$r = \frac{\text{cov}(Z_1, Z_2)}{\sqrt{\text{var}(Z_1)\,\text{var}(Z_2)}} = \text{var}(\tilde{X}) - \text{var}(\epsilon)$$

$$= 2\rho^2 - 1,$$

which is negative for $\rho^2 < 0.5$, a high value for any regression model in psychology, let alone a factor model.

Guttman argued that two equally plausible values of X that correlated negatively would cast doubt on the whole factor model, and he coined the term "factor indeterminacy" for this aspect of the factor model. Because the primary role of the factor model was to make statements about individual unobserved abilities, Guttman concluded that the model could not be used in this way except for models with very high variable–factor score correlations. Factor analysis was based on a shaky assumption.

The Bayesian framework helps to understand why this criticism was overstated. The essential feature of Bayesian analysis is that the information about the model parameters and any other unobserved quantities is expressed through posterior distributions, conditional on the observed data. This applies to the unobserved factor variables, and provides a very natural conditional distribution for an individual subject's factor score. The regression estimate—the mean of this conditional distribution—is indeed an unsuitable summary represention of the factor score because it suppresses the conditional variance, and more generally the whole conditional distribution, of the factor score.

Guttman's criticism, viewed in this light, makes just this point—that the variance is being overlooked: Conditional means cannot be used as a surrogate for the true values without some way of representing the conditional uncertainty. But this failure to represent correctly the uncertainty about factor scores does not cast doubt on the factor model, merely on the technical tools with which the uncertainty in factor scores is represented.

One such representation would be to present the plug-in conditional variance as well as the plug-in conditional mean. The Bayesian representation is more informative however; it gives the full distribution of the uncertain factor score, and

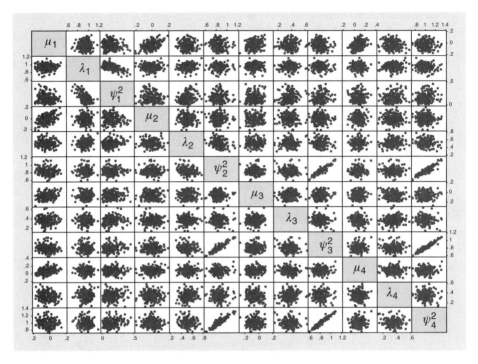

FIG. 8.4. Scatter plots of all parameters.

allows properly for the estimation of the parameters on which this distribution is based. The uncertainty in the factor loading and specific variance parameters is also correctly represented in a much richer way than by the MLE and information matrix.

The simulation approach is even more general than we have demonstrated; it can be applied to differences among individuals in ability by simply computing the M values of any comparison $x_i - x_{i'}$ of interest. Such comparisons are widely used in "small-area estimation" and other empirical Bayes applications in multilevel models where differences among regions, areas, or centers are of importance. Such differences are always overstated by empirical Bayes methods because of the systematic underestimation of variability from the use of plug-in ML estimates.

The full joint posterior distribution of the model parameters provides even more information, for which there is no frequentist equivalent. Figure 8.4 is a composite plot of each parameter against every other for a random subsample of 200 values drawn from the 1,000 (the subsampling is necessary for clarity). It is immediately clear that correlations are very high between the three smaller variances and that the factor loading and specific variance for Y_1 are highly negatively correlated. The correlation matrix of the parameters (from the full 1,000 values) shown in Table 8.2 bears this out.

TABLE 8.2

Correlation Coefficients of the Parameters

	μ_1	λ_1	ψ_1	μ_2	λ_2	ψ_2	μ_3	λ_3	ψ_3	μ_4	λ_4
λ_1	−0.022										
ψ_1	0.013	−0.715									
μ_2	0.452	0.047	−0.038								
λ_2	0.026	0.127	0.228	0.036							
ψ_2	0.003	0.077	−0.061	−0.009	−0.190						
μ_3	0.355	0.057	−0.009	0.142	0.082	0.045					
λ_3	0.007	0.016	0.141	−0.025	0.097	−0.076	0.040				
ψ_3	−0.017	−0.006	0.077	0.005	−0.043	0.912	0.053	−0.157			
μ_4	0.281	−0.060	0.079	0.190	0.024	0.042	0.128	0.003	0.080		
λ_4	−0.075	0.029	0.118	0.024	0.132	−0.076	−0.068	−0.005	−0.055	−0.060	
ψ_4	0.004	−0.047	0.117	0.006	−0.047	0.914	0.061	−0.076	0.957	0.078	−0.142

CONCLUSION

The data augmentation algorithm, and more general Markov chain Monte Carlo methods, provide the Bayesian analysis of the factor model. No new issues arise in the general multiple-common-factor case except for the rotational invariance problem—given a fixed covariance matrix for the factors, their posterior distribution can be simulated in the same way as for a single factor.

The computing time required for the full Bayesian analysis is substantial, but the richness of information from the full joint posterior distribution more than compensates for the computational effort.

MCMC packages like BUGS (Bayesian inference using Gibbs sampling) are widely available: we can look forward confidently to their future use with factor models, and other latent variable models, of much greater complexity than the simple model discussed here.

ACKNOWLEDGMENTS

We have benefited from discussions with our colleague Darren Wilkinson, and from editorial suggestions from Albert Maydeu-Olivares.

REFERENCES

Guttman, L. (1955). The determinacy of factor score matrices with applications for five other problems of common factor theory. *British Journal of Statistical Psychology, 8*, 65–82.

Martin, J. K., & McDonald, R. P. (1975). Bayesian estimation in unrestricted factor analysis: A treatment for Heywood cases. *Psychometrika, 40*, 505–517.

McDonald, R. P. (1974). The measurement of factor indeterminacy. *Psychometrika, 39*, 203–222.

Press, S. J., & Shigemasu, K. (1989). Bayesian inference in factor analysis. In L. J. Gleser, M. D. Perlman, S. J. Press and A. R. Sampson; *Contributions to probability and statistics: Essays in honor of Ingram Olki* (pp. 271–287). New York: Springer-Verlag.

Press, S. J., & Shigemasu, K. (1997). *Bayesian inference in factor analysis—revised* (Technical Rep. No. 243). University of California, Riverside, Department of Statistics.

Rowe, D. B. (2002). *Multivariate Bayesian statistics: Models for source separation and signal unmixing*. Boca Raton, FL: CRC Press.

Rubin, D. B., & Thayer, D. (1982). EM algorithms for ML factor analysis. *Psychometrika, 47*, 69–76.

Tanner, M. A. (1996) *Tools for statistical Inference: Methods for the exploration of posterior distributions and likelihood Functions*. Springer, New York.

Tanner, M. A., & Wong, W. H. (1987). The calculation of posterior distributions by data augmentation. *Journal of the American Statistical Association, 82*, 528–540.

III

Structural Equation Models and Related Methods

Many of the seminal contributions of Roderick P. McDonald come from his work in structural equation modeling (SEM). His early contributions in this area (McDonald, 1969; McDonald & Swaminathan, 1972) were brought to the forefront in his covariance structure analysis (COSAN) model (McDonald, 1978) and the freely available computer program (developed with Colin Fraser). The COSAN model is known for its great flexibility, and reflects McDonald's deep understanding of the mathematical and statistical basis of SEM. Extensions of this logic are presented both in McDonald (1985) and in his Psychometric Society presidential address (McDonald, 1986). In more recent work, Rod has extended SEM in many ways, including theoretical work with Jack McArdle on RAM notation (McArdle & McDonald, 1984) and with Harvey Goldstein on multilevel SEM (McDonald & Goldstein, 1989), and in his continuing efforts to make SEM more widely available and understandable (e.g., McDonald, 1997, 2002).

This part of the book starts with a chapter by **Jack McArdle** describing the initial development of RAM rules for latent variable structural equation modeling. This chapter discusses the interplay between general SEM models (e.g., LISREL and COSAN), as well as the important personal contributions of Rod McDonald to progress in this area.

The next three chapters are devoted to important statistical issues in SEM. The broad problem of goodness of fit in SEM is an important topic taken up by **Herbert Marsh**, **Kit-Tai Hau**, and **David Grayson**. This is a description of contributions of many behavioral scientists to this vexing problem, and Rod McDonald's work is clear and evident. **Wolfgang Hartmann**, known as the creator of SAS PROC CALIS, discusses the practical and theoretical basis of resampling methods in SEM. This chapter leaves no doubt about the important future of this topic.

Jim Steiger details an important and often overlooked problem in basic SEM statistical tests—the comparison of correlations between and within independent samples. Steiger shows why this problem is initially difficult and how it can be easily solved using SEM.

The last two chapters of this part expand the current SEM in important directions. **Michael Browne** and **John Nesselroade** discuss the represention of psychological processes with dynamic factor models based on ARMA time-series models. **Harvey Goldstein** and **William Browne** discuss multilevel factor analysis models and show how they can be used with both continuous and discrete data. Both chapters are filled with interesting modeling ideas that will be widely used in future SEM research.

REFERENCES

McArdle, J. J., & McDonald, R. P. (1984). Some algebraic properties of the reticular action model for moment structures. *British Journal of Mathematical and Statistical Psychology, 37*, 234–251.

McDonald, R. P. (1969). A generalized common factor analysis based on residual covariance matrices of prescribed structure. *British Journal of Mathematical Statistical Psychology, 22*, 149–163.

McDonald, R. P. (1978). A simple comprehensive model for the analysis of covariance structures. *British Journal of Mathematical and Statistical Psychology, 31*, 59–72.

McDonald, R. P. (1985). *Factor analysis and related methods.* Hillsdale, NJ: Lawrence Erlbaum Associates, Inc.

McDonald, R. P. (1986). Describing the elephant: Structure and function in multivariate data. *Psychometrika, 51*, 513–534.

McDonald, R. P. (1997). Haldane's lungs: A case study in path analysis. *Multivariate Behavioral Research, 32*, 1–38.

McDonald, R. P. (2002). What can we learn from the path equations? Identifiability, constraints, equivalence. *Psychometrika, 67*, 225–249.

McDonald, R. P., & Goldstein, H. (1989). Balanced versus unbalanced designs for linear structural relations in two-level data. *British Journal of Mathematical and Statistical Psychology, 42*, 215–232.

McDonald, R. P., Ho, M.-H., & Ringo, A. F. (2002). Principles and practice in reporting structural equation analyses. *Psychological Methods, 7*, 64–82.

McDonald, R. P., & Swaminathan, H. (1972). *Structural analyses of dispersion matrices based on a very general model with a rapidly convergent procedure for the evaluation of parameters.* Toronto: University of Toronto, Ontario Institute for Studies in Education, Department of Measurement, Evaluation and Computer Applications.

9

The Development of the RAM Rules for Latent Variable Structural Equation Modeling

John J. McArdle
University of Virginia

This chapter describes the original basis of the Reticular Action Model (RAM) approach to structural equation modeling (SEM). The RAM rules were initially presented (1978–1981) to simplify and unify structural equation models based on path analysis graphics. The mathematical representation of RAM is presented as a second-order moment structure model that includes two parameter matrices, one of which is a patterned inverse. The graphic representation of RAM is presented through a series of definitions and axioms that provide a complete and concise isomorphism between graphics and algebra. Comparisons to other traditional models, such as those of multiple linear regression, path analysis, and factor analysis, show how these models may be easily and economically represented using RAM rules. Two other general modeling foundations, LISREL and COSAN, are presented as special cases and, somewhat paradoxically, as generalizations of RAM. These results are then used to develop some important technical features of the RAM rules, including efficient algorithmic estimation procedures and the further development of statistical indicators. Issues of conceptual representation are provided from a general systems perspective. Finally, some of the current limitations and benefits of the RAM rules are considered.

INTRODUCTION

Researchers interested in structural equation modeling often face the same questions that were apparent 25 years ago: (a) What analyses can I do with SEM? (b) How do I do these SEM analyses? (c) Why should I do these SEM analyses? Various answers to these questions have been refined over the last several decades, and expert treatments of these topics are available (e.g., Loehlin, 1987, 1998; McDonald, 1986, 1995). However, a substantial part of the debate and confusion about these key questions emanates from the fundamental frame used to describe SEM. To deal with these questions, I revive ideas surrounding what were termed "general models" for SEM. In the early 1970s the question of SEM generality was a major issue for both SEM developers and users. Two seminal developments along these lines included the creation of the linear structural relations (LISREL) program by Jöreskog (1973b) and the creation of the covariance structure analysis (COSAN) program by McDonald (1978). I used these classical ideas to develop a simple notation termed the reticular action meta-model (RAM; McArdle & McDonald, 1984) that renders some of these controversies and problems moot.

The SEM problems discussed here often arise when we deal with practical problems, for example, when we use SEM with longitudinal data with more than two occasions, with any models including incomplete data patterns, and with any models based on atypical representations of latent variables (e.g., Horn & McArdle, 1980; McArdle, 2001). A recent model including this kind of complexity is the latent variable SEM presented in Fig. 9.1; this is the precise path-graph representation of a bivariate difference score model for longitudinal twin data (McArdle & Hamagami, 2003). Of course, any sensible researcher may ask, "Why would anyone want to fit such a model?" Although this is a reasonable question, this is not the focal topic here. Instead we presume a model of this complexity is of substantive interest. This leads the researcher to ask, "Can this model be fitted with my favorite SEM program?" If so, "How can we actually fit this model?" One purpose of this chapter is to provide practical answers to questions of this nature. To do this I will show that the RAM rules are based on the *necessary and sufficient* features required for a general SEM notation.

To begin this task, it is useful to recognize that many researchers rely on the dominant SEM notation termed linear structural relations (LISREL; e.g., Jöreskog & Sörbom, 1979). This elegant notation was developed by merging concepts from a psychometric common factor "measurement model" combined with an econometric "structural model" (Jöreskog, 1973b; Wiley, 1973). In this form LISREL creates restrictive hypotheses about the manifest covariance structure, so this two-part distinction is often seen as a fundamental SEM requirement (e.g., Bollen, 1989; Hayduk, 1987). On the surface, this also seems to imply that LISREL cannot deal with some important analytic problems: (a) path models with no latent variables, (b) correlations among the specific factors across blocks of variables, (c) estimation of standard deviations rather than variances, (d) direct arrows from manifest to

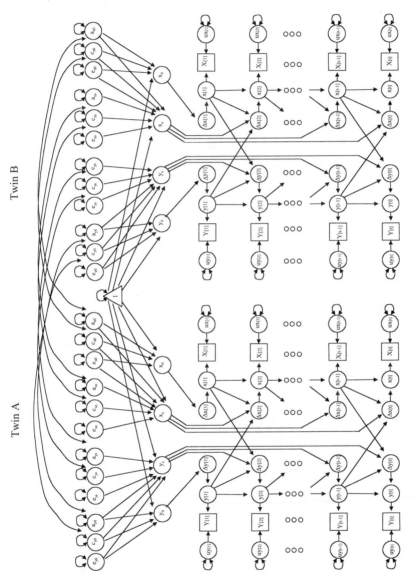

FIG. 9.1. An example of a contemporary path diagram. *Note:* From *Structural equation models for evaluating dynamic concepts within longitudinal twin analyses* by J. J. McArdle & F. Hamagami (2003). *Behavior Genetics, 33*(3), 137–159. Copyright 2003 by Springer Science+Business Media. Inc. Reprinted with permission.

latent variables, (e) higher order factors within each set, (f) more than two sets of variables (e.g., X, Y, and Z), (g) means and intercept terms in the equations, and (h) allowing correlations between predictors and disturbance terms. However, in an illuminating series of reports, Jöreskog and Sörbom (1979) demonstrated how the LISREL program could be reparametrized, or "tricked," into handling these problems. These SEM possibilities still create confusion among the expert and novice alike, but the flexibility of the computational algorithm (combined with the use of the LISREL **B** matrix) leads to an interesting result: *The LISREL model is a general organizing principle but actually poses no restrictive hypotheses about any covariance structure.*

At about the same time, McDonald (1978) developed an algebraic model and implemented a computer program, termed COSAN, which used a higher order structure that seemed to be flexible enough to carry out all SEM analyses. McDonald (1978, p. 61) basically showed that symmetric matrices at each level of a latent variable higher order system were not needed. Any symmetric matrix could essentially be "carried up" from one level to the next by using a series of latent variables with no variance, that is, fixed linear combinations. This mathematical simplicity led to a series of elegant statistical features described by McDonald (1978, 1979, 1980; McDonald & Swaminathan, 1972). This use of flexible programming in place of substantive concepts made COSAN much different from the basic concepts of the prior models (Bentler, 1976).

As a postgraduate user of both programs, I found myself spending a great deal of time studying the ways that these programs were dealt with both standard models and special cases. I learned the differences in the input scripts required for these programs. This allowed me to represent the output of both programs as path diagrams. It was at this output stage that I noticed the communalities among all such programs. I found I could obtain exactly the same path analysis results from both programs. The special cases I was studying were precursors to models such as those of Fig. 9.1, and that did not seem to fit easily into either program (e.g., Horn & McArdle, 1980). The success of these analyses led me to the unusual conclusion that *there were no real differences between LISREL and COSAN.*

My initial publications were suggestions to use a slightly new set of rules for complete path analysis diagrams (McArdle, 1978, 1979b, 1979c). However, this approach also highlighted an algebraic paradox: These graphics showed not only that LISREL and COSAN were identical in applications, but that they also had the same algebraic limits, and each could do the same analyses with far less matrix algebra. In essence, *LISREL and COSAN were special cases of each other and themselves.* This suggestion contested most previous work on this topic, and these paradoxical ideas were dealt with in different ways by different researchers. In general, this was not a critical issue to most SEM researchers because both LISREL and COSAN worked exceptionally well. However, it was also clear that that any advances in this area were thought to be found in extensions of LISREL and COSAN. For example, Bentler (1976) proposed an extension of COSAN as a higher order common factor model, and his student Weeks (1978) completed a doctoral dissertation on an entirely new program based on this logic. In a public presentation (McArdle, 1978), I demonstrated how higher order factor models could already be programmed in both LISREL and COSAN, and this meant that new computer programs were not necessary for this or other problems. In a series of subsequent presentations, Bentler and Weeks (1979, 1980) altered the previous general representation of Bentler (1976) in a radical fashion to account for this new finding.

At this time one of the key developers in this field, Roderick P. McDonald (who I had not yet met) tried to understand my paradoxical conclusions. Rod's willingness to work with me was most helpful in the early days of the basic RAM rules. Under Rod's guidance, I improved the original 1978 manuscript and circulated it in 1981 under the title, "The Reticular Action Meta-model: A Simplified Representation for Structural Equation Modeling." This manuscript was difficult to publish, partly due to the confusing paradoxes and the controversy over its development. After several years of rejection, the key algebraic aspects of this RAM presentation were published in McArdle and McDonald (1984). Some key graphic principles of RAM were published in the RAMpath program by McArdle and Boker (1990) and Boker, McArdle, and Neale (2002). The original and complete development of RAM is published here for the first time as a small tribute to Roderick P. McDonald.

To preserve some key historical aspects of this treatment, the next six sections appear in the exact form as the initial presentation of March 1981. An inital historical account of research on general SEM concepts (ca. 1981) is followed by a description of the mathematical basis of RAM notation (with Greek notation where appropriate), a description of the graphic basis of RAM notation as derived from the mathematics (with highlights where appropriate), and a comparison of RAM notation to several alternatives, which leads to an exposition of the paradoxical interrelationships among general systems, especially LISREL and COSAN, in both graphic and algebraic terms. Then some computational features are added to suggest how RAM notation could be used as the generic basis of future computer programs. This is followed by a discussion of the conceptual utility of RAM, including the freedom to use SEMs that do not seem to fit into any more specific schema (e.g., Fig. 9.1). In the concluding section, I offer an overview of the first 25 years of the RAM rules.

HISTORICAL INTRODUCTION
(CIRCA 1981)

There has recently been some interest in the relationships among models that have been proposed for the structural analysis of covariance matrices and mean vectors (i.e., moment structures). Not surprisingly, in the chronological sequence of development in this area one seems to find a progression from special to more general models that subsume their predecessors. Broadly, the early sequence is from Spearman's (1904) classical one-factor model, through Thurstone's (1947) multiple-factor model, to the beginnings of the treatment of the restricted oblique common factor model by Anderson and Rubin (1956). These seminal developments led to Bock and Bargmann's (1966) introduction of a group of models for the analysis of covariance structures, which was later expanded into the general analysis of covariance structures (ACOVS) model of Jöreskog (1970). The ACOVS model is essentially a second-order common factor model in which the matrices may be *patterned*; that is, the elements of any matrix could be prescribed constants, parameters that are free to be individually estimated, or parameters that are constrained to be equal to one or more other parameters. These provisions supplied a remarkably flexible model for the analysis of covariance structures (Jöreskog, 1973a).

There have been several more recent attempts (*sie*) to develop these ideas further. For example, Bentler (1976) recommended the development of a straightforward generalization of ACOVS to what might be called an *m*th-order common factor model. However, neither Jöreskog's ACOVS model nor Bentler's *m*th-order counterpart of it made provision for specifying the parameters of the inverse of a matrix in the model. Subsequently, Keesling and Wiley (see Wiley, 1973) showed a patterned inverse was necessary in a general-purpose model for multivariate analysis and Jöreskog (1973b) used this in his model for linear structural relations (LISREL). We may loosely describe LISREL as a third-order restricted factor model in which the inverse of one of the three factor loading matrices is patterned. Because a patterned matrix does not in general have an inverse of the same pattern, specific provision for patterned inverses is thus seen to be necessary in the analysis of moment structures. Jöreskog and Sörbom (1980) programmed a version of this model (LISREL-IV) that allowed patterned residual covariances, as in McDonald (1969), and multiple independent groups, as in Jöreskog (1971).

McDonald (1978) described an *m*th-order model in which the inverse of any matrix of the model can be patterned as desired. As a consequence, McDonald's model, COSAN, yields the ACOVS model of any order when no inverse matrix is patterned, and also models of the LISREL type with a mixed sequence of patterned matrices and patterned inverses. McDonald obtained some simplification of the *m*th-order model by an algebraic device that allowed it to be written as though it contained no residual covariance matrices. This meant that an *m*th-order factor model would contain only $m + 1$ matrices instead of $2m + 1$, thus providing a remarkable economy of representation that simplified the programming of the model and certain of its properties.

In a general sense, then, the chronological sequence that has just been outlined shows a broad tendency toward increasing complexity of the matrix representation of the models accompanying an apparent increase in generality. In direct contrast, however, McArdle (1978, 1979b, 1979c, 1980; Horn & McArdle, 1980) presented a path-graphic formulation termed RAM, which showed that all of the foregoing models for the structural analysis of multivariate data could be represented extremely economically by using only a second-order model with an inverse feature. This model also demonstrated a paradoxical set of interrelationships among the models and rendered meaningless any question of determining which model is a "special case" of which other from their matrix specification alone.

A specialized version of McArdle's general result was quoted without proof by Bentler and Weeks (1979, Equations 5 and 6). The account given by Bentler and Weeks of this representation is far from complete and at several points might be misleading. For example, Bentler and Weeks dismiss the simple RAM representation as being "not as convenient for comparative purposes" (p. 172) as, for example, the Bentler (1976) mth-order representation. Thus, the object of this chapter is to fully develop the RAM representation of multivariate moment structures in a formal fashion at several levels of representation; including mathematical, graphic, comparative, technical, and conceptual. This discussion will serve to both clarify the relations between RAM and the main models in this field and show how the simple principles of RAM provide a *necessary and sufficient foundation for traditional* structural equations models.

ALGEBRAIC REPRESENTATION

Let $\mathbf{v}$ be a $t \times 1$ vector of random *variables*, and let

$$\mathbf{v} = \mathbf{A}\,\mathbf{v} + \mathbf{u}, \tag{1}$$

where $\mathbf{A}$ is a square matrix of structural weights of $\mathbf{v}$ on itself so that any element α_{ij} represents a *directed* or *asymmetric* relationship from column variable $\mathbf{v}_j$ to row variable $\mathbf{v}_i$. In the typical case where a variable is not directed onto itself, Equation 1 is similar to the basic regression equation of image theory as treated by Guttman (1957); $\mathbf{A}$ represents the regression of each of the t variables on the other $t - 1$ variables; $\mathbf{u}_i$ represents the residual or anti-image of $\mathbf{v}_i$; and the corresponding diagonal α_{ii} is zero. If all regression coefficients on other variables are zero (e.g., $\alpha_{ij} = 0$, $j = 1, \ldots, t$), then the variable $\mathbf{v}_i$ is considered the same as its own residual $\mathbf{u}_i$.

We also define the $t \times t$ matrix

$$\mathbf{\Omega} = E\{\mathbf{u}\,\mathbf{u}'\}, \tag{2}$$

where E denotes the expectation operator, so that any element ω_{ij} represents an *undirected* or *symmetric* structural relation among residual variables $\mathbf{u}_i$ and $\mathbf{u}_j$. If there is no relationship among the $\mathbf{u}_i$ and $\mathbf{u}_j$, it follows that $\omega_{ij} = 0$ ($i = 1, \ldots, t$; $j = 1, \ldots, t$).

The structural parameters of $\mathbf{A}$ and $\mathbf{\Omega}$ are presumed to be associated with a set of numerical values. In terms of model specification, we will permit any of these parameters to take on one of three different settings: (a) *fixed* at some prescribed constant (e.g., zero or unity), (b) *free* to be estimated in some prescribed fashion, and/or (c) *constrained* to be a linear function of one or a set of other parameters (e.g., equal to another). More details on the estimation of these values are discussed in a later section.

To define the overall moments among variables in terms of structural parameters, we define the $t \times t$ symmetric matrix

$$\mathbf{\Sigma} = E\{\mathbf{v}\,\mathbf{v}'\}, \tag{3}$$

where each element σ_{ij} represents the overall *association* between variables $\mathbf{v}_i$ and $\mathbf{v}_j$. Using these basic definitions, it follows that Equation 1 can be rewritten as

$$\mathbf{u} = \mathbf{v} - \mathbf{A}\mathbf{v} = (\mathbf{I}_t - \mathbf{A})\mathbf{v}, \tag{4}$$

where $\mathbf{I}_t$ is a $t \times t$ identity matrix, whence it follows that

$$\mathbf{\Omega} = (\mathbf{I}_t - \mathbf{A})\mathbf{\Sigma}(\mathbf{I}_t - \mathbf{A})'. \tag{5}$$

Perhaps more important, we may now also write all variables in terms of the residual structural relations as

$$\mathbf{v} = (\mathbf{I}_t - \mathbf{A})^{-1}\mathbf{u}, \tag{6}$$

which yields the *moment structure model* for all variables as

$$\mathbf{\Sigma} = (\mathbf{I}_t - \mathbf{A})^{-1}\mathbf{\Omega}(\mathbf{I}_t - \mathbf{A})^{-1'}. \tag{7}$$

For purposes of empirical utility, we now let $\mathbf{v}$ be partitioned into two subvectors $\mathbf{m}$, of j components, and ℓ, of k components. That is, $t = j + k$ and

$$\mathbf{v}' = [\mathbf{m}, \ell]'. \tag{8}$$

The j components of $\mathbf{m}$ may be considered observed or *manifest* variables, and the k components of ℓ may be considered unobserved or *latent* variables. To distinguish these variables we define the $j \times t$ matrix

$$\mathbf{F} = [\mathbf{I}_j : {}_j\mathbf{O}_k], \tag{9}$$

where ${}_j\mathbf{O}_k$ is a $j \times k$ null matrix, so that

$$\mathbf{m} = \mathbf{F}\mathbf{v}. \tag{10}$$

Thus, $\mathbf{F}$ is a fixed known matrix of prescribed unity and zero constants that acts to select or *filter* the manifest variables out of the full set of manifest and latent variables. If, for any reason, the components of $\mathbf{v}$ are permuted to some mixed order, the columns of $\mathbf{F}$ can be correspondingly permuted.

We now write the $j \times j$ symmetric matrix

$$\Sigma_{mm} = E\{\mathbf{m}\mathbf{m}'\} \tag{11}$$

as a general raw product–moment matrix without correction for means. Of course, with a choice of scale such that all manifest variables have zero means, Σ_{mm} will be a covariance matrix. From Equations 5 and 12 we may also write

$$\mathbf{m} = \mathbf{F}(\mathbf{I}_t - \mathbf{A})^{-1}\mathbf{u}, \tag{12}$$

whereby we may finally write the moment structure among manifest variables as

$$\Sigma_{mm} = \mathbf{F}\Sigma\mathbf{F}' = \mathbf{F}(\mathbf{I}_t - \mathbf{A})^{-1}\Omega(\mathbf{I}_t - \mathbf{A})'^{-1}\mathbf{F}'. \tag{13}$$

The resulting equation completely specifies the expectations for the manifest variable moments Σ_{mm} in terms of the fundamental RAM structural parameters $\mathbf{A}$ and Ω.

In most applications the model matrices for RAM are usually somewhat large and sparse when compared with the traditional algebraic forms. This will generally be true for parameter matrices $\mathbf{A}$ and Ω as well as resultant matrices $(\mathbf{I} - \mathbf{A})$ and Σ. However, to represent all features of any model with sparse matrices we need only (a) provide the relevant manifest j and latent k matrix dimensions, (b) reorganize any long column vectors into transposed row vectors, and (c) use block-partitioned row and column subscripts to refer only to the nonzero subpartitions of $\mathbf{A}$, Ω, and resultant Σ.

The matrix representations of Equations 6 and 7 make the assumption that matrix $\mathbf{I} - \mathbf{A}$ is nonsingular, and it may be useful to more explicitly define

$$\mathbf{E} = (\mathbf{I} - \mathbf{A})^{-1} = \sum_{i=0}^{\infty}\mathbf{A}^i = \mathbf{I} + \mathbf{A}^1 + \mathbf{A}^2 + \cdots$$

$$= \prod_{i=0}^{\infty}\mathbf{A}^i = [\mathbf{Cof}(\mathbf{I} - \mathbf{A})]|\mathbf{I} - \mathbf{A}|^{-1}, \tag{14}$$

where $\mathbf{E}$ represents a matrix of total effects and $\mathbf{Cof}(\cdot)$ represents the matrix of cofactors. These inverse representations, which may all be verified through multiplication by $(\mathbf{I} - \mathbf{A})$, prove particularly useful in the elemental structural decomposition of the association matrix Σ. Following Bock (1975), we may write the determinant of any square matrix as the algebraic sum of all possible products of elements in the matrix; each product is formed in such a way so that one and only one element from each row and column appears in the product. In the specific case of Equation 14, we may expand the determinant as the elemental products

$$|E| = |\mathbf{I} - \mathbf{A}| = \sum_{i=1}^{t^2!} (-1)^s \varepsilon_{1x} \varepsilon_{2y} \cdots \varepsilon_{(tz)}^2, \tag{15}$$

where $\varepsilon_{ij} = (-\alpha_{ij})$ for $i \neq j$ or $(1 - \alpha_{ij})$ for $i = j$; $s = +1$ or -1 depending on whether the natural permutation order of the row subscripts is odd or even, respectively; and $x, y, \ldots, z$ represent the permutations of natural order from 1 to t. The element in the kth row and jth column of the cofactor matrix in Equation 8 may now be written as the determinant of a minor matrix whose jth row and kth column have been removed. These algebraic relationships show that any specific element σ_{ij} of the overall association matrix Σ, when calculated as the bilinear form of Equation 7, may be decomposed into (a) a row sum of signed products based on ε_{ig}, (b) the multiplication of an element $\mathbf{u}_{gh}$, and (c) the postmultiplication by a transposed row sum of signed products based on ε_{hj}. (Of course, as Equation 14 shows, if $|\mathbf{I} - \mathbf{A}| \neq 1$, these cofactors must all be scaled accordingly.) For purposes of *exposition as path-graphic tracing rules*, we later write the resultant algebra of Σ in this full determinant–product decomposition. Specific examples using this more compact notation are presented when useful.

GRAPHIC REPRESENTATION

A critically important aspect in the development of RAM theory is the precise one-to-one relationship between the algebraic form just described and a formal graphic system. Some of our earlier work (Horn & McArdle, 1980; McArdle, 1978, 1980) emphasized the development of the algebra as a direct result of the graphics. Let us first present the properties of any general structural system by offering a series of definitions that describe its primitive features, the axioms that relate the algebra directly to the graphics, and a set of figures that illustrate our major points.

Definition 1. A finite collection of t *points* or vertices or nodes in any space is contained in set $\mathbf{v}$.

Axiom 1. Points may be used to represent variables $\mathbf{v}$. Figure 9.2a illustrates this use of variables as points. These are circled and labeled $\mathbf{v}_1, \mathbf{v}_2, \ldots, \mathbf{v}_t$.

Definition 2. A finite collection of z *lines* or edges that connect each pair of points is contained in set Σ.

Axiom 2. Lines between points may be used to represent the associations between variables in matrix Σ. Figure 9.2b presents an example of these as associations as lines, and shows the line between points $\mathbf{v}_i$ and $\mathbf{v}_j$ labeled as σ_{ij}.

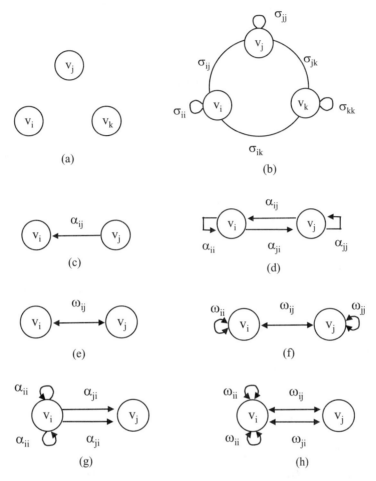

FIG. 9.2. Basic graphic elements of the reticular action meta-model. (a) Variables as points in space, (b) associations as lines between points, (c) a directed arrow, (d) a full set of directed arrows, (e) an undirected turn, (f) a full set of undirected turns, (g) inconsistent arrows, (h) inconsistent turns.

Definition 3. A collection of x directed arrows between pairs of points is contained in set **A**. In any pair of points, one point will be the *input*, or starting point of the directed arrow, and the other will be the *output*, or ending point.

Axiom 3. Directed arrows from one point to another may be used to represent the coefficients of matrix **A**. For any arrow, the input variable is indexed in the column of **A** and the output variable is indexed in the row of **A**. Figure 9.2c presents a simple case of this kind, which shows that the most crucial graphic aspects of an arrow are its direction and value. Figure 9.2d is slightly more complex because it illustrates that a directed arrow may be simultaneously drawn between any two edges of any point, including the possibility of a reflexive "self-loop" arrow from a point back to itself (Heise, 1975). *This self-loop is a novel feature of path graphics that emerges from the algebraic definitions.*

Definition 4. A collection of y undirected *turns* or *slings* between pairs of points is contained in set Ω.

Axiom 4. Undirected slings between points may be used to represent the elements in matrix Ω. In any specific sling, both variables are indexed by the respective row and column entries of Ω. Figure 9.2e illustrates that the undirected sling between the pair of points v_i and v_j is drawn as a line with two arrowheads and labeled as ω_{ij}. Figure 9.2f illustrates that the complete set of slings can include the possibility of a "self-sling" with itself (i.e., ω_{ii} and ω_{jj}) as well as with other points (i.e., ω_{ij}). *This self-sling is a novel feature of path graphics that emerges from the algebraic definitions.*

Definition 5. Parallel elements are pairs of lines, pairs of arrows, or pairs of turns that span the same pair of points and, in the case of arrows, point in the same direction. Only *nonparallel* elements may be contained within set Σ, A, or Ω.

Axiom 5. Parallel arrows, turns, and lines are not permitted because only one value can be placed in any single row and column location of the matrix Σ, A, or Ω. Figure 9.2g illustrates the inconsistent condition of two parallel sets of arrows, those for α_{ji} and those for α_{ii}. Figure 9.2h illustrates the inconsistent condition of two parallel turns, those for ω_{ij} and those for ω_{ii}. Alternatively, we note that the condition where $\alpha_{ij} \neq 0$ and $\omega_{ij} \neq 0$ does not represent a parallelism and may be consistent.

Definition 6. Every element in set A and Ω may take on a symbolic or numeric *value*. Under the condition that the specific value is symbolically null or numerically zero, that specific element will not be drawn. Under the condition that the specific value is symbolically or numerically unit valued, that specific element will not be labeled.

Axiom 6. The value of any line, arrow, or turn may be entered, either symbolically or numerically, in the corresponding row and column location of Σ, A, or Ω. All elements that are not drawn are assumed to be null.

Definition 7. A *graph* is a collection of t points v, x directed arrows A, and y undirected slings Ω, whose values may be used to determine the corresponding values for the z lines in Σ.

Axiom 7. A graph is a precise representation of a structural *model*. The value of the arrows in A and the turns in Ω may be used to provide a "structure" for the values in Σ according to Equation 7. For this reason, we may now say that the arrows in $\mathbf{A}$ and the turns in Ω provide a "structure" for the lines in Σ. It also follows from these definitions that any graph is composed of nonzero values for $0 \leq x \leq t^2$ arrows in $\mathbf{A}$ and $0 \leq y \leq t(t+1)/2$ turns in Ω, which are used to determine the values of the $0 \leq z \leq t(t+1)/2$ nonzero lines in Σ.

Definition 8. A *pathway*, termed $\pi(ij)$, in any graph is any collection of b backward-directed arrows, one turn, and f forward directed arrows, which start at one point $\mathbf{v}_i$ and end at one point $\mathbf{v}_j$. The value of a pathway $\pi(ij)$ is the *product* of the value of its associated $\mathbf{A}$ and Ω elements.

Axiom 8. A pathway $\pi(ij)$ may be used to represent the product of (a) a single b-termed element of $\mathbf{E}$, (b) a single element of Ω, and (c) a single f-termed element of $\mathbf{E}'$. The number of product terms required to make up each specific element of $\mathbf{E}$ is based on the nonzero configuration of elements in $\mathbf{A}$.

Figure 9.3a presents the general form of a pathway $\pi(i \mathinner{..} j)$ from point $\mathbf{v}_i$ to point $\mathbf{v}_j$. This pathway is initiated from point $\mathbf{v}_i$ and flows backward along a set of b directed arrows. These arrows must all point backward, connecting $b+1$ distinct points, and terminate at some point $\mathbf{v}_g$. At point $\mathbf{v}_g$, a single undirected turn toward a forward flow is made through a two-headed ω_{gh} between $\mathbf{v}_g$ and $\mathbf{v}_h$. This single turn from backward to forward arrowhead direction is the only consistent way to alter the pathway direction. Flow then proceeds from $\mathbf{v}_h$ along a set of f forward-directed arrows, passing through $f+1$ total points, until final destination point $\mathbf{v}_j$ is reached. It may be useful to label this general pathway as $\pi(ik \ldots gh' \ldots \ell' j')$, where the transpose is used to designate forward flow. *The definition of a pathway "tracing rule" emerges as a direct interpretation of the algebraic decomposition* (Equations 7 and 14).

This general expression now permits the statement of any specific pathway through a reorientation of pathway points, and this highlights unusual pathways. For example, by letting $i = j$ in the foregoing general expression, we find that the initial starting point is also the final end point and the total pathway is considered a "circuit." A specific example of this type is presented as pathway $\pi(123'1')$ in Fig. 9.3b. As another example, we now let $i = g$ and $b = 0$, so the pathway starts backward with a turn between variables 1 and 2. This case is depicted by $\pi(12'3')$ in Fig. 9.3c. Of course, the same logic would apply to a model where $h = j$ and $f = 0$, where pathway $\pi(12'3')$ would end on the forward flow of a turn. Figure 9.3d illustrates the case where $g = h$ and the self-turn is used as the turning point in $\pi(122'3')$. Figure 9.3e assumes $i = j$, $g = h$, and $b = f = 0$, so the entire pathway reduces to a self-turn denoted by $\pi(11')$. As an example of the pathway value calculation, we simply note that the value of $\pi(123'1')$, as presented in Fig. 9.3b, would be symbolically given as the three-term product $\alpha_{12}\omega_{23}\alpha'_{31}$. Alternatively, the value of $\pi(12'3')$ of Fig. 9.3c is given as the two-term product $\omega_{12}\alpha'_{23}$.

Definition 9. Two pathways are parallel if they contain an identical set of $\mathbf{A}$ arrows and Ω slings in an identical order. This implies that all points are identical also.

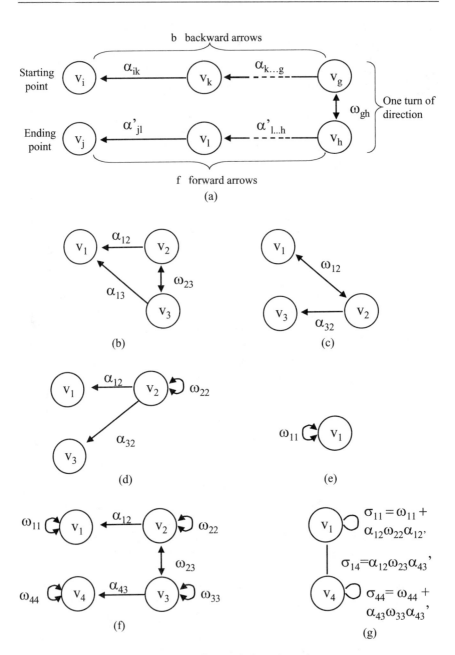

FIG. 9.3.   Decomposition of association via pathway representation. (a) General expression of a single pathway $\pi(i..j)$, (b) a circuit
as a full pathway, (c) starting (or ending) on a turn.

The total value of any association between any starting point and any ending point is the total *sum* of the values of the *nonparallel* pathways between these two points.

Axiom 9.   The line of association between row variables and column variables may be used to represent the overall sum that is created as the bilinear form of Equation 7. In the diagonal and the lower symmetric quadrant of **A**, the row variable is the starting point and the column variable is the ending point.

Figure 9.3f illustrates a simple model with multiple pathways with simple labels. In this figure there is only one consistent pathway between variables 1 and 4; namely the pathway product $\alpha_{12}\omega_{23}\alpha'_{43}$. However, there are two consistent pathways each for the circuits from variables 1 and 4, the two pathways ω_{11} and $\alpha_{12}\omega_{22}\alpha'_{12}$ for variable 1 and the pathways labeled ω_{44} and $\alpha_{43}\omega_{33}\alpha'_{43}$ for variable 4. The lines of total association σ_{ij} are formed as the sum of these pathway products and drawn as Fig. 9.3g.

Definition 10.   Nonoverlapping subclasses of points may be distinguished by their representation as geometric figures—*squares* for the j points labeled $\mathbf{m}_j$, *circles* for the k points labeled ℓ_k, etc.

Axiom 10.   The graphic distinction between squares and circles may be used to represent the presence of a one or zero in the matrix **F** (see Equation 11).

Figure 9.4 presents an overall summary of the key features of the RAM graphics. Structural relations among these points are denoted by lines connecting these

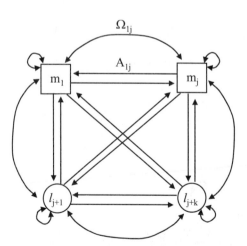

FIG. 9.4.   An overview of reticular action meta-model graphics. Squares represent manifest variables and circles represent latent variables.

points, with directed arrows distinguished from undirected turns. The careful reader will note that this figure does not contain all possible structural relationships or the respective values. Whereas there exist many other graphic possibilities, only those explicitly described here are required for our further development.

As a brief example of the useful features of this isomorphism, consider that the model depicted in Fig. 9.3f may be simply translated into the RAM matrix algebra of

$$
v = \begin{bmatrix} v_1 \\ v_2 \\ v_3 \\ v_4 \end{bmatrix}, \quad A = \begin{bmatrix} 0 & \alpha_{12} & 0 & 0 \\ 0 & 0 & 0 & 0 \\ 0 & 0 & 0 & 0 \\ 0 & 0 & \alpha_{43} & 0 \end{bmatrix} \quad \text{and}
$$

$$
u = \begin{bmatrix} u_1 \\ v_2 \\ v_3 \\ u_4 \end{bmatrix}, \quad \Omega = \begin{bmatrix} \omega_{11} & & & sym. \\ 0 & \omega_{22} & & \\ 0 & \omega_{23} & \omega_{33} & \\ 0 & 0 & 0 & \omega_{44} \end{bmatrix}, \tag{16}
$$

where the elements of u are either labeled as residuals u_i or as the original variables v_i depending on the elements of A (i.e., if v_i is an outcome of any variable v_j). We may now also write

$$
E = (I - A)^{-1} = \begin{bmatrix} 1 & 0 & 0 & 0 \\ 0 & 1 & 0 & 0 \\ 0 & 0 & 1 & 0 \\ 0 & 0 & 0 & 1 \end{bmatrix} + \begin{bmatrix} 0 & \alpha_{12} & 0 & 0 \\ 0 & 0 & 0 & 0 \\ 0 & 0 & 0 & 0 \\ 0 & 0 & \alpha_{43} & 0 \end{bmatrix} = \begin{bmatrix} 1 & \alpha_{12} & 0 & 0 \\ 0 & 1 & 0 & 0 \\ 0 & 0 & 1 & 0 \\ 0 & 0 & \alpha_{43} & 1 \end{bmatrix}, \tag{17}
$$

which may be verified by $(I - A)$ multiplication, so that

$$
\Sigma = (I_t - A)^{-1} \Omega (I_t - A)^{-1'}
$$

$$
= \begin{bmatrix} 1 & \alpha_{12} & 0 & 0 \\ 0 & 1 & 0 & 0 \\ 0 & 0 & 1 & 0 \\ 0 & 0 & \alpha_{43} & 1 \end{bmatrix} \begin{bmatrix} \omega_{11} & 0 & 0 & 0 \\ 0 & \omega_{22} & \omega_{32} & 0 \\ 0 & \omega_{23} & \omega_{33} & 0 \\ 0 & 0 & 0 & \omega_{44} \end{bmatrix} \begin{bmatrix} 1 & 0 & 0 & 0 \\ \alpha_{12'} & 1 & 0 & 0 \\ 0 & 0 & 1 & \alpha_{43'} \\ 0 & 0 & 0 & 1 \end{bmatrix} \tag{18}
$$

$$
= \begin{bmatrix} \omega_{11} + \alpha_{12}\omega_{22}\alpha_{12'} & & & sym. \\ \omega_{22}\alpha_{12'} & \omega_{22} & & \\ \omega_{23}\alpha_{12'} & \omega_{23} & \omega_{33} & \\ \alpha_{43}\omega_{32}\alpha_{12'} & \alpha_{43}\omega_{32} & \alpha_{43}\omega_{33} & \omega_{44} + \alpha_{43}\omega_{33}\alpha_{43'} \end{bmatrix}
$$

as illustrated in Fig. 9.3g. Although no distinction between circles and squares is made in Fig. 9.3f, any such distinction would merely require a subpartitioning of this Σ to obtain Σ_{mm}. For example, under the assumption that v_1 and v_4 were drawn in Fig. 9.3f as squares, we could write nonzero $\mathbf{f}_{11} = 1$ and $\mathbf{f}_{24} = 1$, and this would essentially filter out the associations given as Fig. 9.3g. This can be written in algebraic form as

$$\Sigma_{mm} = \mathbf{F}\Sigma\mathbf{F}'$$

$$= \begin{bmatrix} 1 & 0 & 0 & 0 \\ 0 & 0 & 0 & 1 \end{bmatrix} \begin{bmatrix} \omega_{11} + \alpha_{12}\omega_{22}\alpha_{12'} & & & sym. \\ \omega_{22}\alpha_{12'} & \omega_{22} & & \\ \omega_{23}\alpha_{12'} & \omega_{23} & \omega_{33} & \\ \alpha_{43}\omega_{32}\alpha_{12'} & \omega_{43}\omega_{32} & \alpha_{43}\omega_{33} & \alpha_{43}\omega_{32}\alpha_{12'} \end{bmatrix} \begin{bmatrix} 1 & 0 \\ 0 & 0 \\ 0 & 0 \\ 0 & 1 \end{bmatrix} \quad (19)$$

$$= \begin{bmatrix} \omega_{11} + \alpha_{12}\omega_{22}\alpha_{12'} & sym. \\ \alpha_{43}\omega_{32}\alpha_{12'} & \alpha_{43}\omega_{32}\alpha_{12'} \end{bmatrix}$$

Because we always employ the same matrix operations, we can create various simple devices to convey this information. For example, any graph may be even more simply translated into a compact RAM notation by including only the salient nonnull *list operator* $\mathbf{L}\{*\}$ where elements of Equations 16–19 are listed as

$$\mathbf{L}\{\mathbf{v}\} = \{\mathbf{v}_1, \mathbf{v}_2, \mathbf{v}_3, \mathbf{v}_4\}, \qquad \mathbf{L}\{\mathbf{A}\} = \{\alpha_{12}, \alpha_{43}\},$$

$$\mathbf{L}\{\mathbf{u}\} = \{\mathbf{u}_1, \mathbf{u}_2, \mathbf{u}_3, \mathbf{u}_4\}, \qquad \mathbf{L}\{\Omega\} = \{\omega_{11}, \omega_{22}, \omega_{33}, \omega_{44}, \omega_{34}\}, \quad (20)$$

$$\mathbf{L}\{\mathbf{E}\} = \{1_{11}, 1_{22}, 1_{33}, 1_{44}, \alpha_{12}, \alpha_{43}\}, \qquad \mathbf{L}\{\mathbf{F}\} = \{1_{11}, 1_{44}\}.$$

The resultant RAM algebra can always be summarized in list form as in Equations 20, and the elements of Σ in Equation 18 or elements of Σ_{mm} in Equation 19 could also be listed by row and column entries. These lists $\mathbf{L}$ may be most useful for computer input and output (as described in a later section).

This simple example illustrates the presence of at least one critical distinction between the algebra and the graphs. The inclusion of the self-loop and self-sling (see Figs. 9.2 and 9.3) illustrates that we have not provided a separate "point-in-space" representation for structural residual variables $\mathbf{u}$. As will be shown later, this representation turns out to be redundant in both graphic and algebraic terms, so, although possible, *it is not necessary to draw such residuals.* In graphs, or selected portions of graphs, where there are no directed inputs to a specific variable $\mathbf{v}_i$, the variable $\mathbf{v}_i$ is considered the same as its own residual $\mathbf{u}_i$, and the undirected turn represents relationships among $\mathbf{v}_i$ and other variables. However, directed arrows do end on $\mathbf{v}_i$; then v_i *is not the same as* u_i, and the undirected turn represents relationships among $\mathbf{u}_i$ and other points. In general graphic or algebraic terms, the interpretation of any structural arrow or turn always requires reference to the full graph or model.

COMPARATIVE REPRESENTATION

We now show how some popular models for moment structures may be completely specified under the simple RAM rules. We use both algebraic proofs and graphic presentation to further illustrate the general isomorphism between RAM algebra and graphics.

The models presented in Fig. 9.5 illustrate concepts revolving around the structure of relationships among manifest variables. Let us write a vector model for multiple linear regression as

$$y = Bx + e, \tag{21}$$

where y is a $q \times 1$ vector of endogeneous variables, x is a $p \times 1$ vector of exogeneous variables, and e is a $q \times 1$ vector of residuals. For simplicity, let us also assume that y and x are rescaled to have zero mean, so that B is a $q \times p$ matrix of raw regression coefficients for y regressed on x. Let us further assume model covariances

$$E\{\mathbf{xx'}\} = \Sigma_{xx} \quad \text{and} \quad E\{\mathbf{ee'}\} = \Sigma_{ee}, \tag{22}$$

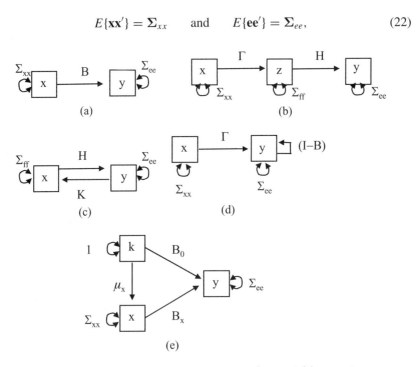

FIG. 9.5. Models of structure among manifest variables. (a) General linear regression, (b) chain or nested regression, (c) feedback or nonrecursive regression, (d) general econometric regression, (e) means and intercepts in a linear regression.

so that the covariance structure of $\mathbf{y}$ is obtained as

$$E\{\mathbf{y}\mathbf{y}'\} = \Sigma_{yy} = E\{(\mathbf{B}\mathbf{x} + \mathbf{e})(\mathbf{B}\mathbf{x} + \mathbf{e})'\} = \mathbf{B}E\{\mathbf{x}\mathbf{x}'\}\mathbf{B}'E\{\mathbf{e}\mathbf{e}'\} = \mathbf{B}\Sigma_{xx}\mathbf{B}' + \Sigma_{ee}.$$
(23)

In many familiar cases such as analysis of variance and covariance, we may wish to assume that Σ_{xx} is fully or partially represented in terms of fixed design parameters. However, in general, we can initially write the model without any additional restrictions.

This linear regression model may now be represented in RAM graphic terms as in Fig. 9.5a. Here it should be clear that the directed arrow represents the regression coefficients B, whereas the undirected turns represent covariance Σ_{xx} and residual covariances Σ_{ee} (not necessarily diagonal). *The latent variable e could be explicitly included in this diagram but it is not necessary* (e.g., Fig. 9.6c). By following the explicit graphic pathway rules, we can state the structure of the model-predicted associations among all variables in Equation 23 without further recourse to the matrix algebra. However, we can write this model in the compact form of *supervectors are with nonzero elements*

$$j = t = p + q, \qquad \mathbf{v}' = [\mathbf{y}'\mathbf{x}'], \qquad \mathbf{u}' = [\mathbf{e}'\mathbf{x}']$$

$$\mathbf{F} = \begin{bmatrix} \mathbf{I} & \mathbf{O} \\ \mathbf{O} & \mathbf{I} \end{bmatrix}, \qquad \mathbf{A} = \begin{bmatrix} \mathbf{O} & \mathbf{B} \\ \mathbf{O} & \mathbf{O} \end{bmatrix}, \qquad \Omega = \begin{bmatrix} \Sigma_{ee} & sym. \\ \mathbf{O} & \Sigma_{xx} \end{bmatrix},$$
(24)

so

$$\mathbf{E} = (\mathbf{I} - \mathbf{A})^{-1} = \begin{bmatrix} \mathbf{I} & \mathbf{B} \\ \mathbf{O} & \mathbf{I} \end{bmatrix}.$$

In general, we can simply state $\mathbf{F} = \mathbf{I}$ is assumed by $j = t$ (i.e., no explicit latent variables; see Equation 9), and the only nonzero subpartitions are those in row 1 and column 2 of $\mathbf{A}$ ($\mathbf{A}_{yx} = \mathbf{B}$) and in the ith row and ith column of Ω ($\Omega_{ii} = [\Sigma_{xx}\Sigma_{ee}]$). This yields the associations as

$$\Sigma = (\mathbf{I}_t - \mathbf{A})^{-1}\Omega(\mathbf{I}_t - \mathbf{A})^{-1'}$$
$$= \begin{bmatrix} \mathbf{I} & \mathbf{B} \\ \mathbf{O} & \mathbf{I} \end{bmatrix}\begin{bmatrix} \Sigma_{ee} & \mathbf{O} \\ \mathbf{O} & \Sigma_{xx} \end{bmatrix}\begin{bmatrix} \mathbf{I} & \mathbf{O} \\ \mathbf{B}' & \mathbf{I} \end{bmatrix} = \begin{bmatrix} \Sigma_{ee} + \mathbf{B}\Sigma_{xx}\mathbf{B}' & sym. \\ \Sigma_{xx}\mathbf{B}' & \Sigma_{xx} \end{bmatrix}.$$
(25)

Obviously this result is equivalent to the covariance structure of Equations 22 and 23.

Let us now consider writing models for some traditional extensions of this general linear model. One model that stems from path-analytic research (Duncan, 1975) is a "nested" set of manifest variables, which may be written as

$$z = \Gamma x + e, \qquad y = Hz + f,$$
(26)

where we assume x, y, and z are manifest and e and f are residuals. We note that this model implies no direct structural regression between x and y, and for this reason z is termed a mediator and the model is termed a "chain" (Wold, 1960). This model is drawn in compact form as in Fig. 9.5b and written in the abbreviated RAM notation as

$$j = t, \quad \mathbf{v}' = [x'z'y'], \quad \mathbf{u}' = [x'e'f'],$$

$$\mathbf{F} = \begin{bmatrix} I & O & O \\ O & I & O \\ O & O & I \end{bmatrix}, \quad \mathbf{A} = \begin{bmatrix} O & O & O \\ \Gamma & O & O \\ O & H & O \end{bmatrix}, \tag{27}$$

$$\Omega = \begin{bmatrix} \Sigma_{xx} & & sym. \\ O & \Sigma_{ee} & \\ O & O & \Sigma_{ff} \end{bmatrix}, \quad \mathbf{E} = (\mathbf{I} - \mathbf{A})^{-1} = \begin{bmatrix} I & O & O \\ \Gamma & I & O \\ \Gamma H & H & I \end{bmatrix}.$$

where the parameter matrices are in the lower diagonal of $\mathbf{A}$ (and $\mathbf{E}$) due to the ordering of the variables in $\mathbf{v}$. This expression leads to the nonzero association submatrices written as

$$\Sigma_{xz} = \Sigma_{xx}\Gamma,$$

$$\Sigma_{zz} = \Sigma_{ee} + \Gamma\Sigma_{xx}\Gamma',$$

$$\Sigma_{yx} = H\Gamma\Sigma_{xx}, \tag{28}$$

$$\Sigma_{yz} = H\Gamma\Sigma_{xx}\Gamma' + H\Sigma_{ee},$$

$$\Sigma_{yy} = H\Gamma\Sigma_{xx}\Gamma'H' + H\Sigma_{ee}H' + \Sigma_{ff} = H(\Gamma\Sigma_{xx}\Gamma' + \Sigma_{ee})H' + \Sigma_{ff}.$$

Another model that has been studied extensively in path-analytic research is the feedback model (Heise, 1975), which may be written in terms of the nonrecursive equations

$$y = Hz + f, \quad z = Ky + s, \tag{29}$$

where both y and z are manifest and f and s are residuals. This model is drawn as Fig. 9.5c and can be written as

$$j = t, \quad \mathbf{v}' = [z'y'], \quad \mathbf{u} = [f's'],$$

$$\mathbf{F} = \begin{bmatrix} I & O \\ O & I \end{bmatrix}, \quad \mathbf{A} = \begin{bmatrix} O & K \\ H & O \end{bmatrix}, \quad \Omega = \begin{bmatrix} \Sigma_{ff} & sym. \\ O & \Sigma_{ss} \end{bmatrix}, \quad so \tag{30}$$

$$\mathbf{E} = (\mathbf{I} - \mathbf{A})^{-1} = \begin{bmatrix} \Xi & K\Xi \\ H\Xi & \Xi \end{bmatrix},$$

where $\Xi = (I - HK)^{-1}$, so that nonzero submatrices yield a complementary co-variance structure,

$$\Sigma_{zz} = \Xi\Sigma_{ff}\Xi' + H\Xi\Sigma_{ss}\Xi'H'$$

$$\Sigma_{zy} = K\Xi\Sigma_{ff}\Xi' + \Xi\Sigma_{ss}\Xi'H' \qquad (31)$$

$$\Sigma_{yy} = \Xi\Sigma_{ff}\Xi' + K\Xi\Sigma_{ff}\Xi'K'.$$

It becomes obvious that the pathway termed Ξ, often considered as a feedback loop, is most crucial in this model. A complete decomposition of the separate pathways within this feedback requires the infinite sum of pathway products of ever-increasing length (see Equation 8 for a general representation). However, both algebraic and graphic forms are still equivalent; backward entry is possible only through Ξ and forward outcome only through Ξ' (Kenny, 1979, p. 100).

A general representation that permits this kind of feedback, as well as other structures, has been of particular interest to econometric research (Wold, 1960) in the form of nonrecursive equations, classically written as

$$By = \Gamma x + z \qquad \text{or} \qquad y = (I - B)y + \Gamma x + z, \qquad (32)$$

where $(I - B)$ is now a $q \times q$ matrix of regression weights for y on itself. This expression is drawn as Fig. 9.5d and written as

$$j = t = q + p, \qquad \mathbf{v}' = [y'x'], \qquad \mathbf{u}' = [z'x'],$$

$$\mathbf{F} = \begin{bmatrix} I & O \\ O & I \end{bmatrix}, \qquad \mathbf{A} = \begin{bmatrix} (I - B) & O \\ \Gamma & O \end{bmatrix}, \qquad \Omega = \begin{bmatrix} \Sigma_{zz} & sym. \\ O & \Sigma_{xx} \end{bmatrix}, \qquad \text{so} \qquad (33)$$

$$\mathbf{E} = (\mathbf{I} - \mathbf{A})^{-1} = \begin{bmatrix} B^{-1} & O \\ B^{-1}\Gamma & I \end{bmatrix},$$

with the resulting expectations

$$\Sigma_{yy} = B^{-1}\Sigma_{xx}B^{-1'} + B^{-1}\Gamma\Sigma_{zz}\Gamma'B^{-1'} = B^{-1}(\Sigma_{xx} + \Gamma\Sigma_{zz}\Gamma')B^{-1'},$$

$$\Sigma_{yx} = \Sigma_{zz}\Gamma'B^{-1'}. \qquad (34)$$

Once again, the feedback matrix $(I - B)$ among the $\mathbf{y}$ variables is seen as a crucially important part of the structural associations.

Let us finally consider a manifest variable model that includes both first and second moments for j variables with means and covariances. One simple approach is to write a linear regression model, such as Equation 16, with the explicit inclusion of means as

$$y = B_0 + B_x x + e, \qquad (35)$$

where B_0 is a $p \times 1$ vector of regression coefficients representing the regression of y on the unit vector $k = 1$ (i.e., the mean intercepts). Let us also define

$$E\{x\} = \mu_x, \qquad E\{e\} = 0, \qquad \text{so} \qquad E\{y\} = B_0 + B_x\mu_x,$$

$$E\{k\} = 1, \qquad E\{kk'\} = 1.$$

(36)

To write this model in RAM notation, we require the explicit inclusion of a design structure where the last row, labeled 1 here, contains all unit values. Now we write the model

$$j = t = p + q + 1, \qquad v' = [y'x'k'], \qquad u' = [e'x'k'],$$

$$\mathbf{F} = \begin{bmatrix} I & O & O \\ O & I & O \\ O & O & I \end{bmatrix}, \qquad \mathbf{A} = \begin{bmatrix} O & B_x & B_0 \\ O & O & M_x \\ 0 & 0 & 0 \end{bmatrix}, \Omega = \begin{bmatrix} \Sigma_{ee} & & sym. \\ O & \Sigma_{xx} & \\ 0 & 0 & 1 \end{bmatrix}$$

(37)

so

$$\mathbf{E} = (\mathbf{I} - \mathbf{A})^{-1} = \begin{bmatrix} I & B_x & B_0 \\ O & I & (B_0 + B_x\mu_x) \\ 0 & 0 & 1 \end{bmatrix},$$

and the matrices of expectations are written in submatrices

$$\Sigma^*_{yy} = \Sigma_{ee} + B_x\Sigma_{xx}B'_x + (B_x\mu_x + B_0)(B_x\mu_x + B_0)',$$

$$\Sigma^*_{yx} = \Sigma_{xx}B'_x + \mu_x(B_x\mu_x + B_0)',$$

$$\Sigma^*_{xx} = \Sigma_{xx} + \mu_x\mu'_x, \qquad \Sigma^*_{yk} = (B_x\mu_x + B_0),$$

$$\Sigma^*_{xk} = \mu_x, \qquad \Sigma^*_{kk} = 1.$$

(38)

As Fig. 9.5e shows, when the means are represented as regressions from a constant they follow all algebraic and graphic rules. A moment matrix that is augmented by a unit constant Σ^* of order $j^* = j + 1$ permits the complete separation of first and second moments. In general, all moment structure models may be written and interpreted in this way. Because unit constants are treated in this special fashion, highlighting these "defined" constants in the graphic (e.g., as a triangle) may be useful.

The models presented in Fig. 9.6 illustrate concepts based on the structure of *relations including latent variables*. One such model that has been of general interest in psychological research is the traditional model of common factor analysis (Thurstone, 1947), usually written as

$$y = \Lambda f + s,$$

(39)

where y is a $p \times 1$ vector of observed variables, f is an $r \times 1$ vector of unobserved common factors, and s is a $p \times 1$ vector of unobserved unique factors (i.e., specific factors plus errors). Let us again assume that these variables have mean zero,

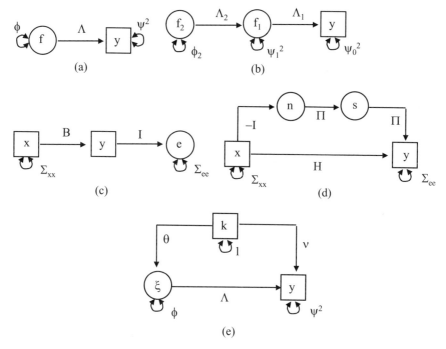

FIG. 9.6. Models of structure among both manifest and latent variables. (a) Traditional common factor model, (b) higher order factor model, (c) explicit inclusion of the residual in the regression, (d) linear constraints in the regression, (e) means and intercepts in a common factor model.

so that Λ is a $p \times r$ matrix of common factor loadings. Under these traditional assumptions, we may draw a general RAM model as in Fig. 9.6a and write

$$j = p, \qquad k = r, \qquad \mathbf{v}' = [\mathbf{y}'\mathbf{f}'], \qquad \mathbf{u}' = [\mathbf{s}'\mathbf{f}'],$$

$$\mathbf{F} = \begin{bmatrix} \mathbf{I} & \mathbf{O} \end{bmatrix}, \qquad \mathbf{A} = \begin{bmatrix} \mathbf{O} & \Lambda \\ \mathbf{O} & \mathbf{O} \end{bmatrix}, \qquad \Omega = \begin{bmatrix} \Psi^2 & sym. \\ \mathbf{O} & \Phi \end{bmatrix}, \qquad \text{so} \qquad (40)$$

$$\mathbf{E} = (\mathbf{I} - \mathbf{A})^{-1} = \begin{bmatrix} \mathbf{I} & \Lambda \\ \mathbf{O} & \mathbf{I} \end{bmatrix},$$

and we obtain the expectations

$$\Sigma_{yy} = \Psi + \Lambda\Phi\Lambda',$$

$$\Sigma_{yf} = \Phi\Lambda', \qquad (41)$$

$$\Sigma_{ff} = \Phi.$$

The overall associations include the traditional factor model as well as the factor structure associations. Now, however, due to the fact that we are explicitly including latent variables, we must also write the filter $\mathbf{F} = [I : 0]$ to subpartition Σ into $\Sigma_{yy} = \mathbf{F}\Sigma\mathbf{F}'$.

The basic concept involved in nested sets of latent variables forms the basis of hierarchical factor analysis models (Schmid & Leiman, 1957). We consider a model written as

$$\mathbf{y} = \Lambda_1\mathbf{f}_1 + \mathbf{s}_1, \qquad \mathbf{f}_1 = \Lambda_2\mathbf{f}_2 + \mathbf{s}_2, \tag{42}$$

where $\mathbf{f}_1$ is an $r \times 1$ vector of first-order latent common factors, $\mathbf{f}_2$ is a $q \times 1$ vector of second-order latent common factors, $\mathbf{s}_1$ and $\mathbf{s}_2$ are first- and second-order unique factors, respectively, and Λ_1 and Λ_2 are first- and second-order factor loading matrices, respectively. This model may be simply drawn as in Fig. 9.6b and written as

$$j = p, \qquad j = r + q, \qquad \mathbf{v}' = [\mathbf{y}'\mathbf{f}_1'\mathbf{f}_2'], \qquad \mathbf{u}' = [\mathbf{s}_1'\mathbf{s}_2'\mathbf{f}_2'],$$

$$\mathbf{F} = \begin{bmatrix} I & O & O \end{bmatrix}, \qquad \mathbf{A} = \begin{bmatrix} O & \Lambda_1 & O \\ O & O & \Lambda_2 \\ O & O & O \end{bmatrix}, \qquad \Omega = \begin{bmatrix} \Psi_1^2 & & sym. \\ O & \Psi_2^2 & \\ O & O & \Phi_2 \end{bmatrix} \tag{43}$$

so

$$\mathbf{E} = (\mathbf{I} - \mathbf{A})^{-1} = \begin{bmatrix} I & \Lambda_1 & \Lambda_1\Lambda_2 \\ O & I & \Lambda_2 \\ O & O & I \end{bmatrix},$$

with the resulting expectations

$$\begin{aligned}
\Sigma_{yy} &= \Psi_1^2 + \Lambda_1\Psi_2^2\Lambda_1' + \Lambda_1\Lambda_2\Phi_2\Lambda_2'\Lambda_1' \\
&= \Psi_1^2 + \Lambda_1\left(\Psi_2^2 + \Lambda_2\Phi_2\Lambda_2'\right)\Lambda_1' \\
\Sigma_{y,f1} &= \Psi_2^2\Lambda_1' + \Lambda_2\Phi_2\Lambda_2\Lambda_1', \\
\Sigma_{f1,f1} &= \Psi_2^2 + \Lambda_2\Phi_2\Lambda_2', \\
\Sigma_{y,f2} &= \Phi_2\Lambda_2'\Lambda_1', \\
\Sigma_{f1,f2} &= \Phi_2\Lambda_2', \\
\Sigma_{f2,f2} &= \Phi_2.
\end{aligned} \tag{44}$$

These associations represent a nested set of factor analysis structures for both first and second orders. Additional hierarchical structures (e.g., Bentler, 1976) merely require repeated sets of latent variables nested in this fashion and do not require special programming (Weeks, 1978).

To illustrate some further concepts in RAM theory, let us once again consider a model that is equivalent to the linear regression model of Fig. 9.5a, but that *now* *explicitly includes the residual **e** as a special latent variable.* We may write this model as

$$j = p + q, \quad k = q, \quad \mathbf{v}' = [\mathbf{y}'\mathbf{x}'\mathbf{e}'], \quad \mathbf{u}' = [\mathbf{y}^{*\prime}\mathbf{x}'\mathbf{e}'],$$

$$\mathbf{F} = \begin{bmatrix} \mathbf{I} & \mathbf{I} & \mathbf{O} \end{bmatrix}, \quad \mathbf{A} = \begin{bmatrix} \mathbf{O} & \mathbf{B} & \mathbf{O} \\ \mathbf{O} & \mathbf{O} & \mathbf{I} \\ \mathbf{O} & \mathbf{O} & \mathbf{O} \end{bmatrix}, \quad \Omega = \begin{bmatrix} \mathbf{O} & & sym. \\ \mathbf{O} & \Sigma_{xx} & \\ \mathbf{O} & \mathbf{O} & \Sigma_{ee} \end{bmatrix}, \tag{45}$$

so there is a zero main diagonal element to signify the lack of any Ω parameter for the **u** associated with this y variable. Here we obtain

$$\Sigma_{yy} = \mathbf{B}\Sigma_{xx}\mathbf{B}' + \Sigma_{ee},$$

$$\Sigma_{yx} = \Sigma_{xx}\mathbf{B}', \quad \Sigma_{ye} = \mathbf{I}\Sigma_{ee}\mathbf{I}'. \tag{46}$$

Now, by a comparison of Σ in Equations 46 with Σ from the original linear regression model of Equation 25, we can see that this new model generates associations that are simply redundant with parameters already available in the model (i.e., the last row of Σ filled with Σ_{ee}). Also, because e is now explicitly written as a latent variable, we must now write a subpartitioned **F** to filter out these redundancies. In this algebraic sense, then, it is unnecessary to explicitly include latent residuals with unit regressions. The model of Fig. 9.6c *is a consistent expression and may be useful for didactic purposes* (i.e., for clarity of $E\{\mathbf{x}\mathbf{e}'\} = 0$).

At this point, however, we can also consider some nonredundant uses of the explicit inclusion of latent residuals. For example, the linear regression model drawn in Fig. 9.6c may now be altered to a model where we add a diagonal matrix T of regressions for **y** on **e** by writing

$$j = p + q, \quad k = q, \quad \mathbf{v}' = [\mathbf{y}'\mathbf{x}'\mathbf{e}'], \quad \mathbf{u}' = [\mathbf{y}^{*\prime}\mathbf{x}'\mathbf{e}'],$$

$$\mathbf{F} = \begin{bmatrix} \mathbf{I} & \mathbf{I} & \mathbf{O} \end{bmatrix}, \quad \mathbf{A} = \begin{bmatrix} \mathbf{O} & \mathbf{B} & \mathbf{O} \\ \mathbf{O} & \mathbf{O} & \mathbf{T} \\ \mathbf{O} & \mathbf{O} & \mathbf{O} \end{bmatrix}, \quad \Omega = \begin{bmatrix} \mathbf{O} & & sym. \\ \mathbf{O} & \Sigma_{xx} & \\ \mathbf{O} & \mathbf{O} & \mathbf{I} \end{bmatrix}, \tag{47}$$

so by this substitution of T (and the removal of Σ_{ee}) we obtain

$$\Sigma_{yy} = \mathbf{B}\Sigma_{xx}\mathbf{B}' + \mathbf{T}\mathbf{T}',$$

$$\Sigma_{yx} = \Sigma_{xx}\mathbf{B}', \quad \Sigma_{ye} = \mathbf{I}\mathbf{T}', \quad \Sigma_{ee} = \mathbf{T}\mathbf{T}'. \tag{48}$$

Although this model has similar properties to the previous one, it exhibits one important distinction; the residual variance $\Sigma_{ee} = \mathbf{T}\mathbf{T}'$ elements are now constrained to be nonnegative because the square roots (deviations) T are structured instead of

Σ_{ee}. This model, then, places a nonnegative constraint on the variance term and may be useful in practice (van Driel, 1978).

Several other forms of general linear *constraints* may be modeled in precisely this fashion. Let us consider a linear regression model with constraints on the B coefficients drawn as in Fig. 9.6d and written as

$$j = p + q, \qquad k = p + p, \qquad \mathbf{v}' = [y'x'n's'], \qquad \mathbf{u}' = [z'x'n's'],$$

$$\mathbf{F} = \begin{bmatrix} I & O & O & O \\ O & I & O & O \end{bmatrix}, \qquad \mathbf{A} = \begin{bmatrix} O & H & -I & O \\ O & O & O & O \\ O & \Pi & O & O \\ O & O & \Pi & O \end{bmatrix}, \qquad (49)$$

$$\Omega = \begin{bmatrix} \Sigma_{ee} & & & sym. \\ O & \Sigma_{xx} & & \\ O & O & O & \\ O & O & O & O \end{bmatrix},$$

where s and n are latent vectors with expectation zero and the regression matrix Π is diagonal, so that $\Sigma_{yx} = (H - \Pi\Pi) = B^*$ and

$$\Sigma_{yy} = \Sigma_{ee} + B^*\Sigma_{xx}B^{*'},$$
$$\Sigma_{yx} = \Sigma_{xx}B^{*'}. \qquad (50)$$

The key result here is that this model yields structural associations that are equivalent to the linear regression model given in Equation 25 except for the fact that we have restructured B with $B^* = (H - \Pi\Pi)$. Now, because Π is structured in this way, the value $\Pi\Pi \geq 0$ and this model *constrains the value $B^* \leq H$, where H may be any fixed at a known value or the value of another parameter*. The fact that neither n nor s has any has associated expectation, and thus is "not variable," poses no problems for the RAM representation. In such cases we will just label n and s as *nodes* (following Horn & McArdle, 1980). The utility of the explicit inclusion of such nodes is that they clearly permit the direct representation of this variety of model constraint, as well as other more complex combinations that follow directly. On the other hand, we also recognize that not all nonlinear model constraints may be accomplished in this simple fashion (McDonald, 1980).

Given these basic relations, we can now consider more general linear structural models. Following Sörbom (1974; also Jöreskog & Sörbom, 1980), we may wish to write the factor analysis model with means as

$$y = v + \Lambda\eta + \epsilon, \qquad E\{\eta\} = \theta, \qquad E\{\epsilon\} = 0, \qquad \text{so} \quad E\{y\} = v + \Lambda\theta, \quad (51)$$

where v represents manifest variable mean intercepts and θ represents the means of common factors η. This model, presented in Fig. 9.6e, may be represented in a fashion equivalent to the mean regression model given in Fig. 9.5e. That is, we create a constant unit vector k (now ordered as the first variable) and we write

$$j = 1 + p, \qquad k = r, \qquad \mathbf{v}' = [k'y'\eta'], \qquad \mathbf{u}' = [k'\epsilon'\eta'],$$

$$\mathbf{F} = \begin{bmatrix} 1 & O & O \\ 0 & I & O \end{bmatrix}, \qquad \mathbf{A} = \begin{bmatrix} 0 & O & O \\ \nu & O & \Lambda \\ \theta & O & O \end{bmatrix}, \qquad \Omega = \begin{bmatrix} 1 & & sym. \\ O & \Psi^2 & \\ O & O & \Phi \end{bmatrix}, \qquad (52)$$

so

$$\mathbf{E} = (\mathbf{I} - \mathbf{A})^{-1} = \begin{bmatrix} 1 & O & O \\ (\nu + \Lambda\theta) & I & O \\ \theta & O & I \end{bmatrix},$$

where the constant k is not filtered, so

$$\Sigma^*_{kk} = 1, \qquad \Sigma_{ky} = (\nu + \Lambda\theta)$$

$$\Sigma^*_{yy} = \Psi + \Lambda\Phi\Lambda' + (\nu + \Lambda\theta)(\nu + \Lambda\theta)', \qquad (53)$$

$$\Sigma^*_{k\eta} = \theta, \qquad \Sigma^*_{y\eta} = \Phi\Lambda + \theta(\nu + \Lambda\theta)', \qquad \Sigma^*_{\eta\eta} = \Phi + \theta\theta'.$$

In general, any regression from the constant vector is scaled in terms of first moments for either manifest or latent variables, or both simultaneously (Sörbom, 1978).

INTERRELATIONSHIPS AMONG GENERAL PURPOSE MODELS

Let us now turn to a consideration of some important principles involving the *interrelationships among the general purpose models* presented in Fig. 9.7. The first model to be considered is the recent, but very popular modeling foundation presented by Jöreskog (1973b) as the linear structural relations (LISREL) model (also see Jöreskog & Sörbom, 1980; Wiley, 1973). This model, when drawn as in Fig. 9.7a, can clearly be seen as a combination of the econometric nonrecursive model given in Fig. 9.5c and the psychometric factor analysis model given in Fig. 9.6a. This model is usually written as

$$x = \Lambda_x\xi + \delta, \qquad y = \Lambda_y\eta + \epsilon, \qquad \text{and} \qquad B\eta = \Gamma\xi + \zeta, \qquad (54)$$

where x $(p \times 1)$ and y $(q \times 1)$ represent observed variables, $\xi\,(n \times 1)$ and $\eta\,(m \times 1)$ represent unobserved common factors, δ and ϵ represent unique factors, and ζ represents a structural residual variable. Here, Λ_x and Λ_y are factor pattern matrices, and B and Γ are structural regression coefficient matrices. As

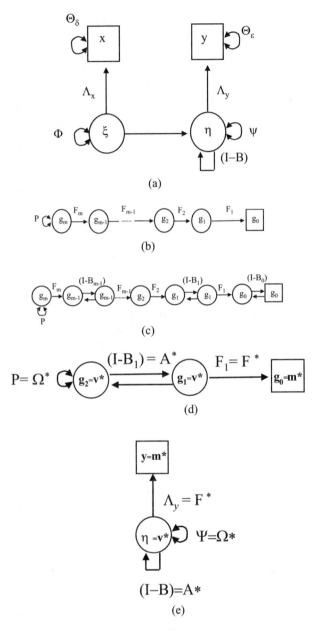

FIG. 9.7. General models represented in reticular action meta-model (RAM) notation. (a) The standard linear structural relations (LISREL) model, (b) the standard covariance structure analysis (COSAN) model, (c) the complete COSAN model, (d) the RAM–COSAN interface, (d) the RAM–LISREL interface.

McArdle (1978) showed, we can write this model in RAM notation as

$$j = p + q, \quad k = n + m, \quad \mathbf{v}' = [\mathbf{y}'\mathbf{x}'\boldsymbol{\eta}'\boldsymbol{\xi}'], \quad \mathbf{u}' = [\boldsymbol{\epsilon}\boldsymbol{\delta}'\boldsymbol{\zeta}'\boldsymbol{\xi}'],$$

$$\mathbf{F} = \begin{bmatrix} I & O & O & O \\ O & O & O & O \end{bmatrix}, \quad \mathbf{A} = \begin{bmatrix} O & O & \Lambda_y & O \\ O & O & O & \Lambda_x \\ O & O & (I-B) & \Gamma \\ O & O & O & O \end{bmatrix}, \tag{55}$$

$$\Omega = \begin{bmatrix} \Theta_{\varepsilon\varepsilon} & & & sym. \\ O & \Theta_{\delta\delta} & & \\ O & O & \Psi & \\ O & O & O & \Phi \end{bmatrix},$$

so

$$\mathbf{E} = (\mathbf{I} - \mathbf{A})^{-1} = \begin{bmatrix} I & O & \Lambda_y B^{-1} & \Lambda_y B^{-1}\Gamma \\ O & I & O & \Lambda_x \\ O & O & B^{-1} & B^{-1}\Gamma \\ O & O & O & O \end{bmatrix},$$

and so

$$\begin{aligned}
\Sigma_{yy} &= \Lambda_y \Sigma_{\eta\eta} \Lambda_y' + \Theta_\varepsilon, \\
\Sigma_{yx} &= \Lambda_x B^{-1}\Gamma\Phi\Lambda_y', \\
\Sigma_{xx} &= \Lambda_x \Phi\Lambda_x' + \Theta_\delta', \\
\Sigma_{y\eta} &= \Sigma_{\eta\eta}\Lambda_y', \\
\Sigma_{x\eta} &= \Sigma_{\eta\eta}\Phi\Lambda_x' \\
\Sigma_{\eta\eta} &= B^{-1}\Gamma\Phi\Gamma'B^{-1'} + B^{-1}\Psi B^{-1'} = B^{-1}(\Gamma\Phi\Gamma' + \Psi)B^{-1'}, \\
\Sigma_{y\xi} &= \Phi\Sigma_{\eta\eta}\Lambda_y', \\
\Sigma_{x\xi} &= \Phi\Lambda_x', \quad \Sigma_{\eta\xi} = \Phi B^{-1}\Gamma, \quad \Sigma_{\xi\xi} = \Phi.
\end{aligned} \tag{56}$$

This moment structure is equivalent to the manifest variable covariance structure proposed by Jöreskog (1973b, p. 87) and Wiley (1973, p. 80), and also includes all other latent and manifest variable associations. These matrices also demonstrate models that LISREL is not directly designed to fit (i.e., the zero locations in matrixes $\mathbf{A}$ and Ω).

We may also wish to develop the association matrix for multiple groups (as in Jöreskog, 1971; Sörbom, 1974, 1978) using a similar device. In the case of equal sample sizes we could simply create a matrix Σ^* that is appropriately subpartitioned into main diagonal block $\Sigma_1, \Sigma_2, \ldots, \Sigma_g$, with zero off-diagonal blocks denoting independence between groups, and with all matrices scaled by the appropriate sample sizes. This supermatrix could then be analyzed under alternative structural representations of $\mathbf{A}$ and Ω with appropriate constraints. It follows that Sörbom's (1978) inclusion of latent variable means combined within a multiple group LISREL model may be accomplished by including a constant variable, as in Fig. 9.6e.

Another general model, first proposed by McDonald (1978; see also McDonald, 1980; McDonald & Swaminathan, 1972), is the covariance structure analysis (COSAN) model, which may be described as

$$g_0 = \left(\prod_{j=1}^{m} F_j \right) g_m, \tag{57}$$

where g_0 is an $h_0 \times 1$ vector of manifest variables, g_m is an $h_m \times 1$ vector of latent variables, and F_j is an $h_{j-1} \times h_j$ matrix of coefficients. By also writing the $h_m \times h_m$ symmetric matrix

$$E\{g_m \, g_m'\} = P, \tag{58}$$

we may describe the manifest variable moment structure of COSAN as

$$\Sigma = E\{g_0, g_0'\} = F_1 F_2 \cdots F_m P F_m' \cdots F_2' F_1' = \left(\prod_{j=1}^{m} F_j \right) P \left(\prod_{j=1}^{m} F_j \right)'. \tag{59}$$

When described in this direct hierarchical fashion, COSAN may be written in RAM algebra as

$$j = h_0, \qquad k = \sum_{j=1,m} h_j, \qquad v' = [g_0' g_1' g_2' \cdots g_m'],$$

$$u' = [g_0^{*'} g_1^{*'} g_2^{*'} \cdots g_m'], \qquad A_{(j,j+1)} = F_j, \qquad \Omega_{ii} = [0, 0, 0, \ldots, P]. \tag{60}$$

Figure 9.7b graphically shows that these general equations represent an mth-level latent hierarchy with $m - 1$ latent nodes.

This interrelationship would be complete except for the fact that COSAN also permits the representation of any model where

$$F_j = B^{-1} \qquad \text{and/or} \qquad P = Q^{-1}, \tag{61}$$

where B and/or Q may be directly patterned (Bentler & Weeks, 1979, p. 176). This extension of COSAN to include patterned inverses at any hierarchical order provides for much more complex models, such as LISREL (McDonald & Swaminathan, 1972). However, McArdle and McDonald (1984) showed that it is also possible to represent any COSAN model with patterned F_j inverses as a RAM model where

$$A_{(j,j+1)} = L_j \quad \text{for } j = 1, \ldots, m \quad \text{and}$$
$$A_{(i,i)} = I - B_i \quad \text{for } i = 0, \ldots, m - 1. \tag{62}$$

That is, patterned matrices such as L_i in Equations 62 should appear on the superdiagonal of $\mathbf{A}$, and patterned inverses $\mathbf{B}_i$ should appear on the main diagonal of $\mathbf{A}$. This mixed-sequence arrangement can now yield any COSAN model by appropriately setting particular $\mathbf{L}_j$ or $\mathbf{B}_i$ equal to an identity matrix. The general form of this RAM–COSAN interchange is drawn as a path diagram in Fig. 9.7c.

As a specific example of this interchange, let us write a second-order COSAN model as

$$\Sigma = \mathbf{L}_1 \mathbf{B}_1^{-1'} \mathbf{P} \mathbf{B}_1^{-1'} \mathbf{L}_1' \tag{63}$$

by initially writing a RAM model where

$$\mathbf{A}_{12} = \mathbf{L}_1, \qquad \mathbf{A}_{11} = \mathbf{I} - \mathbf{B}_0, \qquad \text{and} \qquad \mathbf{A}_{22} = \mathbf{B}_1, \tag{64}$$

so that by setting $\mathbf{B}_0 = \mathbf{I}$, we obtain $\Sigma = \mathbf{A}_{11}$ equivalent to Equation 63. However, as McArdle (1978) showed, now it is possible to write a COSAN model where we set

$$m = 2, \qquad h_0 = j^*, \qquad h_1 = h_2 = t^*, \qquad g_0 = \mathbf{m}^*, \qquad g_1 = g_2 = \mathbf{v}^*,$$
$$\mathbf{F}_1 = \mathbf{F}^*, \qquad \mathbf{F}_2 = \mathbf{B}_2^{-1} = (\mathbf{I} - \mathbf{A}^*)^{-1}, \qquad \text{and} \qquad \mathbf{P} = \Omega^*, \tag{65}$$

where asterisks are used to denote RAM vectors and matrices, and the substitution of Equations 65 into the COSAN result in Equation 59 yields the original RAM equation 13. This specific COSAN model is depicted in Fig. 9.7d.

This result naturally leads us to pursue the interrelationships between RAM and COSAN and the LISREL foundation. Specifically, we now know that we may write nonzero LISREL variables and parameter matrices as

$$q = j^*, \qquad m = t^*, \qquad y = \mathbf{m}^*, \qquad \eta = \mathbf{v}^*, \qquad \zeta = \mathbf{u}^*,$$
$$\Lambda_y = \mathbf{F}^*, \qquad \mathbf{B} = (\mathbf{I} - \mathbf{A}^*), \qquad \Psi = \Omega^*, \tag{66}$$

where asterisks are used to denote RAM vectors and matrices and the substitution of Equations 66 into the LISREL Equations 54–58 also yields the RAM model of Equation 13. This LISREL model of RAM is presented in Fig. 9.7e. More details of the proof of this RAM–COSAN–LISREL interchange are presented by McArdle and McDonald (1984) and will be discussed in the last section.

COMPUTATIONAL REPRESENTATION

Due to the previous proof of the RAM–COSAN–LISREL interchange, theory concerning estimation, identification, and asymptotic testing of hypotheses in RAM can be taken directly from McDonald's (1978) COSAN or Jöreskog and Sörbom's (1978) LISREL. This is critical because, as McDonald (1978) said, "a convenient simplification of the consequent mathematics...would be illusory if it did not carry over into the arithmetic of the estimation procedures" (p. 70). Technical results are presented here to illustrate how such simplifications are made possible through the use of RAM theory.

Directly paraphrasing McDonald (1978), let us say that the moment structure Σ is a prescribed function f of p mathematically independent parameters in $\mathbf{A}$ and Ω. Most specifically, we can say that the parameter estimates for $\mathbf{A}$ and Ω are found among the solutions of the first-order partial derivatives for any RAM model listed as

$$\partial f(\mathbf{S}, \Sigma)/\partial \mathbf{A} = \mathbf{I} - 2Vec\,([\mathbf{FE}]'\mathbf{G}[\mathbf{FE}\Omega\mathbf{E}]) = 0,$$
$$\partial f(\mathbf{S}, \Sigma)/\partial \Omega = Vec\,([\mathbf{FE}\Omega]'\mathbf{G}[\mathbf{FE}\Omega]) = 0, \tag{67}$$

where $\mathbf{S}$ is the sample moment matrix from a sample size N, $f(\mathbf{S}, \Sigma)$ is any loss function, $\mathbf{E} = (\mathbf{I} - \mathbf{A})^{-1}$ in as before, $Vec\,(\cdot)$ represents a matrix operator that lexically realigns all matrix elements into a vector, and $\mathbf{G} = \partial f/\partial \Sigma$ is based on the explicit choice of a loss function. Note the $\partial \Sigma/\partial \mathbf{A}$ and $\partial \Sigma/\partial \Omega$ may be easily written in the same fashion.

From a practical standpoint we can now develop a general algorithm for solving these equations merely by using the general techniques of nonlinear optimization. That is, following McDonald and Swaminathan (1972), we can write a general quadratic form of a Newton-based optimization scheme for the sth iterative step in a direct RAM solution as

$$P(\mathbf{A}, \Omega)^{s+1} = P(\mathbf{A}, \Omega)^s - d^s(\mathbf{M}^{-1})\mathbf{G}^s, \tag{68}$$

where $P(\mathbf{A}, \Omega)^k$ represents a vector of estimated values for $\mathbf{A}$ and Ω parameters estimated at the kth step; the changes at each iteration are defined by a scaling constant d^s whose value is usually chosen in the interval $(0, 1)$ to prevent descent divergence; $\mathbf{M}$ is a square symmetric positive-definite matrix; and $\mathbf{G}$ is the gradient vector. It is well known that the choice of correction elements in $\mathbf{M}$ may be defined in many ways to yield differential performance. For example, setting $\mathbf{M} = \mathbf{H}$ yields the classic Newton–Raphson procedure, which is known to behave quite well in the vicinity of the true solution. It is now a simple matter to write the second-order partial derivatives for RAM following McDonald (1978, pp. 68–69) as

$$\partial^2 f/\partial \mathbf{A}^2 = ([\mathbf{FE}]' \otimes [\mathbf{FE}\Omega\mathbf{E}]')\mathbf{JHJ}([\mathbf{FE}] \otimes [\mathbf{FE}\Omega\mathbf{E}])$$
$$+ 2([\mathbf{FE}]'\mathbf{G}[\mathbf{FE}] \otimes [\mathbf{E}\Omega\mathbf{E}']$$
$$+ \{\mathbf{E}' \otimes [\mathbf{FE}\Omega\mathbf{E}']'\mathbf{G}[\mathbf{FE}] + [\mathbf{FE}]'\mathbf{G}[\mathbf{FE}\Omega\mathbf{E}'] \otimes \mathbf{E}\}\mathbf{J}\}$$
$$\partial^2 f/\partial \Omega^2 = ([\mathbf{FE}\Omega]' \otimes [\mathbf{FE}\Omega]')\mathbf{H}([\mathbf{FEU}] \otimes [\mathbf{FEU}]), \tag{69}$$
$$\partial^2 f/\partial \Omega \partial \mathbf{A} = -\{([\mathbf{FE}\Omega]' \otimes [\mathbf{FE}\Omega]')\mathbf{HJ}([\mathbf{FE}] \otimes [\mathbf{FE}\Omega\mathbf{E}'])$$
$$+ 2[\mathbf{FE}\Omega]'\mathbf{G}[\mathbf{FE}] \otimes [\mathbf{E}\Omega]',$$

where $\mathbf{H} = \partial^2 f / \partial \Sigma^2$ is also based on the choice of a loss function, $\otimes$ denotes the right-hand Kronecker product, and $\mathbf{J}$ is a permutation matrix of prescribed unity and zero values. Note that $\partial^2 \Sigma / \partial \mathbf{A}^2$, $\partial^2 \Sigma / \partial \Omega^2$, and $\partial^2 \Sigma / \partial \mathbf{A} \, \partial \Omega$ may be written in the same fashion. In any case, it should be obvious that *these equations are simplifications of the general treatments* of McDonald (1978) and Jöreskog and Sörbom (1978), yet they can be used to yield identical results. Alternative algorithmic solutions that have been shown to exhibit good comparative performance and do not require these second order derivatives include the Gauss–Newton method (Dennis & Moré, 1978; Lee, 1977) and the Davidon–Fletcher–Powell method (Jöreskog & Sorbom, 1978).

The practical efficiency of a general algorithm is of major concern. This turns out to be a critical issue in RAM theory due to the fact that a general solution for the RAM model will require the repetitive matrix multiplication and inversion of many large and sparse matrices. For this reason, the use of specialized routines for *sparse matrix operations* (Gustavson, 1978) and matrix storage (Duff & Reid, 1979) will no doubt be a required feature of any generally practical algorithm. In all cases, the calculation of $\mathbf{A}$ should be done noting the symmetry of Ω, and, due to the unusually simple pattern inherent in $\mathbf{F}$, the calculation of Σ from $\mathbf{A}$ should be done without direct multiplication by $\mathbf{F}$.

The use of the current sparse matrix algorithm for the repetitive calculation of $\mathbf{E} = (\mathbf{I} - \mathbf{A})^{-1}$ will, for the most part, be an attempt to translate the expensive inverse calculations into a series of much more efficient sparse matrix multiplications. This is usually done by searching for specific patterns (e.g., diagonal block) in the original sparse matrix (Gustavson, 1978). It follows that the more efficiently such patterns are found, the more efficient the overall algorithm will perform. In a large variety of problems it will be possible to simply reorder the vector $\mathbf{v}$ so that $\mathbf{A}$ is upper or lower triangular, and the inverse may be calculated on a single pass of a sweep operation (Jennrich, 1977).

A practical solution to this problem is now possible using RAM theory; the computational inversion of $(\mathbf{I} - \mathbf{A})$ may capitalize on the fundamental relationships among the general models previously described to gain some efficiency in programming. That is, we can now create an algorithm that will (a) efficiently describe the patterns in the RAM matrix $\mathbf{A}$, (b) directly translate these patterns into a series of smaller sparse matrix multiplications using COSAN calculations, and (c) directly translate final estimates back to the RAM notation. The most crucial step in this new algorithm is the direct translation of any arbitrary RAM $\mathbf{A}$ and Ω matrices into an equivalent series of COSAN $\mathbf{F}_j$ and P matrices. Equation 62 illustrates some of the basic principles in the interface between RAM and COSAN, but it does not provide a direct answer to the reverse problem of going from RAM parameters to COSAN parameters. The main steps in a translation from a RAM model to a COSAN model are direct, merely requiring the repetitive search through $\mathbf{A}$ and Ω for specific patterns. However, the complete details of this algorithmic pattern search are too lengthy to detail here (McArdle & Horn, 1981).

To illustrate the possible efficiency of this RAM–COSAN interchange, let us now reconsider the multiple linear regression model of RAM Equations 24 and 25 expressed as a COSAN model in abbreviated notation as

$$m = 1, \quad g_0' = [y'x'], \quad g_1' = [e'x'],$$

$$F_1 = L_1 = \begin{bmatrix} I & B \\ O & I \end{bmatrix}, \quad P = \begin{bmatrix} \Sigma_{ee} & sym. \\ O & \Sigma_{xx} \end{bmatrix}. \tag{70}$$

This model, as may be verified by substitution in COSAN Equation 59, yields a moment structure that is equivalent to Equation 24. This translation to COSAN requires several elemental numerical operations based on the size of y and x, but the COSAN formulation now does not require the repetitive inversion of any model matrix. Thus, we have now effectively replaced the iterative calculation of $E = (I - A)^{-1}$ with a single multiplication problem of an equivalent size that is more easily handled by sparse matrix routines. This exact result applies for the factor analysis model written as Equations 39–41 and the model with the explicit inclusion of errors written as Equations 45 and 46.

As another example, we can translate the linear nested equation path model of RAM Equations 27 and 28 into a COSAN model of

$$m = 2, \quad g_0' = [x'y'z'], \quad g_1' = [x'y'f'], \quad g_2' = [x'q'f'],$$

$$F_1 = L_1 = \begin{bmatrix} I & O & O \\ O & I & O \\ O & H & I \end{bmatrix}, \quad F_2 = L_2 = \begin{bmatrix} I & O & O \\ \Gamma & I & O \\ O & O & I \end{bmatrix}, \tag{71}$$

$$P = \begin{bmatrix} \Sigma_{xx} & & sym. \\ O & \Sigma_{ee} & \\ O & O & \Sigma_{ff} \end{bmatrix}.$$

This type of model now reduces the complex inverse of $(I - A)$ into a much simpler series of sparse matrix multiplications. The other models with nested regressions (hierarchical factors in Equations 42–44 and path constraints in Equations 49 and 50) may be accomplished in similar fashion.

As a final example, let us consider that the general econometric nonrecursive model of RAM Equations 33 and 34 may be translated into an equivalent COSAN model given as

$$m = 2, \quad g_0' = [x'y'], \quad g_1' = [x'y'], \quad g_2' = [x'z']$$

$$F_1 = B_1^{-1} = \begin{bmatrix} I & O \\ O & (I - B) \end{bmatrix}, \quad F_2 = L_2 = \begin{bmatrix} I & O \\ G & I \end{bmatrix}, \tag{72}$$

$$P = \begin{bmatrix} \Sigma_{zz} & sym. \\ O & \Sigma_{xx} \end{bmatrix}.$$

This COSAN model still requires an inversion at the first order, but this inverse problem is now well defined in a block-diagonal form that sparse matrix routines can more easily recognize and evaluate.

The major benefits of an algorithm with the features just defined are relatively easy to describe. First, this algorithm capitalizes on the simplicity of model specification using RAM $\mathbf{A}$ and Ω parameters. These may be input either in compact elemental notation or block matrix form. Any alteration in model input, such as with canonically nested alternatives, requires only minimal additions or subtractions that will be transparent to the user. Second, the algorithm automatically creates the optimally efficient COSAN model for any RAM model by avoiding unnecessary inversion. This internal use of COSAN capitalizes on the general mathematical and algorithmic features of COSAN and permits the general calculation of estimates for any well defined loss function. Finally, the algorithm permits a direct translation back to the simple RAM notation for ease and flexibility of output [see McArdle & Horn (1981) for more details on the available algorithm].

The use of RAM theory as a modeling foundation leads to several other results of theoretical interest. For instance, unique estimates for $\mathbf{A}$ and Ω parameters can only be obtained if the model is identified. General conditions for global model identification can now be simply described by writing a RAM model as

$$\Sigma = \mathbf{FE}^*\Omega^*\mathbf{E}^{*\prime}\mathbf{F}', \tag{73}$$

where $\mathbf{E}^* = (\mathbf{I} - \mathbf{A})^{-1}\,\mathbf{T}$, $\Omega^* = \mathbf{T}^{-1}\Omega$, and $\mathbf{T}$ is any nonsingular transformation matrix (compare Bentler & Weeks, 1980, p. 295). This shows that any RAM model with an $\mathbf{F}$ prescribed by the variables in the model but with unknown $\mathbf{A}$ and Ω parameters is globally identified if and only if $\mathbf{T} = \mathbf{I}$. This condition, of course, is quite difficult to verify for any problem of reasonable complexity. Therefore, although we have reduced the identification problem to a single $\mathbf{T}$-matrix form, the nonlinearity of $\mathbf{E} = (\mathbf{I} - \mathbf{A})^{-1}$ still requires detailed study of the alternative $\mathbf{T}$-matrix properties. Alternatively, it is still quite useful to note that any model is at least locally identified if $\mathbf{M} = \mathbf{H}$ (Equation 68) of full rank in large samples (McDonald & Krane, 1979).

These technical results have been written to be general for any given loss function f, but the statistical properties of the estimators for $\mathbf{A}$ and Ω must be considered under the specific objective loss function defined by f, $\mathbf{G}$, and $\mathbf{M} = \mathbf{H}$ (Krane & McDonald, 1978; McDonald, 1978). In any case, the statistical problem considered here concerns making inferences about overall model fit from sample to population and determining the saliency of estimators. For any specific RAM model, we can write degrees of freedom (df) equal to

$$df = r(\mathbf{S}) - r(\mathbf{A}, \Omega), \tag{74}$$

where $r(\mathbf{S}) = j(j + 1)/2$, the rank of sample moment matrix $\mathbf{S}$, and $r(\mathbf{A}, \mathbf{\Omega})$ equals the rank of the matrix of first derivatives for $\mathbf{A}$ and $\mathbf{\Omega}$ with respect to $\mathbf{\Sigma}$ evaluated at some solution point. Under certain loss functions, such as the generalized least squares or maximum likelihood criteria (Browne, 1977; Lee & Jennrich, 1979), *asymptotic* properties of the estimators prove useful; the estimators are consistent, normally distributed, efficient, and scale invariant, and $N f_m$ is distributed as χ^2. This result yields the general comparison of other canonically nested models as a simple difference of

$$\chi_d^2 = \chi_h^2 - \chi_a^2, \quad \text{with} \quad df_d = df_h - df_a, \tag{75}$$

where subscript h denotes a hypothesized model, subscript a denotes a more global alternative, and subscript d denotes the difference of these two models (Pesaran & Deaton, 1978). The comparison of any model against the trivial alternative where $\mathbf{\Sigma}$ is precisely equal to $\mathbf{S}$ with $df = j(j + 1)/2$ yields a general statistical test for the global adequacy of model fit. The saliency of any individual parameter may now be determined from the calculation of standard errors for each parameter from $diag\,[2/N(\mathbf{H}^{-1})]$.

Many other useful indices that relate directly to goodness of fit and the general process of statistical model building (Saris et al., 1978; Sörbom, 1975) may be developed from RAM theory. For example, consider that the generalized least squares criterion for any RAM model may be explicitly written

$$f = 1/2\,tr[\{\mathbf{S}^{-1}(\mathbf{S} - \mathbf{F}(\mathbf{I} - \mathbf{A})^{-1}\mathbf{\Omega}(\mathbf{I} - \mathbf{A})^{-1\prime}\mathbf{F}')\}^2]. \tag{76}$$

We can now see that the function f may itself be elementally decomposed into residual elements, each of which is in turn based on sums of pathway products of $\mathbf{A}$ and $\mathbf{\Omega}$ elements that make up the $\mathbf{A}$ elements. In this way the weighted effect on any function value may now be calculated for each *individual* structural parameter. Another way to use this logic is to write an index of the model-fitting residuals,

$$g = (|\mathbf{F}(\mathbf{I} - \mathbf{A})^{-1}\mathbf{\Omega}(\mathbf{I} - \mathbf{A})^{-1\prime}\mathbf{F}'| - |\mathbf{S}|)/|\mathbf{S}|. \tag{77}$$

This index, based on the concept of a determinant as a measure of generalized variance, can be interpreted as an overall ratio of variance in the data explained by the model (Specht, 1975), and g can also be decomposed with elemental contributions of $\mathbf{A}$ and $\mathbf{\Omega}$ parameters. Similar concepts have been studied by Montanelli (1974) and Horn and Engstrom (1979), and associated statistical tests for these residual indicators have been studied by McDonald (1975). Of importance here may be the evaluation of the separate contributions of $\mathbf{A}$ and $\mathbf{\Omega}$ parameters, say in $|\mathbf{\Sigma}|$, and their relation to overall model fit. However, these issues are far too complex to be discussed in detail here (Horn & McArdle, 1980).

CONCEPTUAL REPRESENTATION

The mathematical development of RAM is clearly based on the previous treatments of Jöreskog (1973b), Wiley (1973), McDonald (1978), and Sörbom (1978). An especially heavy emphasis has been placed on some of the statistical and algorithmic possibilities (e.g., fixed vs. free parameters). In this sense, we recognize that RAM is not at all new, or even novel. Perhaps RAM is best considered as a consolidation of the basic ideas of the LISREL model, or the complete mathematical simplification of the COSAN model. However, we have also shown that this consolidation is illusory in many theoretical and practical ways. For example, it is clear that the current popularity of the LISREL model is in some part due to its theoretical development as a psychometrically based "measurement" model combined with an econometrically based "structural" model (Jöreskog & Sörbom, 1980). There is no doubt that the distinction between the measurement and structural components of a model is both practically and conceptually useful, especially when statistical issues of parameter estimation are considered. However, the algebraic basis of RAM clearly shows that these kinds of distinctions are not mathematically essential for full model development in terms of specification, estimation, evaluation, or even simulation (McArdle, 1980). Furthermore, these distinctions can breakdown when, for example, dealing with mean structures and/or complex model constraints (see Fig. 9.6).

The graphic development of RAM is clearly based on a combination of concepts in diagraph theory (Christofide, 1975; Harary, 1973) with those of traditional path-analytic diagrammatic representation (Wright, 1934, 1964; see also Li, 1975). Once again, most of the RAM ideas are not at all new, but represent a consolidation of traditional ideas. However, RAM graphics attempt to extend traditional path diagrams in two important ways. First, the RAM formulation requires the explicit definition of all undirected turning paths, even those associated with a single point (e.g., variances), whereas more traditional representations only require undirected turns between two sets of points (e.g., covariance or correlation). This explicit representation of all undirected slings is required simply because these slings are critical elements of the Σ associations. The second major difference between RAM graphics and traditional path diagrams is in the implicit representation of the residual variables **u**. In RAM, latent residual variables with unit weights are not explicitly included, whereas in more traditional representations these are included, albeit not rigorously or consistently. Although it is possible to explicitly include these variables, as latent variables with fixed, unity paths (see Fig. 9.6c), this is unnecessary because it leads to redundancy in the associated algebra (see Equations 43 and 44). In general, the early work in path analysis did not entertain some possibilities that we wish to study with RAM, including models for covariances and means, as well as models with more complex latent common factor networks. Thus, the graphic alterations that we propose here are not arbitrary but are specifically designed to deal with these more general linear algebraic structures. Of course, these new alterations also directly lead to the formal proof of the algebraic–graphic isomorphism.

The theoretical results on the RAM–COSAN–LISREL interchange are surprisingly complex; RAM, COSAN, and LISREL each may be considered as subsets of one another. An important feature of this interchange arises when we consider that the general RAM, COSAN, and LISREL models may each be written as more deeply subpartitioned sets of one another or themselves in an infinite series of translation (Hofstadter, 1979). This paradoxical interchange among general modeling foundations, first described by McArdle (1978, 1979b), and remarked on by Bentler and Weeks (1979), has important implications for structural modeling. For example, this demonstration on the equivalence of these models directly rejects earlier claims about one model being "more general" than another (Bentler, 1976; Bentler & Woodward, 1978; Weeks, 1978; cf. McDonald, 1978, 1979). Also, as can be seen from the RAM–COSAN interchange algorithm, each general modeling system, including LISREL, has potentially different and important theoretical and practical virtues. This emphasis on the important individual features of any modeling system is muddled, if not lost completely, in the search for a "most general" superstructure. Our emphasis here has been to show that RAM representation in Equations 1–15 is the only model that is based solely on the *necessary and sufficient* features required for a general linear structural equation system of the type we have described.

As we have attempted to illustrate, RAM theory also has much practical utility. For instance, in any specific application, RAM can simplify model specification, in terms of algebra or graphics, as well as provide a simplified statistical and algorithmic estimation and testing procedure. These, in turn, lead to several new results that have heretofore not been utilized. Alternatively, we have not pursued other practical algorithmic features for specific models (Wermuth, 1980; Wold, 1980), especially those related to computational graphics (Chachra, Prabhakar, & Moore, 1979; Heap, 1972), or the many other mathematical developments that require detailed study.

The conceptual basis of RAM, though decidedly less formal, is as critical as any other representation herein. Most certainly, the final form of Equation 15 or the isomorphic representation provided by Fig. 9.4 presents possibilities for many alternative abstract formulations. Among these, the one that seems most parallel to RAM theory is the "input/output" logic offered by a general systems philosophy (Rapoport, 1972). Under this logic, we define a "system" simply as "a set of variables and the relationships among them." We ignore several critical features of any specific system until these features prove necessary or useful in the conceptualization of that system. For instance, in this development we initially described only general features of variables until we wished to move toward a model for manifest moment structures, at which point it was necessary to distinguish between manifest and latent variables. Critically, this distinction among variables does not immediately demand any further restrictions on the kind of relationships possible, such as only latent variables can be directed at manifest variables. It is conceivable that another practically useful distinction would be between endogenous (e.g., dependent) and exogenous (e.g., independent) system variables (compare Bentler & Weeks, 1980). However, once again, this would strictly require reference to a specific set of directed relationships that, from our general systems point of view, is unnecessarily artificial at this point in model development (Rozeboom, 1978). The logical extension of this system development is the expression of RAM in COSAN terms when estimation is at issue.

In many senses, RAM can also be considered as a general foundation of system *limits* on model conceptualization. As such, RAM theory provides a generally abstract *meta*-model from which more practical and theoretically interesting forms can emerge. In this presentation, we have chosen not to discuss philosophical notions of *causality*, although clearly these require further discussion (McArdle, 1980; Roozeboom, 1978; Wold, 1954) and have a clear relevance to our general systems perspective. Instead, as Fig. 9.4 shows, the general nature of RAM is just that of a relatively free-form *network* of interrelationships among points in space. The inclusion of the directed/undirected relationship distinction, along with the additional restrictions on pathway information flow throughout this network, denotes the importance of *action* or momentum between points in space. The inclusion of the manifest/latent variable distinction emphasizes the importance of the manifest moment structure as an empirical representation of the overall system action. In the recent psychometric literature, only Cattell (1978) has previously proposed such a general "reticule of interlocking influences" (p. 200; compare Fig. 9.4). To emphasize the importance of this theoretical conception, we have chosen the term *Reticular Action Meta-model*, with the mnemonic *RAM*, to represent both our algebra and our graphics.

A CONTEMPORARY VIEW OF THE RAM RULES

The previous six sections described the origins of the concepts that have come to be known as the RAM rules. At the time these ideas were first being circulated (1978–1981) I was excited by the possibility that I had found something simple about the complex world of general SEM. I was also unsure whether these rules would ever be useful and unsure about how they would be received. In looking back on this treatment, it is now clear that few changes have been required in the original RAM rules. From my point of view, the RAM rules have created both benefits and problems. I now conclude by taking a brief look at what has happened to the RAM rules during the last 25 years after I first wrote the previous sections.

The use of path diagrams has become a common device for the communication of both simple and complex structural models. There are so many applications where SEMs have been depicted as path diagrams that we can select many as exemplars where they had not been used before (e.g., McDonald, 1985). On a more theoretical level, path-diagram graphics assisted in the development of several interesting SEM issues, including exploratory model search strategies (e.g., Glymour et al., 1987; Spirtes et al., 1993), the improved understanding of equivalent structural models (e.g., Lee & Hershberger, 1990; Luijben, 1991; MacCallum et al., 1993; Raykov & Marcoulides, 2002), and the clearer delineation of unambiguous causal inference (McDonald, 1997; Pearl, 2000).

In this same sense RAM suggested the requirement *to diagram every parameter in the model*. On the surface, this does not seem to be an unusual rule, and many researchers apparently believe they are following this rule. However, as witnessed by the current SEM literature, this part of the RAM rules has not yet caught on; most articles on path analysis still do not include all model parameters in their diagrams (McDonald & Ho, 2002). The publication standard of path models seems to have emerged as a mixture of diagramming techniques based on graphics used by Sewell Wright (1921, 1934, 1964, 1983) mixed with the treatment of unobservables in MIMIC models by Hauser and Goldberger (1971). To be sure, Sewell Wright anticipated most every aspect of current diagrams (McArdle & Aber, 1990), but he only made path diagrams as models of correlations. (As an aside, Hauser and Goldberger used circles for manifest variables and squares for latent variables.) However, as the models began to be based on covariances (due to equality constraints) and subsequently included means and intercepts, Wright's classic diagramming conventions prove inadequate in a fundamental way—incomplete diagrams do not allow the reader to count the parameters or to reproduce the model expectations using the tracing rules (Loehlin, 1998).

One oversight in most current published path diagrams is the lack of any self-slings (ω_{ii}) even though these are essential to the scaling of any predictor or latent variables and the subsequent interpretation of the other parameters. Many researchers do not label the residual disturbances or unique factor scores, and this makes it difficult to understand whether variances or deviation terms were fitted (and this can make a difference, see Equation 47). Only a few recent researchers include the means and intercepts in a fashion consistent with the tracing rules of cross-products (e.g., Equations 35–38), and some of these researchers do not include the average cross-product sling (labeled 1) on the constant (possibly due to the common misinterpretation of "slings as variances"). Some recent diagrams intended to reflect mixed-effect or multilevel models have drawn what is described as a "path into a path" (e.g., Muthén & Muthén, 2002, p. 245). Whereas this diagram may be useful in conveying the overall intention of the analysis, it is not a valid path diagram, in that it violates the rules for reproducing the expectations via tracing rules (for multilevel path diagrams, see McArdle & Hamagami, 1996).

The RAM rules are not fully documented in the major programs of SEM, such as LISREL or COSAN. This is no surprise, because these programs were developed using a different algebraic basis. However, the value of using RAM in LISREL programming had been demonstrated and used by McArdle (1978, 1979b, 1979c,

1980; Horn & McArdle, 1980) and subsequently observed by Graff and Schmidt (1982), among others. The use of RAM rules in computer programs without some provision for sparse matrix algebra slows down the calculation at each iteration (i.e., a patterned inverse is always used even if it is not needed; e.g., Equation 70). Nevertheless, whereas a RAM-based LISREL analysis would not be the fastest way for LISREL to do computer calculations, it turns out to be far easier to set up and debug for almost any problem (e.g., consider Fig. 9.1 as LISREL matrices).

In most recent versions of LISREL, a fixed "IZ" and a "No-X" model have been added as general options, and this makes RAM-type analysis far easier to use with the LISREL program (Jöreskog & Sörbom, 1999; McArdle, 2001). In one sense, the RAM rules do not exactly highlight key benefits of the standard LISREL approach, that is, "You may completely ignore five of the eight LISREL matrices here and still generate the same answer!" (e.g., Equations 55–56). Nevertheless, the more user-friendly version of the LISREL manual now recognize that a "No-X, No-ε" 3-matrix LISREL model can precisely match, iteration by iteration, any analysis that a full (now 12-matrix) LISREL model can accomplish. In the many complex applications where LISREL is most useful, the measurement–structural model separation is not the most critical feature, and the standard LISREL matrices have no substantive meaning (e.g., again see Fig. 9.1).

One clear benefit of the RAM rules is that they are not limited to any specific SEM program. As long as a SEM program permits the flexibility of a fixed **F**, a patterned inverse of regression parameters **A**, and a patterned symmetric Ω, this program can fit most any model (e.g., Fig. 9.1). This gives the user the flexibility to choose a program that is most appropriate for the specific problem at hand. In publications, it is possible to simply list all routines that produce similar results (and most do). These conceptual features continue to make RAM-based SEM programming an effective way to begin to use the fundamental and extensive features of excellent programs like LISREL and COSAN. My colleagues and I created our own computer program for model fitting based on the RAM–COSAN interface described here (e.g., RAMIT). The program we published was a subsection based on the tracing rules of path diagrams, RAMpath, by McArdle and Boker (1990; Boker et al., 2002).

Some problems are now outdated because several elegant new computer programs do emphazise RAM rules in their manuals. This started with the RAMONA program by Browne and Mels (1999), which was entirely based on the RAM algebra of Equations 1–15, and the R-SEM package by Fox (2002). Other programs with general matrix algebra have provisions for the RAM rules, including SAS PROC CALIS with the use of the RAMLIST (Hatcher, 1994) and the current Mx program by Neale et al. (1999). Mx is a freeware program that also includes a graphical user interface where a latent variable path model can be drawn and automatically turned into RAM matrices for model fitting and then turned back into presentation-style diagrams (following an algorithm devised by Boker; see Boker et al., 2002). Apparently the AMOS program (Arbuckle & Wotke, 1999) uses the

RAM rules and techniques, but the internal calculations of the AMOS program are not as transparent as those of the Mx program, and the path diagram output does not completely follow the RAM rules presented here (e.g., no self-loops are output, although this would be an easy alteration).

Most benefits of RAM have accrued from novel but practical applications. Our first set of applications included using SEM to deal with fairly complex developmental systems analyses, including *nonlinear constraints on age, time, and cohort* (Horn & McArdle, 1980; McArdle, 1981). In this work, our nonstandard use of "nonvariable" nodes anticipated the subsequent popularity of "phantom" variables by Rindskopf (1984; personal communication, 1986). This represented the beginning of our SEM re-interpretation of the then-new statistical models for dealing with incomplete data simply by writing different filter matrices ($\mathbf{F}^{(g)}$) for groups defined by the patterns of available data (using MAR assumptions; McArdle, 1994; McArdle & Anderson, 1990; McArdle & Hamagami, 1992). Based on the RAM rules, these complex incomplete data concepts were relatively easy to program and apply, and far easier than a standard LISREL approach (e.g., Allison, 1987).

A second set of applications came in the form of *novel behavioral genetics twin analyses* using existing SEM software (e.g., LISREL and COSAN; McArdle, 1986; McArdle, Connell, & Goldsmith, 1980; McArdle & Goldsmith, 1984, 1990). It seemed natural to show how RAM-based twin and family models could be expanded to include common factors, means and intercepts, and various forms of longitudinal data. This use of LISREL-based SEM was not the standard at the time, but appears now to be common (e.g., Henderson, 1992; McArdle & Prescott, 1996).

A third set of applications emerged when we ran across the classical *latent growth models* defined in SEM terms by Meredith and Tisak (1990). Based on RAM rules, these models were easy to represent as nonstandard but complete path diagrams for means and covariances that then could be fitted easily with any SEM software (McArdle, 1988; McArdle & Aber, 1990; McArdle & Epstein, 1987). The mixture of incomplete longitudinal data using simple filter matrices again proved to be a natural feature of RAM analyses (e.g., McArdle & Bell, 2000; McArdle & Hamagami, 1992; McArdle & Woodcock, 1997).

A final set of applications comes from our analyses of longitudinal data using *dynamic time-series models* for individuals and groups (McArdle, 1982; Nesselroade & McArdle, 1986; Nesselroade et al., 2002; Wood, 1988). These concepts led to the more recent representation of longitudinal data using latent difference scores (Hamagami & McArdle, 2000; McArdle, 2000; McArdle & Hamagami, 2001; McArdle & Nesselroade, 1994) and differential equations models (Boker, 2001). This accumulation of prior RAM-based work represents the building blocks for our recent dynamic analyses of incomplete longitudinal multivariate twin data based on models like Fig. 9.1.

Many of us have been able to teach SEM to students using these rules and have found that RAM simplifies many tedious tasks. We recognize that the majority of SEM researchers still rely on the measurement–structural LISREL logic in presentations defined as "fundamental for beginners" (e.g., Bollen, 1988; Byrne, 1998; Mueller, 1996; Raykov & Marcoulides, 2000; Schumacker & Lomax, 1996). Alternatively, using the RAM rules, we can start with a graphic logic, sometimes termed the "RAM Game"(C.E. McArdle, Personal Communication, April, 1987): "Draw circles or squares, one-headed arrows, or two-headed slings." "If you can draw the diagram, you can automatically write the matrices." "Any program can generate the expectations." This starting point allows us to move on to the real hard questions of SEM, such as "What is your model?" This didactic aspect of the RAM rules should not be understated because it is often the novice who uses and appreciates RAM rules and the RAM Game. This approach also led to the development of new teaching tools, such as the automatic generation of SEM expectations and tracing rules using the new MAPLE and Mathematica programs.

Other benefits of RAM rules have been created by other researchers. Of course, many people now use RAM rules in their own presentations (e.g., Browne & Nesselroade, chap. 13, this volume; Loehlin, 1998; McDonald, 1995), and many have commented on their own approach to the RAM rules (e.g., "RAM is not wrong"; M. Browne, personal communication, October 2002). Indeed, Rod Mc-Donald has extended this theory in several directions, including elegant studies in path analysis (McDonald, 1985, 1986, 1997; McDonald & Ho, 2002; McDonald, Parker, & Ishizuka, 1993) the creation of a "bi-level RAM" (Goldstein & McDonald, 1988; McDonald, 1994; McDonald & Goldstein, 1989), and the automatic generation of starting values for any SEM (Fox, 2002; McDonald & Hartman, 1992).

In this same sense, I hope I have demonstrated that RAM is a derivative work that stems from the fundamental flexibility of the original LISREL and COSAN concepts. As I look back on this work, I am not surprised that researchers who were invested in finding a more general system considered that this could only be done by expanding on these matrix representations (e.g., Bentler, 1976) and by creating new and complex programs for higher order systems (e.g., Weeks, 1978). Nor should it be any surprise that coming at the same problem from a different viewpoint—path graphics for SEM programs—could create an alternative view of the flexibility of SEM. I am grateful to those who have considered and improved on these ideas, so, after 25 years, I can use current vernacular and simply restate the simple principle, "RAM Rules."

ACKNOWLEDGMENTS

This research was initially supported by NSF-RIAS grant SER77-06935 and by NIA grant R01-AG02695. Special thanks go to colleagues who have contributed in ways too numerous to detail here, especially John L. Horn, Steven M. Boker, Roderick P. McDonald, Colin Fraser, Michael Browne, William Meredith, John R. Nesselroade, Fumiaki Hamagami, Kevin Grimm, Keith Widaman, and Albert Maydeu-Olivares for their advice and support. Requests for reprints should be sent to the author at jjm@virginia.edu reprints can also be downloaded at http://kiptron.psyc.virginia.edu.

REFERENCES

Circa 1981

Anderson, T. W., & Rubin, H. (1956). Statistical inference in factor analysis. In J. Neyman (Ed.): *Proceedings of the Third Berkeley Symposium on Mathematical Statistics and Probability* (pp. 111–150). Berkeley: University of California Press.

Bentler, P. M. (1976). Multistructure statistical model applied to factor analysis. *Multivariate Behavioral Research, 11,* 3–25.

Bentler, P. M., & Woodward, J. A. (1978). A head start reevaluation: Positive effects are not yet demonstrable. *Evaluation Quarterly, 2,* 493–510.

Bentler, P. M., & Weeks, D. G. (1979). Interrelations among models for the analysis of moment structures. *Multivariate Behavioral Research, 14,* 169–186.

Bentler, P. M., & Weeks, D. G. (1980). Linear structural equations with latent variables. *Psychometrika, 45*(3), 289–308.

Bock, R. D., & Bargmann, R. E. (1966). Analysis of covariance structures. *Psychometrika, 1966, 31,* 507–533.

Bock, R. D. (1975). *Multivariate statistical methods in behavioral research.* New York: McGraw-Hill.

Browne, M. W. (1977). Generalized least-squares estimators in the analysis of covariance structures. In D. J. Aigner & A. S. Goldberger (Eds.), *Latent variables in socio-economic models* (pp. 205–226). Amsterdam: North-Holland.

Cattell, R. B. (1978). *The scientific use of factor analysis in behavioral and life sciences.* New York: Plenum Press.

Chachra, V., Prabhakar, M. G., & Moore, J. M. (1979). *Applications of graph theory algorithms.* New York: North-Holland.

Christofide, N. (1975). *Graph theory: An algorithmic approach.* New York: Academic Press.

Dennis J. E., & Moré, J. J. (1977). Quasi-Newton methods, motivation and theory. *SIAM Review, 19*(1), 46–89.

Duff, I. S., & Reid, J. K. (1979). Some design features of a sparse matrix code. *ACM Transactions on Mathematical Software, 5*(1), 18–35.

Duncan, O. D. (1975). *Introduction to structural equation models.* New York: Academic Press.

Gustavson, F. G. (1978). Two fast algorithms for sparse matrices: multiplication and permuted transposition. *ACM Transactions on Mathematical Software, 4*(3), 250–269.

Guttman, L. (1957). Simple proofs of relations between the communality problem and multiple correlation. *Psychometrika, 22,* 147–158.

Hanushek, E. A., & Jackson, J. E. (1977). *Statistical methods for social scientists.* New York: Academic Press.

Harary, F. (1973). *New directions in the theory of graphs.* New York: Academic Press.

Harary, F., Norman, R. Z., & Cartwright, D. (1965). *Structural models: An introduction to the theory of directed graphs.* New York: Wiley.

Heise, D. R. (1975). *Causal analysis.* New York: Wiley Press.

Heap, B. R. (1972). The production of graphs by computer. In R. C. Read (Ed.), *Graph Theory and Computing* (pp. 10–15). New York: Academic Press.

Hofstadter, D. R. (1979). *Goedel, Escher, Bach: An Eternal Golden Braid.* NY: Basic Books.

Horn, J. L., & Engstrom, R. (1979). Cattell's scree test in relation to Bartlett's chi-square test and other observations on the number of factors problem. *Multivariate Behavioral Research, 14*, 283–300.

Horn, J. L., & McArdle, J. J. (1980). Perspective on mathematical and statistical model building (MASMOB) in aging research. In L. W. Poon (Ed.), *Aging in the 1980's* (pp. 503–541). Washington, D.C.: American Psychological Association.

Jennrich, R. I. (1977). Stepwise Regression. In K. Enslein, I. Ralston & H. W. Wilf (Eds.), *Statistical methods for digital computers-Vol III* (pp. 18–25). New York: Wiley Press.

Jöreskog, K. G. (1970). A general method for the analysis of covariance structures. *Biometrika, 57*, 239–251.

Jöreskog, K. G. (1971). Simultaneous factor analysis in several populations. *Psychometrika, 36*(4), 409–426.

Jöreskog, K. G. (1973a). Analysis of covariance structures. In A. S. Goldberger & O. D. Duncan (Eds.), *Structural equation models in the social sciences* (pp. 53–68). New York: Seminar Press.

Jöreskog, K. G. (1973b). A general method for estimating a linear structural equation system. In A. S. Goldberger & O. D. Duncan (Eds.), *Structural equation models in the social sciences* (pp. 85–112). New York: Seminar Press.

Jöreskog, K. G. (1971). Simultaneous factor analysis in several populations. *Psychometrika, 36*, 409–426.

Jöreskog, K. G., & Sörbom, D. (1980). *Simultaneous analysis of longitudinal data from several cohorts. (Research Report 80-5)*. Uppsala, Sweden; University of Uppsala, Department of Statistics.

Jöreskog, K. G., & Sorbom, D. (1979). *Advances in factor analysis and structural equation models.* Cambridge, MA: Abt Assoc.

Jöreskog, K. G., & Sörbom, D. (1978). LISREL-IV: *Analysis of linear structural relationships by the method of maximum likelihood.* Chicago: National Educational Resources.

Kenny, D. A. (1979). *Correlation and causality.* New York: Wiley.

Krane, W. R., & McDonald, R. P. (1978). Scale invariance and the factor analysis of correlation matrices. *British Journal of Mathematical Statistical Psychology, 31*, 218–228.

Lee, S. Y., & Jennrich, R. I. (1979). A study of algorithms for covariance structure analysis with specific comparisons using factor analysis. *Psychometrika, 44*, 99–113.

Li, C. C. (1975). *Path analysis.* Pacific Grove, CA: Boxwood Press.

McArdle, J. J. (1978). *A structural view of structural models.* Paper presented at the Winter Workshop on Latent Structure Models Applied to Developmental Data. University of Denver.

McArdle, J. J. (1979). *A SYSTEMatic view of structural equation modeling.* Paper presented at the Psychometric Society Annual Meeting, Monterey, California.

McArdle, J. J. (1979). *Reticular Analysis Modeling (RAM) theory: the simplicity and generality of structural equations.* Paper presented at the American Psychological Association Annual Meeting, New York.

McArdle, J. J. (1979). The development of general multivariate software. *Proceedings of the Association for the Development of Computer-Based Instructional Systems* (pp. 824–862). Akron, Ohio: University of Akron Press.

McArdle, J. J. (1980). Causal modeling applied to psychonomic systems simulation. *Behavior Research Methods and Instrumentation, 12*, 193–209.

McArdle, J. J., & Horn, J. L. (1981). *MULTITAB 81: Computer programs for multivariate data analysis.* Department of Psychology, University of Denver.

McArdle, J. J., & McDonald, R. P. (1980). *A note on some properties of the Reticular Action Model for moment structures.* Department of Psychology, University of Denver.

McDonald, R. P. (1969). A generalized common factor analysis based on residual covariance matrices of prescribed structure. *British Journal of Mathematical Statistical Psychology, 22*, 149–163.

McDonald, R. P. (1975). A note on Rippe's test of significance in common factor analysis. *Psychometrika, 40*(1), 117–119.

McDonald, R. P. (1978) A simple comprehensive model for the analysis of covariance structures. *British Journal of Mathematical Statistical Psychology, 31*, 59–72.

McDonald, R. P. (1979). The structural analysis of multivariate data: A sketch of a general theory. *Multivariate Behavioral Research, 1979, 14*, 21–28.

McDonald, R. P. (1980). A simple comprehensive model for the analysis of covariance structures: some remarks on application. *British Journal of Mathematical Statistical Psychology, 33*, 161–183.

McDonald, R. P., & Krane, W. R. (1979). A Monte Carlo study of local identifiability and degrees of freedom in the asymptotic likelihood ratio test. *British Journal of Mathematical Statistical Psychology, 32*, 121–132.

McDonald, R. P., & Swaminathan, H. (1972). *Structural analyses of dispersion matrices based on a very general model with a rapidly convergent procedure for the evaluation of parameters.* Informal publication of M.E.C.A., O.I.S.E, Toronto.

Montanelli, R. G. (1974). The goodness of fit of the maximum-likelihood estimation procedure in factor analysis. *Educational and Psychological Measurement, 34*, 547–562.

Pesaran, M. R., & Deaton, A. S. (1978). Testing non-nested nonlinear regression models. *Econometrika, 46*, 677–694.

Rapoport, A. (1972). The uses of mathematical isomorphism in general systems theory. In G. J. Klir (Ed.), *Trends in general systems theory* (pp. 1–10). New York: Wiley.

Rozeboom, W. W. (1978). *General Linear Dynamic Analysis (GLDA).* Paper presented at the Winter Workshop on Latent Structure Models Applied to Developmental Data, University of Denver.

Saris, W. E., dePijper, M., & Zewaart, P. (1978). Detection of specification errors in linear structural equation models. In K. F. Schuessler (Ed.), *Sociological methodology* (pp. 187–197). San Francisco: Jossey Bass.

Schmid, J., & Leiman, J. (1957). The development of hierarchical factor solutions. *Psychometrika, 22*, 53–61.

Sörbom, D. (1974). A general method for studying differences in factor means and factor structure between groups. *British Journal of Mathematical Statistical Psychology, 27*, 229–239.

Sörbom, D. (1978). An alternative to the methodology for analysis of covariance. *Psychometrika, 43*, 381–396.

Spearman, C. (1904). General intelligence objectively determined and measured. *American Journal of Psychology, 15*, 201–293.

Specht, D. A. (1975). On the evaluation of causal models. *Social Science Research, 4*, 113–133.

Thurstone, L. L. (1947). *Multiple factor analysis.* Chicago: University of Chicago Press.

van Driel, O. P. (1978). On various causes of improper solutions in maximum likelihood factor analysis. *Psychometrika, 43*(2), 225–243.

Weeks, D. G. (1978). *A second order structural equation model of ability.* Paper presented at the Winter Workshop on Latent Structure Models Applied to Developmental Data. University of Denver.

Wermuth, N. (1980). Linear recursive equations, covariance selection, and path analysis. *Journal of the American Statistical Association, 75*, 963–972.

Wiley, D. E. (1973). The identification problem for structural equation models with unmeasured variables. In A. S. Goldberger & O. D. Duncan (Eds), *Structural equation models in the social sciences* (pp. 69–83). New York: Seminar Press.

Wold, H. O. A. (1954). Causality and econometrics, *Econometrika, 22*, 162–177.

Wold, H. O. A. (1960). A generalization of causal chain models. *Econometrika, 28*, 443–463.

Wold, H. O. A. (1980). Soft modelling: Intermediate between traditional model building and data analysis. *Mathematical Statistics, 6*, 333–346.

Wright, S. (1921). Correlation and causation. *Journal of Agricultural Research, 20*, 557–585.

Wright, S. (1934). The method of path coefficients. *Annals of Mathematical Statistics, 5*, 161–215.

Wright, S. (1964). The interpretation of multivariate systems. In O. Kempthorne, T. A. Bancroft, J. W. Gowen & J. L. Lush (Eds.), *Statistics and mathematics in biology* (pp. 100–112). New York: Hafner.

Circa 2004

Allison, P. D. (1987). Estimation of linear models with incomplete data. In C.C. Clogg (Ed.), *Sociological Methodology 1987*, San Fran.: Jossey-Bass, 71–103.

Arbuckle, J. L., & Wotke, W. (1999). AMOS 4.0 User's Guide. Chicago: Smallwaters.

Boker, S. M. (2001). Differential models and differential structural equation modeling of intraindividual variability. In L. M. Collins & A. G. Sayer (Eds.), *New methods for the analysis of change* (pp. 5–27). Washington DC: APA.

Boker, S. M., McArdle, J. J., & Neale, M. (2002). An algorithm for the hierarchical organization of path diagrams and calculation of components of expected covariance. *Structural Equation Modeling, 9*, 174–194.

Bollen, K. A. (1989). *Structural equations with latent variables*. New York: Wiley.

Browne, M. W., & Mels, G. (1999). Path Analysis (RAMONA). In SYSTAT 10, Statistics II [Computer software and manual] (pp. II-233–II-291). Chicago: SPSS Inc.

Byrne, B. (1998). *Structural equation modeling with LISREL, PRELIS, and SIMPLIS. Basic concepts, applications, and programming*. Mahwah, NJ: Erlbaum.

Fox, J. (2002). *SEM (Structural Equation Modeling) for R*. CRAN (the Comprehensive R Archive Network). R Foundation for Statistical Computing, Vienna University of Technology (Technische Univasitat Wien).

Glymour, C., Scheines, R., Spirtes, P., & Kelly, K. (1987). Discovering causal structure: Artifical intelligence, philosophy of science, and statistical modeling. New York: Academic Press.

Goldstein, H., & McDonald, R. P. (1988). A general model for the analysis of multilevel data. *Psychometrika, 53*, 455–467.

Graff, J., & Schmidt, P. (1982). A general model for the decomposition of effects. In K. G. Jöreskog & H. Wold (eds.), *Systems under indirect observation: Causality, structure, prediction* (pp. 131–148). North-Holland.

Hamagami, F., & McArdle, J. J. (2000). Advanced studies of individual differences linear dynamic models for longitudinal data analysis. In G. Marcoulides & R. Schumacker (Eds.), *Advanced structural equation modeling: Issues and techniques* (pp. 203–246). Mahwah, NJ: Erlbaum.

Hatcher, L. (1994). *A step-by-step approach to using the SAS system for factor analysis and structural equation modeling*. Cary, NC: SAS Publishing.

Hauser, R. M., & Goldberger, A. S. (1971). The treatment of unobservable variables in path analysis. In H. L. Costner (Ed.), *Sociological Methodology, 1971* (pp. 81–117). San Francisco: Jossey-Bass.

Hayduk, L. (1987). *Structural equation modeling with LISREL: Essentials and Advances*. Baltimore: John Hopkins University Press.

Henderson, N. D. (1982). Human behavior genetics. *Annual Review of Psychology, 33*, 403–440.

Jöreskog, K. G., & Sörbom, D. (1999). LISREL 8.30: *LISREL 8: Structural equation modeling with the SIMPLIS command language*. Hillsdale, NJ: Scientific Software International.

Lee, S., & Hershberger, S. (1990). A simple rule for generating equivalent models in covariance structure modeling. *Multivariate Behavioral Research, 25*, 313–334.

Luijben, T. C. W. (1991). Equivalent models in covariance structure modeling. *Psychometrika, 56*, 653–665.

Loehlin, J. C. (1987, 1998). *Latent variables: an introduction to factor, path, and structural analysis*. Mahwah, NJ: Laurence Erlbaum Associates.

MacCallum, R. C., Wegener, D. T., Uchino, B. N., & Fabrigar, L. R. (1993). The problem of equivalent models in applications of covariance structure analysis. *Psychological Bulletin, 114*, 185–199.

McArdle, J. J. (1982). Structural Equation Modeling of an Individual System: Preliminary Results from "A Case Study of Episodic Alcoholism." Department of Psychology, University of Denver, Research report to the *National Institute of Alcoholism and Alcohol Abuse*.

McArdle, J. J. (1988). Dynamic but structural equation modeling of repeated measures data. In J. R. Nesselroade & R.B. Cattell (Eds.), *The Handbook of Multivariate Experimental Psychology, Volume 2* (pp. 561–614). New York, Plenum Press.

McArdle, J. J. (1986). Latent variable growth within behavior genetic models. *Behavior Genetics, 16*(1), 163–200.

McArdle, J. J. (1994). Structural factor analysis experiments with incomplete data. *Multivariate Behavioral Research, 29*(4), 409–454.

McArdle, J. J. (2001). A latent difference score approach to longitudinal dynamic structural analyses. In R. Cudeck, S. du Toit, & D. Sörbom (Eds.), *Structural Equation Modeling: Present and future* (pp. 342–380). Lincolnwood, IL: Scientific Software International.

McArdle, J. J., & Aber, M. S. (1990). Patterns of change within latent variable structural equation modeling. In A. von Eye (Ed.), *New Statistical Methods in Developmental Research* (pp. 151–224). New York: Academic Press.

McArdle, J. J., & Anderson, E. (1990). Latent variable growth models for research on aging. In J. E. Birren & K.W. Schaie (Eds.), *The Handbook of the Psychology of Aging* (pp. 21–43). New York: Plenum Press.

McArdle, J. J., & Bell, R. Q. (2000). Recent trends in modeling longitudinal data by latent growth curve methods. In Little, T. D., Schnabel, K. U., & Baumert, J. (Eds.), *Modeling longitudinal and multiple-group data: practical issues, applied approaches, and scientific examples* (pp. 69–108). Mahwah, NJ: Erlbaum.

McArdle, J. J., & Boker, S. M. (1990). *RAMpath: A Computer Program for Automatic Path Diagrams*. Hillsdale, NJ: Lawrence Erlbaum Publishers.

McArdle, J. J., Connell, J., & Goldsmith, H. H. (1980). Latent variable approaches to measurement, structure, longitudinal stability, and genetic influences: Preliminary results from the study of behavioral style. *Behavior Genetics, 10*, 609.

McArdle, J. J., & Epstein, D. B. (1987). Latent growth curves within developmental structural equation models. *Child Development, 58*(1), 110–133.

McArdle, J. J., & Goldsmith, H. H. (1984). Multivariate biometric models of the WAIS. *Behavior Genetics, 14*, 609.

McArdle, J. J., & Goldsmith, H. H. (1990). Some alternative structural equation models for multivariate biometric analyses. *Behavior Genetics, 20*(5), 569–608.

McArdle, J. J., & Hamagami, E. (1992). Modeling incomplete longitudinal and cross–sectional data using latent growth structural models. *Experimental Aging Research, 18*(3), 145–166.

McArdle, J. J., & Hamagami, F. (1996). Multilevel models from a multiple group structural equation perspective. In G. Marcoulides & R. Schumacker (Eds.), *Advanced Structural Equation Modeling Techniques* (pp. 89–124). Hillsdale, NJ: Erlbaum.

McArdle, J. J., & Hamagami, F. (2001). Linear dynamic analyses of incomplete longitudinal data. In L. Collins & A. Sayer (Eds.), *Methods for the Analysis of Change* (pp. 137–176). Washington, DC: APA Press.

McArdle, J. J., & Hamagami, F. (2003). Structural equation models for evaluating dynamic concepts within longitudinal twin analyses. *Behavior Genetics, 33*(3), 137–159.

McArdle, J. J., & McDonald, R. P. (1984). Some algebraic properties of the Reticular Action Model for moment structures. *British Journal of Mathematical & Statistical Psychology, 37*(2), 234–251.

McArdle, J. J., & Nesselroade, J. R. (1994). Structuring data to study development and change. In S. H. Cohen & H. W. Reese (Eds.), *Life-Span Developmental Psychology: Methodological Innovations* (pp. 223–268). Hillsdale, NJ.: Erlbaum.

McArdle, J. J., & Prescott, C. A. (1996). Contemporary models for the biometric genetic analysis of intellectual abilities. In D. P. Flanagan, J. L., Genshaft, & P. L. Harrison (Eds.), *Beyond traditional intellectual assessment: Contemporary and emerging theories, tests and issues* (pp. 403–436). New York: Guilford Press.

McArdle, J. J., & Woodcock, J. R. (1997). Expanding test–rest designs to include developmental time–lag components. *Psychological Methods, 2*(4), 403–435.

McDonald, R. P. (1985). *Factor Analyses and Related Methods*. Mahwah, NJ: Lawrence Erlbaum Associates, Inc.

McDonald, R. P. (1986). Describing the elephant: Structure and function in multivariate data. *Psychometrika, 41*,(4) 513–534.

McDonald, R. P. (1994). The bilevel reticular action model for path analysis with latent variables. *Sociological Methods and Research, 22*, 399–413.

McDonald, R. P. (1997). Haldane's lungs: a case study in path analysis. *Multivariate Behavioral Research, 32*, 1–38.

McDonald, R. P., & Hartman, W. M. (1992). A procedure for obtaining initial values of parameters in the RAM model. *Multivariate Behavioral Research, 27*, 57–76.

McDonald, R. P., & Goldstein, H. (1989). Balanced versus unbalanced designs for linear structural relations in two-level data. *British Journal of Mathematical & Statistical Psychology, 42*, 215–232.

McDonald, R. P., & Ho, M. R. (2002). Principles and practice in reporting structural equation analyses. *Psychological Methods, 7*(1), 64–82.

McDonald, R. P., Parker, P. M., & Ishizuka, T. (1993). A scale-invariant treatment for recursive path models. *Psychometrika, 58*, 431–443.

Meredith, W., & Tisak, J. (1990). Latent curve analysis. *Psychometrika, 55*, 107–122.

Mueller, R. O. (1996). *Basic principles of structural equation modeling: An introduction to LISREL and EQS.* New York: Springer-Verlag.

Muthén, L. K., & Muthén, B. O. (1998). *Mplus, the comprehensive modeling program for applied researchers user's guide.* Los Angeles, CA: Muthén & Muthén.

Neale, M. C., Boker, S. M., Xie, G., & Maes, H. H. (1999). Mx: Statistical Modeling. Box 126 MCV, Richmond, VA: Department of Psychiatry.

Nesselroade, J. R., & McArdle, J. J. (1986). Multivariable causal modeling in alcohol use research. *Social Biology, 33*(4), 272–296.

Nesselroade, J. J., McArdle, J. J., Aggen, S. H., & Meyers, J. (2001). Dynamic factor analysis models for multivariate time series analysis. In D. M. Moskowitz & S. L. Hershberger (Eds.), *Modeling individual variability with repeated measures data: Advances & Techniques* (pp. 233–266). Mahwah, New Jersey: Erlbaum.

Pearl, J. (2000). *Causality: Models Reasoning, and Inference.* Cambridge: Cambridge University Press.

Raykov, T., & Marcoulides, G. A. (2000). *A first course in structural equation modeling.* Mahwah, NJ: Erlbaum.

Raykov, T., & Marcoulides, G. A. (2002). Can there be infinitely many models equivalent to a given structural equation model? *Structural Equation Modeling, 8*, 142–149.

Rindskopf, D. (1984). Using phantom and imaginary latent variables to parameterize constraints in linear models. *Psychometrika, 49*, 37–47.

Schumacker, R. E., & Lomax, R. G. (1996). *A beginner's guide to structural equation modeling.* Mahwah, NJ: Erlbaum.

Spirites, P., Glymour, C., & Scheines, R. (1993). *Causation, Prediction, and Search.* New York: Springer-Verlag.

Wood, P. K. (1988). Dynamic factor analysis as reformulated under the Reticular Action Model. Paper presented at the annual meetings of the *American Educational Research Association*, New Orleans, LA.

Wright, S. (1983). Path analysis in epidemiology: A critique. *Amer. Jour. Human Genetics, 35*, 757–768.

10

Goodness of Fit in Structural Equation Models

Herbert W. Marsh
University of Western Sydney, Macarthur

Kit-Tai Hau
The Chinese University of Hong Kong

David Grayson
University of Sydney

PREFACE

Some of Rod McDonald's most widely cited articles (McDonald, 1989; McDonald & Marsh, 1990; also see Marsh, Balla, & McDonald, 1988) deal specifically with assessing goodness of fit (GOF) and related earlier work on unidimensionality and the nonrelation between coefficient alpha and dimensionality (e.g., McDonald, 1981)—despite his expressed ambivalence about the use of GOF indices. Indeed, their continuing popularity may have more to do with the Zeitgeist that existed in structural equation modeling research—and continues to exist today—than in his enthusiasm for their routine application. Rod was dragged, somewhat reluctantly, into this area of inquiry by one of his former PhD students (John Balla), who had been enticed by another Australian colleague (H. W. Marsh) to this topic. Applying diligence, imagination, lateral thinking, and a bit of naivete, Marsh and Balla were able to find or devise a plethora of alternative goodness-of-fit indices—32 of them—and a preliminary classification schema (absolute, Type 1 incremental, and Type 2 incremental) for generating and classifying these indices. Because many of these indices were not readily amenable to mathematical scrutiny, they constructed a simulation study (based on real data, and artificial data fit to "true" and misspecified models) to evaluate properties of this remarkably large set of indices.

Instilling some rigor and a critical devil's advocate perspective into this research program, Rod contributed substantially to this research (Marsh et al., 1988).

Recognizing the potential usefulness of simulation studies, Rod had a preference for mathematical derivation. Following from the Marsh et al. (1988) research, Rod pursued an analytical approach based on noncentrality (McDonald, 1989). He then (McDonald & Marsh, 1990) derived many of the goodness-of-fit indices described by Marsh et al. (1988) in terms of noncentrality. This elucidated their mathematical properties and provided mathematical explanations for some of their numerical results, which proposed new indices based on noncentrality. In one of life's many ironies, the initial papers leading to the McDonald and Marsh (1990) and the Bentler (1990) publications arrived in the editorial office of the *Psychological Bulletin* on almost exactly the same day. Although there are certainly important differences in the two papers, there was also substantial overlap, particularly in the emphasis on noncentrality. Indeed, both articles, proposed new incremental indices based on noncentrality—the comparative fit index (CFI) and the relative noncentrality index (RNI)—that were essentially identical (except for truncation when the value of RNI goes outside the 0–1 range due to sampling). Both manuscripts were sent to the same reviewers, who recommended that both articles should be published back to back in the same issue of the *Psychological Bulletin*.

Despite his important contributions to the development and application of goodness-of-fit indices, Rod retained scepticism about their routine, mechanistic application. Marsh et al. (1988), although largely uncritical of the logic underlying goodness-of-fit testing, stressed that "the promise of an externally meaningful, well-defined, absolute scale does not appear to be fulfilled by most of the fit indices considered in the present investigation," and that evaluation of fit was only one component in the broader issue of model evaluation. McDonald and Marsh (1990) emphasized that "in applications no restrictive model fits the population, and all fitted restrictive models are approximations and not hypotheses that are possibly true" (p. 247). Thus, even if the populations were known, there would remain the inevitable nonstatistical conflict between good approximation (population goodness of fit) and simplicity (low complexity), which must be decided by theoretical considerations related to substantive interpretability. Expressing a growing concern about the misuse of goodness-of-fit indices, McDonald and Marsh concluded that "Although experience can suggest a recommendable cutoff point for use by those who fear the 'subjectivity' of judgment, such a cutoff must itself remain inevitably subjective as only the saturated model is true" (p. 254). Following this classic publication, Rod essentially retired from this area of research to pursue other areas, which are well represented in this book.

McDonald and Ho (2002) reviewed structural equation modeling (SEM) studies in psychological journals to evaluate what constitutes current practice. Not surprisingly, all 41 studies in their review reported a global χ^2 test as well as at least one GOF index. The most popular index was the CFI or RNI (21 studies), followed by the root mean square error of approximation (RMSEA; 20 studies), the goodness-of-fit index (GFI; 15 studies), the Tucker–Lewis index or nonnormal fit index (TLI and NNFI, respectively; 13 studies), and the normed fit index (NFI; 9 studies), as well as others. Researchers typically reported more than one GOF index. Standards of an acceptable fit were typically .9 or better for those indices designed to vary on a 0 to 1 scale (e.g., RNI, CFI, GFI, TLI, NFI), whereas RMSEA values of less than 0.05 were interpreted as a "good" fit and those of less than 0.08 were interpreted as an acceptable fit. In addition, a majority (33) of the studies also used χ^2 difference tests to choose the best model from among nested models. Rod also noted his current thinking about global GOF, indicating that "there is no established empirical or mathematical basis for their use" (McDonald & Ho, 2002, p. 72) and they do not allow the researcher "to judge whether a marginal or low index of fit is due to a correctable misspecification of the model, or to a scatter of discrepancies, which suggests that the model is possibly the best available approximation to reality" (p. 73). On this basis, McDonald and Ho concluded:

> Our comments on this issue might seem intended to discourage the use of fit indices. Our intention is, instead, to warn that the issue is unsettled. More constructively, but tentatively, we offer some recommendations as follows: It is our belief that no global index of fit (together with a criterion for its acceptability) can substitute for a detailed examination of the discrepancies. However, if inspection shows that these are well scattered, they are adequately summarized in the root mean square residual (RMR), which is an immediately interpretable measure of the discrepancies. (McDonald & Ho, 2002, p. 73)

McDonald and Ho then went onto to suggest that indices that can be expressed in terms of noncentrality and shown to be free of sampling bias (as in McDonald & Marsh, 1990) can also be used to supplement—not replace—good judgment.

In summary, Rod has had a profound impact on the development and application of goodness-of-fit indices as one basis for model evaluation. However, simultaneously he is deeply sceptical of the increasingly prevalent, mechanistic application of GOF indices in relation to prescribed cutoff values as a substitute for good judgment based on the complicated interplay among goodness of fit, substantive interpretability, theory, and empirical considerations. In this chapter we summarize recent (and some not so recent) research covering a selection of theoretical, philosophical, substantive, and pragmatic issues related to goodness of fit, while doing justice to McDonald's impact and healthy scepticism for the use and misuse of goodness of fit.

INTRODUCTION

As emphasized in McDonald's research (Marsh et al., 1988; McDonald & Marsh, 1990; McDonald & Ho, 2002), important, unresolved issues in structural equation modeling are how to evaluate a model and how to select among competing models.

On the basis of theory, previous research, and knowledge of the data, the researcher typically posits at least one or preferably a set of alternative models to explain relations among the measured variables. Models are typically posited a priori, but may also be a posteriori. Model selection and evaluation are based on a subjective combination of substantive issues, inspection of parameter estimates, goodness of fit, parsimony, interpretability, and a comparison of the performances of competing models.

One component of this overall process of model evaluation that has received considerable attention is the evaluation of the goodness of fit between observed data and predictions based on posited models of the data. Whereas the evaluation of fit has a long and controversial history (e.g., Bentler, 1990; Bentler & Bonett, 1980; Bollen, 1989b; Cudeck & Browne, 1983; Gerbing & Anderson, 1993; Jöreskog, 1993; Marsh et al., 1988; Marsh, Balla, & Hau, 1996; McDonald & Marsh, 1990; Mulaik et al., Steiger & Lind, 1980; Tanaka, 1993; Tucker & Lewis, 1973), it continues to be a contentious topic that has not been resolved.

Following the introduction, we divide the discussion of goodness of fit into three broad sections. In the first and the most substantial (in terms of length) section, we provide a technical summary of the GOF literature. In this section we take a reasonably uncritical perspective on the role of GOF testing, providing an almost encyclopedic summary of GOF indices and their behavior in relation to a variety of criteria. Then we introduce some complications related to GOF testing that have not been adequately resolved and may require further research. In the final section, we place the role of GOF within the broader context of model evaluation. Taking the role of devil's advocate, we challenge the appropriateness of current GOF practice, arguing that current practice is leading SEM research into counterproductive directions that run the risk of undermining good science and marginalizing the usefulness of SEM as a research tool.

GOODNESS-OF-FIT INDICES AND THEIR BEHAVIOR

Classification Schemes

For the purpose of this chapter we constructed a compendium of indices considered in the literature, which we categorized into functional families. In the Appendix we provide a definition of each index and many of the alternative names that have been ascribed to each. Whereas Bollen and Long (1993) recommended that researchers use indices representing different families of measures, the development of different classification schemes has only been moderately successful.

Marsh et al. (1988) proposed a preliminary classification schema. In their schema, stand-alone indices are ones based on only the fit of a target model. Type 1 and Type 2 incremental fit indices are based on the difference between the fit of a target model and an alternative model, usually a null model in which $\hat{\Sigma}_k$ is a diagonal matrix (Bentler & Bonett, 1980). Marsh et al. (1988; also see Gerbing & Anderson, 1993; Marsh & Balla, 1986) noted that incremental fit indices can typically be expressed in one of two general forms, which they called Type 1 and Type 2 incremental indices:

- Type I: $|I_T - I_O|/\text{Max}(I_O, I_T)$, which can be expressed as (a) $= (I_O - I_T)/(I_O)$ or (b) $= (I_T - I_O)/(I_T)$.
- Type 2: $|I_T - I_O|/|E(I_T) - I_O|$, which can be expressed as (a) $= (I_O - I_T)/[I_O - E(I_T)]$ or (b) $= (I_T - I_O)/[E(I_T) - I_O]$.

where I_O and I_T are values of an "absolute" (stand-alone or nonincremental) index for an appropriately defined baseline model (typically a null model, which assumes that all measured variables are uncorrelated) and the target model, respectively, and $E(I_T)$ is the expected value for the absolute index for a "true" target model that is correctly specified so that there is no misspecification. Variations a and b are appropriate for stand-alone indices in which poorer fits are reflected by larger values (e.g., χ^2) and by smaller values, respectively. Thus, for example, the TLI can be expressed as a Type 2 index where I is of the form χ^2/degrees of freedom (df); so TLI can be represented as χ^2/df-I2. Similarly, χ^2/df-I1, χ^2-I2, and χ^2-I1 represent the relative fit index (RFI), the incremental fit index (IFI), and the NFI, respectively (also see Marsh & Balla, 1986).

Marsh et al. (1988) evaluated a wide variety of Type 1 and Type 2 incremental fit indices. Their results suggested that incremental Type 1 indices were normed in the sample but had values that were systematically related to sample size. In contrast, Type 2 indices were not normed and were not systematically related to sample size. These conclusions, however, were premature. In a trivial sense they were wrong in that some absolute indices have expected values of 0, so that the Type 1 and Type 2 forms are equivalent. McDonald and Marsh (1990) subsequently evaluated the mathematical properties of a number of these indices of fit by expressing them in terms of the population noncentrality parameter for a target model. In particular, they showed mathematically that the incremental Type 2 index based on the χ^2-I2 (referred to as the IFI in the Appendix) is positively biased for small N.

The Type 1 and Type 2 forms of incremental fit indices proposed by Marsh et al. (1988) were a heuristic basis for generating a large number of different incremental indices, and some of these indices have subsequently been proposed by other researchers with different names. However, subsequent research—particularly that by McDonald and Marsh (1990)—indicated that not all Type 2 indices are unbiased, thus undermining some of the usefulness of the Type 1 and Type 2 distinction. Nevertheless, similar classification systems continue to be used or adopted in recent research. For example, Hu and Bentler (1998, 1999) also categorized different indices as absolute (stand-alone) indices, Type 1 incremental, and Type 2 incremental indices, although their definitions of these categories differed slightly from those of Marsh et al. (1988). However, recognizing the importance of incremental fit indices based on noncentrality, they also placed these indices in an additional category that they called Type 3 incremental indices. Fan, Thompson, and Wang (1999) classified GOF indices into four categories: (a) covariance matrix reproduction indices, which assess the extent to which the reproduced matrix based on the targeted model has accounted for the original sample matrix (e.g., GFI, adjusted GFI [AGFI]); (b) comparative model fit indices, which compare a target model with a null model (e.g., NFI, TLI, CFI); (c) parsimony weighted indices, which impose penalties for more elaborated models (e.g., the parsimony relative noncentrality index [PRNI], the parsimony unbiased goodness-of-fit index [PGFI]); and (d) noncentrality statistics indices, which are based on the noncentral parameter (e.g., RNI, CFI). Perhaps recognizing potential limitations in the Type 1 and Type 2 distinction, McDonald and Ho (2002) only distinguished between two broad classifications of indices: absolute indices, which are a function of discrepancies (and, perhaps, sample size and degrees of freedom), and relative fit indices, which include both Type 1 and Type 2 incremental fit indices. However, with the possible exception of the two-category classification used by McDonald and Ho, each of the schemes suffers because the categories are not mutually exclusive. For example, most of the indices can be expressed in terms of noncentrality and could be put into this category. Recognizing the limitations of any such classification scheme, we classified GOF indices into three broad categories (absolute, incremental, and parsimony) and grouped functionally related indices into families within each of these broad categories (see the Appendix).

Components of Fit: Estimation and Approximation Discrepancy

For present purposes, given a set of measured variables, it is relevant to distinguish among the following:

- Σ_0, the true population covariance matrix
- S, the sample covariance matrix
- Σ_k, the fitted covariance matrix derived from Σ_0 for the "best-fitting" parameters based on the approximating model k that is being tested
- $\hat{\Sigma}_k$, the fitted covariance matrix derived from S, where S is an unbiased estimate of Σ_0, and $\hat{\Sigma}_k$ is an unbiased estimate of Σ_k
- Δ_{est}, the estimation discrepancy, the difference between $\hat{\Sigma}_k$ and Σ_k, which reflects sampling fluctuations
- Δ_{pop}, the population misfit due to approximation discrepancy, the difference between Σ_0 and Σ_k
- Δ_{emp}, the empirical discrepancy, the difference between $\hat{\Sigma}_k$ and S, which reflects population model misfit and estimation discrepancy.

The problem of goodness of fit is how to decide whether $\hat{\Sigma}_k$ and S are sufficiently similar to justify the conclusion that the specific model used to generate $\hat{\Sigma}_k$ adequately fits a particular set of data. Following Cudeck and Henly (1991), it is useful to distinguish among *empirical discrepancy* (the difference between $\hat{\Sigma}_k$ and S), *estimation discrepancy* (the difference between $\hat{\Sigma}_k$ and Σ_k, which reflects sampling fluctuations), and *approximation discrepancy* (the difference between Σ_0 and Σ_k, which reflects population model misfit). As sample size increases, S approaches Σ_0, so that the estimation discrepancy approaches zero. Approximation discrepancy, however, only involves Σ_0 and Σ_k, so that its value does not vary with N. This distinction is important because some indices estimate discrepancy due to approximation, which is independent of N, whereas others reflect the combined influences of approximation discrepancy and estimation discrepancy, which vary systematically with N.

As suggested by Cheung and Rensvold (2001; also see Cudeck & Henly, 1991), researchers seek to determine whether their model is an appropriate representation of the operating model, which can be seen as either a representation of the relations among the population variables or the processes that produce those relations. Whereas the form of the operating (or true) model is unknown in practice, the researchers posit one model k (or a set of alternative approximating models) on the basis of theory and prior empirical results. Model k implies an approximate covariance matrix Σ_k. If the discrepancy Δ_{pop} between Σ_0 and Σ_k meets certain criteria, the representation is deemed to be satisfactory. Specification error occurs because the approximating model differs from the true operating model, so that there is approximation discrepancy (the difference between Σ_0 and Σ_k, Δ_{pop}). However, many researchers argue that the intent of an approximating model is to provide a simplified, parsimonious representation of the more complex operating model, which actually generates the population covariance matrix Σ_0. Indeed, it might be reasonable to argue that the only "model" that is able to exactly reproduce the population covariance ($\Delta_{\text{pop}} = 0$) would be an unrestricted, saturated model with zero degrees of freedom. Because population data are not available, sample data are used to infer empirical discrepancy (Δ_{emp}, the difference between $\hat{\Sigma}_k$ and S), which reflects a combination of approximation discrepancy and estimation discrepancy (the difference between $\hat{\Sigma}_k$ and Σ_k due to sampling fluctuations).

Possibly Desirable Characteristics for Goodness-of-Fit Indices

Goodness of fit is evaluated in part with an overall χ^2 test. As typically employed, the posited model is rejected if the χ^2 is large relative to the degrees of freedom (df) and accepted if the χ^2 is small or nonsignificant. The χ^2 tests the null hypothesis that all empirical discrepancies (the difference between $\hat{\Sigma}_k$ and S) are simultaneously zero or, equivalently, that the hypothesized model is "true." This classical form of statistical hypothesis testing is generally inappropriate for evaluating the size of the empirical discrepancy. The failure to obtain a nonsignif-icant χ^2 may reflect a poorly specified model, the high power of the test, or the failure to satisfy other assumptions underlying the statistical test. Hypothesized models such as those considered in confirmatory factor analysis (CFA) are best regarded as approximations to reality rather than exact statements of truth, so that any model can be rejected if the sample size is sufficiently large. In particular, even very small, trivial differences between the hypothesized model and the data would be statistically significant given a sufficiently large sample size. Conversely, almost any model will be "accepted" if the sample size is sufficiently small be-cause even meaningful large discrepancies would not be statistically significant for small sample sizes. From this perspective Cudeck and Browne (1983) argued that it is preferable to depart from the hypothesis-testing approach that assumes that any model will exactly fit the data. Similarly, McDonald and Marsh (1990) emphasized that "in applications no restrictive model fits the population, and all fitted restrictive models are approximations and not hypotheses that are possibly true" (p. 247). Accordingly, a large number of fit indices that are functions of the empirical discrepancy have been proposed for evaluating fit and comparing alternative models.

Different researchers have proposed a variety of desirable characteristics for indices of fit that may be useful in the evaluation of GOF indices. Here we discuss the most widely recommended of these criteria including the effect of sample size, appropriate penalties for model complexity and rewards for model parsimony, sampling fluctuations, and interpretable metrics.

Model Parsimony and Penalties for Model Complexity

The inclusion of additional parameters, particularly when based on a posteriori criteria and tested with the same data, may provide an "illusory" improvement in fit due to "capitalizing on chance." Researchers have approached this problem from different perspectives. Steiger (1989; Steiger & Lind, 1980) noted that indices that fail to compensate for model complexity inevitably lead to the selection of the most complex model even when simpler models fit the data nearly as well. James, Mulaik, and Brett (1982, p. 155) asked "how efficient is the increase in fit going from the null model with many degrees of freedom to another model with just a few degrees of freedom in terms of degrees of freedom lost in estimating more pa-rameters?" Jöreskog and Sörbom (1981, p. I.40) noted that when the change in χ^2 is close to the difference in degrees of freedom due to the addition of new parame-ters, then the "improvement in fit is obtained by 'capitalizing on chance,' and that the added parameters may not have real significance and meaning." Cudeck and Browne (1983) described the method of cross-validation to determine the ability of a set of parameter estimates to adequately describe data based on new observa-tions from the same population. Cudeck and Browne also used variants of the AIC

(Akaike, 1974) and SC (Schwartz, 1978) indices for this purpose and derived a single-sample cross-validation index (Browne & Cudeck, 1989). Bozdogan (1987) noted that model selection requires researchers to achieve an appropriate balance between problems associated with "overfitting" and "underfitting" the data, and that different fit indices vary in the balance of protection that they offer from these competing risks. McDonald and Marsh (1990) noted the need to strike a balance between badness of fit and model complexity or, equivalently, between goodness of fit and model parsimony.

In the GOF literature, parsimony is typically operationalized as the ratio of degrees of freedom in the model being tested to that in the null model (McDonald & Marsh, 1990; Mulaik et al., 1989). Conversely, model complexity can be defined as 1 minus the parsimony ratio. Penalties for model complexity have different implications for fitting a known population covariance matrix Σ_0 and a sample covariance matrix S. Even if Σ_0 is known, freeing enough parameters still leads to a perfect fit (i.e., in some sense the saturated model with zero degrees of freedom is always able to fit the data). Researchers have routinely recommended indices that control for model complexity and reward model parsimony (e.g., Bollen, 1989a, 1989b, 1990; Bollen & Long, 1993; Bozdogan, 1987; Browne & Cudeck, 1989; Cudeck & Browne, 1983; Gerbing & Anderson, 1993; Marsh & Balla, 1994; Mulaik et al., 1989; Steiger & Lind, 1980; Tanaka, 1993; but for possibly alternative perspectives see Bentler, 1992; McDonald & Marsh, 1990; Marsh & Balla, 1994; Marsh & Hau, 1996). There is, however, room for disagreement as to their interpretation. McDonald and Marsh (1990) discussed some of the relevant theoretical issues, and other perspectives are offered by Mulaik et al. (1989), Bentler (1990), Bozdogan (1987), Cudeck and Henly (1991), Cudeck and Browne (1983; Browne & Cudeck, 1989), and Steiger (1989, 1990). It could be claimed that all models estimating parameters known to be zero in the population beyond those of the most restrictive true model are equally capable of fitting the data and should therefore result in equal estimates of fit. In particular, at the population level the inclusion of additional parameters known to be zero in the population will not improve population misfit. Hence, it follows that the approximation discrepancy at the population level will be the same for all such "overfit" models. Conversely, it could be claimed that a goodness-of-fit index that decreases with the addition of parameters known to be zero is penalizing model complexity appropriately. As noted by McDonald and Marsh (1990), the compromise between goodness of fit (approximation discrepancy) and parsimony is not an issue of sampling in that even if Σ_0 is known, an appropriate compromise is still required. Consistent with this perspective, we reserve the term *parsimony penalty* to refer to penalties for lack of parsimony (or model complexity) that are applied to indices based on unbiased estimates of approximation discrepancy (between Σ_0 and Σ_k) and do not vary with N. They are intended to achieve a compromise between model parsimony and complexity at the population level. It is important to distinguish between these and *estimation penalties*, which are designed to compensate for capitalizing on chance by the inclusion of additional parameters. When population parameters are estimated from a finite S, parameter estimates tend to fit the data used to estimate the parameters better than they fit the data derived from a cross-validation sample or from the population from which the sample came. This is an issue of sampling fluctuations because estimation discrepancy is zero when a model is fit to a true population covariance matrix and tends to zero as N increases sufficiently for estimates based on sample data. For present purposes we use the term estimation penalty to refer to penalties for model complexity that reflect estimation discrepancy (between $\hat{\Sigma}_k$ and Σ_k) and that vary systematically with N. Parsimony penalties are directed at approximation discrepancy and population misfit, whereas estimation penalties are directed at estimation discrepancy and sampling fluctuations. Different indices considered here are designed to facilitate a compromise between model complexity and goodness of fit through the application of parsimony penalties or estimation penalties. An examination of the behavior of these different indices based on results from the GOF literature demonstrates that there are substantial differences in the behavior of these penalty functions.

The issues related to goodness of fit and penalties for model complexity have been blurred in practice because Σ_0 is not known and it has been difficult to operationalize terms such as over- or underparametrization. However, these terms can easily be operationalized for simulated data derived from a known Σ_0 in which some of the population parameters are defined to be zero. If a model is fit to Σ_0, allowing these parameters to differ from zero will not improve the fit. When the model is fit to a finite S, however, allowing these parameters to differ from zero will improve the fit. For purposes of their simulation study, Marsh and Balla (1994; Marsh et al., 1996) operationalized overparametrization as estimating parameters known to be zero in the population and underparametrization as fixing at zero parameter estimates known to be nonzero in the population. Hence, with the use of simulated data, the effects of over- and underparametrization could be evaluated in relation to alternative fit indices.

Sample Size Dependence

Researchers (e.g., Bentler, 1990; Bollen, 1990; Bollen & Long, 1993; Gerbing & Anderson, 1993; MacCallum, Widaman, Zhang, & Hong, 1999; Marsh et al., 1988; McDonald & Marsh, 1990) have routinely proposed that a systematic relation between sample size and the values of a GOF index is undesirable. For example, Bollen and Long (1993) recommended the use of indices "whose means of their sampling distribution are unrelated or only weakly related to the sample size" (p. 8), whereas Gerbing and Anderson (1993) suggested that an ideal fit index should be independent of sample size in that higher or lower values should not be obtained simply because the sample size is large or small. This characteristic was evaluated in detail in studies such as those by Marsh et al. (1988) and McDonald and Marsh (1990), as well as by much subsequent research (e.g., Fan et al., 1999;

Hu & Bentler, 1998). McDonald and Ho (2002) asserted that GOF indices that are relatively free of sampling bias (McDonald & Marsh, 1990) can be used to supplement good judgment.

Following from Marsh et al. (1988) and McDonald and Marsh (1990), we reassert that one useful characteristic for a fit index of empirical discrepancies between S and $\hat{\Sigma}_k$ based on sample data is to provide an unbiased estimate of the corresponding approximation discrepancies between Σ_0 and Σ_k in the population. If the expected value of a sample statistic varies systematically with N, then the statistic provides a biased estimate of the corresponding population parameter. Bias in a fit statistic is undesirable because, on average, tests of a given model for given variables might yield radically different conclusions for different sample sizes, and decisions based on sample data may differ systematically from those based on the population. This influence of N can be demonstrated empirically as by Marsh et al. (1988) and elsewhere or mathematically as by McDonald and Marsh (1990), who demonstrated that many indices based on finite N are biased estimates of their asymptotic limits where the size of this bias is a systematically decreasing function of N. For some indices the direction of this bias was positive, but for others it was negative.

Marsh et al. (1988) examined the influence of sample size on a large number of fit indices in a Monte Carlo study using seven different sample sizes and a variety of different true and misspecified models based on real and simulated data. This study differed from previous research in that it considered a much larger number of fit indices, a larger range of sample sizes, and misspecified (false) models as well as true models (i.e., the approximating model and generating model were or were not the same). They considered results from 31 indices, including many that had not been previously described. This perhaps foretold the plethora of indices (see Appendix) that were to be used in future studies and included in SEM statistical packages. Their most important finding was that the TLI was the only widely used index that had values relatively independent of sample size. This was surprising because many of the indices considered had been explicitly or implicitly claimed to be independent of sample size in the literature. Marsh et al. were particularly concerned with the metric underlying fit indices and the promise of an externally meaningful, well-defined, absolute metric that could be used to evaluate the fit of different models. They suggested that absolute guidelines about what constitutes an acceptable fit were apparently unjustified for any index whose values varied systematically with sample size.

There is, however, an important counterperspective on the sample size dependence in indices that are used to evaluate model fit (Browne, 2000; also see Bozdogan, 1987; Browne & Cudeck, 1989; Cudeck & Browne, 1983; Cudeck & Henly, 1991) that is embodied in what we refer to as "information criterion" indices (see Appendix). Browne (2000) specifically countered McDonald and Marsh's concern that indices like AIC are sample size dependent, arguing that the sample size dependence is appropriate from a cross-validation perspective. Browne emphasized that the AIC and related cross-validation procedures are not appropriate for selecting a best-fitting model in the population that is independent of sampling error, and instead are designed to select the model whose parameter estimates are most trustworthy for a particular sample size. The rationale for this family of indices is that the appropriate level of model complexity and goodness of fit depends on sample size. When N is small, so that sampling error is large, parsimonious models based on relatively fewer estimated parameters will cross-validate better than more complex models based on a relatively larger number of estimated parameters. However, as N increases, so that sampling error is small, increasingly complex models will provide more accurate cross-validation. This rationale is embodied in the information criterion indices that are used to select the "best" model from a series of alternative models [best in terms of accuracy of cross-validation; for an alternative, but compatible, Baysian perspective, see Bozdogan (2000)]. Hence, in this sense the best model would typically be more parsimonious when sample size is small and would be increasingly complex as the sample size increased. Whereas this rationale works well when researchers have a set of competing, alternative models (as in the number-of-factors problem), the indices are idiosyncratic to particular applications so that they do not provide any basis for evaluating GOF along an interpretable metric nor provide an index of a good fit except in relation to other models being considered. Browne (2000) concluded that "In summary, cross-validation says nothing about any best model for the population. What it does consider is to what extent a model has to be oversimplified to avoid the effect of random fluctuations due to small sample size" (p. 115). We agree entirely with Browne that it is inappropriate to criticize AIC-like indices for being sample size dependent when this is an a priori rationale for their design. However, as emphasized by Browne and others, their intent is quite different from the other GOF indices considered here that are designed to aid in the selection of a most appropriate model in the population., and from parsimony corrections embodied in some indices that are intended to penalize *approximation discrepancy* (the difference between Σ_0 and Σ_k) rather than *estimation discrepancy* (the difference between $\hat{\Sigma}_k$ and Σ_k, which reflects sampling fluctuations). However, there has been some confusion about the AIC as balancing against parsimony clarified by McDonald (1989; McDonald & Marsh, 1990). For this reason, we have chosen to treat information-based indices as a separate family of indices.

Reliability of Estimation and Sensitivity to Misspecification

Reliability of estimation (i.e., precision of estimation and a relative lack of sampling fluctuations) is an important characteristic of incremental fit indices that has not been given sufficient attention. In Monte Carlo studies, this feature is typically represented by the within-cell standard deviation of the estimates for a particularly index (i.e., variation in estimated values based on different samples within the same cell of the simulation study). Based on this criterion, many researchers (e.g., Bentler, 1990; Bollen & Long, 1993; Gerbing & Anderson, 1993) recommended that the TLI should be considered cautiously due to the apparently large sampling fluctuations found in simulation studies. The appropriateness of this conclusion rests in part on the implicit assumption that all the incremental fit indices vary along the same underlying metric (i.e., a 0–1 metric in which some value such as .90 or .95 reflects an acceptable fit).

Following from Marsh et al. (1988), Marsh and Balla (1994; also see Gerbing & Anderson, 1993; Marsh et al., 1996; Marsh & Hau, 1996) proposed that a more appropriate criterion was the ability to distinguish between correctly specified models and models with varying degrees of misspecification. Whereas estimation reliability is a desirable characteristic that is reflected in part by within-cell standard deviations, this is not a fully appropriate basis for evaluating the relative precision of estimation in different indices. If, for example, two indices vary along a different metric, then within-cell standard deviations are not comparable. Two trivial examples demonstrate some of our concerns: (a) if an index has a constant value (say, 1.0) for all correctly and incorrectly specified models, then it will have no within-cell variation, and (b) if an index is multiplied by a constant, then the within-cell standard deviation must vary accordingly. A more appropriate measure of reliability of estimation should reflect the relative sizes of within-cell variation compared to between-cell variation due to systematic differences in model misspecification. This situation is analogous to the estimation of reliability as a ratio of true score variance to total variance and not just (raw score) error variance. Marsh and Balla proposed that one approach is to evaluate the proportion of variance due to systematic differences in model misspecification. Hence, for example, no variation due to model misspecification is explained by an index with a constant value in example (a), and variance explained is not affected by multiplication by a constant in example (b). From this perspective, the minimum condition necessary for evaluating reliability of estimation is to test a variety of different models that vary systematically in terms of model misspecification including, perhaps, a true model with no misspecification. Marsh and Balla argued that because most previous simulation studies had considered only true models and apparently none had evaluated some index of variance explained due to systematic variation in model misspecification as an indication of reliability of estimation, conclusions based on this previous research must be evaluated cautiously (see further discussion by Marsh & Balla, 1994). More recently, Hu and Bentler (1998, 1999) also argued that the relative sensitivity of different GOF indices to underparametrized model misspecification had been largely neglected in the evaluation of fit indices. Similar to Marsh and Balla, they evaluated different GOF indices according to variance explained in terms of models differing in level of misspecification and recommended that indices that were not sufficiently sensitive to model misspecification should not be used.

Interpretable Metric and Cutoff Values

Starting with early work by Tucker and Lewis (1973) and particularly Bentler and Bonett (1980), the basic goal of particularly the family of incremental fit indices was to provide an index of goodness of fit that varied along an interpretable metric that provided absolute cutoff values of acceptable levels of fit. In particular, incremental fit indices offered what appeared to be a straightforward evaluation of the ability of a model to fit observed data that varied along an easily understood, 0 to 1 scale. Based on intuition and a limited amount of empirical research, Bentler and Bonett proposed that incremental fit indices of .90 or higher reflected acceptable levels of fit. Other research stemming from early work by Steiger and Lind (1980) argued for the usefulness of indices based on a standardized measure of *empirical discrepancy* (the difference between $\hat{\Sigma}_k$ and S) such as RMSEA. Whereas such indices have no clearly defined upper limit, the lower limit is zero in the population. A combination of intuition and experience led researchers (e.g., Browne & Cudeck, 1993; also see Jöreskog & Sörbom, 1993) to suggest that RMSEAs less than 0.05 are indicative of a "close fit" and that values up to 0.08 represent reasonable errors of approximation. In more recent work, Hu and Bentler (1998, 1999) used the ability of indices to discriminate between correct and misspecified models as a basis for recommending that the cutoff value of .95 for a variety of indices that vary along a 0 to 1 scale and 0.06 for RMSEA. In evaluating GOF indices in relation to this criterion, two quite different questions are relevant. One possible criterion of an interpretable metric is to establish the extent to which an index is able to reflect the relative degree of model misspecification in a set of competing models that might include, for example, the null and saturated models as the endpoints of the continuum. A much more demanding criterion that seems to be driving current practice is the extent to which existing research provides a sufficient basis to specify generalizable cutoff values (e.g., RNI > .95) that apply across a wide variety of different applications.

Goodness-of-Fit Indices: Behavior of Selected Indices

The purpose of the present section is to briefly review results of some large-scale simulation studies that sought to evaluate the behavior of GOF indices, and then evaluate and make recommendations about the appropriate use of GOF indices that are organized in relation to the broad categories presented in the Appendix. (In this section, distinctions between N and $N - 1$ in some formulas are ignored, for the sake of clarity of discussion.) The evaluation of these indices relied heavily on McDonald's research (Marsh et al., 1988; McDonald, 1989; McDonald & Ho, 2002; McDonald & Marsh, 1990) and subsequent research pursuing these issues (Marsh & Balla, 1994; Marsh et al., 1996; Marsh & Hau, 1996), but also incorporates a broad cross section of other research and indices developed by other researchers.

GOF indices considered here (Appendix) have been evaluated primarily through the systematic application of large-scale simulation studies. Gerbing and Anderson (1993) evaluated the design of Monte Carlo studies of goodness-of-fit indices and reviewed results from this research with the primary aim "of providing the substantive researcher with guidance regarding the choice of indices to use" (p. 40). They reviewed the initial research by Bentler and Bonett (1980), the Marsh et al. (1988) classification of Type 1 and Type 2 indices, Bollen's (1986, 1989a) indices, and the comparison of CFI and RNI indices. In their evaluation of fit indices, they emphasized sample size effects, appropriate corrections for model complexity, and distributional properties of fit indices. They also stressed that whereas most early simulation studies evaluated only true models in which data were generated by the model to be tested, they emphasized the need to evaluate incorrect models to test the sensitivity of indices to misspecification. Early simulation studies reviewed by Gerbing and Anderson (1993) evaluated the ability of true models to fit data varying systematically in sample size (e.g., Anderson & Gerbing, 1984; Boomsma, 1982). For example, Anderson and Gerbing (1984) found that the NFI was systematically affected by sample size, whereas the TLI was not, but that the TLI had much larger within-cell standard deviations. Gerbing and Anderson noted that Marsh et al. (1988) replicated these trends.

Marsh and Balla (1994) evaluated the influence of sample size N and model parsimony on a set of 22 goodness-of-fit indices, including those typically used in confirmatory factor analysis and some recently developed indices. They considered sample data simulated from two known population data structures that differed in complexity. The authors fit an extensive set of eight models, including the true, population-generating model, overparametrized models (which included parameter estimates of parameters known to be zero in the population), and under-parametrized models (which fix to zero parameters known to be nonzero in the population). Values for 6 of 22 fit indices were reasonably independent of N and were not significantly affected by the addition of freely estimated parameters known to have zero values in the population. Indices recommended for evaluating goodness of fit were (a) the measure of centrality (Mc) and the rescaled noncentrality parameter (Dk), two indices based on noncentrality described by McDonald (1989); (b) RNI, an incremental index based on noncentrality (Bentler, 1990; McDonald & Marsh, 1990); (c) unbiased estimates of goodness of fit GFI*, AGFI*, and RMSEA developed by Steiger (1989), which are based on noncentrality; and (d) the widely known relative index developed by Tucker and Lewis (1973). Penalties for model complexity designed to control sampling fluctuations and to facilitate the inevitable compromise between goodness of fit and model parsimony were evaluated.

In a particularly influential and ambitious program of simulation study, Hu and Bentler (1998; also see Hu & Bentler, 1999) systematically evaluated the behavior of a representative selection of widely endorsed GOF indices under conditions of different sample sizes, different degrees of model misspecification (underparametrization, but not overparametrization), varying degrees of violation of multivariate normality assumptions, and different estimation procedures. Whereas the performance of different indices under different methods of estimation were not easily summarized, Hu and Bentler found the indices based on maximum likelihood (ML) typically outperformed those based on generalized least squares (GLS) or asymptotically distribution free (ADF) estimation procedures. For ML and GLS estimation procedures, they recommended the use of the standard root mean square residual (SRMR), supplemented by the TLI, IFI, RNI, CFI, GFI*, Mc, or RMSEA (but noted that TLI, Mc, and RMSEA were less preferable at small sample sizes). Indices not recommended by the authors were information indices (the cross-validation index [CK] and the expected cross-validation index [ECVI]), the critical N (CN), LISREL's goodness-of-fit indices (GFI, AGFI), and several older incremental fit indices (NFI and RFI) because they were not sufficiently sensitive to model misspecification but were sample size dependent. Of particular relevance to practice, they argued against traditional cutoff criteria of a good fit as .90 for incremental fit indices and 0.05 values of RMSEA. Emphasizing the difficulty in establishing absolute cutoff values that are broadly generalizable, Hu and Bentler recommended cutoffs of close to .95 for ML-based estimates of TLI, IFI, RNI, CFI, and GFI*; a cutoff of close to .90 for Mc; a cutoff of close to 0.08 for SRMR; and a cutoff of 0.06 for RMSEA. Finally, they noted that at small sample sizes ($N < 250$), TLI, Mc, and RMSEA tend to overreject true-population models and so are less preferable. These results have been highly influential in that the accepted standards of a "good fit" based on incremental fit indices have largely shifted from the .90 cutoff value recommended by Bentler and Bonett (1980) to the new, more stringent cutoff value of .95 recommended by Hu and Bentler.

Incremental Fit Indices

Whereas incremental fit indices represent only a portion of the indices summarized in the Appendix, the history of research based on these indices is central to understanding GOF evaluation. Arguably, Bentler and Bonett (1980) is the most important study in this area of research and one of the most highly cited articles in all of psychology. In that research they developed the prototype for incremental fit indices that were specifically designed to provide an index of goodness of fit that was relatively independent of sample size and varied along an interpretable metric that provided absolute cutoff values of acceptable levels of fit. Hence, it is appropriate to evaluate incremental fit indices in relation to our "desirable criteria." Despite the initial appeal of the 0–1 continuum and the .90 cutoff offered by incremental fit indices, subsequent research indicated that the interpretation of incremental fit indices was more complicated than initially anticipated. In response to real or apparent problems in existing incremental fit indices and the desire to incorporate other desirable features, the number of incremental indices proliferated. With this proliferation came a lack of standardization in the names assigned to the same index, including the independent rediscovery or simultaneous discovery of the same index by different researchers. Hence, we seek to more clearly delineate the incremental fit indices in popular use and to evaluate these indices in relation to desirable criteria for these indices (see Appendix). We begin with a brief historical overview.

Bentler and Bonett's (1980) Indices. Bentler and Bonett (1980) popularized the use of incremental fit indices. Based in part on earlier work by Tucker and Lewis (1973), they argued that it was desirable to assess goodness of fit along a 0 to 1 continuum in which the zero point reflects a baseline or worst-possible fit and one reflects an optimum fit. They suggested that a "null" model, in which all the measured variables were posited to be mutually uncorrelated, provided an appropriate basis for defining the zero point. Whereas other researchers have argued that other, more realistic models may provide a better baseline against which to evaluate target models (Marsh & Balla, 1994; Sobel & Bohrnstedt, 1985), these alternative baseline models are typically idiosyncratic to a particular application and have not been widely accepted. More generally, Marsh et al. (1996) argued that it is important to include a set of alternative competing models—including those that Sobel and Bohrnstedt (1985) suggested as alternative baseline models—that are all evaluated in relation to where they fall along the 0–1 scale that is defined by the null and saturated models.

Bentler and Bonett (1980) proposed two incremental indices: the nonnormed fit index based on the work by Tucker and Lewis (1973; here referred to as the TLI; see Appendix) and their new normed fit index (NFI). The major distinction between these two indices emphasized by Bentler and Bonett was that the NFI was strictly normed to fall on a 0–1 continuum, whereas the TLI could fall outside of the 0–1 range due to sampling fluctuations. Bentler and Bonett suggested that values greater than .90 may constitute an "acceptable" fit, and this somewhat arbitrary "rule of thumb" was widely applied. This guideline as to what constitutes an apparently acceptable fit seems to be an important contributor to the popularity of the incremental fit indices. Byrne (2001) noted that NFI was the index of choice for nearly a decade. However, despite the initial and continued popularity of the NFI, subsequent research (e.g., Bentler, 1990; Bollen, 1989a, 1989b; Gerbing & Anderson, 1993; Hu & Bentler, 1998; Marsh et al., 1988) demonstrated that NFI estimates were biased by sample size, a feature deemed to be undesirable for incremental fit indices. In particular, NFI tended to underestimate fit (was overly conservative) when N was small. Although NFI is still widely used, typically it has not been among the recommended indices in more recent reviews (e.g., Bollen, 1989b; Bollen & Long, 1993; Gerbing & Anderson, 1993; Hu & Bentler, 1999; Marsh et al., 1988; McDonald & Marsh, 1990).

Indices Proposed by Marsh, Balla, and McDonald (1988). Marsh et al. (1988) evaluated a wide variety of new and existing Type 1 and Type 2 incremental fit indices (also see earlier discussion of this classification schema) in relation to sample size dependence for different models based on real and simulated data. The

Type 1 and Type 2 forms of incremental fit indices proposed by Marsh et al. were a heuristic basis for generating a large number of different incremental indices, and many of the indices have subsequently been proposed by other researchers. However, subsequent research indicated that not all Type 2 indices were unbiased, thus undermining some of the usefulness of the Type 1 and Type 2 distinction.

Indices Proposed by Bollen (1986, 1989a, 1989b). Bollen (1986, 1989b, 1990; Bollen & Long, 1993) emphasized the usefulness of indices whose estimated values were unrelated or only weakly related to sample size and that provided a correction for model complexity. Bollen (1986) suggested that the TLI was a function of sample size and proposed the RFI to correct this problem. McDonald and Marsh (1990, p. 249), however, showed mathematically that the TLI "should not exhibit any systematic relation to sample size," a conclusion that was consistent with Monte Carlo results (e.g., Anderson & Gerbing, 1984; Bentler, 1990; Bollen, 1989a, 1989b; Marsh et al., 1988). Marsh et al. (1988, Appendix 1; also see Marsh & Balla, 1986) also demonstrated that the RFI was a variation of their general form of Type 1 incremental indices based on the χ^2/df ratio. Values for RFI were shown to vary systematically with N in Monte Carlo research (Marsh et al., 1988) and by its mathematical form (McDonald & Marsh, 1990). The usefulness of RFI is undermined by the fact that it is biased by N (i.e., N is systematically related to the means of its sampling distribution). Bollen (1989a, 1989b, 1990) subsequently proposed the IFI (which he called $\Delta 2$), a new fit index that was intended to correct this problem of sample size dependence and provide a correction for degrees of freedom. Although derived independently by Bollen (1990, footnote 1), Marsh et al. (1988) had previously described the same index as Type 2 incremental fit index for the χ^2. McDonald and Marsh (1990) subsequently evaluated the mathematical properties of the IFI index in terms of noncentrality estimate (d_T), as shown by the following expression, where $E(\chi^2)$ for a true target model is the degrees of freedom for the model (df_T):

$$
\begin{aligned}
\text{IFI} &= \left(\chi_N^2 - \chi_T^2 \right) \big/ \left(\chi_N^2 - df_T \right) \\
&= [(Nd_N + df_N) - (Nd_T + df_T)]/[(Nd_N + df_N) - df_T] \\
&= [(d_N - d_T) + (df_N - df_T)/N)]/[d_N + (df_N - df_T)/N] \\
&= 1 - \{d_T/[d_N + (df_N - df_T)/N]\}.
\end{aligned}
$$

McDonald and Marsh (1990) noted that "it may be verified that this quantity approaches its asymptote from above, overestimating it in small samples" (p. 250), and that this overestimation tends to disappear as misspecification approaches zero. Hence, the IFI should approach its asymptotic value from above (i.e., become systematically less positively biased for increasing Ns), but the size of the bias should decrease as the degree of misspecification approaches zero. Bollen (1989a) and Bentler (1990) demonstrated that the index was unbiased in Monte

Carlo studies of a correctly specified ("true") model. However, because the index is not biased when there is no misspecification, these were not critical tests of IFI. Bentler also evaluated a slightly misspecified model and reported that IFI was relatively unrelated to N. Marsh (Marsh et al., 1996; Marsh & Hau, 1996), however, noted that whereas the differences reported by Bentler were small, there appeared to be a systematic pattern of effects that was consistent with McDonald and Marsh's suggestions. Gerbing and Anderson (1993) reviewed Marsh et al. (1988) and McDonald and Marsh (1990), but apparently did not realize that IFI had been previously proposed by Marsh et al. under a different name and criticized by McDonald and Marsh. Based on their review of Monte Carlo studies, Gerbing and Anderson recommended the IFI because it was apparently unbiased and provided an apparently appropriate adjustment for degrees of freedom that penalized a lack of parsimony. However, the more critical evaluation of IFI offered by McDonald and Marsh suggests that Gerbing and Anderson's recommendation may have been premature. However, Hu and Bentler (1998, 1999) again recommended the IFI (which they called BL89). On the basis of their research, they concluded that it was reasonably independent of sample size and reasonably sensitive to model misspecification. As is evident in several simulation studies, the undesirable characteristics of the IFI shown in the mathematical derivations by McDonald and Marsh (1990) are not sufficiently strong to be readily apparent.

Marsh et al. (1996), expanding on observations by McDonald and Marsh (1990), provided a more appropriate test of IFI than previous simulation research. In particular, they included a wider variety of underparametrized misspecified models than other evaluations of IFI (IFI is only biased by sample size for underparametrized misspecified models) and included overparametrized models (with superfluous parameters that have zero values in the population-generating model) to evaluate its penalty for model complexity. Based on their empirical results and consistent with the mathematical derivations by McDonald and Marsh, they concluded that the (a) IFI was positively biased for misspecified models and this bias was larger for small N (most indices that are biased are negatively biased so that they provide conservative estimates of fit); (b) IFI was empirically inappropriate in that it penalized model parsimony and rewarded model complexity (it is supposed to reward model parsimony and penalize model complexity); and (c) the inappropriate penalty for parsimony and reward for model complexity are larger for small N. Because of these undesirable properties, the IFI does not achieve its intended goals or claims by its proponents. Hence, even though the sample size dependence is not large, we do not recommend the IFI for routine use.

Incremental Indices Based on Noncentrality. Incremental fit indices are based on the noncentrality parameter from the noncentral χ^2 distribution (e.g., Bentler, 1990; McDonald, 1989; McDonald & Marsh, 1990; Steiger & Lind, 1980) and its sample estimate. Bentler (1990) and McDonald and Marsh (1990) both emphasized that the noncentrality parameter reflects a natural measure of model misspecification. McDonald and Marsh (1990) derived expressions of NFI, TLI, RFI, and IFI in terms of noncentrality, degrees of freedom, and sample size. In this form they demonstrated that TLI should be independent of sample size, whereas values for the other three indices should vary systematically with sample size. They also demonstrated that the most important distinction between the NFI and the TLI is that the TLI is an unbiased estimate of a quantity that incorporates a correction for model complexity, whereas the NFI is a biased estimate of a quantity that does not.

McDonald and Marsh (1990) proposed the RNI, which provides an unbiased estimate of the asymptotic values estimated (with bias) by the NFI and the IFI, and concluded that researchers wanting to use an incremental fit index should logically choose between the RNI and the TLI. Working independently from a similar perspective, Bentler (1990) proposed a new incremental fit index called the CFI that is identical to the RNI except it is "normed"; values falling outside of the 0–1 range are truncated so that the CFI is strictly bounded by 0 and 1 in samples as well as in the population. Consistent with conclusions by McDonald and Marsh (1990), Bentler suggested that the TLI reflects the relative reduction in noncentrality per degree of freedom, so that "it does appear to have a parsimony rationale" (p. 241). Bentler argued that the RNI was better behaved than the TLI in that (a) sampling fluctuations are greater for the TLI than the RNI, (b) the TLI estimates are more likely to be negative, and (c) when the TLI exceeds 1, the RNI will exceed 1 by a smaller amount. He then pointed out that the standard deviation of estimates for the CFI must be less than or equal to that of the RNI. This led Bentler to prefer the CFI to the RNI, and the RNI to the TLI. The reasons for this preference for the CFI and the RNI over the TLI, however, did not seem to reflect that the TLI is a qualitatively different index from the RNI and the CFI.

Bentler (1990) also demonstrated the behavior of the NFI, TLI, IFI, RNI, and CFI in a simulation study in which a true and slightly misspecified model were fit to the same data varying in sample size. He emphasized that the sample size effect evident in the NFI was not evident in any of the other indices. Consistent with previous research, he reported that the range of the TLI (0.570–1.355 for the true model with $N = 50$) was very large and that the within-cell standard deviations (SDs) for TLI values were consistently much larger than for the other indices. Focusing on results based on small samples ($N = 50$) using a true model, Bentler noted that the SD for the CFI was smaller than for any of the other indices. However, the CFI SDs are expected to be substantially smaller for true models (where half the values of the CFI would be expected to exceed 1.0 if the values were not truncated) and smaller sample sizes. Thus, for the slightly misspecified model the SDs for the NFI and the IFI tended to be as small as or smaller than those for the CFI (particularly for $N > 50$). However, the TLI SDs were still substantially larger than for the other indices. Bentler also noted that for the slightly misspecified model the TLIs (mean = .892) were consistently lower than for the other indices (mean = .95). These results led Bentler to prefer the CFI, noting, however, that its advantages were at the expense of a slight downward bias (due to the truncation of values greater than 1.0).

Marsh (Marsh et al., 1996; Marsh & Hau, 1996) reported that the RNI was not systematically related to sample size, had mean values of approximately 1.0 for true approximating models, and appropriately reflected systematic variation in model misspecification. In this respect, it was successful in relation to its intended goals. The only substantial limitation for this index, perhaps, was its failure to penalize appropriately for model complexity (i.e., RNIs were larger for overfit models with superfluous parameter estimates) and its failure to reward model parsimony (i.e., RNIs were smaller for the parsimonious models that imposed equality constraints known to be true in the population). There is, however, room for disagreement on the interpretation of even this one apparent limitation. Whereas many researchers agree that penalties for model complexity and rewards for model parsimony are desirable, some argue otherwise. Thus, for example, Bentler (1992) recognized the importance of this feature but preferred not to mix the separate characteristics of fit and parsimony in a single index. Marsh and Balla (1994) offered related advice in their discussion of model complexity penalties and sample estimation penalties. Because the RNI was well behaved in relation to its intended goals and most of the desirable criteria proposed here, the RNI (or, perhaps, its normed counterpart, the CFI) is recommended for continued use.

In practice, the distinction between the CFI and the RNI is not very important because such extreme values are rare, values of RNI > 1 or CFI = 1 both lead to the conclusion that the fit is excellent, and values of RNI < 0 or CFI = 0 both lead to the conclusion that the fit is very poor. In a comparison of the RNI and the CFI, Goffin (1993) concluded that the RNI might be preferable for purposes of model comparison, whereas the CFI may be preferred with respect to efficiency of estimation. In Monte Carlo studies, however, the difference between the CFI and the RNI is particularly important when "true" models (i.e., population misfit = 0) are considered. For such models, the expected value of the RNI is 1.0 (i.e, approximately half the sample estimates will be above 1 and half below) and this value should not vary with N. The expected value of CFI, however, must be less than 1.0 for any finite N (because CFI is truncated not to exceed 1.0) and the size of this negative bias should be a systematically decreasing function of N. For this reason, it may be desirable to consider the RNI in addition to, or instead of, the CFI, at least for Monte Carlo studies in which a "true" model is fit to the data. Similarly, McDonald and Ho (2002) suggested that reporting RNI > 1 may be more informative than reporting CFI = 1.0.

Further Consideration of TLI. TLI has the longest history of any of the incremental fit indices, but it also seems to be the most misunderstood and inappropriately maligned. Bollen (1986) suggested that by its algebraic form the TLI would be influenced by sample size and argued that the RFI should be independent of sample size. However, further clarification of the meaning of the sample size effect (e.g., Bollen, 1989b, 1990) and a growing body of empirical research showed that values of the RFI are systematically related to N, whereas those of the TLI are not. Bentler and Bonett (1980) favored their NFI over the TLI in part because sample values of the NFI were normed, whereas those for the TLI were not. However, McDonald and Marsh (1990; also see Bentler, 1990) demonstrated that when the TLI was expressed in terms of the noncentrality estimate and the parsimony ratio (see later discussion), it became apparent that the TLI was qualitatively different from other incremental fit indices such as the NFI and the RNI. The TLI, by its mathematical form (McDonald & Marsh, 1990) and on the basis of Monte Carlo results (Marsh & Balla, 1994), provides a parsimony correction, a penalty for model complexity:

$$\begin{aligned} \text{TLI} &= (d_N/df_N - d_T/df_T)/(d_N/df_N) \\ &= 1 - [(d_T/df_T)/(d_N/df_N)] \\ &= 1 - [(d_T/df_T) \times (df_N/d_N)] \\ &= 1 - [(d_T/d_N) \times (df_N/df_T)], \end{aligned}$$

where df_T/df_N is the parsimony ratio recommended by Mulaik et al. (1989). Hence it is clear that the TLI incorporates the parsimony ratio recommended by Mulaik et al. (1989) and satisfies preferences by Bollen and Long (1993), Gerbing and Anderson (1993), Tanaka (1993), and others for fit indices that control for model complexity by taking into account the degrees of freedom of a model. The form of this adjustment for degrees of freedom is appropriate in that model complexity is penalized.

Marsh (Marsh et al., 1996; Marsh & Hau, 1996) suggested that this parsimony property of the TLI might be particularly useful in tests of nested models. Thus, for example, the inclusion of additional parameters (decreases in df_T) can result in a *lower* TLI when the improvement in fit (decreases in d_T) is sufficiently small even though indices such as the RNI that do not contain a penalty for lack of parsimony can never be smaller. Conversely, the TLI rewards model parsimony. Thus, for example, the imposition of equality constraints to test the invariance of solutions over multiple groups may actually result in a higher TLI even though the RNI can never be higher (e.g., Marsh & Byrne, 1993; Marsh, Byrne, & Craven, 1992). Similarly, a higher order factor model that is nested under the corresponding first-order measurement model can have a higher TLI even though the RNI can never be higher. This feature of the TLI provides one potentially useful decision rule ("accept the more parsimonious model if its TLI is equal to or better than that of the less parsimonious model") for concluding that the difference between a more complex model and a more parsimonious model is not substantively important, a feature that differentiates it from many indices that are monotonic with model complexity. In an empirical test of this feature of the TLI, Marsh (Marsh et al., 1996; Marsh & Hau, 1996) demonstrated that the introduction of equality constraints (which were known to be true in the population-generating model) resulted in higher TLIs even though it led to lower RNIs. Similarly, the introduction of superfluous parameters led to poorer TLIs even though there was an increase in RNIs.

The major criticism of the TLI has been because of its large sampling fluctuations. However, interpretations of previous research must be made cautiously because of the apparently overly simplistic manner in which reliability of estimation has been assessed, and this concern will be an important focus of the present investigation. However, such claims are typically based on comparisons of within-cell standard deviations or $SS_{residuals}$ from studies that included only true models. However, Marsh (Marsh et al., 1996; Marsh & Hau, 1996) demonstrated empirically that whereas both the TLI and the RNI have values of about 1 for a true model, TLIs are progressively much lower than RNIs for increasingly misspecified models. Hence, it is evident that the metrics underlying the TLI and RNI are qualitatively different, so that within-cell standard deviations and $SS_{residuals}$ based on raw scores are not comparable. Using a more appropriate approach to assessing the reliability and sensitivity to misspecification requires researchers to evaluate a series of models in which misspecification is systematically varied (Marsh & Balla, 1994; also see Hu & Bentler, 1998). Whereas Marsh and Balla found the $SS_{residuals}$ were substantially larger for the TLI than the RNI, the etas associated with the effects of model misspecification were nearly as high for the TLI as for the RNI.

It is also apparent, however, that the TLI is unstable in some situations. Thus, for example, Anderson and Gerbing (1984) reported extreme TLIs far in excess of 1.0 when sample size was very small. As noted by McDonald and Marsh (1990), inspection of the definition of TLI (Appendix and foregoing equation) demonstrated that the index is undefined due to division by zero when $d_O = 0$ (i.e., the null model is able to fit the data) or $df_T = 0$ (i.e., the target model is the saturated model), and is likely to be very unstable in situations approximating these conditions. Whereas it would be extremely unlikely for population values of noncentrality to approach zero for the null model (i.e., for the null model to be "true"), this can happen for sample estimates based on small Ns (e.g., $N \leq 50$), and this apparently accounts for the extremely large values of the TLI reported in some simulation studies. Marsh (Marsh et al., 1996; Marsh & Hau, 1996) proposed a viable strategy for avoiding such extreme values and associated problems with large sampling fluctuations by using a normed counterpart of the TLI (NTLI) such that NTLI is strictly normed for sample and population values, is defined when TLI is undefined (i.e., $d_o = 0$ and for the saturated model with $df_T = 0$), and takes on its maximum value of 1.0 whenever $d_T \leq 0$. This strategy is somewhat analogous to the comparison of the RNI and its normed counterpart CFI. In the case of the TLI, however, the advantages of a normed counterpart are likely to be much greater because extreme values of the TLI are apparently much more likely than those for the RNI. Thus, anyone preferring the normed CFI over the RNI, its unnormed counterpart, should also prefer the normed version of the TLI over the unnormed version, which has been so severely criticized for problems related to sampling fluctuations.

Absolute Indices

Fit Function-Based Indices (FF; LHR; χ^2; p value; χ^2/df ratio). χ^2
works very well as a GOF index when the model being tested is the same as the
known population-generating model, but this only happens in simulation studies.
When this is not the case, there is a substantial interaction between sample size and
the degree of misspecification, which renders the χ^2 problematic as a GOF index.
χ^2 is very responsive to underparametrization misspecification of (i.e., parameters
with nonzero values in the population-generating model that are specified to be
zero in the approximating model). Even when the model being tested is "true"
(i.e., population misfit is zero because all nonzero parameter estimates in the
population are freely estimated) there are additional effects associated with overparametrization misspecification, rewarding model complexity (i.e., lower values
for the model with superfluous parameters known to be zero in the population-
generating model). Like the χ^2, the minimum fit function (FF) and likelihood ratio
(LHR) are highly discriminating between correctly and misspecified models that
are underparametrized, but there is also a substantial sample size effect that varies
with the degree of misspecification. There are also biases favoring more-complex
models and against parsimonious models that are larger when N is small. The p
value for χ^2 is very useful in simulation studies in which the model being tested is
the same as the known population-generating model, in that there is no sample size
effect, it controls for complexity, and it is highly discriminating between correctly
specified and misspecified models.

The χ^2/df works well for true models, but it has the same problems as χ^2
for misspecified models. It differs from the χ^2 in that it has a correction for
model complexity. For example, for the misspecified models in the Marsh and
Balla (1994) study, it consistently led to the selection of models with appropriate
equality constraints (i.e., constraining parameters to be equal that were known
to be equal in the population-generating model) and to the selection of models
without superfluous parameters (i.e., fixing to be zero selected parameters known
to be zero in the population), showing that it rewarded model parsimony. Although
there was a long history of reporting "acceptable" cutoff values as low as 2.0 or
as high as 5.0, the substantial sample size dependence of this index renders any
absolute cutoff value as inappropriate for all but correctly specified models. As
noted by Steiger (2000), suggestions that χ^2/df has a stable implication are "a
remnant of an earlier time, when the relationships between the likelihood ratio
statistic, population badness of fit, and the noncentral chi-square distribution were
not yet fully understood" (pp. 156–157). Hence, χ^2/df is not recommended for
use as a routine stand-alone GOF index. It is, however, potentially useful as a
basis for comparing between alternative, competing models of the same data in
that it corrects for model complexity (also see related discussion of the TLI and
information criteria indices). In summary, with the possible exception of χ^2/df,
these χ^2-based indices are not particularly useful as GOF indices according to the

criteria considered here, and it is the dissatisfaction with the χ^2 as a GOF index that led to the development of other indices.

Noncentrality Based Indices (Dk, PDF, Mc).   McDonald (1989) noted that a problem with many other fit indices is that the value of the index and model selection based on it are dependent on sample size. He suggested Wald's noncentrality parameter (also see Steiger, 1989; Steiger & Lind, 1980), rescaled to be independent of sample size, as an index of fit (see Dk in the Appendix). A nontechnical interpretation of the noncentrality parameter is as a suitably weighted sum of squares of discrepancies between the parameters of the unrestricted model yielding Σ_0 and the parameters of the approximating model. McDonald further noted that Dk could be transformed to yield Mc, a measure of centrality that is a consistent estimator of the population discrepancy function, scaled to be independent of sample size. It is in the metric of the LHR and bears the same relation to Dk as the LHR does to FF (see Appendix). Mc is scaled to lie on the interval zero to unity with unity representing a perfect fit, though sampling error may produce values outside of this range.

Not surprisingly, Marsh and Balla (1994) found that the population discrepancy function (PDF) and Dk were nearly indistinguishable ($r = .999$) as would typically be the case, particularly for real data. They differ only in that PDF is "normed," whereas Dk is not. For this reason, Marsh and Balla found that PDF was slightly sample size dependent, whereas Dk was not. In general, normed indices tend to be sample size dependent, particularly for simulated data that contain estimates based on the true (population-generating) model. However, both PDF and Dk were equally sensitive to model misspecification. Dk may be preferable in simulation studies in which "true" models are fit, but in practice there would typically be no difference between them. Both are substantially biased toward more-complex models and against more-parsimonious models, particularly when N is small.

Mc is a potentially useful rescaling of Dk so that it varies along a 0 to 1 scale (within sampling error). Marsh and Balla (1994) indicated that it worked well in that it was reasonably independent of sample size and differentiated well between correctly specified and misspecified models, but suggested that it had not been used sufficiently to evaluate its interpretability. In subsequent research Hu and Bentler (1998; also see Fan et al., 1999) also reported that it was relatively independent of sample size and sensitive to model misspecification and suggested that values of Mc greater than .90 were indicative of an acceptable GOF.

Error-of-Approximation Indices (SRMR, RMR, RMS, RMSEA, MSEA, RMSEAP).   The root mean residual (RMR) represents the average empirical discrepancy and can only be interpreted in relation to the variances and covariances of the observed variables (S). The RMR and the SRMR differ only in that the latter is standardized (in a correlational metric), whereas the former is not. Thus,

SRMR is strictly bound by 0 and 1, whereas RMR has a lower bound of zero but no upper bound. In general, the standardized version should be more interpretable and more comparable across different applications, although the two will produce the same rank order of alternative models fit to the same data. Marsh and Balla (1994) found that RMR was highly sensitive to model underparametrization misspecification. However, consistent with results from Marsh et al. (1988), they also found that it was substantially related to sample size and for this reason, they did not recommend its use. However, Hu and Bentler (1998, 1999) recommended that SRMR should be used because it was both sensitive to underparametrization misspecification and only moderately affected by N. However, their results for SRMR varied substantially with the type of underparametrization misspecification. Of their recommended indices, SRMR was least affected by sample size and most sensitive to model misspecification for their "simple" misspecification, but was most affected by N and least sensitive to misspecification for their "complex" misspecification. Because of this apparent disagreement in the usefulness of SRMR in relation to the extent of its sample size dependence and its variation along an underlying metric that is comparable in different contexts, we recommend caution in its use pending research with a wider variety of misspecified models [also see our subsequent discussion of the Hu & Bentler (1999) study of cutoff values for this index].

Steiger and Lind (1980; Steiger, 1989) noted Dk (see later discussion) was not in the metric of the original parameters and may not compensate for model complexity. Steiger and Lind (1980) proposed the Steiger–Lind adjusted root mean square index (RMS) index (see Appendix), which subsequently became known as the RMSEA. Steiger (1990, p. 81) suggested that "Values below .10 indicate a good fit, values below .05 a very good fit. Point estimates below .01 indicated an outstanding fit, and are seldom obtained." The RMSEA is undefined due to division by zero for the saturated model with zero degrees of freedom (see Appendix). Even when degrees of freedom approaches zero, it is a noncontinuous step function that is specific to the particular application and the indices may be unstable (Bentler, 1990). Marsh and Balla (1996) reported a small relation between N and the RMSEA that required further consideration. The RMSEA was based on the square root of Dk "to return the index to the same metric as the original parameters" (Steiger, 1989, p. 81). Because Dk can be negative due to sampling fluctuations, Steiger (1989; see Appendix) set negative values of Dk equal to zero for purposes of defining the RMSEA. However, the negative values of Dk are likely to be more negative on average for small N than for large N, so that Steiger's decision rule results in a more substantial truncation of the negative tail of the distribution of Dk values for small N. Consistent with this observation, for all true models (i.e., approximation discrepancies $= 0$) the RMSEA is systematically related to N even though Dk is not (Marsh & Balla, 1994). The size of the bias, although clearly evident in simulation studies based on "true" models, is likely to be unimportant in practice, and Steiger (2000; also see Bentler, 2000) argued that truncation of this sort is justified because the true population value is necessarily nonnegative so that truncation reduces sampling error and provides more accurate estimates of the corresponding population value. Compared to the RMR, Marsh and Balla (1994) found that the RMSEA was slightly more sensitive to model underparametrization, substantially less affected by N, and relatively unaffected by model overparametrization. The mean square error of approximation (MSEA) and the RMSEA are essentially the same index except that the RMSEA is truncated to be nonzero, whereas the MSEA is not (see related distinction for PDF and Dk), and the MSEA varies along a squared deviation metric. This distinction is only important for simulation studies in which the model being tested is the same as the population-generating model, where the RMSEA is modestly related to sample size (Marsh & Balla, 1994; also see Fan et al., 1999). Because the RMSEA meets the criteria that we specified for GOF indices, we recommend its routine use.

Information Indices (ECVI, Ck, AIC, CAIC). Akaike (1974, 1987) and Schwartz (1978) each proposed fit indices that incorporate estimation penalties for model complexity to be used in comparing alternative models. The development of AIC is based on the Kullback–Leibler information quantity, which reflects the amount of information that would be required to distinguish between distributions based on a hypothesized and a true model, although related derivations have been proposed from Baysian and cross-validation perspectives. In practice, AIC is used to distinguish between different models fit to the same data so that the saturated model is a constant. Using this feature, it is possible to derive a simpler value for AIC that rank orders the alternative models under consideration. Cudeck and Browne (1983, p. 154) and Steiger (1989) considered rescaled versions of these indices that are considered here (see Appendix). Steiger (1989, p. 87) indicated "we rescale the criterion (without affecting the decisions it indicates) so that it remained more stable across differing sample sizes." Because this is considered a desirable feature in the context of the present investigation, we have included the rescaled versions of these indices in the Appendix. The development of the information criterion indices has taken place primarily within the context of selecting a "best" model from a sequence of nested models in which model complexity varies substantially from some minimal level to that of the saturated model [e.g., the "number-of-factors" problem, in which a nested sequence of unrestricted factor analysis models posits between 1 and the maximum number of factors (or the saturated model)]. As noted earlier, the AIC and related cross-validation procedures are designed to select the model whose parameter estimates are most trustworthy for a particular sample. Thus, more-parsimonious models will cross-validate better when N is small (and sampling error is large), whereas more-complex models will cross-validate better when N is large, as will be illustrated.

AIC* (and AIC), SC, and Ck incorporate estimation penalties intended to appropriately balance the risks of under- and overparametrized models. Each index has two components, one reflecting approximation discrepancy (Dk), which is monotonically related to model complexity, and an opposing estimation penalty reflecting estimation discrepancy (sampling error):

$$\text{AIC}^* = \text{Dk} + [\text{df}/N + (2K/N)] = \text{Dk} + [(p^* + K)/N], \tag{1}$$

$$\begin{aligned} \text{SC} &= \text{Dk} + \{\text{df}/N + [K \times \ln(N)]/N\} \\ &= \text{Dk} + \{[p^* + K(\ln(N) - 1)]/N\}, \end{aligned} \tag{2}$$

$$\begin{aligned} \text{Ck} &= \text{Dk} + \{\text{df}/N + [2K/(N - p - 2)]\} \\ &- \text{Dk} + \{(p^* - K)/N + [2K/(N - p - 2)]\}, \end{aligned} \tag{3}$$

where K is the number of parameters, p is the number of variables, $p^* = 0.5p \times (p + 1)$, and $\text{df} = 0.5p(p + 1) - K = p^* - K$.

Hence, the estimation penalties for all three indices are a monotonically decreasing function of N, are a monotonically increasing function of K, and have asymptotic values of zero. For most applications the penalty associated with SC will be substantially larger than the other two, whereas the penalty function associated with Ck will always be somewhat larger than that associated with AIC*.

Cudeck and Henly (1991) and Browne (2000) recommended the use of Ck and specifically called into question the claim by Marsh et al. (1988) and McDonald and Marsh (1990) that the influence of sample size is undesirable. However, there seems to be no controversy over the claim that approximation discrepancy should be estimated with an unbiased index such as Dk that is independent of N. Each of the information criterion indices can be expressed as a function of Dk and an estimation penalty based on sampling fluctuations that reflects estimation discrepancy. Hence, the only controversy is the appropriate application of penalties for estimation discrepancy.

The information criterion indices are intended to be an alternative to statistical significance testing. However, McDonald (1989; McDonald & Marsh, 1990) noted that the model selection based on the AIC was often similar to that based on tests of statistical significance. To demonstrate a mathematical basis for this observation, consider the difference between AICs for two nested models where Model 1 is more restrictive than Model 2 (and so the χ^2 and degrees of freedom will be greater for Model 1 because Model 2 has more parameters). $\text{AIC}_{\text{diff}} = \text{AIC}_1 - \text{AIC}_2$ can be written as

$$\text{AIC}_{\text{diff}} = \left(\chi_1^2 - \chi_2^2\right) - 2(\text{df}_1 - \text{df}_2),$$

where both $\chi_{\text{diff}}^2 = \chi_1^2 - \chi_2^2$ and $\text{df}_{\text{diff}} = \text{df}_1 - \text{df}_2$ are positive. In this form it is clear that the underlying AIC_{diff} decision rule is to accept the more restrictive Model 1 if $(\chi_1^2 - \chi_2^2)/(\text{df}_1 - \text{df}_2)$ is less than 2 (i.e., $\text{AIC}_{\text{diff}} < 0$) and to accept Model 2 otherwise. Comparing these values with those in a standard χ^2 table with 0.05 as critical value, we find (a) for $\text{df}_{\text{diff}} < 7$, the AIC_{diff} rule is less conservative than the

χ^2_{diff} test (i.e., less likely to accept the more restrictive model), (b) for $df_{\text{diff}} = 7$ the AIC_{diff} and χ^2_{diff} tests lead to similar conclusions; and (c) for $df_{\text{diff}} > 7$, the AIC_{diff} rule becomes increasingly more conservative than the χ^2_{diff} test (i.e., more likely to accept the more restrictive model). The AIC_{diff} and χ^2_{diff} tests will only lead to substantially different results when the df_{diff} is moderately large, thus explaining why the two decision rules lead to similar decisions in some applications. A similar logic applies to the Ck and SC, except that these tests tend to be more conservative than the AIC.

Each of these indices (ECVI, Ck, AIC, consistent AIC [CAIC]) has a similar rationale in that model complexity is penalized substantially when N is small and not at all when N is sufficiently large. Marsh and Balla (1994) reported that on average, all four led to the selection of more parsimonious models that imposed equality constraints known to be true in the population. In their study, CK and ECVI were nearly indistinguishable ($r = .999$), whereas AIC and CAIC were very similar to each other ($r = .997$) and different from the other two ($rs < .2$). In particular, the two pairs differed in terms of their sample size effect; the sample size effect was substantial and positive for AIC and CAIC, but substantial and negative for ECVI and Ck. This distinction, however, was somewhat illusory in that the indices were each designed to compare alternative models fit to the same data (thus holding sample size constant). Thus, for example, Jöreskog and Sörbom (1993) pointed out that AIC and ECVI rank order alternative models the same when sample size is constant. More importantly, however, Marsh and Balla (1994) reported that none of the information criteria indices considered in their study were particularly sensitive to the model misspecification that was an important feature of their research. In subsequent research, Hu and Bentler (1999) also reported that information indices were not particularly sensitive to model misspecification but were highly sensitive to sample size. Whereas the authors of these indices would contest the relevance of the sample size dependence, the issue of insensitivity of model misspecification is a serious threat to the appropriateness of these indices. On this basis, Hu and Bentler recommended that these indices not be used. Our conclusions, however, are somewhat more circumspect. These information criterion indices have been shown to be very useful when required to distinguish between competing models on the basis of sampling discrepancy, which is their intended purpose. It is only in relation to the desirable criteria associated with other GOF indices like those proposed here—which are not consistent with the intended purpose of the information criterion indices—that they are not recommended. Hence, our recommendation is that these indices should only be used for purposes consistent with their intended purpose and not as a global GOF index.

Goodness-of-Fit Indices (GFI, GFI*, AGFI, AGFI*). Jöreskog and Sörbom (1981) stated that GFI is "a measure of the relative amount of variances and covariances jointly accounted for by the model" and asserted that "unlike χ^2, GFI is independent of the sample size," whereas AGFI "corresponds to using mean squares instead of total sums of squares" (pp. I.40–I.41). Thus AGFI incorporates a penalty function for additional parameters. Jöreskog and Sörbom suggested that GFI and AGFI would generally fall between 0 and 1, but that it is possible for them to be negative. However, several researchers have shown empirically and/or mathematically (e.g., Maiti & Mukherjee, 1991; Marsh et al., 1988; McDonald & Marsh, 1990; Steiger, 1989, 1990) that the GFI and AGFI indices provided by LISREL are negatively biased estimates of their asymptotic population values. Steiger (1989) proved that the population equivalent of the GFI could be expressed as a simple function of the population noncentrality index and that GFI* (see Appendix) was a consistent estimator of this value. Steiger (1989) noted that GFI* continues to improve as more parameters are added and thus does not take into account model complexity. To address this issue, he defined AGFI*, which contains a penalty for model complexity. Steiger (1989, 1990) suggested that GFI* and AGFI* were not systematically related to N, and Marsh and Balla (1994) provided empirical support for this claim. AGFI* penalizes model complexity, whereas GFI* does not. AGFI* is undefined due to division by zero for the saturated model with zero degrees of freedom (see Appendix). Even when degrees of freedom approaches zero, it is a noncontinuous step function that is specific to the particular application, and the indices may be unstable (Bentler, 1990).

Marsh and Balla (1994) found that GFI and AGFI were both substantially related to N, whereas GFI* and AGFI* were not. For small N, GFI and AGFI were negatively biased. However, they reported that GFI and GFI* differentiated to a similar extent between models of varying degrees of underparametrization misspecification. From this perspective GFI* seems preferable, but this suggestion should be evaluated further because there is limited research using GFI*. Marsh and Balla reported that both AGFI and AGFI* controlled for model complexity in that both indices led to the selection of the model with equality constraints known to be true in the population compared to models without these equality constraints, and models with no superfluous parameters (which were zero in the population) over models with superfluous parameter estimates. Both indices led to the selection of models with (true) equality constraints, but increasingly so for more seriously misspecified models. The size of the penalty for AGFI* is a function of misspecification such that there is no penalty for true models (so that mean values are approximately 1.0). Again, AGFI* seems preferable to AGFI, but more work is needed to clarify this. The pattern of results based on GFI and AGFI is consistent with other results (Bollen, 1989b; Fan et al., 1999; Shevlin & Miles, 1998). Hu and Bentler (1998, 2000) also reported that GFI and AGFI were sample size dependent but were not very sensitive to underparametrization misspecification. For this reason, they did not recommend their continued use. Pending the results of further research, we recommend that GFI* and AGFI* should be used instead of GFI and AGFI.

Parsimony Indices (PRNI; PGFI; PNFI; PGFI).*   James et al.'s (1982) parsimony indices combine in one index a measure of goodness of fit and parsimony

defined as the ratio of degrees of freedom in the fitted model to that in an appropriately defined "null" model. Based on simulated data, previous research (e.g.,
Marsh & Hau, 1996) showed that the parsimony indices consistently led to the
selection of more-parsimonious false models over a less-parsimonious true model
for all sample sizes in certain circumstances. For the parsimony normed fit index
(PNFI), this tendency was much larger for small N, which was consistent with
the bias in the NFI, whereas the PRNI did not vary with N. Whereas the PRNI
is apparently more useful than the PNFI, these results indicate that parsimony indices may overpenalize model complexity in some situations in relation to criteria
established here.

In the application of the parsimony indices there is the tradeoff between improved approximation discrepancy and freely estimating additional parameters.
For example, Marsh and Balla (1994) constructed data in which three factors were
defined by three "major factor loadings" and two "minor factor loadings" of .2.
They selected the .2 values to be small, but large enough to be substantively important in many applications. The application of the parsimony indices systematically
led to the acceptance of more-parsimonious false models, in which these minor factor loadings were fixed at zero, over less-parsimonious true models, in which these
minor factor loadings were free to be estimated. Whereas there may be contexts in
which factor loadings of .2 are not substantively important, as implied by the parsimony indices, the basis of this decision should not be a mechanistic application
of parsimony indices. Whereas model parsimony is an important characteristic,
further research is needed on how best to operationalize parsimony, what standards
imply acceptable parsimony, and how to integrate information about parsimony,
approximation discrepancy, and substantive issues.

Mulaik (1991) suggested that one would only claim support for models with
parsimony indices in the .80s or higher. By definition, a parsimony index based on
an index of fit that varies between 0 and 1 can never be greater than the parsimony
ratio. Marsh and Balla (1994) offered the example from their simulation research
of a three-factor model that fits the data perfectly in the population, has RNI values of approximately 1.0 for sample data, and has a very simple structure (each
measured variable loads on one and only one factor) that most would consider
to be "parsimonious." Yet, the PRNI for this model is only .67. The only way to
achieve an acceptable PRNI would be to fix a number of the nonzero parameters
values at or near their population values. Thus, for example, if five of the nine
nonzero factor loadings were fixed at their known population values instead of
being freely estimated, the PRNI would be .8. To further illustrate this potential
problem with the PRNI, consider a one-factor model. When all parameter estimates
are free to be estimated, as is nearly universal in CFA studies, it is not possible
to obtain an "acceptable" PRNI $> .8$ with fewer than 11 or 12 indicators even if
RNI $= 1.0$ (i.e., the fit is perfect). In contrast, for a 10-factor model with 5 indicators per factor and a modest RNI $= .88$, the PRNI is "acceptable." The conventional
guidelines for acceptable models based on relative fit and parsimony indices are

somewhat arbitrary, based on "current practice" and implicit, untested assumptions that are difficult to evaluate. However, the .8 parsimony index rule is dubious if a 10-indicator one-factor model that fits the data perfectly is not "acceptable." Furthermore, parsimony indices based on 1-factor models do not seem comparable with parsimony indices based on 10-factor models. Similar problems would also exist for any fixed values of parsimony indices used to define an acceptable fit.

Importantly, the parsimony indices differ from other GOF indices considered here that also penalize model complexity (e.g., TLI, RMSEA). For the parsimony indices, the penalty for model complexity depends only on the parsimony ratio (df_T/df_N), whereas for the TLI and the RMSEA the penalty for model complexity depends on the parsimony ratio and the level of misspecification. As the level of misspecification approaches zero, the penalty for model complexity in the TLI and the RMSEA also approaches zero. For this reason, the expected value of the TLI is always 1.0 for true models (and approximately 0 for the RMSEA), whereas the expected value of the parsimony indices will differ for each model (as a function of model complexity). In this sense, it does not appear logical to set absolute cutoff values for parsimony indices that are intended to generalize across different applications.

In summary, the metric of parsimony indices and the expected values for true models are likely to be idiosyncratic to each particular application. Furthermore, parsimony indices are likely to penalize model complexity severely, so that the "best" model based on these indices is likely to be much more parsimonious than models selected according to any of the other indices considered, and lead to the selection of models with potentially substantial levels of misspecification. Whereas it might be argued that this is appropriate in some instances, we do not recommend their routine use as a GOF Index.

Other Indices. Critical N (CN).   Hoelter argued that:

> Rather than ignoring or completely neutralizing sample size one can estimate the sample size that must be reached in order to accept the fit of a given model on a statistical basis. This estimate, referred to here as "critical N" (CN), allows one to assess the fit of a model relative to identical hypothetical models estimated with different sample sizes. (Hoelter, 1983, p. 528)

The usefulness of CN rests on the assumption that its value is independent of sample size. Although the rationale for this index is highly heuristic, the logic underlying the operationalization is flawed (Bollen, 1989b). In particular, numerous empirical studies (e.g., Hu & Bentler, 1998; Marsh et al., 1988) have demonstrated that the CN is highly sensitive to N. For this reason, even though it continues to be used, we strongly recommend against the continued use of CN.

Role of Parsimony and Comparing the Fit of Two Models

Role of Parsimony. Many mechanistic rules of thumb for evaluating the goodness of fit of SEMs emphasize model parsimony; all other things being equal, a simpler, more parsimonious model with fewer estimated parameters is better than a more complex model. Whereas this may be good advice in many applications—particularly in research applications where theory is not highly developed—Marsh and Hau (1996, 1998) demonstrated a heuristic counterexample in which parsimony as typically operationalized in indices of fit was undesirable. Specifically, in simplex models of longitudinal data, the failure to include correlated uniquenesses (i.e., correlations among the unique components) relating the same indicators administered on different occasions would typically lead to systematically inflated estimates of stability (e.g., Bollen, 1989b; Jöreskog, 1979). Although simplex models with correlated uniquenesses are substantially less parsimonious and may be unacceptable according to mechanistic decision rules that penalize model complexity, it can be argued a priori that these additional parameter estimates should be included. Marsh and Hau used simulated data to support this claim and evaluated the behavior of a variety of fit indices and decision rules. The results demonstrated the validity of Bollen and Long's (1993) conclusion that "test statistics and fit indices are very beneficial, but they are no replacement for sound judgement and substantive expertise" (p. 8).

Marsh and Hau (1996) compared two different sets of decision rules—those based on evaluating the acceptability of the parsimonious model (without correlated uniquenesses) alone and those based on the comparison of the parsimonious model and the unparsimonious model (with correlated uniquenesses). When the size of the correlated uniquesses was relatively large, typical decision rules based on most of the GOF indices led to the rejection of this model. However, when the correlated uniquenesses were moderate, many of the indices failed to reject the (false) parsimonious model, which resulted in a systematic bias in the size of the estimated test–retest path coefficients. The pattern of results was more complicated for decision rules used to compare the parsimonious and nonparsimonious models. Marsh and Hau first considered indices that incorporated a parsimony penalty (i.e., penalties for model complexity that are applied to indices based on unbiased estimates of approximation discrepancy between Σ_0 and Σ_k and do not vary with N). Results from these indices fell into two broad categories. In the first category, the AGFI, TLI, IFI, RFI, χ^2/df ratio, AGFI*, MSEA, and, perhaps, RMSEA were about equally likely to lead to the selection of the parsimonious and nonparsimonious models when there were no correlated uniquenesses. This trend was consistent with the attempt by these indices to "neutralize" the improved fit attributable to parameters that have a zero value in the population. These indices were increasingly likely to select—appropriately—the nonparsimonious model as the size of the correlated uniqueness increased. In the second category, the parsimony indices (PGFI, PNFI, and PRNI) so severely penalized model complexity that they tended to select the parsimonious model in all situations, even when the correlated uniquenesses were substantial. Next Marsh and Hau considered indices that incorporated penalties for model complexity that reflected estimation discrepancy that varied systematically with N—the information criteria indices (AIC, Ck, CAIC, ECVI). The likelihood of appropriately selecting the nonparsimonious model varied directly with the sizes of the correlated uniquenesses and the sample size. Three of the information criteria indices (ECVI, AIC, Ck) performed similarly, whereas CAIC was more likely to inappropriately lead to the selection of the parsimonious model. However, particularly when the sample size and the size of the correlated uniqueness were small, all of these indices led to the inappropriate selection of the nonparsimonious model a substantial portion of the time.

In addition to specific concerns about parsimony, Marsh and Hau's (1996) results illustrated a more general concern about the efficacy of *decision rules* based on evaluation of a single solution (e.g., accept if χ^2/df ratios <2.0, error approximation estimates <.05, incremental fit indices >.90, and parsimony indices >.8), which may be useful in some situations, but ultimately seemed to be placing undue emphasis on arbitrary cutoff values whose appropriateness was likely to vary substantially in different applications. Particularly when two a priori nested models have been posited to explain the data, it is a more useful exercise to compare solutions based on the two models than to evaluate the acceptability of any one solution in isolation. For indices that are monotonic with model complexity (e.g., RNI, GFI*) it is unlikely that any generally applicable decision rule can be developed about when the improvement in fit is large enough to justify acceptance of the more-complex model. This is not to say, of course, that it is not useful to compare the values for such indices based on alternative models.

The results of the Marsh and Hau (1996) demonstrated a surprising similarity in the decision rules based on comparison of two competing models using χ^2/df ratios, RMSEA, MSEA, AGFI, AGFI*, TLI, IFI, and RFI. For each of these indices, the parsimonious and nonparsimonious models were selected about equally often when population discrepancy was zero (i.e., there are no correlated uniquenesses). Even when there were only small correlated uniquenesses in the population, these indices correctly identified the inappropriateness of the parsimonious model most of the time. The explanation for this apparent paradox is that many of the limitations of these indices are minimized when comparing two models fit to the same data. Thus, for example, the effect of sample size and its interaction with model complexity are largely nullified when comparing alternative models fit to the same data (and, necessarily, the same sample size). Nevertheless, the authors expressed a preference for the routine use of decision rules based on indices recommended for evaluating single models that also incorporated penalties for parsimony (e.g., χ^2-difference test, χ^2/df ratio, RMSEA, and TLI).

Raykov and Penev (1998) developed an alternative approach to the comparison of two nested models based on differences in fit as indexed by noncentrality differences, a confidence interval for the difference in fit, and a power analysis of the ability of the test to detect meaningful differences in fit. Following from seminal work by Browne and Du Toit (1992), Steiger (1989, 1990; Steiger & Lind, 1980), and others, Raykov and Penev combined the notions of a "close fit" enshrined in the RMSEA and the classical hypothesis-testing approach based on the χ^2 test. A critical feature of this development was the argument that under many conditions the most restrictive of the nested models would be sufficiently unacceptable that the standard χ^2-difference test was not appropriate (see Steiger, Shapiro, & Browne, 1985; also see Jöreskog & Sörbom, 1988), whereas confidence intervals based on the difference in fit using noncentrality indices would provide useful information about the plausibility of the nesting constraints in the two nested models. Hence, the focus of their study was on the plausibility of the nesting restrictions per se, rather than the acceptability of either of the models being considered (although the authors implied that their procedure will break down if either of the models is grossly misspecified, as might be the case for the traditional "null model" used in incremental fit indices). A critical feature in their development was the assumption that differences in the fit corresponding to RMSEA values of less than 0.05 and greater than 0.08 are indicative of a good fit and an unacceptable fit, respectively. In this sense, Raykov and Penev proposed what is likely to be a more generous decision rule for accepting the more-restrictive model than suggested by Marsh and Hau (1996). Raykov and Penev also noted, however, that the development of confidence intervals for nested models based on indices that include a penalty for model complexity, such as the RMSEA, are likely to be much more complicated in that the relation between the noncentrality parameter and the index that takes into account model complexity. Although the focus of goodness-of-fit evaluation on the difference between two nested models is a critical issue, considerable experience is needed to determine the range of applicability of their procedure (relative to the more widely used χ^2-difference test) and whether the actual cutoff values proposed by Raykov and Penev are applicable and broadly generalizable (as is the case with all cutoff values).

Summary of Behavior of Goodness-of-Fit Indices

Communication in this area can be improved by making clear distinctions among approximation discrepancy, estimation discrepancy, parsimony penalties for model complexity applied to indices of approximation discrepancy that are independent of N, and estimation penalties that reflect estimation discrepancy and vary inversely with N. In relation to criteria specified earlier, we found support for Dk (or PDF), RMSEA (or MSEA) Mc, GFI*, AGFI*, TLI (or NTLI), and RNI (or CFI).

Dk, Mc, and GFI* are stand-alone indices that are monotonically related to model complexity. They are particularly useful when the intent is to compare the fits of a relatively small number of a priori models that have a well-defined theoretical rationale. Because these indices are monotonically related to model complexity, caution is needed in evaluating and selecting alternative models. For example, if the a priori models are nested, then each of these indices will automatically select the most complex model.

The RNI is an incremental index that is also monotonically related to model complexity. When used in conjunction with a suitably defined null model, RNI scales goodness of fit along a 0–1 continuum. An apparent advantage of the RNI is that "experience" suggests that RNIs > .90 or, more recently, > .95, constitute an "acceptable fit," although there is apparently no rigorous defense of this guideline. It is also possible to define the RNI in terms of models of intermediate complexity instead of the null and the saturated models. This is not particularly useful, however, because the RNIs are strictly additive. That is, the RNI based on two models of intermediate complexity is merely the difference in RNIs of the same two models that are defined in relation to the saturated and null models. Also, guidelines for interpreting acceptable fits are no longer appropriate if the RNI is not defined in relation to the null and saturated models.

Dk for the null model is a constant for any given sample, so that the RNI is a linear transformation of Dk in any particular sample and the difference in RNIs for any two models is a linear transformation of the difference in Dks. Hence the main advantage for the use of the RNI apparently rests on the suggestion that the absolute values of RNIs are easier to interpret than those of Dk. Given the wide use of implicit guidelines of appropriate cutoff values prompted by Bentler and Bonett's (1980) seminal article, and given its adoption as one of the two most frequently reported indices in SEM research (McDonald & Ho, 2002), it is disappointing that limited research has evaluated this guideline. Whereas we recommend the use of incremental fit indices like the RNI, this is based in large part on the unsubstantiated belief that guidelines used to evaluate their absolute size (e.g., guidelines such that only models with RNIs > .95 are "acceptable") are meaningful. Otherwise, there may be no advantage of the incremental indices over Dk or suitable transformations of it such as Mc.

The TLI and the AGFI* differ from the other recommended indices in that they contain a parsimony penalty for model complexity. The size of the penalty varies inversely with approximation discrepancy, so that it typically has limited effect on models with small Dks or "acceptable" RNIs greater than .95. These indices have the disadvantage of being undefined for the saturated model and may be unstable when the degrees of freedom is close to zero or when the sample size is very small. The TLI is an incremental index in that it varies along a 0 to 1 scale (except for sampling fluctuations) in which the endpoints are defined by the fit of a null model and a "perfect" fit. The parsimony penalty may, however, complicate the typical interpretation of incremental fit indices like the TLI. Thus, for example, the TLI may be maximized for a model of intermediate complexity so that TLIs are not strictly additive. The TLI and AGFI* indices are most useful in comparing the fit of a priori models that differ substantially in the number of estimated parameters. Particularly when degrees of freedom or N is small, these indices are likely to be unstable.

Both the parsimony indices and the information criterion indices are designed to penalize for model complexity. Their rationales are, however, very different. The parsimony indices incorporate a parsimony penalty for model complexity that does not vary with N, whereas the information criterion indices incorporate an estimation penalty that is a monotonically decreasing function of N to control for sampling fluctuations. Model parsimony may be an important criterion, particularly in the early stages of research when theory is still emerging. Whereas this is the explicit intent of the parsimony indices, the specific form of combining information on goodness of fit and parsimony embodied in the parsimony indices seems to lack a clear rationale and in some instances may be inappropriate. Although we do not recommend the routine use of parsimony indices (Appendix), reporting parsimony ratios along with other fit indices would be useful for facilitating integration of parsimony into the evaluation and selection of models.

Cudeck and Browne (1983) rejected the usefulness of the χ^2 test, and proposed the use of information criterion indices as an alternative indicator of fit. The sample size dependence of these indices is often seen as an important limitation (e.g., McDonald & Marsh, 1990), but alternative perspectives are plausible (Browne, 2000). Nevertheless, when N is small and the number of estimated parameters is large, it is important that sampling fluctuation is considered in the evaluation of models. This could be accomplished by presenting separate estimates of approximation discrepancy and estimation discrepancy implicit in the information criterion indices. Alternatively, it may be more useful to present confidence intervals about unbiased estimates of approximation discrepancy such as Dk as recommended by Steiger and Lind (1980; Steiger, 1990). In either case, we do not recommend that the estimates of approximation discrepancy and estimation discrepancy be combined in a single index that confounds the two sources of discrepancy.

Model evaluation inevitably requires a subjective integration of statistical and nonstatistical criteria, but an unbiased estimate of how well a model would fit population data should be one of these considerations. Other information such as parsimony, sampling fluctuations, comparative fit, interpretability, substantive issues, and theory should all be considered. We remain sceptical about indices that seek to transform the art of model evaluation into a set of mechanistic rules and absolute cutoff values that are uniformly applied in all situations. The relentless quest by GOF researchers for a "golden rule"—a GOF index with an absolute cutoff that "works" in all situations—remains as elusive as the even more widely celebrated quest for the fountain of youth, but limited success does not seem to extinguish continued attempts.

COMPLICATIONS IN THE PURSUIT
OF "GOOD" GOODNESS OF FIT

In this section we introduce some complications related to GOF testing that have
not been adequately resolved and may require further research.

Violations of Multivariate Normality and
Asymptotic Conditions

The development of GOF indices typically is largely based on ML estimation,
which assumes multivariate normality and asymptotic conditions. There is limited
work and no clear consensus about the behavior of indices in other conditions.
However, there has been considerable research into alternative estimation procedures and adjustments to the χ^2 test statistic in terms of statistical significance
testing (e.g., Nevitt, 2000). In analyses with nonnormal variables, rating scales
with few categories, or small to moderate sample sizes (i.e., nonasymptotic conditions), the assumptions underlying ML estimation are violated. This problem is
very common. For example, all of the 440 large-sample achievement and psychometric measures reviewed by Micceri (1989) were found to violate assumptions of
univariate normality. West, Finch, and Curran (1995) further warned that the violations would be more serious if more demanding tests of multivariate normality
were pursued.

One approach to this problem has been to develop alternative estimation procedures such as asymptotic distribution free (ADF; Browne, 1984) that do not have
distribution assumptions. However, because ADF involves the calculation of the
fourth-order sample moments, it yields asymptotically unbiased and consistent
estimates only with very large N (usually $N > 5,000$) and with small models (Hu,
Bentler, & Kano, 1992; Muthen & Kaplan, 1992). With moderate sample sizes
or large numbers of measured variables, ADF estimation has serious problems
including nonconvergence, improper solutions, and too frequently rejecting the
null hypothesis. Thus, ADF estimation is not particularly useful for most applied
research. Work by Yuan and Bentler (1997, 1998a, 1998b) has been directed at the
development of test statistics that are better behaved, but these tend to overreject
correct models for small to moderate Ns. Alternatively, Satorra and Bentler (SB)
(1988, 1994) developed corrected normal-theory test statistics (CHI SB), or substituted these into the formulas of other GOF indices (Nevitt & Hancock, 2000),
which have been found to be better than previous robust test statistics (Anderson,
1996; Chou, Bentler, & Satorra, 1991; Hu et al., 1992). Though CHI SB outperformed CHI ML at moderate sample sizes, CHI SB was still found to break down
with smaller sample sizes (Bentler & Yuan, 1999). It should also be noted that for
two nested models, the difference between two CHI SB-corrected test statistics

does not have a χ^2 distribution, although Satorra and Bentler (2001) recently provided additional procedures to calculate the SB scaled difference test. Whereas there is considerable research into the behavior of different estimation procedures and appropriate test statistics, it seems likely that applied researchers will continue to rely heavily on the robustness of ML procedures.

Although ML estimation continues to be the most popular estimation method, there have been systematic comparisons of the fit indices under different estimation methods (e.g., generalized least squares [GLS], weighted least squares [WLS], ADF). The efficiency of alternative estimators has been compared in terms of their behavior under true versus misspecified models, various sample sizes, and degree of nonnormality. The performances of ADF and WLS that aimed to handle nonnormal data have been particularly unimpressive unless huge sample sizes were used (Olsson, Foss, Troye, & Howell, 2000; Olsson, Troye, & Howell, 1999). Generally, the effects of estimators on GOF vary with the degree of misspecification and with the particular index being chosen. Though most of the indices were found to be affected by the estimator effect, some were affected more than the others (e.g., Ding, Velicer, & Harlow, 1995). For example, CFI, NFI, IFI, RFI, and RNI were found to be more affected by the choice of estimators than GFI, AGFI, Mc, TLI, and RMSEA (Ding et al., 1995; Fan et al., 1999; Fan & Wang, 1998; Hu & Bentler, 1998; La Du & Tanaka, 1989, 1995; Maiti & Mukherjee, 1991; Sugawara & MacCallum, 1993), and the effects generally tended to become more severe with increasing model misspecification. Other modeling techniques and estimation procedures have been developed by Muthen (2001; Muthen & Satorra, 1995) in an attempt to provide a general model in handling a mixture of dichotomous, ordered categorical and continuous measures as well as other associated growth and multilevel models. The related analyses have also been made possible through the provision of the commercially available software Mplus (Muthen & Muthen, 1998).

In summary, there appears to be no broadly accepted consensus about what alternative estimation procedures and adjustments to the ML χ^2 are practically and generally appropriate. Given this situation, it is likely that practice will continue to rely heavily on the robustness of the ML procedures. Although there has been some limited work to evaluate the behavior of GOF indices in relation to these different estimation procedures and adjustments (e.g., Hu & Bentler, 1998), this area of research is largely fragmentary and ad hoc, even in relation to the mathematical derivation of the appropriateness of different indices based on other than the ML χ^2 test statistic (e.g., the difference between two robust χ^2 variates typically does not have a χ^2 distribution). Based on our review, we recommend that GOF indices should be based on ML estimation. For this reason we have not systematically pursued the evaluation of GOF indices based on other estimation procedures, but note that this is a potentially important area for further research.

Emphasis on Multiple Steps and the Comparison of Alternative Models

Following Anderson and Gerbing (1988), McDonald (2000; also see McDonald & Ho, 2002), and many others, we find it useful to separate the overall model into two main parts: a measurement model and a structural path model. The measurement model consists of a set of p observed variables, typically multiple indicators of a smaller set of m latent variables, which are usually common factors; the relations between the observed variables and their latent constructs; and possibly covariances between measured variable uniqueness terms. The structural path model describes relations, some of which are hypothesized to be in some sense causal, between the latent variables. In special cases there may only be a measurement model (as in CFA studies) or, perhaps, only a structural path model (when there are not multiple indicators of the latent variables). Also consistent with McDonald and Ho, we assume that in many SEM applications the main substantive purpose is to evaluate support for a priori hypotheses about the structural model and that the evaluation of the measurement model should be subservient to this aim. Hence, it is reasonable to provide a separate evaluation of the fit of these two components of the overall structural model.

Although Anderson and Gerbing (1988) are typically interpreted as recommending a two-step approach, their actual recommendations are that researchers should develop a priori a detailed set of nested or partially nested models. Bentler (1990; Bentler & Bonett, 1980) noted the usefulness of testing a series of nested models $M_0, \ldots, M_i, \ldots, M_j, \ldots, M_k, \ldots, M_s$ in which M_0 is a suitably defined null model (e.g., a model in which each measured variable is an independent factor so that $\hat{\Sigma}_k$ is diagonal), M_s is the saturated model with zero degrees of freedom, and M_i, M_j, and M_k are models with positive degrees of freedom of intermediate complexity. Any two models are nested when the set of parameters estimated in the more restrictive model is a subset of the parameters estimated in the less restrictive model. Hence, it is possible to have a set of partially nested models in which, for example, two models (M_l, M_m) have no nesting relation to each other, but each is nested under some less restrictive model (M_k), and some more restrictive model (M_n) is nested under both of them.

Multitrait–Multimethod Data

Marsh (1989; also see Marsh & Bailey, 1991) and Widaman (1985) posited a partially nested set of competing models that reflect various combinations of correlated trait factors, uncorrelated trait factors, correlated method factors, uncorrelated method factors, and method effects as correlated uniquenesses. The comparison of the fit of models with and without method factors, for example, provides an index of the size of the method factor.

Multiple-Group Comparisons

Following seminal work by Jöreskog (1971), Byrne, Shavelson, and Muthen (1989), Marsh and Hocevar (1985; also see Marsh, 1994), and others developed a partially nested set of competing models to evaluate the invariance of parameter estimates across multiple groups. The partially nested sequence typically begins with a model with no invariance constraints and then moves to a model with the invariance of factor loadings, and ends with a model positing the invariance of all parameter estimates. If theoretical interest is solely in the extent to which interpretations based on an instrument generalize across multiple groups, the set of partially nested models may focus only on the measurement side of the model. If, however, theoretical interest is also in the structural path component of the model, then the set of nested models can also be expanded to include structural path coefficients. Marsh and Grayson (1994) demonstrated a related sequence of partially nested models to evaluate invariance over time based on multiple waves of responses from a single group of respondents on different occasions.

Higher Order Factor Structures

Higher order factor models are typically nested between two first-order models, one positing that first-order factors are completely uncorrelated and one positing that first-order factors are freely correlated (e.g., Marsh & Hocevar, 1985). Recognizing the critical importance of these two models, Marsh and Hocevar developed specific indices of fit in which the 0 to 1 continuum is defined by the model of uncorrelated first-order factors (the higher order conformatory factor analysis (HCFA) equivalent of the null model) and the model of freely correlated first-order factors (the HCFA equivalent of the saturated model). Between these extremes, it is typically possible to develop a partially nested set of a priori models that is intended to evaluate theoretical issues of importance to a particular application.

In summary, there is much potential value in developing an a priori set of partially nested models that is designed to interrogate the data in relation to specific issues of theoretical interest that may be idiosyncratic to a particular application. One model within the set may be the "target" model—the one that the researcher predicts will be "best." Nevertheless, the detailed comparison of viable competing models provides a much stronger basis for evaluating a particular model than does the attempt to argue that the fit of a "false" model (i.e., one whose χ^2 value is statistically significant) is sufficiently "good" in relation to some ultimately arbitrary guideline of what constitutes an "acceptable" fit. Although the focus of this approach is on the evaluation of multiple, competing a priori models, it also provides a potentially valuable structure for determining why there is a difference between two a priori models. In many cases, this can be determined by an appropriate evaluation of parameter estimates (e.g., the correlation between mathematics self-concept and self-esteem is higher for boys than for girls, so that factor covariances are not invariant over multiple gender groups). In other instances it may require the specification of a posteriori models designed to further interrogate the data in relation to particular issues raised by results from the a priori models (e.g., that physical appearance self-concept and body image measured by the same method do not constitute separate factors in a particular multitrait–multimethod (MTMM) study, so that a new model is posited in which these two factors are combined). Whereas there are always dangers associated with expost facto tinkering with a priori models, the inevitable pursuit of this task in many studies is usually more disciplined when conducted within the structured framework of a detailed set of partially nested models, than might otherwise be the case.

Under appropriate assumptions, the difference in χ^2s between two nested models has a χ^2 distribution and so can be tested in relation to statistical significance. Although Anderson and Gerbing (1988), Bentler (1990), and others focused extensively on tests of statistical significance between nested models, this significance test of the difference between two nested models has essentially the same strengths and weaknesses of the χ^2 test applied to any one model. For this reason, Bentler (1990) recommended that goodness of fit be scaled along a 0–1 continuum in which the endpoints are defined by M_0 and M_S, respectively. This provided a potentially useful frame of reference against which to evaluate the fit of any one model or the difference between a pair of models. Hence, we do not recommend undue reliance on the χ^2-difference test to evaluate differences in fit between competing models (for similar reasons that we do not recommend undue reliance on the χ^2 test to evaluate the fit of any one model). In particular, we find curious the apparent "current practice" of completely dismissing χ^2 tests of a single model but emphasizing the χ^2-difference test as the primary basis of comparing two nested models (also see discussion by Jöreskog & Sörbom, 1988; Raykov & Penev, 1998). The well-founded concerns about overreliance on the χ^2 test for a single model also apply to the χ^2-difference test. Thus, when applied to real data, a hypothesis that the less complex of two nested models is able to fit the data as well as the more-complex model is a priori false and would be shown to be false with a sufficiently large sample size. In this sense the researcher is still left the ultimately subjective decision of whether the improvement attributable to the more complex model justifies the rejection of the simpler model.

Importantly, this focus on multiple competing models opens a new and largely unexplored area of research for the evaluation of GOF indices. Whereas researchers who have relied on GOF indices have typically focused on the evaluation of fit for a single model, there has been surprisingly little work on the usefulness of GOF indices for the comparison of multiple competing models of the same data. Whereas exploration of these implications is clearly beyond the scope of this chapter, we note a few areas that might be important to pursue.

1. Information criterion indices, unlike most that we have considered, do focus specifically on the comparison of multiple competing models of the same data.

Nevertheless, the strengths and weaknesses of this approach noted earlier still apply in that the implicit penalty for model complexity is based on sampling error, such that it would typically lead to the selection of increasingly complex models as sample size increased. Even when choosing between multiple, competing models and recognizing the dangers of overinterpreting results based on modest sample sizes, we are uncomfortable with procedures that might result in radically different conclusions based on different sample sizes.

2. We distinguished between models that impose penalty functions and those that do not. This distinction has not been emphasized in the application of GOF indices previously, but is critically important when using these indices to compare models.

a. Indices that do not penalize model complexity and are additive provide a potentially useful metric for comparing the fit of competing models. For nested models, the more complex model must necessarily fit the data as well as or better than the less-complex models. Hence, the ultimately subjective evaluation of the "best" model must be based in part on whether the difference in fit between two competing models is sufficiently large to be substantively important or sufficiently small to be substantively trivial. Recent proposals by Raykov and Penev (1998) provide a basis for establishing confidence intervals for such differences, but these are ultimately based on sampling error rather than approximation discrepancy and the reasonableness of their proposed cutoff values that have not been broadly evaluated in practice (for further discussion, see Steiger et al., 1985).

b. Indices that penalize complexity are not additive in the sense that a less-complex model in a nested sequence can result in a better fit than a more-complex model. For some, this might be an unfortunate complication (e.g., see discussion by Hu & Bentler, 1998), whereas as for others it offers an alternative perspective to comparing the fit of competing models. Thus, for example, Marsh and Hau (1996) developed a set of decision rules for comparing nested models based on indices that incorporated a penalty for model complexity (approximation discrepancy) such that the less-complex model was preferred when its fit was as good or better than that of the more-complex model. Thus, for example, if the TLI associated with tests of invariance of factor loadings in a multiple-group comparison is higher than the TLI for the model with no invariance constraints, then there is support for the invariance of factor loadings. Although potentially useful, the appropriateness of using specific penalties embodied in different GOF indices for this purpose requires further exploration. For example, as noted earlier, the penalty function based on some GOF indices (e.g., the TLI) varies inversely with the level of misspecification such that the penalty function approaches zero as misspecification approaches zero. Whereas this may be a reasonable feature (in contrast, for example, to the parsimony indices), this also requires further research.

3. The comparison of multiple, competing a priori models will inevitably create conflicts between the strategy of model comparison and the evaluation of a single

model in relation to absolute cutoff values dictated by current practice. Thus, for example, the detailed comparison of trait and method effects in the partially nested set of MTMM models may provide a clear interpretation consistent with a priori predictions even when none of the models achieves an acceptable level of fit (e.g., TLI > .90 or .95). The resolution as to the relative importance of goodness of fit compared to support for substantive predictions based on a priori predictions is a key issue that has been given surprisingly little critical attention in the substantial literature on GOF indices and goes to the heart of the appropriate role of GOF in the broader context of model evaluation.

Rationales for Establishing Good-of-Fit Cutoff Values

How good is good enough? There is an implicit assumption in the GOF research that sufficiently high levels of GOF (higher than a prescribed cutoff value) are necessary for establishing the validity of interpretations of a model. Although nobody seriously argues that high GOF is sufficient for concluding that a model is valid, current practice seems to treat high GOF as if it were both necessary and sufficient. Clearly, a high GOF is not a sufficient basis for establishing the validity of interpretations based on the theory underlying the posited model. To make this clear, assume a population-generating model in which all measured variables were nearly uncorrelated. Almost any hypothesized model would be able to fit these data because most of the variance is in the measured variable uniqueness terms and there is almost no covariation to explain. In a nonsensical sense, a priori models positing one, two, three, or more factors would all be able to "explain" the data (as, indeed, would a "null" model with no factors). The problem with the interpretation of this apparently good fit would be obvious in an inspection of the parameter estimates in which all factor loadings and factor correlations were close to zero. Using a less extreme example, we can see that if theory predicts that a path coefficient should be positive whereas the observed results show that it is negative, high levels of GOF are not sufficient to argue for the validity of predictions based on the model. Without belaboring the point further, we conclude that high levels of GOF are not a sufficient basis for model evaluation.

Next we pursue the question of whether high levels of GOF are even a necessary condition for valid interpretations of the data. More specifically, in relation to existing practice, we question whether valid interpretations require that GOF indices meet current standards of acceptability in relation to prescribed cutoff values. In exploring this issue, we briefly digress to the somewhat analogous situation of evaluating reliability estimates, because GOF indices were historically developed as a measure of the reliability of a model (Tucker & Lewis, 1973). There is no universal consensus about what is an "acceptable" level of reliability, but there are at least three different approaches to pursuing this issue: ambit suggestions, a criterion reference approach, and a normative reference approach. Although there are ambit suggestions based on intuition and accepted wisdom that reliability should be at least .70 or at least .80, there is general agreement that—all other things being equal—more reliability is better. In an attempt to provide a more solid basis for establishing acceptable levels of reliability, Helmstadter (1964) described criterion and normed reference approaches to the issue. In the criterion reference approach, he argued that a reliable test should be able to discriminate between scores differing by one fourth of a standard deviation with an 80% probability. Using this standard, we have acceptable levels of reliability of roughly .50 for the comparison of two group means, .90 for group mean scores based on the same group on two occasions, .94 for two different individuals, and .98 for two scores by the same individual. Using a normed reference approach, Helmstadter reported that median reliabilities for different types of tests varied from as low as .79 (attitude scales), .84 (interest inventories), and .85 (personality tests) to as high as .92 (achievement batteries) .90 (scholastic ability), and .88 (aptitude batteries). However, in each of these different content areas, the highest reliabilities varied from .93 to .98. Thus, he concluded that reliability coefficients should be evaluated in relation to the purpose of a test, the content area, and the success of other instruments. In addition to establishing minimum conditions of acceptable reliability, it is also important to ensure that increased reliability is not achieved at the expense of construct validity. Thus, for example, elimination of indicators based solely on item statistics may distort the meaning of scores based on the remaining items, so that the increased reliability may be at the expense of construct validity.

Analogous to the situation in evaluating level of reliability, no one would argue that GOF has to be perfect (e.g., population misfit = 0) to be able to make valid interpretations on the basis of a model. There was a period before we understood the nature of what we were doing when researchers thought that they had to have nonsignificant chi-squares to make valid interpretations of their models. Faced with this impossible task, researchers resorted to counterproductive procedures such as limiting analyses to relatively small sample sizes so that there was not sufficient power to reject the null hypothesis. Fortunately, current practice has largely left behind those ideas and now indicates that incremental fit indices of .90 or even .95 are needed to make valid interpretations based on the model. Analogous to the reliability issue, we argue that all things being equal—which is rarely the case—it is better to have higher GOF indices, but that it is only when GOF indices approach some lower bound (GOF = 0) that valid interpretation of the models is necessarily precluded. Furthermore, some of the behaviors that researchers use to try to achieve GOF indices of .90 or .95 are likely to undermine valid interpretations of their model. From this perspective, the appropriate concern is what are acceptable levels of GOF. Again, using evaluation of reliability as a heuristic analogy, we can make ambit claims about what levels are required, we can establish well-defined criteria of what GOF indices are trying to accomplish and what levels of GOF are needed to satisfy these aims (a criterion reference approach), or we can look to see what levels of GOF are achieved in current "best" practice (a norm reference approach). It is our contention that the .90 and .95 criteria are masquerading as a criterion reference but mostly represent ambit claims.

Analogous to the situation in reliability, rules of thumb about acceptable levels of GOF (e.g., incremental fit indices $>.9$) have traditionally been ambit claims based on intuition and accepted wisdom. Is it reasonable or even desirable to make the cutoff values more definitive? Whereas we agree that a complete lack of GOF precludes valid interpretations of the data in relation to a priori predictions, it is unlikely that any universal cutoff values for GOF indices would be appropriate for all applications. In support of this claim we review some attempts to establish appropriate cutoff values for GOF indices in relation to criterion and normed reference perspectives.

A Criterion Reference Rationale for Cutoff Values Based on Hu and Bentler (1999)

There has been some systematic research attempting to validate GOF indices from a criterion reference approach. Marsh and Balla (1994; Marsh (Marsh et al., 1996; Marsh & Hau, 1996)) constructed a nested series of alternative models that systematically varied in terms of misspecification (and overparametrization) and evaluated GOF indices in terms of how sensitive they were in reflecting misspecification. They did not, however, systematically evaluate specific cutoff values. More recently, Hu and Bentler (1998, 1999) argued that GOF testing has focused too much on the evaluation of true population models. They proposed that absolute cutoff values for GOF indices could be established in relation to an objective criterion of sensitivity to model misspecification. Due to the importance of this issue to this chapter and the influence of the Hu and Bentler's (1998, 1999) articles on current practice, we review this research in detail.

An important basis for the popularity of GOF indices is the elusive promise of absolute cutoff values—a golden rule that will allow researchers to decide whether a model adequately fits the data—one that has broad generality across different conditions and different sample sizes. Because of the substantial relation between N and the ML χ^2 test for even modestly misspecified models, researchers have discarded the χ^2 as an appropriate index of fit (other than in simulation studies). As emphasized by McDonald and Marsh (1990) and many others, the traditional cutoff values (e.g., incremental fit indices $>.90$) amounted to little more than rules of thumb based largely on intuition and have little statistical justification. Hu and Bentler (1999; also see Hu & Bentler, 1998) addressed this issue in a highly influential study that has had a substantial effect on current practice. This effect has been twofold in that it is substantially responsible for providing an apparently much stronger empirical basis for the validity of decisions based on cutoff values and proposed substantially more stringent cutoff values (i.e., raised the bar) for an acceptable fit (e.g., Bryne, 2001).

In addressing the "cutoff" problem, Hu and Bentler argued that:

> An adequate cutoff criterion should result in a minimum Type I error rate (i.e., the probability of rejecting the null hypothesis when it is true) and Type II error rate (the probability of accepting the null hypothesis when it is false) (Hu & Bentler, 1999, p. 5).

In pursuing this issue, the seven best GOF indices recommended in earlier research (Hu & Bentler, 1998) were evaluated in relation to traditional and new cutoff criteria. In the Hu and Bentler (1999) study there were two different population-generating CFA models—a simple structure (five indicators for each of three correlated factors) and a complex structure that differed only in that there were three additional cross-loadings in addition to the 15 factor loadings in the simple structure. Hence, the simple population-generating structure had 33 nonzero parameter estimates, whereas the complex model had 36 nonzero parameter estimates. For each model type, one "true" and two underparametrized, misspecified models were tested. For the misspecified models evaluated in relation to the simple structure, one or two of the factor correlations were fixed to be zero. For the complex structure, the misspecified models had one or two of the three (nonzero) cross-loadings fixed to be zero. The design also included seven distributional conditions and six sample sizes.

The specific paradigm proposed by the Hu and Bentler (1998, 1999) is a traditional hypothesis-testing scenario in which values of the best GOF indices were used to accept or reject models known a priori to be true or false in relation to the population-generating model. Unfortunately, the researchers did not include tests of statistical significance based in the ML χ^2 test statistic as a basis of comparison for the different GOF indices. A long history of research shows that the ML χ^2 does very well in this situation and would apparently have outperformed all of the GOF indices in relation to the criteria proposed by Hu and Bentler. This implies either that we should discard all GOF indices and focus on test statistics or that the paradigm used to evaluate GOF indices by Hu and Bentler was inappropriate. In fact, the reason why the χ^2 test statistic is not a good GOF index is precisely the reason why it would perform so well in the hypothesis-testing situation proposed by Hu and Bentler. The expected value of the ML χ^2 varies directly with N for misspecified models. Whereas this may be undesirable in terms of evaluating approximation discrepancy, it is precisely the type of behavior that is appropriate for optimization of decision rules in a traditional hypothesis-testing situation.

There is, however, an apparent problem in their application of the traditional hypothesis-testing approach. To illustrate this problem, consider, for example, the results for RNI = .95 with the simple structure for small ($N \leq 250$), medium ($N = 500$), and large ($N \geq 1,000$) N values (Hu & Bentler, 1999, Table 2, p. 13). Ideally, one might want a decision rule that was reasonably consistent across N for acceptance of the true model, but the results show that the true model was incorrectly rejected 25%, 3.6%, and 0.1% of the time at small, medium, and large N, respectively. Ideally, one might want false models to be more likely to be rejected when N increases, whereas the actual pattern of results was exactly the opposite. The least misspecified model was correctly rejected 47.2%, 30.1%, and 4.7% of the time at small, medium, and large N respectively. For the seriously misspecified model, the corresponding values were 59.8%, 45.7%, and 19.4%, respectively. Hence, according to the recommended decision rule for the RNI, the likelihood of correctly rejecting a false model is substantial for small N and very small for large N. Clearly, this is not a desirable behavior for a decision rule, and, importantly, this is not an isolated example. For all of the recommended cutoff values for each of the seven GOF indices, the probability of correctly rejecting a false model is lower for large N than for small N for at least one of the misspecified models.

The explanation for this aberrant behavior of the decision rules recommended by Hu and Bentler (1999) lies in the inappropriate use of an estimate of population approximation discrepancy—an estimate of effect size that does not vary with N—as a test statistic. Appropriately behaved test statistics applied to false models should vary with N so that the probability of correctly rejecting a false model increases with increasing N. Why then does the probability of correctly rejecting a false model *decrease* with N so often in the Hu and Bentler study? The answer lies in the combination of only slightly misspecified models and the use of cutoff values that differ from—are somewhat more misspectified than—the expected values for the true model. Imagine, for example a "slightly misspecified" model in which the expected value of RNI is .975 with a cutoff value .95. Based on population parameters, this model should not be rejected in relation to a cutoff value of .95. Due to sampling error, this model will be rejected more frequently for sufficiently small N, less frequently for a moderate N, rarely for sufficiently large N, and not at all for population values. Conversely, suppose that the misspecified model has "large" misspecification, with expected RNI of .925, in relation to a "critical value" of .95. Here, as we increase N, "power" does increase, even though the Type I error rate is "uncontrolled," decreasing as N increases. This perspective implies that many of the misspecified models considered by Hu and Bentler provided a sufficiently good fit to be acceptable, even according to their new, more stringent cutoff criteria. Their slightly misspecified models should *not* have been rejected based on population values of approximation discrepancy that are supposed to be the basis of the GOF indices considered by Hu and Bentler (1999). In this sense, rejection of these slightly misspecified models constituted a Type I error (incorrectly rejecting an "acceptable" model) rather than a correct decision. Hence, the logic of the Hu and Bentler's evaluation of decision rules seems to be flawed in relation to the cutoff criteria that they proposed (for further discussion, see Marsh, Hau, & Wen, 2004).

All GOF indices considered by Hu and Bentler were specifically designed to reflect approximation discrepancy at the population level and to be independent of sample size. However, Hu and Bentler's (1999) approach to evaluating these indices used a hypothesis-testing approach that is based substantially on estimation discrepancy and is primarily a function of sampling fluctuations. Hence, there is a logical inconsistency between the intended purposes of the GOF indices and the approach used to establish cutoff values. The only GOF indices that clearly embody this principle are the family of information criterion indices that Hu and Bentler (1998) rejected because they were sample size dependent.

Four of the recommended indices evaluated by Hu and Bentler (1999) were incremental fit indices. By assigning the same cutoff values for each of these indices, there is an implicit assumption that each index varies along a similar 0–1 continuum. Earlier discussion of these indices—particularly the comparison of the TLI (which penalizes for model complexity) and the RNI (which does not penalize for model complexity)—shows that this is not the case (also see results presented by Hu & Bentler, 1998). This problem is also evident in results by Hu and Bentler (1999). To the extent that the percentage of rejections for a misspecified model decreases with N, the extent of misspecification must be sufficiently small that the population-approximating model should be classified as "acceptable." For the TLI cutoff value of .95, both of the "simple" misspecified models were apparently "acceptable," whereas both the complex models were apparently unacceptable. For the RNI cutoff value of .95, only the most misspecified complex model was unacceptable. For each of the five cutoff values evaluated by Hu and Bentler (1999), the percentage of rejection for misspecified models was consistently higher for the TLI than for the RNI. Thus, for example, for large N the cutoff of .90 resulted in 97.5% rejections for the most misspecified complex model for TLI, but only 19.7% rejection for the RNI. These results are consistent with earlier discussion in this chapter indicating that misspecified models typically had systematically lower TLIs than RNIs (or CFIs). In a related issue, MacCallum and Hong (1997) demonstrated that the mapping of recommended cutoff values for simulated data with known levels of population misfit based on RMSEA, GFI, and AGFI resulted in highly inconsistent conclusions.

In the comparison of their behavior, each of the seven indices was quantitatively different in relation to the percentage rejection of true and misspecified models, whereas the SRMR was qualitatively different from the others. In particular, for six of the seven indices, the two complex misspecified models led to higher percentage of rejection than the two simple misspecified models. In contrast, the SRMR led to much higher rejections of the simple misspecified model than the complex misspecified model. For example, for a 0.10 cutoff value and large N, SRMR led to 100% rejection of both simple misspecified models and less than 1% rejection of both complex misspecified models. As concluded by Hu and Bentler, this implies that SRMR is clearly sensitive to different sorts of misspecification than the other GOF indices. Although Hu and Bentler evaluated different types of misspecification, most parameters in their simulated data were known to be equal to zero in the population-generating model and all estimated parameters perfectly reflected the population-generating model with the exclusion of a few key parameter estimates that led to the models being misspecified. Although relevant for purposes of evaluating the behavior of GOF indices in relation to varying degrees of misspecification, the misspecified models studied by Hu and Bentler are clearly not representative of typical application. The results show that different decision rules do not generalize very well across even the two types of misspecified models considered by Hu and Bentler (1998). However, despite clear warnings in relation to this concern by Hu and Bentler (1998), current practice seems to have incorporated their new recommended guidelines of acceptable fit without the appropriate cautions, even though these guidelines were based on simulation studies in which only a very limited range of misspecification was considered. Apparently consistent with limitations recognized by Hu and Bentler, it seems that much more research with a wider variety of different types of misspecified models and under different conditions (e.g., varying N) is needed before we adequately understand the behavior of rules of thumb or decision rules based on absolute cutoff values.

Hu and Bentler (1998) specifically noted that they were only concerned about the evaluation of the goodness of fit of a single model in isolation, not the comparative fit of alternative, nested models. This is unfortunate in that their data apparently demonstrated that, on average, all the GOF indices were very good at distinguishing between the more- and less-misspecified models within each misspecification (simple and complex) type. Whereas there might be minor differences in the performances of different indices at small N and under different distributional conditions, the indices are apparently better at distinguishing between degrees of misspecification than providing a golden rule about the acceptability of a particular model or whether the extent of difference in misspecification between two models is substantively meaningful. Although disappointing to researchers in quest of a golden rule, we contend that interpretations of the degree of misspecification should ultimately be evaluated in relation to substantive and theoretical issues that are likely to be idiosyncratic to a particular study.

In summary, there are important logical problems underlying the rationale of the new cutoff values proposed by Hu and Bentler (1998). The intent of the GOF indices was to provide an alternative to traditional hypothesis testing approaches based on traditional test statistics (e.g., ML χ^2). However, Hu and Bentler specifically evaluated the GOF indices in relation to a traditional hypothesis-testing situation in which the ML χ^2 test (if it had been considered) would have outperformed all of the GOF indices. Importantly, many of the misspecified models considered by Hu and Bentler provided a sufficiently good fit in relation to population approximation discrepancy that they should have been classified as "acceptable" models even according to the more stringent cutoff values proposed by Hu and Bentler. Hence, rejection of these "acceptable" models should have constituted a Type I error (incorrectly rejecting an "acceptable" model). Whereas Hu and Bentler recommended the same cutoff values for different indices (e.g., the TLI and the RNI), their results, consistent with previous research, showed that TLI values for misspecified models were systematically lower than those for the RNI. Based on only two types of misspecification (simple and complex), there were quantitative and qualitative differences in the behaviors of different GOF indices. This implies that decision rules based on any one situation are unlikely to have broad generalizability across the different types of misspecification likely to be encountered in SEM application. In contrast to decisions based on comparisons with a golden rule, all of the indices seemed to be more effective at identifying differences in misspecification based on a comparison of nested models. Consistent with our earlier discussion, we interpret the Hu and Bentler (1999) results to indicate that rigid decision rules about the acceptability of SEM models based on GOF indices are clearly premature and unlikely to ever provide a golden rule that is a viable alternative to good judgment based on a careful evaluation of the results.

A Normed Reference Rationale for Cutoff Values

Attempts have been limited in validating GOF cutoff values in relation to a norm reference criterion. However, Marsh (2001; SEMNET@UA1vm.ua.edu; also see Marsh, Hau, & Wen 2004) argued that current cutoff values of .90 (and particularly .95) were inappropriate in relation to values likely to be achieved in "best practice." Specifically, he posted the following email to all members of the SEMNET:

> Let me begin with an ambit claim: Conventional CFA goodness of fit criteria are too restrictive when applied to most multifactor rating instruments. It is my experience that it is almost impossible to get an acceptable fit (e.g., CFI, RNI, TLI > .9; RMSEA < .05) for even "good" multifactor rating instruments when analyses are done at the item level and there are multiple factors (e.g., 5–10), each measured with a reasonable number of items (e.g., at least 5–10/per scale) so that there are at least 50 items overall. If this is the case, then I argue that "conventional" rules of thumb about acceptable fit are too restrictive (even though there has been a recent push for even stricter standards). Researchers seem very inventive about ways to get around this apparently inherent problem with conventional fit criteria. Unfortunately, at least some of these behaviors might be counterproductive in terms of good measurement practice (e.g., using only two indicators per factor). In response to this claim, I have twice invited the collective membership of the SEMNET listserve to provide me with any published counter-examples to my claim.[1]

Although a number of interesting points were raised in response to this "ambit claim," no one offered a published counterexample in which any well-established

[1]This claim by Marsh was based on the incremental fit indexes computed with the minimum fit function chi-square, the usual ML chi-square that had been the basis of most research at the time the claim was made. However, in version of 8.54 of LISREL, the default is the normal theory weighted least-squares chi-square (called C2). It appears that incremental fit indexes are systematically higher when based on the normal theory weighted least-squares chi-square—due in large part to substantial difference in the computation of the values for the null model. Hence, this claim and guidelines based on the usual ML chi-square (called C1 in LISREL, version 8.54) may no longer apply to indexes based on the normal theory weighted least-squares chi-square (i.e., C2).

existing instrument with 5 to 10 factors each assessed with 5 to 10 items/scale so that there were at least 50 items was able to achieve even minimally acceptable conventional standards of fit. On this basis it is at least reasonable to conclude that in relation to actual practice, the "old" conventional standards of fit are rarely met. Indeed, many of the large number of responses to Marsh's email argued that support for Marsh's claim merely reflects that there are few, if any existing acceptable instruments. Indeed, the prevailing sentiment was an extreme reluctance to modify existing (new) standards simply because they are not readily obtainable in practice. A substantial tangent to this discussion questioned whether it was even reasonable or appropriate to expect a factor to be represented by more than 2 or 3 items (or, perhaps, more than a single item). Our response is that it may be unreasonable to have more than 2 or 3 items per factor if researchers hope to achieve GOF indices of .95, but that it is highly desirable if researchers want to have measures with good construct validity. As was the case when researchers resorted to counterproductive procedures to achieve nonsignificant χ^2 values when that was the accepted standard of a good fit, it appears that researchers are again resorting to dubious practice to achieve inappropriately high GOF standards.

In conclusion, existing cutoff values of GOF indices are based substantially on ambit claims. There is limited attempt to provide either objective criteria against which to validate current practice or justification for the claim that the same cutoff values are broadly generalizable across all SEM studies. It appears that there are few if any examples of rating instruments with 5 to 10 factors each assessed with 5 to 10 items/scale that are able to achieve even minimally acceptable conventional standards of fit. To insist that the validity of all such research is dubious in relation to questionable cutoff values applied in SEM research seems premature at best and runs the risk of further marginalizing SEM research and the contribution that it can make to mainstream psychological and social science research.

An alternative conclusion is that SEM researchers have placed too much emphasis on goodness-of-fit indices treating them as pseudo-tests of statistical significance, pseudo-objectifying interpretations by specifying cutoff values, trying to establish absolute pseudo-criteria of fit that are appropriate under all circumstances, misinterpreting them as pseudo-tests of underlying theory, and focusing on global measures of fit when our focus should be on specific components of the model (e.g., variance explained in critical outcome variables, specific parameter estimates that are central to theoretical predictions, particularly large discrepancies, which indicate potential problems in the ability of the model to fit the data). In line with this perspective, Kaplan (2000) noted that econometricians use similar statistical procedures, but have never put anywhere near as much emphasis on goodness of fit as have psychometricans. In a related perspective, McDonald and Ho (2002) argued for the need to separate fit for the measurement model and the structural model and suggested that the only metacriterion we can use to evaluate fit is the principle that a model is acceptable if the discrepancies are too small to support a more complex model. They concluded that no global index of fit (together with a criterion for its acceptability) could substitute for a detailed examination of the discrepancies in relation to theory and common sense.

THE ROLE OF GOODNESS-OF-FIT EVALUATION IN THE BROADER CONTEXT OF SCIENTIFIC EVALUATION

In this final section, we address the following question: In evaluating a particular scientific application, what role does GOF play? A particular piece of scientific work is, one hopes original, creative, multifeatured, and probably complex. In evaluating its contribution, a single judgment seems somehow to be called for: Is this a "good" piece of research, the conclusions or implications of which we should allow to alter our understanding or perception of the phenomenon under investigation?

There are no golden rules for such a judgement, and each of us has the right to differ in our evaluations. Ultimately, such judgements are possibly even aesthetic. Indeed, it seems important and healthy for the social and organic practice of science that members of the scientific community span the spectrum of evaluative perspectives, some being positive and forward looking, with others being critical and more difficult to please. Presumably in those scientific areas where a phenomenon under investigation clearly asserts or presents itself, our evaluations will reach some sort of consensus, the evidence becoming overwhelming by almost anyone's standards. Even then, the history of science is not free of cases where progress has occurred with the overturning of strong consensus. This act of evaluation is personal, and should not be proscribed:

> Hitherto the user has been accustomed to accept the function of probability theory laid down by the mathematicians; but it would be good if he could take a larger share in formulating himself what are the practical requirements that the theory should satisfy in application. (E. S. Pearson, 1947)

> I believe each scientist and interpreter of scientific results bears ultimate responsibility for his own concepts of evidence and his own interpretation of results. (A. Birnbaum, 1962)

> We have the duty of formulating, of summarizing, and of communicating our conclusions, in intelligible form, in recognition of the right of *other* free minds to utilize them in making *their own* decisions. (R. A. Fisher, 1955)

> Principles for reporting analyses using structural equation modelling are reviewed ... so that readers can exercise independent critical judgement. (R. P. McDonald and M. R. Ho, 2002)

In such a context, the social sciences have not had a particularly proud history. Disquiet with the significance test orthodoxy that has dominated research methods in the social sciences since the 1940–1950s has a long but ineffective history (Carver, 1978; Gigerenzer et al., 1989; Meehl, 1978; Rozeboom, 1960). It recently came to something of a head (Cohen, 1994; Schmidt, 1996). The issues raised there might still not have been central (Grayson, 1998), and the outcome of this disquiet seems unclear, although the call for the "banning" of the significance test met the fate it arguably deserved. One worrying feature of this activity is the orthodoxy and institutionalization that this history reveals, both in the way that universal golden rules have undoubtedly been used in the past as a substitute for the difficult task of personal evaluation, and in the reactive attempt to replace them with other golden rules proscribing how we should evaluate scientific applications and evidence.

In the present SEM context, the role of GOF indices is not dissimilar to the unhealthy role that significance testing has played (and is still playing?). This GOF index versus that GOF index, this level of cut-point versus that one, parsimony or not—all these discussions seem predicated on a belief that we can find a good golden rule in the SEM area that can be used to tell us whether to believe that a particular application provides good or poor scientific evidence about the phenomenon being studied and our latest theoretical speculations. In this sense, it is a saving grace in the SEM area that the area is unsettled. Were it to become settled, there appears to be no shortage of users ready to blindly adopt expert-recommended numerical criteria in lieu of deeper scientific evaluation, and no shortage of journal editors who would advise, or even insist, that they do so.

If we accept that the desire for orthodoxy and golden rules is itself a problem in the supposedly creative scientific enterprise, then the temptation to use GOF indices as a technical panacea (in much the same way as the significance test has been used), a panacea to the difficult and aesthetic judgment of research applications, then we can ask: Where do GOF indices fit in the bigger picture of scientific evaluation? What other aspects of a scientific application than data-fit might play a role in evaluation?

From this perspective, there are many other aspects than GOF that should play a role in the evaluation a piece of scientific research.

Explained Variability

An SEM model can have perfect fit (ideal GOF index), yet still be a very poor scientific model in terms of scientific explanation. For example, a model with a "structural" portion where the disturbance terms' variances are relatively large (or where the "measurement" portion has very large uniqueness-or-specific variances) may well fit the current data perfectly, but it need not be a good scientific model. In regression, and path analysis, a small R^2 is an indicator that all relevant predictors have not been taken into account, and we would not expect such models to hold up in further research in other contexts, because they are seemingly incomplete. That is, scientific evaluation of unexplained variance can be as important a criterion as GOF in some applications.

GOF Versus Scientific Sense

The essential role of GOF indices is in relation to the basic scientific principle that data will disprove a wrong model. An analogy might be made with the psychometric concepts of reliability and validity. Whereas the complete unreliability of a measure implies it can have no validity, high reliability does not ensure validity. Similarly, a high GOF does not entail the scientific plausibility of such a model. Indeed, it can be misleading. Consider the following multiple linear regression example (a simple SEM). In a particular population, suppose we seek to understand the determinants of some y variable. We arbitrarily select several x predictors, with no scientific rationale whatsoever. We can then fit a perfect regression equation $y = E(y|x) + r$, which may even be linear, $y = \beta'x + r$, with corresponding perfect GOF to the y data. But it will be devoid of scientific meaning.

Data, Model, Theory, Truth

There is a wide range of views and philosophies about just what it is we are attempting to achieve when we "do science." They range from the most instrumentalist (operationalist? positivist?) perspective, that we are simply trying to predict "data" (what data?), to the almost metaphysical view that we are trying to uncover the "truth" in terms of scientific laws and their underlying dynamics. If one adopts the former stance, then GOF would seem to be a more important criterion (possibly the only one) than if one adopts the latter view. As is well discussed by Roberts and Pashler (2000), other evaluative criteria emerge when one perceives the task of science as more than simply "data" and its sterile prediction:

1. How well do the data in question challengingly test the scientific theory under investigation?
2. How easily could alternative scientific theories account for the same data?

The role of "models" in this context can be very slippery. The word "model" has connotations ranging from "a good-fitting account of the current data" alone, to—following Popper—"the latest approximation to the truth, a truth that we seek to approach by further challenging our latest model with new data designed to refute this latest model if wrong." To different researchers, and in different applications, a "model" can be anything from a complete end in itself, to quantitative instantiation of some richer theory that is the prime scientific concern. The apparent confusion—referred to earlier with regard to the Hu and Bentler (1999) approach—between a misspecified model and a "good enough" model (e.g., RNI in excess of .95) may well reflect the importance of this issue.

Exploratory Versus Confirmatory

In the exploratory, model/theory formulation stages of research, typically a broad theoretical context would not exist, and GOF alone might well be the major aspect of evaluation, even for "realist" scientists who believe in an ultimate empirical truth. The same researcher with the same attitudes to the task of science might well relegate GOF to a secondary status as a criterion in evaluating research at a later (dis-) confirmatory stage, where other theoretical concerns achieve much higher salience.

Parsimony

The role of the concept of parsimony in GOF indices seemed far stronger than might be warranted. Perhaps parsimony is a relevant concern in a very exploratory stage of research in some area, where "all other considerations are equal" simply because there are few "other considerations" as yet. However, this situation would seem to be rare. The belief that a simpler model is better in part because it is simpler is not easily sustained from a realist perspective. The better model is the true model, and whether it is simpler is an empirical issue of fact; why one might expect it actually to be simpler in the first place is odd.

Parsimony adjusting indiscriminately for each parameter seems very superficial, in that there would hardly be an SEM application where each parameter plays an equal role in the overall scientific evaluation. In many applications, there would be a majority of parameters not necessarily of main scientific interest that nonetheless have to be estimated: for instance, a large measurement model imposed on a small structural model that is the main current scientific focus, the latter having far fewer but far more important parameters to be estimated. If the model is too complex to interpret, then we have not gained real understanding. However, a similar concern exists with models that are too simplistic.

Global Identification and Equivalent Models

McDonald and Ho (2002) raised the issue of global identification. This seems to be a fundamental issue in evaluation from the wider scientific perspective. If there are several SEM models that fit current data to the same satisfactory level of GOF, then it would seem quite likely (almost certain) that they would have quite different scientific interpretations, interpretations that would be inconsistent. Whereas the task of investigating identification of a model with the current data structure at hand will be highly specific to each distinct and highly structured SEM application, some feeling for the significance of this issue can be gained from the history of exploratory factor analysis (EFA). From the current perspective, EFA models are SEM models, with some identification constraints (the transformation of factors is constrained, specific factors are constrained to be orthogonal). Anderson and Rubin (1956) provided conditions sufficient to ensure global identification when the number of indicators p is more than twice the number of factors q: $p \geq 2q + 1$; however, the conditions where we know that multiple solutions do exist are not known (the conditions whose negations are the necessary conditions for global identification). Even these sufficient conditions do not apply when $p = 2q$, and Wilson and Worcester (1939) provided instances where two quite different solutions existed on the same six-indicator data set for three-factor EFA models. That is, in the EFA case, the issue of global identification is still not understood well (see Bekker & Ten-Berge, 1997). It is therefore quite possible that many reported EFA analyses have exhibited one empirical interpretation of the data where others, with identical GOF, exist with quite different empirical implications. With such a widely used method as EFA, we simply do not yet know how to unambiguously demonstrate that the data structures we use have a single empirical FA interpretation. It may well be that the EFA global identification problem is technically far more difficult to address than is the same problem in other more highly constrained SEM models, but this issue is seldom addressed or discussed in applications, and it goes to the heart of the science we are attempting to perform. The numerical algorithms we use to fit our SEM models will usually warn us when local identification fails, but will provide us with a solution when local identification pertains, a solution that may not be unique.

CONCLUSION

We discussed some of the issues and criteria that a researcher may want to contemplate when evaluating a particular SEM application. There may be other issues. Other researchers in forming their own evaluation of the same application may apply different weights to the same spectrum of issues, and the same researcher may shift his or her evaluative style in relation to a different SEM application. Against this background, overemphasis on any GOF statistic as the primary index of "good research" and a "good model" seems unwarranted.

APPENDIX: GOODNESS-OF-FIT INDICES

Absolute indices

A. Fit-function-based indices

1. Fit Function (FF)[A,L] Minimum fit Function Value[L], FMIN[A].
   $$FF = CHI / (N - 1)$$

2. Likelihood ratio $LHR = e^{-1/2FF}$.

3. CHI[A,E,L] Chi-square[E]; CMIN[A], minimum fit function chi-square[L]:
   $$CHI = \chi^2 = tr(E^{-1}S - I) - \log | E^{-1} S | = (N - 1)FF$$

4. PVALUE[A,E,L] p value of chi-square[E], P[A,L]

5. CHI/DF[A] Chi-square/df ratio, CMIN/DF[A] (AMOS): CHI/DF = CHI/df

B. Noncentrality-based indices

6. Dk[a,b] Rescaled noncentrality parameter (McDonald & Marsh, 1990):
   $$Dk = FF - df/(N - 1) = (CHI - df)/(N - 1)$$

7. PDF[A,L,b] Population discrepancy function (Dk normed to be nonnegative) (Steiger & Lind, 1980), F0[A,L]:
   $$PDF = MAX[FF - df/(N - 1), 0] = MAX[(CHI - df)/(N - 1), 0]$$

8. Mc[E,a] Measure of centrality (McDonald, 1989), CENTRA, noncentrality index, McDonald fit index (MFI)[E]:
   $$Mc = exp(-Dk/2) = exp\{-(CHI - df)/[2(N - 1)]\}$$

9. NCP[A,L] Noncentrality parameter (Steiger, 1980; Steiger et al., 1985):
   $$NCP = (CHI - df)$$

C. Error of approximation indices

10. RMSEA[A,L,b,c] Root mean square error of approximation, RMS (Steiger & Lind, 1980; Steiger, 1989):
    $$RMSEA = SQRT[PDF/df] = SQRT \{MAX[(CHI - df)/(N - 1), 0]/df\}$$

11. MSEA[b] Mean square error of approximation (unnormed version of RMSEA):
    $$MSEA = Dk/df = (CHI - df)/[(N - 1)df]$$

12. RMSEAP[A,E,L] Root mean square error test of close fit (Browne & Cudeck, 1993), RMSEA < 0.05[L], PCLOSE[A]

13. RMR[A,E,L] Root mean residual (Jöreskog & Sörbom, 1988):
    $RMR = \{2\Sigma_{ij}(s_{ij} - e_{ij})^2/[p(p + 1)]\}^{1/2}$, where s_{ij} and e_{ij} are elements in S and E, respectively.

14. SRMR[E,L] Standardized root mean residual (Jöreskog & Sörbom, 1988), SRMS, STDRMR: $SRMR = SQRT \{2 \Sigma(s_{ij} - \sigma_{ij})^2/[p(p + 1)]\}$, where $s_{ij} - \sigma_{ij}$ are the residuals for the sample and fitted correlation matrix.

D. Information indices

15. ECVI[A,L] Expected Cross Validation Index (Cudeck & Browne, 1983), CAK.
    $$ECVI = 1/(N - 1)(AIC) = CHI/(N - 1) + 2k/(N - 1)$$
    $$= FF + 2K/(N - 1)$$
    where AIC is the Akaike information criterion

16. Ck[a] Cross-validation index (an alternative form of ECVI) (Browne & Cudeck, 1989): Ck = CHI/(N - 1) + 2K/(N - p - 2)

18. AIC[A,E,L] Akaike information criterion for model (Akaike, 1974, 1987):
    $$AIC = CHI + 2K = CHI + p(p + 1) - 2 df$$

19. AIC* Rescaled AIC (Steiger, 1989). AIC* = FF + 2K/N

20. CAIC[A,E,L] Consistent Akaike information criterion for model (Bozdogan, 1987).
    $$CAIC = CHI + (1 + lnN)K = CHI + (1 + lnN)[0.5p(p + 1) - df]$$

21. SC Rescaled Schwartz Index (Steiger, 1989): SC = FF +(K × ln(N))/N

(Continued)

22. BCC^A	Brown–Cudeck criterion (Brown & Cudeck, 1989):
	BCC = CHI + $2kp(N - 1)(p + 3)/[p(N - p - 2)(p + 3)]$
23. BIC^A	Baysian information criterion, Schwarz criterion (Schwarz, 1978):
	BIC = $-2 \log L + p \log n$ = CHI + $K \ln\{N[0.5p(p + 1)]\}$
24. MECVI^A	Model expected cross-validation index (Browne & Cudeck, 1989; Arbuckle & Wothke, 1999):
	MECVI = $[1/(N - 1)]$ (BCC)

E. Goodness-of-fit indices

25. GFI^{A,E,L}	Goodness-of-fit index (Jöreskog & Sörbom, 1988), Gamma, LISREL GFI^E:
	GFI = $1 - \text{tr}[(\hat{\Sigma}_k^{-1}S - I)^2]/\text{tr}[(\hat{\Sigma}_k^{-1}S)^2]$, where S and $\hat{\Sigma}_k$ are the sample and fitted covariance matrices, respectively
26. GFI^{*c}	Unbiased goodness-of-fit index (Steiger, 1989), Gamma hat:
	GFI$^* = p/(2Dk + p) = p/[2(CHI - df)/(N - 1) + p]$
27. AGFI^{A,E,L}	Adjusted goodness of fit index (Jöreskog & Sörbom, 1988), LISREL AGFI^E:
	AGFI = $1 - [p(p + 1)/2df](1 - GFI)$
28. AGFI^{*c}	Unbiased adjusted goodness-of-fit index (Steiger, 1989):
	AGFI$^* = 1 - [p(p + 1)/2df](1 - GFI^*)$

H. Other indices

29 CN^{A,L}	Critical N (Hoelter, 1983); Hoelter index^A (AMOS):
	CN = $\{[z_{\text{crit}} + (2 \times df - 1)^{1/2}]^2/[2 \times CHI/(N - 1)]\} + 1$, where z_{crit} is the critical value from a normal curve table for a given probability level.

Incremental (relative) indices

F. Incremental indices (no correction for model complexity)

30. RNI^{a,b}	Relative noncentrality index (McDonald & Marsh, 1990), unbiased relative fit index (URFI):
	RNI = $1 - Dk_T/Dk_N = 1 - (CHI_T - df_T)/(CHI_N - df_N)$, where Dk_N is the rescaled noncentrality parameter (NCP) for the null model
31. CFI^{A,E,L,b}	Comparative fit index (normed version of RNI) (Bentler, 1990):
	CFI = $1 - \text{MAX}(CHI_T - df_T, 0)/\text{MAX}(CHI_N - df_N,$ $CHI_N - df_N, 0] = 1 - \text{MAX}(NCP_T, 0)/\text{MAX}(NCP_N, 0)$
32. NFI^{A,E,L}	Normed fit index (Bentler & Bonett, 1980); Bentler–Bonett index (BBI); Bentler–Bonett normed fit index (BBNFI)^E; DELTA1 (Δ1): NFI = $1 - FF_T/FF_N = (CHI_N - CHI_T)/CHI_N$

G. Incremental indices (with adjustment for model complexity)

33. TLI^{A,E,L}	Tucker–Lewis index (Tucker & Lewis, 1973), nonnormed fit index (NNFI)^L (Bentler & Bonett, 1980), Bentler–Bonett nonnormed fit index (BBNNFI)^E, RHO2: TLI = $(FF_N - FF_T)/(FF_N - 1)$
	= $(CHI_N/df_N - CHI_T/df_T)/(CHI_N/df_N - 1)$
34. NTLI	Normed Tucker–Lewis index (Marsh & Balla, 1996):
	NTLI = MIN(MAX(0, TLI), 1); NTLI = 0 if $d_O \le 0$; TLI = 1 if $d_T \le 0$ (including $df_T = 0$ and both d_T and $d_O \le 0$)
35. IFI^{A,E,L}	Incremental fix index (Bollen, 1989a), DELTA2 (Δ2), BL89:
	IFI = $[(N - 1)FF_N - (N - 1)FF_T]/[(N - 1)FF_N - df_T]$ = $(CHI_N - CHI_T)/(CHI_N - df_T)$
36. RFI^{A,L}	Relative fit index (Bollen, 1986), RHO1, BL86:
	RFI = $(FF_N - FF_T)/FF_N = (CHI_N/df_N - CHI_T/df_T)/(CHI_N/df_N)$

(Continued)

Parsimony indices

H. Parsimony indices

37. PRNI[A,a]   Parsimony relative noncentrality index (McDonald & Marsh, 1990),
PCFI[A] (see slight difference from PRNI in CFI):
$PRNI = (df_T/df_N)RNI = \{df_T/[0.5p(p-1)]\}RNI$

38. PGFI*[a]   Parsimony unbiased goodness-of-fit index (Mulaik et al., 1989):
$PGFI^* = (df_T/df_N)GFI^* = \{df_T/[0.5p(p-1)]\}GFI^*$

39. PNFI[A,L]   Parsimony normed fit index (James et al., 1982):
$PNI = (df_T/df_N)PNI = \{df_T/[0.5p(p-1)]\}NFI$

40. PGFI[A,L,d]   Parsimony goodness-of-fit index (Mulaik et al., 1989):
$PGFI = \{df_T/[0.5p(p+1)]\}GFI$

Note. Most indices are provided by popular software packages: A = AMOS 4.0 (Arbuckle & Wothke, 1999), E = EQS 5.6 (Bentler & Wu, 1995; some indices have to be obtained using the /PRINT fit = all option), and L = LISREL 8 (Jöreskog & Sörbom, 1993). p = Number of variables; K = number of free parameters = $0.5p(p+1) - df_T$; df_T = degree of freedom of the target model; df_N = degree of freedom of the null model = $0.5p(p+1) - p$; N = number of cases; FF = maximum likelihood fitting function for the target model; FF_N = fitting function for the null model; CHI_N = chi-square for the null model defined as a model of independent or uncorrelated measured variables.

[a] Indices discussed by McDonald and Marsh (1990).

[b] Several pairs of indices differ in that one is "normed" to be nonnegative whereas the second is not (PDF vs. Dk; RMSEA vs. MSEA) or one is "normed" not to exceed 1.0 whereas the other is not (CFI vs. RNI). Similarly, the square root operation is not applied in the MSEA, so that the index can take on negative values, whereas the RMSEA is undefined (and operationally defined to be zero) when the MSEA is negative. Because the distribution of the "normed" versions of these indices are truncated, the normed versions are slightly biased. Although the size of this bias is typically trivial, it may be of moderate size in simulation studies in which the "true" models that can perfectly reproduce the population data are considered.

[c] Indices presented by Steiger (1990).

[d] Parsimony indices are determined by multiplying any index (e.g., RNI) by a parsimony ratio defined as the ratio of the degrees of freedom of the target model divided by that of the null model $[p(p-1)/2$, where p is the number of measured variables]. In LISREL8 (Jöreskog & Sörbom, 1993), however, the parsimony ratio for just the PGFI is defined as the ratio of the degrees of freedom of the target model divided by $p(p+1)/2$.

ACKNOWLEDGMENTS

The research was funded in part by grants from the Australian Research Council. The authors would like to acknowledge helpful comments from Rod McDonald, James Steiger, Cameron McIntosh, Peter Bentler, Zhonglin Wen, and others, but emphasize that our conclusions may not represent the perspectives of these helpful colleagues.

REFERENCES

Akaike, H. (1974). A new look at the statistical model identification. *IEEE Transactions on Automatic Control, 19*, 716–723.

Akaike, H. (1987). Factor analysis and AIC. *Psychometrika, 52*, 317–332.

Anderson, R. D. (1996). An evaluation of the Satorra–Bentler distributional misspecification correction applied to the McDonald fit index. *Structural Equation Modeling, 3*, 203–227.

Anderson, J. C., & Gerbing, D. W. (1984). The effect of sampling error on convergence, improper solutions, and goodness-of-fit indices for maximum likelihood confirmatory factor analysis. *Psychometrika, 49*, 155–173.

Anderson, J. C., & Gerbing, D. W. (1988). Structural equation modeling in practice: A review and recommended two-step approach. *Psychological Bulletin, 103*, 411–423.

Anderson, T. W., & Rubin, H. (1956). Statistical inference in factor analysis. In *Proceedings of the Third Berkeley Symposium* (vol. 5, pp. 111–150). Berkeley: University of California Press.

Arbuckle, J. L., & Wothke, W. (1999). *Amos 4.0 user's guide.* Chicago: SmallWaters.

Bekker, P. A., & Ten-Berge, J. M. F. (1997). Genetic global identification in factor analysis. *Linear Algebra And Its Applications, 264*, 255–263.

Bentler, P. M. (1990). Comparative fit indices in structural models. *Psychological Bulletin, 107*, 238–246.

Bentler, P. M. (1992). On the fit of models to covariances and methodology to the *Bulletin. Psychological Bulletin, 112*, 400–404.

Bentler, P. M., & Bonett, D. G. (1980). Significance tests and goodness of fit in the analysis of covariance structures. *Psychological Bulletin, 88*, 588–606.

Bentler, P. M., & Wu, E. J. C. (1995). *EQS for Windows user's guide.* Encino, CA: Multivariate Software.

Bentler, P. M., & Yuan, K. (1999). Structural equation modeling with small samples: Test statistics. *Multivariate Behavioral Research, 34*, 181–197.

Birnbaum, A. (1962). On the foundations of statistical inference. *Journal of the American Statistical Association, 57*, 269–326.

Bollen, K. A. (1986). Sample size and Bentler and Bonett's nonnormed fit index. *Psychometrika, 51*, 375–377.

Bollen, K. A. (1989a). A new incremental fit index for general structural equation models. *Sociological Methods and Research, 17*, 303–316.

Bollen, K. A. (1989b). *Structural equations with latent variables.* New York: Wiley.

Bollen, K. A. (1990). Overall fit in covariance structure models: Two types of sample size effects. *Psychological Bulletin, 107*, 256–259.

Bollen, K. A., & Long, J. S. (1993). Introduction. In K. A. Bollen & J. S. Long (Eds.), *Testing structural equation models* (pp. 1–9). Newbury Park, CA: Sage.

Boomsma, A. (1982). Robustness of LISREL against small sample sizes in factor analysis models. In K. G. Jöreskog & H. Wold (Eds.), *Systems under indirect observation: Causality, structure, prediction* (Part I, pp. 149–173). Amsterdam: North-Holland.

Bozdogan, H. (1987). Model selection and Akaike's information criterion (AIC): The general theory and its analytical extensions. *Psychometrika, 52*, 345–370.

Bozdogan, H. (2000). Akaike's information criterion and recent developments in information complexity. *Journal of Mathematical Psychology, 44*, 62–91.

Browne, M. W. (1974). Gradient methods for analytic rotation. *British Journal of Mathematical and Statistical Psychology, 27*, 115–121.

Browne, M. W. (1984). Asymptotically distribution-free methods for the analysis of covariance structures. *British Journal of Mathematics and Statistical Psychology, 37*, 62–83.

Browne, M. W. (2000). Cross-validation methods. *Journal of Mathematical Psychology, 44*, 108–132.

Browne, M. W., & Cudeck, R. (1989). Single-sample cross-validation indices for covariance structures. *Multivariate Behavioral Research, 24*, 445–455.

Browne, M. W., & Cudeck, R. (1993). Alternative ways of assessing model fit. In K. A. Bollen & J. S. Long (Eds.), *Testing structural equation models* (pp. 136–162). Newbury Park, CA: Sage.

Browne, M. W., & Du Toit, S. H. C. (1992). Automated fitting on nonstandard models. *Multivariate Behavioral Research, 27*, 269–300.

Byrne, B. M. (2001). *Structural equation modeling with AMOS: Basic concepts, applications and programming.* Mahwah, NJ: Lawrence Erlbaum Associates, Inc.

Byrne, B. M., Shavelson, R. J., & Muthen, B. (1989). Testing for the equivalence of factor covariance and mean structures: The issue of partial invariance. *Psychological Bulletin, 105,* 456–466.

Carver, R. P. (1978). The case against statistical significance testing, *Harvard Educational Review, 48,* 378–399.

Cheung, G. W., & Rensvold, R. B. (2001). The effects of model parsimony and sampling error on the fit of structural equation models. *Organizational Research Methods, 4,* 236–264.

Chou, C.-P., Bentler, P. M., & Satorra, A. (1991). Scaled test statistics and robust standard errors for nonnormal data in covariance structure analysis: A Monte Carlo study. *British Journal of Mathematical and Statistical Psychology, 44,* 347–357.

Cohen, J. (1994). The Earth is round ($p < .05$), *American Psychologist, 49,* 997–1003.

Cudeck, R., & Browne, M. W. (1983). Cross-validation of covariance structures. *Multivariate Behavioral Research, 18,* 147–167.

Cudeck, R., & Henly, S. J. (1991). Model selection in covariance structures analysis and the "problem" of sample size: A clarification. *Psychological Bulletin, 109,* 512–519.

Ding, L., Velicer, W. F., & Harlow, L. L. (1995). The effects of estimation methods, number of indicators per factor and improper solutions on structural equation modeling fit indices. *Structural Equation Modeling, 2,* 119–144.

Fan, X., Thompson, B., & Wang, L. (1999). Effects of sample size, estimation methods, and model specification on structural equation modeling fit indices. *Structural Equation Modeling, 6,* 56–83.

Fan, X., & Wang, L. (1998). Effects of potential confounding factors on fit indices and parameter estimates for true and misspecified SEM models. *Educational and Psychological Measurement, 58,* 701–735.

Fisher, R. A. (1955). Statistical methods and scientific induction. *Journal of the Royal Statistical Society, 17,* 69–78.

Gerbing, D. W., & Anderson, J. C. (1993). Monte Carlo evaluations of goodness-of-fit indices for structural equation models. In K. A. Bollen & J. S. Long (Eds.), *Testing structural equation models* (pp. 40–65). Newbury Park, CA: Sage.

Gigerenzer, G., Swijtink, Z., Porter, T., Daston, L, Beatty, J., & Krüger, L. (1989). *The empire of chance.* Cambridge: Cambridge University Press.

Goffin, R. D. (1993). A comparison of two new indices for the assessment of fit of structural equation models.. *Multivariate Behavioral Research, 28,* 205–214.

Grayson, D. A. (1998). The frequentist facade and the flight from evidential inference. *British Journal of Psychology, 89,* 325–345.

Helmstader, G. (1964). *Principles of psychological measurement.* New York: Appleton-Century-Crofts.

Hoelter, J. W. (1983). The analysis of covariance structures: Goodness-of-fit indices. *Sociological Methods and Research, 11,* 325–344.

Hu, L., & Bentler, P. M. (1998). Fit indices in covariance structure modeling: Sensitivity to underparametrized model misspecification. *Psychological Methods, 3,* 424–453.

Hu, L., & Bentler, P. M. (1999). Cutoff criteria for fit indices in covariance structure analysis: Conventional criteria versus new alternatives. *Structural Equation Modeling, 6,* 1–55.

Hu, L., Bentler, P. M., & Kano, Y. (1992). Can test statistics in covariance structure analysis be trusted? *Psychological Bulletin, 112,* 351–362.

James, L. R., Mulaik, S. A., & Brett, J. M. (1982). *Causal analysis. Assumptions, models, and data.* Beverly Hills, CA: Sage.

Jöreskog, K. G. (1971). Statistical analysis of sets of congeneric tests. *Psychometrika, 36,* 409–426.

Jöreskog, K. G. (1979). Statistical estimation of structural models in longitudinal investigations. In J. R. Nesselroade & B. Baltes (Eds.), *Longitudinal research in the study of behavior and development* (pp. 303–351). New York: Academic.

Jöreskog, K. G. (1993). Testing structural equation models. In K. A. Bollen & J. S. Long (Eds.), *Testing structural equation models* (pp. 294–316). Newbury Park, CA: Sage.

Jöreskog, K. G., & Sörbom, D. (1981). *LISREL: User's guide*. Chicago: International Education Services.

Jöreskog, K. G., & Sörbom, D. (1988). *LISREL 7—A guide to the program and applications* (2nd ed.). Chicago: SPSS.

Jöreskog, K. G., & Sörbom, D. (1993). *LISREL 8: Structural equation modeling with the SIMPLIS command language*. Chicago: Scientific Software International.

Kaplan, D. (2000). *Structural equation modeling: Foundations and extensions*. Newbury Park, CA: Sage.

Kumar, A., & Sharma, S. (1999). A metric measure for direct comparison of competing models in covariance structure analysis. *Structural Equation Modeling, 6*, 169–197.

La Du, T. J., & Tanaka, J. S. (1989). Influence of sample size, estimation method, and model specification on goodness-of-fit assessments in structural equation models. *Journal of Applied Psychology, 74*, 625–635.

La Du, T. J., & Tanaka, J. S. (1995). Incremental fit index changes for nested structural equation models. *Multivariate Behavioral Research, 30*, 289–316.

MacCallum, R. C., & Hong, S. (1997). Power analysis in covariance structure modeling using GFI and AGFI. *Multivariate Behavioral Research, 32*, 193–210.

MacCallum, R. C., Widaman, K. F., Zhang, S., & Hong, S. (1999). Sample size in factor analysis. *Psychological Methods, 4*, 84–99.

Maiti, S. S., & Mukherjee, B. N. (1991). Two new goodness-of-fit indices for covariance matrices with linear structures. *British Journal of Mathematical and Statistical Psychology, 44*, 153–180.

Marsh, H. W. (1989). Confirmatory factor analyses of multitrait–multimethod data: Many problems and a few solutions. *Applied Psychological Measurement, 13*, 335–361.

Marsh, H. W. (1994). Confirmatory factor analysis models of factorial invariance: A multifaceted approach. *Structural Equation Modeling, 1*, 5–34.

Marsh, H. W., & Bailey, M. (1991). Confirmatory factor analyses of multitrait–multimethod data: A comparison of alternative models. *Applied Psychological Measurement, 15*, 47–70.

Marsh, H. W., & Balla, J. R. (1986, February). *Goodness-of-fit indices in confirmatory factor analysis: The effect of sample size* (ERIC Document Reproduction Service No. ED 267 091).

Marsh, H. W., & Balla, J. R. (1994). Goodness-of-fit indices in confirmatory factor analysis: The effect of sample size and model complexity. *Quality and Quantity, 28*, 185–217.

Marsh, H. W., Balla, J. R., & Hau, K. T. (1996). An evaluation of incremental fit indices: A clarification of mathematical and empirical processes. In G. A. Marcoulides & R. E. Schumacker (Ed.), *Advanced structural equation modeling techniques* (pp. 315–353). Hillsdale, NJ: Lawrence Erlbaum Associates, Inc.

Marsh, H. W., Balla, J. R., & McDonald, R. P. (1988). Goodness-of-fit indices in confirmatory factor analysis: The effect of sample size. *Psychological Bulletin, 103*, 391–410.

Marsh, H. W., & Byrne, B. M. (1993). Confirmatory factor analysis of multitrait–multimethod self-concept data: Between-group and within-group invariance constraints. *Multivariate Behavioral Research, 28*, 313–349.

Marsh, H. W., Byrne, B. M., & Craven, R. (1992). Overcoming problems in confirmatory factor analysis of MTMM data: The correlated uniqueness model and factorial invariance. *Multivariate Behavioral Research, 27*, 489–507.

Marsh, H. W., & Grayson, D. (1994). Longitudinal stability of latent means and individual differences: A unified approach. *Structural Equation Modeling, 1*, 317–359.

Marsh, H. W., & Grayson, D. (1995). Latent-variable models of multitrait–multimethod data. In R. H. Hoyle (Ed.), *Structural equation modeling: Issues and applications* (pp. 177–198). Thousand Oaks, CA: Sage.

Marsh, H. W., & Hau, K. T. (1996). Assessing goodness of fit: Is parsimony always desirable? *Journal of Experimental Education, 64*, 364–390.

Marsh, H. W., & Hau, K. T. (1998). Is parsimony always desirable: Response to Hoyle, Sivo & Willson, Markus, Mulaik, Tweedledee, Tweedledum, the Cheshire Cat, and others. *Journal of Experimental Education, 66*, 274–285.

Marsh, H. W., Hau, K. T., & Wen, Z. (2004). In search of golden rules: Comment on hypothesis-testing approaches to setting cutoff values for fit indexes and dangers in overgeneralizing Hu and Bentler's (1999) findings. *Structural Equation Modeling, 11*, 320–341.

Marsh, H. W., & Hocevar, D. (1985). The application of confirmatory factor analysis to the study of self-concept: First and higher order factor structures and their invariance across age groups. *Psychological Bulletin, 97*, 562–582.

Maiti, S. S., & Mukherjee, B. N. (1991). Two new goodness-of-fit indices for covariance matrices with linear structures. *British Journal of Mathematical and Statistical Psychology, 44*, 153–180.

McDonald, R. P. (1981). The dimensionality of tests and items. *British Journal of Mathematical and Statistical Psychology, 34*, 100–117.

McDonald, R. P. (1989). An index of goodness-of-fit based on noncentrality. *Journal of Classification, 6*, 97–103.

McDonald, R. P. (2000). *Test theory: A unified approach*. Mahwah, NJ: Lawrence Erlbaum Associates, Inc.

McDonald, R. P., & Ho, M. R. (2002). Principles and practice in reporting structural equation analyses. *Psychological Methods, 7*, 64–82.

McDonald, R. P, & Marsh, H. W. (1990). Choosing a multivariate model: Noncentrality and goodness-of-fit. *Psychological Bulletin, 107*, 247–255.

Meehl, P. E. (1978) Theoretical risks and tabular asterisks: Sir Karl, Sir Ronald, and the slow progress of soft psychology. *Journal of Consulting and Clinical Psychology, 46*, 806–834.

Micceri, T. (1989). The unicorn, the normal curve, and other improbably creatures. *Psychological Bulletin, 105*, 156–166.

Mulaik, S. A. (October, 1991). *Clarifying misconceptions about parsimony adjustments of goodness of fit indices*. Paper presented at the Annual Meeting of the Society of Multivariate Experimental Psychology, Colorado Springs, CO.

Mulaik, S. A., James, L. R., Van Alstine, J., Bennett, N., Lind, S., & Stilwell, C. D. (1989). Evaluation of goodness-of-fit indices for structural equation models. *Psychological Bulletin, 105*, 430–445.

Muthén, B. (2001). Second-generation structural equation modeling with a combination of categorical and continuous latent variables: New opportunities for latent class-latent growth modeling. In L. M. Collins and A. G. Sayer (Eds.), *New methods for the analysis of change. Decade of behavior* (pp. 291–322). Washington, DC: American Psychological Association.

Muthén, B., & Kaplan, D. (1992). A comparison of some methodologies for the factor analysis of non-normal Likert variables: A note on the size of the model. *British Journal of Mathematical and Statistical Psychology, 45*, 19–30.

Muthén, L. K., & Muthén, B. (1998). *M-plus user's guide*. Los Angeles: Muthen & Muthen.

Muthén, B. O., & Satorra, A. (1995). Technical aspects of Muthen's LISCOMP approach to estimation of latent variable relations with a comprehensive measurement model. *Psychometrika, 60*, 489–503.

Nevitt, J. (2000, April). *Evaluating small sample approaches for model test statistics in structural equation modeling*. Paper presented at the Annual Meeting of the American Educational Research Association, New Orleans.

Nevitt, J., & Hancock, G. R. (2000). Improving the root mean square error of approximation for nonnormal conditions in structural equation modeling. *Journal of Experimental Education, 68*, 251–268.

Olsson, U. H., Foss, T., Troye, S. V., & Howell, R. D. (2000). The Performance of ML, GLS, and WLS estimation in structural equation modeling under conditions of misspecification and nonnormality. *Structural Equation Modeling, 7*, 557–595.

Olsson, U. H., Troye, S. V., & Howell, R. D. (1999). Theoretical fit and empirical fit: The performance of maximum likelihood versus generalized least squares estimation in structural equation models. *Multivariate Behavioral Research, 34*, 31–58.

Pearson, E. S. (1947). The choice of statistical tests illustrated on the interpretation of data classed in a 2 × 2 table. *Biometrika, 34*, 139–167.

Raykov, T., & Penev, S. (1998). Nested structural equation models: Noncentrality and power of restriction test. *Structural Equation Modeling, 5*, 229–246.

Roberts, S., & Pashler, H. (2000). How persuasive is a good fit? A comment on theory testing. *Psychological Review, 107*, 358–367.

Rozeboom, W. W. (1960). The fallacy of the null-hypothesis significance test, *Psychological Bulletin, 57*, 416–428.

Satorra, A., & Bentler, P. M. (1988). Scaling corrections for chi-square statistics in covariance structure analysis. In *ASA 1988 Proceedings of the Business and Economic Statistics Section* (pp. 308–313). Alexandria, VA: American Statistical Association.

Satorra, A., & Bentler, P. M. (1994). Corrections to test statistic and standard errors in covariance structure analyses. In A. von Eye & C. C. Clogg (Eds.), *Analysis of latent variables in developmental research* (pp. 399–419). Newbury Park, CA: Sage.

Satorra, A., & Bentler, P. M. (2001). A scaled difference chi-square test statistic for moment structure analysis. *Psychometrika, 66*, 507–514.

Schmidt, F. L. (1996). Statistical significance testing and cumulative knowledge in psychology: Implications for training of researchers. *Psychological Methods, 1*, 115–129.

Schwarz, G. (1978). Estimating the dimension of a model. *Annals of Statistics, 6*, 461–464.

Shevlin, M., & Miles, J. N. (1998). Effects of sample size, model specification and factor loadings on the GFI in confirmatory factor analysis. *Personality and Individual Differences, 25*, 85–90.

Sobel, M. E., & Bohrnstedt, G. W. (1985). Use of null models in evaluating the fit of covariance structure models. In N. B. Tuma (Ed.), *Sociological methodology 1985* (pp. 152–178).

Steiger, J. H. (1989). *EzPATH: A supplementary module for SYSTAT and SYSGRAPH*. Evanston, IL: SYSTAT.

Steiger, J. (1990). Structure model evaluation and modification: An interval estimation approach. *Multivariate Behavioral Research, 25*, 173–180.

Steiger, J. H. (2000). Point estimation, hypothesis testing, and interval estimation using the RMSEA: Some comments and a reply to Hayduck and Glaser. *Structural Equation Modeling, 7*, 149–162 .

Steiger, J. H., & Lind, J. C. (1980, May). *Statistically-based tests for the number of common factors*. Paper presented at the Psychometrika Society Meeting, Iowa City.

Steiger, J. H., Shapiro, A., & Browne, M. W. (1985). On the multivariate asymptotic distribution of sequential chi-square statistics. *Psychometrika, 50*, 253–264.

Sugawara, H. M., & MacCallum, R. C. (1993). Effect of estimation method on incremental fit indices for covariance structure models. *Applied Psychological Measurement, 17*, 365–377.

Tanaka, J. S. (1993). Multifaceted conceptions of fit in structural equation models. In K. A. Bollen & J. S. Long (Eds.), *Testing structural equation models* (pp. 10–39). Newbury Park, CA: Sage.

Tucker, L. R., & Lewis, C. (1973). The reliability coefficient for maximum likelihood factor analysis. *Psychometrika, 38*, 1–10.

West, S. G., Finch, J. F., & Curran, P. J. (1995). Structural equation models with nonnormal variables: Problems and remedies. In R. H. Hoyle (Ed.), *Structural equation modeling: Concepts, issues, and applications* (pp. 56–75). Thousand Oaks, CA: Sage.

Widaman, K. F. (1985). Hierarchically nested covariance structure models for multitrait–multimethod data. *Applied Psychological Measurement, 9*, 1–26.

Wilson, E. B., & Worcester, J. (1939). The resolution of six tests into three general factors. *Proceedings of the National Academy of Sciences of the USA, 25*, 73–77.

Yuan, K. H. B., & Bentler, P. M. (1997). Mean and covariance structure analysis: Theoretical and practical improvements. *Journal of the American Statistical Association, 92*, 767–774.

Yuan, K., & Bentler, P. M. (1998a). Robust mean and covariance structure analysis. *British Journal of Mathematical and Statistical Psychology, 51*, 63–88.

Yuan, K., & Bentler, P. M. (1998b). Normal theory based test statistics in structural equation modeling. *British Journal of Mathematical and Statistical Psychology, 51*, 289–309.

11

Resampling Methods in Structural Equation Modeling

Wolfgang M. Hartmann
SAS Institute, Inc.

INTRODUCTION

In the social sciences it has become customary to denote by structural equation modeling (SEM) the area that focuses on estimating models involving systems of equations that include latent variables, measurement errors, multiple indicators, and so on. Most often such models are estimated by specifying the covariance structure implied by the model and estimating the model parameters by minimizing a discrepancy function between the observed covariance matrix and the sample covariance matrix. Thus, covariance structure modeling is a special case of structural equation modeling. For a good overview of structural equation modeling the reader may consult Bollen (1989), Browne and Arminger (1995), Bentler and Dudgeon (1996), and Yuan and Bentler (1997).

This chapter focuses on covariance structure modeling with a single population where the model parameters are estimated using maximum likelihood (ML). Thus, in the following, based on an $n \times n$ covariance matrix $\mathbf{S} = (s_{ij})$ among n variables, a vector $\hat{\theta}$ of parameter estimates is computed optimizing a maximum likelihood estimation function. Here we are confronted with two data situations:

1. The raw data $\mathbf{X}$ are available. This is a $N \times n$ matrix where the N rows correspond to independent observations (cases, subjects) and the n columns correspond to variables (attributes, properties).
2. The raw data are not available. Only the symmetric $n \times n$ covariance matrix $\mathbf{S}$ and the number N of observations are available.

The results presented here can be extended (with different degrees of difficulty) to other areas of structural equation modeling, such as the following:

- Other estimation functions, such as generalized least squares (GLS) or weighted least squares (WLS), and specifically asymptotic distribution free (ADF) estimation.
- What is known as *multiple sample* modeling in SEM, where M data sets, each for one group of subjects, are given and models are specified individually with parameter constraints across groups.
- Mean and covariance structure models, correlation structure models, models with categorical dependent variables, and so on.

MODELS AND ESTIMATION METHODS FOR STRUCTURAL EQUATION MODELING

We denote the *model* covariance matrix that is obtained by plugging the parameters $\theta = (\theta_1, \ldots, \theta_p)$ into the (usually very sparse) model matrices by $\Sigma = \Sigma(\theta)$. There exist several popular model specifications in SEM. For instance, the covariance structure analysis (COSAN), linear structural relations (LISREL), Bentler–Weeks, and recticular action (RAM) models. McArdle (2003, Chapter 9, this volume) provides a detailed account of the RAM model. Here we mention only the COSAN model (McDonald, 1978, 1980) and the LISREL model (Jöreskog, 1973; Jöreskog & Sörbom, 1988).

From the author's point of view, the COSAN model is very much preferred for model specification because it uses the same matrix formulation that is commonly used in publications in this area, and does not need the knowledge of very specific matrices (like the LISREL formulation) or the structure of parts of a large block matrix (like the RAM model).

The COSAN Model

The COSAN model is a simple symmetric matrix model of the form

$$\Sigma = \mathbf{F}_1 \mathbf{P}_1 \mathbf{F}_1^T + \cdots + \mathbf{F}_m \mathbf{P}_m \mathbf{F}_m^T,$$

where each matrix $\mathbf{F}_k, k = 1, \ldots, m$, is the product of $n(k)$ matrices $\mathbf{F}_{k_1}, \ldots, \mathbf{F}_{k_{n(k)}}$, and each matrix $\mathbf{P}_k$ is symmetric, that is,

$$\mathbf{F}_k = \mathbf{F}_{k_1} \cdots \mathbf{F}_{k_{n(k)}} \qquad \text{and} \qquad \mathbf{P}_k = \mathbf{P}_k^T, \qquad k = 1, \ldots, m.$$

The matrices $\mathbf{F}_{k_j}$ and $\mathbf{P}_k$ can be written as

$$\mathbf{F}_{k_j} = \begin{cases} \mathbf{G}_{k_j} \\ \mathbf{G}_{k_j}^{-1} \\ (\mathbf{I} - \mathbf{G}_{k_j})^{-1} \end{cases} \quad j = 1, \ldots, n(k) \qquad \text{and} \qquad \mathbf{P}_k = \begin{cases} \mathbf{Q}_k \\ \mathbf{Q}_k^{-1} \end{cases}$$

and the matrices $\mathbf{Q}_k, k = 1, \ldots, m$, must be symmetric and positive definite. The COSAN model was first implemented in the COSAN computer program (Fraser, 1980) and later in PROC CALIS (Hartmann, 1990). It can also be specified with the sem function in CMAT (Hartmann, 2002). Using a second (unsymmetric) matrix expression, we can easily extend the COSAN model to specify a mean structure.

The LISREL Model

Given a set of l endogenous latent variables η, a set of m exogenous latent variables ξ, a set of p endogenous manifest variables y, and a set of q exogenous manifest variables x, the LISREL model assumes

$$\eta = \mathbf{B}\eta + \mathbf{\Gamma}\xi + \zeta$$

$$y = \mathbf{\Lambda}_y \eta + \epsilon$$

$$x = \mathbf{\Lambda}_x \xi + \delta,$$

where ζ, ϵ, and δ denote vectors of disturbances, and $\mathbf{B}$, $\mathbf{\Gamma}$, $\mathbf{\Lambda}_y$, and $\mathbf{\Lambda}_x$ denote coefficient matrices of direct effects among the different sets of variables.

The model further assumes that $\mathcal{E}\{\xi\zeta^T\} = 0, \mathcal{E}\{\xi\} = 0, \mathcal{E}\{\epsilon\} = 0, \mathcal{E}\{\delta\} = 0, \mathcal{E}\{\eta\epsilon^T\} = 0, \mathcal{E}\{\xi\delta^T\} = 0, \mathcal{E}\{\eta\} = 0$, and $\mathcal{E}\{\xi\} = 0$. With these assumptions, the covariance matrix Σ of the $n = p + q$ manifest variables y and x is then

$$\Sigma = \mathbf{J}(\mathbf{I} - \mathbf{A})^{-1}\mathbf{P}(\mathbf{I} - \mathbf{A})^{-T}\mathbf{J}^T,$$

$$\mathbf{A} = \begin{pmatrix} 0 & 0 & \mathbf{\Lambda}_y & 0 \\ 0 & 0 & 0 & \mathbf{\Lambda}_x \\ 0 & 0 & \mathbf{B} & \mathbf{\Gamma} \\ 0 & 0 & 0 & 0 \end{pmatrix} \qquad \text{and} \qquad \mathbf{P} = \begin{pmatrix} \mathbf{\Theta}_\epsilon & & & \\ & \mathbf{\Theta}_\delta & & \\ & & \mathbf{\Psi} & \\ & & & \mathbf{\Phi} \end{pmatrix},$$

with selection matrix $\mathbf{J} = (\mathbf{I}_{p+q} \; \mathbf{0}_{l+m})$, $\mathbf{\Phi} = \mathcal{E}\{\xi\xi^T\}$, $\mathbf{\Psi} = \mathcal{E}\{\zeta\zeta^T\}$, $\mathbf{\Theta}_\delta = \mathcal{E}\{\delta\delta^T\}$, and $\mathbf{\Theta}_\epsilon = \mathcal{E}\{\epsilon\epsilon^T\}$.

Estimation Methods

Now, given a model and N observations on the n manifest variables, we can obtain estimates $\hat{\theta}$ for the model parameters by optimizing one of several estimation criteria.

- Maximum likelihood (ML) estimation:

$$F_{\mathrm{ML}}(\mathbf{S}, \boldsymbol{\Sigma}) = \ln|\boldsymbol{\Sigma}| - \ln|\mathbf{S}| + \mathrm{tr}(\mathbf{S}\boldsymbol{\Sigma}^{-1}) - p.$$

- Generalized least squares (GLS) estimation:

$$F_{\mathrm{GLS}}(\mathbf{S}, \boldsymbol{\Sigma}) = \frac{1}{2}\,\mathrm{tr}(\mathbf{S}^{-1}(\mathbf{S} - \boldsymbol{\Sigma}))^2$$

- Weighted least squares (WLS) estimation:

$$F_{\mathrm{WLS}}(\mathbf{S}, \boldsymbol{\Sigma}) = \mathrm{vec}(s_{ij} - \sigma_{ij})\mathbf{W}^{-1}\,\mathrm{vec}(s_{ij} - \sigma_{ij}),$$

where $\mathrm{vec}(s_{ij} - \sigma_{ij})$ denotes the vector of the $n(n+1)/2$ elements of the lower triangle of the symmetric matrix $\mathbf{S} - \boldsymbol{\Sigma}$. With a specific choice of $\mathbf{W}$, the WLS method can be called asymptotic distribution free (ADF; Browne, 1982, 1984).

After estimating the model we often wish to draw statistical inferences on the parameter estimates (or functions of them), as well as to draw statistical inferences about the goodness of fit of the model. Most frequently, statistical inferences in SEM are based on the assumption that the observed data are multivariate normal (MVN), although we can proceed under less restrictive assumptions (Browne, 1984). Regardless of whether MVN is assumed, statistical inferences in SEM on model fit, individual parameters, and functions of model parameters are all based on asymptotic theory. That is, the standard errors obtained, as well as the confidence intervals and p values, are correct provided the sample size is large enough. However, the finite-sample behavior of these methods is unknown and can only be studied on a case-by-case basis by means of simulation studies. In other words, in small samples, standard errors, confidence intervals, and p values obtained using asymptotic methods may be inaccurate, particularly so when MVN is not assumed, because the ADF method requires far larger samples than estimation under MVN.

Resampling methods are a "natural" alternative to the use of asymptotic methods for statistical inference. Resampling methods have a long history in statistics (see, e.g., Quenouille, 1949), and have received considerable attention after Efron's (1979) introduction of the bootstrap method. Their introduction to SEM is more recent. In this chapter we describe in some detail how resampling methods can be used to obtain standard errors, confidence intervals, and p values for the estimated parameters and for functions of these, such as indirect effects, and goodness-of-fit indices. Before discussing resampling methods, we briefly describe asymptotic methods for obtaining standard errors and confidence intervals.

Statistical Inference Using Asymptotic Theory: Goodness of Fit, Standard Errors, and Confidence Intervals

For ease of exposition we describe in this section only asymptotic methods for ML estimation under MVN. Within this setting, a goodness-of-fit statistic χ^2 can be computed as a simple function of the optimal F_{ML} value, $\chi^2 = NF_{\mathrm{ML}}(\hat{\theta})$, and an asymptotic p value for this statistic can be obtained by asymptotic theory.

Now, the computation of asymptotic standard errors (SEs) $\hat{\eta}_j$, $j = 1, \dots, p$, of the parameter estimates $\hat{\theta}$ involves the diagonal entries v_{jj} of the $p \times p$ asymptotic covariance matrix of the parameter estimates $\mathbf{V}(\theta)$,

$$\mathbf{V}(\theta) = \frac{\kappa}{N-1}\mathbf{G}^{-1}(\theta),$$

where $\kappa = 2$ for ML and GLS and $\kappa = 1$ for WLS estimation. Here, $\mathbf{G}(\theta)$ is an (approximate) matrix of second derivatives of the fit function $F(\theta)$,

$$\mathbf{G} = (g_{ij}), \qquad \text{where} \quad g_{ij} = \frac{\partial^2 F}{\partial \theta_i \partial \theta_j}$$

(Hessian matrix) evaluated at the optimal parameter estimates $\hat{\theta}$. With $\mathbf{V} = (v_{ij})$ we obtain

$$\hat{\eta}_j = \sqrt{v_{jj}}, \qquad j = 1, \dots, p.$$

The limits of asymptotic (Wald) confidence intervals $[\theta^{\mathrm{low}}, \theta^{\mathrm{upp}}]$ for the parameter estimates are computed from the asymptotic SEs as follows:

$$\hat{\theta}_j{}^{\mathrm{low}} = \hat{\theta}_j - Q(1 - \alpha/2)\hat{\eta}_j$$

$$\hat{\theta}_j{}^{\mathrm{upp}} = \hat{\theta}_j + Q(1 - \alpha/2)\hat{\eta}_j,$$

where $Q(p)$ is the pth quantile from the standard normal distribution (probit () function in SAS language) for probability $p = 1.0 - \alpha/2$. The Wald confidence limits are symmetric with respect to the estimates $\hat{\theta}$ and assume a symmetric and approximative quadratic behavior of the fit function $F(\theta)$ in a small but finite neighborhood of the optimal estimates. This assumption is likely to be unrealistic when the observed data are not multivariate normal. Even for MVN distributed data, the likelihood function must be symmetric only in a *sufficiently small* neighborhood of the optimal estimates $\hat{\theta}$. More realistic confidence intervals (CIs) for maximum likelihood parameter estimates can be obtained using the so-called *profile likelihood* (PL) method (Meeker & Escobar, 1995). In Appendix A we provide algorithmic details for computing profile likelihood CIs.

Often in SEM one wants to obtain confidence intervals not only for parameter estimates, but also for an r vector of functions $f = f(\hat{\theta})$ of the parameter estimates θ. For instance, the indirect and total effects of the different sets of variables in the LISREL model are functions of the parameter estimates.

Given the $p \times p$ covariance matrix $\mathbf{V}(\theta)$ of the p parameter estimates, we can obtain asymptotic confidence intervals for $f = f(\theta)$ using the *delta method* (Sobel, 1986; also see Bollen, 1987, p. 61). To do so, we compute the $r \times p$ Jacobian matrix $\mathbf{J}_f = (\partial f_i / \partial \theta_j)$ of first-order derivatives of $f(\theta)$. Then, under appropriate assumptions, the $r \times r$ covariance matrix $\mathbf{U}$ of $f(\theta)$ is defined as

$$\mathbf{U} = \mathbf{J}_f \mathbf{V} \mathbf{J}_f^T,$$

and the asymptotic standard errors of the effects (r entries of f) are defined as the square roots of the diagonal elements of covariance matrix $\mathbf{U}$.

The delta method will not work well for nonlinear functions (where the second and further derivatives are nonzero) because only the first derivatives (Jacobian) are used. Another problem with the delta method is that even for linear functions it may be difficult to specify the correct analytic Jacobian matrix for the functional relationship.

Uses of Resampling Methods in Structural Equation Modeling

The following are major applications of jackknife and bootstrap methods in SEM:

- The Bollen–Stine bootstrap method for computing the p value of the χ^2 statistic and for computing confidence intervals of goodness-of-fit indices.
- The estimation of SEs and CIs for the optimal parameter estimates $\hat{\theta}$ substituting for the common *Wald* and *PL* methods assuming MVN.
- The estimation of SEs and CIs for indirect and total effects substituting for the *delta* method.
- The estimation of otherwise difficult-to-obtain SEs and CIs for statistics, such as standardized solutions, covariances and correlations between manifest and latent variables, and those among latent variables.
- Using jackknife for stepwise identifying and removal of outliers ("model misfits").

It is important to point out to be able to use most of the resampling methods described here the $N \times n$ raw data matrix $\mathbf{X}$ must be available. Also, we assume that the N rows are independent. In what follows we use $x_i, i = 1, \ldots, N$, to denote the rows (observations) and x_j, $j = 1, \ldots, n$, for the columns (variables) of $\mathbf{X}$. If only the covariance (or correlation matrix) is available, then the only feasible resampling method is the parametric bootstrap.

DESCRIPTION OF JACKKNIFE AND BOOTSTRAP ALGORITHMS

We assume the p vector of parameter estimates $\hat{\theta}$ is available. For the bootstrap t method additionally a p vector of estimates $\hat{\eta}$ of standard errors is required. The methods in this chapter are concerned with the variability and robustness of parameter estimates $\hat{\theta}$ and/or functions of those (like goodness-of-fit measures) with respect to data sampling.

Jackknife

The conceptually simplest resampling method that can be used to investigate the variability and robustness of parameter estimates $\hat{\theta}$ and/or functions of those (like goodness-of-fit measures) with respect to data sampling is the *delete-1* jackknife first introduced by Quenouille (1949).

After estimating the base model using the complete $N \times n$ data set, N analyses are performed based on $(N - 1) \times n$ data sets $\mathbf{X}_i$, where each $\mathbf{X}_i$ is the same as $\mathbf{X}$ except that just one observation x_i, $i = 1, \ldots, N$, is deleted. In the data-mining literature the *delete-1* jackknife is called *leave-one-out* or *Loo* analysis. The following pseudo-code describes the *delete-1* jackknife:

```
for i=1,...,N
   obtain X_i by deleting observation x_i in X
   compute theta_i by analyzing X_i
end
```

Because the N sample data sets $\mathbf{X}_i$ are very similar to $\mathbf{X}$, the results of each analysis will be very similar to those of the base model except when the observation x_i is an influential outlier.

If the model estimation is based on time-expensive computation, sometimes one-step numerical approximation techniques are used for obtaining the N approximate jackknife results θ_i^*. One of those is a simple Newton step, which uses the base estimates $\hat{\theta}$ and the derivatives $(\mathbf{G}_i, g_i)$ *downdated* with respect to observation x_i,

$$\theta_i^* = \hat{\theta} - \mathbf{G}_i^{-1} g_i, \qquad i = 1, \ldots, N,$$

where the $p \times p$ matrix $\mathbf{G}_i$ is the downdated Hessian matrix (second derivatives) and g_i the downdated gradient vector (first derivatives). A similar approximation, but where the observationwise downdate is replaced by a parameterwise downdate, is used for obtaining the so-called modification indices in SEM. Normally, downdating derivative information is much faster than estimating a model from scratch, which may need several iterations of an optimization technique. Some numerical techniques for using jackknife for confidence intervals in general nonlinear L_p regression are illustrated in Gonin and Money (1989, p. 207).

The *delete-1* can be extended to the *delete-K* jackknife methods, sometimes called *grouped jackknife* (Efron, 1994,). Here, it is assumed that $N = KM$, where M is the size of each sample. Already Qucnouille (1949) considered the *half-sample* case where $N(N - 1)/2$ analyses have to be performed, one for each sample of size $M = N/2$. For $K > 2$ there exist $\binom{N}{K}$ different samples, which means the grouped jackknife could be very time-consuming.

K-Fold Cross-Validation

K-fold cross-validation is very closely related to the *delete-K* jackknife. Cross-validation is rarely found with SEM, but is frequently used in *predictive modeling*. In predictive modeling, one or more response variables y are predicted via a model $f(\ )$ from a set of n predictor variables $x_i, i = 1, \ldots, n$,

$$y = f(x_1, \ldots, x_n) + \epsilon, \qquad \text{where} \quad \epsilon \text{ is some estimation error.}$$

Predictive modeling consists of two basic steps:

1. Estimate model parameters so that the model fits well to a given *training* data set.
2. Compute score values $\hat{y}$ for data that are not necessarily the training data by using the model parameters from the first step.

For this process *test validity* is necessary, which means that the model is not only valid for the training data, but will also be valid for data not being used in the training of the model.

Predictive modeling suffers from the *overfitting* dilemma:

1. Too few model parameters result in bad goodness of fit and can result in large goodness-of-fit error based on residuals ϵ.
2. Too many model parameters reduce test validation, that is, the model specification becomes too specific for a different sample from the same population and may result in erroneous predictions $\hat{y}$.

Cross-validation prevents overfitting by evaluating the goodness of fit of a model not on its training data, but on data that are not used for the modeling.

In K-fold cross-validation, the original $N \times n$ data set is (approximately) equally divided into K parts, each with $M = N/K$ observations. In K analyses, each of these parts is once left out from the data and training is performed on the remaining $(N - M) \times n$ subset. After each model is estimated, the predicted outcomes of all, including the left-out, observations are computed. In cross-validation, the goodness of fit is based on predicted values $\hat{y}$ of the left-out observations. After the K cross-validation modeling analyses we have exactly N predicted values of the left-out observations, which can be used for residuals $r_i = y_i - \hat{y}_i$ in goodness-of-fit tests. Using the predicted values of data not used in the training of the model keeps the fit from becoming unlimitedly better for an increasing number of model parameters. In most applications there will be a well-defined optimum of goodness-of-fit values for a moderate number of parameters.

There are different forms of K-fold cross-validation depending on the method used for selecting the deleted observations at each of K modeling runs:

Block: A block of N/K adjacent observations is left out of the training data.
Split: N/K (approximately) equally distant observations are left out of the training data sample.
Random: N/K randomly selected observations are left out of the training sample.

At the end of the K modeling runs each of the N observations is left out exactly once. For example, for $N = 100$ and *10-fold block* cross-classification the following 10 data sets each with 90 observations are analyzed:

$$(x_{11}, \ldots, x_N), \quad (x_1, \ldots, x_{10}, x_{21}, \ldots, x_N), \quad (x_1, \ldots, x_{20}, x_{31}, \ldots, x_N),$$

$$(x_1, \ldots, x_{30}, x_{41}, \ldots, x_N), \quad (x_1, \ldots, x_{40}, x_{51}, \ldots, x_N),$$

$$(x_1, \ldots, x_{50}, x_{61}, \ldots, x_N), \quad (x_1, \ldots, x_{60}, x_{71}, \ldots, x_N),$$

$$(x_1, \ldots, x_{70}, x_{81}, \ldots, x_N), \quad (x_1, \ldots, x_{80}, x_{91}, \ldots, x_N), \quad (x_1, \ldots, x_{90})$$

Block cross-validation can work badly when the data set is sorted. For *split* cross-classification the following 10 sets of observations are left out of the 10 training runs:

$$(x_1, x_{11}, \ldots, x_{91}), \quad (x_2, x_{12}, \ldots, x_{92}), \ldots, \quad (x_9, \ldots, x_{99}), \quad (x_{10}, \ldots, x_{100}).$$

With SEM, observationwise predicted values $\hat{y}_i$ cannot be computed and cross-validation is not being used as in predictive modeling. However, an obvious analogy exists, which could be used for determining the correct number of factors or a suitable amount of sparsity in modeling to avoid overfitting.

Bootstrap Methods

The bootstrap was invented by Efron (1979). Bootstrap methods are widely used for computing confidence intervals of parameter estimates in the more difficult situations of statistical modeling. The simplicity of bootstrap can tempt a statistician to use it in quite inappropriate situations. See Young (1994) for some problems with bootstrap applications. In addition to Efron and Tibshirani (1993), reading of Shao and Tu (1995) is highly recommended. Davison and Hinkley (1997) have a more applied approach with many *S-PLUS* program listings. Shao and Tu (1995, p. 106) compare jackknife and bootstrap for moment estimators and correlation coefficients.

Whereas for jackknife the size of the sampled data sets is smaller than that of the original data set, for the common bootstrap the sampled data sets have the same number of observations as the original data set. There are situations where bootstrap with sample sizes of less than N observations may be appropriate (Bickel, Götze, & van Zwet, 1994), but we think that these situations would be rare in typical SEM applications. On the other hand, the jackknife deals with a fixed number of samples, for example, N samples for the *delete-1* jackknife, whereas the bootstrap can deal with any number L of samples $\mathbf{X}_l, l = 1, \ldots, L$.

There are two general types of applications where the bootstrap outperforms the *delete-1* jackknife (Shao & Tu, 1995, p. 49):

1. Jackknife estimates can be inconsistent, for example, for sample quantiles, like the median. For the jackknife to be consistent the functional must be smooth.
2. Jackknifing does not provide estimates of the entire sampling distribution of a random variable. On the other hand, the L vectors (values) of a bootstrapped statistics $f_l^* = f(\theta_l^*)$ form a so-called *empirical distribution function* (EDF) having moments like mean, variance, skewness, and kurtosis.

The *delete-K* jackknife, however, overcomes both of these deficiencies of the *delete-1* jackknife.

Naive Bootstrap Sampling

With the use of a uniform random generator the following pseudo-code describes the ordinary method of uniform bootstrap sampling (Gleason, 1988):

```
for l=1,...,L
  for i=1,...,N
    l = ceil(N * ranuni(0,1))
    use observation x_l from X for
    observation i in bootstrap sample
  end
  analyze the bootstrap sample X_l,
  i.e. estimate theta_l
end
```

Here, `ranuni` denotes a uniform pseudo-random generator returning values in $(0, 1]$ and the `ceil(x)` function defines the smallest integer not less than x. The observations in each of the bootstrap samples proceed from the original data matrix $\mathbf{X}$. However, in any given sample $\mathbf{X}_l$, some observations may not be used, whereas others may be used multiple times.

Any computer program performing bootstrap analyses should (have an option to) report the following statistics of the distribution of the L bootstrap estimates θ_l^* (each a p-vector):

1. Mean, variance, skewness, and kurtosis
2. Minimum, maximum, median, and quartiles
3. $100\alpha\%$ and $100(1 - \alpha)\%$ percentiles.

Additionally, a histogram drawing of the distribution of each bootstrapped statistic is recommended to give a feeling about the shape of the EDF.

Balanced Bootstrap Sampling

The balanced bootstrap sampling is like uniform sampling with the additional constraint that after a previously specified number L of data sets is sampled, each of the N observations x_i is used exactly L times in those samples. Davison et al. (1986) first introduced balanced bootstrap and demonstrated that this method can reduce bootstrap bias and variance considerably. Balanced bootstrap is possible only for the common situation where the size of the sampled data set is the same as that of the original data set, that is, equal to N. See Appendix 2 in Hall (1992) for some discussion of balanced bootstrap.

For an understanding of how this constraint could be realized, let us create an index vector with L replications of the numbers $1, \dots, N$ and randomly permute the LN entries. After that we again divide the index vector into L successive parts of N indices, which are used to define the bootstrap samples. The following pseudo-code describes the simple form of balanced bootstrap sampling (Gleason, 1988):

```
form J = {I,...,I} where I=(1,2,...,N)
for i=1,...,L*N
    j = ceil(LN * ranuni(0,1))
    swap entry J_j with J_i
end
for l=1,...,L
  analyze the bootstrap data X_l,
  where X_l = (x[l*N+1],...,x[l*(N+1)])
end
```

In practice, this approach could be difficult to realize because a vector of LN integers may need too much memory for large L and N. A much more memory-efficient implementation of balanced bootstrap was developed by Gleason (1988). Even though balanced sampling is much more computer intensive than uniform sampling, for applications like SEM or general nonlinear regression, this difference is not noteworthy. Shao and Tu (1995, sect. 6.2.3) report on approximate balanced resampling methods. Such techniques may be necessary for balanced repeated replication (BRR).

Weighted Likelihood Bootstrap

In the common bootstrap each observation x_i of an $N \times n$ data set is selected with a weight of $w_i = 1/N$. For general nonlinear regression the maximum likelihood function can be expressed as a sum of contributions of each observation to the likelihood function. Here, the sampling weights w_i of the observations x_i can depend on those observationwise contributions to the likelihood function. For SEM the ML function is defined in terms of the covariance matrix (rather than observationwise), which makes it more difficult to apply this kind of sampling.

Parametric Sampling: Multivariate Normal

Fishman (1996, chap. 3) presents many algorithms for univariate and multivariate sampling. Here we concentrate on sampling from a multivariate normal distribution $\mathcal{N}(\mu, \Sigma)$.

For a specified mean n-vector μ and $n \times n$ full-rank covariance matrix Σ we want to create the N rows (observations) of an $N \times n$ matrix (data set) $\mathbf{X}$ that is MVN distributed with $\mathcal{N}(\mu, \Sigma)$. The following algorithm (Fishman, 1996, p. 223) can be used:

1. We compute the (unique) upper triangular matrix $\mathbf{U}$ of Σ, which is defined by

$$\Sigma = \mathbf{U}^T \mathbf{U},$$

   where the lower triangular matrix $\mathbf{U}^T$ is also called the Cholesky factor[1] of Σ.

2. Inside a loop for i=1,...,N:

   (a) Generate an n-vector y_i of $\mathcal{N}(0, 1)$ univariate normal distributed values.
   (b) Compute row x_i of $\mathbf{X}$ with

$$x_i = \mathbf{U}^T y_i + \mu.$$

For the univariate case ($n = 1$) a large number of normal random generators are available in *statlib* and *netlib*.

---

[1]We changed the common notation of the Cholesky factorization $\Sigma = \mathbf{L}\mathbf{L}^T$, where $\mathbf{L}$ is a lower triangular matrix, to $\Sigma = \mathbf{U}^T\mathbf{U}$ with an upper triangular $\mathbf{U}$ because we use the letter L for the number of sampling replications.

Parametric multivariate normal $\mathcal{N}(\mu, \Sigma)$ sampling is often used in SEM when no raw data and only a covariance matrix and mean vector are given. The following pseudo-code describes how parametric bootstrap is used in SEM:

```
(1) for given mean vector mu and covariance matrix Sigma
    compute the Cholesky factor U' of Sigma
(2) analyze L sample data (mu_1,Sigma_1):
    for l=1,...,L
        (2.1) obtain sample matrix Z_l with:
              for i=1,...,N
                generate univariate normal y_i and compute
                z_i = U' y_i + mu
              end
        (2.2) compute mean vector mu_1 and covariance
              matrix Sigma_1 of data matrix Z_l
        (2.3) analyze the bootstrap sample Z_l,
              i.e. estimate theta_1
    end
```

Estimation of Bias Correction and Standard Errors

To be able to use the resampling methods (jackknife and bootstrap) discussed here to estimate the sampling variability of the parameter estimates (and their functions such as goodness-of-fit indices), it is necessary to remove the estimation *bias* of the resampling methods.

Jackknife estimates are biased. For instance, the mean of the jackknife estimates of a statistic does not coincide with the mean of the (unknown) distribution function of the statistic.

A first-order estimation of the bias B of the delete-1 jackknife was given by Quenouille (1949)

$$\hat{B}(\hat{\theta}) = (N-1)(\bar{\theta}^* - \hat{\theta}), \qquad \text{with} \quad \bar{\theta}^* = \frac{1}{N} \sum_{i=1}^{N} \theta_i^*.$$

Therefore the *bias-corrected jackknifed estimate* is

$$\tilde{\theta} = N\hat{\theta} - (N-1)\bar{\theta}^*.$$

This means that whereas the original estimator $\hat{\theta}$ is biased with $O(1/N)$, the first-order bias-corrected estimator $\tilde{\theta}$ is biased with only $O(1/N^2)$. Higher order estimates of the bias use, in addition to the mean, also the variance, skewness, and so on of the jackknifed estimators. However, in practice, higher order bias estimation is very rare.

Bootstrap estimates are also biased. In fact, the amount of mean and variance bias introduced by the bootstrap can be much larger than that of the delete-1 jackknife. In applications of bootstrap methods it is extremely important that the EDF of the statistic is close to the (unknown) distribution function of the statistic $f(\theta)$. Differences in the mean can be compensated by first-order bias correction. The BCa method (see later discussion) also tries to compensate for differences in the skewness.

The first-order estimate of the bootstrap bias (mean bias) for L samples is defined as

$$\hat{B}(\theta) = \bar{\theta}^* - \hat{\theta}, \qquad \text{with} \quad \bar{\theta}^* - \frac{1}{L}\sum_{i=1}^{L}\theta_i^*,$$

which defines the *mean bias-corrected estimator*,

$$\tilde{\theta} = 2\hat{\theta} - \bar{\theta}^*.$$

Here I would like to cite Efron and Tibshirani (1993, p. 138) in a slightly modified form: "There is a tendency ... to think of $\bar{\theta}^*$ itself as the bias corrected estimate. Notice that the last equation says that if $\bar{\theta}^*$ is *greater* than $\hat{\theta}$, then the bias corrected estimate $\tilde{\theta}$ should be *less* than $\hat{\theta}$."

Note that the BC and BCa methods for confidence intervals correct for *median bias* rather than for *mean bias*. The bootstrap median bias is

$$B_j^{\mathrm{med}} = Q\left(\frac{1}{L}\sum_{l=1}^{N}t_{lj}\right), \qquad \text{where} \quad t_{lj} = \begin{cases} 1. & \text{for } \theta_{lj}^* < \hat{\theta}_j \\ 0. & \text{for } \theta_{lj}^* > \hat{\theta}_j , \\ .5 & \text{for } \theta_{lj}^* = \hat{\theta}_j \end{cases}$$

where $Q(p)$ is the p quantile from the standard normal distribution (probit() function in SAS language).

Bootstrap Methods for Confidence Intervals

Given a set of bootstrap estimators θ^*, where θ is a p-vector, different methods have been proposed to obtain confidence intervals for the parameter estimates. These are based on the bootstrap estimator of the standard errors of the parameter estimates. The latter are obtained by computing the $p \times p$ covariance matrix $\mathbf{V}$ of the bootstrap estimates,

$$\mathbf{V}(\theta^*) = \frac{1}{L-1}\sum_{l=1}^{L}(\theta_l^* - \bar{\theta}^*)(\theta_l^* - \bar{\theta}^*)^T.$$

The L bootstrap estimators $\hat{\eta}_l^*$ of standard errors for the p entries of $\hat{\theta}$ are the square roots of the diagonal entries of $\mathbf{V}(\theta^*)$.

Some computer programs compute estimates of the standard error of the *standardized* regression coefficients $\hat{\theta}_{yx}(s_y/s_x)$ as the square root of

$$s_x^2/s_y^2 \, \mathrm{var}(\hat{\theta}_{yx})$$

(Bollen & Stine, 1990, p. 121).

(Bias-Corrected) Normal Method

In this method, the lower and upper *normal* confidence limits are defined as

$$\hat{\theta} \pm Q(1 - \alpha/2)\hat{\eta}^*,$$

respectively, where $Q(p)$ is the p quantile from the standard normal distribution (probit() function in SAS language). The *bias-corrected normal* confidence limits are

$$\hat{\theta} - B \pm Q(1 - \alpha/2)\hat{\eta}^*.$$

The Percentile Method

This method is called "percentile" by Efron and Tibshirani (1993) and Shao and Tu (1995), "other percentile" by Hall (1992), and "Efron's backwards percentile" by Hjorth (1994).

The percentile method uses the α and $1 - \alpha$ percentiles of the bootstrap distribution of the θ_l^*, $l = 1, \ldots, N$, for the lower and upper confidence limits, respectively. Assuming the L bootstrap estimates θ_{lj}, $j = 1, \ldots, p$, are sorted in ascending order (separate for each j) in the vector $T_j = (t_{1j}, \ldots, t_{Lj})$, then we obtain the confidence limits with

$$\hat{\theta}_j^{\text{low}} = T_j[N\alpha/2]$$
$$\hat{\theta}_j^{\text{upp}} = T_j[N(1 - \alpha/2)],$$

where $T_j[k]$ denotes the entry of array T_j with index k. The percentile method works well for unbiased statistics and nearly symmetric sampling distributions. A major advantage is that this method (like the BC and BCa mehods discussed later) is equivariant with respect to some parameter transformations. (Quantiles are sensitive only to the rank order of the parameters.)

The Hybrid Method

This method is called "hybrid" by Shao and Tu (1995), "percentile" by Hall (1992) and "simple" by Hjorth (1994). It is in some sense the inverse of the percentile method. Assuming the L bootstrap estimates θ_{lj}, $j = 1, \ldots, p$, are sorted in ascending order (separate for each j) in the vector $T_j = (t_{1j}, \ldots, t_{Lj})$ then we obtain the confidence limits with

$$\hat{\theta}_j^{\text{low}} = 2\hat{\theta}_j - T_j[N(1 - \alpha/2)]$$
$$\hat{\theta}_j^{\text{upp}} = 2\hat{\theta}_j - T_j[N\alpha/2].$$

The Bias-Corrected Method

The bias-corrected (BC) method uses the percentile interval that is corrected for *median* bias B_j^{med} (see earlier discussion):

$$\beta^{\text{low}} = P(2B^{\text{med}} + Q(\alpha/2))$$
$$\beta^{\text{upp}} = P(2B^{\text{med}} + Q(1 - \alpha/2)),$$

where

$$P(x) = \frac{1}{\sqrt{2\pi}} \int_{-\infty}^{x} e^{-t^2/2} \, dt$$

is the probability for a normal distributed t with $t < x$ (probnorm() function in SAS language). The BC method uses β^{low} and β^{upp} as percentiles of the bootstrap distribution of the θ_l, $l = 1, \ldots, N$, for the lower and upper confidence limits, respectively:

$$\hat{\theta}_j^{\text{low}} = T_j[N\beta^{\text{low}}]$$
$$\hat{\theta}_j^{\text{upp}} = T_j[N\beta^{\text{upp}}].$$

The Accelerated Bias-Corrected Method

This method is called "BCa" by Efron and Tibshirani (1993), Shao and Tu (1995), and Hjorth (1994), and is called "ABC" by Hall (1992).

The BCa method uses the same percentile interval as the percentile method but corrects the percentiles for median bias and skewness. Normally a jackknife analysis must be performed prior to the bootstrap sampling to compute the skewness of the jackknife distribution of the θ_i^*, $i = 1, \ldots, N$, which is used for computing the "acceleration". Assuming γ_j is the unbiased univariate skewness for parameter $j = 1, \ldots, p$ of the N jackknife estimates, we then compute the *acceleration* κ_j with (Efron & Tibshirani, 1993, p. 186)

$$\kappa_j = -\frac{N - 2}{6N\sqrt{N - 1}} \gamma_j$$

$$\delta^{\text{low}} = P\left(B^{\text{med}} + \frac{B^{\text{med}} + Q(\alpha/2)}{1. - \kappa(B^{\text{med}} + Q(\alpha/2))}\right)$$

$$\delta^{\text{upp}} = P\left(B^{\text{med}} + \frac{B^{\text{med}} + Q(1 - \alpha/2)}{1. - \kappa(B^{\text{med}} + Q(1 - \alpha/2))}\right),$$

where

$$P(x) = \frac{1}{\sqrt{2\pi}} \int_{-\infty}^{x} e^{-t^2/2} \, dt$$

is the probability for a normal distributed t with $t < x$ (`probnorm()` function in SAS language). The BCa method uses δ^{low} and δ^{upp} as percentiles of the bootstrap distribution of the θ_l, $l = 1, \ldots, N$, for the lower and upper confidence limits, respectively:

$$\hat{\theta}_j^{\text{low}} = T_j[N\delta^{\text{low}}]$$

$$\hat{\theta}_j^{\text{upp}} = T_j[N\delta^{\text{upp}}].$$

This method may perform poorly if the "acceleration" is computed incorrectly. For large values of the acceleration and α the CI may be too short (Hall, 1992).

The Bootstrap-t Method

This method is called "bootstrap-t" by Efron and Tibshirani (1993) and Shao and Tu (1995), "studentized" by Hall (1992), and "percentile-t" by Hjorth (1994). The t method is similar to the hybrid method, but it, needs in addition to the parameter estimates θ_l^* a vector η^* of L estimates of standard errors η_l^* for each bootstrap sample.

Using the L pairs of bootstrap estimates (θ_l^*, η_l^*), $l = 1, \ldots, L$, we obtain the vector v^* of corrected estimates

$$v_l = (\theta_l^* - \hat{\theta})/\eta_l^*.$$

Assuming the L values v_{lj}, $j = 1, \ldots, p$, are sorted in ascending order (separate for each j) in the vector $S_j = (s_{1j}, \ldots, s_{Lj})$, then we obtain the confidence limits with

$$\hat{\theta}_j^{\text{low}} = \hat{\theta}_j - S_j[N(1 - \alpha/2)]\hat{\eta}_j$$

$$\hat{\theta}_j^{\text{upp}} = \hat{\theta}_j - S_j[N\alpha/2]\hat{\eta}_j.$$

Remarks

It is not easy to know in advance which kind of bootstrap method will work well for a specific application. This is especially true for small-N data. For very large N *and* very large number of replications L, usually all methods will result in very similar standard errors and CIs. Many times a *trial and error* method must be applied. However, some remarks on this issue can be made (Sarle, 2000):

1. The normal bootstrap CIs will only be appropriate for approximately normal EDFs.
2. For the bootstrap-t, the BC, and the BCa methods, larger L (e.g., $L \geq 1,000$) are necessary than for other methods, where sometimes $L = 500$ may be enough.
3. The BCa and t methods should work better than other methods, but also need more memory and computer time. In SEM the t method can only be used for confidence intervals of direct effects or in connection with the delta method also for total and indirect effects.
4. The BCA method is not monotone with respect to α. Especially for large α and large acceleration (skewness) the CIs can be too short.
5. The percentile method amplifies the bias.
6. The hybrid method seems to be the most stable in difficult situations.

For more comparisons between the methods see Shao and Tu (1985) and Hall (1992).

NUMERICAL APPLICATIONS OF BOOTSTRAP IN STRUCTURAL EQUATION MODELING

In SEM only the mean vector μ and covariance matrix $\mathbf{S}$ of the data set are used for estimating the model parameters θ. Therefore, the common jackknife and naive bootstrap methods are applicable only to those SEM applications where a raw data matrix $\mathbf{X}$ is given. If the only data are covariance or correlation matrices (together with mean vectors), only parametric bootstrap methods are possible. On the other hand, the parametric bootstrap usually assumes multivariate normality in that it uses the mean vector and covariance matrix to sample approximately multivariate normal data. It is therefore valid only for ML and GLS estimation and not for WLS (or ADF) estimation, which does not assume this data distribution.

When using jackknife for SEM, normally (except for outliers) the estimates θ_i^* are very close to the $\hat{\theta}_i$, and jackknife could be numerically very fast. Whereas for jackknife with large samples sizes N a *one-step approximation* for estimating

θ_l^* from $\hat{\theta}$ could be appropriate, for bootstrap and small sample sizes, a *one-step approximation* should be ruled out.

Jacknife is obviously not used for confidence intervals in SEM practice. It is, however, used in nonlinear regression, especially in robust, least-absolute-value regression. Some numerical techniques for using jackknife for confidence intervals in general nonlinear L_p regression are illustrated by Gonin and Money (1989, p. 207).

For small N, naive bootstrap methods may become numerically unstable and very biased when applied to SEM due to the following fact: In bootstrap sampling, some of the observations of the original data set $\mathbf{X}$ are not used in the $\mathbf{X}_i$, whereas other observations are used multiple times. This means that for small N this may yield considerable changes in the mean vector and covariance matrix resulting in discontinuous changes in the model specification. The amount of information provided by the data is reduced and the covariance matrix could even become singular. If N is not much larger than the number of parameters p, then there will be an increasing chance that the SEM model fit will not be successful for some of the $\mathbf{X}_i$. On the other hand, jackknife is much more robust with respect to small N. The (sometimes only slightly modified) estimates $\hat{\theta}$ of the original data $\mathbf{X}$ are normally used as good starting values for the bootstrap analyses. For small N, the quality of those starting values is much worse, which is illustrated by the total number of iterations and function calls needed for convergence of the optimization process. With much more details this is also shown by the simulation results of Ichikawa and Konishi (1995).

Bootstrapping Confidence Intervals for Parameter Estimates

Both naive and parametric bootstrap can be used. When ML and GLS estimation is performed under MVN assumptions, Wald and PL CIs of course assume MVN. Furthermore, MVN normality is used to construct parametric bootstrap CIs. In contrast, naive bootstrap CIs do not rely on an MVN assumption. As pointed out, bootstrap CIs can be obtained using the bootstrap standard errors. These bootstrap standard errors are simply the square root (standard deviation) of its diagonal entries of the covariance matrix of the bootstrap sample distribution (see Statistical Inferences, page 345, or Bollen & Stine, 1990).

It is of interest that profile likelihood and all bootstrap methods are able to show an unsymmetric behavior of the likelihood function. The normal-theory Wald confidence limits are based only on the value of the asymptotic standard errors and are always symmetric. They obviously require stronger assumptions to be valid. For more details on profile likelihood intervals see Meeker and Escobar (1995).

To illustrate numerically the present discussion, we applied naive and parametric bootstrap techniques to two different data sets, a small one and a large one:

1. Example 1: The "industrialization and political democracy" example with $N = 75$ reported in Bollen (1989; see also Bollen & Stine, 1992). There are two models, Model A, with large p value ($\chi_A^2 = 39.6$, $df_A = 38$, $p_A = .40$), and Model B, with very small (highly significant) p value ($\chi_B^2 = 73.6$, $df_B = 44$, $p_B < .01$).
2. Example 2: A previously unpublished example of "sexual risk behavior" data (Coyle, Kirby, Marin, Gomez, & Gregorich, 2002) with $N = 2,151$ and $n = 15$ manifest ordinal variables (data and model were contributed by Steve Gregorich). The model is a confirmatory factor model with five first-order and two second-order factors where the data were treated as continuous.

Appendix B shows the Wald and profile likelihood confidence limits, and those computed by naive and parametric bias-corrected bootstrap, for Models A and B of the industrialization and political democracy example with $N = 75$. From Bollen and Stine (1992) we know that this data set is not close to multivariate normality and has some outliers. Therefore, we cannot trust the Wald confidence intervals. Appendix B also shows the corresponding confidence limits for the large sexual risk behavior data set by Coyle et al. (2002) with $N = 2,151$. We observe that the confidence limits for the large data set agree much more than those of the small data set. In addition, the bootstrap bias is much smaller for the application with large N. The bootstrap CI computations are based on $L = 500$ samples.

A small simulation will show how close the confidence intervals of different bootstrap methods are to the Wald and profile likelihood intervals. Because the raw data are given, we do not report the results for parameteric bootstrap. First we compute the Wald and the profile likelihood confidence intervals as shown in Appendix B. Then, for different seed values of the random generator we compute 50 replications of bootstrap CI computations for $L = 250$ and $L = 500$. Therefore, we obtain 50 pairs of confidence limits for each of the five bootstrap methods, percentile, hybrid, BC, BCa, and t. For all pairs of limits (lower and upper) and all method pairs (a, b), where $a = $ Wald and PL, and $b = $ Perc, Hybrid, BC, BCa, and t, we compute the absolute distances

$$\frac{1}{50} \sum_{i=1}^{50} \sum_{j=1}^{p} \left[\left(x_j^{a,\text{low}} - x_j^{b,\text{low}} \right) \right]^2 + \left[\left(x_j^{a,\text{upp}} - x_j^{b,\text{upp}} \right) \right]^2$$

of the corresponding interval limit values, and obtain the results shown in Table 11.1.

This table shows for Example 1 with small N that percentile and hybrid CIs are in average closer to the Wald CIs; however, hybrid, BC, and BCa CIs are closer to the more-valid unsymmetric profile likelihood CIs. We also note that the hybrid,

TABLE 11.1
Absolute Distance of Bootstrap to Wald and Profile Likelihood (PL) Confidence Intervals (CIs)

	Example	L	Perc	Hybrid	BC	BCa	t
Wald CI	1A	250	1.55959	1.55959	2.91470	4.99362	9.77796
PL CI	1A	250	3.96751	3.67990	2.46934	2.58409	3.62079
Wald CI	1B	250	1.1303	1.1303	2.4544	4.0054	11.3023
PL CI	1B	250	3.03807	2.72473	1.70315	1.64461	4.56019
Wald CI	1A	500	1.27496	1.27496	2.19321	3.71297	4.11391
PL CI	1A	500	2.12675	1.11851	1.06932	1.65149	1.52087
Wald CI	1B	500	0.74834	0.74834	0.81990	1.60358	4.58960
PL CI	1B	500	2.06498	0.43384	0.43914	0.38295	1.51627
Wald CI	2	250	0.03850	0.03850	0.04669	0.04666	0.03491
PL CI	2	250	0.03424	0.04118	0.04185	0.04174	0.03044
Wald CI	2	500	0.04148	0.04148	0.04573	0.04623	0.03611
PL CI	2	500	0.03622	0.04470	0.04022	0.04062	0.03198

Note: L, Number of samples; Perc: percentile; BC, bias corrected; BCa, accelerated bias corrected.

BC, and BCa confidence limits become closer to the profile likelihood CIs for the larger $L = 500$. Furthermore, for a large number of observations N, as with Example 2, the bootstrap-t CIs seems to become better due to the fact that the standard error estimates are more accurate.

The absolute distances between Wald and PL confidence intervals are as follows:

Example 1A: Distance $= 2.4728$.
Example 1B: Distance $= 2.1600$.
Example 2: Distance $= 0.001356$.

This confirms that for a small number of observations the discrepancies between different kinds of CIs tend to be larger, maybe due to violations of distributional assumptions. We also note that for the large-N example, Example 2, the distance between Wald and profile likelihood CIs is smaller than the distances of all bootstrap CIs to each of them. There were no failing optimizations in any of these runs. Each optimization was continued until the largest gradient element was smaller than 1e-4 in magnitude.

Bollen–Stine Bootstrap of the p Value of χ^2

This section describes the Bollen and Stine (1992) algorithm for obtaining the p value of the χ^2 goodness-of-fit test statistic. This statistic is a simple rescaling of the F value of the fit criterion

$$\chi^2 = (N - 1)F(\hat{\theta}), \qquad \text{where} \quad F(\hat{\theta}) = F_{\text{ML}}, F_{\text{GLS}},$$

which provides a likelihood ratio test of the null hypothesis that the predicted (model) matrix $\Sigma(\hat{\theta})$ has the specified model structure against the alternative that $\Sigma(\hat{\theta})$ is unconstrained. Under normality assumptions, the χ^2 statistic is asymptotically distributed as a chi-square.

Bollen and Stine (1992) show that the common *naive bootstrapping* will provide incorrect p values for the χ^2 statistic and other functions of the covariance matrix: This is because the empirical distribution function obtained by naive bootstrapping differs very significant from a χ^2 distribution due to the fact that the EDF includes both model misfit and sampling variation. Beran and Srivastava (1985) proposed to transform the data $\mathbf{X}$ in such a way as to exclude the model misfit,

$$\mathbf{Z} = \mathbf{Y}\mathbf{S}^{-1/2}\Sigma^{1/2}(\hat{\theta}),$$

where $\mathbf{Y}$ is the centered original data set

$$\mathbf{Y} = \mathbf{X} - J \otimes \bar{x} \qquad \text{and} \qquad J = (1, \dots, 1)^T,$$

and therefore $\mathbf{S} = [1/(N-1)]\mathbf{Y}^T\mathbf{Y}$. When $\mathbf{Z}$ (instead of the original data set $\mathbf{X}$) is used in naive bootstrap the model misfit is excluded. Then the covariance matrix of $\mathbf{Z}$ is equal to Σ. Therefore, when $\mathbf{S}$ is replaced by the covariance matrix of $\mathbf{Z}$ we obtain $F(\theta) = 0$. Using $\mathbf{Z}$ for naive bootstrap, we now obtain the means and variances of the distribution function of the L bootstrapped χ_l^{2*} as

$$E^*(\chi^{2*}) \approx df \qquad \text{and} \qquad \text{VAR}^*(\chi^{2*}) \approx 2df$$

(Bollen & Stine, 1992, p. 121). This means that the empirical distribution function of the naive bootstrap with the transformed data set $\mathbf{Z}$ will be approximately χ^2 distributed. The bootstrapped p value is the ratio between the number of bootstrapped χ^{2*} greater than or equal to the $\hat{\chi}^2$ value of the parent data $\mathbf{X}$ and the total number L of successful bootstrap replications.

To illustrate this discussion, we applied the Bollen–Stine bootstrap to the two data sets described in the previous subsection. The SEM computer program AMOS and the sem function in CMAT (Hartmann, 2002) perform Bollen–Stine bootstrap. The latter was used here.

For Model 1A of the industrialization and political democracy example with $N = 75$ we obtain the following table of goodness-of-fit measures:

```
Chi-square (df = 38). . . . . . 39.6438 Prob>chi**2 = 0.3966
Null Model Chi-square (df = 55) . . . . . . . .       720.9120
Bollen-Stine p Value  . . . . . . . . . . . .          0.3440
RMSEA Estimate  . . . . . 0.0242  90%C.I.[ 0.0000,  0.0862]
```

For this example, the bootstrapped $p = .3440$ value confirms the normal-theory $p = .3966$ value. The difference is relatively small.

For Model 1B of the industrialization and political democracy example we obtain the following table of goodness-of-fit measures:

```
Chi-square (df = 44). . . . . . 73.6230 Prob>chi**2 = 0.0034
Null Model Chi-square (df = 55) . . . . . . . .    720.9120
Bollen-Stine p Value  . . . . . . . . . . . . .      0.0320
RMSEA Estimate  . . . . . 0.0954  90%C.I.[0.0550,   0.1326]
```

In this application, the asymptotic and bootstrapped p values differ nearly by a factor of 10, which is significant for this application.

Finally, for Model 2 [a second-order confirmatory factor analysis model by Coyle et al. (2002)] with $N = 2,151$, we obtain the following table:

```
Chi-square (df = 84). . . . . 415.9598 Prob>chi**2 = 0.0000
Null Model Chi-square (df = 105). . . . . . . .   9554.1731
Bollen-Stine p Value  . . . . . . . . . . . . .      0.0000
RMSEA Estimate  . . . . . 0.0429  90%C.I.[0.0388,   0.0470]
```

In this case the normal-theory and the bootstrapped p values are very small. For this large sample size, this is not very surprising.

It is interesting to note that for Example 1B, Bollen and Stine (1992) reported a bootstrapped value of $p = .055$ using $L = 250$. When we ran the same example with $L = 250$ we found a bootstrapped value $p = .032$. This rather large difference is obviously based on the variance of the bootstrap estimates $\hat{\theta}_l^*$, $l = 1, \ldots, L$, which is revealed by using different seed values of the random generator.

To have an idea of the precision of the bootstrap for a given L, we ran the bootstrap 100 times with different seed values of the random generator and determined the range and the moments of the univariate distribution of the 100 bootstrapped p values. We used $L = 250$ and $L = 500$ for each bootstrap. We assumed that the increase in L will reduce the size of the ranges of bootstrap values. The results obtained are provided in Table 11.2.

This table shows that even for $L = 500$ bootstrap samples the Bollen–Stine p value may not be very precise. There were no failing optimizations in any of these runs.

TABLE 11.2
Range of p Values for Repeated Bollen–Stine Bootstrap

Example	L	p_{mod}	$[p_{min}, p_{max}]$	Mean	Variance	Skew	Kurtosis
1A	250	0.3966	[0.3440 0.5160]	0.432	0.001	0.351	0.136
1B	250	0.0034	[0.0200 0.0800]	0.051	0.000	−0.028	−0.864
1A	500	0.3966	[0.3620 0.4940]	0.432	0.001	−0.231	0.094
1B	500	0.0034	[0.0260 0.0780]	0.052	0.000	0.161	1.096
2	250	0	[0.,0.]	0.	0.	0.	−3.0
2	500	0	[0.,0.]	0.	0.	0.	−3.0

In closing this section, we point out the following. Consider a test statistics T that becomes larger with the amount of model misfit, like the χ^2 value. How would the value of T be distributed for the unmodified data? For a unique relationship between data and model, we will obtain a small T value only for the original data set. The range of the $T_l, l = 1, \ldots, L$, values for the resampled data will cover a region of much larger values, especially for small to medium size N. Then, if the range of resampling values T_l covers an area containing the original T value well in its interior, there could be problems with the model specification. Perhaps jackknife and bootstrap could be used to compute sensitivity intervals of goodness-of-fit indices that indicate this unique relationship between data and model. The sem function in CMAT can be used to determine such sensitivity intervals for a set of goodness-of-fit indices for this reason.

Bootstrapping Confidence Intervals of Indirect and Total Effects

Both naive and parametric bootstrap can be used. There is a large amount of literature on bootstrapping standard errors and CIs for indirect and total effects in SEM. Sobel (1982, 1986), Bollen (1987), and Bollen and Stine (1990) recommend both the delta method and the bootstrap for standard errors and confidence intervals.

The original parameter estimates $\hat{\theta}$ are also called *direct effects*. The *total effects* are the sum of indirect and direct effects. For the LISREL model in SEM

$$\eta = \mathbf{B}\eta + \mathbf{\Gamma}\xi + \zeta$$
$$x = \mathbf{\Lambda}_x\xi + \delta$$
$$y = \mathbf{\Lambda}_y\eta + \epsilon.$$

Table 11.3 gives formulas for the effects (Bollen, 1987).

TABLE 11.3
Direct, Indirect, and Total Effects of ξ and η

	Effect on η	Effect on y	Effect on x
Effect of ξ			
Direct	$\mathbf{\Gamma}$	$\mathbf{0}$	$\mathbf{\Lambda}_x$
Indirect	$(\mathbf{I} - \mathbf{B})^{-1}\mathbf{\Gamma} - \mathbf{\Gamma}$	$\mathbf{\Lambda}_y(\mathbf{I} - \mathbf{B})^{-1}\mathbf{\Gamma}$	$\mathbf{0}$
Total	$(\mathbf{I} - \mathbf{B})^{-1}\mathbf{\Gamma}$	$\mathbf{\Lambda}_y(\mathbf{I} - \mathbf{B})^{-1}\mathbf{\Gamma}$	$\mathbf{\Lambda}_x$
Effect of η			
Direct	$\mathbf{B}$	$\mathbf{\Lambda}_y$	$\mathbf{0}$
Indirect	$(\mathbf{I} - \mathbf{B})^{-1} - \mathbf{I} - \mathbf{B}$	$\mathbf{\Lambda}_y(\mathbf{I} - \mathbf{B})^{-1} - \mathbf{\Lambda}_y$	$\mathbf{0}$
Total	$(\mathbf{I} - \mathbf{B})^{-1} - \mathbf{I}$	$\mathbf{\Lambda}_y(\mathbf{I} - \mathbf{B})^{-1}$	$\mathbf{0}$

Source: Bollen (1987).

For the simpler EQS model $\eta = \mathbf{B}\eta + \Gamma\xi$, where the manifest variables of x and y are stacked into ξ and η, only the first column of the table is relevant. Both the delta method and the bootstrap have problems with small sample sizes N. In addition, the approximations for standard errors of the standardized effects may require adjustments that are not necessary when bootstrapping. Bollen and Stine (1990) used percentile CIs for L $\geq$ 1,000 samples. With three examples, two of them with small N, they illustrated the advantage of the bootstrapped CIs compared to those computed by the delta method. In connection with the delta method the bootstrap-t method can also be used for total and indirect effects. To our knowledge, however, no current computer program implements this idea.

There are also a number of papers by David MacKinnon and his coworkers about bootstrapping the indirect and total effects (Lockwood & MacKinnon, 1998; MacKinnon, 1992; MacKinnon & Wang, 1989).

The SEM computer program AMOS offers bootstrapped CIs for indirect and total effects. The sem function in CMAT (Hartmann, 2002) computes estimates for SEs and CIs for indirect and total effects using the naive and the parametric bootstrap. AMOS also uses naive and parametric bootstrap to compute CIs for standardized solutions and variances between latent and manifest variables and the variances among latent variables.

Using Jackknife for Outlier Identification

The jackknife (leave-one-out) process can be used for a table of N goodness-of-fit values (e.g., χ^2 values) to illustrate how much the removal of one observation would improve or reduce the model fit. The observation that corresponds to the largest improvement can be a model outlier ("misfit"). By a stepwise removal of such outlier observations the model fit will be improved.

We illustrate the results using an example from the *EQS Manual* (Bentler, 1989). The $N = 50$-observation artificial data set with one huge outlier as observation 50 shows a χ^2 value

```
Normal Th. Chi-square (df = 8). 16.6917 Prob>chi**2 = 0.0335
```

Analyzing the data without the outlier observation 50 shows the much smaller χ^2 value

```
Normal Th. Chi-square (df = 8).  2.7012 Prob>chi**2 = 0.9517
```

The *EQS Manual* illustrates how to identify the outlier observation with its contribution to the kurtosis. The approach here is more general in that it is able to identify outliers that are *model misfits* that still fit in the multivariate normal distributed range and must not have excessive kurtosis nor skewness.

The sem function in CMAT can be used for identifying a set of model misfits in such a way. The following tables show the output by the sem function:

```
              Rank Order of Outlier Observations
              **********************************

        Function=0.3406 Chisquare=16.69 Pvalue= 0.0335

        Rank     Nobs     OptCrit   Chi-square      pval
          1       50    0.05627578    2.70123733  0.95169
          2       15    0.31474078   15.1075576   0.05709
          3       43    0.31556869   15.1472972   0.05634
          4       12    0.31656969   15.1953451   0.05546
          5        8    0.32461098   15.5813270   0.04878
          6        6    0.32480679   15.5907262   0.04863
          7       13    0.32613436   15.6544493   0.04760
          8       37    0.32654850   15.6743280   0.04729
          9        7    0.32752192   15.7210520   0.04655
         10       31    0.32778227   15.7335490   0.04636
```

It is interesting to note that after removing the strong outlier observation 50 in the second step, observation 28 is considered the worst outlier. Observation 28 did not even occur in the rank order of the 10 largest outliers in the first step. That obviously has to do with the well-known masking effect in stepwise outlier procedures.

```
        ***********************************************
        Rank Order of Outlier Observations (Nobs=49)
        ***********************************************

        Function=0.05628 Chisquare=2.701 Pvalue= 0.9517

        Rank     Nobs     OptCrit   Chi-square      pval
          1       28    0.04358613    2.04854810  0.97949
          2        7    0.04428755    2.08151505  0.97841
          3       36    0.04519250    2.12404738  0.97697
          4        9    0.05043014    2.37021647  0.96751
          5        5    0.05175661    2.43256083  0.96480
          6       17    0.05252000    2.46843989  0.96319
          7       35    0.05275171    2.47933054  0.96269
          8       30    0.05349017    2.51403776  0.96107
          9       16    0.05366883    2.52243518  0.96068
         10        3    0.05370540    2.52415363  0.96060
```

```
**********************************************
Rank Order of Outlier Observations (Nobs=48)
**********************************************

Function=0.04359 Chisquare=2.049 Pvalue= 0.9795

   Rank    Nobs     OptCrit   Chi-square       pval
      1      36  0.03219261  1.48086016  0.99302
      2      16  0.03842558  1.76757676  0.98733
      3       7  0.03866238  1.77846955  0.98707
      4      47  0.03886566  1.78782016  0.98684
      5      27  0.03946553  1.81541450  0.98616
      6       8  0.04062435  1.86872009  0.98478
      7      44  0.04081860  1.87765569  0.98454
      8      24  0.04116463  1.89357288  0.98410
      9      14  0.04148702  1.90840294  0.98369
     10      10  0.04159397  1.91332281  0.98355
```

This a very tempting feature, because it allows us to increase p values of a model by a stepwise removal of observations. Of course there may be very strong ethical restrictions on removing "model misfits" from the analysis. The sem function therefore does not remove those observations in reality, it only shows the theoretical behavior of the change in the goodness of fit.

It is interesting to note that the existence of strong outliers in the data contributes considerably to the computational cost (number of iterations and function calls until convergence). After removing the outlier 50 we notice much faster optimizations to fit the model.

CONCLUSION

Classically, structural equation modeling relies on asymptotic methods and MVN assumptions for obtaining confidence intervals and p values. One possible approach when MVN does not hold is to employ WLS estimation with a weight matrix based on higher order moments (ADF). However, a very large sample size N is necessary to employ this approach, which often cannot be achieved in practical behavioral science applications. Two alternatives have been proposed for obtaining confidence intervals and p values without MVN assumptions when the necessary sample size to use ADF estimation is not available:

- Modifications of the χ^2 test statistics and of the asymptotic standard errors (Satorra & Bentler, 1994; see also Shapiro & Browne, 1985).
- Resampling methods.

In this chapter we discussed in some detail the use of resampling methods in SEM. In particular, we described a variety of methods that can be used to investigate the sampling variability of the statistic of interest. We also described a variety of methods that can be used to obtain confidence intervals given a set of resampled statistics.

In the SEM literature resampling methods have been used to obtain confidence intervals and p values for parameter estimates (i.e., direct effects), indirect effects, and total effects as well as for overall goodness-of-fit statistics. All three of these applications were described here. In addition, we discussed the use of resampling methods for outlier detection. We did consider other applications of resampling methods that have been discussed in the literature. For instance, Enders (2002) presented an extension of the Bollen-Stine bootstrap method for the case of expectation-maximization estimation of SEM with missing data. Yung and Bentler (1994) used bootstrap methods in an attempt to obtain a more stable behavior of ADF estimation fit statistics at its tails, obtaining encouraging results only for large sample sizes and nearly multivariate normal data.

In closing, it is important to bear in mind that resampling methods are not a panacea for inference problems in SEM. If the sample size is too small, naive bootstrapping will not provide correct confidence intervals nor p values. On the other hand, if the sample size is very large, naive bootstrapping may be rather time-consuming. Finally, parametric bootstrap using MVN assumptions may yield considerably biased results if the raw data do not meet the MVN assumptions.

APPENDIX A: PROFILE LIKELIHOOD CONFIDENCE INTERVALS

Profile likelihood confidence intervals were first described in the context of maximum likelihood. Let $F(>\theta_k<)$ be the value of the ML fit function for a fixed value of θ_k and estimates θ_j, $j = 1, \ldots, k-1, k+1, \ldots, p$, that optimize $F(\theta)$ subject to the fixed θ_k. This implies that we have to obtain $F(>\theta_k<)$ for a specific value of θ_k optimizing the fit function with respect to the remaining $p-1$ parameters θ_j, $j \neq k$. Then, the *profile-likelihood confidence region* C_k for parameter θ_k is

$$C_k = \{\theta_k: \quad F(>\theta_k<) \leq F(\hat{\theta}) + Q_{\text{chi1}}(1 - \alpha)\},$$

where $Q_{\text{chi1}}(1 - \alpha)$ is the $(1 - \alpha)$th quantile of the χ^2 distribution with one degree of freedom. If the confidence region is finite, the two endpoints $\{\theta_k^{\text{low}}, \theta_k^{\text{upp}}\}$ of the profile likelihood confidence interval for parameter θ_k are defined as the farthest points left and right of the estimate $\hat{\theta}_k$ where the function $F(>\theta_k<)$ cuts the constant threshold of $F(\hat{\theta}) + Q_{\text{chi1}}(1 - \alpha)$,

$$F(>\theta_k<) \approx F(\hat{\theta}) + Q_{\text{chi1}}(1 - \alpha).$$

The following pseudo-code describes an algorithm for obtaining the lower end point θ_k^{low} of the profile likelihood confidence interval of parameter θ_k. With only a few modifications, an analogous algorithm for the upper end point θ_k^{upp} can be obtained. For simplicity of notation we replace here θ by x.

1. Assuming that we have maximized a likelihood function L(x) for p estimates $(x_1, \ldots, x_p)$ and we have obtained optimal parameter estimates $(\hat{x}_1, \ldots, \hat{x}_p)$ and the optimal likelihood value $\hat{f} = L(\hat{x}_1, \ldots, \hat{x}_p)$, we define a threshold $f^{\text{thr}} = \hat{f} - q(p)$, where $q(p)$ is a quantile of a given probability p that defines the ranges of the CI. We also define a stepsize delta > 0 and two small positive values feps and xeps for termination tests.

2. The following algorithm uses a subroutine

$$f = \text{optim}(L, k, x_k),$$

which, for a specified likelihood function L, an index k, and a fixed estimate $x_k = c$ optimizes L with respect to a constant $x_k = c$ and $p - 1$ unknown estimates x_j, $j \neq k$, and returns the optimal function value f (and the $p - 1$ optimal estimates x_j, $j \neq k$). This subroutine optim is essentially the same as that used in the first step of this algorithm, except that the parameter x_k is here constrained to be constant at a given value.

```
(1) Finding a bracket for the left side range x_k^low:
    Assume delta > 0 and set x_k^0 = x_k^hat - delta.
    Obtain f^0 = optim(L,k,x_k^0).
    If f^0 < f^thr we have a bracket [x_k^0,x_k^hat]
    and proceed with (2).
    Otherwise, we repeat for i=1,...,Ni:
    (1.1) Set x_k^i = x_k^(i-1) - delta and
          compute f^i = optim(L,k,x_k^i).
    (1.2) If f^i < f^thr then proceed with (2).
          Otherwise set i=i+1.
    (1.3) If i < Ni then return to (1.1). Otherwise,
          no bracket was found and we terminate
          with error.

(2) Bisection algorithm (shrinking the bracket):
(2.1) Now we have a bracket [x_k^i,x_k^(i-1)] with
      f^i < f^thr < f^(i-1).
      Compute the midpoint: y = (x_k^(i-1) + x_k^i)/2.
      If x_k^(i-1) - x_k^i < xeps or f^(i-1) - f^i < feps,
      then the bracket is small enough and we
      terminate with x_k^low = y.

(2.2) Otherwise we compute f = optim(L,k,y).
      If f > f^thr then we set: x_k^(i-1) = y and f^(i-1) = f
      otherwise we set: x_k^i = y and f^i = f
      and return to (2.1).
```

Choosing good values for `Ni` and `delta` for finding a bracket is very important. If Wald confidence limits are known, a good choice for `delta` may be the distance between $\hat{x}$ and the corresponding Wald limit. In practice we have found applications where a bracket at least for one side of the CI could not be found even for very large `Ni`. In such cases, the quantile $q(p)$ was just too large, that is, f^{thr} was too small. Because many optimizations may be necessary to find only one range of the interval, the speed of the algorithm depends crucially on providing good starting values for the optimization.

Profile likelihood confidence intervals do not assume that the likelihood function is symmetric with respect to each parameter θ in a small but finite neighbourhood of the optimal estimate $\hat{\theta}$. The graphical inspection of each one-dimensional profile likelihood graph also gives some useful insight about violations of ML theory. Thus, these CIs are more realistic than Wald CIs in *real-world* applications, and some SEM programs already implement them. For example, the SEM computer programs MX (Neale, 1997) and PROC CALIS (Hartmann, 1990), and the `sem` function in CMAT (Hartmann, 2002) offer profile likelihood confidence intervals.

APPENDIX B: CONFIDENCE INTERVALS

Industrialization and Political Democracy Model 1A

The following table contains, for the parameters of Model 1A, (a) the parameter estimates, (b) the Wald confidence intervals (based on the Jacobian), (c) the profile likelihood confidence intervals, (d) the *bias-corrected* naive confidence intervals based on $L = 500$ replications, and (e) the *bias-corrected* parameteric confidence intervals based on $L = 1,000$ replications. The differences between the bootstrap and the Wald CIs are especially large for the variance parameters `zeta1`, `zeta2`, and `zeta3`.

Par	Est	Jac CL Low	Jac CL Upp	PL CL Low	PL CL Upp	naive CL Low	naive CL Upp	param CL Low	param CL Upp
L2	1.19	0.92	1.47	0.93	1.50	0.89	1.47	0.86	1.53
L3	1.17	0.94	1.41	0.95	1.44	0.95	1.48	0.94	1.44
L4	1.25	1.02	1.48	1.03	1.53	0.99	1.57	0.98	1.56
L6	2.18	1.91	2.45	1.92	2.49	1.93	2.57	1.83	2.49
L7	1.82	1.52	2.12	1.53	2.14	1.54	2.09	1.50	2.14
G1	1.47	0.70	2.25	0.71	2.28	0.78	2.14	0.66	2.33
B	0.87	0.72	1.01	0.72	1.02	0.71	0.99	0.70	1.04
G2	0.60	0.16	1.05	0.13	1.09	0.17	1.17	0.07	1.19
E1	1.88	1.01	2.75	1.09	3.00	1.02	2.93	1.04	3.16

```
C15    0.59 -0.12  1.30 -0.07  1.45 -0.34  1.46 -0.19  1.44
E2     7.68  4.95 10.4   5.43 11.0   4.97 10.2   5.23 10.4
C24    1.46  0.08  2.84  0.21  3.11  0.05  3.16  0.24  3.41
C26    2.21  0.74  3.69  0.91  3.97  0.68  4.13  0.83  3.93
C48    0.37 -0.52  1.26 -0.51  1.43 -0.42  1.43 -0.45  1.39
E5     2.34  1.39  3.30  1.54  3.55  1.33  3.72  1.48  3.43
E6     5.04  3.19  6.88  3.53  7.22  3.52  6.94  3.37  7.20
D3     0.47  0.29  0.65  0.32  0.69  0.34  0.67  0.32  0.67
C68    1.39  0.24  2.54  0.36  2.77  0.15  3.41  0.12  2.71
D1     0.08  0.04  0.12  0.05  0.13  0.05  0.12  0.05  0.13
E3     5.02  3.11  6.94  3.44  7.43  3.16  7.18  3.23  7.51
E8     3.35 1.945  4.76  2.13  5.08  1.77  5.59  2.15  5.07
C37    0.72 -0.50  1.94 -0.47  2.15 -0.55  1.87 -0.33  2.09
E4     3.27  1.82  4.71  1.98  5.06  1.92  5.13  1.90  5.21
E7     3.61  2.19  5.03  2.38  5.44  2.66  5.37  2.29  5.37
D2     0.12 -0.02  0.26 -0.02  0.28 -0.02  0.29 -0.01  0.28
ZETA1  3.93  2.20  5.66  2.46  6.15  2.55  5.93  2.32  6.03
ZETA2  0.17 -0.29  0.62 -0.28  0.72 -0.30  0.68 -0.34  0.85
ZETA3  0.45  0.28  0.63  0.31  0.67  0.32  0.64  0.31  0.66
```

Industrialization and Political Democracy Model 1B

The following table shows parameter estimates and confidence intervals of Model 1B:

Par	Est	Jac CL Low	Jac CL Upp	PL CL Low	PL CL Upp	naive CL Low	naive CL Upp	param CL Low	param CL Upp
L2	1.29	1.05	1.52	1.06	1.56	0.99	1.62	0.95	1.62
L3	1.17	0.96	1.39	0.97	1.41	0.98	1.46	0.96	1.45
L4	1.30	1.10	1.50	1.10	1.54	1.04	1.60	1.03	1.60
L6	2.18	1.91	2.46	1.93	2.49	1.93	2.57	1.85	2.50
L7	1.82	1.52	2.12	1.53	2.14	1.54	2.10	1.50	2.14
G1	1.46	0.71	2.22	0.72	2.25	0.78	2.11	0.65	2.30
B	0.89	0.74	1.03	0.74	1.04	0.74	1.00	0.73	1.09
G2	0.46	0.02	0.90	0.01	0.93	0.04	0.96	-0.12	0.96
E1	1.95	1.17	2.72	1.28	2.94	1.24	2.76	1.26	3.09
E2	6.71	4.34	9.08	4.72	9.75	3.75	9.14	4.49	9.66
E3	5.39	3.48	7.31	3.81	7.82	3.47	7.70	3.76	7.85
E4	2.96	1.74	4.17	1.88	4.52	2.01	4.77	1.78	4.51
E5	2.41	1.52	3.30	1.67	3.56	1.46	3.65	1.63	3.57
E6	4.40	2.80	6.01	3.04	6.46	2.92	6.31	2.88	6.28
E7	3.65	2.32	4.99	2.52	5.37	2.64	5.03	2.48	5.31
E8	2.98	1.80	4.15	1.93	4.51	1.63	4.81	1.85	4.53

D1	0.08	0.04	0.12	0.05	0.13	0.05	0.12	0.05	0.13
D2	0.12	-0.02	0.26	-0.02	0.28	-0.02	0.29	-0.01	0.27
D3	0.47	0.29	0.65	0.32	0.70	0.34	0.67	0.32	0.68
ZETA1	3.84	2.22	5.47	2.49	5.92	2.61	5.68	2.35	5.92
ZETA2	0.12	-0.29	0.54	-0.27	0.64	-0.32	0.55	-0.28	0.72
ZETA3	0.45	0.28	0.62	0.31	0.67	0.32	0.64	0.30	0.66

Sexual Risk Behavior Model 2

The following table shows parameter estimates and confidence intervals for the data and model of Coyle et al. (2002). Because of restrictions on space we do not show the bootstraped asymptotic standard errors (ASEs) and the bias estimate. What is remarkable, however, is that the bias values of the parameters of Example 2 are much smaller than the bias values of Examples 1A and 1B. Obviously this can be expected with the much larger number of observations of Example 2.

		Jac CL		PL CL		naive CL		param CL	
Par	Est	Low	Upp	Low	Upp	Low	Upp	Low	Upp
L021	0.95	0.87	1.03	0.87	1.03	0.85	1.04	0.88	1.02
L031	1.05	0.96	1.14	0.96	1.15	0.91	1.18	0.95	1.16
L041	1.16	1.06	1.26	1.06	1.26	1.03	1.30	1.05	1.29
L062	1.25	1.12	1.37	1.13	1.38	1.14	1.39	1.13	1.37
L072	1.33	1.20	1.46	1.21	1.47	1.20	1.48	1.18	1.49
L082	1.33	1.20	1.46	1.20	1.47	1.19	1.46	1.19	1.47
L103	0.98	0.91	1.06	0.91	1.06	0.88	1.11	0.92	1.06
L124	0.90	0.83	0.98	0.83	0.98	0.82	1.00	0.84	0.97
L145	1.32	1.21	1.43	1.21	1.44	1.17	1.50	1.20	1.45
L155	1.28	1.19	1.38	1.19	1.39	1.14	1.44	1.19	1.40
L176	1.10	0.92	1.28	0.93	1.30	0.93	1.35	0.92	1.32
L197	1.37	1.27	1.49	1.27	1.49	1.23	1.58	1.27	1.49
L207	1.05	0.96	1.15	0.96	1.16	0.92	1.22	0.94	1.14
U1	0.20	0.18	0.21	0.18	0.21	0.17	0.22	0.18	0.22
U2	0.18	0.17	0.20	0.17	0.20	0.16	0.21	0.17	0.19
U3	0.26	0.24	0.28	0.24	0.28	0.24	0.29	0.24	0.29
U4	0.28	0.26	0.30	0.26	0.30	0.24	0.31	0.26	0.30
U5	0.49	0.46	0.53	0.46	0.53	0.46	0.52	0.46	0.53
U6	0.33	0.30	0.35	0.30	0.35	0.29	0.35	0.30	0.35
U7	0.26	0.24	0.28	0.24	0.28	0.23	0.29	0.23	0.28
U8	0.33	0.31	0.35	0.30	0.35	0.30	0.36	0.30	0.35
U9	0.06	0.06	0.07	0.06	0.07	0.05	0.08	0.06	0.07
U10	0.06	0.05	0.06	0.05	0.06	0.05	0.07	0.05	0.06
U11	0.09	0.08	0.10	0.08	0.10	0.07	0.11	0.07	0.10
U12	0.17	0.16	0.18	0.16	0.18	0.15	0.20	0.16	0.18
U13	0.11	0.11	0.12	0.11	0.12	0.10	0.13	0.11	0.12
U14	0.17	0.16	0.18	0.16	0.18	0.15	0.19	0.16	0.19

U15	0.08	0.07	0.09	0.08	0.09	0.07	0.10	0.08	0.09
C1	0.03	0.01	0.04	0.01	0.04	0.01	0.05	0.01	0.05
C2	0.03	0.01	0.05	0.01	0.05	0.01	0.05	0.01	0.05
C3	0.01	0.01	0.01	0.01	0.01	0.00	0.02	0.01	0.01
C4	0.03	0.02	0.04	0.02	0.04	0.02	0.05	0.02	0.04
C5	0.01	0.00	0.01	0.00	0.01	0.00	0.02	0.00	0.01
C6	0.11	0.09	0.13	0.09	0.13	0.08	0.14	0.09	0.13
C67	0.03	0.03	0.04	0.03	0.04	0.02	0.04	0.03	0.04
C7	0.06	0.05	0.06	0.05	0.06	0.04	0.07	0.05	0.06

ACKNOWLEDGMENTS

I thank Werner Wothke, Steve Gregorich, and especially Alberto Maydeu-Olivares for very useful discussions, which greatly helped to improve this chapter.

REFERENCES

Arbuckle, J. (1995). *Amos user's guide*. Chicago: Small Waters.

Bentler, P. M. (1989). *EQS, structural equations, program manual* (Program Version 3.0). Los Angeles: BMDP Statistical Software.

Bentler, P. M., & Dudgeon, P. (1996). Covariance structure analysis: Statistical practice, theory, and directions. *Annual Review of Psychology, 47*, 563–592.

Beran, R., & Srivastava, M. S. (1985). Bootstrap tests and confidence regions for functions of a covariance matrix. *Annals of Statistics, 13*, 95–115.

Bickel, P. J., Götze, F., & van Zwet, W. R. (1994). Resampling fewer than *n* observations: Gains, losses, and remedies for losses. In *Diskrete Strukturen in der Mathematik*. Bielefeld, Germany: Universität Bielefeld.

Bollen, K. A. (1987). Total, direct, and indirect effects in structural equation models. In C. Clogg (Ed.), *Sociological methodology* (pp. 37–69). Washington, DC: American Sociological Association.

Bollen, K. A. (1989). *Structural Equations with Latent Variables*, New York: Wiley.

Bollen, K. A., & Stine, R. A. (1990). Direct and indirect effects: Classical and bootstrap estimates of variablity. In C. Clogg (Ed.), *Sociological methodology* (pp. 115–140). Washington, DC: American Sociological Association.

Bollen, K. A., & Stine, R. A. (1992). Bootstrapping goodness-of-fit measures in structural equation models. In K. A. Bollen & J. S. Long (Eds.), *Testing structural equation models*. Newbury Park, CA: Sage.

Browne, M. W. (1974). Generalized least squares estimators in the analysis of covariance structures. *South African Statistical Journal, 8*, 1–24.

Browne, M. W. (1982). Covariance structures. In D. M. Hawkins (Ed.), *Topics in multivariate analyses* (pp. 72–141). Cambridge: Cambridge University Press.

Browne, M. W. (1984). Asymptotically distribution-free methods for the analysis of covariance structures. *British Journal of Mathematical and Statistical Psychology, 37*, 62–83.

Browne, M. W., & Arminger, G. (1995). Specification and estimation of mean and covariance structure models. In G. Arminger, C. C. Clogg, & M. E. Sobel (Eds.), *Handbook of statistical modeling for the social and behavioral sciences* (pp. 185–249). New York: Plenum Press.

Browne, M. W., & Cudeck, R. (1989). Single sample cross-validation indices for covariance structures. *Multivariate Behavioral Research, 24*, 445–455.

Cook, R. D., & Weisberg, S. (1990). Confidence curves for nonlinear regression. *JASA, 85*, 544–551.

Coyle, K., Kirby, D., Marin, B., Gomez, C., & Gregorich, S. (2002). *Draw the Line/Respect the Line: A randomized trial of a middle school intervention to reduce sexual risk behaviors.* Submitted for publication.

Cudeck, R., & Browne, M. W. (1984). Cross-validation of covariance structures. *Multivariate Behavioral Research, 18*, 62–83.

Davison, A. C., & Hinkley, D. V. (1997). *Bootstrap methods and their application.* Cambridge: Cambridge University Press.

Davison, A. C., Hinkley, D. V., & Schechtman, E. (1986). Efficient bootstrap simulation. *Biometrika, 73*, 555–566.

Efron, B. (1979). Bootstrap methods: Another look at the jackknife. *Annals of Statistics, 7*, 1–26.

Efron, B. (1982). *The jackknife, the bootstrap, and other resampling methods.* philadelphia: SIAM.

Efron, B. (1994). Missing data, imputation, and the bootstrap. *JASA, 89*, 463–479.

Efron, B., & Tibshirani, R. J. (1993). *An introduction to the bootstrap.* New York: Chapman & Hall.

Enders, C. (2002). Applying the Bollen–Stine bootstrap for goodness-of-fit measures to structural equation models with missing data. *Multivariate Behavioral Research, 37*, 359–377.

Fishman, G. S. (1996). *Monte Carlo: Concepts, algorithms, and applications.* New York: Springer-Verlag.

Fraser, C. (1980). *COSAN user's guide.* Toronto: Ontario Institute for Studies in Education.

Gleason, J. R. (1988). Algorithms for balanced bootstrap simulations. *American Statistician, 42*, 263–266.

Gonin, R., & Money, A. H. (1989). *Nonlinear L_p-norm estimation.* New York: Dekker.

Hall, P. (1992). *The bootstrap and Edgeworth expansion.* New York: Springer-Verlag.

Hartmann, W. (1990). *The CALIS procedure: Release 6.11, extended user's guide.* Cary, NC: SAS Institute.

Hartmann, W. (2002). *CMAT extension of C language: Matrix algebra, nonlinear optimization and estimation, User's Manual, Release 3.*

Hjorth, J. S. U. (1994). *Computer intensive statistical methods.* London: Chapman & Hall.

Ichikawa, M., & Konishi, F. (1995). Application of the bootstrap methods in factor analysis. *Psychometrika, 60*, 77–93.

Jöreskog, K. G. (1973). A general method for estimating a linear structural equation system. In A. S. Goldberger & O. D. Duncan (Eds.), *Structural equation models in the social sciences* (85–112). New York: Academic Press.

Jöreskog, K. G. (1978). Structural analysis of covariance and correlation matrices. *Psychometrika, 43*, 443–477.

Jöreskog, K. G. (1982). Analysis of covariance structures. In C. Fornell (Ed.), *A second generation of multivariate analysis.* New York: Praeger.

Jöreskog, K. G., & Sörbom, D. (1988). *LISREL 7: A guide to the program and applications.* Chicago: SPSS.

Lambert, Z. V., Wildt, A. R., & Durand, R. M. (1991). Approximating confidence intervals for factor loadings. *Multivariate Behavioral Research, 26*, 421–434.

Lockwood, C., & MacKinnon, D. P. (1998). *Bootstrapping the standard error of the mediated effect.* Paper presented at the 23rd Annual SAS Users Group International Conference, Cary, NC.

MacKinnon, D. P. (1992). Statistical simulation in CALIS. In *Proceedings of the 17th annual SAS Users Group International Conference* (pp. 1199–1203). Cary, NC: SAS Institute.

MacKinnon, D. P., & Wang, E. (1989). A SAS/IML program to estimate indirect effects and their standard errors. In *SUGI 14 Proceedings of the Statistical Analysis System Conference* (pp. 1151–1156). Cary, NC: SAS Institute.

Marn, B. V., Kirby, D. B., Hudes, E. S., Gomez, C., & Coyle, K. (2002). *Youth with older boyfriends and girlfriends: Associations with sexual risk.* Submitted for publication.

Marsh, H. W., Balla, J. R., & McDonald, R. P. (1988). Goodness-of-fit indices in confirmatory factor analysis. The effect of sample size. *Psychological Bulletin, 103,* 391–410.

McArdle, J. J., & McDonald, R. P. (1984). Some algebraic properties of the reticular action model. *British Journal of Mathematical and Statistical Psychology, 37,* 234–251.

McDonald, R. P. (1978). A simple comprehensive model for the analysis of covariance structures. *British Journal of Mathematical and Statistical Psychology, 31,* 59–72.

McDonald, R. P. (1980). A simple comprehensive model for the analysis of covariance structures: Some remarks on applications. *British Journal of Mathematical and Statistical Psychology, 33,* 161–183.

McDonald, R. P. (1984). Confirmatory models for nonlinear structural analysis. In E. Diday et al. (Eds.), *Data analysis and informatics, III.* Amsterdam: Elsevier.

McDonald, R. P. (1985). *Factor analysis and related methods.* Hillsdale, NJ: Lawrence Erlbaum Associates, Inc.

McDonald, R. P. (1989). An index of goodness-of-fit based on noncentrality. *Journal of Classification, 6,* 97–103.

McDonald, R. P., & Hartmann, W. (1992). A procedure for obtaining initial values of parameters in the RAM model. *Multivariate Behavioral Research, 27,* 57–76.

McDonald, R. P., & Marsh, H. W. (1988). *Choosing a multivariate model: Noncentrality and goodness of fit.* Unpublished manuscript.

McDonald, R. P., Parker, P. M., & Ishizuka, T. (1993). A scale-invariant treatment of recursive path models. *Psychometrika, 58,* 431–443.

Meeker, W. Q., & Escobar, L. A. (1995). Teaching about approximate confidence regions based on maximum likelihood estimation. *American Statistician, 49,* 48–53.

Neale, M. C. (1997). *MX. Statistical modeling.* Richmond, VA: Virginia Commonwealth University, Department of Psychology.

Quenouille, M. (1949). Approximate tests of correlation in time series. *Journal of Royal Statistical Society, B, 11,* 18–44.

Sarle, W. (2000). Jackknife and bootstrap analysis. (Technical Rep.). Cary, NC: SAS Institute.

Satorra, A., & Bentler, P. M. (1994). Corrections to test statistics and standard errors in covariance structure analysis. In A. von Eye & C. Clogg (Eds.), *Latent variables analysis* (pp. 399–419). Thousand Oaks, CA: Sage.

Shao, J., & Tu, D. (1995). *The jackknife and bootstrap.* New York: Springer-Verlag.

Shapiro, A., & Browne, M. (1987). Analysis of covariance structures under elliptical distributions. *JASA, 81,* 142–149.

Sobel, R. A. (1982). Asymptotic confidence intervals for indirect effects in structural equations. In S. Leinhardt (Ed.), *Sociological methodology* (pp. 290–312). Washington, DC: American Sociological Association.

Sobel, R. A. (1986). Some new results on indirect effects and their standard errors in covariance structure models. In N. B. Tuma (Ed.), *Sociological methodology* (pp. 159–186). Washington, DC: American Sociological Association.

Steiger, J. H., Shapiro, A., & Browne, M. W. (1985). On the Multivariate Asymptotic Distribution of Sequential Chi-Square Statistics. *Psychometrika, 50,* 253–264.

Stine, R. A. (1989). An introduction to bootstrap methods: Examples and ideas. *Sociological Methods and Research, 18,* 243–291.

Venzon, D. J., & Moolgavkar, S. H. (1988). A method for computing profile-likelihood-based confidence intervals. *Applied Statistics, 37,* 87–94.

Young, G. A. (1994). Bootstrap: More than a stab in the dark. *Statistical Sciences, 9,* 382–415.

Yuan, K. H. B., Bentler, P. M. (1997). Mean and covariance structure analysis: Theoretical and practical improvements. *Journal of the American Statistical Association, 92*, 767–774.

Yung, Y.-F., & Bentler, P. M. (1994). Bootstrap-corrected ADF test statistics in covariance structure analysis. *British Journal of Mathematical and Statistical Psychology, 47*, 63–84.

Yung, Y.-F., & Bentler, P. M. (1996a). Bootstrap-corrected ADF statistics in covariance structure analysis. *British Journal of Mathematics and Statistical Psychology, 47*, 63–84.

Yung, Y.-F., & Bentler, P. M. (1996b). Bootstrapping techniques in analysis of mean and covariance structures. In G. A. Marcoulides & R. E. Schumacker (Eds.), *Advanced structural equation modeling: Issues and techniques* (pp. 195–226). Mahwah, NJ: Lawrence Erlbaum Associates, Inc.

12

Comparing Correlations: Pattern Hypothesis Tests Between and/or Within Independent Samples

James H. Steiger
Vanderbilt University

Many years ago, a psychologist colleague approached me with a question about how to compare two dependent correlations. He was puzzled because equations in two of the few papers then available on the topic seemed to disagree (actually, both contained minor typographical errors). I found the topic fascinating, and got deeply involved in related research of my own. Reviewing the literature, I saw a paper by Rod McDonald (1975) on testing pattern hypotheses on correlations, which discussed a general method for comparing correlations, and alluded to the availability of some computer software he had produced for performing the analyses. At the time, Rod and I were engaged in a spirited (to put it mildly) debate on factor indeterminacy, and it was with some trepidation that I sent him a letter asking if I could acquire the software he had produced. Rod responded quickly and graciously with the requested materials, which saved me a substantial amount of time producing a Monte Carlo study I was working on (Steiger, 1980b). This is only one of the ways that my work (like that of countless others) has been influenced positively by interactions with Rod over the years.

INTRODUCTION

Normal Theory Pattern Hypothesis Tests

A *pattern hypothesis* on a set of statistical parameters specifies that sets of parameters are equal to each other or to specified numerical values. Pattern hypotheses on elements of one or more correlation coefficients have wide application in the analysis of social science data. Unfortunately, the general statistical theory necessary for such comparisons was not made widely available in textbooks prior to 1970, and seemed generally unknown to social scientists at that time. A classic paper by Olkin and Siotani (1964/1976) gave examples of several interesting comparisons, and several subsequent papers (Dunn & Clark, 1969; Neill & Dunn, 1975) by Dunn and her students raised awareness of the fact that correlations may be compared either within or between samples. McDonald (1975) gave a concise description of a general approach to testing pattern hypotheses in a single sample, using the method of maximum likelihood, which assumed a Wishart distribution for the observed covariance matrix. This approach, a special case of the analysis of covariance structures, modeled the covariance matrix of the observed variables as

$$\Sigma = \Delta P(\gamma)\Delta, \tag{1}$$

where $P(\gamma)$ is a patterned correlation matrix that is a function of a vector of free parameters γ, and Δ is a diagonal matrix of free scale factors that are, in this application, generally considered nuisance parameters. This model is a special case of all of the commonly employed structural equation models, including the LISREL model. Consequently, maximum likelihood and generalized least squares (GLS) estimates (and their associated test statistics) may be obtained iteratively using standard methods for nonlinear optimization.

   Browne (1977) presented a generalized least squares procedure for testing any correlational pattern hypothesis in a single sample. Browne's development had a significant advantage over the maximum likelihood approach because the generalized least squares estimators are available in closed form, so nonlinear optimization routines and their attendant convergence problems could be avoided with little apparent loss of efficiency or accuracy. Browne (1977) gave an example of how to fit a perfect circumplex model as a correlational pattern hypothesis. Steiger (1980a, 1980b) reviewed the preceding work, and suggested a modification of Browne's (1977) approach that used the inverse hyperbolic tangent ("Fisher transform") to improve small-sample performance. Steiger (1979) implemented his approach in the freeware program *MULTICORR*. McDonald (1975) showed that ordinary least squares (OLS) estimates are available in closed form when a correlational pattern hypothesis is expressed as a covariance structure model. Browne (1984) showed how to construct an asymptotic chi-square statistic using OLS estimates. The approaches of Browne (1984) and McDonald (1975) may thus be combined to yield a noniterative chi-square test using OLS estimates.

Asymptotically Distribution Free Procedures

Although it is seldom mentioned in textbooks, many standard correlational tests are not robust to violations of the assumption of multivariate normality, and are especially sensitive to kurtosis. Layard (1972, 1974) discussed robust tests for comparing covariance matrices and functions of their elements. Browne (1982, 1984) developed general robust methods for the analysis of covariance structures, and coined the term *asymptotically distribution free* (ADF) to describe the procedures. Browne discussed the use of ADF analysis of covariance structures to test correlational pattern hypotheses.

Steiger and Hakstian (1982) presented expressions for the asymptotic distribution of correlations under very general distributional assumptions, and suggested that this result be used to modify the GLS approaches, thus yielding robust tests of correlational pattern hypotheses.

Comparing Functions of a Correlation Matrix

The approaches of McDonald (1975), Browne (1977), and Steiger (1980a) concentrated on tests involving simple Pearson correlations. Olkin and Siotani (1964/1976) also discussed the use of the multivariate delta method to perform statistical pattern hypotheses tests on multiple and partial correlations. Steiger and Browne (1984) developed an alternative approach that allowed comparison of multiple, partial, and/or canonical correlations using a minor modification of GLS and ADF methods for testing simple correlations. Olkin and Press (1995) gave detailed examples of the use of the delta method for comparing correlations of various kinds.

The work discussed above allows tests on single samples, which may be conceptualized as *N* observations on a vector of *p* random variables in one population. This includes the case where the same variables are sampled on the same subjects several times. For example, this theory can be used to test the hypothesis that a matrix of correlations measured several times on the same individuals has remained stable over time (Steiger, 1980a). However, the foregoing papers do not deal with the case where several *independent samples* (possibly of different size) are taken and correlations need to be compared across the samples with the full range of pattern hypotheses. For example, although a normal theory test for comparing independent correlation matrices is discussed by Jennrich (1970) and a similar ADF test was developed by Modarres and Jernigan (1993), these tests cannot be computed by Steiger's (1979) *MULTICORR*.

The present chapter extends previously available results in several ways:

1. I extend previous theoretical work by Steiger (1980b) in a fairly obvious way to the case of several independent samples, and I provide computer software for performing the analyses.

2. I discuss Steiger's (1980c) observation that unconstrained correlations (those elements of the correlation matrix not constrained to be equal to other correlations or specified numerical values) need not be included in the null-hypothesis specification, thereby reducing computational effort in testing some hypotheses. I then prove the surprising result that eliminating these unconstrained correlations has no effect on the chi-square test statistic, parameter estimates of constrained correlations, or their estimated standard errors.

3. I demonstrate how the chi-square statistic and parameter estimates may be obtained without inverting the estimated covariance matrix of correlations *in both the normal theory and ADF cases, and regardless of whether all correlations are included in the null hypothesis specification.*

PATTERN HYPOTHESIS NOTATION

Let $\mathbf{x}_1, \mathbf{x}_2, \ldots, \mathbf{x}_A$ be A independent random vectors, of (possibly unequal) order p_a, $a = 1, 2, \ldots, A$, having continuous distributions with mean vectors $\boldsymbol{\mu}_a$, $i = 1, 2, \ldots, A$, and variance–covariance matrices $\boldsymbol{\Sigma}_a$, $a = 1, 2, \ldots, A$. Define $\mathbf{P}_a$, $a = 1, 2, \ldots, A$, with typical element $\rho_{ij}^{(a)}$, as the population (Pearson product–moment) correlation matrix of $\mathbf{x}_a$. Let $\boldsymbol{\rho}_a$ be the $v_a \times 1$ vectors whose elements are selected lower triangular elements of the $\mathbf{P}_a$, arranged, for all a, in some consistent fashion. If all nonredundant elements of $\mathbf{P}_a$ are in ρ_a (and they need not be), then $v_a = (p_a^2 - p_a)/2$. Define V as

$$V = \sum_{a=1}^{A} v_a. \tag{2}$$

A *pattern hypothesis* on the $\mathbf{P}_a$ is a hypothesis that sets of their elements are equal to each other or to specified numerical values. Let there be q subsets of the elements of the $\mathbf{P}_a$ that are hypothesized to (within a subset) take on the same unspecified value γ_i, $i = 1, 2, \ldots, q$, and/or possibly w other correlations hypothesized to have a specific numerical value. A convenient notation for expressing such hypotheses is as follows:

$$H_0: \quad \boldsymbol{\rho} = \begin{bmatrix} \boldsymbol{\rho}_1 \\ \boldsymbol{\rho}_2 \\ \vdots \\ \boldsymbol{\rho}_A \end{bmatrix} = \boldsymbol{\Delta\gamma} + \boldsymbol{\rho}^*, \tag{3}$$

where $\boldsymbol{\gamma}$ is a $q \times 1$ vector of common but unspecified correlations, $\boldsymbol{\rho}^*$ is a $V \times 1$ vector containing w numerically specified values (possibly zero), where appropriate, and zeros elsewhere, and $\boldsymbol{\Delta}$ is a $V \times q$ matrix of zeros and ones with typical element

$$\delta_{ij} = \partial\rho_i / \partial\gamma_j. \tag{4}$$

Δ is of rank q.

Consider the following simple example. Suppose $A = 2$, $p_1 = p_2 = 3$, and one hypothesizes that $\mathbf{P}_1 = \mathbf{P}_2$, that is, that the two 3×3 correlation matrices are equal. The null hypothesis may then be written in the notation of Equations 1 through 3 as

$$
\begin{bmatrix}
\rho_{21}^{(1)} \\
\rho_{31}^{(1)} \\
\rho_{32}^{(1)} \\
--- \\
\rho_{21}^{(2)} \\
\rho_{31}^{(2)} \\
\rho_{32}^{(2)}
\end{bmatrix}
=
\begin{bmatrix}
1 & 0 & 0 \\
0 & 1 & 0 \\
0 & 0 & 1 \\
------ \\
1 & 0 & 0 \\
0 & 1 & 0 \\
0 & 0 & 1
\end{bmatrix}
\begin{bmatrix}
\gamma_1 \\
\gamma_2 \\
\gamma_3
\end{bmatrix}
+
\begin{bmatrix}
0 \\
0 \\
0 \\
- \\
0 \\
0 \\
0
\end{bmatrix}. \tag{5}
$$

ASYMPTOTIC SAMPLING THEORY

Following Steiger and Browne (1984), let x_i, x_j, x_k, and x_h be random variables with a multivariate distribution having finite fourth-order moments. Define

$$\mu_i = E(x_i) \tag{6}$$

$$\sigma_{ij} = E(x_i - \mu_i)(x_j - \mu_j) \tag{7}$$

$$\sigma_{ijkh} = E(x_i - \mu_i)(x_j - \mu_j)(x_k - \mu_k)(x_h - \mu_h) \tag{8}$$

$$\rho_{ij} = \sigma_{ij}(\sigma_{ii}\sigma_{jj})^{-1/2}. \tag{9}$$

Next consider samples of $N = n + 1$ independent observations on variates x_i, x_j, x_k, and x_h. We define the sample statistic

$$m_i = N^{-1} \sum_{r=1}^{N} x_{ri} \tag{10}$$

$$s_{ij} = n^{-1} \sum_{r=1}^{N} (x_{ri} - m_i)(x_{rj} - m_j) \tag{11}$$

$$s_{ijkh} = n^{-1} \sum_{r=1}^{N} (x_{ri} - m_i)(x_{rj} - m_j)(x_{rk} - m_k)(x_{rh} - m_h) \tag{12}$$

$$z_{ri} = (x_{ri} - m_i) s_{ii}^{-1/2} \tag{13}$$

$$r_{ij} = s_{ij}(s_{ii}s_{jj})^{-1/2} = n^{-1} \sum_{r=1}^{N} z_{ri}z_{rj} \tag{14}$$

$$r_{ijkh} = s_{ijkh}(s_{ii}s_{jj}s_{kk}s_{hh})^{-1/2} = n^{-1} \sum_{r=1}^{N} z_{ri}z_{rj}z_{rk}z_{rh}. \tag{15}$$

Let $\mathbf{R}_a$, $a = 1, 2, \ldots, A$, be A sample correlation matrices, each based on N_a independent observations. Let the vectors $\mathbf{r}_a$, $a = 1, 2, \ldots, A$, be composed (analogously to the $\boldsymbol{\rho}_a$ in the preceding section) of the lower triangular elements of the $\mathbf{R}_a$. Define $\mathbf{r}_a^*$ as $\mathbf{r}_a^* = n_a^{1/2}(\mathbf{r}_a - \boldsymbol{\rho}_a)$. It has been established (Hsu, 1949; Isserlis, 1916; Steiger & Hakstian, 1982) that under very general conditions $\mathbf{r}_a^*$ has an asymptotic distribution that is $\mathcal{N}(\mathbf{0}, \ \boldsymbol{\Psi}_a)$ (i.e., multivariate normal with a null mean vector and covariance matrix $\boldsymbol{\Psi}_a$). $\boldsymbol{\Psi}_a$ has typical element $\psi_{ij,kh}^{\langle a \rangle} = \mathrm{Cov}(r_{ij}^{*\langle a \rangle}, \ r_{kh}^{*\langle a \rangle})$ given by

$$\psi_{ij,kh}^{\langle a \rangle} = \rho_{ijkh}^{\langle a \rangle} + \frac{1}{4}\rho_{ij}^{\langle a \rangle}\rho_{kh}^{\langle a \rangle}\left(\rho_{iikk}^{\langle a \rangle} + \rho_{jjkk}^{\langle a \rangle} + \rho_{iihh}^{\langle a \rangle} + \rho_{jjhh}^{\langle a \rangle}\right)$$
$$- \frac{1}{2}\rho_{ij}^{\langle a \rangle}\left(\rho_{iikh}^{\langle a \rangle} + \rho_{jjkh}^{\langle a \rangle}\right) - \frac{1}{2}\rho_{kh}^{\langle a \rangle}\left(\rho_{ijkk}^{\langle a \rangle} + \rho_{ijhh}^{\langle a \rangle}\right). \tag{16}$$

If the x's have an elliptical distribution with common relative kurtosis coefficient η, then Equation 16 becomes

$$\psi_{jk,hm}^{\langle i \rangle} = \frac{1}{2}\eta \left\{ \begin{array}{l} \left(\rho_{jh}^{\langle i \rangle} - \rho_{jk}^{\langle i \rangle}\rho_{kh}^{\langle i \rangle}\right)\left(\rho_{km}^{\langle i \rangle} - \rho_{kh}^{\langle i \rangle}\rho_{hm}^{\langle i \rangle}\right) + \left(\rho_{jm}^{\langle i \rangle} - \rho_{jh}^{\langle i \rangle}\rho_{hm}^{\langle i \rangle}\right)\left(\rho_{kh}^{\langle i \rangle} - \rho_{kj}^{\langle i \rangle}\rho_{jh}^{\langle i \rangle}\right) \\ + \left(\rho_{jh}^{\langle i \rangle} - \rho_{jm}^{\langle i \rangle}\rho_{mh}^{\langle i \rangle}\right)\left(\rho_{km}^{\langle i \rangle} - \rho_{kj}^{\langle i \rangle}\rho_{jm}^{\langle i \rangle}\right) + \left(\rho_{jm}^{\langle i \rangle} - \rho_{jk}^{\langle i \rangle}\rho_{km}^{\langle i \rangle}\right)\left(\rho_{kh}^{\langle i \rangle} - \rho_{km}^{\langle i \rangle}\rho_{mh}^{\langle i \rangle}\right) \end{array} \right\}. \tag{17}$$

The multivariate normal distribution is a member of the elliptical class with $\eta = 1$. Substituting this value in the foregoing equation yields the special-case formula (Hsu, 1949; Olkin & Siotani, 1976; Pearson & Filon, 1898) for the covariances of correlations based on observations from a multivariate normal distribution.

Define $\mathbf{r}^*$ as

$$\mathbf{r}^* = \mathbf{r} - \boldsymbol{\rho} = \begin{bmatrix} \mathbf{r}_1^* \\ \mathbf{r}_2^* \\ \vdots \\ \mathbf{r}_A^* \end{bmatrix} = \begin{bmatrix} \mathbf{r}_1 \\ \mathbf{r}_2 \\ \vdots \\ \mathbf{r}_A \end{bmatrix} - \begin{bmatrix} \boldsymbol{\rho}_1 \\ \boldsymbol{\rho}_2 \\ \vdots \\ \boldsymbol{\rho}_A \end{bmatrix}, \tag{18}$$

and let $\mathbf{N}$ be a diagonal matrix of the form

$$
\mathbf{N} = \begin{bmatrix}
n_1 \mathbf{I}_{v_1} & \mathbf{0} & \mathbf{0} & \mathbf{0} \\
\mathbf{0} & n_2 \mathbf{I}_{v_2} & \mathbf{0} & \mathbf{0} \\
\vdots & \vdots & \ddots & \vdots \\
\mathbf{0} & \mathbf{0} & \cdots & n_A \mathbf{I}_{v_A}
\end{bmatrix},
\tag{19}
$$

with $\mathbf{I}_{v_a}$ an identity matrix of order $v_a \times v_a$.

It follows immediately from well known theory on linear composites that $\mathbf{N}^{1/2}\mathbf{r}^*$ has an asymptotic distribution that is $\mathcal{N}(\mathbf{0}, \mathbf{\Psi})$, where $\mathbf{\Psi}$ is a symmetric block-diagonal covariance matrix with the form

$$
\mathbf{\Psi} = \begin{bmatrix}
\mathbf{\Psi}_1 & \mathbf{0} & \mathbf{0} & \cdots & \mathbf{0} \\
\mathbf{0} & \mathbf{\Psi}_2 & \mathbf{0} & \cdots & \mathbf{0} \\
\mathbf{0} & \mathbf{0} & \mathbf{\Psi}_3 & \cdots & \mathbf{0} \\
\vdots & \vdots & \vdots & \ddots & \vdots \\
\mathbf{0} & \mathbf{0} & \mathbf{0} & \cdots & \mathbf{\Psi}_A
\end{bmatrix}.
\tag{20}
$$

ESTIMATION THEORY AND SIGNIFICANCE TESTS

In practice, estimates of the elements of $\mathbf{\rho}$ under the null hypothesis of Equation 3 are restricted in that estimates of correlations that are hypothesized to be equal are required to be equal in value, and estimates of correlations that are hypothesized to be equal to some numerical value are restricted to be equal to that numerical value. Consequently, $\hat{\mathbf{\rho}}$, the vector of estimates of the elements of $\mathbf{\rho}$ under H_0, may be written as

$$
\hat{\mathbf{\rho}} = \mathbf{\Delta}\hat{\mathbf{\gamma}} + \mathbf{\rho}^*,
\tag{21}
$$

and so the problem of estimating $\mathbf{\rho}$ for a given pattern hypothesis can be reduced to finding an estimate $\hat{\mathbf{\gamma}}$ for $\mathbf{\gamma}$.

The "best" estimates are those that minimize an appropriately chosen discrepancy function. The most commonly used discrepancy functions are OLS, GLS, and maximum likelihood. I deal with OLS and GLS estimators here because they can be expressed compactly in closed form.

OLS estimators, in the specialized sense I define them here, minimize the sum of squared discrepancies between the vectors $\mathbf{r}_a$ and estimates $\hat{\mathbf{\rho}}_a$, where, in the multiple-sample case with unequal sample sizes, each squared discrepancy is weighted by n_a. The OLS estimator of $\mathbf{\gamma}$ thus minimizes the discrepancy function

$$
F_{\text{OLS}}(\mathbf{r}, \mathbf{\gamma}) = (\mathbf{r} - \mathbf{\Delta}\mathbf{\gamma} - \mathbf{\rho}^*)' \mathbf{N}(\mathbf{r} - \mathbf{\Delta}\mathbf{\gamma} - \mathbf{\rho}^*),
\tag{22}
$$

where $\mathbf{N}$ is as defined in Equation 19.

$\hat{\boldsymbol{\gamma}}_{OLS}$ is given by

$$\hat{\boldsymbol{\gamma}}_{OLS} = (\boldsymbol{\Delta}'\mathbf{N}\boldsymbol{\Delta})^{-1}\boldsymbol{\Delta}'\mathbf{N}(\mathbf{r} - \boldsymbol{\rho}^*). \tag{23}$$

With $A = 1$, or with equal n_a, $\mathbf{N}$ may be factored out of this expression, and $\hat{\boldsymbol{\gamma}}_{OLS}$ is equivalent to the ordinary (unweighted) least squares estimator discussed by previous authors that is, $\hat{\boldsymbol{\gamma}}_{UOLS} = (\boldsymbol{\Delta}'\boldsymbol{\Delta})^{-1}\boldsymbol{\Delta}'(\mathbf{r} - \boldsymbol{\rho}^*)$. The OLS estimator of $\boldsymbol{\rho}$ is computed from that of $\boldsymbol{\gamma}$ via Equation 21.

Define $\hat{\boldsymbol{\Psi}}$ as a consistent estimator of $\boldsymbol{\Psi}$ under the null hypothesis. We then define the generalized least squares estimator $\hat{\boldsymbol{\gamma}}_{GLS}$ as that which minimizes the discrepancy function

$$F_{GLS}(\mathbf{r}, \boldsymbol{\gamma}) = (\mathbf{r} - \boldsymbol{\Delta}\boldsymbol{\gamma} - \boldsymbol{\rho}^*)'\,\hat{\boldsymbol{\Omega}}^{-1}\,(\mathbf{r} - \boldsymbol{\Delta}\boldsymbol{\gamma} - \boldsymbol{\rho}^*), \tag{24}$$

where

$$\hat{\boldsymbol{\Omega}} = \mathbf{N}^{-1/2}\hat{\boldsymbol{\Psi}}\mathbf{N}^{-1/2}, \tag{25}$$

and $\mathbf{N}^{-1/2}$ is the inverse square root matrix of the matrix $\mathbf{N}$ defined in Equation 19.

This estimate is given by

$$\hat{\boldsymbol{\gamma}}_{GLS} = \left(\boldsymbol{\Delta}'\,\hat{\boldsymbol{\Omega}}^{-1}\boldsymbol{\Delta}\right)^{-1}\boldsymbol{\Delta}'\,\hat{\boldsymbol{\Omega}}^{-1}(\mathbf{r} - \boldsymbol{\rho}^*). \tag{26}$$

We now sketch a proof that F_{GLS} has an asymptotic distribution that is χ^2_{v-q}, and thus provides a significance test of "badness of fit" of the pattern hypothesis. In what follows, the notation $\mathbf{N} \to \infty$ indicates that $\forall a,\ N_a \to \infty$. First, we recall the following lemma (Timm, 1975, p. 132) on the distribution of quadratic forms.

Lemma. Let $\mathbf{y}$ be a random vector having a multivariate normal distribution with mean $\boldsymbol{\mu}$ and covariance matrix $\boldsymbol{\Sigma}$. Then the quadratic form $\phi = \mathbf{y}'\mathbf{A}\mathbf{y}$ has a chi-square distribution with v degrees of freedom and noncentrality parameter $\lambda = \boldsymbol{\mu}'\mathbf{A}\boldsymbol{\mu}$ if and only if $\mathbf{A}\boldsymbol{\Sigma}$ is idempotent and of rank v.

The lemma will apply to asymptotically multinormal variates if $\text{plim}_{N\to\infty}\,\mathbf{A}\boldsymbol{\Sigma}$ is idempotent and of rank v. To apply the lemma, we rewrite F_{GLS} as

$$F_{GLS}(\mathbf{r}, \hat{\boldsymbol{\gamma}}) = \mathbf{y}'\hat{\boldsymbol{\Psi}}^{-1}\mathbf{y}, \tag{27}$$

with

$$\mathbf{y} = \mathbf{N}^{1/2}(\mathbf{I} - \boldsymbol{\Delta}\hat{\mathbf{Q}})(\mathbf{r} - \boldsymbol{\rho}^*) = \mathbf{N}^{1/2}(\mathbf{r} - \boldsymbol{\Delta}\hat{\boldsymbol{\gamma}} - \boldsymbol{\rho}^*) = \mathbf{N}^{1/2}\mathbf{e}, \tag{28}$$

where $\mathbf{e}$ represents the fitted residuals, and

$$\hat{\mathbf{Q}} = (\boldsymbol{\Delta}' \hat{\boldsymbol{\Omega}}^{-1} \boldsymbol{\Delta})^{-1} \boldsymbol{\Delta}' \hat{\boldsymbol{\Omega}}^{-1}. \tag{29}$$

The consistency of $\hat{\boldsymbol{\Psi}}$ implies that

$$\operatorname*{plim}_{N \to \infty} \hat{\boldsymbol{\Psi}} = \boldsymbol{\Psi}, \tag{30}$$

and hence

$$\operatorname*{plim}_{N \to \infty} \hat{\mathbf{Q}} = \mathbf{Q} = (\boldsymbol{\Delta}' \boldsymbol{\Omega}^{-1} \boldsymbol{\Delta})^{-1} \boldsymbol{\Delta}' \boldsymbol{\Omega}^{-1}. \tag{31}$$

To apply the lemma, we need to find the asymptotic distribution of $\mathbf{y}$. From Equations 28 and 31, it follows that $\mathbf{y}$ has the same asymptotic distribution as

$$N^{1/2} (\mathbf{I} - \boldsymbol{\Delta}\mathbf{Q})(\mathbf{r} - \boldsymbol{\rho}^*) = N^{1/2}\mathbf{z}. \tag{32}$$

Under a true null hypothesis, $\boldsymbol{\rho}^* = \boldsymbol{\rho} - \boldsymbol{\Delta}\boldsymbol{\gamma}$, and we have

$$\begin{aligned}
\mathbf{z} &= \mathbf{r} - \boldsymbol{\Delta}\mathbf{Q}(\mathbf{r} - \boldsymbol{\rho}^*) - \boldsymbol{\rho}^* \\
&= \mathbf{r} - \boldsymbol{\Delta}\mathbf{Q}(\mathbf{r} - \boldsymbol{\rho} + \boldsymbol{\Delta}\boldsymbol{\gamma}) - \boldsymbol{\rho} + \boldsymbol{\Delta}\boldsymbol{\gamma} \\
&= \mathbf{r} - \boldsymbol{\rho} - \boldsymbol{\Delta}\mathbf{Q}(\mathbf{r} - \boldsymbol{\rho}) - \boldsymbol{\Delta}\mathbf{Q}\boldsymbol{\Delta}\boldsymbol{\gamma} + \boldsymbol{\Delta}\boldsymbol{\gamma} \\
&= \mathbf{r} - \boldsymbol{\rho} - \boldsymbol{\Delta}\mathbf{Q}(\mathbf{r} - \boldsymbol{\rho}) - \boldsymbol{\Delta}\boldsymbol{\gamma} + \boldsymbol{\Delta}\boldsymbol{\gamma} \\
&= \mathbf{r} - \boldsymbol{\rho} - \boldsymbol{\Delta}\mathbf{Q}(\mathbf{r} - \boldsymbol{\rho}) \\
&= (\mathbf{I} - \boldsymbol{\Delta}\mathbf{Q})(\mathbf{r} - \boldsymbol{\rho}).
\end{aligned} \tag{33}$$

Consequently, $\mathbf{y}$ has the same asymptotic distribution as

$$\begin{aligned}
N^{1/2}\mathbf{z} &= N^{1/2}(\mathbf{I} - \boldsymbol{\Delta}\mathbf{Q})(\mathbf{r} - \boldsymbol{\rho}) \\
&= N^{1/2}(\mathbf{r} - \boldsymbol{\rho}) - N^{1/2}\boldsymbol{\Delta}\mathbf{Q}(\mathbf{r} - \boldsymbol{\rho}) \\
&= N^{1/2}(\mathbf{r} - \boldsymbol{\rho}) - N^{1/2}\boldsymbol{\Delta}(\boldsymbol{\Delta}'\boldsymbol{\Omega}^{-1}\boldsymbol{\Delta})^{-1}\boldsymbol{\Delta}'\boldsymbol{\Omega}^{-1}(\mathbf{r} - \boldsymbol{\rho}) \\
&= N^{1/2}(\mathbf{r} - \boldsymbol{\rho}) - N^{1/2}\boldsymbol{\Delta}(\boldsymbol{\Delta}'\boldsymbol{\Omega}^{-1}\boldsymbol{\Delta})^{-1}\boldsymbol{\Delta}'N^{1/2}\boldsymbol{\Psi}^{-1}N^{1/2}(\mathbf{r} - \boldsymbol{\rho}) \\
&= (\mathbf{I} - \mathbf{V})N^{1/2}(\mathbf{r} - \boldsymbol{\rho}),
\end{aligned} \tag{34}$$

with

$$\mathbf{V} = N^{1/2}\boldsymbol{\Delta}(\boldsymbol{\Delta}'\boldsymbol{\Omega}^{-1}\boldsymbol{\Delta})^{-1}\boldsymbol{\Delta}'N^{1/2}\boldsymbol{\Psi}^{-1}. \tag{35}$$

From the result of Equation 34 and standard results on the expected value and the variance of linear composites, it immediately follows that $\mathbf{y}$ has an asymptotic distribution that is $\mathcal{N}(\mathbf{0}, (\mathbf{I} - \mathbf{V}) \, \boldsymbol{\Psi} \, (\mathbf{I} - \mathbf{V})')$. To show that F_{GLS} is asymptotically χ^2_{V-q}, we must show that $\boldsymbol{\Psi}^{-1} (\mathbf{I} - \mathbf{V}) \, \boldsymbol{\Psi} \, (\mathbf{I} - \mathbf{V})'$ is idempotent and of rank $V - q$. Following some substitution and recombination, we find that

$$\boldsymbol{\Psi}^{-1} (\mathbf{I} - \mathbf{V}) \, \boldsymbol{\Psi} \, (\mathbf{I} - \mathbf{V})' = (\mathbf{I} - \mathbf{V})' . \tag{36}$$

Idempotency of $(\mathbf{I} - \mathbf{V})'$ is established easily by substitution, and the rank property follows from the rank of $\boldsymbol{\Delta}$, which is q. This completes the proof.

Special cases of Equations 26 through 29 may be obtained by selecting different estimators for $\boldsymbol{\Psi}$ (and hence $\boldsymbol{\Omega}$). Under multivariate normal theory, one may obtain a "single-stage GLS" (GLS) estimator by substituting sample correlations for ρ_{ij} in the following equation to obtain estimates of the elements of $\boldsymbol{\Psi}$,

$$\psi^{\langle i \rangle}_{jk,hm} = \left(\rho^{\langle i \rangle}_{jh} - \rho^{\langle i \rangle}_{jk} \rho^{\langle i \rangle}_{kh} \right) \left(\rho^{\langle i \rangle}_{km} - \rho^{\langle i \rangle}_{kh} \rho^{\langle i \rangle}_{hm} \right) + \left(\rho^{\langle i \rangle}_{jm} - \rho^{\langle i \rangle}_{jh} \rho^{\langle i \rangle}_{hm} \right) \left(\rho^{\langle i \rangle}_{kh} - \rho^{\langle i \rangle}_{kj} \rho^{\langle i \rangle}_{jh} \right)$$
$$+ \left(\rho^{\langle i \rangle}_{jh} - \rho^{\langle i \rangle}_{jm} \rho^{\langle i \rangle}_{mh} \right) \left(\rho^{\langle i \rangle}_{km} - \rho^{\langle i \rangle}_{kj} \rho^{\langle i \rangle}_{jm} \right) + \left(\rho^{\langle i \rangle}_{jm} - \rho^{\langle i \rangle}_{jk} \rho^{\langle i \rangle}_{km} \right) \left(\rho^{\langle i \rangle}_{kh} - \rho^{\langle i \rangle}_{km} \rho^{\langle i \rangle}_{mh} \right) ,$$

$$\tag{37}$$

then using the resulting $\hat{\boldsymbol{\Psi}}$ in Equations 26 through 29. However, the null hypothesis may be incorporated into the estimates of the elements of $\boldsymbol{\Psi}$ by using OLS estimates for the ρ_{ij} instead of sample correlations in Equation 37. The resulting estimates are referred to as "two-stage GLS" (TSGLS) estimators. In a similar vein, one may compute "single-stage ADF" (ADF) estimators by constructing $\hat{\boldsymbol{\Psi}}$ with sample correlations and standardized fourth-order moments in Equation 16, and "two-stage ADF" (TSADF) estimators by using OLS estimates instead of sample correlations. Steiger and Hakstian (1982) gave an example of the calculation of a test statistic for comparing two dependent correlations using the TSADF approach.

Define $\mathbf{e}$ as the fitted residuals, that is,

$$\mathbf{e} = \mathbf{r} - \boldsymbol{\Delta} \hat{\boldsymbol{\gamma}} - \rho^* . \tag{38}$$

Estimates of the covariance matrix of the fitted residuals may be calculated as

$$\widehat{\text{Var}}(\mathbf{e}) = \mathbf{N}^{-1/2} (\hat{\boldsymbol{\Omega}} - \boldsymbol{\Delta} (\boldsymbol{\Delta}' \hat{\boldsymbol{\Omega}}^{-1} \boldsymbol{\Delta})^{-1} \boldsymbol{\Delta}') \mathbf{N}^{-1/2} . \tag{39}$$

ASYMPTOTICALLY DISTRIBUTION FREE PROCEDURES

The generalized least squares testing procedures described in the preceding sections, in particular the test statistic of Equation 24, holds so long as $\mathbf{r}$ is an asymptotically unbiased and multinormal estimate of ρ and the estimated variance–covariance matrix (i.e., $\hat{\boldsymbol{\Omega}}_{\text{OLS}}$ in Equation 24) is consistent. If the population distribution departs from multivariate normality, $\mathbf{r}$ will, under very general conditions, remain asymptotically normal, but the matrix $\boldsymbol{\Psi}$ with elements defined as in Equation 37 will no longer be correct. As Steiger and Hakstian (1982) pointed out, this problem can be alleviated by substituting, in place of Equation 37, a more general formula, Equation 16, which holds whether or not the population distribution is multivariate normal. This formula, which yields the *asymptotically distribution free* correlational procedures, should be employed with caution because it requires sample estimates of fourth-order moments. These estimates have large standard errors at small-to-moderate sample sizes, so convergence of the ADF test statistic to its asymptotic distribution is often considerably slower than the normal theory variant. Employing the ADF formula when it is not needed (i.e., when the population distribution *is* multivariate normal) may result in a considerable loss of power.

It should be noted that, with $k > 1$, $\boldsymbol{\Delta}$ of the form in Equation 40,

$$\boldsymbol{\Delta} = \begin{bmatrix} \mathbf{I} \\ \mathbf{I} \\ \vdots \\ \mathbf{I} \end{bmatrix}, \tag{40}$$

and TSGLS estimates, a slight modification of the statistic F_{GLS} (produced by using N_a rather than $n_A = N_A - 1$ in the matrix $\mathbf{N}$) is equivalent to the one given by Jennrich (1970) for testing the equality of two or more correlation matrices. If all elements of $\mathbf{P}$ (including those that are not constrained by the null hypothesis) are included in the hypothesis vector, then F_{GLS} is formally equivalent to the statistic developed by Browne (1977) (although the computational formulas differ, and the relative computational efficiency depends on a particular application).

COMPUTATIONAL CONSIDERATIONS

Interpreted literally, the equations for the chi-square statistics discussed earlier would appear to require, for larger problems, very large amounts of computational space. The difficulties stem from the fact that as the order of a correlation matrix increases, the number of nonredundant elements grows very rapidly. For example, a 20×20 correlation matrix has 190 nonredundant correlations. If $A = 3$ and all correlations are involved in the null hypothesis, the matrix $\boldsymbol{\Psi}$ would then be a block-diagonal matrix of order 570×570. Each of the three 190×190 blocks would contain 17,955 nonredundant elements. Inverting such a matrix involves significant computational effort. In view of such facts, it is important to consider methods for eliminating unnecessary computations.

Discussion of all nontrivial aspects of computational optimization for pattern hypothesis tests is beyond the scope of this chapter. Here I consider aspects of optimization that are related primarily to the statistical theory discussed in this chapter rather than the niceties of programming in any specific computer language. With respect to the latter, let us simply say that (a) some model matrices are sparse, and can be stored very efficiently (as I will illustrate in the case of Δ), and (b) computational efficiency can be improved in many places by careful employment of specialized routines for storing and manipulating symmetric matrices.

I now discuss theoretical developments that are particularly relevant to computational efficiency. First, I point out distinctions between the theory for GLS procedures as presented here and in Steiger (1980b, 1980c), and that given by Browne (1977). In Browne's (1977) derivation of single-sample procedures, the vector ρ is assumed to contain all $(p^2 + p)/2$ elements of $\mathbf{P}$. The theory presented in this chapter, and in Steiger (1980b, 1980c) requires only the *restricted* elements of $\mathbf{P}$ to be included in ρ, although unrestricted elements may be included. For some types of hypotheses, this difference can lead to substantial differences in computational effort. On the other hand, Browne (1977) contained computational simplifications that can yield greater efficiency than the methods discussed here when many of the elements of the correlation matrix are constrained.

Jennrich (1970) presented methods that allow the computation of $\hat{\Omega}^{-1}$ without directly inverting $\hat{\Omega}$, but instead inverting two $p \times p$ matrices. This method can produce substantial gains in computing time. The method, however, assumes that all elements of the correlation matrix being tested are included in ρ, and, moreover, only handle the normal theory case, so that they are not applicable to the method discussed in the preceding paragraph. In what follows, I present an alternative approach that allows computation of $\hat{\Omega}^{-1}$ without directly inverting $\hat{\Omega}$, but which can be applied either in the normal theory or ADF case, and whether or not all correlations are included in ρ.

In the earlier development in this chapter I assumed for clarity of exposition that the correlations included in the null-hypothesis specification were sorted by group, that is, all elements from Group 1 were first, followed by elements from Group 2, etc. However, this assumption is actually not necessary. Two simple adjustments in the notation are needed: (a) The matrix $\mathbf{N}$ in Equation 19 is redefined to be a diagonal matrix with each diagonal element the sample size N (instead of $n = N - 1$) on which the corresponding correlation is based, and (b) the matrix Ψ has elements that are zero if the correlations come from different samples (because they are then independent), and otherwise are as defined previously. Formulas for the estimators and test statistics are otherwise unchanged.

I now demonstrate how GLS estimators, and the associated chi-square statistic, may be obtained without inverting the estimated covariance matrix of correlations (or transformed correlations.) Rather than discuss equations specific to the three chi-square statistics I presented, I give these results in terms of a general computational form applicable, with minimal effort, to all three cases. The following result is needed:

Lemma (Khatri, 1966). Suppose that $\mathbf{S}$ is a $p \times p$ positive-definite matrix. If $\mathbf{A}$ (of order $p \times m$) and $\mathbf{B}$ [of order $p \times (p - m)$] are of ranks m and $(p - m)$, respectively, and if

$$\mathbf{B}'\mathbf{A} = \mathbf{0}, \tag{41}$$

then

$$\mathbf{B}(\mathbf{B}'\mathbf{SB})^{-1}\mathbf{B}' = \mathbf{S}^{-1} - \mathbf{S}^{-1}\mathbf{A}(\mathbf{A}'\mathbf{S}^{-1}\mathbf{A})^{-1}\mathbf{A}'\mathbf{S}^{-1}. \tag{42}$$

Recall that expressions for GLS estimators are of the form

$$\hat{\boldsymbol{\gamma}} = (\boldsymbol{\Delta}'\mathbf{U}^{-1}\boldsymbol{\Delta})^{-1}\boldsymbol{\Delta}'\mathbf{U}^{-1}(\mathbf{r} - \boldsymbol{\rho}^*). \tag{43}$$

This can be rewritten as

$$\hat{\boldsymbol{\gamma}} = (\boldsymbol{\Delta}'\boldsymbol{\Delta})^{-1}\boldsymbol{\Delta}' \left\{ \boldsymbol{\Delta} (\boldsymbol{\Delta}'\mathbf{U}^{-1}\boldsymbol{\Delta})^{-1}\boldsymbol{\Delta}' \right\} \mathbf{U}^{-1}(\mathbf{r} - \boldsymbol{\rho}^*), \tag{44}$$

which, upon application of Khatri's (1966) lemma, becomes

$$\hat{\boldsymbol{\gamma}} = (\boldsymbol{\Delta}'\boldsymbol{\Delta})^{-1}\boldsymbol{\Delta}'\{\mathbf{U} - \mathbf{U}\boldsymbol{\Phi}(\boldsymbol{\Phi}'\mathbf{U}\boldsymbol{\Phi})^{-1}\boldsymbol{\Phi}'\mathbf{U}\}\mathbf{U}^{-1}(\mathbf{r} - \boldsymbol{\rho}^*) \tag{45}$$

$$= (\boldsymbol{\Delta}'\boldsymbol{\Delta})^{-1}\boldsymbol{\Delta}'\{(\mathbf{r} - \boldsymbol{\rho}^*) - \mathbf{z}\},$$

where

$$\mathbf{z} = \mathbf{U}\boldsymbol{\Phi}(\boldsymbol{\Phi}'\mathbf{U}\boldsymbol{\Phi})^{-1}\boldsymbol{\Phi}'(\mathbf{r} - \boldsymbol{\rho}^*), \tag{46}$$

and $\boldsymbol{\Phi}$ is a matrix that satisfies Equation 34 with respect to $\boldsymbol{\Delta}$, that is, if $\boldsymbol{\Delta}$ is of order $V \times q$, then $\boldsymbol{\Phi}$ is of order $V \times (V - q)$, and

$$\boldsymbol{\Phi}'\boldsymbol{\Delta} = \mathbf{0}. \tag{47}$$

Equation 45 shows that GLS estimators can be computed without inverting the matrix $\mathbf{U}$. It also shows that GLS estimators may be thought of as OLS estimators based on an "adjusted" correlation matrix.

An efficient computational approach is as follows:

1. Construct the matrix $\boldsymbol{\Phi}$.
2. Compute the matrix $\boldsymbol{\Phi}'\mathbf{U}\boldsymbol{\Phi}$. To avoid unnecessary multiplication by zeros in the A-sample case, take advantage of the block-diagonal structure of $\mathbf{U}$ by row partitioning $\boldsymbol{\Phi}$ into A submatrices of order $v_i \times (V - q)$. Then use the equality

$$\boldsymbol{\Phi}'\mathbf{U}\boldsymbol{\Phi} = \sum_{i=1}^{A} \boldsymbol{\Phi}_i'\mathbf{U}_i\boldsymbol{\Phi}_i. \tag{48}$$

3. Solve the linear equation system

$$(\Phi'U\Phi)y = \Phi'r = b \tag{49}$$

for y. Then compute z in Equation 46 as $z = U\Phi y$.
4. Compute the vector $r - \rho^* - z$.
5. Compute $\hat{\gamma}$ from Equation 45, keeping in mind that neither the matrix Δ nor, for that matter, $(\Delta'\Delta)^{-1}\Delta'$ need be computed or stored in matrix form because Δ has at most one nonzero element in each row, and that nonzero element is always 1. An efficient internal representation of Δ is an integer vector containing the column index of the 1 in each row of Δ (or a zero if the row is null).

In the course of computing $\hat{\gamma}$, we obtain the quantities y and b. From these, the χ^2_{V-q} test statistic may be obtained using the computational form

$$
\begin{aligned}
\hat{F} &= (r - \rho^* - \Delta\hat{\gamma})'U^{-1}(r - \rho^* - \Delta\hat{\gamma}) \\
&= (r - \rho^*)'\{I - U^{-1}\Delta(\Delta'U^{-1}\Delta)^{-1}\Delta'\}U^{-1}\{I - \Delta(\Delta'U^{-1}\Delta)^{-1}\Delta'U^{-1}\}(r - \rho^*) \\
&= (r - \rho^*)'\{U^{-1} - U^{-1}\Delta(\Delta'U^{-1}\Delta)^{-1}\Delta'U^{-1}\}(r - \rho^*) \tag{50} \\
&= (r - \rho^*)'\Phi(\Phi'U\Phi)^{-1}\Phi'(r - \rho^*) \\
&= b'y.
\end{aligned}
$$

A consistent estimate of the asymptotic variances and covariances of the parameter estimates can be obtained without inverting U using the following result:

$$
\begin{aligned}
\Theta &= \overset{\wedge}{\text{Cov}}(\hat{\gamma}, \hat{\gamma}') = (\Delta'\Delta)^{-1}\Delta'\{\Delta(\Delta'U^{-1}\Delta)^{-1}\Delta'\}(\Delta'\Delta)^{-1}\Delta' \\
&= (\Delta'\Delta)^{-1}\Delta'\{U - U\Phi(\Phi'U\Phi)^{-1}\Phi'U\}(\Delta'\Delta)^{-1}\Delta' \tag{51} \\
&= G'UG - H(\Phi'U\Phi)^{-1}H',
\end{aligned}
$$

where $G = \Delta(\Delta'\Delta)^{-1}$ and $H = G'U\Phi$. Estimated standard errors for the estimates in $\hat{\gamma}$ can be obtained by taking the square root of corresponding diagonal elements of Θ.

I next use the preceding results to demonstrate that elimination of the unconstrained correlations from the null hypothesis specification has no effect on (a) the chi-square test statistic or (b) the estimates of the constrained correlations. First, the following result is needed:

Lemma. If

$$
\Delta = \begin{bmatrix} \Delta_1 & 0 \\ 0 & I \end{bmatrix} \tag{52}
$$

and if

$$\Phi'\Delta = 0, \tag{53}$$

then

$$\Phi = \begin{bmatrix} \Phi_1 \\ 0 \end{bmatrix}. \tag{54}$$

where $\Phi_1'\Delta = 0$.

Proof. Define

$$\Phi = \begin{bmatrix} \Phi_1 \\ \Phi_2 \end{bmatrix}. \tag{55}$$

Then $\Phi'\Delta = [\ \Phi_1'\Delta_1\ \ \Phi_2'\ ] = 0 = [\ 0\ \ 0\ ]$, and hence $\Phi_1'\Delta = 0$ and $\Phi_2 = 0$. ∎

Suppose we consider a case where some of the correlations in the null hypothesis are *not* constrained to be equal to any other correlation or to specific numerical values. We partition ρ as

$$\rho = \begin{bmatrix} \rho_1 \\ \rho_2 \end{bmatrix}, \tag{56}$$

so that all constrained correlations are in ρ_1 and remaining correlations are in ρ_2. In that case, because each unconstrained correlation will be equal to a unique element of γ, Δ will be of the form

$$\Delta = \begin{bmatrix} \Delta_1 & 0 \\ 0 & I \end{bmatrix}, \tag{57}$$

and the null hypothesis may be partitioned as

$$\rho = \begin{bmatrix} \rho_1 \\ \rho_2 \end{bmatrix} = \Delta\gamma + \rho^* = \begin{bmatrix} \Delta_1 & 0 \\ 0 & I \end{bmatrix}\begin{bmatrix} \gamma_1 \\ \gamma_2 \end{bmatrix} + \begin{bmatrix} \rho_1^* \\ 0 \end{bmatrix}. \tag{58}$$

If U (in Equations 43 through 51) is partitioned to correspond with our partition of ρ, that is,

$$U = \begin{bmatrix} U_{11} & U_{12} \\ U_{21} & U_{22} \end{bmatrix},$$

and one applies the facts (easily established by substitution) that

$$(\Delta'\Delta)^{-1} = \begin{bmatrix} (\Delta_1'\Delta_1)^{-1} & 0 \\ 0 & I \end{bmatrix}, \tag{59}$$

$$\Phi'(r - \rho^*) = \Phi_1'(r_1 - \rho_1^*), \tag{60}$$

and

$$\Phi' U \Phi = \Phi_1' U_{11} \Phi_1, \tag{61}$$

then simple substitution and recombination, via Equation 45, establishes that

$$\hat{\gamma}_1 = \left(\Delta_1' U_{11}^{-1} \Delta_1 \right)^{-1} \Delta_1' U_{11}^{-1} (\mathbf{r_1} - \boldsymbol{\rho}_1^*) \tag{62}$$

and that the chi-square test statistic is

$$\hat{F} = (\mathbf{r_1} - \boldsymbol{\rho}_1^* - \Delta_1 \hat{\gamma}_1)' U_{11}^{-1} (\mathbf{r_1} - \boldsymbol{\rho}_1^* - \Delta_1 \hat{\gamma}_1). \tag{63}$$

For example, to prove Equation 62, we combine Equations 45, 46, and 59, obtaining

$$\hat{\gamma} = \begin{bmatrix} \hat{\gamma}_1 \\ \hat{\gamma}_2 \end{bmatrix} = (\Delta' \Delta)^{-1} \Delta' \{ (\mathbf{r} - \boldsymbol{\rho}^*) - \mathbf{z} \}$$

$$= \begin{bmatrix} (\Delta_1' \Delta_1)^{-1} \Delta_1' & \mathbf{0} \\ \mathbf{0} & \mathbf{I} \end{bmatrix} \begin{bmatrix} (\mathbf{r_1} - \boldsymbol{\rho}_1^*) - \mathbf{z_1} \\ \mathbf{r_2} - \mathbf{z_2} \end{bmatrix} \tag{64}$$

$$= \begin{bmatrix} (\Delta_1' \Delta_1)^{-1} \Delta_1' (\mathbf{r_1} - \boldsymbol{\rho}_1^* - \mathbf{z_1}) \\ \mathbf{r_2} - \mathbf{z_2} \end{bmatrix},$$

with

$$\mathbf{z_1} = U_{11} \Phi_1 \left(\Phi_1' U_{11}^{-1} \Phi_1 \right)^{-1} \Phi_1' (\mathbf{r_1} - \boldsymbol{\rho}_1^*)$$

$$= U_{11} \left\{ U_{11}^{-1} - U_{11}^{-1} \Delta_1 \left(\Delta_1' U_{11}^{-1} \Delta_1 \right)^{-1} \Delta_1' U_{11}^{-1} \right\} (\mathbf{r_1} - \boldsymbol{\rho}_1^*) \tag{65}$$

$$= \left\{ \mathbf{I} - \Delta_1 \left(\Delta_1' U_{11}^{-1} \Delta_1 \right)^{-1} \Delta_1' U_{11}^{-1} \right\} (\mathbf{r_1} - \boldsymbol{\rho}_1^*)$$

and

$$\mathbf{z_2} = U_{21} \Phi_1 (\Phi_1' U_{11} \Phi_1)^{-1} \Phi_1' (\mathbf{r_1} - \boldsymbol{\rho}_1^*)$$

$$= U_{21} U_{11}^{-1} \left\{ \mathbf{I} - \Delta_1 \left(\Delta_1' U_{11}^{-1} \Delta_1 \right)^{-1} \Delta_1' U_{11}^{-1} \right\} (\mathbf{r_1} - \boldsymbol{\rho}_1^*). \tag{66}$$

Combining Equations 64 through 66, we find

$$\hat{\gamma}_2 = \mathbf{r_2} - \mathbf{z_2} = \mathbf{r_2} - U_{21} U_{11}^{-1} (\mathbf{r_1} - \Delta_1 \hat{\gamma}_1 - \boldsymbol{\rho}_1^*)$$

$$= \mathbf{r_2} - U_{21} U_1^{11} \hat{\mathbf{e}}, \tag{67}$$

where $\hat{\mathbf{e}}_1$ is the vector of residual correlations, that is, the difference between the estimates and the sample correlations.

The upper partition of Equation 64, when compared to Equation 45, demonstrates that adding unconstrained correlations to the hypothesis specification does not affect the GLS estimates of the constrained correlations in $\hat{\boldsymbol{\gamma}}_1$. It also demonstrates that, in a single sample, GLS estimates may be thought of as OLS estimates computed on an "adjusted" set of sample correlations. When the adjustment is zero, GLS and OLS estimates are identical.

The fact that the chi-square statistic is unchanged by the addition of unconstrained correlations may be proven in a similar manner. From Equations 50, 60, and 61 we have

$$
\begin{aligned}
\hat{F} &= (\mathbf{r} - \boldsymbol{\rho}^*)'\boldsymbol{\Phi}(\boldsymbol{\Phi}'\mathbf{U}\boldsymbol{\Phi})^{-1}\boldsymbol{\Phi}'(\mathbf{r} - \boldsymbol{\rho}^*) \\
&= (\mathbf{r}_1 - \boldsymbol{\rho}_1^*)'\boldsymbol{\Phi}_1(\boldsymbol{\Phi}_1'\mathbf{U}_{11}^{-1}\boldsymbol{\Phi}_1)^{-1}\boldsymbol{\Phi}_1'(\mathbf{r}_1 - \boldsymbol{\rho}_1^*).
\end{aligned}
\tag{68}
$$

Comparing this to the penultimate line of Equation 50 establishes that the chi-square statistic calculated with unconstrained correlations included in the hypothesis statement is equivalent to the statistic without the correlations included.

SOFTWARE FOR PERFORMING PATTERN HYPOTHESIS TESTS

There are several computer programs specifically designed to test correlational pattern hypotheses. Key points of differentiation are (a) whether the software can perform ADF as well as normal theory tests and (b) whether the software can perform tests on more than one sample.

MULTICORR (Steiger, 1979) is a FORTRAN program for testing any pattern hypothesis on a single sample. MULTICORR is freeware, and employs the Fisher transform, as discussed in Steiger (1980a, 1980b). The program is available for download from the website http://www.statpower.net or by e-mail from the author. MULTICORR has some serious limitations, in that it is currently designed to operate on single samples and is limited to correlation matrices no larger than 18×18.

FITCORS (Mels, 2000) is a general program for fitting correlational structures of the form

$$
H_0: \quad \boldsymbol{\rho} = \mathbf{m}(\boldsymbol{\theta}),
\tag{69}
$$

where $\boldsymbol{\theta}$ is a vector of free parameters and $\mathbf{m}$ is a vector model function. Clearly, Equation 69 includes Equation 3 as a special case, so FITCORS can be used to fit correlational models that are not pattern hypothesis tests. However, for models that are neither path models nor correlational pattern hypotheses, the user is required to write and compile a function implementing the model function $\mathbf{m}$. FITCORS implements a variety of estimation methods, including TSGLS, GLS,

ADF, and TSADF chi-square statistics. The program runs under Windows, and is available from its author, Gerhard Mels, whose e-mail address at this writing is mels@ssicentral.com. The program currently performs general tests on one sample only.

WBCORR (within–between correlational tests) for Mathematica is a freeware *Mathematica* package for performing correlational pattern hypothesis tests in one or more samples with possibly unequal sample sizes. The program, which requires the well-known symbolic algebra program *Mathematica*, includes options for analyzing raw data or correlation matrices, and implements TSGLS, GLS, ADF, and TSADF chi-square statistics. WBCORR is available from the author by e-mail, or may be downloaded from his website at http://www.statpower.net.

Other approaches to performing correlational pattern hypotheses are available besides those just discussed. For example, correlational pattern hypothesis tests may be performed with any common covariance structure analysis software program by implementing the method discussed by McDonald (1975). Although these programs are designed primarily to test hypotheses on a covariance matrix, they can be employed to test correlational pattern hypotheses. In particular, my program SEPATH (part of *Statistica*) can perform correlational pattern hypotheses directly on one or more samples by simply selecting "Analyze Correlations" as a program option, and Michael Browne's RAMONA (part of *Systat*) offers similar capabilities for a single sample. Correlation-based methods, i.e., those based on the sampling theory of a correlation matrix, have somewhat different performance characteristics than covariance-based procedures. For a comparison of the relative performance of covariance-based and correlation-based methods for analyzing correlational pattern hypothesis, see Monte Carlo experiments by Steiger (1980b), Fouladi (1996, 2000), and Mels (2000).

SOME NUMERICAL EXAMPLES

The following examples illustrate some of the procedures that can be performed using the theory in this chapter. All these tests can be performed using WBCORR. After loading in the package to *Mathematica* with the command "<<wbcorr.m" the user simply inputs data, specifies a hypothesis, and invokes a single command.

Single-Sample Tests

This section examines hypothesis tests that involve only a single group. The first three examples are based on the raw data shown in Table 12.1.

These data are 25 pseudorandom samples of six independent variates all having a lognormal (0, 1) distribution. The data were rounded at two decimals, and the numbers actually processed are exactly as shown in the table. Assume in

TABLE 12.1
Sample Data Set 1

X_1	X_2	X_3	X_4	X_5	X_6
1.24	2.61	0.26	1.05	7.55	0.20
0.28	2.36	1.19	1.66	0.47	0.46
0.37	0.82	3.23	0.12	4.57	1.84
0.11	5.73	3.04	1.04	0.38	0.35
10.75	2.66	2.62	0.29	4.12	0.38
0.21	0.27	0.42	1.07	1.41	0.24
0.95	0.83	1.00	1.00	1.35	0.90
0.78	0.87	6.99	3.01	2.34	0.41
0.65	0.80	0.70	0.60	2.38	0.49
0.57	0.28	0.55	0.57	0.20	4.60
2.99	0.42	0.34	2.80	0.36	0.67
2.87	1.41	0.49	0.13	3.18	0.53
4.87	2.72	0.39	1.35	1.52	1.89
0.83	2.09	1.00	0.39	0.82	1.80
0.32	3.28	1.91	1.13	1.47	1.44
0.59	5.06	1.07	0.40	3.25	0.57
0.14	0.22	0.25	0.64	0.53	1.07
1.67	1.83	0.85	0.15	0.89	2.39
1.86	0.52	0.14	2.94	1.40	0.97
0.69	0.19	0.46	1.39	4.32	1.51
0.80	4.00	1.90	2.24	2.77	1.31
0.66	0.51	4.52	0.57	4.84	0.82
0.35	0.27	0.78	0.37	0.25	0.72
1.91	1.02	4.32	0.59	1.05	2.35
0.43	0.41	1.67	1.43	0.62	2.64

these examples that the six variables are all observed on the same group of subjects.

Equicorrelation Hypothesis

Suppose that you hypothesize that the first three variables have an *equicorrelation* structure. This structural hypothesis assumes that all off-diagonal elements of the correlation matrix are equal, so the null hypothesis, in the notation of Equation 3, is represented as follows (superscripts being unnecessary when there is only one sample):

$$
\begin{bmatrix} \rho_{21}^{\langle 1 \rangle} \\ \rho_{31}^{\langle 1 \rangle} \\ \rho_{32}^{\langle 1 \rangle} \end{bmatrix} = \begin{bmatrix} 1 \\ 1 \\ 1 \end{bmatrix} \begin{bmatrix} \gamma_1 \end{bmatrix} + \begin{bmatrix} 0 \\ 0 \\ 0 \end{bmatrix} = \begin{bmatrix} \gamma_1 \\ \gamma_1 \\ \gamma_1 \end{bmatrix} + \begin{bmatrix} 0 \\ 0 \\ 0 \end{bmatrix}. \tag{70}
$$

To test this hypothesis with WBCORR, one codes the left and right sides of the
equation into a single hypothesis matrix of the form

$$\begin{bmatrix} 1 & 2 & 1 & 1 & 0 \\ 1 & 3 & 1 & 1 & 0 \\ 1 & 3 & 2 & 1 & 0 \end{bmatrix}. \tag{71}$$

Each row of the hypothesis matrix represents a statement about a correlation that
is constrained by the null hypothesis. The statement is of the form

$$\text{group, row, column, parameter tag, fixed value.} \tag{72}$$

If the correlation is fixed at a specific numerical value, the fixed value is entered
as the ρ^* value (and the parameter tag is 0). If the parameter tag is nonzero, then
the fixed value is not used and is generally entered as zero.

If the raw data are read into *Mathematica* and assigned to a matrix called "data"
and the foregoing hypothesis matrix is assigned to a matrix called "equicorrelationHypothesis," testing the model requires entry of the single command "ComputeChiSquare[{data}, equicorrelationHypothesis, {25}, DataType→RawData]."
WBCORR responds by producing output that describes the results of hypothesis
testing. The typical *Mathematica* session performing the computation for this problem is shown in Appendix A. Scanning the output, we see a number of items that
are common to such analyses. WBCORR is invoked with a single statement of the
form

```
ComputeChiSquare[dataList,hypothesisMatrix,sampleSizeList,
    DataType, EstimationMethod]
```

"dataList" is a *Mathematica* list whose elements are either data matrices or
correlation matrices. "hypothesisMatrix" is a single matrix discussed previously.
"sampleSizeList" is a *Mathematica* list whose elements are the sample sizes for the
data sets. The final two parameters are optional. "DataType" is an option assignment that has two possible values, "RawData" and "CorrelationMatrixData." CorrelationMatrixData is the default, and if a correlation matrix is analyzed, this option
may be omitted. If raw data are analyzed, the option assignment "DataType→
RawData" must be included in the command line. "EstimationMethod" has four
possible values, with the default being "TSGLS" and the others being GLS, ADF,
and TSADF. The EstimationMethod parameter may be omitted if TSGLS is being
performed, otherwise an option assignment like "EstimationMethod→GLS" must
be entered.

After printing the input correlation matrix, WBCORR generates OLS estimates
of the entire input correlation matrix. Note that the estimates for ρ_{21}, ρ_{31}, and ρ_{32} are
all equal to a common value, that is, .0642778. The next output section includes
a list of parameter estimates for the constrained free parameters. In this case,

three correlations are constrained to be equal, and have a parameter tag of 1. The two-stage GLS estimate for the parameter is identical to the OLS estimate. The chi-square test for the null hypothesis, reported under "Significance Test Results," is *not* significant, and so the null hypothesis remains tenable. Note that the tests for multivariate normality based on the Mardia (1970) indices of multivariate skewness and kurtosis are both statistically significant, indicating that the default test (which assumes multivariate normality) may be inaccurate. In such a situation, it is advisable to compute an ADF version of the test statistic. Reanalysis with the two-stage ADF test statistic yields the results shown in the second part of Appendix A. Three important changes can be observed when comparing the two-stage ADF and two-stage GLS results. First, the parameter estimate for the common correlation has changed, and so has its standard error. Second, the value of the chi-square statistic and its associated probability level have changed. In this case, the statistical decision remains the same, that is, not to reject the null hypothesis. However, in many cases shifting to an ADF statistic can change the outcome of a significance test. Third, the parameter estimate for parameter 1 is no longer equal to the corresponding OLS estimate.

One can also employ a range of estimation methods, including two-stage GLS and two-stage ADF, to test the equicorrelation matrix with the freeware program FITCORS (Mels, 2000).

Equality of Two Dependent Correlations

A common pattern hypothesis is to test whether two predictor variables predict a criterion equally well. This is a hypothesis of the form

$$\rho_{21} = \rho_{32} = \rho_1. \tag{73}$$

To test such a hypothesis with WBCORR, one uses the following hypothesis matrix:

$$\begin{bmatrix} 1 & 2 & 1 & 1 & 0 \\ 1 & 3 & 2 & 1 & 0 \end{bmatrix}. \tag{74}$$

Mathematica input and output for such a hypothesis test using the two-stage ADF estimation method are shown in Appendix B.

Perfect Circumplex (Symmetric Circulant) Structure

A perfect circumplex, or symmetric circulant hypothesis (Wiggins, Steiger, & Gaelick, 1981), implies that correlations are exactly equal in diagonal strips, and is a special case of the circumplex model discussed by Browne (1992). For six variables, this model states that the correlation matrix is of the form

$$
P = \begin{bmatrix}
1 \\
\rho_1 & 1 \\
\rho_2 & \rho_1 & 1 \\
\rho_3 & \rho_2 & \rho_1 & 1 \\
\rho_2 & \rho_3 & \rho_2 & \rho_1 & 1 \\
\rho_1 & \rho_2 & \rho_3 & \rho_2 & \rho_1 & 1
\end{bmatrix}. \tag{75}
$$

The WBCORR hypothesis matrix and output for this model are shown in Appendix C. For replicability, we use a random number seed (i.e., 123). Note that, in this case, both tests for multivariate normality have p values close to .50, indicating that there is no evidence for rejecting multivariate normality. Using the two-stage GLS estimation method, we obtain a chi-square test for the circumplex hypothesis that is not significant, indicating that the hypothesis of a perfect circumplex remains tenable for these data.

This example tested the very highly constrained hypothesis of perfect circumplex structure. Browne (1992) discussed more-general circumplex models that are often of significant interest in practical applications. These models require software that can test structural models that are more general than a pattern hypothesis. A freeware computer program (CIRCUM) for fitting these more general models may be obtained from Michael Browne's website.

Equality of Correlation Matrices Over Time

If a set of k variables is observed m times on N individuals, the resulting correlation matrix may be viewed as N observations on km dependent variables. Equality of correlation matrices over time may then be tested by constraining the correlations across the m occasions to be equal to each other. Consider, for example, the correlations among three variables measured on the same individuals on two occasions. In this case, X_1, X_2, and X_3 represent the three variables on the first occasion, and X_4 through X_6 represent the same three variables on the second measurement occasion. Consequently, the hypothesis that the correlations among the three variables have not changed over time is equivalent to the following:

$$
H_0: \quad \rho_{21} = \rho_{54} = \gamma_1, \quad \rho_{31} = \rho_{64} = \gamma_2, \quad \rho_{32} = \rho_{65} = \gamma_3. \tag{76}
$$

In WBCORR, we express such a hypothesis with the following hypothesis matrix:

$$
\begin{bmatrix}
1 & 2 & 1 & 1 & 0 \\
1 & 3 & 1 & 2 & 0 \\
1 & 3 & 2 & 3 & 0 \\
1 & 5 & 4 & 1 & 0 \\
1 & 6 & 4 & 2 & 0 \\
1 & 6 & 5 & 3 & 0
\end{bmatrix}.
$$

TABLE 12.2
Correlations Among Three Variables in Two Groups

	GPA	SAT-V	SAT-M
GPA	1.00	0.44	0.38
SAT-V	0.31	1.00	0.42
SAT-M	0.29	0.24	1.00

Note. Correlations for Group 1, $N = 521$, above the diagonal. Correlations for Group 2, $N = 644$, below the diagonal. GPA, Grade-point average; SAT-V, Scholastic Aptitude Test-Verbal; SAT-M, SAT-Math.

A sample correlation matrix representing measurements on three variables on two separate occasions will be of order 6×6, and may be analyzed with WBCORR, MULTICORR, or FITCORS to test the hypothesis of equality of correlation matrices over time. For brevity, I do not show computer output and input files here (although they are distributed with the WBCORR software).

Multiple-Sample Tests

This section examines hypothesis tests performed on two or more correlation matrices sampled from independent groups. For simplicity, I confine numerical examples to two correlation matrices because the extension to more than two groups is straightforward.

Equality of Independent Correlation Matrices

Table 12.2 shows two correlation matrices, representing correlations between grade-point average (GPA) and Scholastic Aptitude Test (SAT)-Verbal and SAT-Math scores for two groups of unequal size. To test whether the two correlation matrices are equal, we employ the following hypothesis matrix with WBCORR:

$$\begin{bmatrix} 1 & 2 & 1 & 1 & 0 \\ 1 & 3 & 1 & 2 & 0 \\ 1 & 3 & 2 & 3 & 0 \\ 2 & 2 & 1 & 1 & 0 \\ 2 & 3 & 1 & 2 & 0 \\ 2 & 3 & 2 & 3 & 0 \end{bmatrix}.$$

The first three lines of the hypothesis matrix simply establish that the elements of the correlation matrix for the first group are all free parameters, with parameter tags 1, 2, and 3. The next three lines constrain the elements of the correlation matrix in the second group to be equal to those in the first group. WBCORR input and output for the example are shown in Appendix D.

Equality of Predictor–Criterion Correlations in Two Groups

Suppose that, rather than comparing all the correlations for the data in Table 12.2, we wished to compare only the predictor–criterion correlations. For example, we might wish to test whether the correlations between the predictors (SAT-Verbal and SAT-Math) and the criterion (GPA) differed in the two groups. In this case, the hypothesis matrix is

$$
\begin{bmatrix}
1 & 2 & 1 & 1 & 0 \\
1 & 3 & 1 & 2 & 0 \\
2 & 2 & 1 & 1 & 0 \\
2 & 3 & 1 & 2 & 0
\end{bmatrix}.
$$

The TSGLS chi-square statistic is 7.57 with two degrees of freedom ($p = .022721$), and is significant at the .05 level. For brevity, I do not show computer output and input files here (although they are distributed with the WBCORR software).

Equality of Circumplex Structures in Two Groups

One can test the simultaneous hypothesis that two groups have the same correlation matrix *and* that the correlation matrix is a perfect circumplex. Appendix E presents input and output for a demonstration of such calculations, using WBCORR. The first part of the demonstration uses the random number generation capabilities of *Mathematica* to produce two sets of data, with different sample sizes, both of which fit the same circumplex structure perfectly. The second part of the demonstration tests the hypothesis that the two groups have identical circumplex structure, that is, have correlation matrices that are the same *and* that fit a circumplex perfectly. Not surprisingly, the chi-square statistic is not significant.

CONCLUSIONS

This chapter presented a general theory for multiple-sample hypothesis tests on correlations. Using this theory, between- and/or within-sample hypotheses about equality of correlations can be tested. Much of the theory presented in this chapter may be described as a straightforward complement to work by Browne (1977, 1984), McDonald (1975), Steiger (1980b), and Steiger and Hakstian (1982). However, the *Mathematica* software implementation in WBCORR presents a simple, unified method for performing the tests on virtually any number of groups with raw data or correlation matrix input. In addition, researchers may employ WBCORR with *Mathematica's* Monte Carlo sampling capabilities to assess the performance characteristics of these test statistics in any anticipated application.

APPENDIX A: INPUT AND OUTPUT
FOR EQUICORRELATION
HYPOTHESIS EXAMPLE

Two-Stage GLS Analysis

Preliminary Input Lines:

```
In[1]:= << wbcorr.m
In[2]:= data = Import ["EquicorrelationData.csv"];
        Matrixform[data]
Out[2]//MatrixForm=
```

$$
\begin{pmatrix}
1.24 & 2.61 & 0.26 & 1.05 & 7.55 & 0.2 \\
0.28 & 2.36 & 1.19 & 1.66 & 0.47 & 0.46 \\
0.37 & 0.82 & 3.23 & 0.12 & 4.57 & 1.84 \\
0.11 & 5.73 & 3.04 & 1.04 & 0.38 & 0.35 \\
10.75 & 2.66 & 2.62 & 0.29 & 4.12 & 0.38 \\
0.21 & 0.27 & 0.42 & 1.07 & 1.41 & 0.24 \\
0.95 & 0.83 & 1. & 1. & 1.35 & 0.9 \\
0.78 & 0.87 & 6.99 & 3.01 & 2.34 & 0.41 \\
0.65 & 0.8 & 0.7 & 0.6 & 2.38 & 0.49 \\
0.57 & 0.28 & 0.55 & 0.57 & 0.2 & 4.6 \\
2.99 & 0.42 & 0.34 & 2.8 & 0.36 & 0.67 \\
2.87 & 1.41 & 0.49 & 0.13 & 3.18 & 0.53 \\
4.87 & 2.72 & 0.39 & 1.35 & 1.52 & 1.89 \\
0.83 & 2.09 & 1. & 0.39 & 0.82 & 1.8 \\
0.32 & 3.28 & 1.91 & 1.13 & 1.47 & 1.44 \\
0.59 & 5.06 & 1.07 & 0.4 & 3.25 & 0.57 \\
0.14 & 0.22 & 0.25 & 0.64 & 0.53 & 1.07 \\
1.67 & 1.83 & 0.85 & 0.15 & 0.89 & 2.39 \\
1.86 & 0.52 & 0.14 & 2.94 & 1.4 & 0.97 \\
0.69 & 0.19 & 0.46 & 1.39 & 4.32 & 1.51 \\
0.8 & 4. & 1.9 & 2.24 & 2.77 & 1.31 \\
0.66 & 0.51 & 4.52 & 0.57 & 4.84 & 0.82 \\
0.35 & 0.27 & 0.78 & 0.37 & 0.25 & 0.72 \\
1.91 & 1.02 & 4.32 & 0.59 & 1.05 & 2.35 \\
0.43 & 0.41 & 1.67 & 1.43 & 0.62 & 2.64
\end{pmatrix}
$$

$$
In[3]: = \textbf{equicorrelationHypothesis} =
\begin{pmatrix}
1 & 2 & 1 & 1 & 0 \\
1 & 3 & 1 & 1 & 0 \\
1 & 3 & 2 & 1 & 0
\end{pmatrix};
$$

Command Line and Output:

In[4]: = **ComputeChiSquare[{data},equicorrelationHypothesis, {25}, DataType → RawData]**

WBCORR Output

Hypothesis Matrix

Group	Row	Column	Parameter Tag	Fixed Value
1	2	1	1	0
1	3	1	1	0
1	3	2	1	0

Input Correlation Matrix 1 Sample Size = 25

$$
\begin{pmatrix}
1. & 0.108968 & 0.00694539 & -0.0735271 & 0.195968 & -0.116128 \\
0.108968 & 1. & 0.0769198 & -0.0665498 & 0.107224 & -0.239101 \\
0.00694539 & 0.0769198 & 1. & 0.128691 & 0.150023 & -0.0691065 \\
-0.0735271 & -0.0665498 & 0.128691 & 1. & -0.152004 & -0.19305 \\
0.195968 & 0.107224 & 0.150023 & -0.152004 & 1. & -0.322708 \\
-0.116128 & -0.239101 & -0.0691065 & -0.19305 & -0.322708 & 1.
\end{pmatrix}
$$

OLS Estimates of Correlation Matrix 1

$$
\begin{pmatrix}
1. & 0.0642778 & 0.0642778 & -0.0735271 & 0.195968 & -0.116128 \\
0.0642778 & 1. & 0.0642778 & -0.0665498 & 0.107224 & -0.239101 \\
0.0642778 & 0.0642778 & 1. & 0.128691 & 0.150023 & -0.0691065 \\
-0.0735271 & -0.0665498 & 0.128691 & 1. & -0.152004 & -0.19305 \\
0.195968 & 0.107224 & 0.150023 & -0.152004 & 1. & -0.322708 \\
-0.116128 & -0.239101 & -0.0691065 & -0.19305 & -0.322708 & 1.
\end{pmatrix}
$$

Two-Stage GLS Parameter Estimates

Parameter Tag	Estimate	Standard Error
1	0.0642778	0.124453

Significance Test Results

Chi Square	df	plevel
0.140485	2	0.932168

Assessment of Multivariate Normality

	Multivariate Skewness	Chi Square	df	plevel
1	27.3963	114.151	56	7.3502×10^{-6}

	Multivariate Kurtosis	Z	plevel (2-tailed)
1	55.1678	2.77102	0.00558816

Two-Stage ADF Analysis

Command Line and Output:

In[5]:= **ComputeChiSquare[{data}, equicorrelationHypothesis, {25},DataType → RawData,EstimationMethod→ TSADF]**

WBCORR Output

Hypothesis Matrix

Group	Row	Column	Parameter Tag	Fixed Value
1	2	1	1	0
1	3	1	1	0
1	3	2	1	0

Input Correlation Matrix 1 Sample Size = 25

$$
\begin{pmatrix}
1. & 0.108968 & 0.00694539 & -0.0735271 & 0.195968 & -0.116128 \\
0.108968 & 1. & 0.0769198 & -0.0665498 & 0.107224 & -0.239101 \\
0.00694539 & 0.0769198 & 1. & 0.128691 & 0.150023 & -0.0691065 \\
-0.0735271 & -0.0665498 & 0.128691 & 1. & -0.152004 & -0.19305 \\
0.195968 & 0.107224 & 0.150023 & -0.152004 & 1. & -0.322708 \\
-0.116128 & -0.239101 & -0.0691065 & -0.19305 & -0.322708 & 1.
\end{pmatrix}
$$

OLS Estimates of Correlation Matrix 1

$$
\begin{pmatrix}
1. & 0.0642778 & 0.0642778 & -0.0735271 & 0.195968 & -0.116128 \\
0.0642778 & 1. & 0.0642778 & -0.0665498 & 0.107224 & -0.239101 \\
0.0642778 & 0.0642778 & 1. & 0.128691 & 0.150023 & -0.0691065 \\
-0.0735271 & -0.0665498 & 0.128691 & 1. & -0.152004 & -0.19305 \\
0.195968 & 0.107224 & 0.150023 & -0.152004 & 1. & -0.322708 \\
-0.116128 & -0.239101 & -0.0691065 & -0.19305 & -0.322708 & 1.
\end{pmatrix}
$$

Two-Stage ADF Parameter Estimates

Parameter Tag	Estimate	Standard Error
1	0.0806234	0.0942435

Significance Test Results

Chi Square	df	plevel
0.776573	2	0.678218

Assessment of Multivariate Normality

	Multivariate Skewness	Chi Square	df	plevel
1	27.3963	114.151	56	7.3502×10^{-6}

	Multivariate Kurtosis	Z	plevel (2-tailed)
1	55.1678	2.77102	0.00558816

APPENDIX B: COMPARISON OF TWO DEPENDENT CORRELATIONS

Command Statements and Selected Output:

```
<<wbcorr.m
data = Import["EquicorrelationData.csv"];
```
$$\text{hypothesis} = \begin{pmatrix} 1 & 2 & 1 & 1 & 0 \\ 1 & 3 & 2 & 1 & 0 \end{pmatrix};$$

```
ComputeChiSquare[ {data}, hypothesis, {25}, DataType →
   RawData, EstimationMethod → TSADF]
```

WBCORR Output

Hypothesis Matrix

Group	Row	Column	Parameter Tag	Fixed Value
1	2	1	1	0
1	3	2	1	0

Input Correlation Matrix 1 Sample Size = 25

$$\begin{pmatrix}
1. & 0.108968 & 0.00694539 & -0.0735271 & 0.195968 & -0.116128 \\
0.108968 & 1. & 0.0769198 & -0.0665498 & 0.107224 & -0.239101 \\
0.00694539 & 0.0769198 & 1. & 0.128691 & 0.150023 & -0.0691065 \\
-0.0735271 & -0.0665498 & 0.128691 & 1. & -0.152004 & -0.19305 \\
0.195968 & 0.107224 & 0.150023 & -0.152004 & 1. & -0.322708 \\
-0.116128 & -0.239101 & -0.0691065 & -0.19305 & -0.322708 & 1.
\end{pmatrix}$$

OLS Estimates of Correlation Matrix 1

$$\begin{pmatrix}
1. & 0.092944 & 0.00694539 & -0.0735271 & 0.195968 & -0.116128 \\
0.092944 & 1. & 0.092944 & -0.0665498 & 0.107224 & -0.239101 \\
0.00694539 & 0.092944 & 1. & 0.128691 & 0.150023 & -0.0691065 \\
-0.0735271 & -0.0665498 & 0.128691 & 1. & -0.152004 & -0.19305 \\
0.195968 & 0.107224 & 0.150023 & -0.152004 & 1. & -0.322708 \\
-0.116128 & -0.239101 & -0.0691065 & -0.19305 & -0.322708 & 1.
\end{pmatrix}$$

Two-Stage ADF Parameter Estimates

Parameter Tag	Estimate	Standard Error
1	0.0945422	0.0946411

Significance Test Results

Chi Square	df	plevel
0.0190163	1	0.89032

Assessment of Multivariate Normality

	Multivariate Skewness	Chi Square	df	plevel
1	27.3963	114.151	56	7.3502×10^{-6}

	Multivariate Kurtosis	Z	plevel (2-tailed)	
1	55.1678	2.77102	0.00558816	

APPENDIX C: PERFECT CIRCUMPLEX HYPOTHESIS

Preliminary Input Lines and Random Number Generation

```
In[1]:= << wbcorr.m
In[2]:= << Statistics 'DescriptiveStatistics'
In[3]:= << Statistics 'MultinormalDistribution'
In[4]:= << Statistics 'MultiDescriptiveStatistics'
```

$$
In[5]:= \text{circumplexForm6x6} = \begin{pmatrix} 1 & \rho_1 & \rho_2 & \rho_3 & \rho_2 & \rho_1 \\ \rho_1 & 1 & \rho_1 & \rho_2 & \rho_3 & \rho_2 \\ \rho_2 & \rho_1 & 1 & \rho_1 & \rho_2 & \rho_3 \\ \rho_3 & \rho_2 & \rho_1 & 1 & \rho_1 & \rho_2 \\ \rho_2 & \rho_3 & \rho_2 & \rho_1 & 1 & \rho_1 \\ \rho_1 & \rho_2 & \rho_3 & \rho_2 & \rho_1 & 1 \end{pmatrix};
$$

```
In[6]: = populationMatrix = circumplexForm6×6 /. {ρ₃→ .2,
          ρ₂→ .4, ρ₁ → .6}; MatrixForm[populationMatrix]
```

Out[6]//MatrixForm =

$$
\begin{pmatrix}
1 & 0.6 & 0.4 & 0.2 & 0.4 & 0.6 \\
0.6 & 1 & 0.6 & 0.4 & 0.2 & 0.4 \\
0.4 & 0.6 & 1 & 0.6 & 0.4 & 0.2 \\
0.2 & 0.4 & 0.6 & 1 & 0.6 & 0.4 \\
0.4 & 0.2 & 0.4 & 0.6 & 1 & 0.6 \\
0.6 & 0.4 & 0.2 & 0.4 & 0.6 & 1
\end{pmatrix}
$$

```
In[7]: = populationDistribution = MultinormalDistribution
          [{0, 0, 0, 0, 0, 0}, populationMatrix];
In[8]: = SeedRandom [123]
In[9]: = data = RandomArray [populationDistribution, 500];
In[10]:= R = CorrelationMatrix[data]; MatrixForm[R]
```

Out[10]//MatrixForm=

$$
\begin{pmatrix}
1. & 0.598603 & 0.417062 & 0.233987 & 0.415227 & 0.593991 \\
0.598603 & 1. & 0.620032 & 0.417526 & 0.187959 & 0.353934 \\
0.417062 & 0.620032 & 1. & 0.580356 & 0.396385 & 0.199658 \\
0.233987 & 0.417526 & 0.580356 & 1. & 0.616586 & 0.433602 \\
0.415227 & 0.187959 & 0.396385 & 0.616586 & 1. & 0.623676 \\
0.593991 & 0.353934 & 0.199658 & 0.433602 & 0.623676 & 1.
\end{pmatrix}
$$

$$In[11]:= \text{circumplexHypothesis} = \begin{pmatrix} 1 & 2 & 1 & 1 & 0 \\ 1 & 3 & 2 & 1 & 0 \\ 1 & 4 & 3 & 1 & 0 \\ 1 & 5 & 4 & 1 & 0 \\ 1 & 6 & 5 & 1 & 0 \\ 1 & 3 & 1 & 2 & 0 \\ 1 & 4 & 2 & 2 & 0 \\ 1 & 5 & 3 & 2 & 0 \\ 1 & 6 & 4 & 2 & 0 \\ 1 & 4 & 1 & 3 & 0 \\ 1 & 5 & 2 & 3 & 0 \\ 1 & 6 & 3 & 3 & 0 \\ 1 & 5 & 1 & 2 & 0 \\ 1 & 6 & 2 & 2 & 0 \\ 1 & 6 & 1 & 1 & 0 \end{pmatrix};$$

Command Line and Output:

$In[12]:=$ **ComputeChiSquare[{data}, circumplexHypothesis, {500}, DataType → RawData]**

WBCORR Output

Hypothesis Matrix

Group	Row	Column	Parameter Tag	Fixed Value
1	2	1	1	0
1	3	2	1	0
1	4	3	1	0
1	5	4	1	0
1	6	5	1	0
1	3	1	2	0
1	4	2	2	0
1	5	3	2	0
1	6	4	2	0
1	4	1	3	0
1	5	2	3	0
1	6	3	3	0
1	5	1	2	0
1	6	2	2	0
1	6	1	1	0

Input Correlation Matrix 1 Sample Size = 500

$$
\begin{pmatrix}
1. & 0.598603 & 0.417062 & 0.233987 & 0.415227 & 0.593991 \\
0.598603 & 1. & 0.620032 & 0.417526 & 0.187959 & 0.353934 \\
0.417062 & 0.620032 & 1. & 0.580356 & 0.396385 & 0.199658 \\
0.233987 & 0.417526 & 0.580356 & 1. & 0.616586 & 0.433602 \\
0.415227 & 0.187959 & 0.396385 & 0.616586 & 1. & 0.623676 \\
0.593991 & 0.353934 & 0.199658 & 0.433602 & 0.623676 & 1. \\
\end{pmatrix}
$$

OLS Estimates of Correlation Matrix 1

$$
\begin{pmatrix}
1. & 0.605541 & 0.405623 & 0.207201 & 0.405623 & 0.605541 \\
0.605541 & 1. & 0.605541 & 0.405623 & 0.207201 & 0.405623 \\
0.405623 & 0.605541 & 1. & 0.605541 & 0.405623 & 0.207201 \\
0.207201 & 0.405623 & 0.605541 & 1. & 0.605541 & 0.405623 \\
0.405623 & 0.207201 & 0.405623 & 0.605541 & 1. & 0.605541 \\
0.605541 & 0.405623 & 0.207210 & 0.405623 & 0.605541 & 1. \\
\end{pmatrix}
$$

Two-Stage GLS Parameter Estimates

Parameter Tag	Estimate	Standard Error
1	0.605541	0.015424
2	0.405623	0.0245621
3	0.207201	0.0328644

Significance Test Results

Chi Square	df	plevel
6.82337	12	0.869062

Assessment of Multivariate Normality

	Multivariate Skewness	Chi Square	df	plevel
1	0.666646	55.5538	56	0.491696

	Multivariate Kurtosis	Z	plevel (2-tailed)
1	48.3778	0.649714	0.515877

APPENDIX D: EQUALITY OF
INDEPENDENT CORRELATION MATRICES

Input:

```
In[1]: = <<wbcorr.m
```

$$In[2]: = \mathbf{data1} = \begin{pmatrix} 1 & .44 & .38 \\ .44 & 1 & .42 \\ .38 & .42 & 1 \end{pmatrix};$$

```
In[3]: = N1 = 521;
```

$$In[4]: = \mathbf{data2} = \begin{pmatrix} 1 & .31 & .29 \\ .31 & 1 & .24 \\ .29 & .24 & 1 \end{pmatrix};$$

```
In[5]: = N2 =  644;
```

$$In[6]: = \mathbf{hypothesis} = \begin{pmatrix} 1 & 2 & 1 & 1 & 0 \\ 1 & 3 & 1 & 2 & 0 \\ 1 & 3 & 2 & 3 & 0 \\ 2 & 2 & 1 & 1 & 0 \\ 2 & 3 & 1 & 2 & 0 \\ 2 & 3 & 2 & 3 & 0 \end{pmatrix};$$

Command Line and Output:

```
In[7]: = ComputeChiSquare[{data1, data2},hypothesis,{N1,N2}]
```

WBCORR Output

Hypothesis Matrix

Group	Row	Column	Parameter Tag	Fixed Value
1	2	1	1	0
1	3	1	2	0
1	3	2	3	0
2	2	1	1	0
2	3	1	2	0
2	3	2	3	0

Input Correlation Matrix 1 Sample Size = 521

$$\begin{pmatrix} 1 & 0.44 & 0.38 \\ 0.44 & 1 & 0.42 \\ 0.38 & 0.42 & 1 \end{pmatrix}$$

Input Correlation Matrix 2 Sample Size = 644

$$\begin{pmatrix} 1 & 0.31 & 0.29 \\ 0.31 & 1 & 0.24 \\ 0.29 & 0.24 & 1 \end{pmatrix}$$

OLS Estimates of Correlation Matrix 1

$$\begin{pmatrix} 1 & 0.368126 & 0.330241 \\ 0.368126 & 1 & 0.320482 \\ 0.330241 & 0.320482 & 1 \end{pmatrix}$$

OLS Estimates of Correlation Matrix 2

$$\begin{pmatrix} 1 & 0.368126 & 0.330241 \\ 0.368126 & 1 & 0.320482 \\ 0.330241 & 0.320482 & 1 \end{pmatrix}$$

Two-Stage GLS Parameter Estimates

Parameter Tag	Estimate	Standard Error
1	0.368126	0.0253494
2	0.330241	0.0261252
3	0.320482	0.0263114

Significance Test Results

Chi Square	df	plevel
14.5103	3	0.00228681

APPENDIX E: EQUALITY OF CIRCUMPLEX STRUCTURES IN TWO GROUPS

Preliminary Input Lines and Random Number Generation:

```
In[1]: = <<wbcorr.m
In[2]: = <<Statistics 'DescriptiveStatistics'
In[3]: = <<Statistics 'MultinormalDistribution'
In[4]: = <<Statistics 'MultiDescriptiveStatistics'
In[5]: = <<LinearAlgebra 'MatrixManipulation'
```

$$
In[6]: = \text{circumplexForm6} \times 6 = \begin{pmatrix}
1 & \rho_1 & \rho_2 & \rho_3 & \rho_2 & \rho_1 \\
\rho_1 & 1 & \rho_1 & \rho_2 & \rho_3 & \rho_2 \\
\rho_2 & \rho_1 & 1 & \rho_1 & \rho_2 & \rho_3 \\
\rho_3 & \rho_2 & \rho_1 & 1 & \rho_1 & \rho_2 \\
\rho_2 & \rho_3 & \rho_2 & \rho_1 & 1 & \rho_1 \\
\rho_1 & \rho_2 & \rho_3 & \rho_2 & \rho_1 & 1
\end{pmatrix};
$$

```
In[7]: = populationMatrix = circumplexForm6×6 /. {ρ₃→.2,
          ρ₂→.4, ρ₁→.6}; MatrixForm[populationMatrix]

Out[7]//MatrixForm =
```

$$
\begin{pmatrix}
1 & 0.6 & 0.4 & 0.2 & 0.4 & 0.6 \\
0.6 & 1 & 0.6 & 0.4 & 0.2 & 0.4 \\
0.4 & 0.6 & 1 & 0.6 & 0.4 & 0.2 \\
0.2 & 0.4 & 0.6 & 1 & 0.6 & 0.4 \\
0.4 & 0.2 & 0.4 & 0.6 & 1 & 0.6 \\
0.6 & 0.4 & 0.2 & 0.4 & 0.6 & 1
\end{pmatrix}
$$

```
In[8]: = populationDistribution =
          MultinormalDistribution[{0, 0, 0, 0, 0, 0},
          populationMatrix];
In[9]: = SeedRandom[123]
In[10]: = data1 = RandomArray[populationDistribution, 500];
In[11]: = data2 = RandomArray[populationDistribution, 250];
```

Command Line and Output:

```
In[15]: = ComputeChiSquare[{data1, data2},
          circumplexHypothesis, {500, 250}, DataType →
          RawData]
```

WBCORR Output

Hypothesis Matrix

Group	Row	Column	Parameter Tag	Fixed Value
1	2	1	1	0
1	3	2	1	0
1	4	3	1	0
1	5	4	1	0
1	6	5	1	0
1	3	1	2	0
1	4	2	2	0
1	5	3	2	0
1	6	4	2	0
1	4	1	3	0
1	5	2	3	0
1	6	3	3	0
1	5	1	2	0
1	6	2	2	0
1	6	1	1	0
2	2	1	1	0
2	3	2	1	0
2	4	3	1	0
2	5	4	1	0
2	6	5	1	0
2	3	1	2	0
2	4	2	2	0
2	5	3	2	0
2	6	4	2	0
2	4	1	3	0
2	5	2	3	0
2	6	3	3	0
2	5	1	2	0
2	6	2	2	0
2	6	1	1	0

Input Correlation Matrix 1 Sample Size = 500

$$
\begin{pmatrix}
1. & 0.598603 & 0.417062 & 0.233987 & 0.415227 & 0.593991 \\
0.598603 & 1. & 0.620032 & 0.417526 & 0.187959 & 0.353934 \\
0.417062 & 0.620032 & 1. & 0.580356 & 0.396385 & 0.199658 \\
0.233987 & 0.417526 & 0.580356 & 1. & 0.616586 & 0.433602 \\
0.415227 & 0.187959 & 0.396385 & 0.616586 & 1. & 0.623676 \\
0.593991 & 0.353934 & 0.199658 & 0.433602 & 0.623676 & 1.
\end{pmatrix}
$$

Input Correlation Matrix 2 Sample Size = 250

$$
\begin{pmatrix}
1. & 0.612054 & 0.516346 & 0.288556 & 0.436875 & 0.556876 \\
0.612054 & 1. & 0.612947 & 0.351087 & 0.166406 & 0.291171 \\
0.516346 & 0.612947 & 1. & 0.529379 & 0.457793 & 0.155702 \\
0.288556 & 0.351087 & 0.529379 & 1. & 0.624697 & 0.387267 \\
0.436875 & 0.166406 & 0.457793 & 0.624697 & 1. & 0.563182 \\
0.556876 & 0.291171 & 0.155702 & 0.387267 & 0.563182 & 1.
\end{pmatrix}
$$

OLS Estimates of Correlation Matrix 1

$$
\begin{pmatrix}
1. & 0.5981 & 0.406 & 0.205987 & 0.406 & 0.5981 \\
0.5981 & 1. & 0.5981 & 0.406 & 0.205987 & 0.406 \\
0.406 & 0.5981 & 1. & 0.5981 & 0.406 & 0.205987 \\
0.205987 & 0.406 & 0.5981 & 1. & 0.5981 & 0.406 \\
0.406 & 0.205987 & 0.406 & 0.5981 & 1. & 0.5981 \\
0.5981 & 0.406 & 0.205987 & 0.406 & 0.5981 & 1.
\end{pmatrix}
$$

OLS Estimates of Correlation Matrix 2

$$
\begin{pmatrix}
1. & 0.5981 & 0.406 & 0.205987 & 0.406 & 0.5981 \\
0.5981 & 1. & 0.5981 & 0.406 & 0.205987 & 0.406 \\
0.406 & 0.5981 & 1. & 0.5981 & 0.406 & 0.205987 \\
0.205987 & 0.406 & 0.5981 & 1. & 0.5981 & 0.406 \\
0.406 & 0.205987 & 0.406 & 0.5981 & 1. & 0.5981 \\
0.5981 & 0.406 & 0.205987 & 0.406 & 0.5981 & 1.
\end{pmatrix}
$$

Two-Stage GLS Parameter Estimates

Parameter Tag	Estimate	Standard Error
1	0.5981	0.0128252
2	0.406	0.0199668
3	0.205987	0.0267544

Significance Test Results

Chi Square	df	plevel
33.1335	27	0.1927

Assessment of Multivariate Normality

	Multivariate Skewness	Chi Square	df	plevel
1	0.666646	55.5538	56	0.491696
2	1.20136	50.0566	56	0.698181

	Multivariate Kurtosis	Z	plevel (2-tailed)
1	48.3778	0.649714	0.515877
2	47.7694	0.122539	0.902472

ACKNOWLEDGMENT

I am grateful for helpful comments by Michael W. Browne, Albert Maydeu-Olivares, and Rachel T. Fouladi.

REFERENCES

Browne, M. W. (1974). Generalized least squares estimators in the analysis of covariance structures. *South African Statistical Journal, 8*, 1–24.

Browne, M. W. (1977). The analysis of patterned correlation matrices by generalized least squares. *British Journal of Mathematical and Statistical Psychology, 30*, 113–124.

Browne, M. W. (1982). Covariance structures. In D. M. Hawkins (Ed.), *Topics in applied multivariate analysis* (pp. 72–141). Cambridge: Cambridge University Press.

Browne, M. W. (1984). Asymptotically distribution-free methods for the analysis of covarience structures. *British Journal of Mathematical and Statistical Psychology, 37*, 62–83.

Browne, M. W. (1992). Circumplex models for correlation matrices. *Psychometrika, 57*, 469–497.

Dunn, O. J., & Clark, V. A. (1969). Correlation coefficients measured on the same individuals. *Journal of the American Statistical Association, 64*, 366–377.

Fisher, R. A. (1921). On the "probable error" of a coefficient of correlation deduced from a small sample. *Metron, 1*, 1–32.

Fouladi, R. T. (1996). *A study of procedures to examine correlation pattern hypotheses under conditions of multivariate normality and non-normality.* Unpublished doctoral dissertation, University of British Columbia, Vancouver, BC, Canada.

Fouladi, R. T. (2000). Performance of modified test statistics in covariance and correlation structure analysis under conditions of multivariate nonnormality. *Structural Equation Modeling, 7*, 356–410.

Hotelling, H. (1953). New light on the correlation coefficient and its transforms. *Journal of the Royal Statistical Society, Series B, 15*, 193–232.

Hsu, P. L. (1949). The limiting distribution of functions of sample means and applications to testing hypotheses. In *Proceedings of the First Berkeley Symposium on Mathematical Statistics and Probability* (pp. 359–402).

Isserlis, L. (1916). On certain probable errors and correlation coefficients of multiple frequency distributions with skew regression. *Biometrika, 11*, 185–190.

Jennrich, R. I. (1970). An asymptotic χ^2 test for the equality of two correlation matrices. *Journal of the American Statistical Association, 65*, 904–912.

Khatri, C. G. (1966). A note on a MANOVA model applied to problems in growth curves, *Annals of the Institute of Statistics and Mathematics, 18*, 75–86.

Layard, M. W. J. (1972). Large sample tests for the equality of two covariance matrices. *Annals of Mathematical Statistics, 43*, 123–141.

Layard, M. W. (1974). A Monte Carlo comparison of tests for equality of covariance matrices. *Biometrika, 61*, 461–465.

Mardia, K. V. (1970). Measures of multivariate skewness and kurtosis with applications. *Biometrika, 57*, 519–530.

McDonald, R. P. (1975). Testing pattern hypotheses on correlation matrices. *Psychometrika, 40*, 253–255.

Mels, G. (2000). *Statistical methods for correlation structures.* Unpublished doctoral dissertation, University of Port Elizabeth, Port Elizabeth, South Africa.

Modarres, R., & Jernigan, R. W. (1993). A robust test for comparing correlation matrices. *Journal of Statistical Computing and Simulation, 46*, 169–181.

Neill, J. J., & Dunn, O. J. (1975). Equality of dependent correlation coefficients. *Biometrics, 31*, 531–543.

Olkin, I., & Press, S. J. (1995). Correlations redux. *Psychological Bulletin, 188*, 155–164.

Olkin, I., & Siotani, M. (1976). Asymptotic distribution of functions of a correlation matrix. In S. Ideka (Ed.), *Essays in probability and statistics* (pp. 235–251). Tokyo: Shinko Tsusho. (Reprinted from *Asymptotic distribution of functions of a correlation matrix*, Tech. Rep. No. 6, Stanford, CA: Stanford University, Laboratory for Quantitative Research in Education.)

Pearson, K., & Filon, L. N. G. (1898). Mathematical contributions to the theory of evolution. IV. On the probable errors of frequency constants and on the influence of random selection on variation and correlation. *Philosophical Transactions of the Royal Society of London, Series A, 191*, 229–311.

Steiger, J. H. (1979). Multicorr: A computer program for fast, accurate, small-sample tests of correlational pattern hypotheses. *Educational and Psychological Measurement, 39*, 677–680.

Steiger, J. H. (1980a). Tests for comparing elements of a correlation matrix. *Psychological Bulletin, 87*, 195–201.

Steiger, J. H. (1980b). Testing pattern hypotheses on correlation matrices: Alternative statistics and some empirical results. *Multivariate Behavioral Research, 15*, 335–352.

Steiger, J. H. (1980c). *K-sample pattern hypothesis tests for correlation matrices by the method of generalized least squares* (Technical Rep. No. 80-2). Vancouver, Canada: University of British Columbia Institute of Applied Mathematics and Statistics.

Steiger, J. H., & Browne, M. W. (1984). The comparison of interdependent correlations between optimal linear composites. *Psychometrika, 49*, 11–24.

Steiger, J. H., & Hakstian, A. R. (1982). The asymptotic distribution of elements of a correlation matrix: Theory and application. *British Journal of Mathematical and Statistical Psychology, 35*, 208–215.

Timm, N. H. (1975). *Multivariate analysis with applications in education and psychology.* Monterey, CA: Brooks/Cole.

Wiggins, J. S., Steiger, J. H., & Gaelick, L. (1981). Evaluating circumplexity in personality data. *Multivariate Behavioral Research, 16*, 263–289.

13

Representing Psychological Processes With Dynamic Factor Models: Some Promising Uses and Extensions of Autoregressive Moving Average Time Series Models

Michael W. Browne
Ohio State University

John R. Nesselroade
University of Virginia

PROCESS AND CHANGE

Among several key emergent trends in the study of development across the life span were (a) the shift in emphasis from the two–occasion-based measurement of change to the multioccasion focus on change functions and (b) the recognition and separation of intraindividual variability and intraindividual change in the effort to represent concepts of process more fruitfully (Hertzog & Nesselroade, 2003). Psychologists have long been interested in the modeling of process, but the recent psychological literature shows evidence of a more urgent, pervasive commitment to the task. Even in areas with a long-standing tradition of emphasizing stability, for example, research on personality traits, there is an awareness of the need for process-oriented accounts of the linkage between traits and manifest behaviors (e.g., McCrae & Costa, 1996). On the one hand, the emergence of these process-oriented sentiments is highly encouraging, but, on the other, we do not believe that it will suffice. A close examination of the way research questions are framed and the popular methods by which answers are sought does not generate much optimism concerning an impending "great leap forward" in the study of process.

Process Versus Stability Orientation to Research Issues

The critical distinction with which we start this discussion is that between studying process and change from the stasis/equilbrium perspective that has dominated psychology, even developmental psychology (e.g., Gergen, 1977), as well as the natural sciences to some extent (Holling, 1973), versus studying any phenomenon of interest from a process and change perspective. There is a strong parallel here with the distinctions raised by Baltes (1973) in discussing the significance of bringing a "developmental perspective" to bear on research problems—not just developmental research problems, any research problems. At its core, this distinction implies that not only are the methods of data collection and analysis and modeling at issue, but also the very phrasing of the research issues is at stake.

To illustrate the point, consider the differences implicit in asking, "Which of these intelligence tests shows the highest test–retest correlation?" versus "How much more does Anxiety fluctuate than Guilt?" The first is consistent with the prevailing belief in a high level of stability of intelligence as a construct and viewing the amount of departure of the test–retest correlation from 1.00 of the tests used to measure it as primarily indicative of problems with the measurement devices, that is, unreliability. The second question is consistent with a belief that individuals feel more anxious and more guilty at some times than others, but that the nature of the fluctuations is different between attributes. One view is oriented toward stability and equilibrium; the other takes change as a given. The questions are different; the methods of answering them may well need to be, too. How the nature of anxiety fluctuates in adolescence versus adulthood raises the ante even higher with the addition of the concept of developmental change.

The point can be further illustrated by a kind of "half-way between" application. Eizenman, Nesselroade, Featherman, and Rowe (1997) used between-persons differences in the magnitude of week-to-week fluctuations in perceived control to predict mortality 5 years later. Eizenman et al. found that those who showed greater week-to-week fluctuation in control beliefs were at higher risk than those who showed small amounts of week-to-week fluctuation. The predictability was irrespective of the mean level of an individual's beliefs over time. Here the predictor variable was the magnitude of within-person fluctuations, which, on the surface, seems very change oriented. However, the overarching "paradigm" is the traditional one of using putatively stable between-person differences to predict other between-person differences. In this case, the putatively stable between-person differences had to do with within-person changes, but the dominant emphasis was on stable features of these within-person changes.

There are other examples of using interindividual differences in various aspects of intraindividual variability to define key concepts. For example, Shoda, Mischel, and Wright (1993) defined personality "consistency" in terms of the patterning of intraindividual variability in behavior manifested by individuals in moving from one situation to another. Still other researchers invoke the powerful concepts of linear and nonlinear dynamical systems modeling to represent quantitatively the phenomena that they study (e.g., Boker & Graham, 1998; Kelso, 1995; Vallacher & Nowak, 1994).

These few examples illustrate that many behavioral and social scientists have an awareness of intraindividual variation in the way they conceptualize and pursue their research questions. It is in the spirit of these issues, concerns, and perceived shifts in orientation that we take a closer look at certain classes of time series models that we believe can contribute in essential ways to an improved attack on the study of process and change. Many of the methods we will discuss have generally been recommended to behavioral researchers for several decades (e.g., Glass, Willson, & Gottman, 1972), but we will also point toward some needed innovations. For instance, an informative review of issues concerning validity of statistical assumptions in the application of time series methodology to manifest variables in psychological research has been provided by West and Hepworth (1991). This chapter will build on such previous work by concentrating primarily on the modeling of psychological processes by means of time series models.

We begin with a brief overview of how we are thinking about *process* in this context, followed by a review and discussion of some of the basic ideas and models of time series modeling. We then present and differentiate between two types of "dynamic factor analysis model" that are pertinent to representing process, and illustrate their application. The reader will see that we invoke and maintain a fundamental orientation of intraindividual variability and change in the models we discuss.

Modeling Processes

One can use most statistical models, including the familiar multiple regression models in psychology, in highly atheoretical ways, that is, solely for forecasting and prediction. Such pragmatic applications are commonplace in economics, engineering, and environmental science. In these cases, virtually no theoretical meaning need be ascribed to the parameters of the model. What matters is how accurately the model forecasts or predicts, not how well it "squares" with some theory-based set of expectations. This orientation used to be prevalent in psychology, especially among devotees of multiple regression, but many psychologists are uncomfortable with such an atheoretical stance at this point in the history of the discipline. Whether it is in the context of an elaborate structural model or simply a stepwise regression analysis, some "interpretation" of model parameters tends to be undertaken, especially so if theories concerning processes are being developed and refined.

A central premise on which we will anchor the remainder of this discussion is that "process" involves patterns of changes that are defined across variables and organized over time [see, e.g., Nesselroade & Molenaar (2003) for additional discussion of this and related points]. In physics, the label *dynamic* typically pertains to a force or forces that produce motion. In accordance with this usage, we will use the label *dynamic* for a force or forces driving intraindividual change. The variables that are actually being changed will be referred to as the *process* variables. Thus, a model for a dynamic, psychological process should include (a) variables representing the forces that cause change, (b) variables on which the changes (outcomes) are actually manifested, and (c) parameters that define, at least to some extent, a temporal flow in the relationships among and between the two kinds of variables. Thus, the actual values of the model parameters are highly salient to understanding and communicating the nature of process information.

Bear in mind that, in addition to being manifest variables, process variables can be conceptualized as latent variables that are "brought" into the empirical world via a set of manifest or indicator variables. Indeed, in the spirit of the "multivariate orientation" (Baltes & Nesselroade, 1973; Cattell, 1966; Nesselroade & Ford, 1987) we will shift emphasis later in the discussion to the use of latent variables in modeling process. First, however, we explore key aspects of essential time series models at the manifest variable level.

AUTOREGRESSIVE MOVING AVERAGE TIME SERIES MODELS

Because we want to pay explicit attention to the time-ordered nature of the relationships being modeled, in this presentation we are primarily concerned with data that directly represent the time rather than the frequency domain. For our general purposes, probably the most common class of time series models comprises the autoregressive moving average (ARMA) models. Our aim in this section is to introduce ARMA time series and identify some of their more important properties within a process orientation.

In ARMA time series models the random variable providing the dynamic force that changes the process variable is the so-called "white noise" variable. More useful terminology for the present context is "random shock" variable because the values are unpredictable and produce sudden changes in the process variables. If the reader is surprised that "random shock" variables can be conceptualized as "driving" a process, we ask that judgment be suspended on the validity of this point until later. Substantively, Bandura's (1982) discussion of the effects of chance events in the life course rather compellingly illustrates a similar idea.

The random shock variables with which we will be concerned will be denoted as $z_t, t = 1, \ldots, T$, and have the following characteristics:

1. They are latent variables and cannot be directly observed,
2. They are identically distributed with zero means and the same variance ψ, that is, $z_t \sim \mathcal{N}(0, \psi)$ when a normal distribution is assumed.
3. They are independently distributed and consequently are unpredictable.
4. A shock variable at any time point t influences, directly or indirectly, another variable, the process variable, at two or more time points $t, t + 1, \ldots$.

The first three characteristics are also associated with measurement errors. As will be seen, the fourth property distinguishes shock variables from measurement errors.

ARMA models include both process variables and the dynamic variables (random shock variables) that influence them. It is the nature of the persistence of this influence and the locus of any occasion-to-occasion continuity (or lack of it) that distinguishes the various models.

We will first briefly define the moving average (MA) model and the autoregressive (AR) model so that some of their relevant, but more technical properties such as invertibility, the definition of which involves both classes of model, can be discussed precisely. Subsequently both the MA and AR models will be examined in more detail.

The Moving Average Process

The general equation describing a moving average model of order q, MA(q), is

$$y_t = z_t + \beta_1 z_{t-1} + \beta_2 z_{t-2} + \cdots + \beta_q z_{t-q}. \tag{1}$$

where y_t represents the process variable at time t, and $z_{t-j}, j = 0, \ldots, q$, are the random shock variables. In the particular case of a moving average model of order $q = 1$, Equation 1 simplifies to

$$y_t = z_t + \beta_1 z_{t-1}.$$

A path diagram of the MA(1) model in this equation is shown in Fig. 13.1.[1]

Dashed lines refer to the time series prior to the first observation. In this diagram it is apparent that each z_t influences both y_t and y_{t+1}. From Property 4 of a random shock variable it can be seen that the z_t represent random shocks at different time points. The y_t are being changed by the shocks, and therefore represent the corresponding process variable.

---

[1] In Fig. 13.1 the process variable is a manifest or measured variable and is represented as a square. In some later applications, where the process variable is considered a latent, or unmeasured variable, it is shown as a circle.

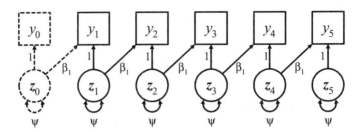

FIG. 13.1. MA(1) process showing missing information.

To illustrate the MA process more concretely, think of the process variable y_t in Fig. 13.1 as daily, self-reported morale and the random shock variable z_t as amount of daily hassle inflicted by the environment. The model of Fig. 13.1 implies that one's self-reported morale is a function of both today's hassles and yesterday's hassles to an extent represented by the magnitude of β_1. According to this model, even if a person experienced no hassles today, his or her self-reported morale would still directly reflect a β_1 worth of the hassles experienced yesterday. Thus, the notion of temporal flow embedded in this model is in the dynamic variable's continuing influence (for up to one lag) on the process variable. An extreme event will still be "felt" by the system at the next time of measurement. The MA model also implies that the amount of hassle experienced today is uncorrelated with the amount experienced yesterday. In some environments this is not a plausible expectation.

As a representation of process the model has obvious limits. There is no temporal flow represented in the sequential values of the z_t. Consider the MA model as a means for representing the influence of parental child-rearing practices on childhood socialization. The idea that parental influence persists over time can be well represented by this model as, for example, an MA(q) where q is very large. However, there is a reasonable presumption of day-to-day continuity in the parental child-rearing practices that the random shocks do not well represent. The MA(q), however, is possibly a very useful model for representing a process where reinforcement and behavior are not contingent on each other, such as in the development of "learned helplessness," where an unpredictability of the shocks to the system is an essential part of the theoretical formulation.

The Autoregressive Process

The general equation describing an autoregressive model of order p, AR(p), is

$$y_t = \alpha_1 y_{t-1} + \alpha_2 y_{t-2} + \cdots + \alpha_p y_{t-p} + z_t. \tag{2}$$

An autoregressive process of order 1 is represented in Fig. 13.2. In this case Equation 2 simplifies to

$$y_t = \alpha_1 y_{t-1} + z_t.$$

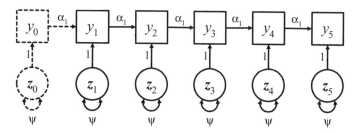

FIG. 13.2.   AR(1) process showing missing information.

In Fig. 13.2 each z_t directly influences y_t. Because y_t influences y_{t+1}, z_t also indirectly influences y_{t+1}. Algebraically this may be represented as

$$y_{t+1} = z_{t+1} + \alpha_1 y_t$$
$$= z_{t+1} + \alpha_1 (z_t + \alpha_1 y_{t-1})$$
$$= z_{t+1} + \alpha_1 z_t + \alpha_1^2 y_{t-1},$$

so that that the contribution of z_t to y_{t+1} is given by $\alpha_1 z_t$. Similarly, z_t also influences y_{t+2} because y_{t+1} influences y_{t+2} and so on. The contribution of z_t to any future observation $y_{t+\ell}$ is $\alpha_1^\ell z_t$. Because the absolute value of α_1 must be less than 1 for stationarity, the contribution of z_t to $y_{t+\ell}$ approaches zero as ℓ increases. Thus z_t indirectly influences all subsequent $y_{t+\ell}$, but to a decreasing extent as the lag ℓ increases. Consequently, z_t represents a shock variable and y_t is a process variable.

As Fig. 13.2 clearly shows, in the case of the AR model, the value of the process variable at earlier times is predictive of its value at later times. The random shock variable, however, has only a concurrent direct effect on the process variable. Something is "added" to the process variable at each instance of random shock, but this addition provides no enhancement of continuity. Here, any sense of temporal flow resides in the process variables themselves. If anything, the effect of the random shocks is to lessen the predictability of current values of the process variable from its earlier values.

More concretely, the AR model seems a potentially valuable representation for a psychological trait where the expectation is "repeatable" behavior from occasion to occasion unless something happens to disrupt it. One tradition in trait theory held the belief that potential disruptions from the environment-dynamic variables have a minimal impact on trait-relevant behaviors, that is, that the latter show a great deal of cross-occasion (transsituation) repeatability. Depending on how "occasion" and "situation" are defined, trait measures show more or less consistency over the relevant units. An illustrative "complicating" of this notion is to conceptualize the process variable—the psychological trait—as a latent variable and allow its indicator variables to be somewhat different from occasion to occasion or situation to situation. This permits the trait to "look different" from one time to another while still manifesting consistency at a "deeper" level (e.g., Bem & Allen, 1974; Brim & Kagan, 1980).

From an explanatory point of view, it is not very satisfying to account for continuity in a process variable at the manifest level simply by relating its current values to its previous values. This is an inherently limiting feature of ARMA models if applied directly to manifest variables and a motivation to apply these models to latent variables. This will necessitate an examination of properties of these models that may be taken into account when deciding on appropriate models for latent processes.

Properties of ARMA Processes

The following three characteristics of ARMA processes particularly concern us here because of their implications for choosing an appropriate model to represent a process:

1. Stationarity, which implies stability of the process over time.
2. Invertibility, which involves a dual relationship between MA and AR processes.
3. The autocovariance function, which yields the covariance between the tth observation and the observation at any arbitrary subsequent lag. Closely related to the autocovariance function is the autocorrelation function or standardized autocovariance function.

A time series is said to be *stationary* if

$$\mathcal{E}(y_t) = \mathcal{E}(y_{t'}),$$

$$\mathrm{Cov}(y_t, y_{t+\ell}) = \mathrm{Cov}(y_{t'}, y_{t'+\ell}),$$

for any t, t', ℓ. Thus, a stationary time series has the same expected value and variance at all time points, and the covariance of $y(t)$ and $y(t + \ell)$ depends only on the lag ℓ and not on the time point t. A consequence of stationarity is that the process variable remains bounded in probability as t increases. With some nonstationary time series the process variable may assume values that are indeterminately large.

An MA(q) time series is said to be *invertible* if it can be expressed as an AR(∞) time series. Conversely, an AR(p) time series is invertible if it can be expressed as an MA(∞) time series. Invertibility is associated with identification of parameters for an MA(q) process and with stationarity of the time series for an AR(p) process.

The *autocovariance function* $\sigma(\ell)$ of a covariance stationary time series yields the covariance between observations at lag ℓ,

$$\sigma(\ell) = \mathrm{Cov}(y_t, y_{t+\ell}),$$

for $\ell = 0, 1, 2, \ldots$, and the corresponding *autocorrelation function* $\sigma(\ell)$ is obtained by rescaling by the variance $\sigma(0)$:

$$\rho(\ell) = \frac{\sigma(\ell)}{\sigma(0)}.$$

In standard usage, where time series are applied to manifest variables, the autocorrelation function may be estimated directly from the data. It is used, together with an estimated partial autocorrelation function, to suggest an appropriate model for the data. When an ARMA process is intended for use with latent variables, substantive considerations regarding the nature of the psychological process will have to be used to choose an appropriate ARMA model from properties of its autocorrelation function. We examine more closely the roles the three characteristics of ARMA processes play in judging the appropriateness of particular ARMA models for modeling psychological process data.

Moving Average Processes

Parameters of a time series are said to be homogeneous over time if they do not change with time. For the MA(1) process in Fig. 13.1, therefore, the two parameters ψ and β_1 are homogeneous over time because neither changes as time t changes. For an MA(2) process, the three parameters, ψ, β_1, and β_2 are homogeneous over time if they remain constant as t changes.

An MA(q) process is stationary whenever its parameters are homogeneous over time, no matter what values these parameters have. Unlike the AR(p) time series, no further constraints on parameters are required for stationarity of the MA process.

Let us examine the substantive implications of stationarity for the representation of process more closely. On the surface, at least, the stationarity property would seem to limit the applicability of MA models to process variables that do not show "dramatic" change over time. However, there are some processes, for example, control processes, in which stationarity can be immediately seen as a desirable manifestation. Even in the case of socialization and parental child-rearing practices mentioned earlier, socialized behavior can be conceptualized not so much as having an amount of some desirable attribute (socialization) as behavior on which limits have been established that the child does not exceed. For instance, expressing disagreement in socially acceptable ways is one thing; throwing a tantrum is something else.

The MA(q) process is invertible if its parameters satisfy certain inequality constraints known as invertibility conditions. It can then be expressed equivalently as an autoregressive (AR) process of infinite order. Thus,

$$\mathrm{MA}(q) = \mathrm{AR}(\infty),$$

if $\beta_1, \ldots, \beta_q$ satisfy certain conditions that restrict their magnitudes. For example, the invertibility condition for an MA(1) process is that $|\beta_1| < 1$. If this is true, then

$$\text{MA(1):} \quad y_t = z_t + \beta_1 z_{t-1}$$

$$= z_t + \alpha_1 y_{t-1} + \alpha_2 y_{t-2} + \cdots + \alpha_\infty y_{t-\infty} \quad :\text{AR}(\infty)$$

where $\alpha_s = (-1)^{s+1} \beta_1^s \to 0$ as $s \to \infty$.

The autocorrelation function for an MA(1) process is

$$\rho(\ell) = \begin{cases} \dfrac{\beta_1}{1 + \beta_1^2}, & \ell = 1, \\ 0, & \ell > 1, \end{cases} \tag{3}$$

so that this process is suitable only for situations where each random shock influences the process over a period of limited duration only. In general, for an MA(q) process, $\rho(\ell) = 0$, $\ell > q$, so that each random shock influences only $q + 1$ observations of the process variable. This highlights again the key role to be played by substantive considerations in modeling process data by ARMA models. Not all psychological processes are construed as endlessly influencing subsequent events, although aspects of the developmental literature suggest otherwise.

Notice that the parameters of an MA(q) process are not identifiable, that is, more than one set of values of the β weights will result in the same autocovariance function and consequently define the same time series. For example, the two MA(1) processes

$$y_t = z_t + \beta_1 z_{t-1}$$

and

$$y_t = z_t + \beta_1^* z_{t-1},$$

where $\beta_1^* = 1/\beta_1$, will yield the exactly the same autocorrelation function

$$\rho(\ell) = \begin{cases} \dfrac{\beta_1}{1 + \beta_1^2} = \dfrac{\beta_1^*}{1 + \beta_1^{*2}}, & \ell = 1, \\ 0, & \ell > 1, \end{cases}$$

and, consequently, fit an observed time series equally well. Consequently, one needs to impose additional constraints to identify the parameters of the model. One set of constraints that results in a unique solution is to choose $\beta_1, \ldots, \beta_q$ so as to satisfy the invertibility conditions. For the MA(1) process this means that requiring β_1 to be less than unity identifies β_1. Unlike the usual situation in the analysis of covariance structures, where equality constraints are used for identification conditions, inequality constraints are required to identify MA weights. The reason for this is that equivalent solutions are finite in number and disjoint for MA models and are usually infinitely many and contiguous in the analysis of covariance structures.

Further details concerning MA(q) processes may be found in Wei (1990, Section 3.2).

Autoregressive Processes

Similar inequality constraints to those applied to β weights for invertibility of an MA(q) process are applied to α weights for invertibility of an AR(p) process when parameters are homogeneous over time. Consider an AR(1) process, for example. If the invertibility condition $|\alpha_1| < 1$ is satisfied then

$$\text{AR}(1): \quad y_t = z_t + \alpha_1 y_{t-1}$$

$$= z_t + \beta_1 z_{t-1} + \beta_2 z_{t-2} + \cdots + \beta_\infty z_{t-\infty} \quad :\text{MA}(\infty)$$

where $\beta_\ell = \alpha_1^\ell \to 0$ as $\ell \to \infty$, so that the AR(1) process has been expressed as an infinite MA process.

The effect of these invertibility conditions on properties of the two processes is different, however. Whereas the invertibility conditions are employed to identify parameters of an MA(q) process, the parameters of an AR(q) process are always identifiable, and no further constraints are required as identification conditions. Unlike an MA(q) process, however, an AR(p) process is not always stationary, even if its parameters are homogeneous over time. The invertibility conditions applied to α weights now are inequality constraints that guarantee stationarity of the AR(p) process. If the α weights do not satisfy the invertibility conditions, the variance of the process variable increases with time, $\text{Var}(y_t) > \text{Var}(y_{t-1})$, and the process variable eventually assumes values that are substantively absurd and too large to handle computationally.

The autocorrelation function of an AR(p) process only exists if the process is invertible. For an invertible AR(1) process, for example, the autocorrelation function is

$$\rho(\ell) = \alpha_1^\ell, \tag{4}$$

so that the lagged correlation $\rho(\ell)$ decays exponentially towards zero as the lag ℓ increases. When α_1 is positive, the lagged correlations are all positive, whereas they alternate between positive and negative values when α_1 is negative.

Thus, an AR(1) time series with a positive weight α_1 is of interest in situations where random shocks have a fairly long influence on the process, but the influence gradually tapers off with time. The duration and extent of the influence depends on the magnitude of α_1: The closer α_1 is to one, the stronger and longer will be the influence of a shock. This is in contrast to the MA(1) series, where the shock has no influence at lags greater than one, no matter how large is the magnitude of β_1.

As was pointed out by Yule (1927), a stationary AR(2) time series

$$y_t = z_t + \alpha_1 y_{t-1} + \alpha_2 y_{t-2},$$

with a positive value for α_1 ($0 < \alpha_1 < 2$) and a negative value for α_2 ($-1 < \alpha_2 < -\alpha_1^2/4$) to yield a damping effect, may be used to model a pendulum subjected to random shocks. In this situation the autocorrelation function follows a damped sine wave (Box & Jenkins, 1976, Section 3.2.4). The AR(2) process may therefore be useful for modeling certain types of mood data. Other quantitative models that may be used in this situation, but do not require equally spaced time points, were presented by Boker and Nesselroade(2002).

Further information concerning AR(p) processes may be found in Wei (1990, Section 3.1)

MIXED AUTOREGRESSIVE MOVING AVERAGE PROCESSES ARMA(p, q)

We turn our attention now to models that combine the features of the MA and AR processes—ARMA models. These models turn out to be particularly promising for representing psychological phenomena. The general equation for an ARMA(p, q) model is

$$y_t = \alpha_1 y_{t-1} + \alpha_2 y_{t-2} + \cdots + \alpha_p y_{t-p} + z_t \qquad (5)$$
$$+ \beta_1 z_{t-1} + \beta_2 z_{t-2} + \cdots + \beta_q z_{t-q}.$$

For an ARMA(1, 1) process, Equation 3 reduces to

$$y_t = \alpha_1 y_{t-1} + z_t + \beta z_{t-1}.$$

Figure 13.3 presents a path diagram for this ARMA(1, 1) model.

Thus, the process variable at time t in an ARMA(p, q) process is not only influenced by its p previous values, but also by the last q random shocks. Consequently, the random shocks influence the future values of the process variable not only indirectly as in an AR process, but also directly as in an MA process.

The ARMA(p, q) process is stationary when the p autoregressive weights $\alpha_1, \ldots, \alpha_p$ satisfy the AR(p) invertibility conditions. Necessary identification conditions are provided by the MA(q) invertibility conditions for $\beta_1, \ldots, \beta_q$. These are not sufficient, however, and parameters may not be identifiable in specific instances where there are certain relationships between the autoregressive weights and moving average weights (Harvey, 1993, pp. 29–30).

The autocorrelation function for an ARMA(1, 1) process is given by

$$\rho\,(\ell) = \begin{cases} \dfrac{(1+\alpha_1\beta_1)(\alpha_1+\beta_1)}{1+2\alpha_1\beta_1+\beta_1^2}, & \ell = 1 \\[2ex] \alpha_1\rho\,(\ell-1), & \ell > 1. \end{cases} \qquad (6)$$

This autocorrelation function reduces to the MA(1) autocorrelation function in Equation 3 when $p = 0$ and to the AR(1) autocorrelation function in Equation 4 when $q = 0$. The moving average weights $\beta_\ell, \ell = 1, \ldots, q$, affect the first q autocorrelation coefficients only, and for $\ell > q$ the recurrence relation for the ARMA(1, 1) process in Equation 6 applies in the same way to the AR(1) process in Equation 4.

Accounting for the Influence of Unobserved Preceding Values in a Time Series

In Figs. 13.1 through 13.3 terms in the time series that precede the first term y_1 are represented by dashed lines. These preceding terms influence the first $q^* = \max(p, q)$ values in the time series (Du Toit & Browne, 2001). If they are disregarded, the estimated time series will not be stationary, initially at least, but may approach stationarity as t increases.

In Fig. 13.3 the first value y_1 of the process variable is influenced both by the preceding unobserved value y_0 of the process variable and the corresponding random shock z_0. It is unnecessary to consider y_0 and z_0 separately. They may be encapsulated in the single "initial state variable"

$$x_1 = \alpha_1 y_0 + \beta_1 z_0, \qquad (7)$$

which is treated as a latent variable with variance θ. This is shown in Fig. 13.4.

If θ is regarded as a free parameter to be estimated, the model shown in Fig. 13.4 is satisfied by any stationary ARMA(1, 1) time series and also by some initially nonstationary ARMA(1, 1) time series. If, however, θ is defined as the appropriate

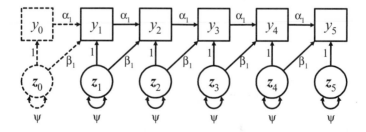

FIG. 13.3. ARMA(1, 1) process showing missing information.

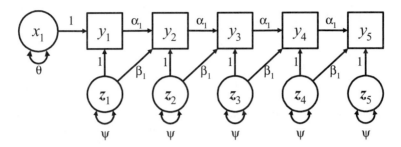

FIG. 13.4.   ARMA(1, 1) process showing the initial state variable.

function of α_1, β_1, and ψ,

$$\theta = \text{Var}(x_1) = \frac{(\alpha_1 + \beta_1)^2 \psi}{1 - \alpha_1^2}, \tag{8}$$

then the model shown in Fig. 13.4 is satisfied only by a stationary ARMA(1, 1) time series.

The initial state variable and its variance for an AR(1) process is obtained by setting $\beta_1 = 0$ in Equations 7 and 8. Corresponding results for an MA(1) process are obtained by setting $\alpha_1 = 0$.

In the case of an ARMA(p, q) time series the terms preceding y_1 may be encapsulated (Du Toit & Browne, 2001)in the $q^* \times 1$ initial state vector $\mathbf{x} = (x_1, \ldots, x_{q^*})'$, with

$$x_1 = \sum_{i=1}^{q^*} (\alpha_i y_{1-i} + \beta_i u_{1-i})$$

$$x_2 = \sum_{i=2}^{q^*} (\alpha_i y_{2-i} + \beta_i u_{2-i})$$

$$\vdots$$

$$x_{q^*} = \alpha_{q^*} y_0 + \beta_{q^*} u_0,$$

where $\alpha_i = 0$ if $i > p$ and $\beta_i = 0$ if $i > q$.

Let

$$\text{Cov}(\mathbf{x}, \mathbf{x}') = \mathbf{\Theta}. \tag{9}$$

Formulas for calculating $\mathbf{\Theta}$ are given by Du Toit and Browne (2001, Proposition 3). In their Figs. 14.1 and 14.2 they provide path diagrams showing the encapsulation of four preceding unobserved terms of an ARMA(2, 2) time series in two initial state variables.

An Alternative Representation of an ARMA(p, q) Process

There is an alternative and equivalent representation of the ARMA(p, q) model that may be more plausible in some circumstances. This is to discard the assumption of independently distributed random shocks, allow them to be correlated at lags $\ell \le q$, and adopt a model similar to that of the AR(p) process:

$$y_t = \alpha_1 y_{t-1} + \alpha_2 y_{t-2} + \cdots + \alpha_p y_{t-p} + \widetilde{z}_t. \tag{10}$$

Equation 10 is almost the same as Equation 2, which defines the AR(p) process. It differs in the definition of the shock term $\widetilde{z}_t$, which replaces $z_t + \beta_1 z_{t-1} + \cdots + \beta_q z_{t-q}$ in Equation 5. To retain the same covariance structure, we must have

$$\mathrm{Cov}(\widetilde{z}_t, \widetilde{z}_{t-\ell}) = \begin{cases} \widetilde{\psi}_\ell & \text{if } 0 \le \ell \le q, \\ 0 & \text{if } \ell > q, \end{cases}$$

where

$$\widetilde{\psi}_\ell = \psi \sum_{j=\ell}^{q} \beta_j \beta_{j-\ell}, \qquad \ell = 0, 1, \ldots, q,$$

with $\beta_0 = 1$. Thus the parameters $\psi, \beta_1, \ldots, \beta_q$ of the usual ARMA(p, q) model in Equation 5 are replaced by the new parameters $\widetilde{\psi}_0, \widetilde{\psi}_1, \ldots, \widetilde{\psi}_q$ of the reparametrized ARMA model in Equation 10. The covariance matrix of the $T \times 1$ redefined shock vector $\widetilde{\mathbf{z}}_t$ is a symmetric Toeplitz matrix of the form

$$\mathrm{Cov}\left(\widetilde{\mathbf{z}}_t, \widetilde{\mathbf{z}}_t'\right) = \begin{bmatrix} \widetilde{\psi}_0 & \widetilde{\psi}_1 & \cdots & \widetilde{\psi}_q & 0 & 0 & \cdots & 0 \\ \widetilde{\psi}_1 & \widetilde{\psi}_0 & \widetilde{\psi}_1 & \cdots & \widetilde{\psi}_q & 0 & \cdots & \cdots \\ \cdots & \widetilde{\psi}_1 & \widetilde{\psi}_0 & \widetilde{\psi}_1 & \cdots & \widetilde{\psi}_q & \cdots & 0 \\ \widetilde{\psi}_q & \cdots & \widetilde{\psi}_1 & \widetilde{\psi}_0 & \widetilde{\psi}_1 & \cdots & \cdots & 0 \\ 0 & \widetilde{\psi}_q & \cdots & \widetilde{\psi}_1 & \widetilde{\psi}_0 & \cdots & \cdots & \widetilde{\psi}_q \\ 0 & 0 & \widetilde{\psi}_q & \cdots & \cdots & \cdots & \widetilde{\psi}_1 & \cdots \\ \cdots & \cdots & \cdots & \cdots & \cdots & \widetilde{\psi}_1 & \widetilde{\psi}_0 & \widetilde{\psi}_1 \\ 0 & \cdots & 0 & 0 & \widetilde{\psi}_q & \cdots & \widetilde{\psi}_1 & \widetilde{\psi}_0 \end{bmatrix}.$$

A path diagram of the alternative representation of an ARMA(1, 1) process is shown in Fig. 13.5.

Environments are not just random configurations. Shocks are often correlated. We pursue this idea more explicitly here and elsewhere. Although the correlated-shock ARMA(p, q) model in Equation 10 is mathematically equivalent to the

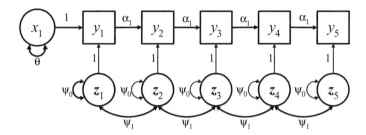

FIG. 13.5.   ARMA(1, 1) process with correlated shock variables.

independent-shock model in Equation 5, the interpretations of the two models differ. As may be seen from Fig. 13.4, on the one hand, each observation of the process variable is regarded as being influenced by more than one random shock in the independent-shock model. On the other hand, Fig. 13.5 illustrates how the correlated-shock model represents each observation as being influenced by a single shock with shocks at lags $\leq q$ being correlated and the rest uncorrelated.

Substantively, the idea of correlated shocks is compatible with, for example, personality concepts such as group dependence in which contextual influences (e.g., peer behavior) impinge on individual behavior or, in child development, with the influence of the kinds of friends with whom the child associates on behavior (e.g., hartup, 1996). A teenager may behave in conformity to the "shocks" provided by his or her current subset of friends. The active subsets of friends change, but with overlapping membership from day to day, thus providing some continuity or correlation of the shocks from one day to the next. Thus, "running with the wrong crowd" does not necessarily mean associating with exactly the same peers from day to day, but it does imply a somewhat correlated set of negative influences over time. The number of lags through which relationships persist will reflect characteristics of the individuals as well as the peer group.

In the subsequent sections, independent random shocks will be employed in ARMA models, and the results will not be duplicated using the correlated-shock representation. It is worth bearing in mind, however, that whenever parameters in the independent random shock ARMA model are estimated, a reparametrization may be carried out to provide corresponding parameters in the correlated-shock model.

THE EFFECT OF MEASUREMENT ERROR ON OBSERVATIONS OF A LATENT TIME SERIES

As has been seen, random shock variables play a key role in the use of time series models to represent change processes. Because of the superficial resemblance of measurement error to random shock variables, it is important to distinguish them from each other and to take a closer look at the effects of measurement error on this modeling approach. Complicating the distinction between the two is the fact that the first three characteristics of independent random shock variables listed earlier also apply to measurement errors:

1. Measurement errors are unobservable.
2. Measurement errors are identically distributed, $u_t, t = 1, \ldots, T \sim \mathcal{N}(0, v)$.
3. Measurement errors are mutually independently distributed, and distributed independently of shock variables. As a result they are unpredictable.
4. A measurement error at any time point t influences another variable, the measured variable, at time t only and at no other time points.

The fourth characteristic alone distinguishes between independent, random shocks and measurement errors. Despite the similarities between statistical properties of independent, random shocks and measurement errors, their substantive interpretations differ entirely. Although differentiating between independent random shocks and measurement errors may be very difficult in practice sometimes, the conceptual distinction between them must be maintained for full understanding of the manner in which psychological process is modeled by a time series.

In situations where correlated random shocks are employed the main distinction between shocks and errors is in the third characteristic, where shocks are allowed to be correlated and errors are not.[2] If correlated shocks are used in ARMA(p, q) models with $p > 0$, the fourth characteristic is still relevant because the autoregressive part of the model implies that the shock term has an indirect effect on future time points.

One of the critical effects of the presence of measurement errors is that they render what would otherwise be a manifest process variable into a latent process variable. Suppose, for instance, that f_t is a process variable in an ARMA(p, q) time series, which is observed subject to measurement error:

$$y_t = f_t + u_t. \tag{11}$$

The situation is analogous to classical test theory with y_t in the role of the observed score, f_t the true score, and u_t the error of measurement. It is in this sense that f_t is a latent variable.

The difficulty is that if f_t in Equation 11 follows an ARMA(p, q) time series, the measurements y_t will follow a different ARMA time series (Box & Jenkins, 1976, Appendix A 4.4; Harvey, 1989, Section 2.5). This time series will be an ARMA(p, q^*), with the same autoregressive order p and a different moving

---

[2]One sometimes sees the term *correlated errors* in contexts such as these involving repeated-measures modeling. We believe that this is an unfortunate contradiction in terms and avoid using it.

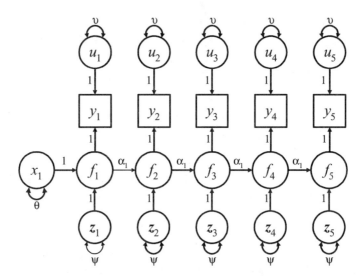

FIG. 13.6. AR(1) process measured subject to error.

average order $q^* = \max(p, q)$. The autoregressive weights $\alpha_1, \ldots, \alpha_q$ are the same for the latent time series of f_t and the observed time series of y_t, but the moving average weights $\beta_1, \ldots, \beta_q$ and shock variance ψ assume new values $\beta_1^*, \ldots, \beta_{q^*}^*$ and ψ^*, respectively, in the presence of measurement error.

These results have implications. Suppose that a latent AR(1) time series for f_t with autoregressive weight α_1 and shock variance ψ is measured, as in Equation 11, subject to error u_t with variance υ. A path diagram of the model is shown in Fig. 13.6.

In this figure, the f_t represent the latent process variable at consecutive time points and the z_t are corresponding random shocks. The f_t are measured subject to error by the manifest variables y_t with errors u_t. Although first examination of the path diagram appears to indicate that the u_t and z_t have similar functions, this is not the case. The effect of u_t on y_t is to partially obscure its measurement of f_t, but u_t has no effect on any other variable in the model. On the other hand, the effect of z_t on f_t is carried through to f_{t+1} and thence to f_{t+2} and all subsequent terms, although the strength of the influence diminishes gradually with time. Thus, z_t affects the time series not only at a single point, but also at all time points after t.

The behavior of systolic blood pressure can be used to illustrate these ideas more concretely. The f_t represent the "true" systolic blood pressure and the y_t represent the systolic blood pressure readings from, say, a pressure cuff. The errors of measurement u_t signify problems with the apparatus, differences in the viewing angle of the technician, and so on. The z_t are the shocks—the events that impinge on the organism and stimulate it to respond by varying systolic blood pressure. The continuity of this system is in the true blood pressure, which further reflects complex central nervous system activity. Whatever continuity is observed in the y_t is due to their being "driven" by the f_t. No continuity is provided by the u_t or the z_t in this model. Continuity introduced through the z_t, for example, would indicate a different model, one with correlated shocks.

We now show how measuring a latent AR(1) process subject to error results in a manifest AR(1, 1) process. Substituting $y_t - u_t$ for f_t in the latent AR(1) model, $f_t = \alpha_1 f_{t-1} + z_t$, gives a correlated-shock representation, $y_t = \alpha_1 y_{t-1} + \tilde{z}_t$, of a manifest ARMA(1, 1) model with shocks defined by $\tilde{z}_t = z_t + u_t - \alpha_1 u_{t-1}$. The shock variance and lagged covariance then are, respectively,

$$\tilde{\psi}_0 = \mathrm{Var}(\tilde{z}_t) = \psi + \left(1 + \alpha_1^2\right) \upsilon,$$
$$\tilde{\psi}_1 = \mathrm{Cov}(\tilde{z}_t, \tilde{z}_{t-1}) = -\alpha_1 \upsilon. \tag{12}$$

This correlated-shock representation is equivalent to the independent-shock representation, $y_t = \alpha_1 y_{t-1} + z_t + \beta_1^* z_{t-1}$, of the manifest ARMA(1, 1) model with

$$\beta_1^* = \frac{\tilde{\psi}_0 - \sqrt{\tilde{\psi}_0^2 - 4\tilde{\psi}_1^2}}{2\tilde{\psi}_1},$$
$$\psi^* = \mathrm{Var}(z_t) = \frac{\tilde{\psi}_1}{\beta_1^*}. \tag{13}$$

Equations 12 and 13 show that the manifest ARMA(1, 1) parameters β_1^* and ψ^* are fairly complicated functions of the latent AR(1) parameters α_1 and ψ_0 and the measurement error variance υ. It can be seen, however, that β_1^* will be opposite in sign to α_1 because $\tilde{\psi}_1$ and α_1 are opposite in sign. The autoregressive weight α_1 remains the same in the latent AR(1) process and the manifest ARMA(1, 1) process. A path diagram of the ARMA(1, 1) representation of the AR(1) process measured with error is shown in Fig. 13.7.

The models shown in the path diagrams in Figs. 13.6 and 13.7 appear very different and have different interpretations, but are mathematically equivalent. There are three free parameters, α_1, ψ, and υ, in the latent AR(1) process with measurement

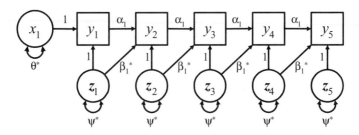

FIG. 13.7.   ARMA(1,1) process equivalent to AR(1) with measurement error.

error, and three parameters, α_1, β_1^*, and ψ^*, in the manifest ARMA(1, 1) process. The two models will fit equally well, and the parameters of one are functions of the parameters of the other. The only choice between them can be on substantive grounds. Reconsider the systolic blood pressure example given earlier. It makes substantive sense to conceptualize a latent variable, systolic blood pressure, and for the continuity of the system to reside in it. Thus, the model shown in Fig. 13.6 seems substantively more apt than that shown in Fig. 13.7.

This mathematical equivalence between a latent AR(p) time series with measurement error and the manifest ARMA(p, q^*) model holds in the current situation where $p = q + 1$, but not always. If $p \neq q + 1$, the two models have different numbers of parameters and cannot be mathematically equivalent.

It is important to bear in mind that the manifest time series y_t is not the same as the latent time series f_t that is measured subject to error. In other words, the manifest time series does not accurately represent the latent time series with respect to the moving average part, although the autoregressive part remains the same.

The differences between the latent time series for the psychological process of interest and the actually observed time series have implications for the methods used to select a model. In most areas of application of time series, a time series for measured variables is of primary interest. Exploratory procedures based on autocorrelation functions and partial autocorrelation functions, estimated without prior information from the data, are used for suggesting an appropriate model. This is not possible when the time series of interest is latent. Applying these exploratory procedures to the manifest time series is not appropriate when the latent time series is of primary interest. Consequently, analyses of latent time series should be based on substantive considerations provided by the user, and will preferably be confirmatory. It is still possible, however, to try several models and choose one, taking both goodness of fit and plausibility into account.

TRENDS: DETERMINISTIC AND RANDOM

The time series models considered up to this point had constant zero means. It is often appropriate to incorporate trends for the mean over time. Two types of model for the mean may be distinguished: models for deterministic trends and models for random trends.

Deterministic trend models for the mean are expressed in the form of a mathematical function $\mu(t, \gamma)$ of time t and a parameter vector γ. They imply that if the parameter vector γ is known, the expected value $\mathcal{E}(y_t)$ of the process variable is known exactly at all t. Models of this type are suitable, for example, for the physical growth of individuals from infancy to adulthood because the general pattern of growth in height has the same general shape for all persons, and differences in parameter values allow for different heights at birth, different heights at adulthood, and different times of onset of the growth spurt at puberty. Suppose that the model employed for a process variable y_t^* is of the form

$$y_t^* = \mu(t, \gamma) + y_t,$$

where y_t has an ARMA time series with zero means. Then the expected value of y_t^* changes in a deterministic manner, but the random fluctuations of y_t^* about this expected value follow the particular ARMA time series. Deterministic polynomial trends for means in single time series were discussed by Wei (1990, Section 4.1.1). Gompertz mean trend curves for repeated ARMA(1, 1) time series in a learning experiment were used by Browne and Du Toit (1991, Section 5). Each subject in a random sample of specified size was assumed to have the same Gompertz mean trend, with deviations about the mean trend according to the same ARMA(1, 1) time series. An alternative approach was considered in Browne (1993, Equation 5.9). Instead of assuming the same expected trend for each person, a latent curve model was used with a different expected trend for each person and with deviations about each expected trend according to the same AR(1) process.

Models for stochastic trends for the mean are are driven by random shocks. Properties of these trends such as onset, rate of change, and change of direction cannot be predicted in advance. When the process variable is manifest and the main purpose of the analysis is short-term prediction, an autoregressive integrated moving average model ARIMA(p, d, q) is often employed (Wei, 1990, section 4.1.2 and 4.2) to model stochastic trends. Stochastic trends in the process variable are induced by assuming an ARMA(p, q) time series for dth-order differences of the process variable, rather than for the process variable itself. This results in nonstationarity both for the mean and the variance of the process variable. In this situation there are no interpretable parameters describing properties of the trend such as the asymptote. The main purpose of the analysis is prediction rather than explanation.

MULTIVARIATE TIME SERIES

We now come to the heart of this chapter. Building on the brief review and summary of ARMA models, we identify and discuss a somewhat more general set of models of process that reflect the multivariate orientation as described by Baltes and Nesselroade (1973), Cattell (1966), and others. Central to this theme is measurement by means of a battery of measures that provides the basis for drawing inferences regarding latent variables (factors) that are presumed to underlie those observed measures. Because these models involve vector analogues of ARMA models, the term VARMA models is used to label them. Although the models we discuss have short histories, they have a relatively long past, which reaches back several decades to the initial P-technique work by Cattell, Cattell, and Rhymer (1947).

Suppose that the process variable $\mathbf{y}_t$ is a $k \times 1$ vector. A vector analogue of the ARMA(p, q) model is VARMA(p, q), defined as

$$\mathbf{y}_t = \mathbf{A}_1\mathbf{y}_{t-1} + \mathbf{A}_2\mathbf{y}_{t-2} + \cdots + \mathbf{A}_p\mathbf{y}_{t-p} + \mathbf{z}_t + \mathbf{B}_1\mathbf{z}_{t-1} + \mathbf{B}_2\mathbf{z}_{t-2} + \cdots + \mathbf{B}_q\mathbf{z}_{t-q}, \quad (14)$$

where $\mathbf{z}_t$ is a $k \times 1$ random shock vector with $\mathbf{z}_t \sim \mathcal{N}(\mathbf{0}, \boldsymbol{\Psi})$; $\mathbf{z}_t$ and $\mathbf{z}_{t+\ell}$, $\ell \neq 0$, are independently distributed; $\boldsymbol{\Psi}$ is a $k \times k$ positive-definite random shock covariance matrix; $\mathbf{A}_1, \ldots, \mathbf{A}_p$ are $k \times k$ autoregressive weight matrices, and $\mathbf{B}_1, \ldots, \mathbf{B}_q$ are $k \times k$ moving average weight matrices. Special cases of the VARMA(p, q) process are the VAR(p) process, where $q = 0$, and the VMA(q) process, where $p = 0$.

Because VARMA processes are generalizations of ARMA processes they have related properties. A brief summary is given here:

1. Invertibility of VAR(p) and VMA(q) processes is defined as before. For VAR(1) all p (complex) eigenvalues of $\mathbf{A}_1$ must be less than one in absolute value for invertibility. All eigenvalues of $\mathbf{B}_1$ must be less than one in absolute value for a VMA(1) process to be invertible.

2. As before, a VAR(p) process is stationary if and only if it is invertible. Invertibility constraints are imposed on the parameter matrices of a VMA(q) process for identification,

3. Identification conditions for VARMA(p, q) processes are substantially more complicated than for ARMA processes. More information may be found in Lütkepohl (1993, Section 7.1) and Wei (1990, pp. 336–337). VAR models, on the other hand, are always identifiable.

4. In general, the multivariate VARMA process poses substantially more problems in identification, interpretation, and computation than the univariate ARMA case.

Further detail may be found in Wei (1990, Chapter 14) and Lütkepohl (1993, Chapter 6).

The autoregressive weight matrices $\mathbf{A}_i$ and the moving average weight matrices $\mathbf{B}_j$ in a k-variable VARMA(p, q) time series are nonsymmetric $k \times k$ matrices. The shock covariance matrix $\boldsymbol{\Psi}$ is a symmetric $k \times k$ matrix, which need not be diagonal. As k increases, the number of parameters in the model consequently increases rapidly. For parsimony and ease of interpretation, therefore, it is advantageous to use one's knowledge of the situation being modeled to fix some parameters to zero when k is not small.

Reducing the number of process variables by treating them as latent variables with manifest indicators will also improve parsimony and ease of interpretation. This is completely in keeping with the multivariate emphasis mentioned earlier.

VARMA Models for Single Time Series

First, we will consider a *single time series*—a sequence of observations on multiple variables on a single case taken at regular intervals over time. For instance, a single time series might consist of T monthly observations made on each of k economic indicators in a single country. Such data are also found in psychology, where they are often referred to as P-technique data (Cattell, 1963; Cattell et al., 1947). In P-technique designs, several tests are given repeatedly to one participant at regular intervals. The number of time points T is typically quite large ($T > 100$), and the number k of tests can be moderately large. Sometimes, several P-technique designs, with multiple participants, are conducted simultaneously to address the matter of generalizability (Jones & Nesselroade, 1990; Zevon & Tellegen, 1982).

Because there is only one observation on each test at a particular time point, the $\mathbf{A}_i$ and $\mathbf{B}_j$ weight matrices are assumed to remain constant from one time point to another to facilitate statistical inference. That is, the set of repeated observations $\mathbf{y}_t, t = 1, \ldots, T$, although they are not independent, may properly be regarded as a sample of size T (not 1) from a distribution with the weight matrices $\mathbf{A}_i$ and $\mathbf{B}_j$ and shock covariance matrix $\mathbf{\Psi}$ as parameter matrices. Provided that the likelihood function is correctly specified to take into account lack of independence of observations, the method of maximum likelihood may be used for estimating the parameters and testing the fit of the model. Standard large-sample theory for maximum likelihood estimation may then be used when T is large. This topic will be considered further in a subsequent section.

If the weight matrices were to differ nonsystematically from one time point t to another, one would then have a single observation $\mathbf{y}_t$ from the k-variate distribution with the parameter matrices appropriate for that particular t. Statistical inference would then be based on a sample of size one and no longer be feasible.

VARMA Models for Repeated Time Series

Next, we examine *repeated time series*—a sequence of observations on k variables at T time points for each of $n = 1, \ldots, N$ subjects. This amounts to $N \times T \times k$ observations in all. Although data of this type are often collected, there are two stringent assumptions underpinning the analysis that are easily violated. The first is that the sequences of observations obtained from different subjects are independent realizations of the same ARMA time series. That is, there are no differences between subjects in either the $\mathbf{A}_i$ and $\mathbf{B}_j$ weight matrices or in the shock covariance matrix $\mathbf{\Psi}$. The second is that all sets of observations on individuals are in phase, or at comparable stages of the process. This is true if the time series is stationary because means, variances, and covariances at specified lags do not change as time progresses. If the time series is not stationary, the starting points for all individuals need to be the same. This could be an acceptable assumption in certain learning experiments, but it is seldom plausible in panel studies.

Standard methodology for the analysis of covariance structures is applicable if N is substantially larger than $T \times k$. Because replicate measurements on the $\mathbf{A}_i$ and $\mathbf{B}_j$ weight matrices are provided by the N subjects, it is no longer necessary to assume that they remain constant as time changes. Changes of the weight matrices between time points implies nonstationarity of the time series, however. Because sequences of observations of the same time series starting at different time points cannot be treated as replications when it changes with time (i.e., is nonstationary), it is now necessary for the starting point of the sequence of observations to be the same for each subject.

The well known quasisimplex model may be regarded as a nonstationary AR(1) model for repeated time series (e.g., Jöreskog & Sörbom, 1977) measured subject to error.[3] When the quasisimplex is used as a model for panel data, therefore, care should be taken that the starting points for all persons in the sample should be "the same" in some sense. This has not always been done in practical applications. It is also a serious consideration for many developmental research designs and models.

The Likelihood Function in Single and Repeated Time Series

A representation of the multivariate normal likelihood function that is employed in structural equation modeling programs for complete data is suitable for repeated time series but not for single time series. Relationships between the likelihood functions for single and repeated time series will therefore be discussed here.

Let the $k \times 1$ vector $\mathbf{y}_{ti}$ represent the scores of subject i on each of k tests at occasion t, and let

$$\mathbf{y}_i = \begin{bmatrix} \mathbf{y}_{1i} \\ \mathbf{y}_{2i} \\ \vdots \\ \mathbf{y}_{Ti} \end{bmatrix}$$

be the $Tk \times 1$ vector of all scores for subject i during all T occasions. Suppose that $\mathbf{y}_i$ has a Tk-variate normal distribution with mean vector

$$\boldsymbol{\mu} = \begin{bmatrix} \mu_1 \\ \mu_2 \\ \vdots \\ \mu_T \end{bmatrix}$$

---

[3]Du Toit (1979) showed that the quasisimplex is equivalent to a nonstationary ARMA(1, 1) model for repeated time series. Equivalently, the equivalence of the path diagrams of Figs. 13.6 and 13.7 also applies in the nonstationary situation where the parameters α_1, β_1, and ψ differ from one time point to another.

and covariance matrix

$$\Sigma = \begin{bmatrix} \Sigma_{11} & \Sigma_{12} & \cdots & \Sigma_{1T} \\ \Sigma_{21} & \Sigma_{22} & \cdots & \Sigma_{2T} \\ \vdots & \vdots & \ddots & \vdots \\ \Sigma_{T1} & \Sigma_{T2} & \cdots & \Sigma_{TT} \end{bmatrix}.$$

The log-likelihood function for the single time series on subject i then is

$$\mathcal{L}_i = -\frac{1}{2}[Tk\ln(2\pi) + \ln|\Sigma| + (y_i - \mu)'\Sigma^{-1}(y_i - \mu)]. \tag{15}$$

The saturated model is the model where all elements of μ and all nonduplicated elements of Σ are regarded as free parameters to be estimated. In this situation, maximization of $\mathcal{L}_i$ to obtain maximum likelihood estimates of μ and Σ would not be feasible because there are too many parameters to be estimated from a single observation y_i.

One may, however, use y_i to estimate parameters in a more restricted model where the elements of μ and Σ are functions of a relatively small number of parameters. Suppose, for example, that each of the k elements of μ_t follows a three-parameter Gompertz trend curve

$$\begin{aligned} m_{tj}(\gamma_{1j}, \gamma_{2j}, \gamma_{3j}) &= \gamma_{1j}\exp\{-\gamma_{2j}\exp[-(t-1)\gamma_{3j}]\}, \\ t &= 1, \ldots, T, \quad j = 1, \ldots, k, \end{aligned} \tag{16}$$

over the T time points. Then

$$\mu = m(\gamma_\mu), \tag{17}$$

where the elements of m are given by Equation 16, and γ_μ is the corresponding $3k \times 1$ parameter vector. Also suppose that deviations from the mean follow the VARMA(p, q) process in Equation 14. The covariance matrix then satisfies the model (Du Toit & Browne, 2001, Proposition 1)

$$\Sigma = T_{-A}^{-1}\{\Theta^* + T_B(I \otimes \Psi)T_B'\}T_{-A}^{-1'}, \tag{18}$$

where T_{-A} is a lower triangular Toeplitz matrix formed from negative autoregressive weight matrices A_i in Equation 14; Θ^* is a matrix of zero elements except for the first $q^* \times q^*$ principal submatrix, which is equal to the initial state covariance matrix Θ in Equation 9; T_B is a lower triangular Toeplitz matrix formed from moving average weight matrices B_j; and Ψ is the shock covariance matrix. Details may be found in Du Toit and Browne (2001). The reduction in the number of parameters now makes it possible to maximize $\mathcal{L}_i$ and obtain estimates of all Gompertz parameters and all VARMA(p, q) parameters. No goodness of fit test is possible, however, because parameters cannot be estimated under the saturated model.

It is possible to test for equality of parameters between several subjects. We consider the null hypothesis that the Gompertz and ARMA(p, q) parameters are the same for each of g subjects $(g \geq 2)$, which is to be tested against the alternative that they are not all the same. Let w be the number of parameters in the likelihood function $\mathcal{L}_i$ for a single subject and let

$$\mathcal{L}_{\text{sum}} = \sum_{i=1}^{g} \mathcal{L}_i,$$

using the same w parameters in $\mathcal{L}_1, \ldots, \mathcal{L}_g$ (see Equation 15). Suppose that $\widehat{\mathcal{L}}_i$ is the maximum of the likelihood function for individual i and that $\widehat{\mathcal{L}}_{\text{sum}}$ is the maximum of the overall likelihood function. Then the likelihood ratio test statistic for testing equality of parameters between subjects is

$$-2 \ln \lambda = -2 \left(\widehat{\mathcal{L}}_{\text{sum}} - \sum_{i=1}^{g} \widehat{\mathcal{L}}_i \right),$$

and the corresponding degrees of freedom are given by

$$\text{df} = (g - 1)\, w.$$

This test is analogous to the test for equality of parameters in several groups in the analysis of covariance structures.

Thus, maximum likelihood estimation may be used in the analysis of single time series even though there is only one case $(N = 1)$. In this situation the number of time points T becomes the effective sample size. Provided that the parameters of the ARMA process satisfy the stationarity requirements and are identifiable, maximum likelihood estimates have the usual desirable asymptotic properties as T increases, and the inverse information matrix may be employed to obtain standard error estimates in the usual manner. There is no likelihood ratio goodness-of-fit test because estimation is not possible under the alternative hypothesis of a saturated model.

In the situation where $N > k \times T$ cases are available, and it is reasonable to assume that the same time series parameters apply to each case, a repeated time series model is appropriate. The log-likelihood function may be expressed in the form

$$\mathcal{L} = \sum_{i=1}^{N} \mathcal{L}_i = -\frac{1}{2} \{ N[Tk \ln (2\pi) + \ln|\Sigma|] + \sum_{i=1}^{N} (y_i - \mu)' \Sigma^{-1} (y_i - \mu) \}.$$

Here $\mathcal{L}$ is defined in terms of the individual observations $\mathbf{y}_i$. An algebraically equivalent, and computationally convenient, form of $\mathcal{L}$ usually employed in structural
equation modeling of complete data is

$$\mathcal{L} = -\frac{1}{2} N \{ Tk \ln{(2\pi)} + \ln|\mathbf{\Sigma}| + (\bar{\mathbf{y}} - \boldsymbol{\mu})'\mathbf{\Sigma}^{-1}(\bar{\mathbf{y}} - \boldsymbol{\mu}) + \text{tr}[\mathbf{S}\mathbf{\Sigma}^{-1}]\},$$

where $\bar{\mathbf{y}}$ is the sample mean, $\mathbf{S}$ is the sample covariance matrix, $\boldsymbol{\mu}$ is a function
of parameters in the model defined by Equations 16, and 17, and $\mathbf{\Sigma}$ is a function
defined by Equation 18. In this situation, $\bar{\mathbf{y}}$ and $\mathbf{S}$ provide maximum likelihood
estimates of $\boldsymbol{\mu}$ and $\mathbf{\Sigma}$ under the saturated model, so that a likelihood ratio goodness-
of-fit test is possible.

DYNAMIC FACTOR ANALYSIS

Finally, we turn to the factor analysis of a single time series. Cattell et al. (1947)
first exemplified the application of the factor model to P-technique data. From the
$T \times k$ matrix of scores resulting from measuring one participant on T successive
days using a test battery consisting of k measures, a $k \times k$ correlation matrix
was computed and subjected to a standard exploratory factor analysis. Since that
initial analysis, this technique has been used successfully in a large number of
studies (for reviews see Jones & Nesselroade, 1990; Luborsky & Mintz, 1972).
P-technique analysis facilitates the examination of differences between subjects
in the way they respond to tests. Although applying standard factor analysis to
P-technique data disregards serial correlation, it will provide a consistent estimate
(as $T \to \infty$) of the factor matrix for a particular subject. The usual goodness-of-fit
tests and standard errors of estimates found in commercial software, however, are
not applicable.

   Anderson (1963), Holtzman (1963), and others (e.g., Molenaar, 1985; Steyer,
Ferring, & Schmitt, 1992) pointed out that information concerning time series
aspects of the data are disregarded in the P-technique approach. Anderson (1963)
discussed how a conventional P-technique factor analysis could first be used to
estimate a factor matrix. After using the factor matrix to estimate factor scores at
each time point, the factor score estimates would be subjected to an ARMA time
series analysis to provide information about changes over time. A difficulty with
this approach is that factor score estimates do not coincide with the latent factor
scores. Because of the effect of measurement error discussed earlier, the time series
analysis of factor score estimates does not convey accurate information about the
latent factors. At the time Anderson (1963) was writing, computers were limited
in capacity and speed and appropriate optimization algorithms were in the early
stages of development, so that better alternatives were not accessible. Methods
for investigating latent time series without computing factor score estimates have
been developed since then (Engle & Watson, 1981; Immink, 1986).

We now examine two general factor analysis models that can be considered to offer at least partial remedies for the shortcomings of ordinary P-technique factor analysis. In the one, the common factors are regarded as process variables. We refer to this model as the *process factor analysis (PFA) model*. In the other, the common factors are regarded as shock variables. This is referred to here as the *shock factor analysis (SFA) model*. Both of these models were assigned the label *dynamic* by their proponents: Engle and Watson (1981) and Immink (1986) for the process factor model, and Geweke (1977), Geweke and Singleton (1981), and Molenaar (1985, 1994) for the shock factor model. Although both models may be regarded as dynamic factor analysis models, they differ substantially in the manner in which a time series model is incorporated to account for interrelationships between manifest variables over time.

The Process Factor Analysis Model

Like the P-technique (Cattell, 1963; Cattell et al., 1947), the process factor analysis model involves a single factor matrix. It further develops the ideas of Anderson (1963) in that the common factors follow a VARMA time series. A special case of this model was treated by Engle and Waston (1981), who considered a single factor with an AR(1) time series and provided a Kalman filter algorithm for obtaining maximum likelihood estimates. Immink (1986) gave an extensive treatment of a generalization of the Engle–Watson model to several independently distributed common factors following VARMA(p, q) processes, with diagonal weight matrices and a diagonal shock covariance matrix. He also used the Kalman filter to obtain estimates and provided several examples of its application.

Parallel work on the PFA model was carried out using a different estimation method. McArdle (1982) considered a PFA model with factors following a VAR time series and applied structural equation modeling methodology to a lagged correlation matrix to obtain estimates. More recently Nesselroade, McArdle, Aggen, and Meyers (2002) defined a two-factor VAR(p) model and showed how parameter estimates could be obtained from the lagged correlation matrix.

We first consider a general PFA model. The manifest variables are assumed to satisfy a factor analysis model:

$$\mathbf{y}_t = \boldsymbol{\mu}_t + \boldsymbol{\Lambda}\mathbf{f}_t + \mathbf{u}_t, \qquad t = 1, \dots, T, \tag{19}$$

where $\mathbf{y}_t$ represents a $k \times 1$ vector of scores on the battery of k tests at time point t; $\boldsymbol{\mu}_t$ is a $k \times 1$ mean vector, which can be constant, $\boldsymbol{\mu}_t = \boldsymbol{\mu}$, or may vary systematically with time such as in Equation 16; $\boldsymbol{\Lambda}$ is a constant $k \times m$ factor matrix; $\mathbf{f}_t$ is an $m \times 1$ vector representing latent common factors at time t; and $\mathbf{u}_t$ is a $k \times 1$ vector representing unique factors at time t. In the most general PFA model the only assumption made about the time series for $\mathbf{f}_t$ is that *it is stationary* with an expected value of zero. Mean trends for the latent process may still be accommodated by taking $\boldsymbol{\mu}_t = \boldsymbol{\Lambda}\boldsymbol{\zeta}_t$, where $\boldsymbol{\zeta}_t$ follows a deterministic trend, and regarding $(\boldsymbol{\zeta}_t + \mathbf{f}_t)$ as representative of the process.

For estimation to be possible, assumptions need to be made about the form of the time series. Previous work has specified either a VARMA(p, q) process (Immink, 1986) for the common factors or the special case of a VAR$(p) =$ VARMA$(p, 0)$ process (Engle & Watson, 1981; McArdle, 1982; Nesselroade et al., 2002). The VARMA(p, q) time series for the common factors is of the form

$$\mathbf{f}_t = \mathbf{A}_1\mathbf{f}_{t-1} + \mathbf{A}_2\mathbf{f}_{t-2} + \cdots + \mathbf{A}_p\mathbf{f}_{t-p} + \mathbf{z}_t + \mathbf{B}_1\mathbf{z}_{t-1} + \mathbf{B}_2\mathbf{z}_{t-2} + \cdots + \mathbf{B}_q\mathbf{z}_{t-q}, \quad (20)$$

where

$$\mathcal{E}(\mathbf{z}_t) = \mathbf{0},$$
$$\mathrm{Cov}(\mathbf{z}_t, \mathbf{z}'_t) = \boldsymbol{\Psi}. \quad (21)$$

We refer to a PFA model given by Equation 19, in which the factors follow the VARMA(p, q) time series in Equation 20, as a PFA(p, q) model. The latent common factor vector $\mathbf{f}_t$ consists of m process variables, which are measured by the $k > m$ manifest variables $\mathbf{y}_t$ subject to contamination by $\mathbf{u}_t$. The elements of $\mathbf{z}_t$ are m random shocks that "drive" the m common factors. Consequently, the principal role of the observed or manifest variables is that of indicator variables for the common factors.

As is the case in the usual factor analysis model, the parameters of the process factor analysis model are not identifiable unless additional constraints are applied. The usual constraints may be applied to the factor matrix $\boldsymbol{\Lambda}$, but those applied to the common factor covariance matrix $\boldsymbol{\Phi} = \mathrm{Cov}(\mathbf{f}_t, \mathbf{f}'_t)$ require different methods because the factors are endogenous. The usual scale determination constraints requiring unit diagonal elements of $\boldsymbol{\Phi}$ now need the imposition of nonlinear equality constraints because $\boldsymbol{\Phi}$ has the VARMA(p, q) structure of the right-hand side of Equation 18. An alternative manner of scale determination for the factors is to fix the variances of the exogenous random shocks to be one (Jöreskog & Goldberger, 1975, Equation 208):

$$\psi_{ii} = 1, \quad i = 1, \ldots, m. \quad (22)$$

It will be convenient for comparative purposes to adopt these identification conditions here because they can also be used for the shock factor model. The process factors will be uncorrelated if all $\mathbf{A}_i$ and $\mathbf{B}_j$ as well as $\boldsymbol{\Psi}$ are diagonal matrices.

It is sometimes reasonable in practice to assume that the unique factor vector $\mathbf{u}_t$ follows a time series. To avoid a complicated exposition, we assume here that the unique factors comprise pure error of measurement, without any specific component that is correlated over time.

A path diagram of a PFA$(1, 0)$ model for the case where there is a single common factor that follows an AR(1) process is shown in Fig. 13.8. It may be seen how

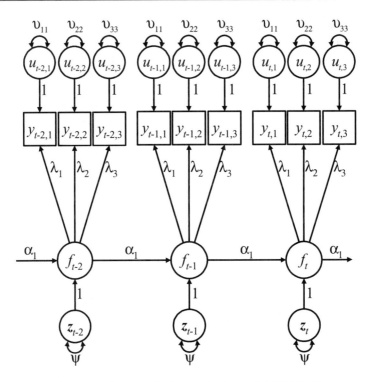

FIG. 13.8. Process factor analysis model: PFA(1, 0).

the factor f_t is a process variable that is driven by the random shock variable z_t, whereas the manifest variables $y_{t,1}$, $y_{t,2}$, and $y_{t,3}$ act only as indicators and are not directly affected by the shocks.

Figure 13.9 shows a path diagram of a PFA(0,1) model where the factor follows an MA(1) model. Again the random shocks do not directly affect the manifest variables, but the effect of each shock on the latent process is limited to two occasions.

This figure will be useful for showing the relationship between process factor models and shock factor models. We note that the restricted possibilities for "continuity" at the process variable level render this model perhaps of less interest to developmentalists, but for those who study affective processes, for example, it would seem to hold a great deal of promise.

The Shock Factor Analysis Model

Brillinger (1975) proposed a principal components procedure for a vector time series involving infinitely many component loading matrices. He transferred his model to the frequency domain for statistical analysis, but stated it originally in the time domain. Geweke (1977) and Geweke and Singleton (1981) proposed a related

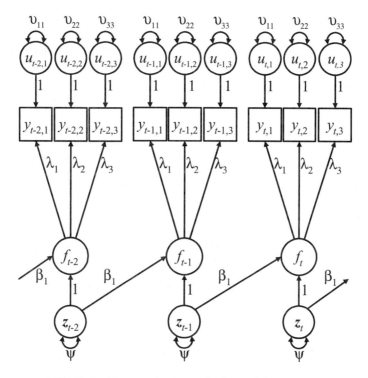

FIG. 13.9. Process factor analysis model: PFA(0,1).

factor analysis model. Again there were infinitely many factor matrices and again the model was stated in the time domain and transferred to the frequency domain for statistical analysis. The main emphasis of the procedure was on hypothesis testing rather than on the estimation of parameters.

The dynamic factor analysis model of Geweke and Singleton (1981) has the form

$$\mathbf{y}_t = \boldsymbol{\mu} + \boldsymbol{\Lambda}_0 \mathbf{z}_t + \boldsymbol{\Lambda}_1 \mathbf{z}_{t-1} + \cdots + \boldsymbol{\Lambda}_\infty \mathbf{z}_{t-\infty} + \mathbf{u}_t, \tag{23}$$

where $\mathbf{u}_t$ is defined as before and the $\mathbf{z}_t$ are regarded as factors but have the properties of random shock variables, being uncorrelated between any two different time periods, $\mathrm{Cov}(\mathbf{z}_t, \mathbf{z}'_{t+\ell}) = \mathbf{0}$, $\ell \neq 0$, identically distributed, and influencing the process variables at a sequence of time points. These process variables now are the manifest variables, and the process is no longer latent. Although Geweke and Singleton (1981) assumed that the elements of $\mathbf{z}_t$ are uncorrelated at any time point, we relax this assumption, assume that $\mathrm{Cov}(\mathbf{z}_t, \mathbf{z}'_t) = \boldsymbol{\Psi}$ as for the PFA(p, q) model, and determine the scale of the random shocks using Equation 22 as before. Thus the random shocks at time point t are now permitted, but not forced, to be correlated with each other. This model is referred to as the shock factor analysis model of infinite order, or SFA(∞).

Molenaar (1985, 1994; see also Wood & Brown, 1994) presented a dynamic factor analysis model as a refinement of P-technique factor analysis that can be viewed as a special case of the SFA(∞) model. He truncated it after a specified number q of terms, thereby making it suitable for use entirely in the time domain. This model is referred to here as the SFA(q) model:

$$\mathbf{y}_t = \boldsymbol{\mu} + \boldsymbol{\Lambda}_0 \mathbf{z}_t + \boldsymbol{\Lambda}_1 \mathbf{z}_{t-1} + \cdots + \boldsymbol{\Lambda}_q \mathbf{z}_{t-q} + \mathbf{u}_t. \tag{24}$$

Molenaar presented various refinements of the model including suggestions for systematically searching for an optimal order q and transforming the solution to induce desirable properties into the factor variables (Molenaar & Nesselroade, 2001)

Figure 13.10 gives a path diagram for the SFA(1) model. Comparison of this path diagram to the path diagram in Fig. 13.9 shows that the PFA(0,1) model is a constrained version of the SF(1) model obtained by imposing the following

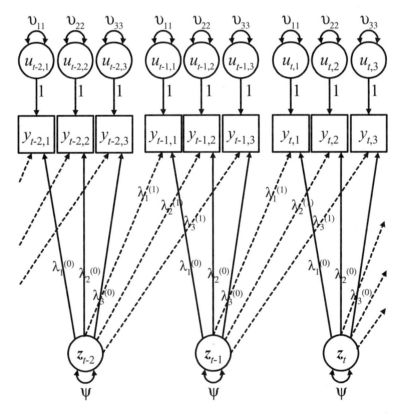

FIG. 13.10. Shock factor analysis model: SFA(1).

restrictions:

$$\left.\begin{array}{l} \lambda_i^{(0)} = \lambda_i \\ \lambda_i^{(1)} = \beta_1 \lambda_i \end{array}\right\} , \quad i = 1, \ldots, 3.$$

This is true in general. If the equation for a VMA(q) process obtained from Equation 20 with $p = 0$ is substituted into Equation 19, one obtains

$$\mathbf{y}_t = \boldsymbol{\mu} + \boldsymbol{\Lambda}\mathbf{z}_t + (\boldsymbol{\Lambda}\mathbf{B}_1)\mathbf{z}_{t-1} + \cdots + (\boldsymbol{\Lambda}\mathbf{B}_q)\mathbf{z}_{t-q} + \mathbf{u}_t, \qquad (25)$$

which is a special case of SFA(q) with $\boldsymbol{\Lambda}_0 = \boldsymbol{\Lambda}$ and $\boldsymbol{\Lambda}_j = \boldsymbol{\Lambda}\mathbf{B}_j$ for $j = 1, \ldots, q$. Thus any PFA($0, q$) model may also be expressed as as a SFA(q) model. The SFA(q) model will have more parameters because the number of elements of $\boldsymbol{\Lambda}_j$ exceeds that of $\mathbf{B}_j$ for each $j = 1, \ldots, q$.

We now consider the most general form of PFA model in which all that is assumed is that the time series of the $\mathbf{f}_t$ should be covariance stationary with zero means. Wold's decomposition (Lütkepohl, 1993, p. 20) then shows that, whether or not this time series is VARMA(p, q), it may be expressed as an infinite vector moving average process VMA(∞). Consequently, a sequence of weight matrices $\mathbf{B}_1^*, \mathbf{B}_2^*, \ldots, \mathbf{B}_\infty^*$ can be found such that

$$\mathbf{f}_t = \mathbf{z}_t + \mathbf{B}_1^*\mathbf{z}_{t-1} + \mathbf{B}_2^*\mathbf{z}_{t-2} + \cdots + \mathbf{B}_\infty^*\mathbf{z}_{t-\infty}, \qquad (26)$$

where $\mathbf{B}_j^* \to \mathbf{0}$ as $j \to \infty$. Equations 19 and 26 now imply that any PFA model may be expressed as a PFA($0, \infty$) model.

We saw in Equation 25 that any PFA($0, q$) model is a constrained SFA(q) model. It follows from Equation 26, therefore, that any PFA model may be expressed as a constrained SFA(∞) model with

$$\boldsymbol{\Lambda}_0 = \boldsymbol{\Lambda} \qquad \text{and} \qquad \boldsymbol{\Lambda}_j = \boldsymbol{\Lambda}\mathbf{B}_j^*, \quad j = 1, \ldots, \infty. \qquad (27)$$

The class of SFA(∞) models therefore not only includes all PFA models, but also includes models that do not fit into the process factor analysis framework at all.

Equation 27 has interesting implications for the simple structure of the factor matrices $\boldsymbol{\Lambda}_0, \boldsymbol{\Lambda}_1, \ldots, \boldsymbol{\Lambda}_\infty$ in the constrained SFA(∞) representation of a PFA(p, q) model. Suppose that all $\mathbf{A}_i$, $i = 1, \ldots, p$, and $\mathbf{B}_j$, $j = 1, \ldots, q$, in the PFA(p, q) model are diagonal matrices. It then follows (Lütkepohl 1993, Equation 6.3.5) that all $\mathbf{B}_j^*$, $j = 1, \ldots, \infty$, are also diagonal. If the PFA(p, q) factor matrix $\boldsymbol{\Lambda}$ has simple structure, it can be seen from Equation 27 that the SFA(∞) factor matrices $\boldsymbol{\Lambda}_0, \boldsymbol{\Lambda}_1, \ldots, \boldsymbol{\Lambda}_\infty$ will satisfy the conditions for parallel proportional profiles (Cattell, 1994) and consequently have the same simple structure when not too close to the limiting value $\boldsymbol{\Lambda}_\infty = \mathbf{0}$. Some of the most interesting applications of the PFA(p, q) model, however, involve cross-lagged effects (Ferrer & Nesselroade, 2003), so that the autoregressive weight matrices are not diagonal. Nonzero off-diagonal elements of either autoregressive or moving average weight matrices can destroy the simple structure in some columns of Λ_i matrices in the constrained SFA(∞) representation of a PFA(p, q) model. For example, if the factor matrix Λ in a PFA(p, 0) model has simple structure and $\mathbf{A}_1$ involves appreciable cross-lagged effects between the first two factors ($[\mathbf{A}_1]_{11} \neq 0, [\mathbf{A}_1]_{12} \neq 0, [\mathbf{A}_1]_{21} \neq 0, [\mathbf{A}_1]_{22} \neq 0$), then only Λ_0 in the constrained SFA(∞) representation will have simple structure in all columns and all remaining shock factor matrices $\Lambda_j, j \geq 1$, will not have simple structure in the first two columns.

We have seen that some dynamic factor analysis models may be expressed either in a form with few parameters or in one with many, possibly infinitely many, parameters. This increase in number of parameters raises the enduring conflict between parsimony and generality (Pitt, Myung, & Zhang, 2002). More-general models are desirable in some ways, but they are also more highly parametrized. Highly parametrized models fitted to small samples give poorer predictions than models with fewer parameters. If all the parameters must be estimated, the more highly parametrized "general" models may be the more suspect and dangerous ones.

It is worth bearing in mind also that the general models PFA($0, \infty$) and SFA(∞) lose their generality when a finite and possibly small order q is employed. For example, the classes of PFA($0, q$) and SFA(q) models will not include a specific PFA(q, 0) model in an exact mathematical sense, and quite possibly not even provide a reasonable approximation.

Estimation

Immink (1986) successfully used the Kalman filter for maximum likelihood analysis of PFA(p, q) models in the special case where all weight matrices and the shock covariance matrix are diagonal. It is also clear that the Fisher scoring approach using likelihood functions of the type specified earlier could be used. This has been done successfully with a model for single time series where the manifest variable covariance matrix is expressed as a direct product between an ARMA(p, q) covariance structure and a factor analysis covariance structure (Hwang & Browne, 1999). No software for dynamic factor analysis by maximum likelihood is readily available.

The alternative of applying readily available structural equation modeling software to lagged correlation matrices is often used. No statistical theory is available. Random sampling experiments (Hamaker, Dolan, & Molenaar, 2002; Molenaar & Nesselroade, 1998) indicated that this approach gives reasonable results in some situations, but not in others.

DISCUSSION AND CONCLUSIONS

The time series models and applications we presented, especially the *dynamic factor models*, can be put to the service of modeling behavioral/psychological processes. Especially valuable and apt for modeling process are three features that have been identified in earlier discussion. First, when dealing with processes, especially complex, psychological ones, multiple variables are almost certainly going to provide a more appropriate measurement basis for capturing their integral features. Multivariate versions of the time series models presented here afford this opportunity. Second, processes, by definition, represent events organized with respect to time. To model them requires longitudinal, repeated measurement data, and time series models are inherently directed at these kinds of data. Third, a focus on process, to be successful, must move beyond behavioral science's historically substantial reliance on stasis/equilibrium models to applications that include model parameters that change with some measure of time (e.g., lags). The time series models we presented contain this property, as has been amply demonstrated.

Clearly, the acquisition of behavioral and psychological data that are suited to time series models places demands on researchers that will tend to discourage their wide use. Much can be done, however, to foster process-oriented, time series-based modeling efforts. Promising avenues include further innovation and improvement of measurement methods such as the use of beepers and Palm Pilots or other personal digital assistants and web-based assessment schemes. The research design lore needs to be augmented with more systematic examinations of the matter of design "tradeoffs," including "juggling" the number of cases and the number of occasions of measurement to maximize the generalizability of findings regarding process. Nesselroade and Molenaar (1999), for example, offered an approach to making data-informed decisions regarding pooling lagged covariance information across subsets of individuals. Such designs, where feasible, permit measuring more people fewer times, which will help with participant recruitment and retention.

Obviously, much additional work is needed, but we have tried to make clear that significant improvements in the systematic modeling of behavioral/psychological process are available and feasible and becoming more widely distributed. The existing modeling possibilities afford a rich variety of representations for rendering operational one's substantive beliefs and considerations regarding process and change. Collecting the appropriate data to capture the nature of process may be demanding, but the prize is bound to be worth the effort.

ACKNOWLEDGMENTS

This chapter reflects the interaction of the ideas of the two authors over several years, with equal contributions to the chapter by each. The order of authership is arbitrary.

We gratefully acknowledge the valuable comments of Kurt Kreppner on an earlier version of this chapter.

Work on this chapter by JRN was supported by grant R01 AG183330-02 from the National Institute on Aging and the Max Planck Institute for Human Development, Berlin, Germany. Work by MWB was supported in part by the Institute for Development and Research Methodology at the University of Virginia.

REFERENCES

Anderson, T. W. (1963). The use of factor analysis in the statistical analysis of multiple time series. *Psychometrika, 28*, 1–24.

Baltes, P. B. (1973). Prototypical paradigms and questions in life-span research on development and aging. *Gerontologist, 1973*, 485–467.

Baltes, P. B., & Nesselroade, J. R. (1973). The developmental analysis of individual differences on multiple measures. In J. R. Nesselroade & H. W. Reese (Eds.), *Life-span developmental psychology: Methodological issues* (pp. 219–249). New York: Academic.

Bandura, A. (1982). The psychology of chance encounters and life paths. *American Psychologist, 37*, 747–755.

Bcm, D. J., & Allen, A. (1974). On predicting some of the people some of the time: The search for cross-situational consistencies in behavior. *Psychological Review, 81*, 506–520.

Boker, S. M., & Graham, J. (1998). A dynamical systems analysis of adolescence substance abuse. *Multivariate Behavioral Research, 33*, 479–507.

Boker, S. M., & Nesselroade, J. R. (2002). A method for modeling the intrinsic dynamics of intraindividual variability: Recovering the parameters of simulated oscillators in multi-wave data. *Multivariate Behavioral Research, 37*, 127–160.

Box, G. E. P., & Jenkins, G. M. (1976). *Time series analysis: Forecasting and control* (rev. ed.). San Francisco: Holden Day.

Brillinger, D. R. (1975). *Time series: Data analysis and theory* (2nd ed.). New York: Holt, Rinehart, & Winston.

Brim, O. G., Jr., & Kagan, J. (Eds.). (1980). *Constancy and change in human development.* Cambridge, MA: Harvard University Press.

Browne, M. W. (1993). Structured latent curve models. In C. Cuadras & C. Rao (Eds.), *Multivariate analysis: Future directions 2* (pp. 171–198). Amsterdam: North-Holland.

Browne, M. W., & Du Toit, S. (1991). Models for learning data. In L. Collins & J. Horn (Eds.), *Best methods for the analysis of change* (pp. 47–68). Washington, DC: American Psychological Association.

Cattell, R. B. (1994). 'Parallel proportional profiles' and other principles for determining the choice of factors by rotation. *Psychometrika, 9*, 267–283.

Cattell, R. B. (1963). The structuring of change by P-technique and incremental R-technique. In C. W. Harris (Ed.), *Problems in measuring change* (pp. 167–198). Madison: University of Wisconsin Press.

Cattell, R. B. (1966). Guest Editorial: Multivariate behavioral research and the integrative challenge. *Multivariate Behavioral Research, 1*, 4–23.

Cattell, R. B., Cattell, A. K. S., & Rhymer, R. M. (1947). P-technique demonstrated in determining psychophysical source traits in a normal individual. *Psychometrika, 12*, 267–288.

Du Toit, S. H. C. (1979). *The analysis of growth curves.* Unpublished doctoral dissertation, University of South Africa, Pretoria.

Du Toit, S., & Browne, M. W. (2001). The covariance structure of a vector time series. In R. Cudeck, & S. H. C. du Toit (Eds.), *Structural equation modeling: Present and future* (pp. 279–314). Lincolnwood, IL: Scientific Software International.

Eizenman, D. R., Nesselroade, J. R., Featherman, D. L., & Rowe, J. W. (1997). Intra-individual variability in perceived control in an elderly sample: The MacArthur Successful Aging Studies. *Psychology and Aging, 12*, 489–502.

Engle, R., & Watson, M. (1981). A one-factor multivariate time series model of metropolitan wage rates. *Journal of the American Statistical Association, 76*, 774–781.

Ferrer, E., & Nesselroade, J. R. (2003). Modeling affective processes in dyadic relations via dynamic factor analysis. *Emotion, 3*, 344–360.

Gergen, K. J. (1977). Stability, change, and chance in understanding human development. In N. Datan & H. W. Reese (Eds.), *Life-span developmental psychology* (pp. 135–158). New York: Academic.

Geweke, J. (1977). The dynamic factor analysis of economic time-series models. In D. Aigner & A. Goldberger (Eds.), *Latent variables in soci-economic models* (pp. 365–383). Amsterdam: North-Holland.

Geweke, J. F., & Singleton, K. J. (1981). Maximum likelihood "confirmatory" factor analysis of economic time series. *International Economic Review, 22,* 37–54.

Glass, G. V., Willson, V. L., & Gottman, J. M. (1972). *Design and analysis of time-series experiments* (Laboratory of Educational Research Report). Boulder: University of Colorado.

Gottman, J. M., McFall, R. M., & Barnett, J. T. (1969). Design and analysis of research using time series. *Psychological Bulletin, 72,* 299–306.

Hamaker, E. L., Dolan, C. V., & Molenaar, P. C. M. (2002). On the nature of SEM estimates of ARMA parameters. *Structural Equation Modeling, 9,* 347–368.

Hartup, W. W. (1996). The company they keep: Friendships and their developmental significance. *Child Development, 67,* 1–13.

Harvey, A. C. (1989). *Forecasting, structural time series models and the Kalman filter.* Cambridge: Cambridge University Press.

Harvey, A. C. (1993). *Time series models* (2nd ed.). Cambridge, MA: MIT Press.

Hertzog, C., & Nesselroade, J. R. (2003). Assessing psychological change in adulthood: An overview of methodological issues. *Psychology and Aging, 18,* 639–657.

Holling, C. S. (1973). Resilience and stability of ecological systems. *Annual Review of Ecology and Systematics, 4,* 1–23.

Holtzman, W. H. (1963). Statistical models for the study of change in the single case. In C. W. Harris (Ed.), *Problems in measuring change* (pp. 199–211). Madison: University of Wisconsin Press.

Hwang, P. M. T., & Browne, M. W. (1999). *Factor analysis of time series.* Unpublished manuscript, Ohio State University, Department of Statistics, Columbus.

Immink, W. (1986). *Parameter estimation in Markov models and dynamic factor analysis.* Unpublished doctoral dissertation, University of Utrecht, Utrecht.

Jones, C. J., & Nesselroade, J. R. (1990). Multivariate, replicated, single-subject designs and P-technique factor analysis: A selective review of the literature. *Experimental Aging Research, 16,* 171–183.

Jöreskog, K. G., & Goldberger, A. (1975). Estimation of a model with multiple indicators and multiple causes of a single latent variable. *Journal of the American Statistical Association, 70,* 631–639.

Jöreskog, K. G., & Sörbom, D. (1977). Statistical models and methods for analysis of longitudinal data. In D. Aigner & A. Goldberger (Eds.), *Latent variables in socioeconomic models* (pp. 285–325). New York: Wiley.

Kelso, J. A. S. (1995). *Dynamic patterns: The self-organization of brain and behavior.* Cambridge, MA: MIT Press.

Larsen, R. J. (1987). The stability of mood variability: A spectral analytic approach to daily mood assessments. *Journal of Personality and Social Psychology, 52,* 1195–1204.

Luborsky, L., & Mintz, J. (1972). The contribution of P-technique to personality, psychotherapy, and psychosomatic research. In R. M. Dreger (Ed.), *Multivariate personality research: Contributions to the understanding of personality in honor of Raymond B. Cattell* (pp. 387–410). Baton Rouge, LA: Claitor's.

Lütkepohl, H. (1993). *Introduction to multiple time series analysis* (2nd ed.). Berlin: Springer-Verlag.

McArdle, J. J. (1982). *Structural equation modeling of an individual system: Preliminary results from "A case study in episodic alcoholism."* Unpublished manuscript, Department of Psychology, University of Denver.

McCrae, R. R., & Costa, P. T. (1996). Toward a new generation of personality theories: Theoretical contexts for the five-factor model. In J. S. Wiggins (Ed.), *The five-factor model of personality: Theoretical perspectives* (pp. 51–87). New York: Guilford.

Molenaar, P. C. M. (1985). A dynamic factor model for the analysis of multivariate time series. *Psychometrika, 50*, 181–202.

Molenaar, P. C. M. (1994). Dynamic latent variable models in developmental psychology. In A. von Eye & C. C. Clogg (Eds.), *Latent variables analysis: Applications for developmental research* (pp. 155–180). Thousand Oaks, CA: Sage.

Molenaar, P. C. M., & Nesselroade, J. R. (1998). A comparison of pseudo-maximum likelihood and asymptotically distribution-free dynamic factor analysis parameter estimation in fitting covariance-structure models to block-Toeplitz matrices representing single-subject multivariate time series. *Multivariate Behavioral Research, 33*, 313–342.

Molenaar, P. C. M., & Nesselroade, J. R. (2001). Rotation in the dynamic factor modeling of multivariate stationary time series. *Psychometrika, 66*, 99–107.

Nesselroade, J. R., & Ford, D. H. (1987). Methodological considerations in modeling living systems. In M. E. Ford & D. H. Ford (Eds.), *Humans as self-constructing living systems: Putting the framework to work* (pp. 47–79). Hillsdale, NJ: Lawrence Erlbaum Associates, Inc.

Nesselroade, J. R., McArdle, J. J., Aggen, S. H., & Meyers, J. M. (2002). Alternative dynamic factor models for multivariate time-series analyses. In D. M. Moskowitz & S. L. Hershberger (Eds.), *Modeling intraindividual variability with repeated measures data: Advances and techniques* (pp. 235–265). Mahwah, NJ: Lawrence Erlbaum Associates, Inc.

Nesselroade, J. R., & Molenaar, P. C. M. (1999). Pooling lagged covariance structures based on short, multivariate time-series for dynamic factor analysis. In R. H. Hoyle (Ed.), *Statistical strategies for small sample research* (pp. 223–250). Newbury Park, CA: Sage.

Nesselroade, J. R., & Molenaar, P. C. M. (2003). Quantitative models for developmental processes. In J. Valsiner & K. Connolly (Eds.), *Handbook of developmental psychology* (pp. 622–639). London: Sage.

Pitt, M. A., Myung, I. J., & Zhang, S. (2002). Toward a method of selecting among computational models of cognition. *Psychological Review, 109*, 472–490.

Shoda, Y., Mischel, W., & Wright, J. C. (1993). The role of situational demands and cognitive competencies in behavior organization and personality coherence. *Journal of Personality and Social Psychology, 65*, 1023–1035.

Steyer, R., Ferring, D., & Schmitt, M. (1992). States and traits in psychological assessment. *European Journal of Psychological Assessment, 8*, 79–98.

Vallacher R. R., & Nowak A. (Eds.). (1994). *Dynamical systems in social psychology*. San Diego, CA: Academic.

Wei, W. W. S. (1990). *Time series analysis: Univariate and multivariate methods*. New York: Addison-Wesley.

West, S. G., & Hepworth, J. T. (1991). Statistical issues in the study of temporal data: Daily experiences. *Journal of Personality, 9*, 609–662.

Wood, P., & Brown, D. (1994). The study of intraindividual differences by means of dynamic factor models: Rationale, implementation, and interpretation. *Psychological Bulletin, 116*, 166–186.

Yule, G. U. (1927). On a method for investigating periodicities in disturbed series with special reference to Wölfer's sunspot numbers. *Philosophical Transactions of the Royal Society of London, Series A, 224*, 267–298.

Zevon, M., & Tellegen, A. (1982). The structure of mood change: Idiographic/nomothetic analysis. *Journal of Personality and Social Pyschology, 43*, 111–122.

14

Multilevel Factor Analysis Models for Continuous and Discrete Data

Harvey Goldstein
University of London

William Browne
University of Nottingham

MULTILEVEL MODELS

The technique of multilevel modeling is now well established and has been incorporated into most standard statistical packages. It is convenient for present purposes to consider educational data that exhibit a hierarchical structure of students nested within classrooms nested within schools—a three-level structure. Other examples are repeated-measures data with occasions nested within subjects, and surveys with people nested within households, both of these being two-level data structures. More-complex data structures such as cross-classifications and multiple-membership structures are extensions for which models have been developed. Goldstein (2003) provided a detailed exposition with references to further application areas.

A general model for the three-level schooling case, assuming normality, can be written as

$$y_{ijk} = (X\beta)_{ijk} + Z_{ijk}^{(3)}w_k + Z_{ijk}^{(2)}v_{jk} + e_{ijk},$$

$$w \sim \text{MVN}(0, \Omega_w), \qquad v \sim \text{MVN}(0, \Omega_v), \tag{1}$$

where the superscripts indicate the level; the more general n-level model can be written compactly as

$$Y = X\beta + Zu + e, \qquad u \sim \text{MVN}(0, \Omega_u), \qquad e \sim N\left(0, \sigma_e^2 I\right).$$

For a generalized linear model, say with a binary response, we correspondingly have

$$g(\pi) = X\beta + Zu, \qquad u \sim \text{MVN}(0, \Omega_u), \qquad Y \sim \text{Bernoulli}\,(1, \pi), \qquad (2)$$

where g is a suitable link function and $X\beta$ refers to the fixed-coefficient (regression) component of the model. We shall assume that the Level 1 residual matrix is diagonal, and this also will apply to our factor models.

First, we review briefly the traditional approach to estimating these models based on maximum likelihood.

MAXIMUM LIKELIHOOD ESTIMATION

For the normal model the standard (twice) the log likelihood is

$$2L(\Omega, \beta) = -\log|V| - \text{tr}(V^{-1}S) = -\log|V| - (Y - X\beta)^T V^{-1}(Y - X\beta),$$
$$S = (Y - X\beta)(Y - X\beta)^T, \qquad V = \text{cov}(Y|X\beta), \qquad (3)$$

where Ω is the set of random parameters comprising the variances and covariances in Equation 1. If we have an ML estimate of β, then

$$2L(\Omega, \hat{\beta}) = -\log|V| - \text{tr}(V^{-1}S) = -\log|V| - (Y - X\hat{\beta})^T V^{-1}(Y - X\hat{\beta}) \quad (4)$$

is the profile likelihood for the random parameters Ω. A convenient algorithm known as iterative generalized least squares (IGLS) alternates between maximizing Equation 4 and then obtaining the conditional ML (GLS) estimate of Ω until convergence.

We can write the extended likelihood, referred to in different contexts as a penalized likelihood or an h-likelihood (Lee & Nelder, 2001), that includes the actual random effects (residuals) as parameters:

$$2L(\Omega, \beta, u) = -\log|R| - (Y - X\beta - Zu)^T R^{-1}(Y - X\beta - Zu)$$
$$-\log|\Omega_u| - u^T \Omega_u^{-1} u, \qquad (5)$$
$$R = \sigma_e^2 I.$$

If we maximize Equation 5 for the random effects, given (β, Ω), we obtain the usual estimator, which can be written conveniently as

$$\hat{u} = \left(Z^T R^{-1} Z + \Omega_u^{-1}\right)^{-1} Z^T (Y - X\beta). \qquad (6)$$

Given Ω and u, the profile likelihood for the fixed effects is thus

$$2L(\hat{\Omega}, \hat{u}) = -\log|\hat{R}| - (Y - X\beta - Z\hat{u})^T \hat{R}^{-1}(Y - X\beta - Z\hat{u})$$
$$-\log|\hat{\Omega}_u| - \hat{u}^T \hat{\Omega}_u^{-1} \hat{u}. \tag{7}$$

Thus, a convenient modification of the IGLS procedure is to iterate between calculating the fixed effects using Equation 7, which, when R is diagonal, is just ordinary least squares (OLS), calculating the random effects from Equation 6 and then the random parameters using the same step as is used in the standard IGLS algorithm.

Expression 3 is known as the *marginal* log likelihood because it is obtained by integrating out the random effects regarded as nuisance parameters.

Because the random effects depend on the random but not the fixed parameters, more generally we can write

$$\log[L(\beta, \Omega, U)] = \sum \{\log[f(Y|U; \beta)] + \log[f(U; \Omega)]\}. \tag{8}$$

The marginal likelihood is thus given by

$$L(\beta, \Omega) = \int f(Y|U; \beta)f(U; \Omega)\, dU, \tag{9}$$

where the first term on the right-hand side is the distribution function for the responses conditional on the random effects, or residuals, U. The second term is the distribution function for the random effects. The first term, given U, depends only on the unknown parameters β, and the second depends only on the unknown parameters Ω. Thus, for example, for a two-level logistic binary response model where the random effects are assumed to be multivariate normal we have, because the random effects are independent across units,

$$L(\beta, \Omega) = \prod_j \int \prod_i \left[(\pi_{ij})^{s_{ij}}(1 - \pi_{ij})^{n_{ij}-s_{ij}}\right] \Phi(u_j; \Omega)\, du_j,$$
$$\pi_{ij} = [1 + \exp(-X_{ij}\beta_j)]^{-1}, \qquad \beta_j = \beta + u_j, \tag{10}$$

where Φ is the multivariate normal density function for the u_j, and n_{ij} and s_{ij} are the number of trials and number of successes, respectively. The integral in Equation 10 can be written in the form $\int_{-\infty}^{\infty} P(u_j)\Phi(u_j)\, du_j$.

Gauss–Hermite quadrature approximates such an integral as

$$\int_{-\infty}^{\infty} P(v)e^{-v^2}\, dv \approx \sum_{q=1}^{Q} P(x_q)w_q, \tag{11}$$

where the right-hand side is a Gauss–Hermite polynomial evaluated at a series of quadrature points indexed by q. Hedeker and Gibbons (1994) gave a detailed discussion and also considered the multicategory (multinomial) response case. This function is then maximized using a suitable search procedure over the parameter space. Rabe-Hesketh, Pickles, and Taylor (2002) used quadrature to fit general multilevel structural equation models with a variety of link functions. An alternative to quadrature is to use simulated maximum likelihood, which is attractive for models with large numbers of random parameters (Goldstein, 2003, Appendix 4.2).

We now look at multilevel factor models. We briefly refer to the maximum likelihood analysis of multilevel factor analysis models and then develop an alternative approach using Markov chain Monte Carlo (MCMC) estimation.

A MULTILEVEL FACTOR MODEL

We begin by considering a simple single-level factor model for continuous responses, which we write as

$$y_{ri} = \lambda_r v_i + e_{ri}, \qquad r = 1, \ldots, R, \qquad i = 1, \ldots, N,$$
$$v_i \sim N(0, 1), \qquad e_{ri} \sim N\left(0, \sigma_{er}^2\right), \tag{12}$$

where r indexes the responses and i indexes individuals. This can in fact be viewed as a two-level model with a single Level 2 random effect (v_i) with variance constrained to 1 and R Level 1 units for each Level 2 unit, each with its own (unique) variance.

If we knew the values of the "loadings" λ_r, then we could fit Equation 12 directly as a two-level model with the loading vector as the explanatory variable for the Level 2 variance, which is constrained to be equal to 1; if there are any measured covariates in the model, their coefficients can be estimated at the same time. Conversely, if we knew the values of the random effects v_i, we could estimate the loadings; this would now be a single-level model with each response variate having its own variance. These considerations suggest that an expectation-maximization algorithm can be used in the estimation where the random effects are regarded as missing data (Rubin & Thayer, 1982). They also motivate the use of MCMC estimation, which we discuss later.

We now add a second level with its own factor structure and write

$$Y = \Lambda_2 v_2 + u + \Lambda_1 v_1 + e,$$
$$Y = \{y_{rij}\}, \qquad u = \{u_r\}, \qquad e = \{e_r\}, \tag{13}$$
$$r = 1, \ldots, p, \qquad i = 1, \ldots, n_j, \qquad j = 1, \ldots, J,$$
$$v_2 \sim N(0, 1), \qquad v_1 \sim N(0, 1), \qquad e_r \sim N\left(0, \sigma_{er}^2\right), \qquad u_r \sim N\left(0, \sigma_{ur}^2\right),$$

where the "uniquenesses" u (Level 2) and e (Level 1) are mutually independent and there are p response measures. Here Λ_1 and Λ_2 are the loading matrices for the Level 1 and Level 2 factors, respectively, and v_1 and v_2 are the independent factor vectors at Level 1 and Level 2, respectively. Note that we can have different numbers of factors at each level. We adopt the convention of regarding the measurements themselves as constituting the lowest level of the hierarchy, so that Equation 13 is regarded as a three-level model. Extensions to more levels are straightforward.

We can write the normal log likelihood for Equation 12 as

$$2L(\Omega, \beta, v) = -\log|R| - (Y - \Lambda v)^T R^{-1}(Y - \Lambda v)$$
$$-\log|\Omega_v| - v^T \Omega_v^{-1} v, \tag{14}$$
$$\Lambda = (\Lambda_1 \, \Lambda_2), \qquad v^T = (v_1 \, v_2), \qquad R = \text{diag}\left(\sigma_{e1}^2, \ldots, \sigma_{ep}^2\right),$$

with corresponding expressions for other link functions. A general approach to estimation is to form the marginal likelihood as described earlier. McDonald and Goldstein (1989) provided an explicit computational algorithm for the normal response model of Equation 13. Longford and Muthen (1992) developed this approach. The latter authors, together with Goldstein (2003, Chapter 7) and Rowe and Hill (1997) and Rowe (2003), also pointed out that consistent estimators can be obtained from a two-stage process as follows. A two-level multivariate response linear model is fitted using an efficient procedure such as maximum likelihood. This can be accomplished, for example, as pointed out earlier by defining a three-level model where the lowest level is that of the response variables (Goldstein, 2003, Chapter 6; also see the model in Equation 15). This analysis will produce estimates for the (residual) covariance matrices at each level, and each of these can then be structured according to an underlying latent variable model in the usual way. By considering the two matrices as two "populations," we can also impose constraints on, say, the loadings using an algorithm for simultaneously fitting structural equations across several populations.

This chapter describes a general approach to the estimation of such multilevel factor analysis models using MCMC. In the standard multilevel model described in Equation 1, MCMC treats the random effects at higher levels as parameters alongside the fixed coefficients, variances, and covariances. The algorithm proceeds in steps where at each step a parameter or set of parameters is updated by sampling from the distribution for those parameters conditional on the current values for all the other parameters, the data, and the prior distributions. For each parameter this results in a chain of correlated values, which, after the chain has become stationary, can be used for inference. Thus, the mean and the standard deviation provide estimates corresponding to the traditional maximum likelihood estimate and its standard error. An advantage of MCMC is that, given a long enough chain, we can obtain exact interval estimates based on quantiles rather than relying on large-sample approximations.

We now describe the details of an MCMC algorithm for the factor analysis model.

MARKOV CHAIN MONTE CARLO ESTIMATION FOR THE FACTOR ANALYSIS MODEL

We first develop our MCMC algorithm for the multivariate normal model. This is followed by an extension to the binary and mixed response cases, where we also give a detailed example. Further discussion of the multivariate normal model can be found in Goldstein and Browne (2002).

To show the steps of the MCMC algorithm we write Equation 13 in the more detailed form

$$y_{rij} = \beta_r + \sum_{f=1}^{F} \lambda_{fr}^{(2)} v_{fj}^{(2)} + \sum_{g=1}^{G} \lambda_{gr}^{(1)} v_{gij}^{(1)} + u_{rj} + e_{rij}, \qquad u_{rj} \sim N\left(0, \sigma_{ur}^2\right),$$

$$e_{rij} \sim N\left(0, \sigma_{er}^2\right), \qquad v_{fj}^{(2)} \sim \text{MVN}_F(0, \Omega_2), \qquad v_{gij}^{(1)} \sim \text{MVN}_G(0, \Omega_1), \quad (15)$$

$$r = 1, \ldots, R, \qquad i = 1, \ldots, n_j, \qquad j = 1, \ldots, J, \qquad \sum_{j=1}^{J} n_j = N.$$

Again we have R responses for N individuals split between J Level 2 units. We have F sets of factors $v_{fj}^{(2)}$ defined at Level 2, and G sets of factors $v_{gij}^{(1)}$ defined at Level 1. We also introduce the fixed part of the model, but for simplicity restrict our algorithm to a single intercept term β_r for each response, although it is easy to extend the algorithm to arbitrary fixed terms. The residuals at Levels 1 and 2, e_{rij} and u_{rj}, respectively, are assumed to be independent.

Although this allows a very flexible set of factor models, it should be noted that for such models to be identifiable, suitable constraints must be put on the parameters. See Everitt (1984) for further discussion of identifiability. These consist in fixing the values of some of the elements of the factor variance matrices Ω_1 and Ω_2 and/or some of the factor loadings $\lambda_{fr}^{(2)}$ and $\lambda_{gr}^{(1)}$.

The algorithms presented will give steps for all parameters, and so any parameter that is constrained will simply maintain its chosen value and will not be updated. We initially assume that the factor variance matrices Ω_1 and Ω_2 are known (completely constrained) and then discuss how the algorithm can be extended to encompass partially constrained variance matrices. The parameters in the following steps are those available at the current iteration of the algorithm.

Prior Distributions

For the algorithm we assume the following general priors:

$$p(\beta_r) \sim N\left(\beta_r^*, \sigma_{br}^2\right),$$

$$p\left(\lambda_{fr}^{(2)}\right) \sim N\left(\lambda_{fr}^{(2)*}, \sigma_{2fr}^2\right), \qquad p\left(\lambda_{gr}^{(1)}\right) \sim N\left(\lambda_{gr}^{(1)*}, \sigma_{1gr}^2\right),$$

$$p\left(\sigma_{ur}^2\right) \sim \Gamma^{-1}\left(a_{ur}^*, b_{ur}^*\right), \qquad p\left(\sigma_{er}^2\right) \sim \Gamma^{-1}\left(a_{er}^*, b_{er}^*\right).$$

Known Factor Variance Matrices

We assume that the factor variance matrices are known, so that we can use a Gibbs sampling algorithm, which involves updating parameters in turn by generating new values from the following eight sets of conditional posterior distributions.

Step 1. Update current value of β_r ($r = 1, \ldots, R$) from the following distribution:

$$p(\beta_r) \sim N\left(D_{br}\left(\frac{\sum_{ij} d_{rij}^\beta}{\sigma_{er}^2} + \frac{\beta_r^*}{\sigma_{br}^2}\right), D_{br}\right),$$

where

$$D_{br} = \left(\frac{N}{\sigma_{er}^2} + \frac{1}{\sigma_{br}^2}\right)^{-1} \qquad \text{and} \qquad d_{rij}^\beta = e_{rij} + \beta_r.$$

Step 2. Update $\lambda_{fr}^{(2)}$ ($r = 1, \ldots, R; f = 1, \ldots, F$, where not constrained) from the following distribution:

$$p\left(\lambda_{fr}^{(2)}\right) \sim N\left(D_{fr}^{(2)}\left(\frac{\sum_{ij} v_{fj}^{(2)} d_{rijf}^{(2)}}{\sigma_{er}^2} + \frac{\lambda_{fr}^{(2)*}}{\sigma_{2fr}^2}\right), D_{fr}^{(2)}\right),$$

where

$$D_{fr}^{(2)} = \left(\frac{\sum_j n_j \left(v_{fj}^{(2)}\right)^2}{\sigma_{er}^2} + \frac{1}{\sigma_{2fr}^2}\right)^{-1} \qquad \text{and} \qquad d_{rijf}^{(2)} = e_{rij} + \lambda_{fr}^{(2)} v_{fj}^{(2)}.$$

Step 3. Update $\lambda_{gr}^{(1)}$ ($r = 1, \ldots, R; g = 1, \ldots, G$, where not constrained) from the following distribution:

$$p\left(\lambda_{gr}^{(1)}\right) \sim N\left(D_{gr}^{(1)}\left(\frac{\sum_{ij} v_{gij}^{(1)} d_{rijg}^{(1)}}{\sigma_{er}^2} + \frac{\lambda_{gr}^{(1)*}}{\sigma_{1gr}^2}\right), D_{gr}^{(1)}\right),$$

where

$$D_{gr}^{(1)} = \left(\frac{\sum_{ij} \left(v_{gij}^{(1)} \right)^2}{\sigma_{er}^2} + \frac{1}{\sigma_{1gr}^2} \right)^{-1} \quad \text{and} \quad d_{rijg}^{(1)} = e_{rij} + \lambda_{gr}^{(1)} v_{gij}^{(1)}.$$

Step 4. Update $v_j^{(2)}$ ($j = 1, \ldots, J$) from the following distribution:

$$p\left(v_j^{(2)}\right) \sim \text{MVN}_F \left(D_j^{(2)} \left(\sum_r \sum_{i=1}^{n_j} \frac{\lambda_r^{(2)} d_{rij}^{(2)}}{\sigma_{er}^2} \right), D_j^{(2)} \right),$$

where

$$D_j^{(2)} = \left(\sum_r \frac{n_j \lambda_r^{(2)} \left(\lambda_r^{(2)} \right)^T}{\sigma_{er}^2} + \Omega_2^{-1} \right)^{-1}$$

and

$$d_{rij}^{(2)} = e_{rij} + \sum_{f=1}^F \lambda_{fr}^{(2)} v_{fj}^{(2)}, \quad \lambda_r^{(2)} = \left(\lambda_{1r}^{(2)}, \ldots, \lambda_{Fr}^{(2)} \right)^T, \quad v_j^{(2)} = \left(v_{1j}^{(2)}, \ldots, v_{Fj}^{(2)} \right)^T.$$

Step 5. Update $v_{ij}^{(1)}$ ($i = 1, \ldots, n_j; j = 1, \ldots, J$) from the following distribution:

$$p\left(v_{ij}^{(1)}\right) \sim \text{MVN}_G \left(D_{ij}^{(1)} \left(\sum_r \frac{\lambda_r^{(1)} d_{rij}^{(1)}}{\sigma_{er}^2} \right), D_{ij}^{(1)} \right),$$

where

$$D_{ij}^{(1)} = \left(\sum_r \frac{\lambda_r^{(1)} \left(\lambda_r^{(1)} \right)^T}{\sigma_{er}^2} + \Omega_1^{-1} \right)^{-1}$$

and

$$d_{rij}^{(1)} = e_{rij} + \sum_{g=1}^G \lambda_{gr}^{(1)} v_{gj}^{(1)}, \quad \lambda_r^{(1)} = \left(\lambda_{1r}^{(1)}, \ldots, \lambda_{Gr}^{(1)} \right)^T, \quad v_{ij}^{(1)} = \left(v_{1ij}^{(1)}, \ldots, v_{Gij}^{(1)} \right)^T.$$

Step 6. Update u_{rj} ($r = 1, \ldots, R; j = 1, \ldots, J$) from the following distribution:

$$p(u_{rj}) \sim N \left(\frac{D_{rj}^{(u)}}{\sigma_{er}^2} \sum_{i=1}^{n_j} d_{rij}^{(u)}, D_{rj}^{(u)} \right),$$

where

$$D_{rj}^{(u)} = \left(\frac{n_j}{\sigma_{er}^2} + \frac{1}{\sigma_{ur}^2} \right)^{-1} \quad \text{and} \quad d_{rij}^{(u)} = e_{rij} + u_{rj}.$$

Step 7. Update σ_{ur}^2 from the following distribution:

$$p\left(\sigma_{ur}^2\right) \sim \Gamma^{-1}(\hat{a}_{ur}, \hat{b}_{ur}),$$

where

$$\hat{a}_{ur} = J/2 + a_{ur}^* \quad \text{and} \quad \hat{b}_{ur} = \frac{1}{2} \sum_j u_{rj}^2 + b_{ur}^*.$$

Step 8. Update σ_{er}^2 from the following distribution:

$$p\left(\sigma_{er}^2\right) \sim \Gamma^{-1}(\hat{a}_{er}, \hat{b}_{er}),$$

where

$$\hat{a}_{er} = N/2 + a_{er}^* \quad \text{and} \quad \hat{b}_{er} = \frac{1}{2} \sum_{ij} e_{rij}^2 + b_{er}^*.$$

Note that the Level 1 residuals e_{rij} can be calculated by subtraction at every step of the algorithm.

Unconstrained Factor Covariances

In the general algorithm we have assumed that the factor variances are all constrained. Typically we will fix the variances to equal 1 and the covariances to equal 0 and have independent factors. This form will allow us to simplify Steps 4 and 5 of the algorithm to univariate normal updates for each factor separately. However, we may wish to consider correlations between the factors. Here we modify our algorithm to allow another special case, where the variances are constrained to be 1 but the covariances can be freely estimated. Where the resulting correlations obtained are estimated to be close to 1 or −1, then we may be fitting too many factors at that particular level. As the variances are constrained to equal 1, the covariances between factors equal the correlations between the factors. This means that each covariance is constrained to lie between −1 and 1. We consider here only the factor variance matrix at Level 2 because the step for the Level 1 variance matrix simply involves changing subscripts. We use the following priors:

$$p(\Omega_{2,lm}) \sim \text{Uniform}(-1, 1) \quad \forall l \neq m.$$

Here $\Omega_{2,lm}$ is the lmth element of the Level 2 factor variance matrix. We update these covariance parameters using a Metropolis step and a normal random walk proposal [see Browne (2003) for more details on using Metropolis–Hastings methods for constrained variance matrices].

Step 9.   At iteration t generate $\Omega_{2,lm}^* \sim N(\Omega_{2,lm}^{(t-1)}, \sigma_{plm}^2)$, where σ_{plm}^2 is a proposed distribution variance that has to be set for each covariance. Then, if $\Omega_{2,lm}^* > 1$ or $\Omega_{2,lm}^* < -1$, set $\Omega_{2,lm}^{(t)} = \Omega_{2,lm}^{(t-1)}$ as the proposed covariance is not valid, else form a proposed new matrix Ω_2^* by replacing the lmth element of $\Omega_2^{(t-1)}$ by this proposed value. We then set

$$\Omega_{2,lm}^{(t)} = \Omega_{2,lm}^* \quad \text{with probability} \quad \min\left(1, p(\Omega_2^*|v_j^{(2)})/p(\Omega_2^{(t-1)}|v_j^{(2)})\right)$$

$$\Omega_{2,lm}^{(t)} = \Omega_{2,lm}^{(t-1)} \quad \text{otherwise.}$$

Here

$$p(\Omega_2^*|v_j^{(2)}) = \prod_j |\Omega_2^*|^{-1/2} \exp\left[\left((v_j^{(2)})^T (\Omega_2^*)^{-1} v_j^{(2)}\right)/2\right]$$

$$p(\Omega_2^{(t-1)}|v_j^{(2)}) = \prod_j |\Omega_2^{(t-1)}|^{-1/2} \exp\left[\left((v_j^{(2)})^T (\Omega_2^{(t-1)})^{-1} v_j^{(2)}\right)/2\right].$$

This procedure is repeated for each covariance that is not constrained.

Missing Data

Where some of the responses are missing, this poses no problem for the MCMC methods if we are prepared to assume missingness is at random or effectively so by design. This is equivalent to giving the missing data a uniform prior. We then have to simply add an extra Gibbs sampling step to the algorithm to sample the missing values at each iteration. As an illustration, we consider an individual who is missing response r. In a factor model the correlation between responses is explained by the factor terms, and conditional on these terms the responses for an individual are independent, and so the conditional distributions of the missing responses have simple forms.

Step 10.   Update y_{rij} $(r = 1, \ldots, R; i = 1, \ldots, n_j; j = 1, \ldots, J; \forall y_{rij}$ that are missing) from the following distribution, given the current values $y_{rij} \sim N(\hat{y}_{rij}, \sigma_{er}^2)$ where

$$\hat{y}_{rij} = \beta_r + \sum_{f=1}^{F} \lambda_{fr}^{(2)} v_{fj}^{(2)} + \sum_{g=1}^{G} \lambda_{gr}^{(1)} v_{gij}^{(1)} + u_{rj}.$$

Goldstein and Browne (2002) discussed the extension of this model to the general structural equation case.

BINARY RESPONSE FACTOR MODELS

Modeling of data that consist of binary or ordered responses to questions in an achievement or similar test instrument has a long history. Goldstein and Wood (1989) described the history of mental testing from the early work of Lawley (1943) and the work of Lord and Novick (1968) on item response models to more recent developments of general factor analysis modeling (Bock, Gibbons, & Muraki, 1988). Rod McDonald made important contributions to this area through his discussions of test item dimensionality and models for nonlinear factor analysis (McDonald, 1981, 1985).

The early work was characterized by "fixed-effect" models of the kind

$$f(\pi_{ri}) = \beta_{0r} + \beta_{1r}\theta_i \qquad (16)$$

relating the probability of a correct response to the rth item for the ith respondent, where typically a logit link function is used for the probability. The most common link function f is a logit or probit. The response y is typically $(0, 1)$, and we have the local, or conditional, independence assumption

$$y_{ij} \stackrel{\text{iid}}{\sim} Bin(1, p_{ij}).$$

This is often referred to, somewhat inaccurately, as a two-parameter model, where in Equation 16 each response is characterized by an intercept β_{0r} and a factor coefficient β_{1r}, and each respondent has a factor value θ_i. This gives rise to a model with $N + 2p$ parameters, where N is the number of respondents and p is the number of items or questions. Extensions to the case where responses are on an ordered scale (a graded response or partial credit model; Baker, 1992) relate the cumulative proportion of success to a linear function via a suitable link function, for example, the cumulative odds model for category h of item r:

$$f\left(\sum_{g=1}^{h} \pi_{gri} \Big/ \sum_{g=h+1}^{t_r} \pi_{gri}\right) = \beta_{0rh} + \beta_{1r}\theta_i, \qquad h = 1, \ldots, t_{r-1}, \qquad (17)$$

where t_r indexes the final category of item r.

Such fixed-effect models have more recently been superseded by "random effects" models (Bartholomew & Knott, 1999), where the individual parameter θ_i is assumed to have a distribution, typically normal, across individuals. This provides both more efficient estimates and straightforward ways of handling missing responses. More important, it allows for the fitting of more than one parameter for individuals, so that we can write down a general multidimensional binary (or ordered) extension of Equation 16,

$$f(\pi_{ri}) = \beta_{0r} + \sum_{h=1}^{q}\beta_{hr}\theta_{hi}, \qquad \theta_i \sim MVN(0, \Omega),$$

$$y_{ri} \overset{iid}{\sim} Bin(1, \pi_{ri}), \tag{18}$$

which is simply a single-level binary response factor model.

Having fitted such a model, we can obtain estimates of factor values, or scores, for each individual on each factor. In practice, models with more than one factor dimension have been used rarely, or typically are covariates incorporated, for example, for gender or other predictors. We explore some of the consequences of this in the analysis of a large-scale data set.

We now introduce a multilevel model, as with the normal response case, that recognizes that groups such as schools may differ in their response probabilities. We write

$$f(\pi_{rij}) = \beta_{0r} + \sum_{h=1}^{q_1}\beta_{hr}^{(1)}\theta_{hij}^{(1)} + \sum_{h=1}^{q_2}\beta_{hr}^{(2)}\theta_{hj}^{(2)} + u_{rj},$$

$$\theta_{ij}^{(1)} \sim MVN(0, \Omega_1), \qquad \theta_j^{(2)} \sim MVN(0, \Omega_2), \tag{19}$$

$$y_{rjk} \overset{iid}{\sim} Bin(1, \pi_{rjk}).$$

We have now added a second set of factors, indexed by the superscript (2), varying at the group Level 2, independent of the individual level factors, indexed by the superscript (1). In contrast to the normal response factor model, the Level 1 variance is constrained by the assumption of binomial variation, and the factor structure has a nonlinear link with the responses. We retain the notational conventions for binary response models, generalized from Equation 17, where we have the following equivalences for the factor structure between Equations 18 and 15:

$$\beta_{hr}^{(1)} \equiv \lambda_{gr}^{(1)}, \qquad \beta_{hr}^{(2)} \equiv \lambda_{fr}^{(2)},$$

$$\theta_{hij}^{(1)} \equiv v_{gij}^{(1)}, \qquad \theta_{hj}^{(2)} \equiv v_{fj}^{(2)}.$$

The Level 2 residuals u_{rj} are assumed independent, $N(0, \sigma_{ur}^2)$.

We show how to specify and fit such a model and use it with a large-scale survey of student achievement.

DATA

The data are taken from the Programme for International Student Assessment (PISA) carried out under the auspices of the Organisation for Economic Co-operation and Development (OECD) in 2000 in 32 industrialized countries

(Organisation for Economic Co-operation and Development, 1999). The data sets, together with full descriptions, are available online (www.pisa.oecd.org). The full data set included a student and school questionnaire together with tests of reading, mathematics, and science. A sample of 14- to 15-year-old school students was selected in each country with a 70% response rate as a minimum requirement for inclusion. The OECD program plans further surveys every 3 years. The major aim of the survey was to develop a "literacy scale" for each of the three areas tested and to compare countries in terms of their average performance on these. The resulting continuous scales had distributions approximately normal with a mean of 500 and a standard deviation 100. Each scale was divided into six "proficiency" categories, each characterized in terms of responses to chosen sample test items. The scores were also analyzed by background factors such as gender and parental education, and a multilevel analysis was also carried out to study variation between schools.

The three OECD literacy scales were constructed using the model of Equation 18 with a single factor. Each scale used only those items designated as Reading, Mathematics, or Science. Factor scores were computed for use in subsequent analyses. For these analyses a multiple imputation procedure was used as follows.

Each student has a factor score based on a linear predictor using his or her individual responses and the estimated model parameters. Under the model assumptions, these scores have an approximate normal distribution, the accuracy of the approximation being a function of the number of item responses for an individual. Using an estimate of the standard error, multiple imputation is used; that is, a set of (typically five) random draws from this estimated normal distribution is made and these are then used for subsequent modeling (Rubin, 1996).

We refer to some of the limitations of this as a general procedure later, but for now note that a key feature is the use of a one-dimensional factor model, and we will discuss the incorporation of further dimensions.

For present purposes we chose the Mathematics test items for two countries, France and England. In total there are 31 Math questions. In fact several questions are grouped in that they all relate to the same problem. For example, one problem described a pattern of trees planted as a set of squares of different sizes, and associated with this problem there were three separate questions. For a model such as that of Equation 18 it is doubtful whether for such questions the local independence assumption will hold, although this was assumed in the OECD analysis. A more satisfactory treatment would be to combine the three separate questions into an ordered scale, for example, by forming an a priori suitably weighted combination of the responses, and treating this as an ordered categorical response as described earlier. For present purposes we selected 15 items, each of which is a response to a different problem, and dichotomized responses into correct/incorrect, treating part-correct answers as correct.

ESTIMATION FOR THE BINARY RESPONSE FACTOR MODEL

The OECD analyses use the logit link function. The probit function generally produces similar results and has certain advantages in terms of computational convenience. One important advantage of the probit is that we can think of the response as a threshold from an underlying (unknown) continuous response, which is normally distributed (Albert & Chib, 1993). We use the Gibbs sampling algorithm for normally distributed responses described earlier and adapted for a probit model as follows.

Assume that we have a binary variable y_i collected for several individuals i, that is, a threshold version of an (unknown) continuous normally distributed variable y_i^*. Now, if we knew the value of y_i^*, then we could fit the standard Gibbs sampling algorithm for normal response models. So we add an extra step to the Gibbs sampling algorithm and generate y_i^* at each iteration from its conditional posterior distribution, which is a truncated normal distribution with mean (in the standard single-level probit model) $X\beta$ and variance one. The truncation point is zero, and if y_i is zero, y_i^* has to be negative, and if y_i is one, y_i^* has to be positive. This step is inserted into the existing algorithm for the normal response factor model. It should be noted that this model can also be updated using Metropolis sampling, but the Gibbs sampling algorithm is faster and produces fewer correlated chains. Consider the standard two-level model

$$Y = X\beta + ZU + e, \qquad e \sim N(0, 1). \tag{20}$$

Given current estimates of parameters and residuals, we have $Y \sim N(XB + ZU, 1)$, and for the probit model the observation of a positive value (>0) on the scale of Y corresponds to the observation of a "success" on the probability scale and the observation of a negative (<0) value corresponds to a "failure." The probit function that determines the underlying chance of a correct response is the cumulative probability given by

$$\int_0^\infty \phi(t)\,dt, \qquad \phi(t) \text{ is pdf of } N(X\beta + ZU, 1),$$

or equivalently

$$\int_{-(X\beta+ZU)}^\infty \phi(t)\,dt, \qquad \phi(t) \text{ is pdf of } N(0, 1). \tag{21}$$

Alternatively, if we write the value of the ijth response as

$$y_{ij} = (X\beta)_{ij} + (ZU)_{ij} + e_{ij},$$

a positive value occurs when $y_{ij} > 0$. We then have

$$\Pr(y_{ij} > 0) = \Pr(e_{ij} > -[(X\beta)_{ij} + (ZU)_{ij}]), \tag{22}$$

which leads to Equation 21.

Thus, given current values of β, U, and the observation for a Level 1 unit (0 or 1), we take a random draw e^*. If we observe a 1, then we draw from the truncated normal distribution $[-X^*, \infty]$, $X^* = (X\beta + ZU)$, and if we observe a 0, we sample from $[-\infty, -X^*]$. This is then applied to Equation 20 to give a new value Y^*. This procedure is applied as an extra step in the factor analysis model, for example, before Step 1, with the remaining steps as before.

This approach is readily extended to the case of ordered categories, which can be applied to "partial-credit" models. We assume that there is an underlying normally distributed response and that for p-category observed responses there are $p - 1$ thresholds. Assume a proportional odds model, where for the sth cumulative probability we have (Goldstein, 2003)

$$\text{probit}\,(\gamma^{(s)}) = \alpha^{(s)} + (X\beta) + ZU,$$

so that corresponding to Equation 21 this gives

$$\int_{-(\alpha^{(s)} + X\beta + ZU)}^{\infty} \phi(t)\, dt,$$

and sampling is conditional, as before, including the current values of the threshold parameters $\alpha^{(s)}$.

RESULTS

The analyses reported here were carried out using MLwiN Beta version 1.2 (Browne, 2004; Rasbash et al., 2000). Table 14.1 shows a basic model in which a simple single-level probit model is fitted for each item allowing for different country means. We see that, of the 10 statistically significant items, France does better on 4 (all free-response items) and worse on 6 (3 free-response and 3 multiple-choice items) than England. The interpretation of the probit function is that it predicts a value from an underlying standard normal distribution with mean zero and standard deviation one. This can be turned into a probability using the Cumulative distribution function of the standard normal distribution. Thus, for example, the French students are, on average, 0.7 standard deviations ahead of the English for item 136Q01 (a free-response Geometry item) but 0.7 standard deviations behind on item 161Q01 (a multiple-choice Geometry item).

We now fit a single factor at each level (the student and the school), with results under Analysis A in Table 14.2. For convenience we present only the estimated factor loadings. At both levels we have a common factor with comparable loadings

TABLE 14.1
Separate Country Analyses With Probit Response Model for Each Item

Item	England	France–England
Student level		
33q01 (MC)	0.80	−0.06 (0.05)
34q01 (FR)	−0.25	0.03 (0.06)
37q01 (FR)	0.65	−0.11 (0.07)
124q01 (FR)	0.01	−0.18 (0.07)
136q01 (FR)	−0.23	0.69 (0.05)
144q01 (FR)	0.16	0.40 (0.05)
145q01 (FR)	0.65	−0.13 (0.06)
150q01 (FR)	0.78	−0.35 (0.06)
155q01 (FR)	0.54	0.27 (0.06)
159q01 (MC)	0.89	−0.24 (0.06)
161q01 (MC)	0.96	−0.70 (0.06)
179q01 (FR)	−0.11	0.64 (0.06)
192q01 (MC)	−0.28	0.07 (0.06)
266q01 (MC)	−0.75	−0.26 (0.06)
273q01 (MC)	−0.04	0.03 (0.06)

Note. Columns show the English mean and the French–English difference between means. Standard errors are shown in parentheses. There are
10,000 Markov chain Monte Carlo iterations with default priors. The type of
item is shown by each item name. MC, Multiple choice; FR, free response.

on each item, although at the student level the multiple-choice items tend to have
smaller loadings. The next model fits a different mean for each item for France
and England, namely

$$\text{probit}(\pi_{rijg}) = \beta_{0r} + \delta_g d_r + \beta_{1r}^{(1)}\theta_{1ij}^{(1)} + \beta_{1r}^{(2)}\theta_{1j}^{(2)} + u_{rj},$$

$$\theta_{1ij}^{(1)} \sim N\left(0, \sigma_{(1)}^2\right), \qquad \theta_{1j}^{(2)} \sim N\left(0, \sigma_{(2)}^2\right),$$

$$y_{rijg} \sim Bin(1, \pi_{rijg}), \qquad g = 1, 2 \tag{23}$$

$$\delta_g = \begin{cases} 0 & \text{if } g = 1, \\ 1 & \text{if } g = 2. \end{cases}$$

Note that in Equation 23, g identifies country and takes the value 1 for England
and 2 for France, and we actually fit a global mean vector plus a difference term,
d_r, which captures the difference between French and English scores. The factor
loadings are virtually unchanged. The means for the two countries, however, do
differ somewhat for certain items. Thus, given the factor values, the French are
somewhat further ahead than before on item 136Q01. This suggests that there may
be different factor structures in the two countries, and we return to this later.

   If we ignore the interaction between country and item, it is possible (but not
otherwise) to use these models for purposes of comparing countries. There are
two natural extensions where we allow the factor means to vary between countries

TABLE 14.2
Factor Loadings With a Single Factor at Each Level

		Analysis B	
Item	Analysis A	Loadings	France–England
Student level			
33q01	0.46 (0.04)	0.46 (0.04)	−0.08 (0.04)
34q01	0.70 (0.04)	0.71 (0.05)	0.01 (0.07)
37q01	0.96 (0.09)	0.92 (0.07)	−0.16 (0.10)
124q01	0.69 (0.07)	0.72 (0.07)	−0.20 (0.10)
136q01	0.69 (0.05)	0.70 (0.06)	0.96 (0.08)
144q01	0.55 (0.05)	0.54 (0.05)	0.46 (0.07)
145q01	0.63 (0.05)	0.62 (0.05)	−0.21 (0.08)
150q01	0.59 (0.05)	0.59 (0.04)	−0.41 (0.07)
155q01	0.51 (0.05)	0.52 (0.04)	0.33 (0.07)
159q01	0.46 (0.04)	0.47 (0.05)	−0.31 (0.07)
161q01	0.30 (0.04)	0.33 (0.04)	−0.78 (0.07)
179q01	0.54 (0.06)	0.52 (0.06)	0.79 (0.08)
192q01	0.68 (0.04)	0.68 (0.05)	0.09 (0.07)
266q01	0.36 (0.05)	0.38 (0.05)	−0.28 (0.07)
273q01	0.47 (0.04)	0.46 (0.05)	0.03 (0.06)
School level			
33q01	0.26 (0.03)	0.26 (0.03)	
34q01	0.39 (0.03)	0.39 (0.03)	
37q01	0.77 (0.06)	0.74 (0.06)	
124q01	0.71 (0.05)	0.71 (0.05)	
136q01	0.49 (0.04)	0.54 (0.04)	
144q01	0.31 (0.04)	0.31 (0.03)	
145q01	0.47 (0.04)	0.48 (0.04)	
150q01	0.41 (0.04)	0.42 (0.04)	
155q01	0.29 (0.04)	0.31 (0.03)	
159q01	0.35 (0.04)	0.36 (0.04)	
161q01	0.23 (0.04)	0.24 (0.03)	
179q01	0.42 (0.05)	0.46 (0.04)	
192q01	0.43 (0.03)	0.43 (0.04)	
266q01	0.33 (0.04)	0.33 (0.04)	
273q01	0.35 (0.03)	0.35 (0.03)	

Note. Analysis A ignores country differences; analysis B fits the model of Equation 23 and shows the loadings together with French–English difference. Factor variances are set equal to 1.

but where the factor structures are the same in each country. Thus we can extend Equation 23 for country g as follows:

$$\text{probit}(\pi_{rijg}) = \beta_{0rg} + \beta_{1r}^{(1)}\theta_{1ijg}^{(1)} + \beta_{1r}^{(2)}\theta_{1jg}^{(2)} + u_{rj},$$
$$\theta_{1ijg}^{(1)} \sim N\left(\mu_g^{(1)}, \sigma_{(1)}^2\right), \qquad \theta_{1jg}^{(2)} \sim N\left(\mu_g^{(2)}, \sigma_{(2)}^2\right) \tag{24}$$
$$y_{rijg} \sim Bin(1, \pi_{rijg}), \qquad g = 1, 2.$$

Typically we would be interested in modeling the same overall shift at each level l, so that we have $\mu_g^{(l)} = \mu_g$. In this case for a single-factor model, we can write Equation 24 in the alternative form

$$\text{probit}(\pi_{rijg}) = \beta_{0r} + \delta_g d\left(\beta_{1r}^{(1)} + \beta_{1r}^{(2)}\right) + \beta_{1r}^{(1)}\theta_{1ij}^{(1)} + \beta_{1r}^{(2)}\theta_{1j}^{(2)} + u_{rj},$$

$$\theta_{1ij}^{(1)} \sim N\left(0, \sigma_{(1)}^2\right), \qquad \theta_{1j}^{(2)} \sim N\left(0, \sigma_{(2)}^2\right) \qquad (25)$$

$$y_{rijg} \sim Bin(1, \pi_{rijg}), \qquad g = 1, 2.$$

Clearly we can extend such a model to other explanatory variables such as gender, in effect obtaining a structural equation model for the factor mean structures. We note that the OECD procedure for country and group comparisons will not in general produce the same inferences because the model that is fitted assumes no differences. Likewise, the OECD model assumes only a single (student) level, with school-level variation estimated in the second-stage analysis. In the case of factor models the OECD approach to group comparisons leads to interpretational difficulties because the factor structure that is fitted, in the presence of real group differences under a model such as Equation 23, is incorrect. We also note that for those with at least one valid mathematics item response (55%), the average number of Mathematics items responded to by students is 12.6, with a range from 1 to 16, so that the normal approximation implicit in the use of plausible values may not be very accurate for some of the students.

The OECD country comparisons for Mathematics show a small difference between England and France, and this is borne out by our results, although we have used a reduced set of items.

An alternative formulation for country and group differences is to write Equation 25 as

$$\text{probit}(\pi_{rij}) = \beta_{0r} + d\delta_g + \beta_{1r}^{(1)}\theta_{1ij}^{(1)} + \beta_{1r}^{(2)}\theta_{1j}^{(2)} + u_{rj},$$

$$\theta_{1ij}^{(1)} \sim N\left(0, \sigma_{(1)}^2\right), \qquad \theta_{1j}^{(2)} \sim \text{MVN}\left(0, \sigma_{(2)}^2\right), \qquad (26)$$

$$y_{rjk} \sim Bin(1, \pi_{rjk}).$$

This model additionally constrains the item differences for each country to be constant. If we estimate the parameter d in Equation 26, we obtain the value 0.02 with standard error 0.05, so that we would conclude that the French–English difference is small and nonsignificant. In Table 14.2, however, we show considerable individual differences. Thus, if we had only fitted Equation 26 representing a simple overall country effect, as in the PISA analysis, we would be missing potentially important differential (interaction) effects.

The next model fits two orthogonal factors at the student level and one at school level. In the present set of analyses we do not report fitting more than one factor at the school level. In Table 14.3 the first factor at the student level is again a general

TABLE 14.3

Loadings for Two Orthogonal Factors at Level 1 and One Factor at Level 2

Item	Factor 1	Factor 2
Student level		
33q01	0.51 (0.06)	0
34q01	0.67 (0.05)	0.22 (0.09)
37q01	0.81 (0.10)	0.42 (0.14)
124q01	0.56 (0.11)	0.80 (0.21)
136q01	0.60 (0.09)	0.47 (0.12)
144q01	0.58 (0.10)	0.08 (0.10)
145q01	0.57 (0.06)	0.19 (0.12)
150q01	0.72 (0.10)	−0.07 (0.18)
155q01	0.44 (0.06)	0.28 (0.10)
159q01	0.50 (0.06)	−0.04 (0.12)
161q01	0.43 (0.07)	−0.27 (0.14)
179q01	0.46 (0.08)	0.46 (0.17)
192q01	0.62 (0.06)	0.28 (0.10)
266q01	0.41 (0.06)	−0.10 (0.09)
273q01	0.42 (0.06)	0.21 (0.12)
School level		
33q01	0.27 (0.03)	
34q01	0.39 (0.04)	
37q01	0.76 (0.06)	
124q01	0.82 (0.10)	
136q01	0.52 (0.05)	
144q01	0.32 (0.04)	
145q01	0.47 (0.04)	
150q01	0.45 (0.05)	
155q01	0.31 (0.04)	
159q01	0.36 (0.04)	
161q01	0.25 (0.04)	
179q01	0.46 (0.05)	
192q01	0.44 (0.04)	
266q01	0.34 (0.04)	
273q01	0.36 (0.03)	

Note. The first loading of factor 2 is constrained to zero. The variances constrained to one.

common factor, and the second factor tends to distinguish the free-response from the multiple-choice items. We also studied three factors at the student level, but the results are not easy to interpret, perhaps unsurprisingly given only 15 binary response variables.

We now fit separate factors for the two countries. Table 14.4 shows the results for a single factor at each level. We see that there are different patterns of loadings at both levels and those for France are much closer to the factor loadings estimated from the combined country data set, perhaps unsurprisingly because there are almost twice as many French students in the combined sample. We computed the

TABLE 14.4

Loadings for Single-Factor Models Separately for Each Country

Item	England	France
Student level		
33q01	0.49 (0.08)	0.46 (0.04)
34q01	0.56 (0.10)	0.75 (0.05)
37q01	0.69 (0.12)	1.09 (0.11)
124q01	0.50 (0.10)	0.82 (0.09)
136q01	0.75 (0.14)	0.71 (0.06)
144q01	0.48 (0.09)	0.58 (0.06)
145q01	0.38 (0.09)	0.68 (0.05)
150q01	0.50 (0.11)	0.62 (0.06)
155q01	0.31 (0.08)	0.59 (0.05)
159q01	0.34 (0.09)	0.51 (0.06)
161q01	0.32 (0.09)	0.33 (0.05)
179q01	0.34 (0.09)	0.62 (0.07)
192q01	0.75 (0.14)	0.68 (0.05)
266q01	0.33 (0.09)	0.41 (0.06)
273q01	0.44 (0.09)	0.48 (0.05)
School level		
33q01	0.36 (0.06)	0.22 (0.04)
34q01	0.46 (0.07)	0.36 (0.04)
37q01	0.73 (0.09)	0.79 (0.08)
124q01	0.80 (0.10)	0.68 (0.06)
136q01	0.75 (0.08)	0.44 (0.04)
144q01	0.41 (0.06)	0.25 (0.04)
145q01	0.72 (0.08)	0.39 (0.04)
150q01	0.44 (0.06)	0.43 (0.04)
155q01	0.23 (0.06)	0.35 (0.04)
159q01	0.47 (0.07)	0.31 (0.04)
161q01	0.27 (0.06)	0.24 (0.04)
179q01	0.50 (0.07)	0.45 (0.05)
192q01	0.42 (0.08)	0.44 (0.04)
266q01	0.38 (0.07)	0.30 (0.05)
273q01	0.41 (0.06)	0.32 (0.04)

factor scores for the English students from the combined and separate analyses and these show a high correlation (.98). This reflects the fact that the factor score is effectively a weighted mean of the item responses, and the two sets of loadings are all positive and comparable in size. It is also inflated because the factor scores are "shrunken" estimates with shrinkage a function of the number of items responded to. A simple comparison of the mean factor scores from the joint analysis with a single factor at each level gives a nonsignificant difference. Thus, whereas a joint analysis will lead to comparable rankings for individuals, as indeed will a simple scoring system using just the average percentage correct (the correlation is .84), the interpretation of factor loadings in the context of group differences will not be the same.

At the school level for France the factor loadings are approximately proportional to those at the school level for the combined analysis, but this is not the case for England, which has different orderings for the loadings. In the pooled analysis the comparison between student and school loadings is more like that for France.

CONCLUSIONS FROM THE ANALYSIS

We have not attempted to study reasons for country differences in any detail in these analyses. Our intention has been to show how multilevel binary factor models can be specified with covariates and group differences. We show that for the purposes of comparing countries it is important to fit a model that explicitly includes country effects. In this case we show that, in the simple case where one general factor is fitted at each level, student and school, the factor structures are somewhat different for each country. Thus, a single "pooled" set of factor loadings used for purposes of country comparisons leads to considerable difficulty in interpreting results because, as in this case, the pooled factors will be influenced by the weightings implicit in the numbers of students in each country. Where several countries are pooled as in the OECD PISA analyses, the factors are even more difficult to interpret, as are resulting country differences. Furthermore, and perhaps more important, we showed that, after fitting a single-factor model there are still differences between countries in item response probabilities (Table 14.2). This implies that the choice of items to use will determine the factor loadings, in that if we choose a majority of items that all load highly on a factor, then that factor will tend to dominate the structure. If those items also happen to favor a particular country then that country will tend to have higher factor scores, but this could only be ascertained by carrying out a multidimensional analysis.

DISCUSSION

The issues that surround the specification and interpretation of single-level factor and structural equation models are also present in our multilevel versions. Parameter identification has already been mentioned; with the ability to include prior distributions we can often treat identification problems with more flexibility. In the traditional model, overparametrization requires setting one or more parameters or functions of parameters to known values. In our case we can obtain estimates by imposing informative prior distributions on each of the parameters, which, when combined with the data, will provide the joint posterior distribution. An example is in the estimation of factor correlations where the assumption of a prior in the interval $(0, 1)$ can allow the joint posterior of all the parameters in an "overidentified" model to be estimated.

Another potential advantage of our approach, common to all MCMC procedures, is that we can make exact inferences based upon the Markov chain values.

This will be a particular advantage for small data sets where we may be unwilling to rely on likelihood-based approximations.

Another issue is the boundary, Heywood case. We observed such solutions occurring where sets of loading parameters tend toward zero or a correlation tends toward 1.0. A final important issue that only affects stochastic procedures is the problem of flipping states. This means that there is not a unique solution even in a one-factor problem because the loadings and factor values may all flip their sign to give an equivalent solution. When the number of factors increases there are greater problems because factors may swap over as the chains progress. This means that identifiability is an important consideration when using stochastic techniques.

We can extend the models considered here to mixtures of binary, ordered, and continuous responses. We have separately discussed all three types of responses. They are linked via the threshold probit model, so that at Level 1 we have a set of independent normal variables (uniquenesses), each one arising from a continuous response, a binary response, or an ordered response. At higher levels the random effects are assumed to have a multivariate normal distribution and the MCMC estimation proceeds in a straightforward fashion.

Such an example might arise in a health application where individuals respond to a health questionnaire at the same time as a set of continuous measurements of health status are made. It might also arise in an educational examination where, for example, some responses are multiple-choice binary questions and some are free responses marked on a continuous scale. Another important application is to questionnaires that contain mixtures of ordered rating scales and binary responses.

A major drawback of current implementations of binary factor (item response) models that attempt to account for multilevel data structures is that they fit a multilevel model in two stages: first estimating a single-level model and then fitting a multilevel model using the estimated factor scores, typically using multiple imputation via plausible values. Such a procedure does not allow the exploration of any factor structure at higher levels. We showed that this may be important, especially when comparing groups or countries.

Finally, we note that all of our models can be extended straightforwardly to more-complex data structures involving cross-classifications and multiple-membership structures (Browne, Goldstein, & Rasbash, 2001).

REFERENCES

Albert, J. H., & Chib, S. (1993). Bayesian analysis of binary and polychotomous response data. *Journal of the American Statistical Association, 88*, 669–679.

Baker, F. (1992). *Item response theory*. New York: Dekker.

Bartholomew, D. J., & Knott, M. (1999). *Latent variable models and factor analysis* (2nd ed.). London: Arnold.

Bock, R. D., Gibbons, R., & Muraki, E. (1988). Full-information item factor analysis. *Applied Psychological Measurement, 12*, 261–280.

Browne, W. J. (2002). *MCMC estimation in MLwiN.* London: Institute of Education.

Browne, W. J. (2004). *MCMC estimation of 'constrained' variance matrices with applications in multilevel modelling.* Manuscript submitted for publication.

Browne, W. J., Goldstein, H., & Rasbash, J. (2001). Multiple membership multiple classification (MMMC) models. *Statistical Modelling, 1,* 103–124.

Everitt, B. S. (1984). *An introduction to latent variable models.* London: Chapman & Hall.

Goldstein, H. (2003). *Multilevel statistical models* (3rd ed.). London: Arnold.

Goldstein, H., & Browne, W. (2002). Multilevel factor analysis modelling using Markov chain Monte Carlo estimation. In G. Marcoulides & I. Moustaki (Eds.), *Latent variable and latent structure models* (pp. 225–243). Mahwah, NJ: Lawrence Erlbaum Associates, Inc.

Goldstein, H., & Wood, R. (1989). Five decades of item response modelling. *British Journal of Mathematical and Statistical Psychology, 42,* 139–167.

Hedeker, D., & Gibbons, R. D. (1994). A random effects ordinal regression model for multilevel analysis. *Biometrics, 50,* 933–944.

Lawley, D. N. (1943). The application of the maximum likelihood method to factor analysis. *British Journal of Psychology, 33,* 172–75.

Lee, Y., & Nelder, J. A. (2001). Hierarchical generalised linear models: A synthesis of generalised linear models, random-effect models and structured dispersions. *Biometrika, 88,* 987–1006.

Longford, N., & Muthen, B. O. (1992). Factor analysis for clustered observations. *Psychometrika, 57,* 581–597.

Lord, F. M., & Novick, M. R. (1968). *Statistical theories of mental test scores.* Reading, MA: Addison-Wesley.

McDonald, R. P. (1981). The dimensionality of tests and items. *British Journal of mathematical and statistical psychology, 34,* 100–117.

McDonald, R. P. (1985). *Factor analysis and related methods.* Hillsdale, NJ: Lawrence Erlbaum Associates, Inc.

McDonald, R. P. (1993). A general model for two-level data with responses missing at random. *Psychometrika, 58,* 575–585.

McDonald, R. P., & Goldstein, H. (1989). Balanced versus unbalanced designs for linear structural relations in two-level data. *British Journal of Mathematical and Statistical Psychology, 42,* 215–232.

Meng, X. L. (1994). Posterior predictive *p*-values. *Annals of Statistics, 22,* 1142–1160.

Organisation for Economic Co-operation and Development. (1999). *Measuring student knowledge and skills: A new framework for assessment.* Paris: Author.

Rabe-hesketh, S., Pickles, A., & Taylor, C. (2000). Sg129: Generalized linear latent and mixed models. *Stata Technical Bulletin, 53,* 47–57.

Rasbash, J., Browne, W., Goldstein, H., Yang, M., Plewis, I., Healy, M., Woodhouse, G., Draper, D., Langford, I., & Lewis T. (2000). *A user's guide to MLwiN* (2nd ed.). London: Institute of Education.

Rowe, K. J., & Hill, P. W. (1997). *Simultaneous estimation of multilevel structural equations to model students' educational progress.* Paper presented at the Tenth International Congress for School Effectiveness and School Improvement, Memphis, TN.

Rowe, K. J. (2003). Estimating interdependent effects among multilevel composite variables in psychosocial research: An example of the application of multilevel structural equation modeling. In S. P. Reise & N. Duan (eds.) *Multilevel modeling: Methodological advances, issues, and applications* (pp. 255–284). Mahwah, NJ: Lawrence Erlbaum Associates, Inc.

Rubin, D. B. (1996). Multiple imputation after 18+ years. *Journal of the American Statistical Association, 91,* 473–489.

Rubin, D. B., & Thayer, D. T. (1982). EM algorithms for ML factor analysis. *Psychometrika, 47,* 69–76.

Spiegelhalter, D., Best, N., Carlin, B. P., & Van der Linde, A. (2002). Bayesian measures of model complexity and fit (with discussion). *Journal of the Royal Statistical Society, Series B, 64,* 583–640.

Zhu, H.-T., & Lee, S.-Y. (1999). Statistical analysis of nonlinear factor analysis models. *British Journal of Mathematical and Statistical Psychology, 52,* 225–242.

IV

Multivariate Analysis

Although Rod McDonald's contributions to general multivariate analysis are less known than his contributions to test theory, factor analysis, or structural equation modeling, they are not less relevant. For instance, the McDonald–Swaminathan (1973) matrix calculus system preceded some of the later (and best known) results in this area (Magnus & Neudecker, 1988; Nel, 1980). Also, his contributions to optimal scaling (McDonald, 1968, 1983; McDonald, Torii, & Nishisato, 1979) lead quite naturally to the integration of optimal scaling and factor analysis (McDonald, 1969), an area that remains virtually unexplored. Finally, but not less importantly, Rod has searched to unify the diversity of models for the analysis of multivariate data under a common umbrella (McDonald, 1979, 1986).

Here, **Shizuhiko Nishisato** discusses how to handle ordinal measurement from a dual-scaling (optimal scaling, correspondence analysis, etc.) perspective. In his chapter he puts forward a thought-provoking recommendation, namely, to break away from the following two major premises: Use only monotonic transformations, and Do not treat ordinal measurement as cardinal numbers.

In the second chapter in this part, **Wayne Velicer** and **Suzanne Colby** approach the important problem of how to tackle model specification and missing data in time series models. They advocate using the Velicer–McDonald (1984) general transformation approach in conjunction with maximum likelihood estimation (MLE). To support their proposal, they report three simulation studies examining the accuracy of the MLE algorithms under violations that are likely to occur in applied behavioral research: (a) model misspecification, (b) systematically missing data vs. randomly missing data, (c) and nonnormality.

Finally, **Lisa Harlow**, very much in the McDonaldian tradition of the "search of an essential unity in multivariate analysis," delineates a set of basic themes that reoccur within statistics, particularly with multivariate procedures, in the hope of making conscious and apprehensible the core tenets, if not axioms, of these methods.

REFERENCES

Magnus, J. R., & Neudecker, H. (1988). *Matrix differential calculus with applications in statistics and econometrics*. Chichester, UK: Wiley.

McDonald, R. P. (1968). A unified treatment of the weighting problem. *Psychometrika, 33*, 351–381.

McDonald, R. P. (1969). The common factor analysis of multicategory data. *British Journal of Mathematical and Statistical Psychology, 22*, 165–175.

McDonald, R. P. (1979). The structure of multivariate data: A sketch of a general theory. *Multivariate Behavioral Research, 14*, 21–38.

McDonald, R. P. (1983). Alternative weights and invariant parameters in optimal scaling. *Psychometrika, 48*, 377–391.

McDonald, R. P. (1986). Describing the elephant: Structure and function in multivariate data. *Psychometrika, 51*, 513–534.

McDonald, R. P., & Swaminathan, H. (1973). A simple matrix calculus with applications to multivariate analysis. *General Systems, 18*, 37–54.

McDonald, R. P., Torii, Y., & Nishisato, S. (1979). Some results on proper eigenvalues and eigenvectors with applications to scaling. *Psychometrika, 44*, 211–227.

Nel, D. G. (1980). On matrix differentiation in statistics. *South African Statistical Journal, 14*, 137–193.

Velicer, W. F., & McDonald, R. P. (1984). Time series analysis without model identification. *Multivariate Behavioral Research, 19*, 33–47.

15

On the Scaling of Ordinal Measurement: A Dual-Scaling Perspective

Shizuhiko Nishisato
Ontario Institute for Studies in Education of the University of Toronto

INTRODUCTION

Dual Scaling and Its Family

This chapter deals with quantification of categorical data, another area in which R. P. McDonald's contribution is well known (e.g., McDonald, 1983; McDonald, Torii, & Nishisato, 1979).

Under the umbrella of quantification theory, many names have been proposed, including optimal scaling, dual scaling, correspondence analysis, biplot, the Gifi system of quantification, and Hayashi's theory of quantification. These methods are all closely related to one another or basically the same. They were proposed for most economical multidimensional decomposition of categorical data, which turned out to be nothing but singular value decomposition (SVD) (Beltrami, 1873; Eckart & Young, 1936; Jordan, 1874; Schmidt, 1907) applied to categorical data. Before introducing SVD, let us look at some familiar problems in which SVD is used.

In mathematics, we talk about *canonical reduction* of a quadratic form, which is nothing but a special transformation of a given rectangular coordinate system, that is, the transformation of

$$aX^2 + 2bXY + cY^2 = k \qquad \text{to} \qquad eX^2 + fY^2 = k. \tag{1}$$

In matrix notation,

$$\begin{bmatrix} X & Y \end{bmatrix} \begin{bmatrix} a & b \\ b & c \end{bmatrix} \begin{bmatrix} X \\ Y \end{bmatrix} \qquad \text{to} \qquad \begin{bmatrix} X & Y \end{bmatrix} \begin{bmatrix} e & 0 \\ 0 & f \end{bmatrix} \begin{bmatrix} X \\ Y \end{bmatrix}. \tag{2}$$

This transformation is said to change the original coordinate system to the principal coordinate system in which the new axes are called *principal axes* and the coefficients e and f are called *eigenvalues*. The dropping of the cross-product bXY from the general expression by canonical reduction amounts to making the shape of the quadratic function symmetric with respect to the new axes X and Y, that is, principal axes. Keep in mind this symmetric or *dual* aspect of SVD.

Let us look at SVD from a different point of view. In statistics, we talk about a linear combination of variables X and Y, $aX + bY$, subject to the condition that $a^2 + b^2 = 1$. When this condition is met and when both X and Y are centered, composite scores by the linear combination can be geometrically expressed as projections of data points onto the axis going through the origin with an angle a/b. So, a linear combination is an axis, and the variance of the linear combination (i.e., composite scores or projections of data points on an axis) changes as the orientation of the axis, which is determined by a and b. When we determine a and b so that the variance of the composite scores is a maximum, that axis is called a principal axis and the variance an eigenvalue.

Let us now formally introduce SVD. Given an n-by-m matrix $\mathbf{F}$, the SVD of $\mathbf{F}$ can be expressed as

$$\mathbf{F} = \mathbf{Y}\Lambda\mathbf{X}', \tag{3}$$

where $\mathbf{Y}'\mathbf{Y} = \mathbf{I}$, $\mathbf{X}'\mathbf{X} = \mathbf{I}$, and $\Lambda = \text{diag}[\lambda_1, \lambda_2, \ldots, \lambda_K]$. Note that $\mathbf{Y} = [\mathbf{y}_1, \mathbf{y}_2, \ldots, \mathbf{y}_K]$ and $\mathbf{X} = [\mathbf{x}_1, \mathbf{x}_2, \ldots, \mathbf{x}_K]$ are matrices of right and left singular vectors, respectively, and Λ is the diagonal matrix of singular values λ_k. From SVD, we obtain a typical expression of eigenvalue decomposition (EVD),

$$[\mathbf{F}'\mathbf{F} - \Lambda^2\mathbf{I}]\mathbf{Y} = \mathbf{O} \qquad \text{or} \qquad [\mathbf{F}\mathbf{F}' - \Lambda^2\mathbf{I}]\mathbf{X} = \mathbf{O}, \tag{4}$$

where λ^2 is the square of the singular value and is called the eigenvalue, and $\mathbf{Y}$ and $\mathbf{X}$ are matrices of left singular vectors (eigenvectors) and right singular vectors (eigenvectors), respectively. From this relation, one can say that SVD is a more general expression of EVD. Both have played very important roles in multivariate analysis, serving as a foundation of modern data analysis. SVD of data can be expressed in many ways, and perhaps the following two sets of expressions are the most relevant to, and best known for, the quantification methods under discussion. One is the bilinear expression, and the other are dual relations or transition formulas, given, respectively, as

$$f_{ij} = \frac{f_{i.}f_{.j}}{f_{..}}(1 + \rho_1 y_{i1}x_{j1} + \rho_2 y_{i2}x_{j2} + \cdots + \rho_K y_{iK}x_{jK}), \qquad (5)$$

$$y_{ik} = \frac{1}{\rho_k}\frac{\sum_{j=1}^{m} f_{ij}x_{jk}}{f_{i.}}, \qquad x_{jk} = \frac{1}{\rho_k}\frac{\sum_{i=1}^{n} f_{ij}y_{ik}}{f_{.j}}. \qquad (6)$$

Multidimensional space, expressed in terms of principal axes, is called principal hyperspace. Principal hyperspace is the preferred coordinate system for many researchers. Pearson (1901) and Hotelling (1933) used principal hyperspace to represent continuous data, now known as principal component analysis (PCA). PCA is a method for calculating projections of data points on principal axes. In PCA, we determine weights for items in such a way that the average of all interitem correlations is a maximum.

When data are discrete, such as multiple-choice data, we want to determine weights for response options (not for items as in continuous data) in such a way that the average interitem correlation is a maximum. This is attained by representing data in principal coordinates, and the analysis is called principal component analysis of categorical data (Torgerson, 1958) or by any one of the following names: the method of reciprocal averages, Hayashi's theory of quantification, Fisher's appropriate scoring and additive scoring, Bock's optimal scaling, French correspondence analysis, Dutch homogeneity analysis, and Canadian dual scaling. Notice that all of these methods are based on SVD, and as such they are mathematically equivalent.

One possible reason so many aliases have been proposed seems to lie in the fact that SVD is a final expression derived from a number of objective functions used in quantification: In determining weights for rows and columns of a data matrix, maximize (a) the product–moment correlation between data weighted by row weights and those by column weights, (b) the correlation ratio expressed by row weights, (c) the correlation ratio expressed by column weights, or (d) canonical correlation between categories of a variable and those of another variable, (e) determine weights for rows and those for columns so as to make the regression of rows on columns and that of columns on rows simultaneously linear, or (f) reciprocate averaging of rows, weighted by column weights and that of columns, weighted by row weights, each time using new row (column) weights to calculate weighted column (row) weights, until convergence is attained.

Noting that maximization of these objective functions (a) through (d), linearization of (e), or convergence of the process (f) leads to SVD, we reach the conclusion that all these quantification methods, under different names, are basically the same, the main difference being in special emphases placed on some aspects of the methods, such as symmetry (duality), maximum variance, homogeneity of variables, low-rank approximation, standardized versus nonstandardized discrete data, or the choice of the units of quantified variates. Dual scaling is thus essentially the same as correspondence analysis/multiple-correspondence analysis, except for its orientation, as will be described further.

Two Types of Categorical Data

There are a number of ways to classify data, such as binary versus polytomous, ordered categories versus unordered categories, similarity, dissimilarity, proximity, and preference data. To adhere to the dual-scaling framework, however, we will follow Nishisato's (1993) classification of categorical data into two types: *incidence data*, where the information is typically given by "presence" or "absence," 1 or 0, or frequencies in categories that may be dichotomous, polytomous, ordered, or unordered; and *dominance data*, where the information is given by "greater than," "equal to," or "smaller than," or ranking, where categories are in general weakly ordered. The two data types have distinct characteristics when subjected to dual scaling, as follows:

Incidence Data:

1. Examples: contingency tables, multiple-choice data, sorting data.
2. A trivial solution, which is independent of data, is involved.
3. A chi-square metric is typically used.
4. The object of quantification is a low-rank approximation to the data.
5. Even when data are of perfect internal consistency, they cannot generally be explained by one solution (dimension).

For points 2 and 4, see Guttman (1941), Nishisato (1980, 1994), Greenacre (1984), and Gifi (1990). For point 3, see Greenacre (1984), Lebart, Morineau, and Warwick (1984), and Nishisato and Clavel (2003). For point 5, see Nishisato (2002, 2003).

Dominance Data:

1. Examples: rank-order data, paired-comparison data, successive-categories data.
2. No trivial solution is involved.
3. A Euclidean metric is typically used.
4. The object of quantification is a low-rank approximation to the inequalities of input data.
5. When data are of perfect consistency, data are explained by one solution.

For point 1, see Guttman (1946), Nishisato (1978, 1980, 1994), Greenacre and Torres-Lacomba (1999), and van de Velden (2000). For point 3, see Nishisato (2003). For points 4 and 5, see Nishisato (1994, 1996). Many terms are too technical to explain in the space available here. However, the references given are sufficient for understanding them.

Correspondence analysis deals mainly with contingency tables, and multiple correspondence analysis with multiple-choice data. Thus, what we call correspondence analysis typically handles incidence data. In contrast, dual scaling was developed for quantifying both incidence data and dominance data from its debut in 1969. For this reason, it must be clear why Meulman (1998) called dual scaling a comprehensive framework for multidimensional analysis of categorical data.

In this chapter we look at the problem of handling ordinal information contained in these two types of categorical data.

TWO MAJOR PREMISES FOR ORDINAL MEASUREMENT

Let us adopt the generally accepted definition of measurement as the assignment of numbers to objects according to certain rules (Bock & Jones, 1968; Torgerson, 1958). For ordinal measurement, the rules are one-to-one correspondence and greater than, equal to, or less than. When we apply this definition to ordinal measurement, we can come up with two premises for scaling ordinal measurement.

Premise 1: Use Only Monotone Transformation

The fundamental aspect of ordinal measurement lies in the fact that measurement reflects only an order relation, hence any transformation applied to ordinal measurement should be restricted to a monotone transformation. An example of this premise is typically found in the quantification of incidence data with ordered categories.

Suppose we have four categories for each variable—never, sometimes, often, and always—and we would like to quantify the data by assigning weights to these ordered categories, x_1, x_2, x_3, and x_4, respectively. According to the first premise, the task of quantification is to maximize the variance of the composite scores in terms of these weights, under the condition that

$$x_1 \leq x_2 \leq x_3 \leq x_4. \tag{7}$$

This task sounds reasonable, and there have been a number of papers published on this task (e.g., Bradley, Katti, & Coons, 1962; Nishisato & Arri, 1975; Tanaka & Asano, 1978; Tanaka & Kodake, 1980; Tsujitani, 1988a, 1988b). But is it always reasonable? We will see a counterexample later. In a lesser degree, we can also mention the Sheppard–Kruskal nonmetric multidimensional scaling (Kruskal, 1964a, 1964b; Sheppard, 1962a, 1962b) as another example in which the transformation is limited to an order-preserving transformation such as monotone regression or isotonic regression and a rank-image method.

Premise 2: Do Not Use Cardinal Numbers

We should not treat ordinal measurement as cardinal numbers. This premise is also reasonable, and in fact a good example can be found in the early work of Coombs's unfolding method (e.g., Coombs, 1950, 1964), and such algorithms as linear programming, Goode's equal-delta algorithm (Goode, 1957), and Phillips's algorithm (Phillips, 1971) were considered for solving the unfolding problem. This problem will be discussed later.

In this chapter we look at the first premise in handling incidence data by dual scaling and the second premise in handling dominance data by dual scaling.

In a typical course on measurement, these premises are taught and the students follow them as rules for ordinal measurement. In fact, the scientific community has accepted these fundamental premises for ordinal measurement for many years without questioning their merits or practical aspects, or more important, their validity.

Are they really acceptable, however? They have affected the directions of data analysis to an unimaginable extent. Positively? No. Negatively? Perhaps yes. This chapter attempts to go against the adage that "what is done cannot be undone." Once we adopt the view that the main purpose of data analysis is to extract as much information as possible from the given data, it follows that these premises must go.

ORDINAL INFORMATION
IN INCIDENCE DATA

Examination of the First Premise

Let us start with the first premise for ordinal measurement. The imposition of a weak order constraint on a set of ordered categories has been investigated by many researchers (e.g., Bradley et al., 1962; Nishisato & Arri, 1975; Tanaka & Asano, 1978; Tanaka & Kodake, 1980; Tsujitani, 1988a, 1988b). Therefore, methods are available. The issue is whether they are necessary for the purpose of information retrieval. We would like to show here that the answer is "not always."

Multiple-Choice Items With
Ordered Categories

Consider the following example of six multiple-choice questions with three ordered response categories per item (Nishisato, 2003):

1. How would you rate your blood pressure? (Low, Medium, High: coded 1, 2, 3, respectively).

2. Do you get migraines? (Rarely, Sometimes, Often: coded 1, 2, 3, respectively).
3. What is your age group? (Young [20 to 34], Middle [35 to 49], Older [50 to 65], coded 1, 2, 3, respectively).
4. How would you rate your daily level of anxiety? (Low, Medium, High: coded 1, 2, 3, respectively).
5. How would you rate your weight? (Light, Medium, Heavy: coded 1, 2, 3, respectively).
6. What about your height? (Short, Medium, Tall: coded 1, 2, 3, respectively).

The data collected from 15 subjects are presented in two distinct formats, one in terms of the chosen option numbers or Likert scores (Likert, 1932), that is, coded scores of 1, 2, or 3, and the other in (1, 0) response patterns, represented in the following way: (100) if the subject chooses the first option, (010) for the choice of the second option, and (001) for the choice of the third option (see Table 15.1). For the details of analysis, see Nishisato (2003).

Format 1. If the first part (15×6) of the data matrix, consisting of 1, 2, and 3, is subjected to singular value decomposition, the results are a principal component analysis in which the data are treated as continuous. Each principal component is the variance-maximized *linear combination of items.*

TABLE 15.1
Likert Scores for Principal Component Analysis and Response Patterns for Dual Scaling

	Principal Components Analysis						Dual Scaling					
Subject	Bpr Q1	Mig Q2	Age Q3	Anx Q4	Wgt Q5	Hgt Q6	Bpr 123	Mig 123	Age 123	Anx 123	Wgt 123	Hgt 123
1	1	3	3	3	1	1	100	001	001	001	100	100
2	1	3	1	3	2	3	100	001	100	001	010	001
3	3	3	3	3	1	3	001	001	001	001	100	001
4	3	3	3	3	1	1	001	001	001	001	100	100
5	2	1	2	2	3	2	010	100	010	010	001	010
6	2	1	2	3	3	1	010	100	010	001	001	100
7	2	2	2	1	1	3	010	010	010	100	100	001
8	1	3	1	3	1	3	100	001	100	001	100	001
9	2	2	2	1	1	2	010	010	010	100	100	010
10	1	3	2	2	1	3	100	001	010	010	100	001
11	2	1	1	3	2	2	010	100	100	001	010	010
12	2	2	3	3	2	2	010	010	001	001	010	010
13	3	3	3	3	3	1	001	001	001	001	001	100
14	1	3	1	2	1	1	100	001	100	010	100	100
15	3	3	3	3	1	2	001	001	001	001	100	010

Note: Bpr, Blood pressure; Mig, migraine; Anx, anxiety; Wgt, weight; Hgt, height.

Format 2. If the second part (15 × 18), consisting of (1, 0) response patterns, is subjected to singular value decomposition, the results are a dual-scaling analysis, in which we obtain the variance-maximized *linear combination of item options*, not that of items. When the number of categories is greater than two, one can consider either an ordered set of categories or a set of unordered categories. In a typical application of dual scaling, categories are not assumed ordered, but of course dual scaling of ordered categories also is an option (Nishisato, 1980).

Let us consider three ways of handling ordered categories:

1. Use the traditional Likert scores 1, 2, and 3 for the three ordered categories of each question, using Format 1.
2. Use monotone transformations for the three categories in Format 2.
3. Use no constraints on categories in Format 2 (as in typical dual scaling).

When we consider maximizing the average interitem correlation under the three cases 1, 2, or 3, these conditions have the effect of placing the data through three kinds of filters, linear, monotone, and nonlinear, respectively, before subjecting the data to SVD. For the first case, the task involves calculating product–moment correlation of Likert scores, the second case is carried out by dual scaling with a weak order constraint on each set of the three ordered categories, and the third task is carried out by dual scaling, without any order constraints on the response options. For the first case, the analysis starts with the left-hand side table of the data, and for the other two cases, the analysis starts with the response pattern table, which is on the right-hand side of the table. The results are as follows:

```
------------------------------------------------------------------
Correlation from Cardinal Numbers
------------------------------------------------------------------
BP      1.00
Mig     -.06    1.00
Age      .66     .23    1.00
Anx      .18     .21     .22    1.00
Wgt      .17    -.58    -.02     .26    1.00
Hgt     -.21     .10    -.30    -.23    -.31    1.00
------------------------------------------------------------------
Monotone Regression (Dual scaling with order constraints)
------------------------------------------------------------------
BP      1.00
Mig      .49    1.00
Age      .74     .39    1.00
Anx      .40     .40     .54    1.00
Wgt      .30     .33     .08    -.36    1.00
Hgt      .21     .29     .29     .26     .30    1.00
```

```
-----------------------------------------------------------------
Correlation under No Restrictions (Typical dual scaling)
-----------------------------------------------------------------
BP      1.00
Mig      .99   1.00
Age      .60    .58   1.00
Anx      .47    .52    .67   1.00
Wgt      .43    .39    .08   -.33   1.00
Hgt      .56    .57    .13    .19    .20   1.00
-----------------------------------------------------------------
```

When we look at the first correlation matrix, we notice something quite revealing. Take a look at the correlation between blood pressure and age (.66) and the correlation between blood pressure and migraines (−.06), together with the corresponding data expressed in the form of contingency tables:

```
-----------------------------------------------------------------
                 Age                             Migraine
Blood      20-34 35-49 50-65   Blood Rarely  Sometimes Often
-----------------------------------------------------------------
High BP      0     0     4     High BP   0        0       4
Mid BP       1     4     1     Mid BP    3        3       0
Low BP       3     1     1     Low BP    0        0       5
-----------------------------------------------------------------
```

We can immediately tell that blood pressure is correlated linearly with age, hence the correlation is .66 (the first correlation matrix), whereas blood pressure is not linearly correlated with migraines, thus the correlation is −.06 (the first correlation matrix), but is nonlinearly correlated with the value of .99 (the third correlation matrix). The same correlation under monotone transformations is .49 (the second correlation matrix). Even without any calculations, it seems obvious that the relation between blood pressure and migraines is stronger than that between blood pressure and age, for the former tells us that when the migraines are frequent the blood pressure is surely either high or low.

To examine the data structure, Likert scores are subjected to PCA, and the other two to dual scaling. To simplify the discussion, let us look at only the first two dimensions. First, the results of PCA with Likert scores are as follows:

```
-----------------------------------------------------------------
PCA of Likert Scores in Two Dimensions
-----------------------------------------------------------------
Blood pressure, age, and anxiety form a cluster.
Blood pressure and migraines are almost orthogonal.
Weight is also almost orthogonal to the above cluster.
Height and migraines are slightly related.
-----------------------------------------------------------------
```

The current algorithm did not provide two components when the monotone constraint was imposed on each category set. It is easy to conjecture, however, that the results would not be much different from the foregoing results of Likert scores. So, let us skip the second case, and look at the third case, that is, dual scaling of response patterns without order constraints:

```
-----------------------------------------------------------------
PCA of Response-Pattern Table without Order Constraints
  (Dual Scaling)
-----------------------------------------------------------------
(Dimension 1)
High blood pressure, low blood pressure, frequent migraines,
high anxiety level, short height are all closely related.
(Dimension 2)
High blood pressure is related to old age, short, heavy,
high anxiety level. Low blood pressure is related to young
age, lean, and light.
-----------------------------------------------------------------
```

What can we conclude from the foregoing comparisons? In spite of the fact that the data clearly indicate the relation between blood pressure and migraines, the Likert scores could not detect the relation, and we can also state without analysis that the same applies to the case of monotone constraints as well. This can be inferred from the category weights obtained from dual scaling:

```
----------------------------------------------------------------
Blood P    Migraine     Age    Anxiety     Weight      Height
----------------------------------------------------------------
L -0.71    Rare   1.04  Y  0.37 L  1.55  L    -0.27  Short -0.56
M  1.17    Some   1.31  M  1.03 M  0.12  Med   0.32  Med    0.83
H -0.86    Often -0.78  O -0.61 H -0.35  Heavy 0.50  Tall  -0.27
----------------------------------------------------------------
```

Under the condition of monotone transformation, the weights for Low and Medium of blood pressure will be equated, and the two categories Rarely and Sometimes of the migraines must be equated to satisfy the monotone relation, thus eliminating the association between low blood pressure and frequent migraines. Similarly, two categories of age, Young (20 to 34 years) and Medium (35 to 49 years), must be equated to satisfy the monotone condition, which reduces its correlation with blood pressure. The variable of height indicates that the categories Medium and Tall must be equated under the monotone condition. All these observations lead us to believe that the monotone condition would not change the problem from that of the linear constraint on categories, that is, the results of PCA with Likert scores. The main conclusion from this example is that ordinal treatment of ordered categories does not allow us to detect any nonlinear relation between variables, and that the ordinal treatment can be a hindrance to the object of analysis, which is to extract as much information from data as possible.

A Conclusion on the First Premise

If the purpose of data analysis is to extract as much information as possible from the data and provide a simple, concise interpretation of the outcome, the conclusion seems to be obvious that we must discard the first premise. By assigning order-preserving weights to the ordered categories, we are essentially filtering only linear or monotone information of the input data into the analytical framework, which is contrary to the aforementioned purpose of data analysis. Once the data are expressed as variables as units, rather than categories of variables as units, the data analysis is doomed to be confined within the realm of linear analysis. The message is then: Do not impose monotone transformations as a requirement in handling ordinal measurement.

ORDINAL INFORMATION
IN DOMINANCE DATA

Coombs's Unfolding Problem

Coombs (1950) proposed a nonmetric scaling method, called the *unfolding technique*, for rank-order data. It was an individual difference ordinal scaling method for rank-order data. His model was simple: Subjects and objects are located along a single continuum, and each subject ranks objects according to the order of their closeness to the subject. When this joint continuum is folded at each subject's position, the objects will appear on the folded continuum in the order in which the subject orders them. Coombs thus considered all rank orders from subjects as folded scales, and his task was to *unfold* a set of the folded scales (i.e., rank orders of objects) to recover the original joint scale. This was his initial unidimensional model, which was soon expanded to a multidimensional model: Both subjects and objects are distributed in multidimensional space, and each subject's decision rule is to rank a set of objects in the order of their closeness to the subject. The multidimensional unfolding problem is how to find such a configuration of subjects and objects that satisfies this decision rule.

The unidimensional unfolding problem was solvable, using linear programming or Goode's method of equal delta (Goode, 1957), later further elaborated by Phillips (1971). Coombs's unfolding technique was unique in the sense that the solution was sought in the context of ordinal measurement, hence exactly within the framework governed by the second premise.

Historical Evidence Against
the Second Premise

Before Coombs's 1950 study, the same problem of finding scale values of object and subject positions in multidimensional space was investigated by Guttman (1946), who presented the famous Guttman quantification of rank-order and paired-comparison data. It is perfectly understandable why Guttman (1967) complained about Coombs's handling of references, the main complaint being that Coombs did not refer to Guttman's earlier studies on handling rank-order data.

Coombs's overlooking of Guttman's work was due to Coombs's adherence only to the nonmetric approach (see also Bennett, 1956), whereas Guttman treated ordinal measurement like cardinal numbers. It is interesting to note some changes in Coombs's standpoint already in the paper by Coombs and Kao (1960). It was around this time that his unidimensional unfolding model was extended to the multidimensional model (Bennett & Hays, 1960; Hays & Bennett, 1961) because a large number of rank orders could not be explained by a unidimensional model. Schönemann's (1970) monumental work on metric multidimensional unfolding opened the gate of the reservoir, and research papers on unfolding flooded the scientific community (e.g., Adachi, 2000; Bechtel, 1968; Davidson, 1973; Gold, 1973; Greenacre & Browne, 1986; Heiser, 1981; Hojo, 1994; Okamoto, 1995; Sixtl, 1973). The most important aspect of this surge of publications, however, was that the researchers abandoned Coombs's original nonmetric approach completely. Thus, the second premise followed by Coombs (1950) did not come to fruition, but researchers interested in Coombs's unfolding method jumped at the opportunity to handle ordinal measurement like cardinal numbers, encouraged by Schönemann's work. This drastic change took place because it was almost impossible to solve the multidimensional unfolding problem in a purely nonmetric way.

The irony of the history is that the very approach by Guttman (1946) that Coombs (1964) ignored came to be alive again, but not in the way Guttman would have wanted. Namely, most researchers who adopted the metric approach kept referring to Coombs's work (1950, 1964) and not to Guttman's (1946) work. As discussed later, the Guttman-type approach offers a solution to Coombs's problem of multidimensional unfolding (Nishisato, 1994, 1996).

A Conclusion on the Second Premise

The least-squares approach to the analysis of rank order used by Guttman (1946) is only possible by discarding the second premise, that is, by handling ordinal measurement like cardinal numbers. Coombs's original intension of solving the problem of multidimensional unfolding in a nonmetric way turned out to be too difficult and was abandoned by many researchers. From the pragmatic point of view, a better approach with no solution is definitely not a choice in the scientific community, which would rather choose a common approach of the least squares residual, which provides a good approximation to the solution. Thus, the second premise is also rejected.

MORE ON DOMINANCE DATA: A CLARIFICATION

Both dominance data (e.g., rank-order data, paired-comparison data) and inci-dence data (e.g., contingency tables, multiple-choice data) have been in the main domain of dual scaling from its beginning in 1969 (the main work is reported in two books (Nishisato, 1980, 1994), whereas correspondence analysis was mostly restricted to incidence data. Recently, nearly 60 years after Guttman (1946) and more than 25 years after Nishisato (1978), Greenacre and Torres-Lacomba (1999) from the University Pompeu Fabra and van de Velden (2000) from the University of Amsterdam extended correspondence analysis to rank-order data by adhering to the framework that correspondence analysis is for nonnegative categorical variates. There was no doubt in my mind, though, that someone in the field of correspon-dence analysis (Benzécri et al., 1973; Greenacre, 1984) would eventually apply singular value decomposition (e.g., Beltrami, 1873; Eckart & Young, 1936; Jordan, 1874; Schmidt, 1907) to rank-order data.

Multidimensional quantification of dominance data was pioneered by Guttman (1946). His method covered a wider range than Coombs's unfolding research, which was restricted to rank-order data. Guttman's approach can be grouped with other studies following his, such as those of Tucker (1960), Slater (1960), Hayashi (1964), Carroll (1972), Schönemann and Wang (1972), de Leeuw (1973), Nishisato (1978, 2000b), Heiser (1981), and Han and Huh (1995). In 1978, Nishisato clarified that methods proposed by Slater (1960), Tucker (1960), and Carroll (1972) were equivalent to Guttman's (1946) method. Since this is important as a historical account, let us recapture the essence of Nishisato's (1978) work first.

Guttman's Formulation

Guttman's formulation (1946) can handle both rank-order data and paired-comparison data. For a pair of two objects (X_j, X_k) judged by Subject i, define

$$_i e_{jk} = \begin{cases} 1 & \text{if Subject i judges } X_j > X_k, \\ 0 & \text{if Subject i judges } X_j < X_k, \end{cases} \tag{8}$$

$i = 1, 2, \ldots, N$; $j, k = 1, 2, \ldots, n$ $(j \neq k)$. Define two variables f_{ij} and g_{ij} as follows:

$$f_{ij} = \sum_{k=1}^{n} {}_i e_{jk}, \qquad g_{ij} = \sum_{k=1}^{n} {}_i e_{kj}. \tag{9}$$

Note that the sum of these variables is always equal to $n - 1$ for every i and every j. Historically, it is interesting to note that Guttman's use of these quantities in 1946 was essentially identical to the concept of "doubling" in correspondence analysis that Greenacre (1984) referred to as a way of handling rank-order data. To determine the weight vector for n objects in such a way that the objects are maximally discriminated, Guttman (1946) solved the following eigenequation:

$$(\mathbf{H}_g - \lambda \mathbf{I})\mathbf{x} = \mathbf{0}, \tag{10}$$

where

$$\mathbf{H}_g = \frac{2}{Nn(n-1)^2}(\mathbf{F}'\mathbf{F} + \mathbf{G}'\mathbf{G}) - \frac{1}{n}\mathbf{1}_n\mathbf{1}_n' \tag{11}$$

and $\mathbf{F} = (f_{ij})$ and $\mathbf{G} = (g_{ij})$.

Nishisato's Alternative Formulation

Nishisato's (1978, 1994) formulation also handles both rank-order data and paired-comparison data. Nishisato introduced the following response variable:

$$_{i}f_{jk} = \begin{cases} 1 & \text{if Subject i judges } X_j > X_k, \\ 0 & \text{if Subject i judges } X_j = X_k, \\ -1 & \text{if Subject i judges } X_j < X_k, \end{cases} \tag{12}$$

$i = 1, 2, \ldots, N; j, k = 1, 2, \ldots, n\, (j \neq k)$. This response variable allows a tied response, a feature that the other formulations described here did not consider. Then, define the dominance number for Subject i and Object j by

$$e_{ij} = \sum_{k=1}^{n} {}_{i}f_{jk}. \tag{13}$$

The judge-by-object table of e_{ij} is called the dominance matrix and is indicated by $\mathbf{E}$. This explanation of the dominance table may not be very clear. So, let us consider a small example of paired-comparison data, say five subjects comparing stimulus pairs (A, B), (A, C), and (B, C). Suppose that a 5×3 data matrix of response variates, say $\mathbf{F}$, and the traditional paired-comparison design matrix (Bock & Jones, 1968) for the three pairs (A, B), (A, C), and (B, C), respectively, are given as follows:

$$\mathbf{F} = \begin{bmatrix} 1 & 1 & -1 \\ 1 & -1 & -1 \\ -1 & 1 & -1 \\ 1 & 1 & 1 \\ 1 & -1 & -1 \end{bmatrix}, \qquad \mathbf{H} = \begin{bmatrix} 1 & -1 & 0 \\ 1 & 0 & -1 \\ 0 & 1 & -1 \end{bmatrix}. \tag{14}$$

Then the dominance matrix $\mathbf{E}$ is given by

$$\mathbf{E} = \mathbf{FH} = \begin{bmatrix} 1 & 1 & -1 \\ 1 & -1 & -1 \\ -1 & 1 & -1 \\ 1 & 1 & 1 \\ 1 & -1 & -1 \end{bmatrix} \begin{bmatrix} 1 & -1 & 0 \\ 1 & 0 & -1 \\ 0 & 1 & -1 \end{bmatrix} = \begin{bmatrix} 2 & -2 & 0 \\ 0 & -2 & 2 \\ 0 & 0 & 0 \\ 2 & 0 & -2 \\ 0 & -2 & 2 \end{bmatrix}. \tag{15}$$

In 1973, de Leeuw proposed the following formula for rank-order data:

$$e_{ij} = n + 1 - 2R_{ij}, \tag{16}$$

where R_{ij} is the rank that Subject i gave to Object j out of n objects. Nishisato (1976) showed that his general formula, developed for both rank-order data and paired-comparison data, is identical to the de Leeuw formula when applied to rank-order data. In Nishisato's formulation, the eigenequation to be solved is given by

$$(\mathbf{H}_n - \lambda\mathbf{I})\mathbf{x} = \mathbf{0}, \tag{17}$$

where

$$\mathbf{H}_n = \frac{1}{Nn(n-1)^2}\mathbf{E}'\mathbf{E}. \tag{18}$$

This problem can be stated, for example, as that of determining weights for subjects (rows) in such a way that the weighted averages for objects (columns) attain the maximal variance. Recall Guttman's definition of two matrices $\mathbf{F}$ and $\mathbf{G}$, and note that Nishisato's matrix $\mathbf{E} = \mathbf{F} - \mathbf{G}$. Then, after a few algebraic manipulations, we reach the conclusion that $\mathbf{H}_n = \mathbf{H}_g$. In other words, Nishisato's formulation is mathematically equivalent to Guttman's.

In 1978, Nishisato further demonstrated the equivalence of the foregoing two formulations to those of Slater (1960), Tucker (1960), and Carroll (1972): Slater's principal component analysis of the row-centered matrix of $\mathbf{F}$ leads to SVD of $\frac{1}{2}\mathbf{E}$, and the other two formulations start with a matrix proportional to $\mathbf{E}$. Greenacre and Torres-Lacomba (1999) and van Velden (2000) presented formulations within their framework of correspondence analysis (i.e., quantification of only nonnegative variates), and both studies arrived at solving an eigenequation involving one of the two doubled matrices:

$$\mathbf{B} = [\mathbf{F}, \mathbf{G}], \qquad \mathbf{C} = \begin{bmatrix} \mathbf{F} \\ \mathbf{G} \end{bmatrix}, \tag{19}$$

where two matrices $\mathbf{F}$ and $\mathbf{G}$ are identical to Guttman's $\mathbf{F}$ and $\mathbf{G}$, respectively. Their formulations lead to SVD of one of the two matrices,

$$c[-\mathbf{E}, \mathbf{E}] \qquad \text{and} \qquad c\begin{bmatrix} -\mathbf{E} \\ \mathbf{E} \end{bmatrix}, \tag{20}$$

where $\mathbf{E}$ is the same as Nishisato's $\mathbf{E}$ and c is a scaling constant. Thus, depending on which of the two matrices they consider for SVD, they obtain either two identical row weight vectors or column weight vectors of opposite signs. Thus their formulations involve extra redundant computations, which the aforementioned formulations by Guttman, Slater, Tucker, Carroll, and Nishisato do not. Their contributions then seem to lie in the fact that the formulations were carried out in the context of correspondence analysis, as noted earlier.

DUAL-SCALING SOLUTION FOR THE UNFOLDING PROBLEM

Mathematically the problem of multidimensional unfolding has been investigated by many researchers, as mentioned earlier. As is well known, in the quantification approach, the space for row variables and the space for column variables of a two-way table are different, which prompted warnings such as "a great deal of caution is needed in interpreting the distance between a variable point and an individual point, because these two points do not belong to the same space" (Lebart et al., 1984, p. 19). Guttman (1946) did not look at his results in terms of a joint display of subjects and objects in the way Coombs would have. This problem of space discrepancy in plotting subjects and objects seems to have escaped the attention of most of the researchers in multidimensional unfolding analysis.

In 1994 and 1996, Nishisato repeatedly discussed the matter, and presented his discovery that the Coombs problem of multidimensional unfolding can be solved if we plot subjects using their normed weights and objects using their projected weights; then the joint configuration provides a solution to the Coombs problem of multidimensional unfolding. In other words, the idea is to project objects onto the space of subjects. Let us look at some illustrations.

Numerical Verifications: Ranking of Six Cars

The following examples are modified outputs from the computer program DUAL3 for Windows (Nishisato & Nishisato, 1994) with some annotations. Unlike some of the other procedures so far proposed, dual scaling can handle rank-order data or paired-comparison data even from only one subject. Let us start with rank-order data from one subject.

```
------------------------------------------------------------
    (a) Data = [ 1 2 3 4 5 6]
        Results: Eigenvalue= 0.4667 (100 per cent)
        Normed weight of subject 1=1.00
        Projected weights of cars:
            A=1.00, B=0.60, C=0.20, D=-0.20, E=-0.60, F=-1.00
------------------------------------------------------------
```

It is obvious that the ranking of the distances from the subject to the cars is exactly the same as the input data. Note that the eigenvalue is equal to $(n + 1)/[3(n - 1)] = 7/15 = 0.4667$, as we will see from the formula later. Let us add the ranking by the second subject to the data set, and analyze the 2×6 data.

```
----------------------------------------------------------------
(b)  Data = 1 2 3 4 5 6
            5 3 6 2 1 4

Results:

    Eigenvalue 1= 0.3333 (71.4 per cent)
    Eigenvalue 2= 0.1333 (28.6 per cent)

Normed weights of subject 1= 1.00(dim 1), -1.00 (dim 2)
Normed weights of subject 2= -1.00 (dim 1), -1.00 (dim 2)
Projected weights of A =  0.80 (dim 1), -0.20 (dim 2)
Projected weights of B =  0.20 (dim 1), -0.40 (dim 2)
Projected weights of C =  0.60 (dim 1),  0.40 (dim 2)
Projected weights of D = -0.40 (dim 1), -0.20 (dim 2)
Projected weights of E = -0.80 (dim 1), -0.20 (dim 2)
Projected weights of F = -0.40 (dim 1),  0.60 (dim 2)
----------------------------------------------------------------
```

Notice that the sum of the eigenvalues is the same as the eigenvalue from the previous case of one subject, that is, .4667. The DUAL3 provides calculations of the distance between each subject and each car. Although this is what is called the between-set distance, there is no problem of the space for rows being different from that for columns because we have projected cars (columns) onto the space of subjects (rows), this scaling being called nonsymmetric scaling. When we use only the first solution to calculate and rank the distances, the resultant ranks are called the rank-one approximation. When the distances are calculated by the first two solutions, it is called the rank-two approximation. These results are as follows:

```
----------------------------------------------------------------
(1)  Subject-Car Squared Distances Based on the First
     Dimension
  Subject    A       B       C       D       E       F
----------------------------------------------------------------
    1       .04     .64     .16    1.96    3.24    1.96
    2      3.24    1.44    2.56     .36     .04     .36
```

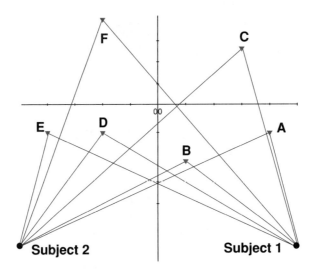

FIG. 15.1. Two-dimensional perfect solution for cars and subjects.

```
-----------------------------------------------------------------
Ranks of the Above Distances (Rank 1 Approximation)
Subject    A        B        C        D         E        F
-----------------------------------------------------------------

   1       1        3        2       4.5        6       4.5
   2       6        4        5       2.5        1       2.5
-----------------------------------------------------------------
(2) Subject-Car Squared Distance Based on Two Dimensions
Subject    A        B        C        D        E        F
-----------------------------------------------------------------

   1      .68     1.00      .12     2.16     3.88     4.52
   2     3.88     1.80     4.52     1.00      .68     2.92
-----------------------------------------------------------------
Ranks of the Distances (Rank 2 Approximation)
Subject    A        B        C        D        E        F
-----------------------------------------------------------------

   1       1        2        3        4        5        6
   2       5        3        6        2        1        4
-----------------------------------------------------------------
```

We can see that the rank-two approximation reproduces the input ranks correctly. See Fig. 15.1. Let us now add one more subject to the data set, and see how these ranks are approximated by solutions 1, 2, and 3.

```
-----------------------------------------------------------------
(c) Data =  1   2   3   4   5   6
            5   3   6   2   1   4
            2   1   3   5   4   6
```

Results:

```
Eigenvalue 1 = 0.3268 (70.0 per cent)
Eigenvalue 2 = 0.1251 (26.8 per cent)
Eigenvalue 3 = 0.0148 ( 3.2 per cent)
```

Normed weights for subjects

```
Subject 1 = -1.15 (dim 1), -0.30 (dim 2), -1.26 (dim 3)
Subject 2 =  0.70 (dim 1), -1.56 (dim 2), -0.27 (dim 3)
Subject 3 = -1.09 (dim 1), -0.69 (dim 2),  1.16 (dim 3)
```

Projected weights for cars

```
A = -0.74 (dim 1),  0.07 (dim 2), -0.14 (dim 3)
B = -0.55 (dim 1), -0.39 (dim 2),  0.12 (dim 3)
C = -0.38 (dim 1),  0.45 (dim 2),  0.08 (dim 3)
D =  0.43 (dim 1), -0.15 (dim 2), -0.20 (dim 3)
E =  0.54 (dim 1), -0.41 (dim 2),  0.09 (dim 3)
F =  0.70 (dim 1),  0.43 (dim 2),  0.05 (dim 3)
```

Again, the sum of the eigenvalues is equal to .4667. Because the rank-one approximation shows substantial discrepancies between the approximated and the input ranks, we look at only the rank-two (see Fig. 15.2) and the rank-three approximations.

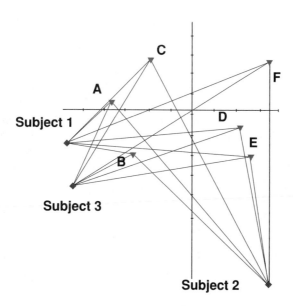

FIG. 15.2.   Two-dimensional approximation to data, cars, and subjects.

```
--------------------------------------------------------------
Subject-Car Squared Distances Based on Solutions 1 and 2
Subject    A       B        C        D        E        F
--------------------------------------------------------------
   1      0.31    0.37     1.16     2.53     2.86     3.96
   2      4.76    2.92     5.24     2.05     1.34     3.98
   3      0.70    0.38     1.80     2.61     2.72     4.46
--------------------------------------------------------------

Ranks of the Above Distances (Rank 2 Approximation)
Subject    A       B        C        D        E        F
--------------------------------------------------------------
   1       1       2        3        4        5        6
   2       5       3        6        2        1        4
   3       2       1        3        4        5        6
--------------------------------------------------------------

Subject-Car Squared Distances Based on Three Solutions
Subject    A       B        C        D        E        F
--------------------------------------------------------------
   1      1.57    2.27     2.96     3.65     4.67     5.68
   2      4.77    3.07     5.36     2.05     1.47     4.08
   3      2.37    1.47     2.96     4.45     3.87     5.68
--------------------------------------------------------------

Ranks of the Above Distances (Rank 3 Approximation)
Subject    A       B        C        D        E        F
--------------------------------------------------------------
   1       1       2        3        4        5        6
   2       5       3        6        2        1        4
   3       2       1        3        5        4        6
--------------------------------------------------------------
```

From the fact that the third eigenvalue is comparatively very small, it is understandable that the rank-two approximation is almost perfect. In comparing the two approximations, we see that there is only one switched pair, the ranks of D and E by Subject 3, that is, 4 and 5 for D and E, respectively, in the rank-two approximation and 5 and 4 for D and E in the rank-three approximation, which is the perfect reproduction of the input ranks. Another output of DUAL3 for Windows is the sums of the squared discrepancies between the input ranks and approximated ranks. In the current example, we obtain the following:

```
--------------------------------------------------------------
Sums of Squared Rank Discrepancies
Subject        Rank 1        Rank 2        Rank 3
--------------------------------------------------------------
   1             0             0             0
   2            20             0             0
   3             4             2             0
--------------------------------------------------------------
```

This table shows that the ranks of Subject 1 were reproduced even with the rank-one approximation, the ranks of Subject 2 were reproduced correctly by the rank-two approximation, and the ranks of Subject 3 were well approximated by the rank-one approximation, but needed the rank-three approximation for perfect reproduction.

Characteristics of Dual-Scaling Solutions

We have seen that dual-scaling solutions provide a joint configuration of subjects and objects from analysis of rank-order data and paired-comparison data, or more generally, dominance data. There are a number of aspects of the solutions one should keep in mind (Nishisato, 2000b).

Total Information in Ordinal Measurement

It would be of interest to assess how much information one can capture from rank-order and paired-comparison data by dual scaling. First, let us define the total information as the sum of squares of all singular values associated with the $N \times n$ dominance table, or the eigenvalues of $n \times n\mathbf{H}_n$.

Then, the total information T is given by

$$T = \text{tr}(\mathbf{H}_n) = \frac{1}{Nn(n-1)^2}\text{tr}(\mathbf{E}'\mathbf{E}). \tag{21}$$

Noting that the elements of $\mathbf{E}$ can be generated by the de Leeuw formula, we can obtain the total information from the trace of $\mathbf{E}'\mathbf{E}$ as

$$\text{tr}(\mathbf{E}\mathbf{E}') = \text{tr}(\mathbf{E}\mathbf{E}') = N\sum_{j=1}^{n}(n+1-2R_j)^2 \tag{22}$$

$$= N\sum[(n+1)^2 - 4(n+1)R_j + 4R_j^2], \tag{23}$$

$$= Nn(n+1)^2 - 4N(n+1)\sum R_j + 4N\sum R_j^2, \tag{24}$$

$$= Nn(n+1)^2 - 4N(n+1)\frac{n(n+1)}{2} + \frac{4Nn(n+1)(2n+1)}{6}, \tag{25}$$

$$= \frac{Nn}{3}(n-1)(n+1). \tag{26}$$

Therefore, the trace of $\mathbf{H}_n$ is given by

$$\text{tr}(\mathbf{H}_n) = \frac{1}{Nn(n-1)^2}\text{tr}(\mathbf{E}\mathbf{E}') = \frac{n+1}{3(n-1)}. \tag{27}$$

Thus, the total information is bounded by

$$\frac{1}{3} \leq \text{tr}(\mathbf{H}_n) \leq 1. \tag{28}$$

The minimal information is obtained when n goes to infinity, and the maximum of 1 is attained when $n = 2$. What does this mean?

Distribution of Information

The last formula for the total information tells us the interesting fact that the total information is solely a function of the number of objects and is independent of the number of judges. This has a number of implications for the distribution of information in rank-order data. Let us start with special cases.

The Case of One Judge.   Dual scaling is a descriptive method, as opposed to an inferential method. As such, the independence of the total information of the number of judges implies that dual scaling has no numerical difficulty in solving the eigenequation when there is only one judge! We already have seen an example of this earlier, in which a single component exhaustively explained the entire data, irrespective of the number of objects. Although one solution exhaustively explains the total information, the eigenvalue varies between one third and one, depending on the number of objects.

The independence of the total information of the number of judges may be why rank order data are called row-conditional, that is, two rank numbers are comparable when they come from a single row (judge) and are not comparable when they come from two different rows (judges).

Dual scaling of data from many judges then is only a matter of calculating differentially weighted configurations of objects coming from individual judges.

One-Dimensional Rank-Order Data.   There are three obvious cases when data can be explained by one dimension: first when there is only one judge, second when there are only two objects, irrespective of the number of judges, and third when all the judges provide the same ranking of objects, irrespective of the number of objects and the number of judges. These are special cases, and serve to show some important differences between Coombs's approach and the quantification approach.

Coombs's Unfolding and Dual Scaling.   The preceding two sections serve the purpose of distinguishing between Coombs's approach and dual scaling. First, when data are collected from a single judge, Coombs's method cannot provide a quantitative scale because a single set of ranks does not provide enough quantitative information.

The concept of dimensionality is a point of departure between the two approaches. In dual scaling, the rank numbers are treated as if they were real numbers of equal units, and as such the dimensionality is defined by the rank of the dominance matrix. In contrast, Coombs's approach is an ordinal approach, in which one can distort a multidimensional configuration in any way one likes so long as ordinal information is retained. In this regard, Coombs's approach is logically more sound than dual scaling as a technique for handling ordinal data, but it encounters difficulty when the data size increases.

If we limit the data size to a size manageable by Coombs's unidimensional model, we can vividly see the difference between the two approaches. Let us look at a numerical example:

```
Coombs's Unidimensional Data      Dual Scaling Results


                  Object


Subject  A  B  C  D  E  F      Solution Eigenvalue   Delta
-----------------------------  ----------------------------
   1     1  2  3  4  5  6          1        0.261      55.45
   2     2  1  3  4  5  6          2        0.107      22.86
   3     2  3  1  4  5  6          3        0.060      12.66
   4     2  3  4  1  5  6          4        0.032       6.74
   5     3  2  4  1  5  6          5        0.011       2.26
   6     3  4  2  1  5  6      ----------------------------
   7     3  4  2  5  1  6                   0.470
   8     3  4  5  2  1  6
   9     3  4  5  2  6  1
  10     4  3  5  2  6  1
  11     4  3  5  6  2  1
  12     4  5  3  6  2  1
  13     5  4  3  6  2  1
  14     5  4  6  3  2  1
  15     5  6  4  3  2  1
  16     6  5  4  3  2  1
-----------------------------
```

This table contains rank-order data that satisfy the conditions of unidimensionality under Coombs's model. Thus, with Coombs's unfolding technique, we can identify a unidimensional continuum from which the foregoing set of rank orders can be generated. Notice how only one pair of adjacent ranks changes as we go down the table from Judge 1 to Judge 16. The table also shows some statistics from dual scaling, where we first note that information is scattered over five dimensions rather than one because of the rank of the corresponding dominance matrix is five. This is so even though Coombs's approach provides a unidimensional scale! Fig. 15.3 is a plot of the first two dual-scaling components, in which we can see that by rotating axes slightly, we may project objects A through F on a single axis with the correct rank order. Typically, Coombs's method does not provide exact locations of subjects, whereas dual scaling yields a joint graph of both objects and subjects. The positions of 16 respondents are shown in Fig. 15.3 without identifications of the subjects.

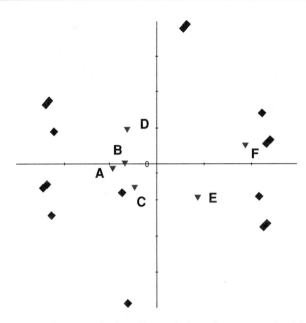

FIG. 15.3.   First two dual-scaling solutions for cars and subjects.

In dual scaling one obtains an approximation to ranks from each judge in terms of the ranking of the distances from each judge to objects. Unfortunately, treating ranks as cardinal numbers would not allow us to further reduce the dimensionality of the space. A serious implication of handling ranks like cardinal numbers is that we must deal with the problem of discrepant spaces: The space for judges and that for objects have different coordinates, and this discrepancy necessitates projecting objects onto the space of judges when we want to explain the relation between objects and judges. This problem of discrepant spaces does not arise with Coombs's method for the reason stated earlier.

Practically speaking, however, dual scaling can handle data collected from any number of judges, even as few as one judge or as many as 10,000, whereas Coombs's approach often encounters the problem of insufficient information in the data or too much information to deal with. As such, dual scaling, or any of the Guttman-type method, is available for any rank-order data without ever facing ill-conditioned data as often seen in the other metric approaches to the Coombs problem of multidimensional unfolding.

Dual scaling is not a model-based approach, but a data-based method with singular value decomposition, an optimal method of mathematical decomposition. Data will guide us to what kind of information it can extract, and no matter what data we may have, it always works.

Goodness of Fit. The traditional statistic of δ, the percentage of the total information explained, is useful in many cases:

$$\delta_j = 100\frac{\lambda_j}{T}, \tag{29}$$

where λ_j is the jth eigenvalue of $\mathbf{H}_n$.

Because we are dealing with rank orders, however, a better statistic than this would be the goodness of fit of recovered ranks to the original ranks. Nishisato (1996) considered two statistics: (a) the sum of squares of rank discrepancies between observed ranks (R_{ij}) and recovered ranks ($R*_{ij}$)for each solution, or multiple solutions, for each judge or all the judges; and (b) the percentage of the foregoing statistic as compared to the worst ranking, that is, the reversed ranking of the observed for each judge, δ_{ij}(rank), or all the judges, δ_j(rank). For the first choice, we should modify it to calculate the average over n objects because the original statistic grows larger as the number of objects increases. We thus obtain the modified first pair of statistics as

$$\delta_i(\text{diff}) = \frac{\sum_{j=1}^{n}(R_{ij} - R_{*ij})^2}{n}, \tag{30}$$

$$\delta(\text{diff}) = \frac{\sum_{i=1}^{N} \delta_i(\text{diff})}{N}, \tag{31}$$

We can also calculate the second pair of statistics as

$$\delta_{ij}(\text{rank}) = 100 - \frac{100\sum_{j=1}^{n}(R_{ij} - R_{*ij})^2}{\sum_{h=0}^{n-1}(n - 2h - 1)^2}, \tag{32}$$

$$\delta_j(\text{rank}) = \frac{\sum_{i=1}^{N} \delta_{ij}(\text{rank})}{N}, \tag{33}$$

Here, we propose yet another statistic, the percentage of the squared discrepancies between the observed ranks and the tied ranks (i.e., all objects being given the same rank), δ_{*ij}(rank), that is, the case of no discrimination:

$$\delta_{*ij}(\text{rank}) = 100 - \frac{\sum_{i=1}^{n}(R_{ij} - R_{*ij})^2}{\sum_{j=1}^{n}[(R_{ij} - (n + 1)/2]^2}, \tag{34}$$

$$\delta_{*j}(\text{rank}) = \frac{\sum_{i=1}^{N} \delta_{*ij}(\text{rank})}{N}. \tag{35}$$

There must be other ways of evaluating the outcome of scaling. An important point is that we can look at the original data with a new perspective gained from scaling.

CONCLUDING REMARKS

The main message of this chapter is that for multiple-choice data we must use a response-pattern format rather than a subjects-by-items score matrix, and that for dominance data we must project objects onto the space of subjects. For the former, it is a problem of retaining as much information in the data as possible, and we must avoid forcing unreasonable constraints on the data processing; in particular, we should avoid the use of a linear filter in pre-data processing. For dominance data, it seems that we should treat ordinal measurement like cardinal numbers to take advantage of the ease with which we can process data with well-established procedures such as the least-squares method. Combining these two, it is the main conclusion of this chapter that dual scaling offers a satisfactory approach to data analysis in general. We need to be free from the shadow of the well-established linear models, which do not seem to capture much information in the data. Because of the limited space available here, we did not discuss how to assess total information contained in both discrete and continuous multivariate data. As with the case of linear models, we are accustomed to defining the total information in terms of the sum of the eigenvalues. We can learn from dual scaling of discretized data that the traditional definition of information is not appropriate for comparison of information from different data sets (Nishisato, 2002, 2003). This is so because the sum of the eigenvalues does not reflect covariances in the data. A detailed discussion of this matter, however, must be left for another place.

ACKNOWLEDGMENTS

This study was supported by a grant from the Natural Sciences and Engineering Research Council of Canada. The paper was written while the author was a visiting professor at the School of Business Administration, Kwansei Gakuin University, Nishinomiya, Japan.

REFERENCES

Adachi, K. (2000). Keiryo tajigen tenkaiho no henryo model [A random effect model in metric multidimensional unfolding]. *Japanese Journal of Behaviormetrics, 27*, 12–23 (in Japanese, with an English abstract).

Bechtel, G. G. (1968). Folded and unfolded scaling from preferential paired comparisons. *Journal of Mathematical Psychology, 5*, 333–357.

Beltrami, E. (1873). Sulle funzioni bilineari [On the linear functions]. *Giornale di Mathematiche, 11*, 98–106.

Bennett, J. F. (1956). Determination of the number of independent parameters of a score matrix from the examination of rank orders. *Psychometrika, 21*, 383–393.

Bennett, J. F., & Hays, W. L. (1960). Multidimensional unfolding: Determining the dimensionality of ranked preference data. *Psychometrika, 25,* 27–43.

Benzécri, J.-P., et al. (1973). *L'analyse des données: II. L'analyse des correspondances* [Data analysis II: Correspondence analysis]. Paris: Dunod.

Bock, R. D., & Jones, L. V. (1968). *Measurement and prediction of judgment and choice.* San Francisco: Holden-Day.

Bradley, R. A., Katti, S. K., & Coons, I. J. (1962). Optimal scaling of ordered categories. *Psychometrika, 27,* 355–374.

Carroll, J. D. (1972). Individual differences and multidimensional scaling. In R. N. Shepard, A. K. Romney, & S. B. Nerlove (Eds.), *Multidimensional scaling: Theory and applications in the behavioral sciences* (Vol. 1, pp. 105–155). New York: Seminar.

Coombs, C. H. (1950). Psychological scaling without a unit of measurement. *Psychological Review, 57,* 145–158.

Coombs, C. H. (1964). *A theory of data.* New York: Wiley.

Coombs, C. H., & Kao, R. C. (1960). On a connection between factor analysis and multidimensional unfolding. *Psychometrika, 25,* 219–231.

Davidson, J. (1973). A geometrical analysis of the unfolding model: General solutions. *Psychometrika, 38,* 305–336.

de Leeuw, J. (1973). *Canonical analysis of categorical data.* Unpublished doctoral dissertation, Leiden University, the Netherlands.

Eckart, C., & Young, G. (1936). The approximation of one matrix by another of lower rank. *Psychometrika, 1,* 211–218.

Gifi, A. (1990). *Nonlinear multivariate analysis.* New York: Wiley.

Gold, E. M. (1973). Metric unfolding: Data requirements for unique solution and clarification of Schönemann's algorithm. *Psychometrika, 38,* 555–569.

Goode, F. M. (1957). *Interval scale representation of ordered metric scale.* Unpublished manuscript, University of Michigan.

Greenacre, M. J. (1984). *Theory and applications of correspondence analysis* London: Academic.

Greenacre, M. J., & Browne, M. W. (1986). An efficient alternating least-squares algorithm to perform multidimensional unfolding. *Psychometrika, 51,* 241–250.

Greenacre, M. J., & Torres-Lacomba, A. (1999). *A note on the dual scaling of dominance data and its relationship to correspondence analysis.* (Working Paper Ref. 430). Universidat Pompeu Fabra, Departament d'Economia i Empresa, Barcelona, Spain.

Guttman, L. (1941). The quantification of a class of attributes: A theory and method of scale construction. In Committee on Social Adjustment (Ed.), *The prediction of personal adjustment* (pp. 319–348). New York: Social Science Research Council.

Guttman, L. (1946). An approach for quantifying paired comparisons and rank order. *Annals of Mathematical Statistics, 17,* 144–163.

Guttman, L. (1967). The development of nonmetric space analysis: A letter to Professor John Ross. *Multivariate Behavioral Research, 2,* 71–82.

Han, S. T., & Huh, M. H. (1995). Biplot of ranked data. *Journal of the Korean Statistical Society, 24,* 439–451.

Hayashi, C. (1964). Multidimensional quantification of the data obtained by the method of paired comparison. *Annals of the Institute of Statistical Mathematics, 16,* 231–245.

Hays, W. L., & Bennett, J. F. (1961). Multidimensional unfolding: Determining configuration from complete rank order preference data. *Psychometrika, 26,* 221–238.

Heiser, W. J. (1981). *Unfolding analysis of proximity data.* Unpublished doctoral dissertation, Leiden University, the Netherlands.

Hojo, H. (1994). A new method for multidimensional unfolding. *Behaviormetrika, 21,* 131–147.

Hotelling, H. (1933). Analysis of a complex of statistical variables into principal components. *Journal of Educational Psychology, 24,* 417–441, 498–520.

Jordan, C. (1874). Mémoire sur les formes bilineares [Notes on bilinear forms]. *Journal de Mathématiques Pures et Appliquées, Deuxiéme Série, 19*, 35–54.

Kruskal, J. B. (1964a). Multidimensional scaling by optimizing a goodness of fit to a nonmetric hypothesis. *Psychometrika, 29*, 1–28.

Kruskal, J. B. (1964b). Nonmetric multidimensional scaling: A numerical method. *Psychometrika, 29*, 115–129.

Lebart, L., Morineau, A., & Warwick, K. M. (1984). *Multivariate descriptive statistical analysis.* New York: Wiley.

Likert, R. (1932). A technique for the measurement of attitudes. *Archives of Psychology, 140*, 44–53.

McDonald, R. P. (1983). Alternative weights and invariant parameters in optimal scaling. *Psychometrika, 48*, 377–392.

McDonald, R. P., Torii, Y., & Nishisato, S. (1979). Some results on proper eigenvalues and eigenvectors with applications to optimal scaling. *Psychometrika, 44*, 211–227.

Meulman, J. J. (1998). Review of W. J. Krzanowski and F. H. C. Marriott. *Multivariate analysis. Part 1. Distributions, ordinations, and inference.* London: Edward Arnold, 1994. *Journal of Classification, 15*, 297–298.

Nishisato, S. (1978). Optimal scaling of paired comparison and rank-order data: An alternative to Guttman's formulation. *Psychometrika, 43*, 263–271.

Nishisato, S. (1980). *Analysis of categorical data: Dual scaling and its applications.* Toronto: University of Toronto Press.

Nishisato, S. (1993). On quantifying different types of categorical data. *Psychometrika, 58*, 617–629.

Nishisato, S. (1994). *Elements of dual scaling: An introduction to practical data analysis.* Hillsdale, NJ: Lawrence Erlbaum Associates, Inc.

Nishisato, S. (1996). Gleaning in the field of dual scaling. *Psychometrika, 61*, 559–599.

Nishisato, S. (2000a). Data analysis and information: Beyond the current practice of data analysis. In R. Decker & W. Gaul (Eds.), *Classification and information processing at the turn of the millennium*, (pp. 40–51). Heidelberg: Springer-Verlag.

Nishisato, S. (2000b). A characterization of ordinal data. In W. Gaul, O. Opitz, & M. Schader, (Eds.), *Data analysis: Scientific modeling and practical applications* (pp. 285–298). Heidelberg: Springer-Verlag.

Nishisato, S. (2002). Differences in data structure between continuous and categorical variables from dual scaling perspectives, and a suggestion for a unified mode of analysis. *Japanese Journal of Sensory Evaluation, 6*, 89–94 [in Japanese].

Nishisato, S. (2003). Geometric perspectives of dual scaling for assessment of information in data. In H. Yanai, A. Okada, K. Shigemasu, Y. Kano, & J. J. Meulman (Eds.), *New developments in psychometrics* (pp. 453–462). Tokyo: Springer-Verlag.

Nishisato, S., & Arri, P. S. (1975). Nonlinear programming approach to optimal scaling of partially ordered categories. *Psychometrika, 40*, 525–548.

Nishisato, S., & Clavel, J. G. (2003). A note on between-set distances in dual scaling and correspondence analysis. *Behaviormetrika, 30*, 87–98.

Nishisato, S., & Nishisato, I. (1994). *The DUAL3 for Windows.* Toronto: MicroStats.

Okamoto, Y. (1995). Unfolding by the criterion of the fourth quantification method. *Journal of Behaviormetrics, 22*, 126–134 [in Japanese with English abstract].

Pearson, K. (1901). On lines and planes of closest fit to systems of points in space. *Philosophical Magazine and Journal of Science, Series 6, 2*, 559–572.

Phillips, J. P. N. (1971). A note on the presentation of ordered metric scaling. *British Journal of Mathematical and Statistical Psychology, 24*, 239–250.

Schönemann, P. (1970). On metric multidimensional unfolding. *Psychometrika, 35*, 167–176.

Schönemann, P., & Wang, M. M. (1972). An individual difference model for the multidimensional analysis of preference data. *Psychometrika, 37*, 275–309.

Schmidt, E. (1907). Zür Theorie der linearen und nichtlinearen Integleichungen Erster Teil. Entwicklung willkürlicher Functionen nach Syetemen vorgeschriebener. *Mathematische Annalen, 63*, 433–476.

Shepard, R. N. (1962a). The analysis of proximities: Multidimensional scaling with an unknown distance function. I. *Psychometrika, 27*, 125–140.

Shepard, R. N. (1962b). The analysis of proximities: Multidimensional scaling with an unknown distance function. II. *Psychometrika, 27*, 219–245.

Sixtl, F. (1973). Probabilistic unfolding. *Psychometrika, 38*, 235–248.

Slater, P. (1960). Analysis of personal preferences. *British Journal of Statistical Psychology, 3*, 119–135.

Tanaka, Y., & Asano, C. (1978). A generalized method of optimal scaling for partially ordered categories. In *Proceedings of the Third Symposium on Computational Statistics* (pp. 324–330). Berlin: Springer-Verlag.

Tanaka, Y., & Kodake, K. (1980). Computational aspects of optimal scaling for ordered categories. *Behaviormetrika, 7*, 35–46.

Torgerson, W. S. (1958). *Theory and methods of scaling*. New York: Wiley.

Tsujitani, M. (1988a). Graphical analysis of association in cross classification having ordered categories. *Behaviormetrics, 24*, 41–53.

Tsujitani, M. (1988b). Optimal scaling of association models when category scores have a natural ordering. *Statistics and Probability Letters, 6*, 175–180.

Tucker, L. R. (1960). Intra-individual and inter-individual multidimensionality. In H. Gulliksen & S. Messick (Eds.), *Psychological scaling* (pp. 155–167). New York: Wiley.

van de Velden, M. (2000). Dual scaling and correspondence analysis of rank order data. In R. D. H. Heijmans, D. S. G. Pollock, & A. Satorra (Eds.), *Innovations in multivariate statistical analysis* (pp. 87–97). Dordrecht: Kluwer.

16

Missing Data and the General Transformation Approach to Time Series Analysis

Wayne F. Velicer
University of Rhode Island

Suzanne M. Colby
Brown University

INTRODUCTION

Time series analysis is a statistical procedure appropriate for repeated observations on a single subject or unit. It can be viewed as an exemplar of longitudinal methods. A practical advantage of the procedure is that it is highly appropriate for the type of data often available in applied settings. A theoretical strength is that the method emphasizes the nature of the change process and is appropriate for assessing the pattern of change over time. The goal of the analysis may be to determine the nature of the process that describes an observed behavior or to evaluate the effects of an intervention. Modern time series analysis and related research methods represent a sophisticated leap in the ability to analyze longitudinal data gathered on single subjects.

A very important practical problem for time series analysis is missing data. Like other statistical procedures, the analytic methods for time series were initially developed under the assumption of complete data. Missing data are an almost unavoidable problem in time series analysis and present a number of unique challenges. Life events will result in missing data even for the most conscientious researchers. Researchers typically employed a number of ad hoc procedures to address the problem of missing data, and the performance of these methods was

509

either unknown or poor, particularly when the percentage of data missing increased. In the last two decades, a number of statistical methods have been developed to provide more-accurate methods to address the missing-data problem (Graham, Cumsille, & Elek-Fisk, 2003; Hall et al., 2001; Little & Rubin, 1987; Schafer, 1997; Schafer & Graham, 2002). The application of these procedures presents several unique challenges.

One of the major characteristics of time series data is the inherent dependence present in a data set that results from repeated measurements over time on a single subject or unit. All longitudinal designs must take the potential relationship between observations over time into account. In many statistical procedures, the structure of the data refers to the relationship between multiple variables all assessed at the same time. In univariate time series analysis, the structure of the data refers to the relationship between the same variable measured on multiple occasions. It must be assessed to account for the dependence in the data. In multivariate time series, structure becomes even more complicated, involving the relationship between variables, between a variable on different occasions, and between the same variables on different occasions.

In an extensive simulation study, Velicer and Colby (in press) compared four different methods of handling missing data in an autoregressive integrated moving average (ARIMA) (1, 0, 0) model: (a) deletion of missing observations from the analysis, (b) substitution of the mean of the series, (c) substitution of the mean of the two adjacent observations, and (d) maximum likelihood estimation (Jones, 1980). The choice of method had a major impact on the analysis. The maximum likelihood procedure for handling missing data outperformed all others. Although this result was expected, the degree of accuracy was very impressive. The Velicer and Colby (in press) study investigated missing-data procedures when all assumptions were met. It is also critical to evaluate the performance of missing-data procedures when violations of the assumptions occur. This chapter addresses that issue.

The chapter unfolds as follows. After a general overview, we provide an introduction to the major concepts, issues, and terminology used in time series analysis, including a specific class of time series known as autoregressive integrated moving average models. Challenges involved with model specification are summarized and alternative procedures for analyzing data without model specification are described. Then we present an overview of missing-data procedures. Little and Rubin (1987), Schafer (1997), and Schafer and Graham (2002) provided thorough theoretical and mathematical coverage of handling missing-data generally; this section reviews the limited literature on missing-data procedures appropriate for time series analysis. We devote a section each to the results of three simulation studies that evaluated an algorithm for missing data in time series analysis, the Jones (1980) maximum likelihood algorithm available in SAS (SAS Institute, 1988). Each study was designed to test the algorithm under violations of assumptions that are likely to occur in applied behavioral research. These include, as discussed in the respective sections, model misspecification, systematically missing data, and nonnormality. The final section provides a summary discussion of the implications of these findings for handling missing data in time series analysis.

OVERVIEW OF TIME SERIES ANALYSIS

Time series analysis involves repeated observations on a single unit (often a single subject) over time. In psychology, the analysis of interest is often an interrupted time series analysis. The interruption corresponds to the occurrence of an intervention, and the goal is to evaluate its effect. Traditional between-groups statistical procedures cannot be employed because repeated observations on the same unit cannot be assumed to be independent. The presence of dependence may substantially bias a statistical test that does not take it into account. The direction of the bias will depend on the direction of the dependence. The most widely employed methods of analysis for time series designs are based on the ARIMA models (Box & Jenkins, 1976; Box, Jenkins, & Reinsel, 1994; Box & Tiao, 1965). These procedures permit the effects of dependence to be statistically removed from the data (Glass, Willson, & Gottman, 1975; Gottman, 1981; Velicer & Fava, 2003).

Time series analysis has generated widespread interest for a number of reasons. First, time series designs are particularly applicable to the study of problems in applied settings where more traditional between-subject designs are often impossible or very difficult to implement. Second, time series designs can make a compelling case regarding causality because of the temporal occurrence of both the intervention and the effect of the intervention. Third, time series designs possess the additional advantage of permitting the study of the pattern of intervention effects across time (i.e., temporary effects vs. permanent effects, changes in slope as well as changes in level) over and above the usual question of the existence of a mean treatment effect.

The employment of time series methods also suffers from several drawbacks. First, generalizability cannot be inferred from a single study, only through systematic replication. Second, traditional measures may be inappropriate for time series designs; measures are required that can be repeated a large number of times on a single subject, usually at short intervals. Third, a large number of observations is required for accurate model specification. Model specification is a necessary step to remove the dependence present in the data. Finally, time series analysis requires complete data for analysis.

ARIMA(p, d, q) Modeling

The most widely used time series analysis procedure is described by Glass et al. (1975), following Box and Jenkins (1976; Box & Tiao, 1965). It involves a two-step process: first, the researcher determines which of a family of ARIMA(p, d, q) models is appropriate for the data; then the researcher employs a specific transformation appropriate to the specified model to transform the dependent observed variable (Z_i) into a serially independent variable (Y_i). Intervention effects can then be evaluated by a general least squares estimate of the model parameters. This procedure suffers from a number of drawbacks including (a) the requirement of a large number of data points for accurate model specification (b) mathematical complexity, and (c) problems with accurately and reliably performing the model specification task, even when the recommended minimum number of observations is obtained (Velicer & Harrop, 1983).

A key concept for time series analysis is dependence. Calculating the autocorrelations for various lags assesses dependence. Whereas correlation coefficient estimates the relationship between two variables measured on a single occasion on multiple subjects, an autocorrelation estimates the relationship between the same variable measured on multiple occasions on a single subject. For example, for a series of observations, if the second observation is paired with the first, the third observation paired with the second, and so on, until the last observation is paired with the second-from-the-last observation, the correlation between the paired observations is the *lag-one autocorrelation*. If the third is paired with the first and each subsequent observation with the observation two occasions behind, the correlation is the *lag-two autocorrelation*. The *lag* of an autocorrelation refers to how far in the past you go. Autocorrelations range between 1.00 and -1.00. In the behavioral sciences, the size of the autocorrelation will typically decrease as the lag increases. The exception is seasonal or cyclic data, which may involve patterns that reflect the day of the week or month when an activity increases or decreases (e.g., an individual who drinks alcohol in a weekly pattern may have a high lag-seven autocorrelation). The pattern of the autocorrelation and the related *partial autocorrelations* at each lag are employed as the basis for determining the specific ARIMA model that best models the data. Plots of the autocorrelations and partial autocorrelations along with the related confidence intervals are provided in the printed output of most time series analysis programs. [Partial autocorrelations are mathematically complex and will not be defined here; see Box et al. (1994) for a detailed description]. A *white-noise model* is one where there is no dependence in the data, that is, the autocorrelations and partial autocorrelations for all lags are zero.

Time Series Model Specification

In interrupted time series analysis, model specification often represents a first step, a preliminary to the ultimate goal of the analysis. The ultimate goal is the estimating and testing of the pre- and postintervention parameters (Box & Jenkins, 1976; Box & Tiao, 1965; Glass, et al., 1975; McCleary & Hay, 1980; Velicer & McDonald, 1984, 1991). However, model specification can also be the primary goal of a time series analysis. Determining the specific ARIMA model can identify a basic process underlying a particular behavior, thereby addressing important theoretical and etiologic issues.

Model specification can be a difficult and problematic procedure. Although an extensive variety of procedures has been developed to identify the model (Glass et al., 1975; Velicer & Fava, 2003), no clear consensus has emerged about which method is best. Model specification has also been problematic because of the large number of data points required, the complexity of the procedures, and problems with accuracy and reliability of some methods, even under ideal circumstances (Velicer & Harrop, 1983). In this section, some procedures and inherent problems in model specification will be described.

Definition of Model Specification

The ARIMA(p, d, q) model represents a family of models with the parameters designating which specific model is involved. The first parameter (p) is the order of the autoregressive parameter and the last parameter (q) is the order of the moving average parameter. The middle parameter (d) represents the presence of instability or stochastic drift in the series. Each of the parameters of the model may be of order 0, 1, 2, 3, or more, although higher order models are unusual in the behavioral sciences (Glass et al., 1975). A parameter equal to zero indicates the absence of that term from the model.

Order refers to how many preceding observations must be considered to account for the dependence in the series. Accuracy is difficult because higher order autocorrelation terms are typically closer to zero than first-order terms and therefore are more likely to be included within the bounds for any error estimate. Order reflects how far into the past one must go to predict the present observation.

Degree of dependence is measured by the autocorrelation coefficients and refers to how large the autocorrelations are on a scale between 0.0 and 1.0. This can be interpreted as the strength of relationship between consecutive measurements. The accuracy of estimation is largely a function of the number of observations. The degree of dependence indicates the extent to which an observation at any point in time is predictable from one or more preceding observations. Autocorrelation in the moving average component of a time series (ARIMA) model is represented by the coefficient θ_i, where i refers to the lag of the autocorrelation. In the autoregressive component of an ARIMA model, autocorrelation is represented by the coefficient ϕ_j, where j refers to the lag of the autocorrelation.

Direction of dependence refers to whether the autocorrelation is positive or negative. This can be determined with a high degree of accuracy when the dependence is clearly nonzero. When the sign of the autocorrelation is negative, a high level for the series on one occasion predicts a low level for the series on the next occasion. When the sign is positive, an above-average level of the series on one occasion predicts a higher than average level on the next occasion.

Interrupted Time Series Analysis

The simplest interrupted time series analysis is a design that involves repeated observations on a single unit followed by an intervention followed by additional observations of the unit. The purpose of the analysis is to determine whether the intervention had an effect. The analysis involves preprocessing of the data to remove the effects of dependence. Several alternative procedures will be described. The analysis then involves a general linear model analysis using a general least squares or Aitken estimator (Aitken, 1934; Morrison, 1983). The intervention can be an experimental manipulation, such as the implementation of some kind of pharmacologic or behavioral treatment, or it can be a naturally occurring event, such as a change in policy or funding for a public program. If the intervention effect is significant, it is of interest to evaluate the nature of the effect.

Box–Jenkins Intervention Analysis

An intervention with a single subject or experimental unit can be evaluated using a Box–Jenkins analysis. The Box–Jenkins procedure (Box & Jenkins, 1976), as adapted by Glass et al. (1975), is a two-step process. As described earlier, the autocorrelations and the partial autocorrelations are calculated for various lags. This information is the basis for specifying the ARIMA model, that is, specifying the values for p, d, and q. Model specification determines the specific transformation matrix to be used. The purpose of this transformation is to remove the dependence from the data so that the data series meets the assumptions of the general linear model (GLM).

The GLM is the general analytic procedure that includes multiple regression, analysis of variance, and analysis of covariance as special cases. Once transformed, the data are analyzed with a modified GLM program, and the parameters are estimated and tested for significance. With the dependence in the data accounted for, the analysis follows standard estimation and testing procedures.

A basic interrupted time series problem would be to determine whether the average level of the series has changed as a result of the intervention. In such an analysis two parameters are estimated: L, the level of the series, and DL, the change in level after intervention. A test of significance would then examine the hypothesis of prime interest, $H_0: DL = 0$. In algebraic terms this can be expressed in terms of the general linear model as

$$\mathbf{Z} = \mathbf{Xb} + \mathbf{a}, \tag{1}$$

where $\mathbf{Z}$ is an $N \times 1$ vector of observed variables, such that N is the total number of observations, with the first $\mathbf{z}_i$ observations occurring prior to the intervention, and $\mathbf{X}$ is an $N \times p$ design matrix, where p is the number of parameters estimated, $\mathbf{b}$ is the $p \times 1$ vector of parameters, and $\mathbf{a}$ is the $N \times 1$ vector of residuals.

The usual least squares solution, which minimizes the sum of the squared errors, is

$$\mathbf{b} = (\mathbf{X}'\mathbf{X})^{-1}\mathbf{X}'\mathbf{Z}, \tag{2}$$

and a test of significance for the null hypothesis H$_0$: $b_i = 0$ is given by

$$t_{bi} = b_i/s_{bi}, \tag{3}$$

where

$$s_{bi}^2 = s_a^2 C^{ii}, \tag{4}$$

and s_a^2 is the estimate of the error variance and C^{ii} is the ith diagonal element of $(\mathbf{X}'\mathbf{X})^{-1}$. The test statistic would have a **t** distribution with degrees of freedom $N - p$. This is the same test of significance that is used for testing whether the regression weight for a predictor is significant in multiple regression.

The general linear model cannot be directly applied to time series analysis because of the presence of dependence in the residuals. It is necessary to perform a transformation on the observed variable Z_t to remove dependence prior to the statistical analysis. A transformation matrix **T** must be found, yielding

$$\mathbf{Y} = \mathbf{TZ}, \tag{5}$$

and

$$\mathbf{X}^* = \mathbf{TX}. \tag{6}$$

The purpose of the model-specification step is to determine the appropriate transformation of **Z** to **Y**. The particular ARIMA(p, d, q) model will determine the specific content of the transformation matrix **T**. Because the correction for dependence involves previous observations, all transformation matrices will have a similar form, a lower triangular matrix.

Given **T**, the estimate of the parameters **b** may be expressed as a general least squares problem, that is,

$$\mathbf{b} = (\mathbf{X}'\mathbf{T}'\mathbf{TX})^{-1}\mathbf{X}'\mathbf{T}'\mathbf{TZ} = (\mathbf{X}^{*'}\mathbf{X}^*)^{-1}\mathbf{X}^{*'}\mathbf{Y}. \tag{7}$$

The Box–Jenkins approach to intervention analysis has several disadvantages. First, the number of observations required for model specification is often prohibitive for research in applied settings. Second, even when the required number of observations has been attained, correct specification is problematic (Velicer & Harrop, 1983). Third, the method is complex, making applications by the mathematically unsophisticated researcher difficult. Two alternative approaches are described in the next section, all of which attempt to avoid the problematic model-specification step.

Simonton First-Order Approach

Simonton (1977) proposed a procedure that avoids the problem of model specification by using an estimate of the variance–covariance matrix based on a pooling of the observations across all subjects observed. This approach, however, requires the basic assumption that all series fit an ARIMA(1, 0, 0) model. Although the assumption is theoretically indefensible, empirical investigations indicate that this procedure works well in a wide variety of cases (Harrop & Velicer, 1985).

Velicer–McDonald General Transformation Approach

Instead of trying to determine the specific transformation matrix (i.e., the one matrix uniquely appropriate for the specific underlying ARIMA model of a series), Velicer and McDonald (1984) proposed a *general transformation matrix* **T**, with the numerical values of the elements of **T** being estimated for each problem. The rationale for a general matrix is that all transformation matrices have an identical form—a lower triangular matrix with equal subdiagonals. Weight vectors with five nonzero weights are accurate for most cases. A greater number of weights can be employed where indicated by appropriate diagnostics (Velicer & McDonald, 1984). The accuracy of this approach has been supported by two simulation studies (Harrop & Velicer, 1985, 1990).

This approach was extended to provide a solution to the problem of pooled time series analysis (Velicer & McDonald, 1991). Pooled time series analysis refers to the problem of combining data from several different units or individuals. In the Velicer–McDonald approach, all observations for all the units are represented in a single vector. This vector contains the set of subvectors for the individual units combined in the form of a single vector rather than a matrix with multiple columns. In this case, the vector **Z** is composed of a subvector of N observations (pre- and postintervention) for each of the experimental units. The method requires the use of a patterned transformation matrix **W** with repeating general transformation matrices in diagonal blocks and null matrices elsewhere. The specific choice of the design matrix **X** and the number of units will be dictated by the particular questions of interest. As with any of the analytic approaches, diagnostic indicators such as the Ljung and Box (1978) test may be used to test the fit of the model [see Dielman (1989) for a more extensive discussion of testing model assumptions].

An advantage of this approach is that it can be adapted with only minor alterations to implement either the Box–Jenkins (1976; Glass et al., 1975) or Simonton (1977) procedures. For the Glass et al. (1975) approach, a specific transformation matrix corresponding to a particular ARIMA(p, d, q) model would replace the general transformation matrix. Following the Simonton (1977) approach, the ARIMA(1, 0, 0) transformation matrix would be used for all cases instead of the general transformation approach. The approach can be implemented by existing computer programs.

MISSING DATA AND TIME SERIES ANALYSIS

Missing data is a common problem when studies are characterized by repeated observations on the same experimental unit, particularly when the experimental unit is a person (Laird, 1988). Thus, time series designs in clinical research are particularly susceptible to missing-data problems, which present a number of unique challenges. Methods for handling missing data in time series analysis vary in terms of their ease of implementation and their appropriateness for time-ordered data.

Missing-Data Procedures

The problem of missing data in time series designs has received little attention in the behavioral sciences area until recently. This reflects the situation in data analysis in general, where ad hoc methods dominated until a new generation of computer-intensive statistical methods were developed. A recent review by Schafer and Graham (2002) provides a guide to recently developed statistical procedures like maximum likelihood estimation and multiple imputation and why these methods are generally superior to either ad hoc procedures or early statistical methods like regression methods.

   The choice of an appropriate method for handling missing data depends in part on why the data are missing, or the missing-data mechanism (Little & Rubin, 1987; Schafer, 1997; Schafer & Graham, 2002). Rubin (1976) developed the following classification.

- Data are *missing completely at random* (MCAR) if the observations with any missing values are a random subsample of the full sample. In this case, the missing-data mechanism is unrelated to the model and is therefore ignorable.
- Data are *missing at random* (MAR) if the pattern for a variable is not a function of its observed values, but it may be a function of other values in the model. For example, a response for annual household income on a survey may be missing for several reasons. One reason is that the respondent may not know his or her household income. The missing-data mechanism may be a function of the respondent's age (e.g., very young respondents often do not know their family's income) but not a function of the respondent's household income. MAR is a less stringent assumption than MCAR.
- Values are classified as *nonignorable* if they are systematically missing from the data set, that is, the missingness is a function of the values that are missing.

For example, in a study of self-monitored standard drinks consumed each day, data may be missing on days for which the value of the observation (number of drinks consumed) is very high due to inability or lack of motivation to record data on those days.

Previous Research on Missing Data in Time Series Analysis

An early study of missing data in time series analysis was conducted by Rankin and Marsh (1985), who assessed the effect of different amounts of missing data for 32 simulated time series, modeled after 16 real-world data examples. They concluded that with up to 20% missing data there was little effect on model selection, but the effect is pronounced when more than 40% is missing.

In a recent simulation study, Velicer and Colby (in press) compared four different techniques of handling missing data. Three were widely employed ad hoc methods: deletion of missing observations from the analysis, substitution of the mean of the series, and substitution of the mean of the two adjacent observations. The fourth was a statistical procedure, a maximum likelihood estimation procedure (Jones, 1980) available in SAS/ETS. These methods were tested using generated time series data with varying levels of autocorrelation, slope, and missing data. It was expected that the statistical procedure would be superior. Therefore, the effect of the different factors manipulated and the effect size were of primary interest.

Overall, the maximum likelihood approach was the most accurate; it led to accurate time series parameter estimates in every condition with up to 40% missing data (the highest level of missing data tested). Substituting the mean of the series was judged unacceptable; use of this technique resulted in huge overestimates of the variance and the level of the series, and led to inaccurate estimation of autocorrelation parameters. These effects were apparent even at low levels of missing data (e.g., 10%). Substitution of the mean of the adjacent observations, although intuitively appealing, led to the least accurate estimates of the autocorrelation parameter. Deletion was acceptable at low levels of missing data (e.g., 10%), but was consistently less accurate than maximum likelihood. The results are consistent with other reviews in the missing-data literature (Graham et al., 2003; Hall et al., 2001; Schater & Graham, 2002), which have recommended the use of maximum likelihood and multiple imputation.

Missing Data and Violations

Whereas the Velicer and Colby (in press) study was helpful in establishing the clear superiority of maximum likelihood estimation of missing data in time series analysis, the study was restricted to ideal situations where the model is known and all the assumptions are met. This represents an unrealistic situation; the performance of statistical procedures like the Jones (1980) maximum likelihood (ML) algorithm in more realistic situations is critical. There are three areas of concern that require attention.

Model Specification

When using the Jones (1980) ML algorithm available in SAS/ETS, it is necessary to first specify the model that underlies the series of data. This model specification is used for both ML estimation of missing values and the time series analysis itself. In the simulation study, the model specification issue was circumvented by generating only ARIMA(1, 0, 0) series and then correctly specifying the model for the SAS/ETS program. All missing-data methods compared in this study had the benefit of correct model specification for time series analysis.

Because the underlying model of a time series cannot be known a priori, except in simulation research, it is important to know the effects of model misspecification on ML estimation of missing data and subsequent time series analysis. It is plausible that the same approaches used to analyze time series data without model specification [e.g., specifying a (1, 0, 0) model for all series or specifying a higher order autoregressive model for all series] may also work for estimating missing time series observations. This is one of the issues that will be addressed in this chapter.

Nonignorable Missingness

The mechanism producing the missing data is critical. If the missing-data mechanism and the value of the missing observations are related, the values would be described as "not MAR".

The Velicer and Colby (in press) study provides empirical support for the accuracy of ML estimation of missing data under the ideal condition of data MCAR. This chapter tests the accuracy of ML estimation under more the common condition of data that are MAR. Missing-data patterns examined are systematic (i.e., consecutively or alternating missing) but independent of the values of the missing observations.

Nonnormality

It is common in applied behavioral research for time series data to be attained on a nonnormally distributed variable. Human addictive behavior is often characterized by long periods of moderate behavior followed by brief periods of extreme (e.g., binge) behavior (Velicer & Colby, 1997). Such patterns of behavior result in data distributions that are characterized by positive skew and kurtosis. Because the general linear model and maximum likelihood approaches to estimation assume normally distributed data, it was considered important to test missing-data estimation algorithms under conditions of nonnormality.

This chapter provides a comparison of the algorithms under violations of assumptions likely in applied research settings. Material contained in this chapter originally appeared in Colby (1996), and additional details about the three studies can be found in that source.

ALTERNATIVE MODEL SPECIFICATION APPROACHES (STUDY 1)

Time series analysis typically assumes that the correct model is known. However, available model-specification procedures are not very accurate, even when an adequate number of observations are available. An insufficient number of observations, either by design or due to missing data, will increase problems with accurate model specification.

In this section, the performance of the maximum likelihood procedure for missing data is evaluated employing simulated data under three conditions. First, the correct model is specified. This provides a benchmark for all other comparisons. Second, the Simonton procedure is evaluated, where a (1, 0, 0) model is specified for all examples. Third, the Velicer and McDonald general transformation approach is evaluated, where a (5, 0, 0) model is specified for all examples. The missing-data mechanism is random and the distribution is normal.

Procedure

First, time series data representing several common ARIMA models were generated. Second, several different amounts of data points were randomly eliminated from the series. Third, ML estimation of the missing data was performed under conditions of correct and incorrect model specifications. Fourth, the resulting parameter estimates were compared across these conditions, as well as with criterion values and analyses based on the original, complete data.

Data Generation

All data generation was performed on an IBM 4381 mainframe computer using the most recent version of a FORTRAN computer program that was originally developed by Padia (1975), revised by Harrop and Velicer (1985), and revised again by Colby (1996). This program generates time series data according to a specified underlying ARIMA model and criterion values of series length, level, change in level, slope, change in slope, error variance, and phi.

Four types of series were generated, which represent four different underlying ARIMA models, and then three different proportions of data were randomly eliminated from each series. The mean of the random component of all series was 0.00, and the variance was 1.00. The magnitude of the change in level from pre- to postintervention was 1.50 standard deviations. All series had a positive slope of 15 deg. There was no change in slope from pre- to postintervention.

Number of Observations

Generated time series had $N_1 = N_2 = 50$ data points, the minimum amount recommended for accurate model specification with complete data (Glass et al., 1975). Whereas shorter series are often found in the applied behavioral literature, such series were not examined in this study because its focus was data estimation in time series that met general requirements for accurate analysis in all respects other than the missing data.

Number of Replications

Ten replications in each condition were generated. The number of replications was chosen based on a power analysis by Harrop and Velicer (1990). A preliminary simulation study was performed to verify the results of their analysis for this study. Five, 10, and 20 replications were compared. It was found that 10 and 20 replications yielded estimates that were more accurate and stable than estimates from 5 replications, but there was little or no improvement in the estimates when using 20 replications as opposed to 10. Based on the effect sizes observed by Harrop and Velicer (1990) and Velicer and Colby (in press), 10 replications provided adequate power to detect even very small effect sizes (Cohen, 1988).

Independent Variables Manipulated

There were four independent variables manipulated, resulting in a total of 72 conditions ($4 \times 3 \times 3 \times 2$) with 10 replications in each condition.

Underlying Time Series Model (Four Levels)

Underlying model was manipulated as a between-groups factor. Four different types of underlying ARIMA models were simulated: (a) autoregressive (1, 0, 0) model, (b) autoregressive (2, 0, 0) model, (c) autoregressive (3, 0, 0) model, and (d) moving-averages (0, 0, 1) model.

Proportion of Missing Data (Three Levels)

Data were randomly eliminated from the time series in varying proportions. In the Velicer and Colby (in press) simulation study, 10%, 20%, 30%, and 40% of the data were eliminated, with complete data (0% eliminated) used for purposes of comparison. Effects of proportion of data missing were linear, with accuracy decreasing steadily as proportion of missing data increased. Because no curvilinear relationships were found, it was decided that in this study only two proportions of data would be eliminated (20% versus 40%), and these would be compared to complete data (0% eliminated).

Data Estimation Technique (Three Levels)

Time series parameters were estimated using the Jones (1980) maximum likelihood algorithm with three different model specifications: (a) Simonton, or first-order autoregressive model (1, 0, 0); (b) Velicer and McDonald, or higher order (5, 0, 0) autoregressive model; and (c) Box–Jenkins, or the correctly specified ARIMA model.

Direction of Dependence in the Data (Two Levels)

Positive and negative dependence in the time series was compared, based on findings by Velicer and Colby (in press). There were four types of positive dependence, each specified with respect to the model: (a) for the ARIMA(1, 0, 0) model, $\phi_1 = 0.60$; (b) for the ARIMA(0, 0, 1) model, $\theta_1 = 0.60$; (c) for the ARIMA(2, 0, 0) model, $\phi_1 = 0.60$ and $\phi_2 = 0.30$; and (d) for the ARIMA(3, 0, 0) model, $\phi_1 = 0.60$, $\phi_2 = 0.30$, and $\phi_3 = -0.15$. There were four types of negative dependence, each specified with respect to the model: (a) for the ARIMA(1, 0, 0) model, $\phi_1 = -0.60$; (b) for the ARIMA(0, 0, 1) model, $\theta_1 = -0.60$; (c) for the ARIMA(2, 0, 0) model, $\phi_1 = -0.60$ and $\phi_2 = -0.30$; and (d) for the ARIMA(3, 0, 0) model, $\phi_1 = -0.60$, $\phi_2 = -0.30$, and $\phi_3 = 0.15$.

Dependent Variables

Time series analyses were performed by Proc ARIMA, version 6.06, of SAS/ETS (SAS Institute, 1988). SAS/ETS uses a nonlinear algorithm for its solution. Analyses used default values for starting estimates and stopping criterion. The maximum number of iterations was set at 100. The conditional least squares (CLS) method of estimation was used. Six dependent variables were observed, corresponding to the parameters of ARIMA interrupted time series models (level, slope, error variance, change in level, change in slope, and autocorrelation).

Level

This statistic is equal to the intercept of the best-fitting straight line through the plotted observations of a series. The criterion value of level L was 0 in all series.

Slope

The presence of slope S in a series may change interpretations of results or speculations about processes of change. The population value of S was 15 deg at both pre- and postintervention. SAS provides an estimate of the tangent of the slope, which is equal to 0.27. It is the tangent of the slope that was used in analyses.

Residual Error Variance

This is a measure of chance variation in a transformed time series (i.e., after the dependence has been removed from the data). In interrupted time series designs, this term is critical in the calculation of tests of significance. The criterion value of error variance was 1.00.

Change in Level

Change in level DL is one of the two parameters that measure intervention effects in an interrupted time series design. The criterion value of DL was 1.5 in all series.

Change in Slope

Change in slope DS is the second parameter that measures intervention effects in an interrupted time series design. However, in these series there was no significant change in slope from pre- to postintervention. The criterion value of DS was 0 in all series.

Autocorrelation Coefficients

Phi (ϕ) represents the degree of dependence in the data when the underlying model is autoregressive. Theta (θ) represents the degree of dependence in the data when the underlying model is moving averages.

Results

For each condition, the mean and standard deviation of the 10 replications were calculated for estimates of level, slope, error variance, change in level, change in slope, and phi or theta. Five separate $4 \times 3 \times 3 \times 2$ (type of underlying model $\times$ missing data estimation technique $\times$ percentage data missing $\times$ direction of dependence) analyses of variance (ANOVAs) were used to examine mean differences for level, slope, error variance, change in level, and change in slope. In this design, the first and last factors were between-subjects factors; the remaining two factors were within-subjects factors. Significant effects ($p < .01$) were followed up with simple effects tests and Tukey tests.

Level, Slope, Error Variance, Change in Level, and Change in Slope

A separate $4 \times 3 \times 3 \times 2$ (model $\times$ technique $\times$ percentage missing $\times$ direction of dependence) ANOVA was used to compare estimates of five dependent measures of level, slope, residual error variance, change in level, and change in slope. Model and direction of dependence were between-subjects factors; technique and percentage missing were within-subjects factors. All of the ML parameter estimates were accurate and did not differ from each other regardless of the different model specifications used [e.g., ARIMA(1, 0, 0), ARIMA(5, 0, 0), or the correct model].

Phi (Autoregressive Models)

Because direction of dependence was also an independent variable in this design, estimates of phi were analyzed in two separate ANOVAs, one selecting series with positive autocorrelation, the other for negatively autocorrelated series. Series with a first-order moving averages model (0, 0, 1) underlying the data were also analyzed separately (see later discussion) because two of the data estimation techniques did not yield phi estimates for (0, 0, 1) models.

Analysis of phi was performed using two separate $3 \times 4 \times 3$ [underlying ARIMA model (including only autoregressive models) $\times$ missing-data estimation technique $\times$ percentage-data missing] analyses of variance. Model was a between-subjects factor and technique and percentage missing were within-subjects factors. For positive autocorrelations, all of the ML estimates were accurate and did not differ from each other regardless of the different model specifications used [e.g., ARIMA(1, 0, 0), ARIMA(5, 0, 0), or the correct model]. For negative autocorrelations, ML phi estimates for the ARIMA(1, 0, 0) model were significantly lower than the ML estimates for the ARIMA(5, 0, 0) model and the correctly specified model. The ML estimates for the ARIMA(5, 0, 0) model and the correctly specified model resulted in phi estimates close to criterion and not different from each other.

Phi (Moving Averages Model)

The correct coefficient for a moving-averages model is theta, so only the two incorrect model methods were evaluated here. Estimates of phi were analyzed in two separate ANOVAs, one for each direction of dependence. These analyses were limited to series with a first-order moving averages ARIMA(0, 0, 1) model underlying the data, and missing data were estimated using the ML approach with either an ARIMA(1, 0, 0) or an ARIMA(5, 0, 0) model specified. These were the only techniques that will yield a phi estimate for the moving-averages model. Analysis of phi was performed using 2×3 (missing-data estimation technique $\times$ percentage data missing) ANOVAs. Both factors were within subjects manipulations.

For the *positive autocorrelation model*, the main effect for technique was the only significant effect in the analysis, $F(1, 9) = 25.13$, $p < .01$, indicating that the ARIMA(1, 0, 0) specification yielded significantly less accurate estimates of phi ($M = 0.434$, $SD = 0.128$) than the ARIMA(5, 0, 0) specification ($M = 0.638$, $SD = 0.149$) (criterion value = .60). For the negative autocorrelation model, none of the effects in the analysis were significant, indicating that estimates of negative phi did not differ significantly by technique used to estimate missing data or by the percentage of data missing.

Theta (Moving Averages Model)

Estimates of theta were analyzed in two separate ANOVAs, one for each direction of dependence. All series had a first-order moving averages model (0, 0, 1) underlying the data. This is the only set of conditions under which a theta estimate was produced. Analysis of theta was performed using 2×3 (missing-data estimation technique $\times$ percentage data missing) ANOVAs. Both factors were within-subjects manipulations. For both the positive and negative autocorrelation models, none of the effects in this analysis were significant, indicating that estimates of negative phi did not differ significantly by technique used to estimate missing data or by the percentage of data missing.

Discussion

The findings from this study were clear and support the use of the general transformation approach [i.e., the ARIMA(5, 0, 0) specification] for time series analysis with missing data. Findings summarized for all dependent variables in this study support the accuracy of ML regardless of model specification under most conditions tested. When differences were observed among the three model specification procedures, the ARIMA(5, 0, 0) specification performed as well as the correct model specification, whereas the ARIMA(1, 0, 0) specification was slightly inaccurate. Differential results were observed primarily with the estimates of autocorrelation. All other dependent variables were accurately estimated by ML irrespective of the model specification was used. Because the Velicer–McDonald general transformation approach does not require accurate model specification, these results support the use of this approach.

THE EFFECTS OF SYSTEMATICALLY MISSING DATA (STUDY 2)

This study compares the accuracy of ML estimation under conditions that represent another real-world problem, data that are missing in a systematic pattern rather than missing completely at random. In this study, first-order autoregressive data series that were simulated for the previous study were again used, but in this study data were eliminated in three different arrangements: (a) systematically missing, with complete data in some parts of the series and alternating observations missing in other parts of the series; (b) systematically missing, with all missing data occurring on consecutive observations; and (c) data missing completely at random, from Study 1. Missing data were then estimated using two of the ML estimation methods employed in the previous study: the correct specification ARIMA(1, 0, 0) and the ARIMA(5, 0, 0) specification. The ARIMA(5, 0, 0) model was so accurate in the previous study that it was retained in this design for comparison. [Because the underlying model was an ARIMA(1, 0, 0) model, ML with an ARIMA(1, 0, 0) specification and the "correct" model specification were equivalent.]

Data Generation

SAS/ETS was used for time series analysis, and parameter estimates resulting from each condition were compared. The conditions of this study are described in greater detail in what follows. Rationales for certain design choices that are redundant with the same choices made for the previous study are not repeated. Generated times series had $N_1 = N_2 = 50$ data points. Ten replications were generated in each of the conditions.

Independent Variables Manipulated

Four independent variables were manipulated in a $3 \times 3 \times 3 \times 2$ factorial design. The factor that is unique to this study is the *missing-data pattern*. Three different missing-data patterns were compared, as a within-groups manipulation. Within each series, pre- and postintervention observations had the same missing-data pattern.

The first missing-data pattern was an *alternating-observations missing-data pattern*. Series at pre- and postintervention were missing data in the following pattern: a run of complete data followed by a run where the series was missing alternating observations. For example, in the 20%-missing condition, observations 1 through 30 were complete; 31 through 50 had even-numbered observations, but odd-numbered observations were missing; observations 51 through 80 were complete; 81 through 100 were missing odd-numbered observations. Observations 1 through 50 were "preintervention"; 51 through 100 were "postintervention."

The second missing-data pattern was a *consecutive missing-data pattern*. In this condition, all missing data were eliminated from a consecutive run of observations in the middle of the series. For example, in the 20%-missing condition, observations 1 through 20 were complete; 21 through 30 were missing; 31 through 50 were complete; 51 through 70 were complete; 71 through 80 were missing; and 81 through 100 were also complete.

The third missing-data-pattern was a pattern of data *missing completely at random*. This served as the comparison condition. Data were eliminated according to a random number generator at both pre- and postintervention.

The other independent variables manipulated were (a) proportion of missing data, where data were eliminated from the time series in the proportions 0% (complete data, for comparison), 20%, and 40%; (b) missing-data approach, where two methods of estimating missing data were compared: ML estimation with the correct model [an ARIMA(1, 0, 0) model specified] and ML with an ARIMA(5, 0, 0) model specified; and (c) direction of autocorrelation, where there were two levels of dependence, or ϕ, in the series for comparison: Half the series had $\phi = 0.60$, the other half had $\phi = -0.60$.

Dependent Variables

Five hundred forty series (3 patterns of missing data × 3 proportions of missing data × 3 methods of missing-data estimation × 2 levels of autocorrelation × 10 replications of each) were input to SAS/ETS for time series analysis. Six dependent variables were obtained, corresponding to parameters of ARIMA(1, 0, 0) models (level, slope, error variance, change in level, change in slope, and phi).

Results

For each condition, the mean and standard deviation of the 10 replications were calculated for estimates of level, slope, error variance, change in level, change in slope, and phi. Five separate 3 × 3 × 2 × 2 (three missing data patterns × three proportions of missing data × two methods of data estimation × two levels of autocorrelation) ANOVAs were used to examine mean differences for the first five dependent variables. Phi was analyzed in two separate 3 × 3 × 2 analyses of variance, one for each level of autocorrelation. Significant effects were followed up with simple effects tests and Tukey tests.

An identical pattern of results was observed for five of the dependent variables, level, slope, error variance, change in level, and change in slope. The ML estimates were accurate and did not differ regardless of the independent variable manipulated, that is, pattern of missing data, estimation method [ARIMA(1, 0, 0) or ARIMA(5, 0, 0)], percentage of data missing, or direction of dependence.

Phi

Because direction of dependence was also an independent variable in this design, estimates of phi were analyzed in two separate ANOVAs, one for each criterion value of phi. Analysis of phi was performed using two separate 3 × 3 × 2 (missing data pattern × percentage data missing × missing-data estimation technique) ANOVAs. All factors in these analyses were within-subjects factors.

Figure 16.1 illustrates the results for the positive autocorrelation comparisons (criterion = .60). There were a total of nine cases created by the pattern of missing data and the percentage missing. For eight of the cases the pattern was clear and consistent: The general transformation model, ARIMA(5, 0, 0), produced more accurate estimation of phi than the correct model, ARIMA(1, 0, 0). For the final case, an alternating pattern with 40% missing, the correct model, ARIMA(1, 0, 0), badly underestimated phi and the general transformation model, ARIMA(5, 0, 0), badly overestimated phi.

Figure 16.2 illustrates the results for the negative autocorrelation comparisons (criterion = −.60). The results were more complex. There were a total of nine

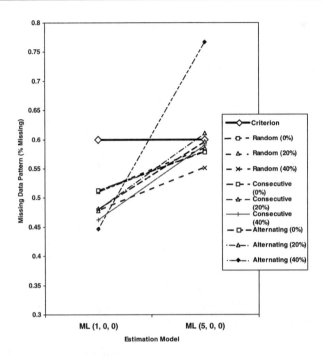

FIG. 16.1.   Estimation of a positive phi coefficient (criterion = .60)
for nine different combinations of pattern of missing data and percentage of data missing.

cases created by the pattern of missing data and the percentage missing. For six of
the cases the pattern was clear and consistent: The two methods produced similar
and generally accurate estimates. For the random pattern with 20% missing, the
general transformation model, ARIMA(5, 0, 0), produced more accurate estimation
of phi than the correct model, ARIMA(1, 0, 0). For the other two cases, the general
transformation model, ARIMA(5, 0, 0), badly overestimated phi in the case of a
random pattern with 40% missing and badly underestimated phi in the case of an
alternating pattern with 40% missing.

Discussion

The results of this study lend further support to the accuracy of the Jones (1980)
ML algorithm. The results also support the use of the Velicer–McDonald general transformation [ARIMA(5, 0, 0)] model specification. Use of the two ML
approaches led to virtually equivalent estimates of all time series parameters except positive phi. The (correct) ARIMA(1, 0, 0) specification sometimes resulted
in underestimates of phi when data were missing in an alternating or consecutive pattern. ML with an ARIMA(5, 0, 0) specification was consistently the most

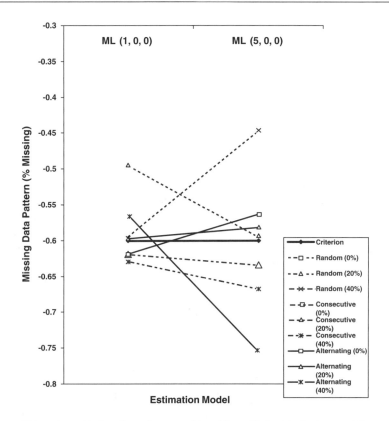

FIG. 16.2. Estimation of a negative phi coefficient (criterion = .60) for nine different combinations of pattern of missing data and percentage of data missing.

accurate approach for data estimation. This finding is particularly striking given that an ARIMA(1, 0, 0) was also the *correct* model specification in this design. The results for a negative phi were inconsistent and deserve further investigation.

THE EFFECTS OF NONNORMALITY (STUDY 3)

This study represents an initial exploration of another potential problem for the ML algorithm, the violation of the assumption of normally distributed data. The practical implications of violating normality assumptions for the accuracy of the algorithm are important to establish because data that violate this assumption are common in the behavioral sciences. However, there is little information available to suggest alternative distributions. Therefore, the study was limited in scope.

Data Generation

SAS/ETS was used for time series analysis, and parameter estimates resulting from each condition were compared. Again, generated times series had $N_1 = N_2 = 50$ data points, and 10 replications were generated.

Independent Variables Manipulated

For this study, all series fit a first-order autoregressive model, ARIMA(1, 0, 0), with moderately positive autocorrelation (.60). Given the more limited scope of this study, it was considered reasonable to restrict inquiry to one ARIMA model and one level of autocorrelation. Three independent variables were manipulated in a $2 \times 3 \times 3$ mixed factorial design. The time series data simulation program drew observations from either a normal or a log-normal distribution. This factor was manipulated as a between-groups factor. Data were randomly eliminated from the time series in the following proportions: 0% (complete data), 20%, and 40%. This variable was manipulated as a within-groups factor. Two methods of estimating missing data were compared as a within-subjects manipulation: ML estimation with an ARIMA(1, 0, 0) model specification and ML estimation with an ARIMA(5, 0, 0) model specification.

Dependent Variables

One hundred eighty series (2 levels of data distribution $\times$ 3 proportions of missing data $\times$ 3 methods of missing data estimation $\times$ 10 replications of each) were input to SAS/ETS for time series analysis. Six dependent variables were obtained, corresponding to parameters of ARIMA(1, 0, 0) models (level, slope, error variance, change in level, change in slope, and phi).

Results

For each condition, the mean and standard deviation of the 10 replications were calculated for all six dependent variables. Six separate $2 \times 3 \times 2$ (two levels of data distribution $\times$ 3 proportions of missing data $\times$ 2 methods of missing data estimation) ANOVAs were used to examine mean differences for each dependent variable. Significant effects were followed up with simple effects tests and Tukey tests.

Level

A $2 \times 3 \times 2$ (distribution $\times$ technique $\times$ percentage missing) ANOVA was used to compare estimates of level. Data distribution was a between-subjects factor; technique and percentage missing were within-subjects factors. There was a significant main effect for distribution. Collapsed across all other conditions, series with log-normal distributions resulted in estimates of level ($M = 4.39, SD = 1.11$) that were significantly higher, and more divergent from the criterion value of zero, than series that were normally distributed ($M = 0.71, SD = 0.39$). The ML estimates were not significantly different from each other at any level of missing data.

Error Variance

A $2 \times 3 \times 2$ ANOVA compared estimates of error variance. There was an expected main effect for data distribution whereby series with log-normal distributions resulted in higher estimates of error variance ($M = 12.51, SD = 2.33$) than series that were normally distributed ($M = 8.70, SD = 1.39$). The ML estimates were not significantly different from each other at any level of missing data.

Slope, Change in Level, Change in Slope, and Phi

Four separate $2 \times 3 \times 2$ ANOVAs were used to compare effects of data normality, missing-data technique, and percentage of missing data on the accuracy of the four different parameter estimates, with no significant effects found. The ML estimates were accurate, and were not significantly different from each other for any of the three conditions manipulated.

Discussion

The results of this study lend further support to the accuracy of the Jones (1980) ML algorithm. The results also support the use of the Velicer–McDonald general transformation ARIMA(5, 0, 0) model specification. Use of the two ML approaches led to virtually equivalent estimates of all time series parameters except positive phi. The correct ARIMA(1, 0, 0) specification sometimes resulted in underestimates of phi when data were missing in an alternating or consecutive pattern. Again, ML with an ARIMA(5, 0, 0) specification was consistently the most accurate approach for data estimation despite the fact that the ARIMA(1, 0, 0) was the *correct* model specification in this study. A third important finding was the absence of any significant effects with respect to the distribution variable. Data distribution only had a significant main effect on estimates of level and error variance, as expected. In these analyses, this effect only reflected the actual differences in the original simulated series, that is, log-normal series had higher levels and greater error variance. However, data distribution did not *differentially* affect data estimation by technique used.

DISCUSSION

The findings reported in this chapter have implications both for missing-data analysis generally and for time series analysis specifically. With respect to missing-data procedures, this chapter extends the previous results with respect to the advantage of statistical procedures for handling missing data over existing ad hoc procedures. Velicer and Colby (in press) demonstrated the superiority of maximum likelihood estimation of missing data in time series analysis under ideal situations, that is, the model is known, the missing data mechanism is missing completely at random, and the variable is normally distributed. This chapter explored the accuracy of the maximum likelihood procedure under violations.

Of the three violations considered, the most unique to time series analysis is model specification. When using the Jones (1980) ML algorithm, it is necessary to specify the type of model that underlies the series of data. The findings provide clear support for the use of the general transformation approach [i.e., the ARIMA(5, 0, 0) specification] for time series analysis with missing data. Findings also support the accuracy of ML regardless of actual model specification under most conditions tested. When differences were observed among the three model specification procedures, the ARIMA(5, 0, 0) specification performed as well as the correct model specification, whereas the ARIMA(1, 0, 0) specification was slightly inaccurate. Differential results were observed primarily with the estimates of autocorrelation. All other dependent variables were accurately estimated by ML irrespective of the model specification used. Because the Velicer-McDonald general transformation approach does not require accurate model specification, these results support the use of this approach.

The other two studies involved violations that are issues with missing data generally. The mechanism producing the missing data is critical. The Velicer and Colby (in press) study provided empirical support for the accuracy of ML estimation of missing data under the ideal condition of data MCAR. This chapter tests the accuracy of ML estimation under the more common conditions of data that are not MCAR. Missing-data patterns in Study 2 are either MCAR or systematic (i.e., consecutively or alternating missing) but independent of the values of the missing observations.

Use of the correct ARIMA(1, 0, 0) and general transformation ARIMA(5, 0, 0) ML approaches led to virtually equivalent estimates of all time series parameters except positive phi. The ARIMA(1, 0, 0) specification sometimes resulted in underestimates of phi when data were missing in an alternating or consecutive pattern. ML with a (5, 0, 0) specification was consistently the most accurate approach for data estimation. The results for a negative phi were inconsistent and deserve further investigation.

There are two limitations on the generalizability of these results. First, only two systematically missing data patterns were compared to completely random data elimination. There are numerous other idiosyncratic patterns of missing data that can occur in applied research. The results may not generalize to other types of missing-data patterns. Second, it is important to note that even though data were eliminated in a systematic pattern, those patterns were *unrelated to* (independent of) the values of the observations missing [i.e., data were MAR according to Rubin's (1976) classification]. It is often the case in applied research that systematic missing-data patterns are related to missing-data values (i.e., "not MAR"). In these cases, the reason the data are missing and the values of the missing data are related. Findings from Study 2 may not generalize to that case of data that are not missing at random.

The third study investigated the effects of violations of the normality assumption. Normality is a typical assumption for maximum likelihood procedures, and the robustness of the procedure under violations is critical. Use of the correct ARIMA(1, 0, 0) and the Velicer–McDonald general transformation ARIMA(5, 0, 0) ML approaches led to virtually equivalent estimates of all time series parameters except positive phi. The ARIMA(1, 0, 0) specification sometimes resulted in underestimates of phi when data were missing in an alternating or consecutive pattern. Again, ML with an ARIMA(5, 0, 0) specification was consistently the most accurate approach for data estimation. Surprisingly, there were no significant effects observed for data nonnormality on missing-data estimation or accuracy of parameter estimation.

An important limitation of the third study was the limited scope. This study provided only an initial exploration into time series data estimation under conditions of nonnormality. It was intended to be a limited probe for problems rather than an exhaustive study of the effects of nonnormality on data estimation for time series data. Future research should test the effects of nonnormality at various series lengths and levels of skew and kurtosis. However, even with the present study's limitations, it still contributes to the current state of knowledge in this area.

These three studies, combined with the results of the Harrop and Velicer (1985, 1990) studies and the Velicer and Colby (in press) study, provide strong support for the regular use of the Velicer–McDonald general transformation approach in time series analysis. Model specification is a difficult and subjective procedure. The Velicer–McDonald approach represents an attempt to avoid this problematic procedure. The results of the simulation studies demonstrate that there is little or no advantage to knowing the correct model compared to using a general transformation approach. Indeed, for some of the parameters estimated under missing-data conditions and violations, the correct model specification produced inferior estimates of the parameters compared to the general transformation approach. In the absence of compelling evidence to the contrary, researchers should employ the general transformation approach for all time series analysis. When data are missing, this procedure combined with the Jones (1980) maximum likelihood procedures should produce the most accurate parameter estimates.

ACKNOWLEDGMENTS

This chapter is based in part on revised material from Velicer and Colby (1997, in press), Velicer and Fava (2003), and Colby (1996). This research was partially supported by grants CA27821, CA63045, CA71356, and CA50087 from the National Cancer Institute.

REFERENCES

Aitken, A. C. (1934). On least squares and lineal combination of observations. *Proceedings of the Royal Society of Edinburg H, 55*, 42–47.

Box, G. E. P., & Jenkins, G. M. (1976). *Time-series analysis: Forecasting and control.* San Francisco: Holden-Day.

Box, G. E. P., Jenkins, G. M., & Reinsel, G. C. (1994). *Time series analysis: Forecasting and control* (3rd ed). Englewood Cliffs, NJ: Prentice-Hall.

Box, G. E. P., & Tiao, G. C. (1965). A change in level of nonstationary time series. *Biometrika, 52*, 181–192.

Cohen, J. (1988). *Statistical power analysis for the behavioral sciences* (2nd ed.). Hillsdale, NJ: Lawrence Erlbaum Associates, Inc.

Colby, S. M. (1996). *Algorithms for missing data replacement in time series analysis.* Unpublished doctoral dissertation, University of Rhode Island, Kingston.

Dielman, T. E. (1989). *Pooled cross-sectional and time series data analysis.* New York: Dekker.

Glass, G. V., Willson, V. L., & Gottman, J. M. (1975). *Design and analysis of time series experiments.* Boulder: Colorado Associated University Press.

Gottman, J. M. (1981). *Time series analysis: A comprehensive introduction for social scientists.* New York: Cambridge University Press.

Graham, J. W., Cumsille, P. E., & Elek-Fisk, E. (2003). Methods for handling missing data. In J. A. Schinka & W. F. Velicer (Eds.), *Research methods in psychology* (pp. 87–114). New York: Wiley.

Hall, S. M., Delucchi, K. L., Velicer, W. F., Kahler, C. W., Ranger-Moore, J., Hedeker, D., Tsoh, J. Y., & Niaura, R. (2001). Statistical analysis of randomized trials in tobacco treatment: Longitudinal designs with dichotomous outcome. *Nicotine and Tobacco Research, 3*, 193–202.

Harrop, J. W., & Velicer, W. F. (1985). A comparison of three alternative methods of time series model identification. *Multivariate Behavioral Research, 20*, 27–44.

Harrop, J. W., & Velicer, W. F. (1990). Computer programs for interrupted time series analysis: II. A quantitative evaluation. *Multivariate Behavioral Research, 25*, 233–248.

Jones, R. H. (1980). Maximum likelihood fitting of ARMA models to time series with missing observations. *Technometrics, 22*, 389–396.

Kohn, R., & Ansley, C. F. (1986). Estimation, prediction, and interpolation for ARIMA models with missing data. *Journal of the American Statistical Association, 81*, 751–761.

Laird, N. M. (1988). Missing data in longitudinal studies. *Statistics in Medicine, 7*, 305–315.

Little, R. J. A. (1988). A test of missing completely at random for multivariate data with missing values. *Journal of the American Statistical Society, 83*, 1198–1202.

Little, R. J. A., & Rubin, D. B. (1987). *Statistical analysis with missing data.* New York: Wiley.

Little, R. J. A., & Rubin, D. B. (1990). The analysis of social science data with missing values. In J. Fox & J. S. Long (Eds.), *Modern methods of data analysis* (pp. 374–409). Newbury Park, CA: Sage.

Ljung, G. M., & Box, G. E. P. (1978). On a measure of lack of fit in time series models. *Biometrika, 65*, 297–303.

Marsh, J. C., & Shibano, M. (1984). Issues in the statistical analysis of clinical time-series data. *Social Work Research and Abstracts, 20*, 7–12.

McCleary, R., & Hay, R. A., Jr. (1980). *Applied time series analysis for the social sciences.* Beverly Hills, CA: Sage.

Morrison, D. F. (1983). *Applied linear statistical methods.* Englewood Cliffs, NJ: Prentice-Hall.

Padia, W. L. (1975). The consequences of model misidentification in the interrupted time-series experiment. *Dissertation Abstracts International, 36*, 4875A (University Microfilms No. 76-3938).

Rankin, E. D., & Marsh, J. C. (1985). Effects of missing data on the statistical analysis of clinical time series. *Social Work Research and Abstracts, 21*, 13–16.

Rubin, D. B. (1976). Inference and missing data. *Biometrika, 63*, 581–592.

SAS Institute. (1988). *SAS/ETS user's guide, version 6.* Cary, NC: Author.

Schafer, J. L. (1997). *Analysis of incomplete multivariate.* New York: Wiley.

Schafer, J. L., & Graham, J. W. (2002). Missing data: Our view of the state of the art. *Psychological Methods, 7*, 147–177.

Simonton, D. K. (1977). Cross-sectional time-series experiments: Some suggested statistical analyses. *Psychological Bulletin, 84*, 489–502.

Velicer, W. F. (1994). Time series models of individual substance abusers. In R. Brown & W. J. Bukoski (Eds.), *Advances in data analysis for prevention intervention research* (pp. 264–301). Washington, DC: National Institute on Drug Abuse. pp. 264–301.

Velicer, W. F., & Colby, S. M. (1997). Time series analysis for prevention and treatment research. In K. J. Bryant, M. Windle, & S. G. West (Eds.), *The science of prevention: Methodological advances from alcohol and substance abuse research* (pp. 211–249). Washington, DC: American Psychological Association.

Velicer, W. F., & Colby, S. M. (in press). *A comparison of missing data procedures in time series analysis.* Manuscript Educational and Psychological measurement publication.

Velicer, W. F., & Fava, J. L. (2003). Time series analysis. In J. Schinka & W. F. Velicer (Eds.), *research methods in psychology* (pp. 581–606). New York: Wiley.

Velicer, W. F., & Harrop, J. W. (1983). The reliability and accuracy of time series model identification. *Evaluation Review, 7*, 551–560.

Velicer, W. F., & McDonald, R. P. (1984). Time series analysis without model identification. *Multivariate Behavioral Research, 19*, 33–47.

Velicer, W. F., & McDonald, R. P. (1991). Cross-sectional time series designs: A general transformation approach. *Multivariate Behavioral Research, 26*, 247–254.

17

Making Meaning of
Multivariate Methods

Lisa L. Harlow
University of Rhode Island

Multivariate methods provide a way of thinking and a set of tools to delineate and uncover the latent order in a specific system of constructs (e.g., McDonald, 1986). I argue that the search for latent order could be made much more attainable with the tools of multivariate statistics.

This chapter overviews several sets of themes that tend to run through most multivariate methods. First, the most salient theme of multivariate methods is to draw on multiple sources in the development of a strong system of knowledge. We are ultimately looking for truth in multiple places and in multiple ways (e.g., multiple theories, empirical studies, measurements, samples, time points, and statistical methods). Second, there are several background themes that pertain to both univariate and multivariate methods. These include issues about data, sample, measurement, variables, assumptions, and descriptive and inferential statistics. Third, central themes are discussed that seem to underlie many of the multivariate methods. These draw on the notions of variance, covariance, ratios of variances and/or covariances, and linear combinations. Fourth, several themes are presented that help in evaluating and interpreting results from multivariate methods. These include macroassessment summarizing significance tests and effect sizes that often examine the essence of shared variance with squared multiple correlations, eigenvalues, traces, and determinants, as well as evaluating results from a microperspective to determine the specific salient aspects of a significant effect. Finally, several multivariate methods will be outlined in several charts that delineate how the major themes pertain to each method.

Quantitative methods have long been heralded for their ability to synthesize the basic meaning in a body of knowledge. Aristotle emphasized meaning through the notion of "definition" as the set of necessary and sufficient properties that allowed an unfolding of understanding about concrete or abstract phenomena; Plato thought of essence or meaning as the basic form (Lakoff & Núñez, 2000). Finding the central meaning is at the heart of most mathematics, which uses axioms and categorical forms to define the nature of specific mathematical systems.

In this chapter, I focus on the delineation of basic themes that reoccur within statistics, particularly with multivariate procedures, in the hope of illuminating the core tenets, if not axioms, of these methods. Before describing these themes, I present a brief definition of multivariate methods and itemize several benefits and drawbacks to developing an understanding of them.

DEFINITION

Multivariate methods are a set of tools for analyzing multiple variables in an integrated and powerful way. By taking several relevant variables into account and acknowledging the relationships among them, often within a single analysis, multivariate methods help us to reduce the chances of making errors, either Type I (rejecting the null hypothesis too easily) or Type II (retaining the null hypothesis too easily). This provides a much more realistic and rigorous framework for analyzing data than with univariate methods.

BENEFITS

Several benefits can be derived from understanding and using multivariate methods. First, our thinking is stretched to embrace a larger context in which we can envision more-complex and more-realistic theories and models than could be rendered with univariate methods. This is important because most phenomena of interest to researchers are elaborate, involving several possible variables and patterns of relationship. Second, understanding multivariate methods helps us to crystallize theory into testable hypotheses and to provide empirical support for our observations. After gaining an overview of various kinds of multivariate statistics (e.g., group difference, prediction, exploratory, structural, and longitudinal methods), we have at our disposal a set of powerful methods for handling large, intricate designs. Third, multivariate statistics allow researchers to examine large sets of variables in a single analysis, thereby controlling for the level of Type I and Type II error rates and also taking correlations among variables into account. This is preferred to conducting a large number of univariate analyses that would increase the probability of making incorrect decisions while falsely assuming that each analysis is orthogonal. Fourth, multivariate methods provide several assessment indices to determine whether the overall or macroanalysis, as well as specific parts or the microanalysis, are behaving as expected. These overall and specific indices are analogous to the omnibus F test and planned comparisons, respectively, in an analysis of variance (ANOVA) design. Fifth, a thorough study of multivariate methods helps in understanding others' research. Even if we never choose to conduct our own analyses, knowledge of multivariate methods opens our eyes to a wider body of research than would be possible with only univariate study. Finally, multivariate participation in the research process engenders more-positive attitudes toward statistics and greater awareness and appreciation of how to use them effectively in furthering scientific research.

DRAWBACKS

Due to the size and complexity of most multivariate designs, several drawbacks may occur. First, statistical assumptions (e.g., normality, linearity, homoscedasticity) must be met for most methods, and less is known about the robustness of these to violations as compared to univariate methods. More is said about assumptions in the section on inferential statistics. Second, many more participants are usually needed to adequately test a multivariate design compared to smaller univariate studies. One rule of thumb suggests having at least 5 to 10 participants per variable or per parameter, though as many as 20 to 40 participants per variable or parameter may be necessary when assumptions are not met (e.g., Bentler, 1995; Tabachnick & Fidell, 2001). Others (e.g., Boomsma, 1983; Comrey & Lee, 1992) recommend having a sample size of 200 to 500, with smaller sample sizes allowed when there are large effect sizes (e.g., Green, 1991; Guadagnoli & Velicer, 1988). Third, interpretation of results from a multivariate analysis may be difficult due to having several layers to examine. These layers will be discussed more specifically later in the chapter when discussing macro- and microassessment. Fourth, some researchers speculate that multivariate methods are too complex to take the time to learn them. This is an inaccurate perception because the basic themes are clear and reoccurring, as we will shortly see. Fifth, after learning and using multivariate methods, it could become increasingly difficult to justify constructing or analyzing a narrow and unrealistic research study. One might even find oneself thinking from a much wider and global perspective.

OVERRIDING THEME OF MULTIPLICITY

The main theme of multivariate thinking is multiplicity, drawing on multiple sources in the development of a strong methodology. We are ultimately looking for truth in multiple places and in multiple ways. We could start by identifying multiple ways of thinking about a system; for example, we could consider how theory, empirical research, and applied practice impinge on our study. If there is a strong theoretical framework that guides our research, rigorous empirical methods with which to test our hypotheses, and practical implications that derive from our findings, contributions to greater knowledge and understanding become much more likely. We could also investigate multiple ways to measure our constructs, multiple statistical methods to test our hypotheses, multiple controls to ensure clear conclusions, and multiple time points and samples with which to generalize our results. In our multivariate venture into knowledge generation, perhaps the most primary goal is to consider several relevant theories that could direct our efforts to understanding a phenomenon.

Theory

Before embarking on a research study, it is essential to inquire about metaframeworks that can provide a structure with which to conduct our research. Are there multiple divergent perspectives to consider? Are any of them more central or salient than the others? Which seem to offer a more encompassing way to view an area of study, while also providing a basis for strong investigations? Meehl (1997) spoke of the need to draw on theory that makes risky predictions that are capable of being highly refuted. These strong theories are much preferred to weak ones that make vague and vacuous propositions. Others concur with Meehl's emphasis on theory. Wilson (1998) discussed theory in reverent words, stating that "Nothing in science—nothing in life, for that matter—makes sense without theory. It is our nature to put all knowledge into context in order to tell a story, and to recreate the world by this means" (p. 56). Theory provides a coherent theme to help us find meaning and purpose in our research. Wheatley (1994) wrote of the power and coherence of theory in terms of providing an overall meaning and focus in our research: "As long as we keep purpose in focus . . . we are able to wander through the realms of chaos . . . and emerge with a discernible pattern or shape" (p. 136). Abelson (1995) posited credible theory as being able to cull together a wide range of findings into "coherent bundles of results" (p. 14), which he called "signatures" (p. 14). Thus, a thorough understanding of the theories that are germane to research provide purpose and direction in the quest to perceive the pattern of meaning present in a set of variables that explain a phenomenon.

Hypotheses

On pondering a number of theories of a specific phenomenon, several hypotheses or predictions will undoubtedly emerge. In everyday life we all formulate predictions and hypotheses, however informal. This can be as mundane as a prediction about what will happen during the day, or about how the weather will unfold. In scientific research, we strive to formalize our hypotheses so that they directly follow from well-thought-out theory. The more specific and precise we make our hypotheses, the more likelihood there is of either refuting them or finding useful evidence to corroborate them (e.g., Meehl, 1997). Wilson (1998) made this clear by stating that theoretical tests of hypotheses "are constructed specifically to be blown apart if proved wrong, and if so destined, the sooner the better" (p. 57). Multivariate statistics allow us to formulate multiple hypotheses that can be tested in conjunction. Thus, we should try to formulate several, pivotal hypotheses or research questions that allow for rigorous tests of our theories, allowing us to hone and fine-tune our theories or banish them as useless. The testing of these hypotheses is the work of empirical research.

Empirical Studies

Having searched for pertinent theories that lead to strong predictions, it is important to investigate what other researchers have found in an area of research. Are there multiple empirical studies that have previously touched on aspects of these theories and predictions? Are there multiple contributions that could be made with new research that would add to the empirical base in this area? Schmidt and Hunter (1997) emphasized the need to accrue results from multiple studies and assess them within a meta-analysis framework. This allows the regularities and consistent ideas to emerge as a larger truth than could be found from single studies. Abelson (1995) described this as the development of "the lore" whereby "well-articulated research . . . is likely to be absorbed and repeated by other investigators" as a collective understanding of a phenomenon (pp. 105–106). No matter what the area of interest, a thorough search of previous empirical research on this topic is a must. After taking into account meaningful theories and empirical studies we are ready to consider the major constructs we plan to include in our research.

Measurement

When conducting empirical research, it is useful to ask about the nature of measurement for constructs of interest (McDonald, 1999). Are there several nuclear constructs that need to be delineated and measured? Are there multiple ways to measure each of these constructs? Are there multiple, different items or variables for each of these measures? *Classical test theory* (e.g., Lord & Novick, 1968) and *item response theory* (e.g., Embretson & Reise, 2000; McDonald, 2000) emphasize the importance of modeling the nature of an individual's response to a measure and the properties of the measures. *Reliability theory* (e.g., Anastasi & Urbina, 1997; Lord & Novick, 1968; McDonald, 1999) emphasizes the need to have multiple items for each scale or subscale we wish to measure. Similarly, statistical analysts conducting principal components or factor analyses emphasize the need for a minimum of three or four variables to anchor each underlying dimension or construct (e.g., Gorsuch, 1983; Velicer & Jackson, 1990). The more variables we use, the more likelihood there is that we are tapping the true dimension of interest. In everyday terms, this is comparable to realizing that we cannot expect someone else to know who we are if we only use one or even two terms to describe ourselves. Certainly, students would agree that if a teacher were to ask just a single exam question to tap all of their knowledge in a topic area, this would hardly cover the subject. Multivariate statistics aid us in this regard, by not only encouraging, but also requiring multiple variables to be examined in conjunction. This makes it much more likely that we will come to a deeper understanding of the phenomenon under study. Having identified several pertinent variables, it is also important to consider whether there are multiple time points across which a set of variables can be analyzed.

Multiple Time Points

Does a phenomenon change over time? Does a certain period of time need to pass before a pattern emerges or takes form? These questions are often important when we want to examine change or stability over time (e.g., Collins & Horn, 1991; Collins & Sayer, 2001; Moskowitz & Hershberger, 2002). Assessing samples at multiple time points aids us in discerning which variables are most likely the causal agents and which are more the receptive outcomes. If the magnitude of a relationship is always stronger when one variable precedes another in time, there is some evidence that the proceeding (i.e., independent) variable may be affecting the other, more-dependent outcome. Having contemplated the possibility of multiple time points, it is important to consider how to build in multiple controls.

Multiple Controls

Perhaps the most trustworthy way to assure causal inferences is to implement controls within a research design (e.g., Pearl, 2000). The three most salient controls involve a test of clear association between variables, evidence of temporal ordering of the variables, and the ability to rule out potential confounds or extraneous variables (e.g., Bullock, Harlow, & Mulaik, 1994). This can be most elegantly achieved with an experimental design that:

1. Examines the association between carefully selected reliable variables.
2. Manipulates the independent variable such that one or more groups receives a treatment, whereas at least one group does not.
3. Randomly selects a sufficient number of participants from a relevant population and randomly assigns them to either the treatment or the control group.

With this kind of design, there is a greater likelihood that nonspurious relation-ships will emerge in which the independent variable can clearly be identified as the causal factor, with potential confounding variables safely ruled out with the random selection and assignment (Fisher, 1925, 1926).

Despite the virtues of an experimental design in ensuring control over one's research, it is often difficult to enact such a design. Variables, particularly those used in social sciences, cannot always be easily manipulated. For example, I would loathe to try to experimentally manipulate the amount of substance abuse that is needed to bring about a sense of meaninglessness in life. These kinds of variables would be examined more ethically in a non- or quasiexperimental design that tried to systematically rule out relevant confounds (e.g., Shadish, Cook, & Campbell, 2002). These latter designs could include background variables (e.g., income, education, age at first substance abuse, history of substance abuse, history of meaninglessness) or covariates (e.g., network of substance users in one's environment, stressful life events) that could be statistically controlled while examining the relationship perceived between independent and dependent variables. Needless to say, it is very difficult to ensure that adequate controls are in place without an experimental design, though the realities of real-world research make it necessary to consider alternative designs. In addition to multiple controls, it is useful to consider collecting data from multiple samples.

Multiple Samples

Are there several pertinent populations or samples from which data could be gathered to empirically study the main constructs and hypotheses? Samples are a subset of entities (e.g., persons) from which we obtain data to statistically analyze. Ideally, samples are randomly drawn from a relevant population, though much research is conducted with convenience samples such as classrooms of students. Samples can also be "purposive" indicating a sample that is purposely heterogeneous or typical of the population from which generalization is possible (Shadish, Cook, & Campbell, 2002). When samples are not drawn at random or purposively, it is difficult to generalize past the sample to a larger population (e.g., Shadish, 1995). Results from a nonrandom sample can offer more descriptive or preliminary information that can be followed up in other research. Procedures such as propensity score analysis (e.g., Rosenbaum, 2002) can be used to identify covariates that can address selection bias in a nonrandom sample, thus allowing the possibility of generalizing to a larger population. The importance of identifying relevant and meaningful samples is pivotal to all research. In multivariate research, samples are usually larger than when fewer variables are examined.

Whether analyzing univariate or multivariate data from a relevant sample, it is preferable to verify whether findings are consistent. Fisher (1935) highlighted the need for replicating results in independent samples. More recent researchers (e.g., Collyer, 1986; Cudeck & Browne, 1983) reiterated the importance of demonstrating that findings can be cross-validated beyond a single sample. Statistical procedures have been developed in several areas of statistics that incorporate findings from multiple samples. For example, Jöreskog (1971) and Sörbom (1974) developed multiple-sample procedures for assessing whether a hypothesized mathematical model holds equally well in more than one sample. These multiple-sample procedures allow for tests of increasing rigor of replication or equality across the samples, starting with a test of an equal pattern of relationships among hypothesized constructs, up through equality of sets of parameters (e.g., factor loadings, regressions, and means) among constructs. If a hypothesized model can be shown to hold equally well across multiple samples, particularly when constraining the parameters to be the same, this provides a strong test of the generalizability of a model (Alwin & Jackson, 1981; Bentler, Lee, & Weng, 1987; Jöreskog, 1971).

Practical Implications

Though research does not have to have an immediately apparent practical need, it is helpful to consider what implications can be derived from a body of research. When multiple variables are examined, there is a greater likelihood that connections among them will manifest in ways that suggest practical applications. For example, research in health sciences often investigates multiple plausible predictors of disease, or, conversely, well-being (Diener & Suh, 2000), that can be used in developing interventions to prevent illness and sustain positive health (e.g., Prochaska & Velicer, 1997; Velicer et al., 2000). Practical applications do not have to originate with initial research in an area. For example, John Nash researched mathematical group theory, which only later was used to understand economics, bringing Nash a Nobel prize (Nash, 2002). Lastly, it is important to consider a number of multivariate methods from which one could select depending on specific research goals.

Multiple Statistical Methods

Are there several analyses needed to address the main questions? What kinds of analyses are needed? It is often important to examine research using several multivariate methods (e.g., Grimm & Yarnold, 1995, 2000). John Tukey (1977) championed the idea of liberally exploring data to find what it could reveal. In this respect, the process is not unlike an artist using several tools and utensils to work with a mound of clay until the underlying form and structure is made manifest. Throughout the chapter, examples are provided about how the themes pertain to various multivariate methods. Here, a brief overview of several sets of multivariate methods is given.

One set of methods focuses on group differences (e.g., Maxwell & Delaney, 1990; Tabachnick & Fidell, 2001). For group-difference methods, the main question is: Are there mean significant differences across groups, over and above what would occur by random chance, and how much of a relationship is there between the grouping and outcome variables? *Analysis of covariance (ANCOVA)* allows examination of group differences on a single outcome after controlling for the effects of one or more continuous covariates. *Multivariate analysis of variance (MANOVA)* is used to examine group differences on linear combinations of several continuous dependent variables. *Multivariate analysis of variance of covariance (MANCOVA)* extends ANCOVA and MANOVA when investigating group differences on multiple dependent variables with one or more covariates. ANCOVA, MANOVA and MANCOVA can be described with a basic model:

$$Y = \text{Grand } M + \tau + [\beta_i C_i +] E \tag{1}$$

where Y is a dependent variable, M is a mean of the Y scores, τ is a treatment mean, $[\beta_1 C_1 +]$ represents a regression slope, β_i, on a covariate, C_i, and E represents error. When not including a covariate the bracketed term drops out (e.g., for MANOVA). For group difference methods, the focus is on *means* across groups. Each of these group-difference methods help us to discern whether the average score between each group is more different than the scores within each group. If the between-group differences are greater than the random differences that are found among scores within each group, we have some evidence that the nature of the group is associated with the outcome scores.

Prediction methods allow us to predict an outcome on the basis of several predictor variables. The main question addressed with these methods is: How much of an outcome can we know given a set of predictor variables, and is the degree of relationship significantly different from zero? When there are multiple predictors and the outcome is a continuous variable, *multiple regression (MR)* (e.g., Cohen, Cohen, West, & Aiken, 2003) is the method of choice. When there are multiple predictors and a categorical outcome, *discriminant function analysis (DFA)* (e.g., Tatsuoka, 1970) can be used. When predictors are mostly categorical, *logistic regression (LR)* (e.g., Hosmer & Lemeshow, 2000) provides a useful method of ascertaining the probability of a categorical outcome. MR, DFA, and LR can be described with some function of the basic model:

$$Y = \alpha + \beta_1 X_1 + \cdots + \beta_p X_p + E \tag{2}$$

where α represents an intercept, X_i stands for the ith independent variable, and Y, β and E are the same as with the group difference model in equation 17.1. For prediction methods, the focus is on *weighted* combination of variables. Each of these predictive methods allows us to assess possible relationships between variables, such that scores increase or decrease in predictable ways. If the pattern of increase and decrease between two sets of scores is almost as large as the average random differences among the scores for each variable, there is some evidence of an association between the pair of variables.

Exploratory dimensional methods delineate the underlying dimensions in a large set of variables or individuals. If the emphasis is on identifying two sets of dimensions to explore the relationships among two sets of variables, *canonical correlation* (CC) is suggested (e.g., Thorndike, 2000). When the goal is to reduce a large set of correlated variables to a smaller set of orthogonal dimensions, then *principal components analysis (PCA)* is appropriate (Velicer & Jackson, 1990). When the focus is on identifying a set of theoretical dimensions that explain the shared common variance in a set of variables, *factor analysis (FA)* can be used (e.g., Gorsuch, 1983; McDonald, 1985). CC, PCA, and FA can be specified by the following correlational structure:

$$(\sigma_{ij})/\sqrt{(\sigma_{ii}^2)\,(\sigma_{jj}^2)} \tag{3}$$

where σ_{ij} is the covariance between variables i and j, and σ_{ii}^2 is the variance for variable i. With each of these methods, the focus is on *correlations* among the variables and dimensions. If there is sufficiently more intercorrelation or similarity within dimensions than across dimensions, and if each measure correlates predominantly with just one dimension, there is greater confidence that the underlying set of dimensions adequately explains the variation and covariation in the set of measures.

Structural equation modeling (SEM) provides a set of methods for examining a complex pattern of hypothesized relationships among a set of variables (e.g., Bollen, 1989; Loehlin, 2004; McDonald, 1978; McDonald, Ho, & Ringo, 2002). The main focus in SEM is to find a close match between a hypothesized theoretical model and the pattern of variation and covariation in a set of data. *Path analysis (PA)* (e.g., McDonald, 1996, 2002) is an appropriate SEM method when the focus is on a multifaceted predictive model with multiple constructs, where all of the variables are single measures. *Confirmatory factor analysis (CFA)* is an SEM method that is useful for examining the relationships among several latent factors and their respective measures. SEM methods can be described by one or both of the following two equations:

$$Y = \lambda\eta + E \tag{4}$$

$$\eta = \beta\eta + \zeta \tag{5}$$

where λ is a factor loading, η is a (latent factor or) dimension, ζ is prediction error, and Y, E, and β are as previously defined. The focus in SEM methods is on understanding the relationships among the variables and latent dimensions. CFA differs from exploratory factor analysis in that CFA hypothesizes and tests a more restrictive pattern of loadings, most often with each variable loading on only one of the underlying factors. *Latent variable modeling (LVM)* combines PA and CFA by allowing hypothesized predictions among several theoretical factors, each of which is measured by several variables.

Finally, there are several longitudinal for examining the pattern of change over time. One longitudinal method, *Time Series*, is useful when exploring the pattern of change in one or more variables over many time points (e.g., Box, Jenkins, & Reinsel, 1994; Velicer & McDonald, 1984, 1991). This method would be useful when data are collected at regular intervals over a long period of time, as in weekly assessments over a 1-year period. Another longitudinal method, *cross-lagged design* (e.g., Burkholder & Harlow, 2003), allows an examination of several constructs over several time points. With this method, causal evidence for temporal ordering can be gained when a construct consistently serves as a stronger predictor of other constructs measured at subsequent time points than when it serves as an outcome of other constructs measured at previous time points. Still another longitudinal method, *latent growth modeling* (e.g., Duncan, Duncan, Strycker, Li, & Alpert, 1999), allows an investigation of the level and rate of change over time. These longitudinal methods can be modeled with one or both of the following two equations:

$$Y = \alpha + \lambda \eta + \mathrm{E} \tag{6}$$

$$\eta = \beta_o + \beta \eta + \zeta \tag{7}$$

where α represents a measurement intercept, β_o stands for a structural intercept, and Y, λ, η, β, and ζ, are as previously defined, and E can have an auto-correlational structure across time points. The focus of longitudinal methods is on the intercepts and slopes to assess changes in means and regressions across time.

Summary of Multiplicity Theme

In the realm of methodology each of these facets of multiplicity coalesce under the effective tools of multivariate statistics to inform us of the fundamental nature of the phenomenon under study. All considered investigation begins with well-reasoned theories, articulate hypotheses, careful empirical research, accurate measurement, representative samples, and relevant statistical methods. When time and multiple controls are also possible, we have the added benefit of discerning the causal nature of the relationships among the variables.

BACKGROUND THEMES

In addition to the overriding theme of plurality that characterizes multivariate thinking, it is helpful to notice several background themes that are essential to an understanding of quantitative methods, whether multivariate or univariate.

Mathematics has long been concerned with noticing the fundamental patterns and connections in an area of study. Devlin (1994) stated, "differential equations describe the very essences of life: growth, development, and decay" (p. 94). Seen from this perspective, the abstract patterns of differential equations do not seem that alien to commonly understood conceptions. In the more applied field of statistics, we can notice some basic themes that tend to permeate quantitative thinking. At least a preliminary understanding of them will help us later when delving into the complexities of specific multivariate methods.

Data

Data constitute the pieces of information (i.e., *variables*) on a phenomenon of interest. Data that can be assigned meaningful numerical values can be analyzed with a number of statistical methods. We usually assign a (numerical) score to each variable for each entity and store this in an *"N by p" data matrix*, where N stands for the number of participants or entities and p stands for the number of variables (predictors or outcomes). A data matrix is the starting point for statistical analysis. It is the large, numerical knowledge base from which we can combine, condense, and synthesize to derive meaningful and relevant statistical nuggets that capture the essence of the original information. Obviously, a data matrix will tend to have more columns (of variables) and most likely more rows (of participants) with multivariate research than with univariate methods. To the extent that the data were collected from a large and representative sample it can offer a strong foundation for subsequent analyses.

Measurement Scales

Variables can be measured on a categorical or a continuous scale. Variables measured on a continuous scale have numerical values that can be characterized by a smooth flow of arithmetically meaningful quantitative measurement, whereas categorical variables take on finite values that are discrete and more qualitatively meaningful. Age and height are examples of continuous variables, which can take on many values that have quantitative meaning. In contrast, variables like gender and ethnicity have categorical distinctions that are not meaningfully aligned with any numerical values. Categorical variables are often used to separate people into groups for analysis with group-difference methods. For example, we may assign participants to a treatment or a control group with the categorical variable of treatment (with scores of $1 = yes$ and $0 = no$). Continuous variables can be used as either predictors or as outcomes (e.g., in multiple regression). As we will see later in the chapter, the choice of statistical analysis is often dependent, at least in part, on the measurement scales of the variables being studied. This is true for both multivariate and univariate methods. If variables are reliably and validly measured, then the results of analyses will be less biased and more trustworthy.

Roles of Variables

Variables can be independent (i.e., perceived precipitating cause), dependent (i.e., perceived outcome), or mediating (i.e., forming a sequential link between independent and dependent variables). In research, it is useful to consider the role that each variable plays in understanding phenomena. A variable that is considered a causal agent is sometimes labeled as *independent* or *exogenous*. It is not explained by a system of variables, but is rather believed to have an effect on other variables. The affected variables are often referred to as *dependent* or *endogenous*, implying that they were directly affected by other, more inceptive variables (e.g., Byrne, 2001).

Variables can also be conceptualized as intermediate, and thus intervene between or change the nature of the relationship between independent and dependent variables. When a variable is conceived as a middle pathway between independent and dependent variables it is often labeled as a *mediating variable* (e.g., Collins, Graham, & Flaherty, 1998; MacKinnon & Dwyer, 1993). For example, Schnoll, Harlow, Stolbach, and Brandt (1998) found that the relationship between the variables age and cancer stage and the variable psychological adjustment appeared to be mediated by coping style. In this model, age and cancer stage, the independent or exogenous variables, were not directly associated with psychological adjustment, the dependent or endogenous variable, after taking into account a cancer patient's coping style, the mediating variable. Instead, cancer patients who were younger and had a less serious stage of cancer had more positive coping styles. Furthermore, those who coped more with a fighting spirit rather than with hopelessness, fatalism, and anxious preoccupation adjusted better. Thus, coping style served as a mediator between demographic/disease variables and psychological adjustment variables.

Variables are referred to as *moderator variables* when they change the nature of the relationship between the independent and dependent variables (e.g., Baron & Kenny, 1986; Gogineni, Alsup, & Gillespie, 1995). For example, teaching style may be a predictor of an outcome, school performance. If another variable is identified, such as gender, that when multiplied by teaching style changes the nature of the predictive relationship, then gender is seen as a moderator variable.

Moderating or mediating variables are also sometimes referred to as covariates.*Covariates* are variables that may correlate with a dependent variable and are ideally *not* correlated with other independent variables. Failing to consider covariates could hinder the interpretation of relationships between independent and dependent variables, especially with nonrandom samples. Covariates help to statistically isolate an effect, especially when random assignment and/or manipulation is not accomplished. When several well-selected covariates (i.e., confounds, extraneous variables) are included in a study, if the relationship between the independent and the dependent variables still holds after controlling for the effects of one or more covariates, we have greater assurance that we have isolated the effect. We should also realize that the designation of a variable as either independent or dependent does not necessarily ensure the associated properties. An experimental design, for example, is usually needed to adequately designate a variable as a causal independent variable. Still, it is important to clearly articulate the intended role of variables in any design, preferably with support and justification from previous theory and empirical research. Finally, we should realize that statistical methods can analyze multiple variables at a time, with multivariate methods allowing larger and more-complex patterns of variables than other procedures.

Descriptive Statistics

Descriptive statistics provide an ungirded view of data. This often involves summarizing the central nature of variables (e.g., average or mean score; midpoint or median score; most frequently occurring or modal score), ideally from a representative or purposive sample. This can also comprise the spread or range of scores, as well as the average difference each score is from the mean (i.e., standard deviation). Thus, descriptive statistics summarize basic characteristics of a distribution such as central tendency and variability. Descriptive statistics can be calculated for large multivariate studies that investigate the relationships among a number of variables, preferably based on a well-selected and abundant sample.

A broader form of descriptive statistics occurs when we synthesize information from multiple variables in a multivariate analysis on a specific nonrandom sample. For example, an instructor may want to describe the nature of class performance from a specific set of variables (e.g., quizzes, tests, projects, homework) and sample (e.g., one classroom). If she wanted to describe group differences between male and female students, she could conduct a multivariate analysis of variance with a categorical independent variable, gender, and the several continuous outcomes she measured from students' performance. Results would not necessarily be generalized beyond her immediate classroom, though they could provide a descriptive summary of the nature of performance between gender groups in her class of students.

Inferential Statistics

Inferential statistics allow us to generalize beyond our sample data to a larger population. With most statistical methods, inferences beyond one's specific data are more reliable when statistical assumptions are met.

Statistical assumptions for multivariate analyses include the use of random samples, an evenly (i.e., normally or bell-shaped) distributed set of scores, linear relationships (i.e., variables that follow a pattern of increasing or decreasing together along a straight line), and homoscedasticity (i.e., similar variance on one variable along all levels of another variable).

Inferential statistics allow estimates of population characteristics from random samples drawn from the population. If we can show that our sample is selected so as to be representative of a larger population of interest, and would not have undue bias or extraneous confounds evident, then we are in a much better position to draw conclusions from our data that most likely will hold in the larger population.

Likewise, if we can show that the data follow expected distributions such that we can rule out random chance with our findings, then results are more conclusive. Finally, variables that covary in linear elliptical patterns allow more straightforward statistical inference than those that follow more complex curvilinear trends (e.g., anxiety and performance rise together until a certain point when the greater anxiety is associated with a decrease in performance). Multivariate research that has these features (i.e., random samples, controlling for confounds, and normally distributed data) can provide a basis for inferences beyond the immediate sample to a large population of interest.

Types of Variables and Choice of Methods

Different types of variables are associated with different types of statistical methods, particularly for inferential statistics.

Group-difference methods usually apply to categorical independent variables and one or more continuous dependent variables (e.g., MANOVA). They can also include one or more (usually continuous) covariates (e.g., confounding variables) to statistically isolate the relationship between the independent and dependent variables (e.g., ANCOVA, MANCOVA).

Predictive methods are most often applied to several predictor variables and a single dependent variable. Choice of prediction method is often based on the nature of the predictor and outcome variables. With all continuous variables, use *multiple regression*. When the predictor variables are continuous and the outcome is categorical, *discriminant function analysis* would be appropriate. When there is a mixture of both categorical and continuous and categorical predictors and a categorical outcome, *logistic regression* is the best choice.

Exploratory or *confirmatory structural methods* assess the underlying dimensions in a large set of (usually continuous) variables. With exploratory methods, we are trying to find which variables interrelate on a smaller set of dimensions that may not be completely known ahead of time. With confirmatory methods, we already have a known set of theoretically defined dimensions and want to verify that hypothesized sets of indicators or measures adequately correlate with each dimension.

Longitudinal methods usually involve the categorical variable of time points, as well as several other variables, often measured on a continuous scale.

Summary of Background Themes

Multivariate statistical methods build on these background themes to allow more-realistic designs among multiple variables than methods that just analyze one (i.e., univariate) or two (i.e., bivariate) key variables. Multivariate methods can help us see relationships that might only occur in combination with a set of well-selected variables.

Background themes involve consideration of the data used to test your hypotheses, the scale of measurement and nature of your variables, both descriptive and inferential statistics, and how the form of your variables often affects your choice of multivariate method for a particular study.

Inherent in all statistical methods is the idea of analyzing *incomplete information,* where only a portion of knowledge is available. For example, we analyze a subset of the data by selecting a sample from the full population because this is all we have available to provide data. We examine only a subset of the potential causal agents or explaining variables because it is nearly impossible to conceive of all possible predictors. We collect data from only a few measures for each variable of interest because we do not want to burden our participants. We describe the main themes in the data (e.g., factors, dimensions) and try to infer past our original sample and measures to a larger population and set of constructs. In each case, there is a need to infer a generalizable outcome from a subset to a larger universe to explain how scores vary and covary. Ultimately, we would like to be able to demonstrate that associations among variables can be systematically explained with as little error as possible. For example, a researcher might find that substance use scores vary depending on the level of distress and the past history of substance abuse. It may be that the higher the level of distress and the greater the past history of substance abuse, the more likely someone is to engage in greater substance use.

It is most likely true that other variables are important in explaining an outcome. Even when conducting a large multivariate study, it is important to recognize that we cannot possibly examine the full set of information, largely because it is not usually known or accessible. Instead, we try to assess whether the pattern of variation and covariation in the data appears to demonstrate enough evidence for statistically significant relationships, over and above what could be found from sheer random chance. Thus, the concepts of variance and covariance are central themes in understanding statistical thinking. Next, these concepts are discussed more fully within a multivariate framework.

CENTRAL THEMES

Just as with basic descriptive and inferential statistics, multivariate methods help us to understand and quantify how variables (co-)vary. Multivariate methods provide a set of tools for analyzing how scores from several variables covary, whether through correlations, group differences, or structural dimensions to explain systematic variance over and above random error variance. Thus, we are trying to explain or make sense of the variance in a set of variables with as little random error variance as possible. Multivariate methods draw on the foregoing background themes with several additional themes. Probably the most central themes for both multivariate and univariate methods involve the concepts of variance, covariance, and ratios of these variances and covariances. We will also examine the theme of creating linear combinations of the variables because this is central to most multivariate methods.

Variance

Variance is the average of the squared difference between a set of scores and their mean:

$$\sigma_x^2 = \sum (X - M)^2 \div (N - 1) \tag{8}$$

where σ_x^2 indicates the variance, X stands for a score, M_x is the mean of the X scores, and N is the number of X scores. With most statistical analyses, we try to explain how things vary. When a variable has a large variance, sample scores tend to be very different, having a wide range. It is useful to try to predict how scores vary, to find other variables that help to explain the variation. Statistical methods help to identify systematic, explained variance, acknowledging that there will most likely be a portion of unknowable and random (e.g., *error*) variance. Variance is what we usually want to analyze with any statistic. The goal of most statistics is to try to explain how scores vary so that we can predict or understand them better. Variance is an important theme particularly in multivariate thinking, and can be analyzed in several ways, as we shall see later in this chapter.

Covariance

Covariance is the product of the average differences between one variable and its mean and a second variable and its mean:

$$\sigma_{xy} = \sum (X - M_x)^*(Y - M_y) \div (N - 1) \tag{9}$$

where σ_{xy} indicates the covariance, X and Y stand for two different variable scores, M_x and M_y are the means of the X and Y scores, respectively, and N is the number of X and Y scores. *Covariance* or *correlation* depicts the existence of a relationship between two or more variables. When variables rise and fall together (e.g., study time and grade point average), they positively covary or co-relate. If scores vary in opposite directions (e.g., greater practice is associated with a lower golf score), negative covariance occurs. The theme of covariation is fundamental to multivariate methods because we are interested in how a set of variables covaries. Multivariate methods most often assess covariance by assessing the relationship among variables while also taking into account the covariation among other variables included in the analysis. Thus, multivariate methods allow a more informed test of the relationships among variables than can be analyzed with univariate methods that expect separate or orthogonal relationships with other variables. Both variances and covariances (see Equations 8 and 9) can be examined more broadly in a multivariate framework by inserting these values in a square matrix with variances along the diagonal and covariances among the variables in the off-diagonals. For a simple example with two variables, the variance-covariance matrix, usually labeled as $\sum_{xy}$ would look like the following:

$$\sum_{xy} = \begin{bmatrix} \sigma_x^2 & \sigma_{xy} \\ \sigma_{yx} & \sigma_y^2 \end{bmatrix} \tag{10}$$

Ratio of (Co-)Variances

Many methods examine a ratio of how much (co)variance there is between variables or groups relative to how much variance there is within variables or within groups:

$$[(\text{Co-})\text{Variance Between}] \div [\text{Variance Within}] \tag{11}$$

When the numerator is large relative to the denominator, we usually conclude that the results are significantly different from those that could be found based on pure chance. The reason for this is that when there is a greater difference across domains than there is within domains, whether from different variables or different groups, there is some indication of systematic shared or associated variance that is not just attributable to random error.

It is useful to see how correlation and ANOVA, two central univariate statistical methods, embody a ratio of variances. Building on Equations 8 and 9, correlation shows a ratio of covariance between variables over variance within variables:

$$(\sigma_{xy}) \div \sqrt{[(\sigma_x^2)^*(\sigma_y^2)]} \tag{12}$$

When the covariance between variables is almost as large as the variance within either variable, this indicates a stronger relationship between variables. With group-difference statistics (e.g., ANOVA), we often form a ratio of how much the group means vary relative to how much variance there is within each group:

$$F = (\text{variance between means}) \div (\text{variance within scores}) \tag{13}$$

where F is the statistical test formed by this ratio that should be significantly greater than 1.0. When the means are much more different across groups (i.e., large variance between groups) than the scores are within each group (i.e., smaller variance within groups), we have evidence of a relationship between the grouping (e.g., categorical, independent) and outcome (e.g., continuous, dependent) variables.

These ratios, whether correlational or ANOVA based, are also found in multivariate methods. In fact, just about every statistical significance test is based on some kind of ratio of variances. Knowing this fact and understanding the nature of the ratio for each analysis help us make much more sense out of our statistical results, whether from univariate or multivariate methods.

Linear Combinations

A basic theme throughout most multivariate methods is that of finding the relationship between two or more sets of variables. This is usually accomplished by forming *linear combinations* of the variables in each set that are additive composites that maximize the amount of variance drawn from the variables. These linear combination scores, which can be thought of as latent dimensions, are then analyzed, thereby summarizing the many variables in a simple, concise form. With multivariate methods, we are often trying to assess the relationship between variables or the shared variance between linear combinations of variables. Several multivariate methods analyze different kinds of linear combinations.

Components

A *component* is a linear combination of variables that maximizes the variance extracted from the original set of variables:

$$V = b_1X_1 + b_2X_2 + \cdots + b_pX_p \tag{14}$$

where V is a linear combination score, b_1 is a weight for variable "i", X_i is a score for variable X_i, and p stands for the number of variables in the linear combination. The concept of forming linear combinations is probably most salient with PCA. With PCA, we aim to find several linear combinations (i.e., components) that help to explain most of the variance in a set of the original variables. MANOVA and DFA also form component-like linear combinations (i.e., discriminant scores) to examine the relationships among the categorical grouping variable(s) and the continuous, measured variables. In each case, the use of components or linear combinations helps to synthesize information by redistributing most of the variance from a larger set of variables, usually into a smaller set of linear combinations.

Factors

We have just seen how linear combinations can be thought of as dimensions that seem to summarize the essence of a set of variables. If we are conducting a factor analysis, we refer to the dimensions as factors. Factors differ from the linear combinations analyzed in PCA, MANOVA, and DFA in that they are more latent dimensions that have separated common, shared variance among the variables from any unique or measurement error variance within the variables. Thus, a factor is sometimes believed to represent the underlying true dimension in a set of variables after removing the portion of variance in the variables that is not common to the others. In fact the linear combination that is modeled in factor analysis is the measured variable that is a function of the underlying factor plus some error (see Equation 4). (Exploratory) factor analysis is an initial method for analyzing factors, though there are several other methods. For example, CFA analyzes the relationships among several well-specified factors, each of which has several reliable measures. LVM also analyzes the relationships among several factors, allowing for theoretically grounded predictions among them.

Summary of Central Themes

In our discussion of central themes, we discussed the pivotal role of variances, covariances, and ratios of these, particularly in multivariate statistics. Ultimately, we are always trying to explain how variables vary and covary, and we do so often by examining a ratio of variances or covariances. The ratio informs us of the proportion of explained variance, which is often used as an indication of effect size. We also described the concept of a linear combination, which incorporates much of the variance from several variables. Many multivariate tools (e.g., CC, PCA, FA, DFA, MANOVA) use linear combinations to summarize information in sets of variables. Depending on the method, linear combinations are referred to with different terms (e.g., components, factors, discriminant functions). Regardless of the label, multivariate linear combinations synthesize the information in a larger set of variables to make analyses more manageable or comprehensible. Now we turn to ways to evaluate and interpret results from multivariate methods, using both a macro- and a microassessment focus.

INTERPRETATION THEMES

When interpreting results and assessing whether an analysis is successful, we should evaluate from several perspectives. Most statistical procedures, whether we are using univariate or multivariate methods, allow a *macroassessment* of how well the overall analysis explains the variance among pertinent variables. It is also important to focus on a *microassessment* of the specific aspects of the multivariate results.

Macroassessment

The first way to evaluate an analysis is at a global or macrolevel, which usually involves a significance test and most likely some synthesis of the variance in a multivariate data set. A *macrosummary* usually depicts whether there is significant covariation or mean differences within data relative to how much variation there is among scores within specific groups or variables.

A *significance test* is usually the first step of macroassessment in a multivariate design. Significance tests tell us whether our empirical results are likely to be due to random chance or not. It is useful to be able to rule out, with some degree of certainly, an accidental or anomalous finding. Of course we always risk making an error no matter what our decision. When we accept our finding too easily, we could be guilty of a Type I error, saying that our research had veracity when in fact it was a random finding. When we are too cautious about accepting our findings, we may be committing a Type II error, saying that we have no significant findings when in fact we do. Significance tests help us to make probabilistic decisions about our results within an acceptable margin of error, usually set at 1% to 5%. We would like to say that we have more reason to believe that our results are true than that they are not true. Significance tests give us some assurance in this regard, and are essential when we have imperfect knowledge or a lack of certainty about an area. We can help to rule out false starts and begin to accrue a growing knowledge base with these tests.

One kind of significance test is a chi-square goodness-of-fit statistic. This is used in SEM methods, among others. In SEM, the goal is to find a small chi-square value relative to the degrees of freedom, thereby indicating that there is no significant difference between a proposed model and the multivariate data on which the model is tested.

Most significance tests involve *a ratio of (co-)variances*. For example, most group-difference methods (e.g., ANOVA, ANCOVA, MANOVA, MANCOVA, DFA) use an F test, which is a ratio of the variance between means over the variance within scores, to assess whether observed differences are significantly different from what we would expect based on chance alone. Correlational methods (e.g., multiple regression) can also make use of an F test to assess whether the covariance among variables is large relative to the variance within variables. When the value of an F test is significantly large (as deemed by appropriate statistical tables), we can conclude that there is sufficient evidence of relationships occurring at the macrolevel. This would suggest that there is a goodness of approximation between the model and the data (McDonald, 1997). When this occurs, it is helpful to quantify the extent of the relationship, usually with effect sizes.

Macro effect sizes (ESs) provide an indication of the magnitude of our findings at an overall level. They are a useful supplement to the results of a significance test. Effect-size calculations often take the form of proportions of shared variance, particularly for multivariate analyses. Shared variance ESs are evaluated as small, medium, and large for values of .02, .13, and .26, respectively (Cohen, 1988; Kirk, 1996).

Shared variance is a common theme throughout most statistical methods. We are always trying to understand how to explain how scores vary. Most always this involves two sets of variables such that the focus is on how much variance is shared between the two sets (e.g., a set of independent and a set of dependent variables, or a set of latent dimensions and a set of measured variables). With multivariate methods, there are several ways to summarize the essence of shared variance; squared multiple correlations, eigenvalues, traces, and determinants are a few of them. Indices of shared variance can inform us of the strength of relationship or effect size (e.g., Cohen, 1988).

Squared multiple correlation, R^2, indicates the amount of shared variance between the variables. It is useful by providing a single number that conveys how much the scores from a set of variables (co-)vary in the same way (i.e., rise and fall together) relative to how much the scores within each variable differ among themselves. A large R^2 value (e.g., .26 or greater) indicates that the participants responses on a multivariate set of variables tend to behave similarly, such that a common or shared phenomenon may be occurring among the variables. For example, research by Richard and Shirley Jessor (e.g., Jessor & Jessor, 1973) and their colleagues demonstrated large proportions of shared variance among alcohol abuse, drug abuse, risky sexual behavior, and psychosocial variables, providing compelling evidence that an underlying phenomenon of "problem behavior" is apparent.

Many statistical methods use the concept of R^2 or shared variance. Pearson's correlation coefficient, r, is an index of the strength of relationship between two variables. Squaring this correlation yields R^2, sometimes referred to as a coefficient of determination, which indicates how much overlapping variance is shared between two variables. In multiple regression (e.g., Cohen et al., 2003), a powerful multivariate method useful for prediction, we can use R^2 to examine how much variance is shared between a linear combination of several independent variables and a single outcome variable. With multiple regression, the linear combination is formed by a "least squares" approach, which minimizes the squared difference between actual and predicted outcome scores. Other multivariate methods use different methods to form linear combinations of variables to examine the relationship or shared variance between variables. One method involves the use of eigenvalues, where *eigenvalues*, λ, are the variances of linear combinations that are formed to maximize the amount of information or variance taken from each of the individual variables to form a composite variable. We can use an analogy with sandboxes to help describe this process. Imagine that the variance for each variable is contained in its own sandbox. When we want to form combinations of several variables to examine relationships between sets of variables, we can visualize a whole row of sandboxes representing the variances for each of the variables with a whole row of empty sandboxes behind them waiting to hold the variances of the new linear combinations that will be formed. Using information from an *eigenvector weight*, b, we take a large portion of sand from each of the first row of sandboxes and place it in the first back-row *linear combination* sandbox. The amount of sand in the first *linear combination* sandbox is indicated by *its eigenvalue* (i.e., the amount of variance in a linear combination). The process continues with more sand being drawn from the first row of sandboxes (i.e., the original variables' variance), which is placed in subsequent back-row *linear combination* sandboxes. These remaining *linear combination* sandboxes contain less and less of the original sand because most of the information is placed in the first few linear combinations.

Several macro-assessment summary indices for MANOVA can be seen as functions of eigenvalues (e.g., greatest characteristic root, Hotelling's trace, Pillai's trace, Wilks' Lambda, each described subsequently). Roy's greatest characteristic root (GCR) is simply the largest eigenvalue of the matrix formed from the ratio of between-group variances, divided by within-group variances. Thus, the GCR is the variance of the largest linear combination for a set of variables. Knowing that an eigenvalue is a variance for a linear combination, it makes sense that the sum of the eigenvalues (also known as the trace) is equal to the sum of the original variances of the variables used in forming the linear combinations.

A *trace of a matrix* is the sum of the values along the diagonal from upper left to lower right. If the matrix is a covariance matrix, the trace provides a sum of all of the variance in the variables. If the matrix is a correlation matrix, the trace is equal to the number of variables because each of the values along the diagonal is equal to 1.0. In both types of matrices, the trace gives us one way to summarize the amount of variance available in the set of variables, ignoring the covariance or correlation among the variables. Thus, the trace may not provide enough information about a set of variables if there is significant covariance among them, though it may be helpful when the variables are relatively orthogonal. In MANOVA, two macroassessment summary indices are often used that incorporate the trace of a variance–covariance matrix. Hotelling's trace is simply the sum of the diagonal elements of the ratio of the between-groups variance matrix over the within-groups variance–covariance matrix. Pillai's trace is the sum of the diagonal elements of the between-groups variance–covariance matrix over the total (i.e., between plus within) variance–covariance matrix.

A *determinant* can be thought of as the generalized variance of a matrix. It consists of a single number, which usually ranges from 0 to 1.0 for a correlation matrix. When variables are highly related, the determinant is close to zero, indicating that there is not much variation between the variables. For example, when examining two completely redundant variables (e.g., degrees Fahrenheit and degrees centigrade), the determinant would equal zero. When examining variables that are very different, the determinant is larger, reflecting the fact that the matrix of variables is widely variant. For example, the determinant of an identity matrix, which would occur if variables were completely orthogonal, is 1.0 for a correlation matrix. A macroassessment index for MANOVA called Wilks's lambda forms a ratio of the determinant of two variance matrices. Wilks (1932) suggested that the determinant of the within-groups variance–covariance matrix over the determinant of the total (i.e., within plus between) variance–covariance matrix indicates how much of the variation and covariation between the grouping variable(s) and the continuous variables was unexplained. Thus, one minus the ratio of Wilks's lambda provides an indication of the shared or explained variance between grouping and continuous variables. This is often labeled as η^2 and can be seen as a multivariate effect size.

Many statistical procedures benefit from assessing the amount of *residual or error variance* in an analysis. In multiple regression or latent variable modeling, we often want to examine prediction error variance (i.e., $1 - R^2$), which is how much variation in the outcome variable was not explained by the predictors. In multivariate analysis of variance, discriminant analysis, and canonical correlation, we can get an indication of the residuals by subtracting η^2 (between variance over total variance) from one.

Microassessment

It is also useful to examine results at a more specific microlevel. *Microassessment* involves examining specific facets of an analysis (e.g., means, weights) to determine specifically what is contributing to the overall relationship. In microassessment we ask whether there are specific coefficients or values that can shed light on which aspects of the system are working and which are not.

Means

With group-difference methods, microassessment entails an examination of the differences between pairs of means. We can accomplish this by simply presenting a descriptive summary of the means and standard deviations for the variables across groups and possibly graphing them to allow visual examination of any trends.

Bonferroni Comparisons

Simply conducting a series of t tests between pairs of groups allows us to evaluate the significance of group means. A Bonferroni approach establishes a set alpha level (e.g., $p = .05$) and then distributes the available alpha level over the number of paired comparisons. Thus, if there were four comparisons and a desired alpha level of .05, each comparison of means could be evaluated with a p value of .0125.

Planned Comparisons

We could also see which pairs of means were statistically different, using a multiple comparison method such as Tukey's (1953) honestly significant difference (HSD) approach, which builds in control of Type I error. Ideally, these microlevel tests should directly follow from the hypotheses, rather than simply test for any possible difference.

Weights

With correlational or structural methods, we often want to examine weights that indicate how much of a specific variable is contributing to an analysis. In multiple regression, we examine least squares regression weights, which tell us how much a predictor variable covaries with an outcome variable after taking into account the relationships with other predictor variables. In an unstandardized metric, it represents the change in an outcome variable that can be expected when a predictor variable is changed by one unit. In a standardized metric, the regression weight, often referred to as a *beta weight*, gives the partial correlation between the predictor and the outcome after controlling for the other predictor variables in the equation. In other multivariate methods (e.g., discriminant function analysis, principal components analysis), the unstandardized weights are actually the eigenvector weights used in forming linear combinations of the variables. These are often standardized to provide an interpretation that is similar to the standardized weight in multiple regression. In factor analysis and structural equation modeling methods, weights are also used. These can indicate the amount of relationship between a variable and an underlying dimension (i.e., a factor loading) or can indicate the amount of association or regression across constructs (i.e., regression coefficient). In all of these instances, the weight informs us of how much a specific variable relates to some aspect of the analysis.

Micro Effect Sizes

Cohen's d (Cohen, 1988) is a useful micro ES to describe the standardized difference between means. Cohen's d is considered as small, medium, and large for values of .2, .5, and .8, respectively. Correlations or standardized weights are also examined as ESs, with values of .1, .3., and .5 seen as small, medium, and large, respectively.

Summary of Interpretation Themes

For most multivariate methods, there are two themes that help us with interpreting our results. The first of these, macroassessment, focuses on whether the overall analysis is significant and how much of an effect size there is. In addition, we often want to examine residuals to assess the nature of unexplained or error variance. Second, microassessment focuses on the specific aspects of an analysis that are important in explaining the overall relationship. These microaspects can be means, particularly with group-difference methods, or weights, particularly with correlational methods.

THEMES APPLIED TO MULTIVARIATE METHODS

Having considered a number of themes that run through multivariate methods, it is instructive to briefly outline how these themes apply to several multivariate methods. To do this, it is helpful to reflect on a set of questions to ask when approaching multivariate research:

1. What is the main question we want answered from our research?
2. What statistical methods are most appropriate to address this question?

TABLE 17.1
Multiplicity, Background, Central, and Interpretation Themes Applied to Group Difference Methods

	ANCOVA	MANOVA	MANCOVA
Multiplicity themes[a]	+*Theory, hypotheses, empirical research* +*Controls*: experimental design, covariate(s) +*Time points*: repeated measures +*Samples*: +groups for IV(s) +*Measurements*: +IVs, 1 DV, and +covariates	+*Theory, hypotheses, empirical research* +*Controls*: experimental design +*Time points*: repeated measures +*Samples*: +groups for IV(s) +*Measurements*: +IVs, +DVs	+*Theory, hypotheses, empirical research* +*Controls*: experimental design, covariate(s) +*Time points*: repeated measures +*Samples*: +groups for IV(s) +*Measurements*: +IVs, +DVs, +covariates
Background themes	*Sample data*: random selection and assignment *Measures*: grouping IVs, continuous covariate(s), continuous DV *Assumptions*: normality, linearity, homosc, homogeneity of regressions *Methods*: inferential with experimental design and assumptions met	*Sample data*: random selection and assignment *Measures*: grouping IVs, no covariate, continuous DV *Assumptions*: normality, linearity, homosc *Methods*: Inferential with experimental design and assumptions met	*Sample data*: random selection and assignment *Measures*: grouping IVs, continuous covariate(s), continuous DVs *Assumptions*: normality, linearity, homosc, homogeneity of regressions *Methods*: inferential with experimental design and assumptions met
Central themes	*Variance*: in DV *Covariance*: between DV and covariate(s) *Ratio*: between groups/within groups	*Variance*: in DVs *Covariance*: among DVs *Ratio*: between groups/within groups	*Variance*: in DV *Covariance*: among DVs and covariate(s) *Ratio*: between groups/within groups
Interpretation themes (questions to ask)	*Macro*: F test, $ES = \eta^2$ *Micro:* means, group comparisons Do groups differ after controlling for covariate? All variables reliable? Low–no correlation between IV and covariates? Correlation between DV and covariates? Are means significantly different, i.e., high between-group variance? Are groups sufficiently homogeneous, i.e., low within-group variance? Can design support causal inference?	*Macro*: F test, $ES = \eta^2$ *Micro:* Means, group comparisons Do groups differ overall and for each DV? Are DVs all needed? Low–no correlation between groups of IV(s)? Low correlation among DVs? Are means significantly different, i.e., high between-group variance? Are groups sufficiently homogeneous, i.e., low within-group variance? Can design support causal inference?	*Macro*: F test, $ES = \eta^2$ *Micro:* Means, group comparisons Do groups differ after considering covariates? All variables reliable? Low correlation between IVs & covariate & between DVs? Correlation between DVs and covariates? Are means significantly different, i.e., high between-group variance? Are groups sufficiently homogeneous, i.e., low within-group variance? Can design support causal inference?

Note: IV = Independent variable; DV = dependent variable; homosc = homoscedasticity.
[a]A plus sign indicates multiplicity of this theme pertains.

3. What are the main multiplicity themes of these statistical methods?
4. What are the main background themes?
5. How do the central themes of variance and covariance relate to these methods?
6. What are the main themes needed to interpret results at the macro- and microlevels?
7. What are some other considerations or next steps after applying these methods?

These questions can help us focus on how the major themes apply to various multivariate methods. In the next section a series of summary charts are organized by the type of research question addressed and the major sets of themes. For example, most methods benefit from considering multiplicity themes of multiple theories, hypotheses, empirical studies, controls, time points, samples, and measures. Similarly, most methods gain from careful attention to background themes concerning data, measurement, assumptions, and inferences. Likewise, most methods focus to some degree on the central themes of variance, covariance, and ratios of (co-)variances. Finally, questions to ask when addressing interpretation themes are provided for each of the methods. This will provide an integrated summary of common and unique aspects of a number of multivariate methods, helping to demystify these procedures and encourage wider application of them.

Group-Difference Methods

Group-difference multivariate methods (e.g., ANCOVA, MANOVA, MANCOVA) examine how the means vary across two or more groups, on one or more dependent variables. Table 17.1 presents a summary of how the main themes (i.e., multiplicity, background, central, and interpretation) apply to each of these group-difference methods.

Prediction Methods

Prediction methods (e.g., multiple regression, discriminant function analysis, and logistic regression) examine how a set of predictors relates to one or more outcome variables. Table 17.2 presents how the main themes apply to several prediction methods.

Exploratory Dimensional Methods

Exploratory dimensional methods allow us to formulate underlying dimensions among a set of variables and to examine relationships among the dimensions. Exploratory structural methods include canonical correlation, principal components analysis, and factor analysis. Table 17.3 lists these exploratory dimensional methods and indicates how the main themes apply to each of them.

TABLE 17.2
Multiplicity, Background, Central, and Interpretation Themes Applied to Prediction Methods

	Multiple Regression	Discriminant Function	Logistic Regression
Multiplicity themes[a]	+*Theory, hypotheses, empirical research* +*Controls*: covariate(s) +*Time points*: IVs and/or DV +*Samples*: cross-validate +*Measurements*: +IVs, 1 DV, +covariates are possible	+*Theory, hypotheses, empirical research* +*Controls*: experimental design +*Time points*: IVs and/or DV +*Samples*: + DV groups, cross-validate +*Measurements*: +IVs, +Groups for DV(s)	+*Theory, hypotheses, empirical research* +*Controls*: covariate(s) +*Time points*: IVs and/or DV +*Samples*: Cross-validate +*Measurements*: +IVs, 1 category DV, (+covariates)
Background themes	*Sample data*: Random selection *Measures*: continuous IVs and covariate(s), continuous DV *Assumptions*: normality, linearity, homosc *Methods*: inferential with assumptions met	*Sample data*: random selection (and assignment) *Measures*: grouping DV, continuous covariate(s), continuous IVs *Assumptions*: normality, linearity, homosc *Methods*: inferential with assumptions met	*Sample Data*: random selection *Measures*: grouping DV, grouping or continuous IVs and covariate(s) *Assumptions*: not needed for descriptive use *Methods*: inferential with assumptions met
Central themes	*Variance*: in DV *Covariance*: between DV and IVs and among IVs *Ratio*: Between variables variance/error variance	*Variance*: in DV *Covariance*: between DV and IVs and among IVs *Ratio*: between groups/within groups variance	*Variance*: in DV *Covariance*: among DV, IVs and covariate(s) *Ratio*: likelihood
Interpretation themes (questions to ask)	*Macro*: F test, $ES = R^2$ *Micro*: Regression weights, t tests Do IVs significantly predict or relate to DV? Are all variables reliable and needed? Low correlations among IVs (i.e., no collinearity)? Significant R^2 or shared variance between IVs and DV? Significant subset(s) of IVs? Which IVs significantly predict DV? Assumptions met? Can design support causal inference?	*Macro*: χ^2, F test, $ES = \eta^2$ *Micro*: discriminate weights, and correct classification Do IVs discriminate among DV groups? Are all variables reliable and needed? Low correlations among IVs (i.e., no collinearity)? Significant η^2 or shared variance between IVs and DV? Correct classification into DV groups by set of IVs? Which IVs significantly discriminate DV groups? Assumptions met? Can design support causal inference?	*Macro*: log-likelihood, ρ^2 *Micro*: coefficients, Wald tests, odds ratios What is probability of DV given set of IVs? Are all variables reliable and needed? Low correlations among IVs (i.e., no collinearity)? Significant ρ^2 or shared variance between IVs and DV? Compare different models to predict DV? Which IVs significantly increase probability of DV? Can design support causal inference?

Note: IV = Independent variable; DV = dependent variable; homosc = homoscedasticity.
[a]A plus sign indicates multiplicity of this theme.

TABLE 17.3

Multiplicity, Background, Central, and Interpretation Themes Applied to
Exploratory Dimensional Methods

	Principal Components	*Factor Analysis*	*Canonical Correlation*
Multiplicity themes[a]	+*Theory, hypotheses, empirical research* *Controls*: few *Time points*: replicate? *Samples*: cross-validate +*measurements*: +DVs, +components	+*Theory, hypotheses, empirical research* *Controls*: few *Time points*: replicate? *Samples*: cross-validate +*measurements*: +DVs, +factors	+*Theory, hypotheses, empirical research* *Controls*: few *Time points*: replicate? +*Samples*: cross-validate +*Measurements*: +IVs, +DVs, +Dimensions
Background themes	*Sample data*: random selection *Measures*: continuous DVs *Assumptions*: normality, linearity, homosc[b] *Methods*: descriptive or may be inferential with theory, random sample, and assumptions met	*Sample data*: random selection *Measures*: continuous DVs *Assumptions*: normality, linearity, homosc[b] *Methods*: descriptive or may be inferential with theory, random sample, and assumptions met	*Sample data*: random selection *Measures*: continuous IVs and DVs *Assumptions*: (normality, linearity, homosc[b] *Methods*: Descriptive or may be inferential with theory, random sample, and assumptions met
Central themes	*Variance*: in DVs explained by components *Covariance*: among DVs *Ratio*: proportion of variance for components	*Variance*: in DVs explained by factors *Covariance*: among DVs and among factors *Ratio*: of factor variance	*Variance*: between dimensions *Covariance*: among IVs and DVs *Ratio*: correlation
Interpretation themes (questions to ask)	*Macro*: PCA structure *Micro:* component loadings Do PCs explain variance? Are all variables reliable and needed? High correlation within components? Low correlations across components? 3+ variables per PC? Which variables load on each component? Assumptions met? Can design support causal inference?	*Macro*: χ^2 test *Micro:* factor loadings Do factors explain much of the variance? Are all variables reliable and needed? High correlation among variables within factors? Low correlations across factors? 3+ variables per factor? Which variables load on each factor? Assumptions met? Can design support causal inference?	*Macro*: F test, $ES = r^2$ *Micro:* canonical weights Number of pairs of canonical dimensions? Do canonical dimension pairs correlate? Are all variables reliable? High correlations within dimensions? Which variables load on each dimension? Assumptions met? Can design support causal inference?

Note: DV = dependent variable; IV = Independent variable; homosc = homoscedasticity; PCA = Principal components analysis; PC = Principal component.

[a]A plus sign indicates multiplicity pertains to this theme.

[b]Assumptions not needed for descriptive use.

TABLE 17.4

Multiplicity, Background, Central, and Interpretation Themes Applied to
Structural Equation Modeling Methods

	Path Analysis	Confirmatory Factor Analysis	Latent Variable Modeling
Multiplicity themes[a]	+*Theory, hypotheses, empirical research* *Controls*: covariates *Time points*: replicate? *Samples*: cross-validate +*Measurements*: +IVs, +DVs	+*Theory, hypotheses, empirical research* *Controls*: few *Time points*: replicate? *Samples*: cross-validate +*Measurements*: +DVs, +factors	+*Theory, hypotheses, empirical research* *Controls*: covariates *Time points*: replicate? +*Samples*: cross-validate +*Measurements*: +IVs, +DVs, +latent variables
Background themes	*Sample data*: large, and random selection *Measures*: continuous IVs and DVs *Assumptions*: normality, linearity, homosc *Methods*: Inferential with theory, random sample, and assumptions met	*Sample data*: large, and random selection *Measures*: continuous DVs and factors *Assumptions*: normality, linearity, homosc *Methods*: inferential with theory, random sample, and assumptions met	*Sample data*: large, and random selection *Measures*: continuous IVs, DVs and LVs *Assumptions*: normality, linearity, homosc. *Methods*: inferential with theory, random sample, and assumptions met
Central themes	*Variance*: in DVs explained by IVs *Covariance*: among IVs and DVs *Ratio*: $(S - \Sigma)/\Sigma$	*Variance*: in DVs explained by factors *Covariance*: among DVs and among factors *Ratio*: $(S - \Sigma)/\Sigma$	*Variance*: in DV factors explained by IV factors *Covariance*: among variables and factors *Ratio*: $(S - \Sigma)/\Sigma$
Interpretation themes (questions to ask)	*Macro*: χ^2 test, $ES = R^2$ *Micro*: Path coefficients, z tests Does model of IVs and DVs fit the data? IVs predict DVs? Are all variables reliable and needed? Low correlations among IVs (i.e., no collinearity)? Significant R^2 or shared variance in DVs by IVs? Significant IVs? Which IVs significantly predict DV? Low residuals? Assumptions met? Can design support causal inference?	*Macro*: χ^2 test *Micro*: Loadings, z tests Does factor model fit the data? Do factors explain much of the variance? Are all variables reliable and needed? High loadings on factors? Low error variances of variables? 3+ variables per factor? Which variables load on each factor? Low residuals? Assumptions met? Can design support causal inference?	*Macro*: χ^2 test, $ES = R^2$ *Micro*: parameter estimates, z tests Does model of IV and, DV factors fit the data? IVs predict DV factors? Are all variables reliable and needed? 3+ variables per factor? Significant R^2 or shared variance in DVs by DVs? Significant loadings and path coefficients? Low measurement and prediction errors? Low residuals? Assumptions met? Can design support causal inference?

Note: IV= Independent variable; DV=dependent variable; homosc=homoscedasticity.
[a]A plus sign indicates multiplicity pertains to this theme.

TABLE 17.5

Multiplicity, Background, Central, and Interpretation Themes Applied to Longitudinal Methods

	Time Series Analysis	Cross-Lagged Design	Latent Growth Modeling
Multiplicity themes[a]	*+Theory, hypotheses, empirical research*	*+Theory, hypotheses, Empirical research*	*+Theory, hypotheses, empirical research*
	Controls: covariates, time ordering	*Controls*: covariates, time ordering	*Controls*: covariates, time ordering
	Time points: multiple points	*Time points*: 2+ time points	*Time points*: 2+ time points
	Samples: cross-validate	*Samples*: cross-validate	*+Samples*: cross-validate
	+Measurements: 1+DVs over + time points	*+Measurements*: 1+IVs and/or 1+DVs	*+Measurements*: +IVs, +DVs, +latent variables
Background themes	*Sample data*: large, and random selection	*Sample data*: large, and random selection	*Sample data*: large, and random selection
	Measures: continuous variables	*Measures*: continuous variables	*Measures*: continuous variables
	Assumptions: normality, linearity, homosc[b]	*Assumptions*: normality, linearity, homosc	*Assumptions*: normality, linearity, homosc.
	Methods: inferential with theory, random sample, and assumptions met	*Methods*: inferential with theory, random sample, and assumptions met	*Methods*: inferential with theory, random sample, and assumptions met
Central themes	*Variance*: in DVs by previous DV	*Variance*: in DVs explained by IVs	*Variance*: in DV factors explained by IV factors
	Covariance: among DVs	*Covariance*: IVs and DVs	*Covariance*: among latent variables
	Ratio: likelihood	*Ratio*: $(S - \Sigma)/\Sigma$	*Ratio*: $(S - \Sigma)/\Sigma$
Interpretation themes (questions to ask)	*Macro:* model fit	*Macro:* χ^2 test, $ES = R^2$	*Macro:* χ^2 test, $ES = R^2$
	Micro: autocorrelations, t tests	*Micro:* path coefficients, z tests	*Micro:* parameters (e.g., intercept, slope, regressions), z tests
	Does time series model adequately explain data?	Does cross-lagged model fit the data?	Does latent growth model fit the data?
	Significant autoregressive parameters, i.e., links between adjacent points?	Significant explained variance across time?	Is intercept parameter significant?
	Significant moving-average parameters, i.e., links between random shocks?	Significant path coefficients?	Is slope parameter significant?
		Significant cross-lags for causal parameters?	Is interaction of intercept and slope significant?
		High reliability across lags?	Are all variables reliable and needed?
	Are all variables reliable and needed?	Are all variables reliable and needed?	Significant R^2?
	Low residuals?	Low residuals?	Low residuals?
	Assumptions met?	Assumptions met?	Assumptions met?
	Can design support causal inference?	Can design support causal inference?	Can design support causal inference?

Note: DV = Dependent variable; IV= independent variable; homosc = homoscedasticity.
[a]A plus sign indicates multiplicity applies to this theme.
[b]Assumptions not needed for descriptive use.

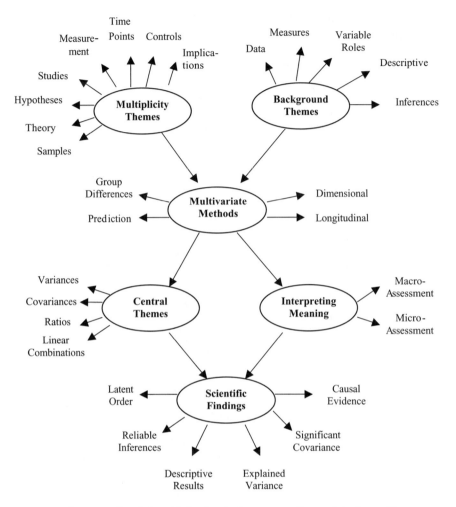

FIG. 17.1. Depiction of the basic themes as they relate to multivariate methods and the uncovering of scientific findings.

Structural Equation Methods

Structural equation methods allow us to simultaneously examine a complex set of hypothesized relationships and assess how well a model of these relationships explains the pattern of variation and covariation in a multivariate data set. Table 17.4 presents several structural equation methods (e.g., path analysis, confirmatory factor analysis, and latent variable modeling) and indicates how the main themes apply to each of them.

Longitudinal Methods

Longitudinal methods incorporate an element of change over time, increasing our ability to temporally order variables. Table 17.5 summarizes how the main themes apply to several longitudinal methods (i.e., time series, cross-lagged panel design, and latent growth modeling).

SUMMARY

In this chapter, several themes were elucidated to describe multivariate methods, which are useful in uncovering truth and underlying meaning in well-constructed research studies. Figure 17.1 presents a summary depiction of the basic themes and how they related to multivariate methods and ultimately, scientific findings.

ACKNOWLEDGMENTS

The chapter draws from an LEA book on *The Essence of Multivariate Thinking* (Harlow, 2005). Support was partially provided by a Fulbright Award while the author was at York University, Toronto, Ontario, Canada; by a National Science Foundation (NSF) grant on Learning Communities in Science, Engineering and Women's Studies; and by an NSF grant on Advancing Women in Science. Thanks are offered to all of the students and faculty at York University, and the University of Rhode Island, and the Cancer Prevention Research Center who generously offered resources, support, and comments. Thanks are also offered to members and affiliates of the Society of Multivariate Experimental Psychology (SMEP), who provide an ongoing forum in which to stay informed and enlightened on state-of-the-art methodology. Finally, thanks are extended to a past president of SMEP, Rod McDonald, who by his incredible insight and productivity serves as a constant source of inspiration and guidance to me and generations of methodologists.

REFERENCES

Abelson, R. P. (1995). *Statistics as principled argument.* Mahwah, NJ: Lawrence Erlbaum Associates, Inc.

Alwin, D. F., & Jackson, D. J. (1981). Applications of simultaneous factor analysis to issues of factorial invariance. In D. Jackson & E. Borgatta (Eds.), *Factor analysis and measurement in sociological research: A multi-dimensional perspective* (pp. 249–279). Beverly Hills, CA: Sage.

Anastasi, A., & Urbina, S. (1997). *Psychological testing.* Upper Saddle River, NJ: Prentice-Hall.

Baron, R. M., & Kenny, D. A. (1986). The moderator–mediator variable distinction in social psychological research: Conceptual, strategic, and statistical considerations. *Journal of Personality and Social Psychology, 51,* 1173–1182.

Bentler, P. M. (1995). *EQS: Structural equations program manual.* Encino, CA: Multivariate Software, Inc.

Bentler, P. M., Lee, S.-Y., & Weng, L.-J. (1987). Multiple population covariance structure analysis under arbitrary distribution theory. *Communications in Statistics—Theory, 16,* 1951–1964.

Bollen, K. A. (1989). *Structural equations with latent variables.* New York: Wiley.

Boomsma, A. (1983). *On the robustness of LISREL (maximum likelihood estimation) against small sample size and nonnormality.* Unpublished doctoral dissertation, University of Groningen, The Netherlands.

Box, G. E. P., Jenkins, G. M., & Reinsel, G. C. (1994).*Time series analysis: Forecasting and control* (3rd ed.). Englewood Cliffs, NJ: Prentice-Hall.

Burkholder, G. J., & Harlow, L. L. (2003). An illustration of a longitudinal cross-lagged design for larger structural equation models. *Structural Equation Modeling Journal, 10,* 465–486.

Bullock, H. E., Harlow, L. L., & Mulaik, S. (1994). Causation issues in structural modeling research. *Structural Equation Modeling Journal, 1,* 253–267.

Byrne, B. M. (2001). *Structural equation modeling with AMOS: Basic concepts, applications, and programming.* Mahwah, NJ: Lawrence Erlbaum Associates, Inc.

Cohen, J. (1988). *Statistical power analysis for the behavioral sciences.* San Diego, CA: Academic.

Cohen, J., Cohen, P., West, S. G., & Aiken, L. S. (2003). *Applied multiple regression/correlation analysis for behavioral sciences* (3rd ed.). Mahwah, NJ: Lawrence Erlbaum Assoicates, Inc.

Collins, L. M., Graham, J. W., & Flaherty, B. P. (1998). An alternative framework for defining mediation. *Multivariate Behavioral Research, 33,* 295–312.

Collins, L., & Horn, J. (Eds.). (1991). *Best methods for the analysis of change.* Washington, DC: American Psychological Association.

Collins, L. M., & Sayer, A. G. (Eds). (2001). *New methods for the analysis of change. Decade of behavior.* Washington, DC: American Psychological Association.

Collyer, C. E. (1986). Statistical techniques: Goodness-of-fit patterns in a computer cross-validation procedure comparing a linear and threshold model. *Behavior Research Methods, Instruments, and Computers, 18,* 618–622.

Comrey, A. L., & Lee, H. B. (1992). *A first course in factor analysis* (2nd ed.). Hillsdale, NJ: Lawrence Erlbaum Associates, Inc.

Cudeck, R., & Browne, M. W. (1983). Cross-validation of covariance structures. *Multivariate Behavioral Research, 18,* 147–157.

Diener, E., & Suh, E. M. (Eds.). (2000). *Culture and subjective well-being: Well being and quality of life.* Cambridge, MA: MIT Press.

Devlin, K. (1994). *Mathematics: The science of patterns. The search for order in life, mind, and the universe.* New York: Scientific American Library.

Duncan, T. E., Duncan, S. C, Strycker, L. A., Li, F., & Alpert, A. (1999). *An introduction to latent variable growth curve modeling.* Mahwah, NJ: Lawrence Erlbaum Associates, Inc.

Embretson, S. E., & Reise, S. P. (2000). *Item response theory for psychologists.* Mahwah, NJ: Lawrence Erlbaum Associates, Inc.

Fisher, R. A. (1925). *Statistical methods for research workers.* Edinburgh: Oliver & Boyd.

Fisher, R. A. (1926). The arrangement of field experiments. *Journal of the Ministry of Agriculture of Great Britain, 33,* 505–513.

Fisher, R. A. (1935). *The design of experiments.* Edinburgh: Oliver & Boyd.

Gogineni, A., Alsup, R., & Gillespie, D. F. (1995). Mediation and moderation in social work research. *Social Work Research, 19,* 57–63.

Gorsuch, R. L. (1983). *Factor analysis* (2nd ed.). Hillsdale, NJ: Lawrence Erlbaum Associates, Inc.

Green, S. B. (1991). How many subjects does it take to do a regression analysis? *Multivariate Behavioral Research, 26,* 449–510.

Grimm, L. G., & Yarnold, P. R. (1995). *Reading and understanding multivariate statistics.* Washington, DC: American Psychological Association.

Grimm, L. G., & Yarnold, P. R. (2000). *Reading and understanding more multivariate statistics.* Washington, DC: American Psychological Association.

Guadagnoli, E., & Velicer, W. F. (1988). Relation of sample size to the stability of component patterns. *Psychological Bulletin, 10,* 265–275.

Hosmer, D. W., Jr., & Lemeshow, S. (2000). *Applied logistic regression.* New York: Wiley.

Jessor, R., & Jessor, S. L. (1973). A social psychology of marijuana use: Longitudinal studies of high school and college youth. *Journal of Personality and Social Psychology, 26,* 1–15.

Jöreskog, K. G. (1971). Simultaneous factor analysis in several populations. *Psychometrika, 57,* 409–426.

Kirk, R. E. (1996). Practical significance: A concept whose time has come. *Educational and Psychological Measurement, 56,* 746–759.

Lakoff, G., & Núñez, R. E. (2000). *Where mathematics comes from: How the embodied mind brings mathematics into being.* New York: Basic Books.

Loehlin, J. C. (2004). *Latent variable models* (4th ed.). Mahwah, NJ: Lawrence Erlbaum Associates, Inc.

Lord, F. M., & Novick, M. R. (1968). *Statistical theories of mental test scores.* Reading, MA: Addison-Wesley.

MacKinnon, D. P., & Dwyer, J. H. (1993). Estimating mediated effects in prevention studies. *Evaluation Review, 17,* 144–158.

Maxwell, S. E., & Delaney, H. D. (2003). *Designing experiments and analyzing data: A model comparison perspective* (2nd ed.). Mahwah, NJ: Lawrence Erlbaum Assocites, Inc.

McDonald, R. P. (1978). A simple comprehensive model for the analysis of covariance structures. *British Journal of Mathematical and Statistical Psychology, 31,* 59–72.

McDonald, R. P. (1985). *Factor analysis and related methods.* Hillsdale, NJ: Lawrence Erlbaum Associates, Inc.

McDonald, R. P. (1986). Describing the elephant: Structure and function in multivariate data. *Psychometrika, 51,* 513–534.

McDonald, R. P. (1996). Path analysis with composite variables. *Multivariate Behavioral Research, 32,* 1–38.

McDonald, R. P. (1997). Goodness of approximation in the linear model. In L. L. Harlow, S. A. Mulaik, & J. H. Steiger (Eds.), *What if there were no significance tests* (pp. 199–219)? Mahwah, NJ: Lawrence Erlbaum Associates, Inc.

McDonald, R. P. (1999). *Test theory: A unified treatment.* Mahwah, NJ: Lawrence Erlbaum Associates, Inc.

McDonald, R. P. (2000). A basis for multidimensional item response theory. *Applied Psychological Measurement, 24,* 99–114.

McDonald, R. P. (2002). What can we learn from the path equations? Identifiability, constraints, equivalence. *Psychometrika, 67,* 225–249.

McDonald, R. P., Ho, M.-H., & Ringo, A. F. (2002). Principles and practice in reporting structural equation analyses. *Psychological Methods, 7,* 64–82.

Meehl, P. E. (1997). The problem is epistemology, not statistics: Replace significance tests by confidence intervals and quantify accuracy of risky numerical predictions. In L. L. Harlow, S. A. Mulaik, & J. H. Steiger (Eds.), *What if there were no significance tests* (pp. 393–425)? Mahwah, NJ: Lawrence Erlbaum Associates, Inc.

Moskowitz, D. S., & Hershberger, S. L. (Eds.). (2002). *Modeling intraindividual variability with repeated measures data: Methods and applications.* Mahwah, NJ: Lawrence Erlbaum Associates, Inc.

Nash, J., Nasar, S., & Kuhn, H. W. (Eds.). (2002). *The essential John Nash.* Princeton, NJ: Princeton University Press.

Pearl, J. (2000). *Causality: Models, reasoning and inference.* Cambridge: Cambridge University Press.

Prochaska, J. O., & Velicer, W. F. (1997). The transtheoretical model of health behavior change. *American Journal of Health Promotion, 12*, 38–48.

Rosenbaum, P. R. (2002). *Observational studies* (2nd ed.). New York: Springer-Verlag.

Schmidt, F. L., & Hunter, J. E. (1997). Eight common but false objections to the discontinuation of significance testing in the analysis of research data. In L. L. Harlow, S. A. Mulaik, & J. H. Steiger (Eds.), *What if there were no significance tests* (pp. 37–64)? Mahwah, NJ: Lawrence Erlbaum Associates, Inc.

Schnoll, R. A., Harlow, L. L., Stolbach, L. L., & Brandt, U. (1998). A structural model of the relationships among disease, age, coping, and psychological adjustment in women with breast cancer. *Psycho-Oncology, 7*, 69–77.

Shadish, W. R. (1995). The logic of generalization: Five principles common to experiments and ethnographies. *American Journal of Community Psychology, 23*, 419–428.

Shadish, W. R., Cook, T. D., & Campbell, D. T. (2002). *Experimental and quasi-experimental designs for generalized causal inference*. Boston: Houghton Mifflin.

Sörbom, D. (1974). A general method for studying difference in factor means and factor structures between groups. *British Journal of Mathematical and Statistical Psychology, 27*, 229–239.

Tabachnick, B. G., & Fidell, L. S. (2001). *Using multivariate statistics* (4th ed.). Boston: Allyn & Bacon.

Tatsuoka, M. M. (1970). *Discriminant analysis*. Champaign, IL: Institute for Personality and Ability Testing.

Thorndike, R. M. (2000). Canonical correlation analysis. In H. E. A. Tinsley & S. D. Brown (Eds.). *Handbook of applied multivariate statistics and mathematical modeling* (pp. 237–263). San Diego, CA: Academic Press, Inc.

Tukey, J. W. (1953). *The problem of multiple comparisons*. Unpublished manuscript, Princeton University.

Tukey, J. W. (1977). *Exploratory data analysis*. Reading, MA: Addison-Wesley.

Velicer, W. F., & Jackson, D. N. (1990). Component analysis versus common factor analysis: Some issues in selecting an appropriate procedure. *Multivariate Behavioral Research, 25*, 1–28.

Velicer, W. F., & McDonald, R. P. (1984). Time series analysis without model identification. *Multivariate Behavioral Research, 19*, 33–47.

Velicer, W. F., & McDonald, R. P. (1991). Cross-sectional time series designs: A general transformation approach. *Multivariate Behavioral Research, 26*, 247–254.

Velicer, W. F., Prochaska, J. O., Fava, J. L., Rossi, J. S., Redding, C. A., Laforge, R. G., & Robbins, M. L. (2000). Using the transtheoretical model for population-based approaches to health promotion and disease prevention. *Homeostasis in Health and Disease, 40*, 174–195.

Wheatley, M. J. (1994). *Leadership and the new science: Learning about organization from an orderly universe*. San Francisco: Berrett-Koehler.

Wilks, S. S. (1932). Certain generalizations in the analysis of variance. *Biometrika, 24*, 471–494.

Wilson, E. O. (1998). *Consilience*. New York: Vintage.

Author Index

Note: Numbers in *italics* indicate pages with complete bibliographic information.

Subject Index

581